Elizabeth Gundrey
of this country's
(*Shoppers' Guide*) l
keen eye for qualit
the subject of travel
has been far the m
each year in new er
this is the ninth. She is also the author of
England by Bus & Coach (Sphere); and
Running your own Bed and Breakfast (Piatkus)
for people who want to start doing this
themselves.

Staying Off the Beaten Track reached the bestseller listings last year for months on end. It is
a book for all seasons.

VOUCHERS WORTH £18

(by courtesy of the houses concerned)

This voucher is worth **£6** at any establishment starred in the list on pages **ix–xviii** provided it is presented **ON ARRIVAL** and not later. It is valid throughout **1990**, and may be used if you stay **3** or more nights. Only one voucher usable per establishment.

This voucher is worth **£6** at any establishment starred in the list on pages **ix–xviii** provided it is presented **ON ARRIVAL** and not later. It is valid throughout **1990**, and may be used if you stay **3** or more nights. Only one voucher usable per establishment.

This voucher is worth **£6** at any establishment starred in the list on pages **ix–xviii** provided it is presented **ON ARRIVAL** and not later. It is valid throughout **1990**, and may be used if you stay **3** or more nights. Only one voucher usable per establishment.

OFFER OF NEXT EDITION

Using an out-of-date edition can lead to costly disappointments. A new edition appears every November, updated, with fresh entries added, some deleted and others revised, and with vouchers valid for the next year. Make sure you are not using an out-of-date edition by sending a stamped self-addressed envelope to Explore Britain, Alston, Cumbria, CA9 3SL, for an order form (UK only) on which you can apply for the 1991 edition even before it reaches the shops. No need for a letter: just put SOTBT 1991 on top left corner of the envelope you send. **New in 1991:** far more about Wales, and many new entries for Cheshire, Derbyshire and Staffordshire (the Peak District), Devon and Cornwall, Durham, East Anglia, Gloucestershire (the Cotswolds), Herefordshire, Kent, Lancashire, Lincolnshire, London, Nottinghamshire and Shropshire.

STAYING OFF THE BEATEN TRACK

ELIZABETH GUNDREY
with Walter Gundrey

A personal selection of moderately priced
inns, small hotels, farms and country houses

NINTH EDITION
1990

ARROW

To Andrew, with love

Arrow Books Limited
62–65 Chandos Place, London WC2N 4NW

A division of Century Hutchinson Limited

London   Melbourne   Sydney   Auckland
Johannesburg and agencies
throughout the world

First published in Great Britain 1982
by Hamlyn Paperbacks
Second edition 1983
Third edition 1984
Fourth edition 1985
Fifth edition 1986
Arrow edition (Sixth edition) 1986
Seventh edition 1987
Eighth edition 1988
Ninth edition 1989

Copyright © 1982, 1983, 1984, 1985, 1986, 1987, 1988, 1989
by Elizabeth Gundrey and Walter Gundrey

Set in Linotron Plantin by
Rowland Phototypesetting Limited
Bury St Edmunds, Suffolk
Printed and bound in Great Britain by
The Guernsey Press Co. Limited, Guernsey, C.I.

Cover picture: **Paradise House**, Bath,
Avon (*rear view*) by Michael Cyprien
(*see page 228*)

British Library Cataloguing in Publication Data
Gundrey, Elizabeth
Staying off the beaten track.—9th ed
1. Great Britain. Hotels and inns
I. Title
647′.944101

ISBN 0-09-961390-5

The author and publishers would like to thank all those
owners who allowed us to use their drawings. Additional
line drawings by David Mostyn, Peter Gregory, Matthew
Doyle, Nicole Tedder, Jeremy Ford, Leslie Dean and
Elizabeth Gundrey

Although every care has been taken to ensure that all
the information in this book is correct and up-to-date,
neither the author nor the publishers can accept respon-
sibility for details which may have changed since the
book went to press.

CONTENTS

TOWNS OF
ENGLAND
which have
'SOTBT' houses
nearby

FOR SCOTLAND
SEE PAGE 360

0   50

miles

N

R WALES

PAGE 346

Acknowledgments

The author and associates acknowledge with much appreciation the assistance of the rest of the 'Staying Off the Beaten Track' team (Michael Cyprien, Jonathan May, Jennifer Christie and – last but far from least – Andrew Cockburn); of editor Jan Bowmer and her colleagues at Arrow Books; and of all the proprietors of houses but for whom this book could never have been written.

The hotels and houses in England appear in alphabetical order later. For convenience in locating them, they are grouped in the following list according to counties. On the left is the nearest town (sometimes distant), with its map reference (see page vii), followed by the house or hotel and its nearest village.

✲ Establishments marked with a star will accept the discount vouchers from page ii. Other discounts to readers are described in the text.

NOTE: The houses in this book have been personally visited by Elizabeth (or in some cases Walter) Gundrey. **At over three-quarters of them you may stay for as little as £9–£16 (for bed-and-breakfast)** although their best rooms may cost more, and their prices may rise in high season. But owners, and prices can change overnight; so check before you book. At many places, you can dine or lunch without staying: see entries under 'dinner'.

COMPLAINTS: I will investigate if you have first taken the matter up with the owners, who are normally anxious to put right anything that is wrong. E.G.

COUNTY LIST OF HOUSES & HOTELS IN ENGLAND

Nearest town	Map reference *(see page vii)*	Address	Page
AVON			
Bath	F.11	(Avonside, *see* Wiltshire)	13
		(Bradford Old Windmill, *see* Wiltshire)	35
		Oldfields	221
		The Orchard, Bathford	223
		Paradise House✳	228
		Parkside	288
		(Pickford House, *see* Somerset)	236
		Somerset House✳	275
		Strathavon✳	288
		(Tumblers, *see* Somerset)	302
Bristol	F.11	Cameley Lodge, Temple Cloud	48
		Dornden, Old Sodbury✳	97
BEDFORDSHIRE			
Bedford	J.10	Church Farm, Roxton	61
		The Grange, Ravensden✳	121
BERKSHIRE			
Hungerford	G.11	Marshgate Cottage, Marshgate	176
Maidenhead	H.11	Inverlodden, Wargrave	148
Newbury	G.11	St Mary's House, Kintbury	263
Reading	H.11	Boot Farm, Bradfield	32
		Bridge Cottage, Woolhampton	32
Windsor	H.11	Bear Farm, Binfield✳	20
BUCKINGHAMSHIRE			
Aylesbury	H.10	Apsley Manor Farm, Marsh	11
		Foxhill, Kingsey✳	117
		Poletrees Farm, Brill✳	240
		Wallace Farm, Dinton✳	310
Beaconsfield	H.11	Old Jordans, Jordans	203
High Wycombe	H.11	White House, Widmer End	329
Milton Keynes	H.10	Richmond Lodge, Mursley	252
		White House, Olney	330
CAMBRIDGESHIRE			
Cambridge	J.9	Coach House, Dry Drayton✳	72
		The Watermill, Hildersham	316
Ely	K.9	Warden's House, Wicken	314
CHESHIRE			
Chester	E.7	Castle House	52
		Duddon Lodge, Tarporley	282
		Hatton Hall, Hatton Heath	133
		Stapleford Hall, Tarvin	282
Nantwich	F.7	Burland Farm, Burland	45
CORNWALL			
Bude	C.12	(Leworthy Farm, *see* Devon)	161
		Manor Farm, Crackington Haven	172

THE PLACES IN BETWEEN

'Green' tourism, some say, is now making rural holidays as popular as visits to famous historic cities.

How much of rural England do you really know? Its variety continues to hold surprises for me.

Tourists still make for the same few areas the names of which are familiar worldwide: the Cotswolds, West Country, New Forest, South Downs and the great national parks such as the Lake District, Norfolk Broads, the Peak District and the Yorkshire Dales and Moors. They blindly pass by places just as attractive which lie between these tourist honeypots.

I invite you to test your own knowledge of England's lesser-known beauty-spots by ticking the following: how many have you explored? (Indeed, do you even know which counties they are all in?) Each one of them would be a good focal point for a two- or three-day break to explore the area in detail: or in some cases an even longer stay. (The names in brackets refer to some houses in SOTBT which are in, or *fairly near*, the area concerned.) A long round-England tour going from one to another could be planned which would avoid all the places that are overcrowded in summer.

Allendale (Eldochan Hall)
Aln Estuary (Westlea)
Amberley Wild Brooks (Rock Windmill)
Arnside & Silverdale (New Capernwray)
Ashdown Forest (Old Place)
Aylesbury, Vale of (Poletrees Farm)
Bagshot Heath (Bear Farm)
Belvoir, Vale of (Langar Hall)
Bere, Forest of (South Farm)
Bewl Water (Newbarn)
Black Down (Woodmans Green Farm)
Blackmoor Vale (Fox Inn)
Blakeney Point (Cley Mill)
Bodmin Moor (Hurdon Farm)
Bowland, Trough of (Clay Lane Head)
Breckland (College Farm)
Bredon Hill (Windrush, Little Comberton)
Brownsea Island (Old Granary)
Charnwood Forest (Wheathill Farm)
Cheviots (Coach House)
Chichester Harbour (White Barn)
Chilterns (Apsley Manor Farm)
Clent Hills (Little Lodge Farm)
Coquetdale (New Moor House)
Cranborne Chase (Fleur-de-Lys Inn)
Danbury and Lingwood Commons (Blackwater Hotel)

Dart Estuary (Wavenden House)
Dean, Forest of (Tudor Farmhouse Hotel)
Deben Estuary (Spion Kop)
Dedham Vale (Dedham Hall)
Delamere Forest (Stapleford Hall)
Eden Valley (Prospect Hill Hotel)
Evesham, Vale of (Mill Hay House)
Fens (Warden's House)
Fontmell Down (Stourcastle Lodge)
Frensham Ponds (Trevena House)
Golden Cap (Chimneys)
Golden Valley (Haven)
Hambleton Hills (St James's House)
Hamsterley Forest (Grove House)
Hatfield Forest (Greys)
Hindhead Common (Woodmans Green Farm)
Holy Island (Lindisfarne Hotel)
Hughenden Valley (White House, Widmer End)
Ilkley Moor (Unicorn Hotel)
Itchen Valley (Yew Tree Cottage)
Kennet Valley (Boot Farm)
Kielder Forest & Water (Pheasant Inn)
Long Mynd (Birches Mill)
Lune Valley (New Capernwray)
Macclesfield Forest (Burland Farm)
Malvern Hills (One Eight Four)

Manifold Valley (White House, Grindon)
Marshwood Vale (Red House)
Matlocks (Shottle Hall)
Mendips (Penscot Farmhouse Hotel)
Mersea Island (Blackwater Hotel)
Nidderdale (Sportsman's Arms)
North Downs, Box Hill, Leith Hill (Bulmer Farm)
Oxney, Isle of (Tighe Farm)
Peckforton Hills (Hatton Hall)
Pewsey, Vale of (Enford Hall)
Piddle Valley (Poachers' Inn)
Poole Harbour (Old Granary)
Purbeck, Isle of (Scott Arms)
Quantocks (Alfoxton Cottage)
Ranmore Common (Clandon Manor Farm)
Ribblesdale (Rowe House)
Rodings (Greys)
Romney Marshes (Old Vicarage, Rye)
Rutland Water (Home Farm)
St Leonards Forest (Brookfield Farm Hotel)
Salcombe Estuary (The Wood)

Scilly Isles (Carnwethers, Coastguards, Bank Cottage)
Selborne Hill (Street Farmhouse)
Severn Valley (Pool House)
Sherwood Forest (Langar Hall)
Taunton Dene (Old Manor Farm, Norton Fitzwarren)
Teesdale (Grove House)
Tennyson Downs (The Nodes)
Thatcham Moors (St Mary's House)
Tunstall Forest (Priory Cottage)
Wareham Forest (Trent Vale Farmhouse)
Weald (Munk's Farmhouse)
Weardale (Pennine Lodge)
West Wight (The Nodes)
White Horse, Vale of (Portwell House)
Wiltshire Downs (Enford House)
Wirral (Castle House)
Wolds (Village Farm)
Wye Valley (Ancient Camp Inn)
Wylye and Nadder Valleys (Mill House, Berwick St James)
York, Vale of (Old Farmhouse, Raskelf)

A number of these scenic areas are in counties which the average tourist wrongly supposes to be uninteresting. But the best parts of (for instance) Essex, Bedfordshire, Lincolnshire, Northamptonshire, Staffordshire, Lancashire, Surrey, County Durham, Cheshire and all the border counties (adjacent to Wales or Scotland) are outstandingly attractive – if you know where to look. And as to the Midlands, this is where to find all the spots mentioned in *The Country Diary of an Edwardian Lady* (see Northleigh House), just south of Birmingham's unlovely bustle!

HOW TO HAVE A GOOD TIME

For months on end in the last two years, this book was either first or second among accommodation guides on the weekly bestseller lists of the book trade. Good news, but it does also mean that as the readership grows so also does the diversity of readers' tastes. My detailed descriptions are meant to help each one pick out the places that suit him or her best; but I still get readers who write to complain about bar noise in inns (so why pick an inn rather than a house without a bar?), the presence of dogs (why go to a house with the code letter **D**, meaning dogs accepted, or to a farm where dogs are almost certainly kept?) and so forth.

Some people have very particular requirements; and it is up to them to discuss these when telephoning to book. Many hosts in this book are more flexible than big hotels, and all are eager to help if they can. I have in mind such things as: a bad back, needing a very *firm mattress*; special *dietary* requirements, and *allergies* to feather pillows or animals; a strong preference for *separate tables* rather than a shared dining-table – or vice versa; *fewer courses* than on the fixed menu; *twin beds* rather than double beds – or vice versa; freedom to *smoke* – or freedom from it; a particular wish for *electric blanket, hot water-bottle*, etc. or a dislike of *duvets*; the need to arrive, depart or eat at *extra-early* or *extra-late* hours; an intention to pay by *credit card* (this should not be taken for granted, particularly at small guest-houses). Houses which ordinarily do not admit non-residents to dine may nevertheless permit you to invite a friend – just ask.

The code letters that appear after the name of each house will help you identify houses suitable for children, dogs, handicapped people, users of public transport, etc.: for full explanation, see page xxvi.

Please also use the 'how to book' checklist on page xxii when telephoning.

And one final tip on ensuring that you get all that you hope for: at the end of each season, throw away *Staying Off The Beaten Track* and get next year's edition (you can soon recoup its cost through using the fresh set of accommodation vouchers it contains). Here's why this is so important. A reader wrote to me as follows: 'The house was dirty; room smelt damp; toilet-seat wobbly and stained; under-pillows had no cases; grubby carpets . . . (etc.)'. The house had changed hands years ago, and been dropped from my book as a consequence; but the reader was using an out-of-date edition. Prices change, so do telephone numbers and much else. Change of owner or grossly inflated prices are the two most common reasons why I drop houses; a third is that I find somewhere better – or of better value – in the neighbourhood.

My own standards (and, indeed, standards generally) have gone up over the years. Value for money remains one of my main criteria. I rate unpretentious hospitality far above outward show.

There is one other, important component in having an enjoyable experience: congenial company. I am struck by the number of readers who comment that, when they stay at a *Staying Off the Beaten Track* house, they find other visitors – from the same source – very agreeable company because they are compatible people. (Just occasionally there is an exception: the one who keeps aloof, or who loudly complains about trivia, for instance.)

TELEPHONING TO BOOK: A CHECKLIST

Book well ahead: many of these houses have few rooms. Further, at some houses, rooms (though similarly priced) vary in size or amenities: early applicants get the best ones. Mention that you are a reader of *Staying Off the Beaten Track*. Telephoning is preferable to writing to enquire about vacancies, but not at mealtimes or late.

1. Ask for the owner by the *name* given in this edition. (If there has been a change, standards may differ.)
2. Specify *your precise needs* such as en suite bathroom, if available: see page xxi. (Do not turn up with children, dogs or disabilities if you have not checked that these are accepted or provided for.) Elderly people may wish to ensure that their room is not on the second floor.
3. Check *prices* – these, too, can change (particularly after spring). Ask whether there are any bargain breaks. All prices quoted in this book are minimum; and at some houses wide variations occur. Be sure that VAT is not extra.
4. Ask what *deposit* to send (or quote a credit card number). There is more about deposits below.
5. State your intended *time of arrival*, and what *meals* are wanted. (If you should then be late, telephone a warning – otherwise your room may be let to someone else.)
6. Ask for precise instructions for *locating the house*, many are remote. Better still, ask for a brochure with map to be posted to you. Check where to park.

> **At houses where dinner is not served, a very good snack or sandwich supper can often be obtained (if ordered in advance).**

YOU AND THE LAW

Once your booking has been confirmed – orally or in writing – a contract exists between you and the proprietor. He is legally bound to provide accommodation as booked; and you are legally bound to pay for this accommodation. If you are unable to take up the booking – even if through sickness – you still remain liable for a very substantial proportion of the charges (in addition to losing your deposit).

If you have to cancel, let the proprietor know as soon as possible; then he may be able to re-let the accommodation (in which case you would be liable to pay only a re-letting cost or forfeit your deposit). Phone if you are going to arrive late.

A note to American readers. It may be an acceptable practice elsewhere to make bookings at several houses for the same date, choosing only later which one to patronize; but this way of doing things is not the British practice and you are legally liable to compensate any proprietors whom you let down in this way – see above.

READER PARTICIPATION

1 It would be very helpful if you will let me know your opinion of places from this book at which you have stayed. Please also tell me if you experience difficulties in making bookings. Please post this to: Elizabeth Gundrey (SOTBT), 19 Fitzjohns Avenue, London NW3 5JY (no phone calls please!). If you wish for an acknowledgment please enclose a stamped addressed envelope.

Names of establishments

Your comments (with date of stay)

2 If you find other places you think I should visit, for possible inclusion in a future edition, please will you either send me their brochure or give your own description (including price and address). No expensive places, please.

Your name and address (capitals): _____

_____

Date: _____ Occupation (optional): _____

READERS' LETTERS:
A SMALL SELECTION

My wife and I have never travelled to England without the latest edition of 'The Bible'; in fact, I purchase a copy even when I can't get away.

Many thanks for providing such a useful book. Thanks to you we have had some really marvellous breaks, comfortable accommodation, good food and reasonably priced.

Such a first-class book – which on several occasions has kept me sane through a very traumatic year.

I now always arrange accommodation through SOTBT.

I have used your book extensively, given copies to others, and recommended it to many more. It is by far the best guidebook available.

My husband and I have been disciples of yours since receiving our copy of 'Staying Off the Beaten Track' – much gratitude to you from both of us.

I look forward to putting you to the test again, though I may say I get nearly as much fun out of browsing through your book as I do out of 'using' it!

I sometimes have to travel to aerospace companies in the U.K. and whenever possible use your excellent book to find suitable accommodation.

We would like to thank you for all the trouble you take over your descriptions, it is much appreciated and we recommend your book to all we meet.

Ever since the publication of the first edition of 'Staying Off the Beaten Track', my wife and I have stayed in many of the places in the book, and without exception have been entirely satisfied. What we have found so interesting is that each one has its own individual character, and in addition we usually find the guests are people of interest.

Having for several years now made great use of your book, I felt I should write and say what pleasure it has given us. We have never been let down.

From Richard T. Quinlan, proprietor of The Mill (Mungrisdale, Cumbria):
The season is going very well with lots of bookings from 'Staying Off the Beaten Track' and without fail, those guests tell us how much they enjoy using your guide and how reliable they find it.

And from Brigitte Skan, proprietor of the prestigious Chewton Glen Hotel (New Milton, Hampshire):
On a cycling tour, we stayed in a couple of b & bs in SOTBT. We have never stayed in private homes and we enjoyed it enormously. Thank you for having advised us so well.

THE WESTERN ISLES (and beyond)

The *Hebridean Princess* is the only hotel ship cruising British waters.

The *Princess* is a luxurious but small ship (two dozen cabins). Cruises are of 3, 4 or 7 days, weaving in and out among Scotland's isles from Arran to the Outer Hebrides and Orkneys. Every view delights: snow tops the far peaks while evening sunlight shines upon colourful waterfront cottages or the grim towers of some lonely castle; against bright blue skies, passing clouds turn the green-gold foothills to purple and back again; wheeling gulls are as snowy white as the spotless paintwork of the ship. A totally serene and relaxing holiday.

The effect is of a 5-star hotel but with much more personal attention, and no affectation. A typical dinner: salmon mousse, pheasant breast in Madeira, soufflé crêpes, and Scottish cheeses. Fish is particularly good. Bread, gâteaux at teatime and petits fours with coffee are all baked in the galley. An occasional barbecue or champagne party are surprise treats. And absolutely no garish entertainments!

In 1990 about six different cruises will be run between spring and autumn. Shore visits are frequent, for sightseeing, walking or birdwatching (usually the ship anchors offshore and one is taken by boat).

Even the simplest cabins ('Yachtsman's') are roomy enough for two beds (not bunks) while at the other extreme is a suite ('Arran') with sitting-room, elegantly draped beds, TV/video, and so forth. All passengers enjoy every amenity – big lounge, well-chosen library, and the company of like-minded people.

Prices range from £225 (3 nights, Yachtsman's cabin, autumn) to £1995 (7 nights, Arran suite, high season). Singles pay no more than a person sharing, if they book a Yachtsman's cabin. And *for SOTBT readers only*, the following voucher can be used for a Yachtsman's cabin.

A colourful 24-page brochure is obtainable from Hebridean Island Cruises, Bank Newton, Skipton, BD23 3NT (tel: 0756 748077).

Book early: cabins are few.

£50 / £25

This voucher is worth £50 per cabin towards payment for 7 nights in a Yachtsman's cabin; or £25 for a 3/4 night cruise.

SPECIAL REQUIREMENTS

(see code letters after names of houses)

C D H PT S S-C X

Code letters after the names of houses indicate which ones are (in alphabetical order) likely to prove suitable for families with *children* (**C**), *dogs* (**D**) or *handicapped people* (**H**); and for those who, being without a car, depend upon *public transport* (**PT**). (In the case of children, a minimum age is sometimes stipulated, in which case this has been indicated by a numeral: thus **C**(5) means children over 5 are accepted.) **S** indicates those that charge singles no more, or only 10% more, than half a double (except, possibly, at peak periods). Some houses additionally have *self-catering* accommodation available (**S-C**); some accept visitors at *Christmas* (**X**), but do not necessarily provide Christmas meals.

In most cases, places that accept *children* (**C**) offer reduced rates and special meals. They may provide cots, high chairs and even baby-listening; or games and sports for older children. Please enquire when booking. And do not expect a toddler to be regarded as a (free) baby.

For *dogs* (**D**) a charge is rarely made, but often it is a stipulation that you must ask before bringing one; and the dog may have to sleep in your car, or be banned from public rooms.

Handicapped people vary in their needs. Wherever I have used the code letter **H**, this indicates that not only is there a ground-floor bedroom and bathroom but that these, and doorways, have sufficient width for a wheel-chair, and that steps are few. For precise details, ask when booking.

It is not necessary to have a car in order to get off the beaten track because public transport is widely available: hotels indicated by the code **PT** have a railway station or coach stop within a reasonable distance, from which you can walk or take a taxi (quite a number of hosts will even pick you up, free, in their own car). The symbol **PT** further indicates that there are also some nearby buses to use for local sightseeing, but these may be few. Ask for details when booking.

ALPHABETICAL DIRECTORY OF HOUSES AND HOTELS IN
ENGLAND

Prices are the **minimum** per person
in a double room, at the beginning of
the year. You may be quoted more
for the best rooms, particularly after
spring.

ABBEY BRIDGE INN

C(5) D PT S X

Lanercost, north of Brampton, Cumbria, CA8 2HG   Tel: 06977 2224

5 bedrooms (single or double) from £16. Rooms have central heating; own bathroom (two); armchairs; views of country or garden. Tea in bed is available.
Dinner A la carte. Vegetarian or special diets if ordered. Lunches, packed lunches, snacks. Coffee, tea, for a charge. Drinks can be ordered.
2 sitting-rooms with central heating, open fire, TV, books; bar.
Nearest main road A69 from Hexham to Brampton.

Where two rivers converge to the sound of rushing water, there is an old hump-backed bridge of red sandstone built in the time of James II. The traffic ignores it, hurrying across over a modern bridge further along. From it you can see part-ruined Lanercost Priory, or leave it to walk along riverside paths. Right here, Mr and Mrs Arthur run the Abbey Bridge Inn. Its name has been changed at least five times – once, when the reforming Countess of Carlisle made it 'dry', it was called the Temperance Hotel.

It's a snug place to stay, particularly when log fires are blazing in the lounges, or after a day's strenuous walking in the Border hills. The bedrooms are simply furnished. The Arthurs' first achievement was the renovation of what was once a blacksmith's forge, dating back to the 17th century, where meals (other than breakfast) are served to residents and non-residents. It is a barn-like building with gnarled rafters and white-painted walls. The bar (with real ale) and sitting-area downstairs are made cosy by a big iron stove. Up a specially made wrought-iron spiral staircase is a gallery where one eats beneath wrought-iron chandeliers with flickering electric candles. You can have either very good bar snacks; or a dinner including home-made pâté, venison and a fruity dessert, for instance.

Drinks or coffee can be enjoyed sitting under sun-umbrellas on the old bridge itself; or in the garden, frequented by the Arthurs' Great Dane. Across the way they have created, in an ancient stone building, a crafts centre with tearoom beneath it.

As well as scenic walks or drives, and the beautiful priory, there is plenty to do or see in the area: 14th-century Naworth Castle, Hadrian's Wall with Roman forts, the Saxon church at Over Denton, and historic villages like Gilsland and Bewcastle with Roman remains. Bewcastle has a decorated stone cross which is one of Britain's greatest Saxon treasures. In the river at Corby Castle on the way to Carlisle are salmon-traps built by 12th-century monks and still in use today. The road from Brampton to Alston is particularly attractive, running alongside the South Tyne River, with views of the northernmost Pennines. There is a good garden centre at Hexham. The new 'dig' at Birdoswald Roman fort is near the inn, a particularly interesting site (with interpretation centre) where one can see the dig in process.

Readers' comments: A wonderful stay. Very high standard, excellent food, thoroughly to be recommended. Exceptional interest in the well-being of guests; outstanding value for money. Well ordered; Mrs Arthur gives a warm welcome and caters for guests as individuals. Quite wonderful.

ABBEY HOUSE

Monk Soham, north-west of Woodbridge, Suffolk, IP13 7EN
Tel: 072882 225

3 bedrooms (double or family) from £15. Less for 6 nights. Rooms have central heating; bathroom (in one); armchairs; tea/coffee facilities; views of country or garden.
Dinner £8.50 for 4 courses and coffee, at 7–8pm. Vegetarian or special diets if ordered. Lunches, packed lunches, snacks. Coffee, tea, free. Drinks can be brought in.
Sitting-room with central heating, open fire, TV, books. Piano in dining-room.
Large garden and meadows with croquet, swimming-pool.
Nearest main road A1120 from Stowmarket to Yoxford.

'Fish, fish, do your duty!' the rector who lived here in the late 19th century used to admonish the inhabitants of his ponds (still there), which had originally provided Friday food for monks at the abbey (long vanished). This and other anecdotes of his life at Abbey House are in a book by his son which Sue Bagnall shows her visitors. It was he who planted the huge oaks, beeches and limes in the grounds. The architect was Teulon, a high Victorian gothicist.

Sue and her husband have made the old mansion comfortable and have furnished it with antiques, but keeping the atmosphere informal. Among fine old features they have restored is a magnificent cast-iron fireplace in the dining-room. Colours are soft (pale buff or shell pink, for instance). Sue, a former nurse, cooks traditional English meals (using their own meat and vegetables) such as artichoke soup, steak-and-kidney pie, lemon ice cream and cheeses. (Not on Sundays.)

Guests are welcome to look at the livestock which includes Jersey cows (calves sometimes), sheep, pigs, turkeys, chickens, ducks, black swans and peafowl.

The Norfolk Broads are within reach; historic Norwich and its cathedral; bird reserves along the coast; old-fashioned seaside towns like Southwold and Aldeburgh; Lowestoft with its sands and its busy fishing port. Inland are famous beauty-spots like the villages of Lavenham and Kersey or Dedham Vale ('Constable country').

Other sights include Somerleyton and Helmingham halls, Framlingham and Orford castles, Bressingham Steam Museum (with gardens), the Otter Trust, wildlife or farm parks, Saxtead windmill, rural crafts, vineyards and inns.

Readers' comments: Delightful.

Nearby is **Monk Soham Hall** (tel: 072 882 358), a very pleasant Tudor farmhouse where in addition to other bedrooms Gay Clarke has created, in a beamed ground-floor room opening on to garden and moat, a bedroom and bathroom fully equipped for disabled people.

rear view

3

ALEXA HOUSE

26 Ripon Road, Harrogate, North Yorkshire, HG2 2JJ Tel: 0423 501988

C H PT S

12 bedrooms (single, double or family) from £18. Much less (outside summer) for 2 nights or bargain breaks. Rooms have central heating or electric heaters; shower or bathroom; TV, armchairs; tea/coffee-making facilities.
Sitting-room with central heating, gas fire, TV, books, record-player; bar.
Small garden
Nearest main road A61 from Leeds to Ripon.

Dating from 1830, this house is typical of many such solidly built and handsome private homes which later became small hotels in Yorkshire's famous spa town. It has been furnished by Marilyn Bateson with an eye to her guests' comfort (generous armchairs in the bedrooms, for instance) more than to elegance.

In the cheerful breakfast-room, Marilyn recently uncovered a pink-and-white marble fireplace, and added silver chandeliers. As to dinner, she gives visitors a street map with nearby recommended restaurants marked on it: Harrogate has a very wide choice.

Behind the house are some small new rooms (very neatly designed) ideal not only for visitors wanting quiet, but also for disabled guests – with sitz baths and grab-rails, for instance. (Marilyn was once a teacher of physically handicapped children, and understands what is needed.)

A clerical visitor wrote to Marilyn after his first stay: 'I have never fared better since I once spent a weekend at Balmoral. Both hostesses proved to be most charming and kind, but I think you have the edge over HM for you did not feel disposed to discuss my sermon with me!'

Elegant Harrogate is full of shops selling antiques and other luxuries. Its award-winning gardens and flowery parks are famous; it has a large, modern entertainments centre; and it is an ideal centre from which to explore the Yorkshire Dales and such famous sights as Fountains Abbey, Ripon Cathedral, Harewood House, Harlow Car gardens and, of course, the city of York as well as Bolton Abbey, Ripley Castle, Newby Hall and Knaresborough.

Readers' comments: Every comfort, and super food. Courteous welcome, we had an excellent time – our stay surpassed all others. Excellent food and facilities. Well furnished, comfortable; quieter at the back. Will return whenever possible; refreshingly friendly atmosphere, staff happy to please.

Inclusive terms for dinner, bed-and-breakfast (particularly for a week) can be much lower than those quoted here for these items taken separately. For short-notice bookings you may be able to get a reduction.

No proprietor wants to have a room standing empty. This particularly applies to Sunday nights. Some hotels make a discount if you want only two courses from a three-course menu.

4

ALFOXTON COTTAGE

Holford, west of Bridgwater, Somerset, TA5 1SG   Tel: 027874 418

4 bedrooms (single or double) from £13. Less for 4 nights. All have central heating and views of sea, country or garden. No smoking. (Washing-machine on request.)
Dinner £12 for 4 courses and coffee, at 7pm. Non-residents not admitted. Vegetarian or special diets if ordered. Tea, coffee, free. Wine can be ordered or brought in.
Sitting-room with central heating, open fire, books, piano, record-player. No smoking.
Small garden
Nearest main road A39 from Bridgwater to Minehead.

The cottage is truly remote, right up in the Quantock Hills with views across the Bristol Channel to Wales. You may believe you are never coming to it as you follow twists and turns up the small wooded lane to the top of the hill.

This little house is now the home of Richard and Angela Delderfield who started Little Byres in Sussex (in previous editions of this book). Rooms are small and low but pleasantly furnished – for instance, bamboo or velvet bedheads; a grandfather clock and flounced armchairs by the log fire in the white sitting-room, from which a door leads to the garden, woods, a trickling stream, donkeys and chickens.

Angela's cooking is one of the main attractions of staying here. She sometimes serves as a starter prawns in a creamy sauce containing whisky, or perhaps chilled lettuce soup. Chicken breasts will be stuffed with cashew and brazil nuts, raisins, herbs and lemon juice. Into her salads may go unusual ingredients such as spinach, sunflower seeds or hot crisp bacon with slivers of avocado. She makes flans of rhubarb and lemon, rum and almonds, or orange and almonds.

All round the cottage are the Quantock Hills and pretty hamlets, the very first area of Britain to get official designation as an area of outstanding natural beauty. Alfoxton House (now a hotel) was tenanted by Wordsworth and his sister in 1797. They frequently walked here on their way to visit Coleridge who was busy writing *The Ancient Mariner* and *Kubla Khan* at Nether Stowey (his cottage now belongs to the National Trust). Some of Wordsworth's best poems, the *Lyrical Ballads*, were inspired by the Quantocks. The area is ideal for walking and for wildlife-spotting (red deer roam here) and wildflowers are abundant. Within a short drive are Exmoor, Dartmoor, the fenland known as the Somerset Levels, and the coast – including Watchet's active little harbour, cliffs and sands (Cleeve Abbey's Norman remains are in this direction). There are idyllic finds to be made up many a secluded lane – for instance, East Quantoxhead's cottages around a duckpond. Nether Stowey has a ruined castle, prehistoric earthworks, two mediaeval mansions and a stream; beyond it is Stogursey with priory church and castle. Let Wordsworth have the last word about Alfoxton:

> 'Through primrose tufts, in that green bower,
> The periwinkle trailed its wreaths;
> And 'tis my faith that every flower
> Enjoys the air it breathes.'

Readers' comments: A wonderful establishment. A lovely home in a beautiful area. Very hospitable, food and service excellent. Friendly and genuine people.

ALMSHOUSE
off The Square, Axbridge, north-west of Glastonbury, Somerset, BS26 2AR
Tel: 0934 732493

3 bedrooms (double or family) from £15. Less for 4 nights. Rooms have central heating and tea/coffee facilities.
Dinner (Friday and Saturday only.) A la carte from 7pm. Snacks. Tea, coffee, extra. Drinks can be ordered.
Sitting-room with central heating, open fire, TV, books; bar.
Nearest main road A38 from Bristol to Bridgwater.

Not long ago this impressive 15th-century building was near collapse. Into its restoration went authentic materials and techniques, and quite a bit of historical research into its origins. As restoration proceeded, mediaeval hearths and a garderobe (toilet) with drains were uncovered. A gallery (made out of old timbers from a church) makes it possible for visitors to get a close-up view of the superb roof timbers. The quarry from which stone for the pointed mullion windows had come five centuries ago provided stone for replacement mullions – the stonemason was a man who has worked on Windsor Castle and Westminster Abbey. The window glass was hand-made, some with heraldic devices of monastic orders associated with the Almshouse. Even the heavy tables in the restaurant, which is what the Almshouse has now become, were hand-made from English oak. At the back is a small courtyard, with white iron tables and chairs for meals.

Resident visitors are accommodated in the adjoining house, the home of the proprietors (Nigel and Janet Hillier). On its ground floor is a long, beamed sitting-room with stone walls, large inglenook fireplace and flagstone floor. Above are bedrooms with brimming window boxes on every sill overlooking The Square.

The beamy restaurant, decorated with an abundance of dried flowers, serves bistro-type snacks mid-week but on Fridays and Saturdays an accomplished chef cooks sophisticated meals. Choices include such things as oak-smoked venison or exotic fruits with lime sorbet to start with; fish such as brill or mullet, or lamb cutlets in a sauce of sorrel, mint, cream and wine (there are always vegetarian alternatives); and guava ice cream.

Pretty little Axbridge is on the edge of the Mendip Hills and very close to the Cheddar Gorge. Around its square are ancient byways, old buildings and a museum of local bygones. The Gorge (for the finest view, approach it from the north) has a number of caves with stalactites, in rich colours; Stone Age men lived in these caves and some of their tools and weapons are on show.

Readers' comments: Delightful accommodation, tastefully decorated. Superb cooking. Terrific value.

For explanation of code letters (**C, D, H, PT, S, S-C, X**) see page xxvi

ANCIENT CAMP INN

Ruckhall, west of Hereford, HR2 9QX   Tel: 0981 250449

3 bedrooms (single, double or family) from £18.75. All have own bath/shower; TV; tea/coffee facilities; phone; central heating; views of country or garden. (Washing-machine on request.)
Dinner A la carte at 7–9.30pm. Vegetarian or special diets if ordered. Lunches, packed lunches, snacks. Drinks can be ordered.
Sitting-room with central heating, TV, books. Large bar area with open fires.
Large garden
Nearest main road A465 from Hereford to Abergavenny.

Few establishments in this book have such a superb view as this one. The inn is perched 80 feet above a bend of the lovely River Wye, with seats on a terrace from which to enjoy the spectacle – drink in hand. A wooded path follows the river for over a mile.

As to the old inn itself, David and Nova Hague have created an excellent atmosphere by blending modern with ancient, and adding personal possessions which contribute to its character. Stone walls and a flagstone floor contrast with green upholstered chairs and soft lighting. There are open fires, pot-plants on barrels, pewter mugs hanging on the beams, photographs of David's sailing boats and a big watercolour of the historic textile mill in Oldham where he used to work. At one end is a carpeted area with sofas. The bedrooms, modern in style, are particularly well equipped and one is a suite – it has its own sitting-room with William Morris sofa and chairs from which to enjoy the river view. The food, too, is rather special: even the bar snacks (for instance, oxtail; or ham and celery au gratin). From the à la carte dinner menu one might choose such dishes as suckling-pig in port sauce, monkfish kebabs or rack of lamb.

Popular though the inn is for meals (and only 10 minutes from the city of Hereford), it is totally silent and secluded at night because no road runs past it. It stands in its own five acres (which include part of the River Wye, with fishing rights), on the site of an Iron Age camp dating from 400 BC, with another in view across the river; and on a wall of the inn is a display explaining the prehistory of the area.

Ruckhall is in one of England's most scenic areas, the lush Golden Valley contrasting with the awesome splendours of the Black Mountains nearby. .

View from Ancient Camp Inn

ANGEL CORNER   C

17 Market Place, Lavenham, north-east of Sudbury, Suffolk, CO10 9RH
Tel: 0787 247168

3 bedrooms (double or family) from £14. Less for 4 nights and bargain breaks. All have tea/coffee facilities; central heating. (Washing-machine on request.)
Dinner £8.50 for 3 courses and coffee, at 7pm or later. Non-residents not admitted. Vegetarian or special diets if ordered. Lunches, packed lunches, snacks. Tea, coffee, free. Drinks can be brought in.
Sitting-room with central heating, open fire, TV, books.
Small garden
Nearest main road A134 from Sudbury to Bury St Edmunds.
Closed in December and January

In the Middle Ages, Suffolk grew rich on wool and woollen cloth. As a result, and in Lavenham above all other villages, the county is full of splendid mediaeval churches and the houses of wealthy merchants.

This house, built in 1482 – the year before Richard III became King – is one of the finest, its name taken from the adjoining Angel Inn to which it was once connected by the round-arched doorways you can still see in its large entrance hall.

To the left of this are the sitting- and dining-rooms, with log fire, beams and quaint carved figures decorating one of the doorways. Here and upstairs are blue-and-white Delft tiles, and views of the informal, brick-walled cottage garden at the back (only one bedroom overlooks the market square and its old preaching cross – busy by day but quiet once the throngs of day-visitors have gone). Beyond an oak-panelled door in the hall are narrow stairs and passages leading to pretty bedrooms.

Although there are a number of eating-places in Lavenham, Maureen Bourne will prepare dinner if this is ordered in advance, cooking such dishes as deep-fried mushrooms (served with cucumber and mint yogurt), chicken breasts in orange sauce, and summer pudding.

Just across the square is the town's great half-timbered Guildhall which houses a museum of wool history. The resplendent Wool Hall where merchants traded is now part of the big Swan Hotel, which has notable music recitals. The church owes much of its splendours to benefactions made as atonement by a cloth-merchant (who, in the reign of Henry VII, got rich by giving short measure and other sharp practices): in return he had his coat-of-arms carved 36 times on the high tower. Constable went to the grammar school in Lavenham; Shilling Street is named for a Flemish weaver who taught the English clothmaking skills (Jane Taylor, who wrote 'Twinkle, Twinkle, Little Star' lived here in the 18th century); Prentice Street is lined with cottages where apprentices lodged. One wanders through lanes of colourful, half-timbered and lopsided houses little changed since the 15th century, some embellished with symbols of the crafts once carried on in them (for instance, the comb of St Blaise – a patron of clothworkers because he was tortured with wool-combs). With the introduction of machine-weaving (powered by coal, which is not found in this region), prosperity deserted Lavenham – which is why, fortunately for us, its ancient buildings were never replaced with 18th- or 19th-century 'improvements'.

APPLETREE COTTAGE

12 Shitterton, Bere Regis, south of Blandford Forum, Dorset, BH20 7HU
Tel: 0929 471686

C S

2 bedrooms (double or family) from £12.50. Less for 4 nights. Rooms have central heating; views of country or garden. Coffee, tea, for a charge.
Sitting-room with central heating, open fire, TV, piano.
Nearest main road A35 from Dorchester to Poole.

rear view

This is a real Hansel-and-Gretel style cottage – thick cob (clay) walls and thatched roof, with honeysuckle clambering round the pink front door. It was built in the 17th century and was a tiny inn when the little lane outside was a coaching road, and is now a listed building.

Inside, all ceilings are low, and walls slope. The breakfast-table is in the sitting-room, which has silky patchwork cushions on the velvet armchairs gathered around the inglenook with log stove. The very modern bathroom (its chocolate-brown suite includes a bidet) is also on the ground floor. Bedrooms have sprigged wallpapers, beams and board doors, and overlook the pretty garden with flagstone steps leading to the lawn. For evening meals, Beryl Wilson recommends two inns in the hamlet, especially the Royal Oak.

Bere is about half way between Poole and Dorchester, the environs of which are described elsewhere in this book. Lulworth Cove, T. E. Lawrence's cottage, Hardy country, good walks, pretty villages like Milton Abbas, a parachute club, seaside resorts and mellow old towns are all within easy reach as well as Bovington Tank Museum, Corfe Castle, Kingston Lacy House (and garden). Garden-lovers will enjoy Abbotsbury, Compton Acres, Athelhampton, and Galtons garden centre. The area has many antique shops, and pick-your-own farms.

Bere Regis is where the d'Urbervilles are buried and 'Tess' was filmed here. Hardy re-named it Kingsbere ('a little one-eyed, blinking sort o' place') and here the story begins with old Farmer Durbeyfield boasting, 'Under the church of that there parish lie my ancestors – hundreds of 'em – in coats of mail and jewels, in gr't lead coffins weighing tons and tons. There's not a man in the county of South Wessex that's got grander and nobler skillentons in his family than I.'

Don't complain if –
- – because you booked at short notice, you do not get the best room
- – because you did not order a meal in advance, you get something plucked from the freezer
- – because you do not arrive on time, your room is let to someone else
- – because you bring a dog without asking, it is refused entry
- – because you don't express your wishes (for more heat, a second helping or whatever), you don't get what you want!

9

APSE MANOR

west of Shanklin, Isle of Wight, PO37 7PN   Tel: 0983 866651

rear view

5 bedrooms (double or family) from £18 **to SOTBT readers** only. Bargain breaks. Rooms have central heating; own bathroom; TV, armchairs; phones; views of country or garden. Four-poster suite.
Dinner £8 for 5 courses and coffee, at 6.45pm. Vegetarian diets can be prepared. Coffee, tea, and drinks can be ordered.

Sitting-room with central heating, open fire, books.
Large garden
Nearest main road A3020 from Shanklin to Newport.

Until recently, this fine Tudor mansion was a farmhouse but it has since been renovated – Sue Boynton will show you her albums of 'before' and 'after' pictures as you sit by the log fire blazing in a huge inglenook that was one of the features uncovered and restored. This is in a great room with coffered ceiling and stone-mullioned windows, the other end of which is used for dining (buttoned banquettes of cream velvet surround tables with lace over crimson cloths).

A corridor, still with a long row of bells to summon servants, leads to bedrooms which have flowery wallpapers and light colour schemes; one has a four-poster. The main entrance hall serves as a bar – you help yourself and write down what you have taken.

The choices at dinner by candlelight may include plaice goujons or home-made pâté to start with; pork cooked with cider, apples and cream; then perhaps crème caramel or profiteroles and cheeses. Sue, who used to do large-scale catering, says she much prefers cooking for smaller numbers to higher standards, often using produce straight from the garden.

The surroundings are attractive, from the flowerbeds by the drive, with cupid statues here and there, to the stone verandah with view of a stream below.

Readers' comments: Very comfortable and well appointed. Friendly hosts, strongly recommended.

About a mile northward is **The Grange**, Alverstone; an immaculate guest-house where Geraldine Watling provides good home cooking (tel: 0983 403729).
Readers' comments: Effortless efficiency. Relaxed and happy atmosphere. Imaginative cooking. Warm and welcoming. Excellent accommodation, wonderful food.

APSLEY MANOR FARM   C S
North Lee Lane, Marsh, south of Aylesbury, Buckinghamshire, HP22 5YA
Tel: 029661 3209

2 bedrooms (single or double) from £15.50. Both have own bath or shower; tea/coffee facilities; central heating; views of country or garden. No smoking.
Sitting-room with central heating and open fire. No smoking.

Large garden
Nearest main road A4010 from High Wycombe to Aylesbury.

The sun was filtering through mossy treetrunks and onto fallen copper leaves (a typical Chilterns scene in autumn) as I made my way to the Perrins' brick-and-timber farmhouse, built in 1486 or earlier. Outside, nerines and jasmine, tubs of lobelias on paving-stones, and a great barn with rust-red roof added their colours to the scene.

Inside are pale carpets, pine bedroom fitments and immaculate paintwork which contrast with ancient features carefully retained – such as chamfered beams in the breakfast-room, old quarry-tiled floors and the log fire. On the walls are views painted by a local artist (these are for sale) and in an alcove the family's silver cups – for riding, sailing and the milking herd. The sitting-room is particularly beautiful. Beyond its sliding glass doors is a paved terrace, lawn with haha to keep the sheep at a respectful distance, and the remains of a moat (home to freshwater mussels) which once went all round the house. Beyond all this and an orchard are splendid views of the Chiltern Hills, topped by a monument and the long-distance Ridgeway Path for keen walkers.

Bed-and-breakfast only: for an outstanding dinner, go to the famous Bell at Aston Clinton; or to local inns.

The country town of Aylesbury must be explored on foot if you want to discover the Tudor lanes and courtyards at its heart, around the old church and market square. It has a part-mediaeval inn (the King's Head) run by the National Trust, with 15th-century stained glass. The Trust also owns property in Long Crendon, a village of rose-covered cottages, a long bridge and several fine houses; while at Waddesdon is the château-like Rothschild mansion on a high hill (from another, at nearby Upper Winchendon, is a fine view of the Thames Valley). Wendover is a quaint, timbered town from which one can get to the summit of Coombe Hill – one of the heights of the Chiltern Hills, celebrated for the copper tints of their beeches in autumn. Princes Risborough is another town with much timbering and thatch surviving in the centre, where there is an arcaded market hall with elegant cupola (the Prime Minister's country house, Chequers, is near here); and Little Missenden is well worth a visit, particularly when marsh marigolds glow along the riverbanks.

ASHLEIGH HOUSE

C(5) **D X**

Whitley Hill, Henley-in-Arden, west of Warwick, Warwickshire, B95 5DL
Tel: 05642 2315

6 bedrooms (double or family) and another 4 in a converted coach house, from £18. Rooms have central heating; shower or bath; TV, armchairs; phones; views of farmland or garden. Tea-making facilities.
Sitting-room with central heating, and reading-room with books.
Large garden
Nearest main road A34 from Stratford-upon-Avon to Birmingham.

This handsome Edwardian mansion, once the home of a Birmingham merchant, stands well back from the road, on top of a hill with fine views. Since Colin Eades, a retired accountant, took it over (together with his partner Francisco Garcia, who used to run a restaurant) it has been immaculately restored and filled with Edwardian – and earlier – antiques as well as flowers. On my last visit, I thought it even better than before: its hospitable owners, the immaculate and handsome rooms, the outstanding garden.

Francisco in particular enjoys spending time with visitors and giving them sound advice on where to go hunting for antiques in this well-supplied area – also on where to dine in Henley or elsewhere (I ate well at Grubb's). Only snack suppers are served.

Every bedroom is furnished in keeping with the style of this spacious, solid house and all the original features have been retained – shuttered bay windows, panelled doors, turned banisters, for example.

There is good walking country all around, an 18th-century canal for boats, historic Henley-in-Arden itself (it has the longest village street in England), Stratford-upon-Avon, great Warwick Castle, Birmingham, the National Exhibition Centre, Ragley Hall, Packwood House, Baddesley Clinton, and all the countryside associated with Edith Holden's *Country Diary of an Edwardian Lady*. Head for the Vale of Evesham if you want pick-your-own fruit farms.

There are many good drives from Henley-in-Arden. For instance, the road to Stratford-upon-Avon goes through Wootton Wawen with a church dating back to the time of King Canute, Aston Cantlow (Shakespeare's parents were married in its church), Great Alne where you can buy stone-ground flour at the watermill, Alcester (at Coughton Court are relics of the gunpowder plotters and of Mary Queen of Scots, and at Ragley Hall an outstanding modern mural in a Palladian setting), Wixford (good food at the riverside Fish Inn), Shottery (Anne Hathaway's cottage) and Wilmcote (where Shakespeare's mother lived): what a lot to see in so few miles.

Readers' comments: Very warm welcome, excellent food. Good value. Converted stables are delightful; breakfast beautifully served; congenial atmosphere. So welcoming and restful.

> Prices are the minimum *per person* in a double room at the beginning of the year.

Limpley Stoke, south of Bath (Avon), Wiltshire, BA3 6EX
Tel: 0225 722547

2 bedrooms (double) from £15. Less for 4 nights. Rooms have central heating and electric heaters; armchairs, views of country and garden.
Dinner £9.50 for 3 courses, wine and coffee, at 8pm. Afternoon tea free. Non-residents not admitted. Drinks can be brought in.

Sitting-room with central heating, open fire, books, piano.
Large garden and orchard, with hard tennis court, croquet and coarse fishing.
Nearest main road A36 from Bath to Warminster.

A typical English country house, built of honey-coloured Bath stone, the Challens' secluded home stands on the banks of the River Avon: walks along it (or the nearby Kennet and Avon Canal) are one of the attractions of staying in this very scenic area.

Ursula has furnished the sitting-room with tangerine or pale lime armchairs, oriental rugs and antiques that show up well against walls painted peach, on which hang many paintings by Peter who, after serving as a major in the Gurkhas, turned to a completely different career as an artist. Through the bay window is a serene view of the well-kept lawn and landscaped grounds.

Other rooms are equally pleasing, with attractive wallpapers and leafy views. The Challens treat visitors as if they were house guests, offering them pre-dinner drinks and wine (no extra charge). Typical of the kind of meal Ursula serves: avocado pâté; roast lamb with quince jelly and vegetables from the garden; a brûlée of brown sugar, cream and yogurt over raspberries. Alternatively, visitors can go out to the excellent Nightingales restaurant in the village or to the Hop Pole inn.

At Bradford-on-Avon several steep roads converge downhill to the mediaeval bridge with domed chapel on it. It takes time to discover all Bradford's handsome houses, Saxon church, vast tithe barn and old inns. A few miles away is Bath, and, northward, such other lovely spots as Corsham, Lacock (mediaeval abbey, and museum of photographic history) and the Chippenham-Calne area. Garden-lovers head for Stourhead, antique-hunters for Bath. Malmesbury (on a hill almost surrounded by the River Avon) has its famous Norman abbey and handsome stone houses from the 17th and 18th centuries lining its streets and market square. Longleat, Dereham Manor and the historic American Museum are popular.

Readers' comments: Wonderful people, very friendly. Elegant; lovely meals. The Challens make one feel like their house guests. Excellent accommodation and food.

BANK COTTAGE

Bryher, Isles of Scilly, TR23 0PR   Tel: 0720 22612

C S PT(boat)

5 **bedrooms** (double or single) from £13. Rooms have central heating or electric heaters; TV, armchairs; own bathroom; views of sea and garden.
Dinner £6 for 4 courses and coffee, at 6.30pm. Special diets if ordered. Lunches, packed lunches, snacks. Coffee, tea, soft drinks, free. Non-residents not admitted. Wine can be ordered.
Sitting-room with TV, books.
Garden with badminton.
Closed in winter

Even a millionaire might have a long search before finding somewhere to stay in quite such an idyllic situation as this little guest-house on Rushy Bay. Visitors here have a superb sandy beach (right outside) virtually all to themselves: when I was there, I encountered only one other couple on the golden, sunny sands. And beyond it is one of England's most beautiful seascapes, dotted with 22 islets.

Mac Mace works as a diver: sometimes diving for lobsters and crabs or for archaeological finds, including Spanish doubloons, on the many nearby wrecks; sometimes for sea urchins, the decorative shells of which are exported by the thousand. He and his wife Tracy take a few guests in their cottage (built at least 300 years ago, but with later additions). The rooms are simple, with low ceilings and thick walls to keep winter's gales at bay. Bedrooms are cheerful and bright.

Many visitors are content just to sit all day in the colourful garden (facing south-west) to enjoy the view of the bay, sheltered by the pink-flowered escallonia hedges; or they can accompany Mac when he is setting nets or fishing. The sunsets are outstanding. A gate opens onto the beach, but although the climate is warm here, the sea is not. There is a badminton lawn. The garden is at its most colourful in early summer (fuchsias, flowering cherries, tulips and arum lilies abound); the islets are best in late spring, when they are smothered in pink sea-thrift.

Vegetables and loganberries are home-grown, rolls home-baked, eggs from the Maces' hens. A typical meal cooked by Tracy may start with fish or fish pâté, followed by a roast or casserole. Tracy particularly enjoys making puddings like banana mousse or sherry trifle and her vegetarian meals are imaginative. Sometimes meals are served outdoors, using the granite barbecue.

Visitors arriving by boat from St Mary's are met and their baggage taken up for them by tractor or Landrover. The boats provide a service throughout winter (which can be mild and sunny, or with dramatic storms), but less frequently. Up to Easter, there are very few visitors; but even in summer Bryher is never crowded.

Readers' comments: Wished we could stay for ever! Felt completely at home; happy and relaxed atmosphere. Comfortable room, excellent food. Simply delighted, a marvellous time. Nothing is too much trouble. Excellent food and accommodation, good hosts. Now a regular and much-loved destination.

14

BANK VILLA

C(5) D

Masham, north-west of Ripon, North Yorkshire, HG4 4DB   Tel: 0765 89605

7 bedrooms (double) from £13.50. Less for 7 nights. Rooms have central heating; shower; armchairs; views of country or garden.
Dinner £11 for 3 courses, at 7.30pm. Vegetarian or special diets if ordered. Coffee, tea, for a charge. Non-residents not admitted. Drinks can be ordered.
2 sitting-rooms with central heating, TV, books.
Terraced gardens
Nearest main road A6108 from Ripon to Leyburn.
Closed in winter

Good food is the principal attraction at Bank Villa, where Phillip Gill (former administrator of York's arts festival) is an inspired cook.

The villa is a late Georgian stone house set back from the busy road, with a steep terraced garden behind it (where there is a sunny summerhouse in which to sit). Here are grown fruit and vegetables for the kitchen.

Dinner is served in a pleasant room – pretty 'Old Colonial' china and rush mats on the pine tables contrast with the deep raspberry walls. Phillip cooks, and his partner Anton serves, such delicious menus as spinach-and-cheese soufflé as a starter, smoked pork cooked with Calvados, and iced Drambuie parfait.

Bedrooms, too, are attractive but not smart, many with floral wallpapers and pine furniture, and some with a glimpse of the River Ure at the foot of the hill.

Masham, a little market town, has a church with interesting features; and, in mid-July, a traction-engine and steam fair. It stands at the beginning of Wensleydale, in an area of great historic as well as very varied scenic interest: within a few miles are two abbeys, three castles, one cathedral and a stately home, as well as the spa towns of Harrogate and Ripon. There are scenic roads, markets, the sight of racehorses exercising, waterfalls, a beautifully restored Georgian theatre (at Richmond) and fine gardens.

Bedale, which has had a market since the 13th century, is a town of pleasing buildings with a very fine church. Don't miss Fountains, finest of all the Yorkshire abbeys. Other nearby sights are Newby Hall, Ripon's cathedral, Middleham Castle, Brimham Rocks and Harlow Car gardens.

If you visit Ripon, you can hardly miss the big inscription over the market square: 'Except ye Lord keep ye cittie, ye Wakeman waketh in vain'. And if you are there at 9pm, you will see and hear the wakeman (i.e., watchman) blowing his buffalo horn and wearing a frock coat, a cocked hat, white gloves and a silver badge on his arm. The office dates back to Alfred the Great, who gave the city its first charter and a horn in AD 886. The wakeman was there to keep an all-night watch for Viking raiders, and he had to blow the horn to let the citizens know that he was on duty. The nocturnal patrol ceased centuries ago, but the horn-blowing continues. The wakeman's house, built in 1250, is now the city's tourist information centre. Below the cathedral is a Saxon crypt, all that remains of Ripon's first Christian church, which was destroyed by those same raiders, and in it is a fine monument to a wakeman of the past.

Readers' comments: A great start to our stages to Scotland: we'll be back. Food as good as in the priciest restaurants. Energetic, cheerful and efficient.

BARK HOUSE
Oakford Bridge, north of Tiverton, Devon, EX16 9HZ   Tel: 03985 236

6 bedrooms (single, double or family) from £17. Less for 7 nights. Some have own bath/shower; TV; central heating; views of river, country, garden. (Washing-machine on request.)
Dinner £11.25 for 3 courses (with choices) and coffee, at 8pm. Non-residents not admitted. Vegetarian or special diets if ordered. Lunches, packed lunches, snacks. Tea, coffee, extra. Drinks can be ordered.
Sitting-room with central heating, open fire, books, bar.
Large garden
Nearest main road A396 from Exeter to Minehead.
Closed in January and February

In a wooded valley through which runs the River Exe is a stone building of unusual origin. It was used as a tannery, the oak bark for which was brought from Exmoor Forest. Today, it has been handsomely converted; and Pauline and Douglas West provide visitors with complete comfort. Books, good pictures, thick Berber carpets, antiques, pot-plants and the flicker of a cheerful log fire set the scene.

In the dining-room brown and pink tablecloths contrast with white walls; around the tables are either pews or Windsor chairs. Every bedroom is different. No. 1 has a bow window with window-seat from which to enjoy the tranquil view; no. 4, art nouveau nymphs on the ceiling – however did *they* get there! No. 6 is a huge family room with its own ancient arched door to a rock garden with pool, and leaded casements.

Dinner may begin with smoked salmon mousse or fish chowder or eggs en cocotte (there are several choices at every course). With a daube of beef will be served potato galette and other vegetables. The fresh peach Melba has an orange-and-raspberry sauce. Because the Wests once lived in Provence, Pauline has many recipes from that region. (Breakfast is continental. English breakfast extra.)

From Bark House there is a particularly scenic route over moors to Minehead in Somerset. Both Exmoor and the sea are near; and so are Exeter, Taunton and Barnstaple, all described elsewhere. The area has a great many stately homes to visit, such as Knightshayes (NT), and gardens (Killerton); as well as churches and castles. Dunster village and Dartington are other popular outings. South Molton, a market town, has a number of good 18th-century buildings and fine views; North Molton likewise (derelict copper mines here); Swimbridge, a particularly rich church; outside Rose Ash is pretty Cuckoo Mill Bridge. The area is one for quiet enjoyment, largely undisturbed by traffic: thatched villages, stone manor houses, woods, cider orchards, trickling streams and lanes that wander up and down.

Readers' comments: Beautiful setting; excellent cooking; friendly and cheerful hosts. Have stayed four times. Charming hotel and surroundings.

BARNFIELD FARM
CS
near Charing, north-west of Ashford, Kent, TN27 0BN   Tel: 023371 2421

4 bedrooms (single, family or double) from £15. Rooms have central heating, electric heaters; armchairs; views of country or garden; tea/coffee facilities on request. (Clothes-washing facilities.) No smoking.

Dinner £8.50 for 3 courses and coffee, at 7pm or by arrangement. Vegetarian or special diets if ordered. Coffee, tea, for a charge. Drinks can be ordered. No smoking.

Sitting-rooms with central heating, open fire, TV, books, record-player. No smoking.

Garden with tennis; farmland.

Nearest main road A20 from Maidstone to Ashford.

This historic farmhouse was built about the time of the Battle of Agincourt (1415). It is so remarkable that sometimes coaches of overseas visitors come to see it; and even individual visitors are given a tour round by Martin Pym, who grew up here, or his wife Phillada.

One steps into a large hall, where the oak framework of the house is exposed to view (draped with hop bines) and a cask holding shepherds' crooks stands in one corner – for outside are sheep pastures, with arable fields beyond. The main sitting-room has an exceptionally large inglenook where logs blaze in front of a Cromwellian fireback; the original pot-hooks, soot-blackened, are still in place. Along one beam hangs a set of handbells, on which Christmas is rung in every year. The dining-room, too, has an open fire and ancient beams, with one especially fine door (linenfold panels contrasting with intricately carved foliage), made from a church chest. There is another sitting/dining-room for guests' use, comfortably furnished with deep cretonne armchairs, plenty of books and – like every room in the house – attractive objects.

The bedrooms are equally agreeable, and in two one can see the construction of the house very clearly: massive treetrunks, rough-hewn to shape, curve up to support the roof. Some overlook the River Stour on its way to Canterbury.

Some of the furnishings were made by Martin's grandmother – for instance, a screen of Victorian scraps in one room, and an intricate embroidery commemorating two Pyms who died in the First World War in another. An old linen-press, chests, rocking-chairs – at every turn of the wandering corridors there is something interesting to see. Outside are lawns, herbaceous borders surrounding a pool guarded by four stone owls, and a lake visited by ducks and Canada geese.

Phillada serves such meals as egg mayonnaise, casseroled lamb cutlets and apple fool with shortbread – loading a hot-tray on the sideboard so that guests can help themselves to as much as they wish.

The most popular nearby sights are Leeds Castle, Canterbury Cathedral, Sissinghurst, Chilham and Dover castles, and Godinton Park. (Bicycles on loan.)

At Charing are remains of the archbishop's palace where Henry VIII stayed en route to the Field of the Cloth of Gold (1520), and from Charing Hill are views across the Weald.

Readers' comments: Enjoyed our stay very much; a warm welcome. Unobtrusive but charming hostess. Delightful house and garden. Excellent meal. Nicely secluded position.

BARROW HILL FARM

Ramsdean, west of Petersfield, Hampshire, GU32 1RW Tel: 073087 340

C(8) D S

rear view

3 bedrooms (single or double) from £15. Less for 4 nights or more. Rooms have central heating or electric heaters; shower or bathroom; armchairs; views of country or garden. Tea, coffee, free.
Sitting-room with central heating, open fire, TV, books.

Garden and farmland.
Nearest main road A272 from Petersfield to Winchester.
Closed in winter

A nearby hill with prehistoric burial-mound gives this beef- and dairy-farm its name. In the opposite direction it has a view of equally ancient Butser Hill, a windswept height well worth a visit.

The tile-hung house itself is beautifully furnished, with Victorian antiques shown at their best against well-chosen colour schemes and fabrics. The beamed sitting-rooms are divided by a see-through fireplace, and on the sills of the big windows all round is a profusion of pot-plants. Breakfast is served at a large oval table of mahogany in the dining-room. Bedrooms are excellent.

Everything is immaculate, outside as well as in, from carefully trained roses climbing up flint walls to the smooth lawns where one can sit to enjoy the setting sun amid the scent of catmint or lavender. Old chimney-pots have been used for planting petunias and lobelias. There are mementoes of Beatrix Potter – the very plates to be seen in the Tiggy-Winkle drawings; Mary's great-aunt was the little girl illustrated in the story.

Mary Luff serves only breakfast, recommending local inns (or Langish House Hotel) for other meals, including those at East Meon, described elsewhere.

Petersfield's 18th-century streets are pleasant; and at Greatham Mill is a lovely garden. All around are hills, woods and tranquil valleys of great beauty: a very agreeable area to explore by car or on foot. Jane Austen's home at Chawton and Gilbert White's at Selborne are only a few miles away. The Queen Elizabeth Country Park is an area of superb scenery.

Readers' comments: Excellent, very comfortable. A pleasant welcome. Huge, comfortable room. A most generous and cheerful hostess.

Some readers tell me they have stayed at lots of places from *Staying Off the Beaten Track*. I wonder who has stayed at most? A free copy of the next edition awaits the reader who sends me his/her comments on the greatest number!

BEANSHEAF   C D H PT S S-C X

Kirby Misperton, north of Malton, North Yorkshire, YO17 0UE

Tel: 065 386 614

17 bedrooms (single, double or family) from £17.50. Less for 2 nights and bargain breaks. All have own bath/shower; TV; tea/coffee facilities; central heating; views of country or garden. No smoking. (Washing-machine on request.)

Dinner £8.50 for 3 courses (with choices) and coffee, at 7–9.30pm. Vegetarian or special diets if ordered. Lunches, packed lunches, snacks. Tea, coffee, extra. Drinks can be ordered.

Sitting-room with central heating, books, record-player; wine bar.

Large garden

Nearest main road A169 from Malton to Pickering.

Michele Sardone trained as a chef in Switzerland before bringing his skills to England. He offers a fixed price menu or a huge à la carte choice with every dish freshly cooked to order: some twenty starters (antipasta pescatore and home-made lasagne are two examples) and even more main courses (from steaks and Barnsley chops to game). Often there are unusual vegetables available – pumpkin, kohlrabi, fennel, ratatouille or cauliflower polonaise, for instance. Michele's specialities include beef with a pork-and-veal stuffing, and kid cooked in an earthenware pot with mushrooms, tomatoes and peppers. He makes a Parmesan-type cheese, using milk from his goats. Meals are served in a pleasant dining-room where Tyrolean-style chairs surround tables laid with pink cloths, overlooking a patio.

The well-equipped bedrooms have good colour schemes, and outstanding bathrooms or showers with such things as navy-and-gold fitments or basins of marble inlay brought from Italy. One pink room has a pine four-poster with a curvaceous and frilly canopy. For quiet, ask for one at the back: the Beansheaf is on a road. There is a sauna and a solarium; a wine bar and coffee shop.

Readers' comments: Superb. The best Italian food we have had in Britain. Friendly service. A little gem. More than pleased. Atmosphere relaxed and pleasant. Staff friendly and helpful.

The cellar bar at the Bell Inn (see page 188)

BEAR FARM   C(4)
Binfield, Bracknell, south-west of Windsor, Berkshire, RG12 5QE
Tel: 0734 343286

2 bedrooms (double or family) from £15. Both have TV; tea/coffee facilities; central heating; view of garden. (Washing-machine on request.)
Dinner £10 for 4 courses, (wine etc.) and coffee, by arrangement. Snacks. Tea, coffee, free.
Sitting-room with central heating, open fire, TV, books, bar
Large garden
Nearest main road M4 (junction 10).

This has one of the prettiest approaches of any farm in this book: a garden with roses and lily-pool; big porch smothered in honeysuckle; lawn, weeping willows and brilliant busy Lizzies. A pantiled barn partly surrounds a sheltered court and what was once the milking-parlour has been turned into attractive and very well-equipped ground-floor bedrooms. Visitors walk across to the house for meals at which Ann Skidmore joins her guests (typically, dinner might comprise a seafood cocktail, roast joint, raspberry pavlova and cheeses – with aperitif and wine included – unless a simple supper of omelette and fruit is preferred). Afterwards, unless tempted to return to the hard tennis court, they relax in deep, cushiony sofas and armchairs around a hearth brimming with her collection of copper wine- and beer-funnels.

The house itself, low-beamed and with leaded casements, is 400 years old. Its name is a corruption of 'bere' meaning 'woodland', for once Windsor Forest covered this area. Today the farm, which concentrates on cereals and beef-cattle, is surrounded by attractive countryside; and yet it is less than an hour from London (and half an hour from Heathrow) on the motorway.

Binfield (where Alexander Pope grew up) is well placed for visiting Windsor, many Thames beauty-spots, Ascot and the little market town of Wokingham. Reading is a big shopping centre; its university has an outstanding museum of rural life, and many river trips start from here. Bagshot Heath is good for picnics and walks; there are country parks (the Wellington park houses a dairy museum, the California country park particularly appeals to children, and Windsor has its safari park). Garden-lovers particularly enjoy Cliveden, Virginia Water, the Savill Garden, and (on the rare May dates when it is open) the garden around the royal mausoleum at Frogmore – with tombs of Victoria and Albert.

Berkshire is a county of contrasts – regal at Windsor, full of Edwardian elegance in its Thames-side houses, more rural as you go further west. Its history goes back to prehistoric times, and great events have been taking place there ever since: for instance, Runnymede is where King John was forced to accept Magna Carta. And it is a particularly good choice for a winter break because there is so much to see which does not depend upon the weather and many sights remain open throughout the year.

All prices are inclusive of any VAT or service charge. They are minimum prices: superior rooms or high-season bookings may cost more.

BEECROFT   C
**Middle Drive, Woolsington, north-west of Newcastle-upon-Tyne,
Tyne & Wear, NE13 8BS**   Tel: 091 2861009

2 bedrooms (single, double or family) from £15. Less for 5 nights. No smoking. (Washing-machine on request.)
Dinner £5.50 for 3 courses and coffee, at 6–8.30pm. Non-residents not admitted. Vegetarian or special diets if ordered. Packed lunches, snacks. Tea, coffee, free. Drinks can be brought in.

Sitting-room with central heating, open fire, TV, books, record-player.
Small garden
Nearest main road A696 from Newcastle to Ponteland.
Closed December–February

Newcastle's airport was built on what was once the great Woolsington estate, of which John Beattie's grandfather was head gamekeeper.

This 17th-century sandstone lodge was his home, and John remembers seeing game hanging and pheasant chicks being reared here. No longer, alas – though there remain the bees that give the house its name and which provide honey for breakfast. John also produces leeks (for which Northumberland is famous – in early September, growers compete at leek shows throughout the county).

Sylvia's soups and pâtés are all home-made; garden vegetables accompany her roasts and casseroles; and then may follow fruit tarts, lemon meringue pie or a cheesecake. (Excellent meals at the price.) All bedrooms are on the ground floor. From the house there are pleasant woodland walks to Woolsington Hall and its lake.

This is obviously a very useful stopover for people using the airport to go to Europe or Canada (the Beatties give free lifts to and from the airport). But it deserves a lingering stay, not least to visit Newcastle itself, ¼ hour by bus. No one driving through this city's one-way maze can guess at its hidden splendours: it needs to be explored on foot. It has some really exceptional Georgian streets.

I recommend starting at the old Blackfriars monastery which has a particularly imaginative museum explaining the city's history, crafts and a good café. Downhill are Dean Street (antiques, crafts and bistros), the cathedral, castle (where Northumbrian pipes are played – different from Scottish bagpipes), quays (markets and a lighthouse museum). All Newcastle's museums are exceptionally good: the Joicey (historical – particularly good on Bewick), the Laing art gallery, the Hancock (natural history) and the Museum of Science and Engineering. Another bus will take you to Gateshead (for the finest park in the north and an excellent art gallery), the metro to Jarrow (where Bede's monastic times are vividly brought to life again). In the Eldon Square shopping centre, Marks & Spencer's first 'penny bazaar' has been recreated. In 1990, the National Gardens Festival takes place at Gateshead.

THE BEEHIVE

C(5) **D S X**

Osmington, north-east of Weymouth, Dorset, DT3 6EL   Tel: 0305 834095

4 bedrooms (single or double) from £12. Much less for 3 nights or bargain breaks. Rooms have central heating; armchairs; views of country or garden; bedboard; tea/coffee facilities. No smoking.
Dinner £6 for 2 courses and coffee, or £9 for 3 courses, at 7.30–8pm. Vegetarian or special diets if ordered. Packed lunches. Coffee, tea, free. Non-residents not admitted. Drinks can be brought in.
Sitting-room with central heating, log fire, TV, books, record-player. No smoking.
Small garden
Nearest main road A353 from Weymouth to the A352.

Mary Kempe's father was Lord of the Manor at Osmington; and this little thatched stone cottage was the holiday home of her childhood. While the manorial lands passed into other hands, she was pursuing an academic career at the universities of Nairobi and London: the former accounts for the presence of African crafts in the old cottage, which is now her permanent home.

It is tucked away – in a pocket-handkerchief garden – down a lane leading to countryside of great beauty, with some lovely walks; to the south fine coast scenery lies only a mile away (shingle beaches closest, sandy ones a little further).

The friendly sitting-room is a place of books and watercolours, lead-paned windows and old cretonne-covered sofas or chairs. Breakfast is served in the big, cork-floored kitchen warmed by a stove (you can buy jars of Mary's home-made jams). She produces, on certain nights only, imaginative dinners with many dishes based on traditional local recipes and produce – for instance, Martlemas (or Michaelmas) beef, which is marinaded in wine and vinegar then rubbed with spices before being baked, or Wessex chicken in a cider sauce. Before this might come Dorset pâté or a soup of carrots or lentils; and after it apple hedgehog, blueberry pie or buttered oranges. Or you can eat well at the nearby Smugglers' Inn. (Ask Mary for an excellent leaflet on where to buy Dorset local foods to take home.) Nearby are good nurseries and garden centres, too.

Birdwatchers go out from here to spend days at Radipole Lake, the Fleet or Studland nature reserve. Others tour the Thomas Hardy sites. Osmington, being roughly midway between Poole at one end of Dorset and Lyme Regis at the other, is a good centre from which to explore all parts of the county: see details elsewhere in this book. And at Osmington Mills are inns overlooking the sea at which crab or lobster are served. Further afield, one can visit such beauty-spots as Lulworth Cove and the Purbeck Hills; T. E. Lawrence's cottage at Clouds Hill; and picturesque villages like Wool which has *Tess of the d'Urbervilles* associations.

Upstairs, among the cottage-style bedrooms (and bathroom decorated with African hippos), Mary has a large collection of maps and books on all aspects of Dorset history and wildlife, and is herself a willing fount of guidance on where to go.

Readers' comments: Superb; delightful haven of peace; a marvellous hostess. One of the best meals we have ever sampled.

BEGGAR BOG

C(5) **H X**

Housesteads, Haydon Bridge, west of Hexham, Northumberland, NE47 6NN
Tel: 04984 320

Some have own bath/shower; TV; tea/coffee facilities; central heating; views of country or garden. (Washing-machine on request.)
Dinner £8 for 3 courses and coffee, at 7pm. Non-residents not admitted. Vegetarian or special diets if ordered. Lunches, packed lunches, snacks. Tea, coffee, free. Drinks can be brought in.
Sitting-room with central heating, open fire, TV, books. No smoking.
Large garden
Nearest main road A69 from Haltwhistle to Haydon Bridge.

4 bedrooms (single, double or family) from £11. Less for 3 nights and bargain breaks.

Opposite the National Trust information centre at Housesteads on Hadrian's Wall stands this solitary stone farmhouse. It is a spick-and-span house with light colour schemes and handsome new pine doors. In the sitting-room, comfortable beige velvet armchairs face a stone fireplace across a brown Axminster carpet, and there are some fine pieces of antique oak furniture about. Some bedrooms give views of the Wall, and all the windows are double-glazed. This makes them quiet, even though the house is quite close to the road. The (relatively) 'beaten track' here is itself of interest, being the Military Road built, like his better-known one across the Highlands, by General Wade to improve communications after the first Jacobite rebellion.

The house is surrounded by trim lawns, garden and the pasture the Huddlestons use for the horses which are a family passion.

The typical farmhouse cooking is of a high standard: home made pâté, stuffed eggs, steak, lasagne, hazelnut meringue and lemon pie are the sort of things visitors might get. Everything is home-made. Incidentally, despite the name of the house, there is no bog now and there never was a beggar ('beggar' is a type of ash tree).

Housesteads is one of the best known sites on the Wall. This is partly because it is one of the most well-preserved of the main forts, where you can see, among other remains, a hospital and a latrine; and partly because the site is so dramatic and the views so spectacular. Not far away is Vindolanda, which stands south of the Wall rather than on it and includes a civilian settlement. It is worth visiting for the sake of its museum and for the reconstructions of a turret, a wooden gatehouse, and the turf wall which preceded the stone one.

Visitors to Beggar Bog will have the advantage of being able to look over Housesteads early in the day, before the crowds of summer. People who walk the length of the Wall, or want to do a sketch of it, find that Beggar Bog and **Holmhead** (a later entry) are a comfortable day's walk apart.

Readers' comments: Beautifully situated. Very friendly and very good cook.

In holiday areas, travel on any day other than a summer Saturday if you can. Make ferry, Motorail or coach/train reservations well in advance if travelling at such periods.

---

37 Bridewell Street, Clare, west of Sudbury, Suffolk, CO10 8QD
Tel: 0787 277538

2 bedrooms (double) from £11.50. TV and central heating. No smoking.
Dinner £7.50 for 3 courses and coffee, at 7pm. Non-residents not admitted. Vegetarian or special diets if ordered. Wine can be brought in. No smoking.
Sitting-room with books. No smoking.
Nearest main road A1092 from Long Melford to the A604.

This small but historic house (once three cottages in a terrace) is filled with antiques, paintings that include family portraits which go back to the 18th century, all kinds of Victoriana and a great many books. At the back is a little paved garden frequented by the Bells' three cats and two dogs. Around the dining-room are ladderback chairs and a pine settle. Bedrooms, too, are cottage-like in their furnishings.

For many years, the Bells used to run a restaurant in nearby Cavendish so cooking here is above average: Gillian serves such meals (if ordered in advance) as fish mousse, chicken provençale and raspberries with home-made ice cream.

Clare is a place to explore on foot, to enjoy all the details of its ancient houses – plasterwork decoration, exuberant inn signs, the old priory. It is close to Cavendish, Sudbury and other attractive places in Suffolk such as Kentwell Hall and gardens, Long Melford, Clare country park, the Colne Valley steam railway, Gainsborough's house, Hedingham Castle and Melford Hall. Bury St Edmunds and its abbey gardens are worth a leisurely visit, and so is Lavenham (both described elsewhere in this book); as well as Beth Chatto's garden and the many nursery gardens of the area, Constable's Flatford Mill, and Cambridge.

In nearby Callis Street is the **Ship Stores** (tel: 0787 277834). Miles from the sea, this one-time inn was originally called the Sheep, not the Ship. Now it is a small shop run by Colin and Deborah Bowles, with a few simply furnished bedrooms and an upstairs sitting-room for guests. Secrets in this building, 400 years old, have been uncovered: fireplaces long boarded up, and the original brick floor downstairs, for instance. It is a place of low beams, creaking floors, undulating roof and pink-plastered front: full of character, but very modest (as are its prices). In

the breakfast-room there is solid elm furniture locally made; and anyone who wants an out-of-the-ordinary breakfast (pâté? sardines? beans?) is welcome to select from the stock in the grocery.

When writing to me, if you want a reply please enclose a stamped addressed envelope.

BERE MARSH HOUSE
Shillingstone, south of Shaftesbury, Dorset, DT11 0QY

C(6) D S

Tel: 0258 861133

2 bedrooms (double or family) from £10.50. Less for 2 nights. Rooms have tea/coffee facilities; central heating; views of country or garden. (Washing-machine on request.)
Dinner £10–£11.50 for 4 courses (with choices) and coffee, at 7.30pm onwards. Vegetarian or special diets if ordered. Tea, coffee, free. Drinks can be ordered.
Sitting-room with central heating, open fire, TV, books, piano, record-player; bar.
Large garden
Nearest main road A357 from Blandford Forum to Sturminster Newton.

It is the food which brings most visitors here, for in the restaurant James and Felicity Roe serve gourmet meals. In the past, Felicity used to cook directors' lunches in London and then worked at the celebrated Peacock Vane hotel on the Isle of Wight during its heyday.

There's a breakfast-room with dried flowers overhead, a conservatory with grapevine (meals are sometimes served here), armchairs surrounding a log stove in the hall of the 18th-century house. In the garden are a tennis court, summer-house overlooking a rock garden in a dell and a big vegetable garden. Beyond are far views over good walking country.

As to the meals, the Roes operate a sensible system. Although their repertoire is very considerable, they let the first party to book dinner choose the menu for that night, for all comers: that way, they can provide dishes from freshly bought and cooked ingredients and (there being no waste) at a very reasonable price. So it pays to make your reservation and study their list of dishes well in advance. Most dishes are such French classics as mushrooms à la grecque, boeuf Stroganoff and crème brûlée.

There are plenty of good drives around here. For instance, one might go via Sturminster Newton and Mere (which has a 16th-century inn that was a Royalist stronghold during the Civil War) to visit the world-famous landscaped gardens and lake of Stourhead and the 18th-century mansion itself (full of art treasures). Alternatively, via Shaftesbury (described elsewhere) one could drive to Tollard Royal on a road of hairpin bends that is an outstanding scenic route with superb views when you get to the top. Along the way, lynchets can be seen – narrow terraces constructed on the steep hillsides to make cultivation possible. This is part of Cranborne Chase, for a thousand years a royal hunting forest: at Tollard Royal the hunting-lodge of King John has been carefully preserved (the village church is also worth a visit, particularly for its effigy of a knight in armour; and also Larmer Grounds park when it is open – there are oriental temples and a wooden theatre).

Other places of interest in the vicinity include the 15th-century manor house at Purse Caundle; Sherborne for its golden abbey and two castles; and Longburton in the church of which is a remarkable painted and canopied tomb.

Book well ahead: many of these houses have few rooms. Do not expect dinner if you have not booked it.

BICKLEIGH COTTAGE

Bickleigh, south of Tiverton, Devon, EX16 8RJ   Tel: 088 45 230

C(8) S PT

9 bedrooms (single or double) from £13.50. Less for 7 nights. Rooms have central heating or electric heaters; tea/coffee facilities. Most have bathrooms and/or river views. **Dinner** £6.50 for 4 courses and coffee, at 7pm. Non-residents not admitted. Drinks can be ordered.

2 sitting-rooms with central heating, TV, books.
Riverside garden
Nearest main road A396 from Exeter to Tiverton.
Closed in winter

Built about 1640 and later extended, this very picturesque thatched cottage has been run as a small hotel by the same family for over 50 years. It stands on a road by the banks of the River Exe, with a foaming weir a few yards downstream: everyone's ideal of a typically Devonian beauty-spot.

The rooms downstairs are full of antiques such as old chests and carved oak chairs, as well as a collection of blue glass and other interesting trifles including articles of Honiton lace made by Mrs Cochrane, which are for sale. The bedrooms (many with river views) are more simply furnished, though one has a four-poster bed. Outside is a pretty riverside garden with a fish-pool and glasshouses containing a collection of cacti and succulents.

Meals are of plain home cooking, a typical menu being smoked mackerel, roast lamb, pineapple meringue and cheeses.

A good day's outing via Tiverton (which has a castle) would be along the Exe Valley (visiting opulent Knightshayes Court, lavishly designed by William Burges in 1869 amid beautiful gardens) to Dulverton – old woodlands giving way to open moors as you travel towards Exmoor. In Dulverton are mediaeval lanes and an ancient bridge, tempting shops, weavers' workshops and Exmoor's interpretation centre. There are good walks in Eggesford Forest on the way to the steep village of Lapford, in the church of which are outstanding Tudor woodcarvings. Crediton's stately church once had cathedral status (built of red sandstone, it has stained glass windows depicting the life of its patron St Boniface). In the vicinity are other stately homes, such as Fursdon (Fursdons have lived in it from the 13th century to the present day) and Bickleigh Castle which, among other unusual exhibits, has espionage gadgets invented by the original 'Q' in the James Bond novels. Bickleigh's watermill houses a craft centre.

Readers' comments: Delightful. A favourite place. Beautiful position, good meals.

For explanation of code letters (**C, D, H, PT, S, S-C, X**) see page xxvi

BIGGIN HALL

C D S S-C

Biggin-by-Hartington, south of Buxton, Derbyshire, SK17 0DH
Tel: 029 884 451

12 bedrooms (single, double or family) from £17.50. Less for 5 nights or bargain breaks. Rooms have central heating and/or electric radiators; bathroom; armchairs; views of country or garden; tea/coffee facilities and TV in some.
2 sitting-rooms with central heating, open fire, TV, books.
Extensive grounds Grassland.
Nearest main road A515 from Ashbourne to Buxton.
Closed November–March.

Charles II was on the throne when this handsome stone house with leaded windows was built, and it has changed little since his day (modern comforts apart). Logs blaze in the great stone fireplace, with cretonne-covered chairs grouped around on a quarry-tiled floor. Another sitting-room has one wall of bookshelves, and glass doors opening onto the garden where children can play on the swing. Upstairs, one oak-panelled room has an oak-panelled half-tester bed (pink lilies on its blue draperies) and another a spectacular four-poster under the exposed beams – its bathroom is huge, carpeted and even equipped with a bidet. There are other rooms in an 18th-century stone annexe: no room service here. The Hall's owners, the Moffetts, used to be antique dealers.

In the dining-room (oriental rugs on flagstones, rush chairs, flowers on each table) breakfast is (unless you pay a little extra) continental-style, but this includes a choice of cereals, fruits and juices followed by home-made brioches, croissants and jams. In winter, cooked breakfast, packed lunch and mulled wine are free.

In front of the house is a small stone-walled garden with poppies and peonies, and an old laburnum bowing low over its iron gates. A serene spot (slightly marred by telephone wires and a bright green plaque) in which to take one's tea or coffee.

Biggin is near the centre of the Peak District, 1000 feet up where the air is pure and fresh. Scenery is the main attraction here, but most visitors also go to see sights like Chatsworth House, Haddon Hall, the Tram Museum at Crich. Cycles can be hired locally, to follow the 'Tissington Trail' or the famous River Dove. Arbor Low has prehistoric remains. Unfrequented walks abound.

Readers' comments: A wonderful weekend; warmly greeted, gorgeous furniture. The Moffetts are friendly, humorous and jovial. Warm and welcoming.

Inclusive terms for dinner, bed-and-breakfast (particularly for a week) can be much lower than those quoted here for these items taken separately. For short-notice bookings you may be able to get a reduction.

No proprietor wants to have a room standing empty. This particularly applies to Sunday nights. Some hotels make a discount if you want only two courses from a three-course menu.

27

BIRCHES MILL

C D PT X

Clun, west of Ludlow, Shropshire, SY7 8NL   Tel: 05884 409

All have central heating; views of river, country or garden. (Washing-machine on request.)

Dinner A la carte or £9 for 3 courses (with choices) and coffee, at 7.30pm. Vegetarian or special diets if ordered. Lunches, packed lunches, snacks. Tea, coffee, extra. Drinks can be brought in.

Sitting-room with central heating, TV, books.

Large garden

3 bedrooms (double or family) from £12. Less for 2 nights and bargain breaks. TV.

Nearest main road A488 from Knighton to Bishops Castle.

On the secluded valley banks of a trout river stands a 17th-century, ivy-covered watermill, its working days long over. Now it is the home of Avis and Peter Ades, beautifully converted to provide accommodation for guests. The sitting-room still has the old flagged floor and stone walls, but now with a thick Indian carpet, and deep leather armchairs drawn up around the fire. Glass doors open onto waterside lawns. The loudest sounds are the slow tick of a grandfather clock within and the frothing weir without. There is a large rock garden (with plants for sale – primulas are a speciality), and all around grow fritillaries, ragged robin, crocuses and orchids. This is an area particularly rich in wildflowers.

In the beamed dining-room there is still an old range in the stone fireplace. Here Avis serves, on handsome Royal Worcester porcelain, meals using organically-grown produce. The choice of dishes is wide and her standards are high. There might be a choice of rabbit pâté or onion soufflé soup to start with, and then saddle of lamb accompanied by an onion soubise. Puddings such as apple pie or brandied prunes (with cream) are followed by cheeses. You can buy some of her pies and cakes to take home.

Attention to detail is evident in everything from freshly squeezed orange juice at breakfast to the lace or crochet trimmed bedlinen. Altogether there is something idyllic about this isolated spot, the old mill and the Ades' hospitality.

Readers' comments: Cared for with consideration, in most congenial surroundings. Very comfortable, many amenities; the peace is so special; delicious cooking. Intend to return. Comfort standards are high, dinners most interesting. Courteous, friendly and helpful.

Billiard room at Stone House Hotel (see page 285)

BLACKWATER HOTEL

C D PT X

Church Road, West Mersea, south of Colchester, Essex, CO5 8QH
Tel: 020638 3338

7 bedrooms (single, double or family) from £18. Less for 7 nights or bargain breaks. Rooms have central heating or electric heaters; shower or bathroom; TV, armchairs; tea/coffee facilities.
Dinner A la carte, at 7–10pm. Special diets if ordered. Lunches, packed lunches, snacks. Coffee, tea and other drinks can be ordered.
Sitting-room with central heating, open fire, books; bar.
Nearest main road A12 from Colchester to Chelmsford.

The coastline here is a wilderness of creeks, islets and estuaries made colourful by the sails of small boats. A causeway now connects Mersea to the mainland, yet it still has the feel of an island with an identity all its own. There are Roman, Saxon and Norman remains – and, of course, the beds of Colchester oysters still flourish as they have done for centuries. Visitors go there, too, for all the usual seaside pleasures, for golf, sea-angling or for riding and walking. At nearby Fingringhoe Wick is an outstanding bird reserve, with hides alongside its lakes.

Down a quiet side-street is the creeper-covered Blackwater Hotel. Downstairs, beams and scarlet gingham tablecloths, copper pans and strings of onions, give the dining-room the informal air of a French bistro – these touches are Monique Chapleo's style. Here and in the small sitting-room with its tub chairs there are bowls of roses and pinks. All the bedrooms are very neat and fresh: wallpaper, curtains and bedspreads in matching sprigged patterns; bedheads of cane. Outside is a lawn with seats.

The food cooked by chef Roudesli is excellent, and the wine list is good. One might start with mushrooms champenoises or local shellfish, to be followed by pigeon pie or guinea-fowl in Marsala sauce and a pudding such as profiteroles or lemon tart. There is a bamboo-and-chintz coffee-room that serves snacks.

Although so near London, there are plenty of rural rides in this part of Essex, and many sights to see within a few miles – such as the timbered village of Coggeshall (with Paycockes, a National Trust house, and antique shops), the historic city of Colchester founded by the Romans before London (castle, museums, old churches, ancient byways and zoo), St Osyth's Priory and East Bergholt (Constable country). Maldon is very near – an old port still frequented by the great sailing-barges. Oyster fishery and museum can be visited (tastings, boat trips – phone 0206 384141).

Readers' comments: Charming hostess, excellent dinner and breakfast superb. Excellent cuisine. A real find – quite simply, perfect; charming patronne; superb meals; I don't think we have ever enjoyed a place so much. Outstanding.

Some hotels and even farms offer special Christmas holidays; but, unless otherwise indicated (by the code letter **X** at top of entry), those in this book will then be closed.

29

BLEA TARN HOUSE D S
Little Langdale, Ambleside, Cumbria, LA22 9PG   Tel: 09667 614

3 bedrooms (small doubles) from £12.50. Rooms have central heating; views of country or garden.
Dinner £6 for 3 courses and coffee, at 6.30pm. Lunches, packed lunches. Coffee, tea, for a charge. Non-residents not admitted. Drinks can be brought in.
Sitting-room with open fire, books.
Nearest main road A593 from Ambleside to Coniston.

'It seemed a home of poverty and toil', said Wordsworth of Blea Tarn House, but it does not seem at all like that any more, for it is warm and cosy and prettily decorated, with an open fire in the corner of the guests' sitting-cum-dining room. Off it is Sheila Myers' kitchen: she likes to talk to guests while she prepares, as it might be, egg mayonnaise, roast beef, and apple or lemon-meringue pie. She serves classic country dishes, always with two vegetables (usually fresh, occasionally frozen, but never tinned) and two sorts of potatoes. In summer, there will be more in the way of salads, and in cooler weather hotpots and cobblers. Upstairs, the bedrooms are small, but they are quaint and pretty.

This is the very heart of the Lake District, for Blea Tarn House sits on its own, high above the Langdales, Great and Little, amid the scenery which has made the area such a draw for centuries – rugged and colourful, and punctuated by famous peaks. Reached by a narrow and twisting road, this is a popular beauty-spot, but it is never excessively crowded with the sightseers who can sometimes detract from such places. From the late afternoon onwards the peace and quiet are unbroken.

A field away from the house is the tarn (small lake) from which it takes its name, where you can bathe or fish. Within a few miles are some of the Lake District's best known villages – Grasmere, Hawkshead, Ambleside and Coniston.

Readers' comments: Comfortable atmosphere, friendliness, good food. Delightful cottage and situation: an experience we would not have missed for anything. Excellent: good food, wonderful views, nice atmosphere. Characterful.

Tongue Ghyll near Grasmere (tel: 09665 571) is more spacious: a 17th-century house once the home of the county's High Sheriff. From Mrs Dixon's rooms and pretty garden (with streams) there are mountain views – a path leads up to Helvellyn. B & b only.

BOLEBROKE MILL C(7)

Edenbridge Road, Hartfield, south-east of East Grinstead, East Sussex, TN7 4JP Tel: 0892 770425

2 bedrooms (double or family) from £17.50. Less for 7 nights and bargain breaks.

Both have own bath/shower; TV; tea/coffee facilities; phone; central heating; views of millpond, country or garden. No smoking. (Washing-machine on request.)
Dinner (by arrangement, in low season only) £15 for 4 courses (with choices) and coffee, at 7.30pm. Vegetarian diets if ordered. Lunches, packed lunches, snacks. Tea, coffee, free. Drinks can be brought in.
Sitting-room with central heating, TV, books. No smoking.
Large grounds
Nearest main road A264 from East Grinstead to Tunbridge Wells.
Closed November–February

Remember that familiar scene? – Pooh, Piglet, Rabbit and Roo playing Pooh-sticks. They leant over one side of the bridge and dropped their sticks in when Rabbit said 'Go!' Then they dashed to the other side of the bridge, and leant over to see whose stick would drift into sight first. On days when the river was slow and lazy, it seemed as if the sticks might never appear from below the bridge.

The river that carried Pooh's sticks away feeds into the Medway as does the millstream that powered the wheel of this ancient mill, first recorded in Domesday Book, refurbished in the 18th-century, and operated right up to the Second World War (when German prisoners-of-war were used to man it).

Visitors who stay here need to be nimble, for when David Cooper restored it he was careful to retain every original feature that he could – steep and narrow stairs to each bedroom, bathrooms tucked into what were once the big corn-bins, for instance. In the large sitting-room there are still millstones, the grain-hopper and overhead gear-wheels to be seen from the comfort of large armchairs or the bed that folds down from a wall. On the beams are hung horse-tack and a boar's head; and through the lattice-paned windows or the stable-type doorway one can watch Muscovy ducks that frequent the willow-fringed millpond beyond which lie woods, orchards and meadows where bullocks graze. The bedrooms above are white and airy, with skylights; dried flowers hang from the rafters.

To get to the dining-room visitors descend through a hatch. Dinner, served at an oak table surrounded by leather chairs, might comprise a vol-au-vent with mussels and scrambled egg; spatchcock, a small chicken with a light mustard sauce; and rum babas. (There are several choices at each course.)

The mill stands in a particularly scenic and historic area. It almost certainly provided flour for the bread eaten by Henry VIII when he came here to hunt the deer – and to court Anne Boleyn, staying at nearby Bolebroke Castle. Winnie the Pooh addicts can see the house where A. A. Milne lived in Upper Hartfield and buy bearish mementoes at Christopher Robin's old sweet-shop, now called (of course) Pooh Corner. In whichever direction you go, the views will be very lovely – eastward to the elegant old spa town of Tunbridge Wells; south to mediaeval Lewes, the Downs and coast at Brighton; north to Sevenoaks and the Weald.

Some visitors combine an overseas holiday with a stay at the mill, finding it cheaper (and possibly safer) to leave their car here, free, and hire taxis to and from Gatwick. Others have chosen it as a romantic venue for a honeymoon.

BOOT FARM

C(10) S

Southend, Bradfield, west of Reading, Berkshire, RG7 6ES
Tel: 0734 744298

3 bedrooms (single, double or family) from £14. Less for 3 (midweek) nights and bar-gain breaks. Some have own bath/shower; TV; tea/coffee facilities; central heating; views of country, garden. No smoking. (Washing-machine on request.)

High tea £3.50 served at 5.30 or 6.30pm. Non-residents not admitted. Vegetarian or special diets if ordered. Packed lunches. Tea, coffee, extra. Drinks can be brought in. **Sitting-room** with central heating, open fire, books.

Large garden

Nearest main road M4 (junction 12).

From this farm comes some of the best cream and butter there is – supplied direct to many top restaurants and hotels. Guests may enjoy these at high tea, a filling and very good value meal of ham salad, omelette or Welsh rarebit followed by home-made cakes and jams. (Patricia Dawes is prepared to cook a full dinner sometimes; otherwise visitors go to The Bladebone or the Royal Oak.)

There is a large and very comfortable sitting-room, William Morris fabrics contrasting with pale walls, a log fire blazing on cold days, casements open to the garden in summer. Bedrooms are attractive and the bathroom is exceptional; toilet as well as bath has a flowery pattern. In the dining-room hand-stitched roses on tapestry chairs are complemented by an all-pink colour scheme.

In addition to farming, the Dawes run a livery stable and riding school and so are able to offer special riding weekends or holidays, popular with Londoners who live under an hour away. Others come for the open-air theatre of Bradfield College, for the trout lakes, or for the many golf courses in the county. East Berkshire has been described under other entries; to the west lies picturesque Hungerford, famous for its scores of antique shops (many open even on Sundays). Nearby are the windswept heights of the Berkshire Downs where racehorses train, and you can walk along the prehistoric Ridgeway Path. The sites of Iron Age forts or burial mounds dot the area. The Kennet Valley is in complete contrast – fertile meadows with birch and oak woods beyond, a great area for birdwatchers. The villages here have flint-and-brick cottages roofed with thatch. In and around both Lambourn and Newbury are historic buildings (the latter has a racecourse and a theatre in a converted watermill), stately homes and pretty villages. In this area is Littlecote (stately home with a Cromwellian armoury, jousting and other sights).

Further south, at Woolhampton is mediaeval **Bridge Cottage** (tel: 0734 713138), so-called because it is right beside a bridge over the old Kennet & Avon Canal. Jill Thornely has furnished the house pleasantly and from its windows you can see the boats going by (or take out Jill's canoes yourself). Breakfast is served in the low-beamed kitchen or in the walled garden. For dinner there is the nearby Rowbarge Inn.

BOUCHERS C(5) S

Bentham, south-west of Cheltenham, Gloucestershire, GL51 5TZ
Tel: 0452 862373

2 bedrooms (double) from £9.50. Rooms have central heating; views of country or garden. No smoking.
Sitting-room with central heating, open fire, TV, books. No smoking.
Large garden
Nearest main road A46 from Cheltenham to Stroud.

Once a farmhouse, Bouchers is still surrounded by hayfields just beyond the garden, where rock doves fly across the lawns to a graceful weeping willow. A sundial on one wall declares the date of the house, 1661, and of the old cider-house which is now Bruce's workshop.

Inside all is immaculate and very comfortable, and you will get a warm welcome from Anne Daniels as you step through the front door straight into the big U-shaped living-room. Here plenty of velvet armchairs are grouped round the hearth where an open fire crackles in winter, and a grandfather clock ticks the time away. Round the other side of the U is the dining-room, for breakfast only (visitors eat other meals at local inns or at one of the innumerable restaurants in Cheltenham, which is also near).

Bentham, on the edge of the Cotsworlds, is close to the route south to Bath. Gloucester with its cathedral, historic Cirencester (don't miss the Roman museum) and the Forest of Dean are all within easy reach, as are Prinknash Abbey and the Wye Valley. Also in the area are Slimbridge Wildfowl Trust, Westonbirt Arboretum, Badminton House (a Palladian mansion, where the Queen is often seen at the spring horse trials), 12th-century Berkeley Castle in its lovely grounds. Cheltenham and Tewkesbury are both near – as are the gardens at Hidcote.

The Cotswolds is a rich hunting-ground for antique collectors and there is an illustrated guide to about 50 of its antique shops (with map, on which to base a tour) obtainable from the Cotswold Antique Dealers Association – tel: 0386 700280. This describes the specialism of each shop, its opening hours and (briefly) the sightseeing possibilities nearby.

Cheltenham has many such shops – and others of every conceivable kind. Its Regency houses date from its heyday as a fashionable spa: the Duke of Wellington regularly came here whenever rheumatism or the affairs of state got him down. The town needs repeated visits to see everything: the birthplace of composer Gustav Holst, the Pump Room (where you still can 'take the waters'), the elegant Promenade and Montpelier area, 14th-century church, distinguished art gallery, very lovely gardens and Pittville Park (costume museum). Racegoers throng here at Gold Cup time; others come for various arts festivals.

Readers' comments: Service excellent – the sort for which you would expect to pay double the price. Will go there again. Very satisfied.

Prices are the minimum *per person* in a double room at the beginning of the year.

BOURNE EAU HOUSE

C PT

Bourne, north of Stamford, Lincolnshire, PE10 9LY   Tel: 0778 423621

3 bedrooms (single, double or family) from £17.50. Less for 4 nights. Rooms have central heating; shower or bathroom; TV, armchairs; views of garden; tea/coffee facilities (Clothes-washing facilities.) **Dinner** £14 for 4 courses and coffee, at 7.30–8pm. Vegetarian or special diets if ordered. Packed lunches, snacks. Coffee, tea, free. Non-residents not admitted. Drinks can be ordered.
2 sitting-rooms with central heating, open fire, books, table tennis, piano.
Large garden
Nearest main road A15 from Peterborough to Sleaford.

There are many good reasons to visit Lincolnshire (a much underrated county), and this exceptional home is one of them. It lies, almost islanded, within a twist of a little river frequented by swans and geese (the 'eau' that gives the house its name), a mixture of Tudor and Georgian architecture. A small wrought-iron footbridge leads to a Norman abbey behind the house; at the front are public gardens and the mound which is all that is left of Hereward the Wake's castle – the last Saxon leader to hold out against William the Conqueror.

To one side of an all-white, tiled hall is a pretty sitting-room where blue velvet chairs, contrasting with aquamarine walls, are grouped around a fireplace and its shining brass fender and firedogs. Through two bay windows are views of the lovely garden, of almond blossom and immaculate lawns. In another room is a concert piano and an ornately carved 17th-century mantelpiece; while the low-beamed, flagstoned dining-room (its floor made of Stamford 'marble') has yet another distinctive fireplace with a hood (depicting a wild man of the woods) made by a fenland blacksmith. Throughout the house there are other interesting features such as lattice window-panes, a cheese cupboard built into a wall, and (in a bedroom) a little cast-iron fireplace with built-in boiler for hot water.

The best bedroom, a suite, has a carved mantelpiece that was once part of an altar – hence the symbols of alpha and omega, barley and vines. The room is decorated in soft pinks and creams, has gros-point cushions and a Kashmiri camphor chest. The carpeted bathroom is equally elegant, in peach and turquoise.

Dawn Bishop's meals fully live up to the standards of the house, and, Lincolnshire being famous for its vegetables, plenty of local produce is served. A typical menu might comprise prawn and avocado salad followed by cauliflower soup with croûtons, then chicken in a ginger and soya sauce (there are always several vegetables interestingly prepared – such as courgettes cooked with paprika), and perhaps a syllabub. Cheeses will include Stilton made in the region.

This part of the country is perhaps at its best in spring when the scudding clouds in blue skies are reflected in the many dykes that drain the land, and the fields of the bulb-growing districts are brilliant with daffodils or tulips – road verges too. Villages of stone and thatch are picturesque, and this is an outstanding area for gardeners who want to go home laden with purchases from the many nurseries.

Readers' comments: House and hosts charming. Excellent accommodation. Care, quality and hospitality can not be beaten. Beautiful house. Charming and caring hosts.

BRADFORD OLD WINDMILL

C(5) PT S X

Masons Lane, Bradford-on-Avon, east of Bath (Avon), Wiltshire, BA15 1QN
Tel: 02216 6842

Some have own bath/shower; TV; all have tea/coffee facilities; central heating; views of country or garden. No smoking. (Washing-machine on request.)
Dinner £12 for 3 courses and coffee, at 8pm. Non-residents not admitted. Vegetarian or special diets if ordered. Packed lunches. Drinks can be ordered.
Sitting-room with central heating, open fire, books, record-player. No smoking.
Small garden
Nearest main road A363 from Bath to Trowbridge.

5 bedrooms (single, double or family) from £15. Less for 3 nights and bargain breaks.

The Napoleonic wars brought prosperity to this area (where cloth for uniforms was woven) but with peace came depression. As a result, the baker who in 1807 had built a windmill here went broke. In 1817 the mill ceased to function, and its sails and machinery were removed. Today its stump is simply a very unusual stone house, perched on a hillside within picturesque Bradford-on-Avon. From it there is a view full of interest, overlooking a higgledy-piggledy array of old roofs.

It is now in the imaginative care of Peter and Priscilla Roberts, a much-travelled couple (engineer and teacher) who have brought back finds from the Far East, New Zealand, Tahiti and Los Angeles which now decorate the rooms – as do pictures and mementoes of their other enthusiasms, from canal boats to whales.

Every circular room has its own character. In the sitting-room, William Morris sofas and furniture of stripped pine face a log fire and there are maps on the walls. One bedroom (with the best roofscape view of all, through a pair of deep-set pointed windows) has a circular bed with a spread of wildflowers and butterflies. In another, there are windmill pictures, arrangements of dried flowers and tea things laid out on top of an old barrel. Draped Tahitian fabrics contrast with a collection of old sewing-machines, Paisley scarves with pieces of driftwood, a figured walnut bed with a bamboo swinging-chair hung from a rafter.

Their cooking, too, is eclectic (even breakfasts are imaginative, with such options as hash browns, muffins or croissants, and home-made yogurts). For dinner, you may be able to try recipes from all over the world – Thailand and Nepal, in particular – and unusual vegetarian dishes, too. If you select a Thai meal you might enjoy a menu that includes eggs in a spicy coconut sauce; aubergines braised in a sauce of beans, garlic and ginger; and 'shrikhand' (cream cheese, cardamom-flavoured and with roast almonds on top). Less exotic dinners are available too. (Order dinner in advance; particularly in summer, when booking rooms well ahead is essential.)

There is a tiny, Victorian-style garden around the foot of the mill stump and from it one gets a good view of Bradford's notable buildings – a panorama that includes a colossal 14th-century tithe barn, river bridge with one-cell prison actually on it, 18th-century cloth mill, and (just beside the Round House) the ruins of an old chapel within which is a swimming-pool!

Readers' comments: Everything you could want. Very friendly, I thoroughly enjoyed my visit.

BRAMWOOD   **C PT S X**
19 Hallgarth, Pickering, North Yorkshire, YO18 7AW   Tel: 0751 74066

rear view

6 bedrooms (double or family) from £11. Less for 7 nights and bargain breaks. Some have own shower; tea/coffee facilities; central heating. No smoking.
Dinner £6.50 for 3 courses and coffee, at 6.30pm. Non-residents not admitted. Vegetarian diets if ordered. Wine can be brought in.
Sitting-room with central heating, open fire, TV, books. No smoking.
Small garden
Nearest main road A170 from Thirsk to Scarborough.

The best approach to this 18th-century guest-house is from the back, through an old archway built for coaches – racks for the horses' tack and an old forge still survive, but beyond what was once the stable yard there is now a pretty and secluded garden, with clematis scrambling up old walls and an apple tree; in one part vegetables are grown for the table.

All the bedrooms are immaculate, some of them spacious, and many have cane rocking-chairs – a nice touch. The white-and-green and cream-and-blue colour schemes downstairs are tranquil and refreshing. Ann Lane, who used to enjoy cooking 'for recreation' has put her enthusiasm to good use here, providing visitors with such meals as garlic mushrooms, pork medallions served with sage-and-apple sauce, and Yorkshire curd tart. She finds old-fashioned puddings are very popular with guests, particularly at the end of a strenuous day's walking, cycling, birdwatching or even gliding. Her home-made chutneys and marmalades are on sale.

In the vicinity are lovely Staindale and many moorland villages tucked away which are well worth seeking. Lastingham, for instance, which has fountain and crypt dating back to the 11th century. Two hundred years ago, its inn, the Blacksmiths' Arms, was run by its curate: when the bishop objected, he said he had thirteen children to support! Thornton Dale is very picturesque: trout swim in the clear stream that curves through the village and under the little footbridges that lead to each 17th- or 18th-century house and its flowery cottage-garden. Hutton-le-Hole, which has the region's folk museum, was once a refuge for persecuted Quakers. Through the middle of its cluster of pale stone houses is a ravine carved by a stream that descends, with cascades, from the high moors near Rosedale Abbey.

This area has some of the most spectacular abbey ruins: Rievaulx, Byland, etc. In 1536 over 800 monasteries flourished in Britain; by 1540 Henry VIII had the whole lot destroyed or closed. In the north's loveliest of solitary places were sited great abbeys built in the Cistercians' heyday (the 12th century). Some were wealthy and owned vast lands, but monastic life was already in decline when Henry helped himself to their properties.

When looking round these ruins it is hard to imagine them bustling with monks, pilgrims and beggars seeking bed and board, scholars in their libraries and schools, and the comings-and-goings of any big property-owning institution – all combined with ceaseless prayer, seven church services a day, and observance of St Benedict's strict Rule (no meat, no baths, no letters, no idleness).

BROADWATER

Woodbridge Road, Framlingham, Suffolk, IP13 9LL   Tel: 0728 723645

Rooms have central heating; shower or bathroom (some); armchairs; views of country or garden; tea/coffee facilities.
Dinner £9 for 3 courses and coffee, at 7pm. Vegetarian or special diets if ordered. Non-residents are not admitted. Drinks can be ordered.
Sitting-room with central heating, open fire, TV, books, piano.
Extensive grounds Wood, garden, paddocks, vineyard.
Nearest main road A1120 from Stowmarket to Yoxford.

6 bedrooms (single, double or family) from £14. Less for 2 nights or bargain breaks.

I came away with a case of white wine – for Broadwater is a name you will find on wine labels: it consists of a vineyard and an 18th-century house, once a shooting-lodge. You can drink the wine at dinner here, in a pleasant green-and-white room. Sheila Stocker serves such meals as courgettes in cheese sauce; fish pie containing smoked haddock and prawns; summer pudding. Vegetables and fruit usually come from the garden. Big cretonne armchairs are grouped round a log fire in the sitting-room, which has windows all round with views of woodland where nightingales sing, occasional rabbits, horses and Jacob sheep. Sheila Stocker's garden is sometimes opened to the public for charity: a 70-year-old yew hedge divides it into rose, iris and well gardens and a 'long walk'.

The bedrooms are well furnished – even the single rooms, which is not always the case – and one has a four-poster bed. One of the toilets is rightly nicknamed 'the throne room': a real museum-piece!

The most popular places to visit near here are Framlingham and Orford castles, Woodbridge, Glemham Hall, Easton Farm Park and Bruisyard vineyard. Notcutts, Helmingham and Charlsfield attract garden-lovers.

If you go further afield, you will find Thetford – its architecture begins with Saxon remains – and the riverside walks here are particularly attractive. Whether shopping for antiques (shops or auctions) or for farm produce, this is a good area. Near Bury St Edmunds are stately homes including Kentwell Hall, Ickworth House and Melford Hall. This area also has several very good garden centres and innumerable antique shops, Snape Maltings, Minsmere bird reserve and the heritage coast. Altogether, a county of great interest and variety.

Inclusive terms for dinner, bed-and-breakfast (particularly for a week) can be much lower than those quoted here for these items taken separately. For short-notice bookings you may be able to get a reduction.

No proprietor wants to have a room standing empty. This particularly applies to Sunday nights. Some hotels make a discount if you want only two courses from a three-course menu.

BROOKFIELD FARM HOTEL

C D H PT X

Plummers Plain, Horsham, West Sussex, RH13 6LO   Tel: 0403 891568

rear view

22 bedrooms (single, double or family) from £17.25. Less for 7 nights or bargain breaks. (Two ground-floor bedrooms. One four-poster room.) Rooms have central heating or electric heaters; shower or bathroom; TV, armchairs; views of country or garden. Tea/coffee facilities downstairs.

Dinner £9 for 3 courses (with choices) and coffee, at 6.15pm onwards. Special diets if ordered. Packed lunches. Coffee, tea, for a charge. Drinks can be ordered.

2 sitting-rooms and a games-room with central heating, open fire, TV, books, billiards, darts, Star Wars, organ, record-player. Sauna and gym. There is a bar.

Garden and lake (with fishing, swimming-pool and boats, croquet, golf-driving, children's play area), farmland and forest.

Nearest main road A281 from Horsham to Brighton.

Although this modernized farmhouse in the Sussex Weald is now a busy guesthouse, it is on a very real farm with hundreds of acres of sheep and cattle.

The picture windows that look out onto the lawn slide right back on warm evenings and there is a paved terrace with seats and lighting outside. There is a tiled, flat roof for sunbathing.

The sitting-room has sofas and armchairs of ample dimensions, a plethora of ornaments, and an open fire for chilly nights. Bedrooms vary in size: some are small.

Adjoining the house is a games room (with bar billiards, darts, video games and so forth); children can ride the donkey; there are pedal-boats and a canoe on the lake (and a watersplash into it); and croquet on the lawn, as well as children's slides and swings, and a golf-driving range.

Walkers can make for St Leonards Forest. Some of the most popular sights of Sussex and Kent are within motoring distance, including Arundel (castle), Chichester (cathedral), Chartwell (Churchill's house) and Hever (stately home).

Gatwick Airport is near, and visitors can be collected from there by car. Some people going on holiday abroad spend a night at Brookfield first and then leave their car here, at far less cost than using an airport car park. A minibus takes them to and from the airport.

Readers' comments: Cheerful surroundings, friendly hospitality.

A sedate Victorian house, **Westlands** at Monk's Gate, has been very well furnished by Kathleen Ticktum, with much emphasis on light colours and complete comfort at moderate prices. (Tel: 0403 891383.) There is a very lovely flower garden with terrace and lily-pool (floodlit at night). A good choice for anyone who values peace, spaciousness and high standards, but only b & b provided: there are nearby inns and hotels for meals. Parking (and taxi-service) available for visitors flying from Gatwick Airport.

Readers' comments: Immaculate. Warm and friendly owners.

38

BROOKLAND

Peacock Lane, Middle Tysoe, south-east of Stratford-upon-Avon, Warwickshire, CV35 0SG 029588 202

3 bedrooms (single, twin or double) from £11.50. Less for 7 nights and bargain breaks. All have own tea/coffee facilities; electric heating; views of country or garden. No smoking. (Washing-machine on request.)
Dinner £7.50 for 3 courses and coffee, at 7pm. Non-residents not admitted. Vegetarian or special diets if ordered. Lunches, packed lunches, snacks. Tea, coffee, free. Drinks can be brought in.
Sitting-room with central heating, open fire, TV, books, record-player.
Small garden
Nearest main road A422 from Stratford-upon-Avon to Banbury.

The first battle of the Civil War was fought nearby at Edgehill (in 1642, not long before this cottage was built), a dramatically sharp ridge on the border of Oxfordshire and a fine car-drive today. Charles I narrowly missed a defeat that could have prevented his army from moving on to London and all the long struggles which followed until he was beheaded in 1649. It is difficult to imagine such violent deeds while enjoying this tranquil spot today.

When I visited Brookland, my first impression was of flowers everywhere, butterflies thronging the tall yellow spires of verbascum, stone troughs brimming with colourful blooms. There is a little sun-lounge where one can sit under a vine to enjoy the morning sunshine, while inside grandfather clocks tick peacefully. The old stone cottage still retains many of its original features, such as the tinderbox cupboard built into an inglenook fireplace; and Topsy Trought has furnished the dining-room with carved, cane chairs in William-and-Mary style.

Topsy makes wedding- and birthday-cakes for local families, but it is Tim who does the elaborate and colourful decorations of sugar fruit and vegetables. The Troughts' niece is Rosemary Nunnely whose cooking (see **Sugarswell Farm**) so many readers of past editions of this book have praised highly; and it seems that good cooking is a family accomplishment. Topsy says her most popular meal is a peach-and-pineapple starter, gamekeeper's casserole and loganberry mousse.

As to sightseeing, most visitors head first – of course – for Stratford-upon-Avon but Warwick and its castle, Leamington Spa and Coventry (for its cathedral) are all near. This is good walking country, too, with footpaths to Edgehill.

In Stratford tourists usually start by visiting Shakespeare's well-preserved birthplace in Henley Street and his grave in Holy Trinity church beside the river and its swans. New Place is the house where he finally lived and wrote 'The Tempest' (a charming Tudor knot garden adjoins it); Hall's Croft, my favourite, was the home of his daughter and son-in-law – a doctor. There is, of course, the Royal Shakespeare Company's theatre; and in the nearby village of Shottery is his wife's childhood home, always known as 'Anne Hathaway's Cottage' even though it is a house of some size. Through it all the Avon winds its way, 'pearl-paved and with blue-eyed deeps' (in the words of Michael Drayton), among willows, watermills and quiet villages.

Readers' comments: Outstanding. Most beautiful and interesting.

BUCKNELL HOUSE

Bucknell, west of Ludlow, Shropshire, SY7 0AD Tel: 05474 248

3 bedrooms (double or family) from £12. Less for 3 nights. All have tea/coffee facilities; central heating; views of country or garden. (Washing-machine on request.)
Sitting-room with central heating, fire, TV, books, piano.

Small garden
Nearest main road A4110 from Hereford to Knighton.

In the early 18th century, the clergy lived well: this huge and handsome house, honeysuckle and wisteria clambering up its walls, was a vicarage then. The vicar would have approved of the equally handsome way in which Brenda Davies has furnished it – the dining-room with Sheraton chairs, a fine wallpaper; the sitting-room with big velvet armchairs, curtains of pale green silk, cream brocade wallpaper and alcoves of fine china; flowers everywhere. Bedrooms are just as good, spacious and with antique furniture. (B & b only.)

The grounds (garden and water meadows) are secluded, looking across the lovely valley of the River Teme to Wales. There are rosebeds, daffodil drive, shrubbery, croquet lawn, a hard tennis court, shooting, and fishing in the river. Woodlands and hills around here are full of wildlife.

Readers' comments: Wonderfully comfortable bed, breakfast an ample repast, some of the most beautiful countryside in England. Such excellence and outstanding amenities; marvellous people. Pleasant welcome. Warmth and comfort.

For those who require dinner there is **Upper Buckton** at Leintwardine, home of Yvonne Lloyd (tel: 05473 634). This is a late 18th-century house at the peaceful centre of a large sheep and cattle farm, with croquet and other garden games, table tennis and snooker in a granary. Antiques furnish the comfortable rooms, fine china the tables; Yvonne is an accomplished cook, serving such starters as bananas and bacon with curry sauce or stuffed mushrooms; then roasts, salmon or chicken with orange and almonds; vacherins or chocolate roulade. (No smoking.)

Readers' comments: Outstanding location, imaginative and generous cooking, most comfortable.

40

BUCKYETTE

Littlehempston, north of Totnes, Devon, TQ9 6ND Tel: 080 426 638

C S S-C

6 bedrooms (double or family) from £11.25. Less for 7 nights. Tea/coffee facilities; night-store heaters in 4; views of country or garden. Two with bathrooms.
Dinner £6.50 for 3 courses (with occasional choices) and coffee, at 6.30pm. Non-residents not admitted. Vegetarian or special diets if ordered. Drinks can be ordered.
Sitting-room with open fire, TV, books, piano.
Small garden
Nearest main road A381 from Newton Abbot to Totnes.
Closed October–April

The curious name of this house appears in the Domesday Book and is believed to be a Saxon word meaning 'head of a spring': the spring is still there, and in use. The present building, made from stone quarried on the farm, dates from 1860. It is on a commanding site with far views, and is furnished with Edwardian pieces suited to the scale of the lofty rooms. In the sitting-room is a log fire for chilly days, and for sunny ones tall French doors open onto a wisteria-hung verandah. The peppermint-pink dining-room has particularly handsome tables, which Roger Miller himself made from timber on the estate, and pictures of theatrical costumes. Bedrooms are not elegant but comfortable.

Elizabeth Miller serves such meals as lentil soup, chicken in a crisp cheese-and-garlic coating and queen of puddings; with home-baked bread. The garden provides asparagus, strawberries and other produce. Everything about the house is solid, comfortable, unpretentious, and very English. Children are particularly welcome.

Littlehempston is well placed for a family holiday because the safe sands of Torbay are so near – as are Paignton's zoo, miniature gardens, a scenic steam railway and river trips. There are plenty of inns, theatres and concerts including those at Dartington's celebrated arts and crafts centres. Totnes has its castle and streets of ancient buildings, with interesting little shops. In the church is an especially fine rood-screen. At Buckfast Abbey the monks sell their wine and honey to visitors; Buckland Abbey was Sir Francis Drake's house. Ashburton is a pretty hill town, with all of Dartmoor beyond – its most famous beauty-spot is Dartmeet where two rivers converge and there is an old 'clapper' bridge of stones by which to cross the water, a typical Devon feature. Widecombe, of 'Uncle Tom Cobleigh' fame, still has its celebrated fair high up on the moor every September. Princetown (large, bleak and weather-beaten) is where the big Dartmoor Prison is, originally built by and for Napoleonic prisoners-of-war. Brixham, Salcombe and Plymouth are described elsewhere.

Readers' comments: Amazingly good welcome. Beautifully served food. Very charming lady – I will go again.

When writing to me, if you want a reply please enclose a stamped addressed envelope.

41

BULMER FARM

C(12) **D S X**

Holmbury St Mary, south-west of Dorking, Surrey, RH5 6LG

Tel: 0306 730210

3 bedrooms (twin-bedded) from £12. Rooms have central heating or electric heaters; views of farm or garden; tea/coffee facilities.

Sitting-room with open fire, TV, books, record-player.

Large garden plus farm.

Nearest main road A25 from Dorking to Guildford.

In the folds of Surrey's high North Downs (most of which are so scenic that they are in National Trust protection) a number of very picturesque villages lie hidden, and Holmbury is one. Near the centre stands Bulmer Farm, built about 1680. One steps straight into the large dining-room, and through this to an attractive sitting-room – a room of pink walls and old beams, chairs covered in cretonne patterned with pink poppies, logs crackling in front of the cherubs and harps of an old iron fireback in the inglenook. It opens onto the large garden.

Upstairs are attractive bedrooms with immaculate paintwork and cottage-style furnishings.

Outdoors (where chickens run free among the old rickstones), a Dutch barn is crammed with hay; across the yard from an ancient byre, the tiles of its long, wobbly roof softened with moss, is a small farm shop from which you can take home Bulmer's own vegetables or eggs, lettuces from the glasshouses, or Gill Hill's home-made marmalade. David will show you the lake he created a few years ago, now a haven for herons, kingfishers, Canada geese, snipe and other wildfowl.

Bed-and-breakfast only, but the area is full of inns offering good meals such as the Royal Oak.

Some tourists find this a good area in which to stay while visiting London – train day-tickets cost very little, and the journey takes three-quarters of an hour (from Dorking).

The surrounding area of woodland and hills is one of the finest beauty-spots near the capital, truly rural, and dotted with stately homes to visit, footpaths to follow, historic churches and villages with craft shops, trout farms, antiques and the like. Dorking and Guildford (the latter with castle ruins, river trips and a good theatre) are each well worth a day's visit. The Royal Horticultural Society's gardens at Wisley are near, too, and so are Box Hill (viewpoint), Leith Hill (walks), Clandon and Polesden Lacey (stately homes). Several fine gardens open to view. Beautiful Shere has monthly antiques' fairs.

Readers' comments: One's every wish is catered for. So warm and friendly. Made so welcome, made to feel like one of the family.

Book well ahead: many of these houses have few rooms. Do not expect dinner if you have not booked it.

BULMER TYE HOUSE C X
Bulmer Tye, south-west of Sudbury, Suffolk, CO10 7ED Tel: 078729 315

4 bedrooms (single, double or family) from £10. Some have own bath; all have central heating and views of garden. No smoking. (Washing-machine on request.)
Dinner £5 for 2 or 3 courses and coffee. Served at time to suit guests. Non-residents not admitted. Vegetarian or special diets if ordered. Tea, coffee, free.
2 sitting-rooms with central heating, open fire, TV, books, piano. No smoking.
Large garden
Nearest main road A131 from Halstead to Sudbury.

One of Gainsborough's most famous paintings is of the Andrews family whom he knew when he lived in Suffolk. It was one of their sons, a parson, who in the 18th century 'modernized' this house, most of which dates back to the reign of Elizabeth I, by putting in huge sash windows and so forth.

Today its old timbers resonate to the sound of music (played by family or guests), for Peter Owen is a maker of very fine clavichords – and of much of the interesting furniture seen in the rooms. A hexagonal table with a complex pattern of end-grain triangles is his; so is a throne-like chair of elm, its joints secured with wood pegs only; and also two dolls' houses – one of which is in fact a scale replica of Bulmer Tye House itself. Little boxes here and there and eggs in decorative woods are his work too.

His wife is an authority on antique furniture, about which she writes articles for specialist magazines (under the name Noël Riley); so not surprisingly there are some unusual period pieces in the house. Instead of using furnishing fabrics with a traditional look, the Owens have contrasted the antiques with strong modern patterns – a Bauhaus design for curtains in one room, an Aztec-style pattern in another, in strong colours such as tangerine and turquoise. A Chinese sunshade, inverted, makes an unusual ceiling light-shade. There is a large Bechstein in one of the sitting-rooms and log fires in both. In one bedroom, with a particularly handsome bed, 19th-century Persian curtains and a Laura Ashley pattern co-exist happily.

The quarry-tiled kitchen is decorated in brilliant primary colours and on one wall screen-printed Spanish tiles give a *trompe l'oeil* effect. Here guests eat with the family round a huge pine table and are apt to get drawn into family life, as well as anything from duets to political debates with Peter. Garden produce often goes into the making of soups and of fruit puddings; wine, lemonade and elderflower cordial are all home-made and Peter bakes the bread. Some of the dishes guests enjoy most are beef-and-lentil flan; Roman cobbler (pork and mushrooms with a topping of semolina and cheese), fish pie and, for vegetarians in particular, a cheesy bread-and-butter pudding served wth stir-fried vegetables. Only a basic continental breakfast is served.

The large garden is notable for its many fine trees (some 200 years old) which include copper beeches, walnuts, cedars and yews, as well as a number of unusual plants. There is a grass tennis court.

Readers' comments: Characterful house, beautiful garden, very informal and friendly.

43

BURGOYNE HOTEL

C D PT S X

Reeth, west of Richmond, North Yorkshire, DL11 6SN   Tel: 0748 84292

THE BURGOYNE HOTEL REETH — SWALE DALE

11 bedrooms (single, double or family) from £15.95. Less for 7 nights and bargain breaks.

Some have own bath/shower; TV; tea/coffee facilities; central heating; views of country or garden. (Washing-machine on request.) **Dinner** £10 for 4 courses (with choices) and coffee, at 7.30pm. Vegetarian or special diets if ordered. Lunches, packed lunches. Tea, coffee, extra. Drinks can be ordered.
2 sitting-rooms with central heating, open fire, TV, books; bar.
Small garden
Nearest main road A6108 from Richmond to Leyburn.
Closed January–February

I have added yet another entry for Swaledale because this is rightly such a very popular area with my readers, the deepest, widest, and one of the loveliest of the Dales. Pat and Steve Foster (both formerly RAF officers) had only recently taken over when I visited the Burgoyne, and were still in the throes of raising the standards of rooms in this handsome 18th-century building at the top of Reeth's steeply sloping green, with an old pump just outside.

One sitting-room has a huge arched door and triple-arched stone fireplace; the other, a stone fireplace carved with Burgoyne family crests. (The most famous of the Burgoynes distinguished himself at a vital battle of the Crimean war, when Sebastopol's fort – guarding the harbour where the Russian fleet lay – was bombarded into submission.) The bedrooms now are very pleasant – for instance, one in powder-blue and white has its shower-room in matching colours, and I liked another with a restful green and grey colour scheme: like most, it has spectacular views. The house is unusually well provided with bathrooms.

There is plenty of choice at dinner, and the dishes include some imaginative options – such as spinach roulade (with Boursin cheese filling), salmon with asparagus sauce, coffee fudge pudding and local cheeses. Vegetables, too, are out-of-the-ordinary – fennel in a sauce, Anna potatoes or peas with tiny onions are examples. With coffee, mint fudge is served.

Reeth was once a busy town, a centre for the local industries which, apart from farming, included lead-mining (the relics of this are now scheduled monuments), hand-knitting stockings (men as well as women did this) and peat-digging (the peat was used for smelting the lead). All of this is recorded in Reeth's folk museum, which takes the area's history back to prehistoric times – there are plenty of earthworks to be seen. Across the river is Grinton and the big church known as the 'Cathedral of the Dales'. All around are stone-walled pastures for the curly-horned Swaledale sheep; a Swaledale tup (ram) is in fact the symbol of the Dales National Park.

It is a short drive south from here to the next big dale: Wensleydale, which – like Swaledale itself – is fully described under other entries. Or head north into Teesdale, past the disused lead mines of Arkengarthdale and over the moors (the Tan Hill Inn is the highest in England) to Barnard Castle.

> All prices are inclusive of any VAT or service charge. They are minimum prices: superior rooms or high-season bookings may cost more.

44

BURLAND FARM

C D X

Wrexham Road, Burland, north-west of Nantwich, Cheshire, CW5 8ND
Tel: 0270 74 210

4 bedrooms (double or family) from £15. All have own bath/shower; TV; tea/coffee facilities; central heating; views of country or garden.
Dinner £10 for 3 courses and coffee, at about 7pm. Vegetarian or special diets if ordered. Lunches, packed lunches, snacks. Tea, coffee, free. Drinks can be brought in.
2 sitting-rooms with central heating, open fire, books, piano.
Small garden
Nearest main road A534 from Nantwich to Wrexham.

This early Victorian house, surrounded by lawn and trees, is in the pretty *cottage ornée* style that was once fashionable: windows are lozenge-paned, the gable is decorated with woodwork, hinges are of wrought iron. (The lozenge panes are to be seen elsewhere in the area – a feature of many houses on the great Tollemache estate.)

The Allwoods' furnishings complement this well. Their huge dining-table and cupboard were made by Michael's great-grandfather from oaks felled on the farm, and other antiques have been added, such as spindleback chairs. Colour schemes are pleasant – a pink and grey bedroom, for instance, with a white tapestry bedspread from Portugal.

Sandra likes having visitors as an excuse to use her talent for 'dinner party' cooking (unless they prefer a cottage-pie supper). She produces such meals as hot chicken mousse (served with a spring-onion sauce), pork fillet in mustard sauce, blackcurrant sorbet accompanied by home-made biscuits, and then cheeses. She usually bakes her own bread, and will make American-style muffins for breakfast if requested.

Nearby Nantwich is an old town where black-and-white Tudor houses jostle one another in picturesque streets such as Welsh Row (the carvings inside the church and on the almshouses are well worth seeing). Its prosperity was founded on salt-mining, salt having been deposited here millions of years ago when the sea covered Cheshire. 'Magpie' houses (timbers painted black and plaster white) are characteristic throughout the great plain of Cheshire, a vast area like an immense park, with cows grazing among buttercups, meres shining, tracts of woodland, and rivers flowing peacefully to the sea. This is a historic area which was well populated even before the Romans came here in strength: on hilltops with far views are traces of prehistoric forts. Throughout the county there are historic towns full of character, such as Macclesfield (hilly streets from which you can see right to the Peak District, and old silk-weaving mills), Knutsford (Mrs Gaskell's 'Cranford') and of course Chester itself, described elsewhere. Near Knutsford is the huge radio telescope of Jodrell Bank (there is a visitor centre here). Macclesfield Forest is a vast wild moor, with crags and narrow valleys; at Anderton a lift raises boats from one canal to another (Cheshire is criss-crossed with canals); and in nearby Northwich houses lean at odd angles because of subsidence caused by salt-mines.

Readers' comments: Warmly recommended, lovely airy room, superb meal.

45

Woolhope, south-east of Hereford, HR1 4RF   Tel: 043277 281

3 bedrooms (double or single) from £16.50. Less for 7 nights or bargain breaks in winter. The rooms have central heating; TV,

armchairs; views of country; tea/coffee facilities; fruit.
Dinner 3-course bar meal, £5.85. Restaurant, à la carte, at 7.30–9.00pm, Wednesdays to Saturdays only. Special diets if ordered. Smoking discouraged. Lunches, packed lunches. Drinks can be ordered.
Lounge bar (open during licensed hours only), with central heating and open fire, books.
Patio garden
Nearest main road A438 from Hereford to Ledbury.

The sun streamed down from a clear blue sky onto the paved garden where I was lunching; a small stream clattered by and birds were singing. Yet it was mid-November!

The half-timbered Butchers Arms, which dates back to the 14th century, stands among fields that are far from any other building. Nevertheless its excellence is well known to scores of people who, though they live some distance away, beat a path to its door; and the bar was crowded. Even the snacks are outstanding, and the small restaurant is of gourmet standard. Breakfasts too are excellent.

William Griffiths offers a wide repertoire of rather unusual dishes to complement the straightforward Herefordshire beef steaks which are also served. From a wide selection one might, for instance, choose fried clams or a terrine made from tongue, chicken livers and brandy to start with; while main courses often include rabbit-and-bacon pie, pigeon with juniper berries and beef bourguignonne. Vegetarian dishes are imaginative.

In the bar, where an open fire crackles, you must duck to avoid low beams. Dining-room and bedrooms (quiet except over the bar) are furnished simply.

Woolhope is in the middle of a particularly scenic area: the Wye Valley and Symonds Yat are only a few miles away; so are the attractive old towns of Ross-on-Wye, Ledbury, and Hereford with its fine cathedral, big garden centre and cider museum. The Welsh borders, Black Mountains, Forest of Dean and Malvern Hills attract walkers as well as those who enjoy touring by car along traffic-free lanes. There is a falconry centre at Newent and gardens at Hergest Croft. Go in late autumn if you want to see a blaze of copper and gold foliage.

Readers' comments: Pleasant comfortable room; excellent staff; food extremely good. One of the nicest holidays in years. Excellent value. Outstanding value; excellent bar meals. Excellent food and service. Highly satisfied. Very good on all points.

Some readers tell me they have stayed at lots of places from *Staying Off the Beaten Track.* I wonder who has stayed at most? A free copy of the next edition awaits the reader who sends me his/her comments on the greatest number!

BUTTONS GREEN FARM

C D PT S

Cockfield, south of Bury St Edmunds, Suffolk, IP30 0JF   Tel: 0284 828229

3 bedrooms (single, double or family) from £12. Less for 2 nights. Rooms have electric heaters; armchairs; views of country or garden; tea/coffee facilities.
Dinner £8 for 3 courses and coffee, at 6.30pm. Special diets if ordered. Coffee, tea, for a charge. Non-residents not admitted. Drinks can be brought in.
Sitting-room with open fire, TV, books.
Garden and farmland.
Nearest main road A1141 from Hadleigh to the A134.
Closed in winter

Behind a big duckpond and masses of roses stands an apricot-coloured house built around 1400, the centre of an 80-acre farm of grain and beet fields. It has mullioned windows and a Tudor fireplace upstairs.

In the sitting-room, with large sash windows on two sides, a pale carpet and silky wallpaper make a light background to the antiques and velvet armchairs grouped round a big log fire. In one window is an epiphyllum which annually produces over 80 huge pink blooms. The dining-room has a log-burning stove in the brick inglenook, and leather-seated chairs are drawn up at a big oak table. Here Margaret Slater serves meals with home-grown or home-made produce, her own chutneys and marmalade. Among her most popular starters are egg mayonnaise and home-made pâté. A chicken or other roast may follow and then, for instance, chocolate soufflé or raspberries and cream.

Twisting stairs lead to big beamed bedrooms with sloping floors, which Mrs Slater has furnished with flowery fabrics, pot-plants and good furniture.

The farm is only a few minutes from Lavenham, one of the county's show villages – very beautiful (but, in summer, often very crowded), with a guildhall owned by the National Trust and a spectacular church. Still further south, in beautiful countryside threaded by rivers with old bridges and water-meadows, are such other historic villages as Bures (where St Edmund was crowned King of East Anglia in 855) and pretty Kersey, full of colourful half-timbered cottages.

Readers' comments: Lovely house. Charming hosts. Good home cooking.

Just the other side of Lavenham is Brent Eleigh and **Street Farm** (tel: 0787 247 271), its apricot walls half-timbered, its garden well-groomed. Inside are beamed ceilings and good furnishings – big velvet armchairs, and Hepplewhite-style chairs in the dining-room, for instance. Bedrooms are spacious. Jean Gage serves breakfast only.

Readers' comments: Very friendly. Comfortable. Beautifully maintained, very quiet.

47

CAMELEY LODGE

Temple Cloud, south of Bristol, Avon, BS18 5AH   Tel: 0761 52790

C(6) **PT S S-C**

rear view

4 bedrooms (single, double or family) from £15. Rooms have central heating; bathroom in some; TV, armchairs; views of country, lake or garden; tea/coffee facilities.
Dinner from £11 for 3 courses and coffee, at 7pm. Special diets if ordered. Lunches, packed lunches, snacks. Coffee, tea, for a charge. Drinks can be ordered.
Sitting-room with central heating, open fire, books; bar.
Grounds trout lake and farmland.
Nearest main road A37 from Bristol to Shepton Mallet.

A huge, stone barn in a superb setting was converted a few years ago into an extremely comfortable guest-house, run by John Harris whose parents own the farm on which it stands. It was built three hundred years ago for hay. Now it has a sitting-room with a bar and log fire, and an airy dining-room with windows overlooking the trout lake below, which is shared by swans, ducks and anglers. The conversion has been done with style: a red pantiled roof was put on, lattice windows inserted and panelled doors hung. Above are pleasantly furnished bedrooms, some with lake views and some looking towards the church.

Unexpectedly, Cameley Lodge is often quite full midweek – for a large number of Bristol businessmen find it a quiet place in which to confer, where they can offer business guests good fly-fishing afterwards (tuition bookable). Meals are based on local produce served in generous quantities (a whole 2lb trout may be offered as one serving). As a starter there might be prawn-and-apple cocktail or kidneys in brandy, before such a main course as suprême of chicken with a Madeira-and-peach sauce and to follow, a deliciously light coffee gâteau.

This is a very scenic area. The limestone Mendip Hills vary from wild ridges to gently rounded foothills, with drystone walls. Caves and gorges (at Cheddar and Wookey, in particular) add to their interest; and the stone, of course, means villages are as beautiful as many in the Cotswolds. The cathedral city of Wells is the region's greatest jewel; but Bristol now is very well worth visiting – its ancient quays restored, many good restaurants and theatres (the Welsh National Opera Company comes here), fine mediaeval church, and Brunel's SS *Great Britain* to visit. Bath is near, and the scenic Chew Valley.

Readers' comments: Good value.

Sitting-room at Low Hall (see page 168)

CARNWETHERS

Pelistry Bay, St Mary's, Isles of Scilly, TR21 0NX   Tel: 0720 22415

rear view

10 bedrooms (single, double or family) from £16. Discounts for payment in advance and 7 days or more. Rooms have central heating or electric heaters; shower or bathroom; armchairs; views of sea, country or garden; tea/coffee facilities; TV.
Dinner £8 for 4 courses (some choice) and coffee, at 6.30pm. No smoking. Packed lunches. Bedtime hot drinks can be ordered. Non-residents not admitted. Drinks can be ordered.
2 sitting-rooms with central heating, TV, books; bar.
Garden with heated pool (75°), croquet, putting, pool table, darts, table tennis.
Closed in winter

St Mary's, the principal island in the Scillies, is only three miles long. Even its centre of action, Hugh Town, can hardly be called busy by mainland standards (though it does receive tides of day-visitors during high summer), and so it is easy to find any number of unfrequented coves or beaches within a mere quarter of an hour or so from Hugh Town. Pelistry Bay is one of these – sheltered from wind, calm and unspoilt. Around it are pines and ferns, coastal footpaths and nature trails.

Carnwethers is more than an ordinary guest-house (and a very good one, at that): it is also a centre for marine studies. Its owner is Roy Graham, well known in the island and beyond as an underwater explorer and photographer, and a marine archaeologist – with 30 years in the Navy before he came here. Even non-experts appreciate his library of books on maritime subjects (wrecks, shipping, fish, wildlife, boats) and his immense knowledge of Scillonian history and ecology. His illustrated lectures in St Mary's twice a week should not be missed. He has assembled a number of videos about the islands which he shows to visitors, and can advise on boating or diving.

As to the house itself, this was once a farmhouse, but has been modernized. It is still surrounded by fields. Every room is as neat as a new pin. There is a bar and lengthy list of good-value wines, a heated 30-foot swimming-pool within sight of the sea itself but sheltered by granite walls and flowering shrubs, solarium, sauna, games room (for table tennis, darts, pool, etc.) and croquet lawn.

Meal times fit in with the times of the buses that take visitors into Hugh Town for evening events: not cinemas and night clubs, but slide shows which are usually packed out, concerts and the pubs.

Local produce is much used by Joyce for meals: fish (obviously), new potatoes, free-range eggs, home-grown vegetables and home-made marmalade, for example. A typical meal might comprise soup (not home-made) or fruit juice, roast turkey, and rolypoly pudding or fudge cake. Breakfasts include options like kedgeree and kippers. The dining-room has hanging plants, a stove for cold days and views of the fields with cows, flowers or potatoes in them according to season. Here and in the sitting-room, there are pictures of ships and seascapes. Bedrooms, too, are agreeably decorated; colours are pretty, cupboards have louvred pine doors, and each has at least its own shower.

The main attractions of the Scillies are their unspoilt beauty, mild climate, low rainfall and pure air. Storms are brief, sunny days long. Visitors to St Mary's get about on foot, by bus, and with hired cars or cycles (no cars on the other islands, which are reached by boats that regularly ply to and fro). Of course, the superb scenery and the solitude are the biggest attractions on all the islands; but in St Mary's, the main island, there are other things of interest: prehistoric villages and burial chambers; old fortifications and watch-tower; a clifftop golf course with arguably the most beautiful setting in England; boat-building, pottery and other crafts to watch (or learn); streams and pools, rock and islets to explore; subtropical flowers growing wild, butterflies, and rare birds that excite the ornithologists. The excellent local museum tells the story of the innumerable wrecks in these waters and of the latest discoveries by underwater archaeologists diving to them. There is the lifeboat station to visit, and weekly races of gigs (a type of rowing-boat peculiar to the Scillies). Penninis Head is infinitely more beautiful than Land's End: just one of the many memorable walks around the varied coastline. Nearly every kind of sea sport, of course; and fish that go straight from sea to saucepan. There is a new heritage/ecology centre with shipwreck museum. Day-trips to each of the other islands are well worth taking. Among these, Tresco is world-famous for its romantic gardens planted with subtropical flowers from every continent; it contains an outdoor museum of ships' figureheads.

There is rarely any rain in summer, and so, all along the wild tracks of the islands, succulents and cacti flourish together with high, blue echiums from New Zealand and the Madeira geranium (magenta in colour, round and bushy). The island is ideal for little ones, as there are safe beaches and lanes; and island children quickly become friends with young visitors. For town children, this is a paradise of wild violets, bumblebees, pennyworts growing on the stone walls and lichens in a dozen colours. Diving, boating and shark fishing can be arranged.

Readers' comments: Happy, friendly atmosphere. Could not ask for more. Lovely situation. Pleasant and helpful hosts.

Nearby is **Carn Vean** (tel: 0720 22462) in a pleasant setting of lawn and trees. Here Laurel Deason provides inexpensive accommodation and meals, as well as running a tea-garden.

CASTLE FARM

CS

Fotheringhay, north-east of Corby, Northamptonshire, PE8 5HZ
Tel: 08326 200

6 bedrooms (single, double or family) from £13. Most have own bath/shower; TV; tea/coffee facilities; central heating; views of river, country or garden. No smoking. (Washing-machine on request.)
Dinner £7.50 for 2 courses and coffee, at 7pm. Non-residents not admitted. Vegetarian or special diets if ordered. Lunches, packed lunches, snacks. Tea, coffee, free. Drinks can be brought in.
Sitting-room with central heating, open fire, TV, books.
Large garden
Nearest main road A605 from Peterborough to Oundle.

In the castle that was once here, Richard III was born – later to gain an infamous and probably unjustified reputation as murderer of 'the princes in the Tower'. Here, too, in that grim keep surrounded by two moats (a maximum-security prison) Mary Queen of Scots was, after many similar imprisonments, confined at the end of her life – to be tried for conspiracy against Elizabeth I. Forget the romantic picture of the lovely young queen. Ageing, lined and bent after long years of captivity, she limped pathetically with rheumatism to her execution on a scaffold she had earlier heard being hammered together in the courtyard, leaving 'this world out of which I am very glad to go' at daybreak on a bright, wintry morning: 8 February 1587. When the executioner lifted her head away from the body (clad in the scarlet of martyrdom), its wig fell off to reveal the balding head beneath. She had wished to be buried in Catholic France; but after interment by night in Peterborough Cathedral her headless corpse was later re-interred by her son, James I, in Westminster Abbey.

Her heart had been secretly buried, however, in the mound on which the castle, now long gone, was built: part of the land belonging to Castle Farm today. The thistles that grow here are called Queen Mary's tears.

At the Victorian farm, one steps straight into Stephanie Gould's huge quarry-tiled kitchen where a pine staircase rises to spacious bedrooms that are spick-and-span, all with good views (one of them looks onto the farmyard in one direction and to the ancient church in the other). There are very good bath- or shower-rooms, and much stripped pine. The big, comfortable sitting-room, too, has a view to enjoy – of the swift River Nene beyond the lawn, and a picturesque bridge. When I visited, the Goulds were in the process of converting outbuildings to make more bedrooms.

Stephanie produces traditional meals of two courses (such as lamb navarin with four vegetables including, for instance, home-grown asparagus, followed by sticky pear-gingerbread) or one can eat outstandingly well at the nearby Falcon Inn.

Fotheringhay Church is particularly fine, and contains interesting tombs. To the south is Oundle, famous for its public school (a delightful little town within a loop of the river, on which you can go boating). The whole area is dotted with the soaring spires of mediaeval churches rising above undisturbed woods and fields watered by the winding rivers. Once, kings hunted deer in Rockingham Forest – stretches of which still survive, together with William the Conqueror's Rockingham Castle. Southward there are some fine panoramas, numerous reservoirs that attract birdwatchers, and buildings of golden stone as fine as any in the Cotswolds.

CASTLE HOUSE

C D PT S X

23 Castle Street, Chester, Cheshire, CH1 2DS   Tel: 0244 350354

5 bedrooms (single, double or family) from £18. Less for 7 nights and bargain breaks. Most have own shower; TV; tea/coffee facilities; phone; central heating; views of garden. (Washing-machine on request.)
Sitting-room with central heating, open fire, books; bar.
Small garden
Nearest main road A41 from Whitchurch to Birkenhead.

Right in the middle of the city but in a quiet by-road, this interesting house has a breakfast-room which dates from 1540 behind an 18th-century frontage and staircase. The arms of Elizabeth I (with English lion and Welsh dragon) are over the fireplace.

It is both the Marls' own home and a guest-house with elegant bedrooms that are exceptionally well furnished and equipped. Bed-and-breakfast only, for Chester has so many good restaurants; but visitors are welcome to use the kitchen. Newspapers and local phone calls are free – as are evening refreshments: Cheshire cheese with a help-yourself drink from a small bar. Coyle Marl, a local business-man, is an enthusiast for Chester and loves to tell visitors about its lesser-known charms.

The city is, of course, of outstanding interest – second only to Bath and York in what there is to see. It is surrounded by ancient walls of red sandstone, just outside of which is a large Roman amphitheatre (more Roman and even older remains are constantly coming to light, the smaller artefacts displayed in the Grosvenor Museum). You can walk all round the top of the ramparts, a 2-mile trek. The most unique feature, however, is The Rows: here steps from street level lead up to balustraded galleries overhanging the pavements, serving a second level of small shops above the ones below. Many of the half-timbered houses have particularly fine carvings. Chester's cathedral of red stone dates back to the 14th century and its zoo is one of Britain's best.

From Chester many visitors head for Wales; but there is a nearby part of Cheshire which should not be ignored – the Wirral. This thumb of land is sandwiched between two estuaries: the Mersey on its industrial side, the Dee on its other, very scenic side – facing Wales. The climate here is so mild that spring comes earlier than in some southern counties, which is why (at Ness) there are such beautiful botanic gardens. Visit little Parkgate for shrimps, sea-birds and Nelson connections; the country park for tranquillity and views; the Victorian fort on a rock at the mouth of the Mersey; the Lady Lever art gallery, containing some of the world's most famous paintings; Port Sunlight – one of the first garden-cities; Ellesmere Port for the canal boat museum – all these are on the Wirral, as is Wallasey, a popular seaside resort with sand dunes, beaches and piers.

To the south lie the Peckforton Hills (with Beeston and Cholmondeley castles), Delamere Forest (dotted with shining meres) and such historic little towns as Malpas and Nantwich.

CATHEDRAL GATE HOTEL   C PT X
36 Burgate, Canterbury, Kent, CT1 2HA   Tel: 0227 464381

25 bedrooms (single, double or family) from £17.50. Some have own bath/shower; TV; tea/coffee facilities; phones; central heating; views of cathedral. (Washing-machine on request.)

Dinner £8 for 3 courses (with choices) and coffee, at 7–9.30pm. Non-residents not admitted. Vegetarian or special diets if ordered. Packed lunches, snacks. Drinks can be ordered.

3 sitting-rooms with central heating, TV (in one); bar. No smoking (in one).

Nearest main road A2 from Dover to the M2 (junction 7).

The cathedral has a great, sculpted, mediaeval gateway. Tucked beside it is a row of shops and restaurants, above part of which is this upstairs guest-house (which has direct access to the cathedral precincts).

Even in Saxon times there was some kind of hospice here; and when the martyrdom of Thomas Becket in 1170 began to bring pilgrims to Canterbury in their thousands, it was in these beamy rooms that many of them stayed.

The spacious bedrooms (and small residents' sitting-rooms) are reached via a maze of narrow corridors and creaking stairways which twist this way and that. All are quiet (for Burgate is now restricted to pedestrians only); and some at the top have superlative views across the cathedral precincts to the great tower and south transept – floodlit at night.

The small hotel was recently taken over by Caroline Jubber and her husband who have greatly improved the bedrooms – some of them reached via a rooftop walkway – while retaining ancient beams, leaded casements and bow windows. There are now three small sitting-rooms, too, which include a bar and a television room. Breakfast (continental, unless you pay extra) is brought to you in one of these or in your bedroom. Formal dinner is not provided because there are so many restaurants close by; but at any hour you can order meals such as spaghetti bolognese or chicken Kiev, or full afternoon teas. Bedrooms are very well equipped and some even have mini-bars. Many look across undulating old roofs and red chimney-pots where chattering starlings perch. The only inconvenience is that cars have to be parked a few minutes' walk away.

It is, of course, the cathedral which brings most visitors to Canterbury: one of Britain's finest and most colourful, with many historical associations. It is the site of Becket's martyrdom (commemorated in some of the finest stained glass in the world) and houses the splendid tomb of the Black Prince, and much more.

The ancient walled city still has many surviving mediaeval and Tudor buildings, the beautiful River Stour, old churches and inns, Roman remains, a very good theatre, and lovely shops in its small lanes. It is in the middle of some of Kent's finest countryside, with a coast of great variety quite near (cliffs, sands or shingle; resorts, fishing harbours or historic ports). It would be very easy to spend a fortnight here without discovering all there is to see in one of England's most beautiful and most historic counties.

Canterbury is a useful place to stay before or after a ferry-crossing to the continent – or as a base from which to explore the historic south Kent coast, the Cinque Ports, Dover Castle and Dover's famous Roman 'Painted House' or the Kent countryside, the garden of England.

53

CAVENDISH HOUSE

Eastmount Road, Shanklin, Isle of Wight, PO37 6DN   Tel: 0983 862460

PT S

3 bedrooms (double) from £14. Less for 7 nights or bargain breaks. Rooms have central heating; shower or bathroom; TV, armchairs; tea/coffee facilities.
Nearest main road A3055 from Shanklin to Sandown.

Although this resort is full of hotels, I had difficulty in finding any with really attractive rooms. Lesley Peters' home is an exception. She has furnished the large Victorian rooms with style – Laura Ashley fabrics and well-chosen colour schemes complementing good antiques. She has made the most of handsome architectural features (for instance, picking out in blue the plasterwork vine of one ceiling and filling an old tiled fireplace with pot-plants). Every room has a table and chairs for breakfast, as there is no dining-room. For dinner, Lesley (once an air stewardess) recommends The Cottage; or you can take the nearby lift to the foot of the cliff and Osborne House Hotel where, after an excellent help-yourself buffet, prepared by Mike Hogarth, you can sit on the flowery, grass-enclosed verandah facing the sea (bedrooms available, but hardly 'off the beaten track').

Shanklin has sandy beaches and a beautiful chine (ravine); the picturesque village of Godshill and its smithy lie inland. In many parts of the island, there are plenty of well-marked footpaths for walkers; and sights to see are described under other entries of which the most popular are Queen Victoria's Osborne House, Carisbrooke Castle, Blackgang Chine, Alum Bay, Barton Vineyard and Arreton Manor.

Although Shanklin itself gets uncomfortably busy in high summer, this house is well away from all the bustle.

Other attractions of the Isle of Wight are described elsewhere.

When to go? Seaside resorts or other places suitable for children will be at their busiest (and dearest) in July–August and during half-term holidays (especially in late May, which is also a bank holiday period). Other peak periods are, of course, Easter, Christmas, New Year and the bank holiday in late August. (The bank holiday in early May is not usually a peak, because it comes rather soon after Easter, but much depends on the weather.) There are local peaks, too (the Gold Cup races at Cheltenham or the regatta at Henley, for instance, are apt to fill hotels for miles around), and local troughs (Brighton, a conference centre, is least busy in high summer). You won't get much personal attention when hotels are full to bursting.

CHAPEL HOUSE

C PT

Friar's Gate, Atherstone, north of Coventry, Warwickshire, CV9 1EY
Tel: 0827 718949

12 bedrooms (single or double) from £18.50. Less for 2 nights at weekend. Rooms have central heating; shower; TV, phone, armchairs; views of garden. (Clothes-washing facilities.)

Dinner £9.95 (weekdays) for 3 courses and coffee, or à la carte, at 7pm. Vegetarian or special diets if ordered. Lunches, packed lunches, snacks. Coffee, tea, for a charge. Drinks can be ordered.

Sitting-room with central heating and open fire, books and a bar.

Walled gardens

Nearest main road A5 from Dunstable to Wales.

Tucked away in a flowery corner just off the Market Square is hidden an elegant 18th-century house, now once again equally elegantly furnished by Pat and David Roberts, both highly expert cooks (David used to teach in a catering college).

It was previously the dower house of Atherstone Hall, home of Selina Bracebridge who in the 1840s was the only friend of young Florence Nightingale to encourage her ambition to become a nurse. The Bracebridges accompanied Florence to the Crimea in 1854 and were her most loyal assistants.

This is why Florence's head ornaments the pelmet in the dining-room. It is a handsome room where the marble fireplace contrasts with walls covered in cocoa hessian, the long curtains are of magnolia chintz and the shield-back chairs are upholstered in velvet. Chapel House is renowned for its gourmet meals, particularly at weekends (the Prince and Princess of Wales were lunched here when attending a civic function at Atherstone).

Through a small conservatory, hung with fuchsias, one reaches a very pretty enclosed garden with tables on the lawn. This is one of three gardens around the house. Another has a high, curved wall behind which lay the one-time friary where Henry VII prayed before he defeated Richard III at the Battle of Bosworth.

The sitting-room (pine-panelled, with an attractive colour scheme of water-melon pink, pale grey and moss green) lies beyond a stone-flagged hall, from which the staircase rises to equally attractive bedrooms – I particularly liked one with a window-seat overlooking the walled garden, but even those on the second floor – under the eaves, furnished in cottage style – are very pretty.

The inclusive terms for residents allow for a 3-course meal (such as potted meat made from rabbit, pork and chicken liver; stuffed pork; chocolate, hazelnut and brandy mousse), with coffee. Five-course à la carte choice on certain evenings.

Atherstone, a pleasant town on the A5 (which is often an agreeable alternative to using the M1 as a way to get from London to the Midlands), is in the northern part of Warwickshire There is wooded countryside, and from here you can visit Sutton Coldfield's 2000-acre natural park. Around are woods, valleys, heather moors, lakes, bird reserves and a championship golf course. The town itself has 17th-century stone houses. Mediaeval Maxstoke Castle and nearby Coleshill; Arbury Hall (near which George Eliot was born); Birmingham's art gallery (strong on pre-Raphaelites) and outstanding botanical gardens; Tamworth for its castle; Lichfield for its 3-spired cathedral and Samuel Johnson's birthplace.

Readers' comments: Beautifully furnished, food superb.

55

CHASE LODGE

C D PT X

Park Road, Hampton Wick, Surrey, KT1 4AS Tel: 01-943 1862

6 bedrooms (double or family) from £15. Less for 3 nights and bargain breaks (and if breakfast or tea/coffee are not wanted). Some have own bath/shower; all have TV; tea/coffee facilities; central heating. (Washing-machine on request.)
Small garden
Nearest main road A308 from Staines to Surbiton.

This is a very handy place at which to stay in order to explore the 'royal' stretch of the Thames Valley (monarchs chose nearby Richmond, Hampton Court, Kew and Windsor for their palaces). It is only half an hour from London in one direction and from Heathrow Airport in the other.

Park Road is in a quiet conservation area, a street of pretty little Victorian villas with cottage-gardens, yet only a minute or two from a railway station, buses and the excellent shops and market of Kingston.

Chase Lodge has been redecorated with interesting pieces of Victorian furniture and decorative trifles in its sitting-room and elsewhere (even a toilet has a tented ceiling of pleated silk). There are African violets and other pot-plants in the bedrooms; and attractive quilted spreads are on some of the beds.

Only breakfast is served as a rule, but there are local restaurants and take-aways. (Denise Dove encourages visitors to use the breakfast-room for snacks.)

At the back of the house is a tiny, sun-trapping patio with a few seats among the petunias and nasturtiums. One bedroom has a tented scarlet-and-green ceiling and a mural of a crusader castle in its bathroom. Another, a four-poster with lace.

I was greatly impressed by Mrs Dove's attention to detail and the immense trouble she takes. Not many far more costly hotels provide room service free, fresh towels and soap daily, fridges with milk and soft drinks in every room.

There is an enormous amount to see and do in the neighbourhood: river trips from nearby Kingston Bridge, walks among the deer and chestnut trees of Bushey Park or along the towpaths, Kew Gardens and Palace, Hampton Court – now with son-et-lumière shows at night – and its gardens (with maze), horse-racing, tennis at Wimbledon, rugby at Twickenham, and any number of regattas and festivals in summer. Richmond deserves at least a day to itself, to explore the byways and curio shops off the green, the stunning river view from the top of the hill, and the 3000 acres of Richmond Park. Windsor has its great castle, royal steam-rail show and safari park (Eton College is close by). There are Georgian villages, and Georgian or earlier mansions in fine grounds (Ham House, Orleans House, Marble Hill, Syon Park, Chiswick House, Hogarth's house and Osterley Park).

A little further west is Staines and at **Thames Side**, Penton Road (tel: 0784 452294), Geraldine Lewin not only provides bed-and-breakfast but also runs a booking service for other private houses nearby: several with gardens by the Thames; some are historic houses and others (including hers) modern; a few provide dinner. If you explain your tastes and needs to her, she will select a house suited to you. In her own house, the guest-room – with shower and toilet – is on the ground floor. Geraldine is a talkative lady and happy to draw everyone into the family's many activities.

(There is the sound of aircraft using Heathrow.)

CHERRYBROOK

Two Bridges, west of Tavistock, Devon, PL20 6SP   Tel: 0822 88260

7 **bedrooms** (single, double or family) from £18.50. Less for 3 nights. Prices go up from Easter. Rooms have central heating; own bathroom; armchairs; views of country or garden; tea/coffee facilities.

Dinner £8.50 for 4 courses and coffee, at 7.30pm. Special diets if ordered. Packed lunches, snacks. Coffee, tea for a charge. Drinks can be ordered.

Sitting-room with central heating, open fire, TV on request, books; bar.

Extensive grounds

Nearest main road A386 from Tavistock to Okehampton.

High up and right in the middle of Dartmoor, this little hotel is full of character. It was built by a friend of the Prince Regent when he acquired farming rights on the moor, and many of the old features are still to be seen – low-beamed ceilings and thick stone walls (now painted white). What was once a cowshed is now a sitting-room, with rugs on floors made of polished slate. On the walls, John Reynolds has hung old peat-digging tools and a pair of Canadian snow shoes (still awaiting sufficient snow to make them useful). There is a log stove and, at one end, a small bar. Pewter mugs hang from a beam; Susan's spinning-wheel stands ready for use.

Bedrooms are pleasantly furnished, with leafy views and no sound louder than the baaing of sheep. Every room is immaculate, and paintwork throughout is pristine. I particularly appreciated the armchairs facing the big windows of bedrooms nos. 1 and 2. This remote house pumps its own pure spring water. Truly 'away from it all'!

There are always choices at each course of dinner, from which one might perhaps choose mushroom soup, chicken casseroled in cider, chocolate sponge and then cheese.

As to sightseeing, apart from the moor itself (a National Park) and all its villages, National Trust houses and gardens, nature reserves and guided walks (of one to six hours), it is possible to visit both north and south coasts of Devon as well as the historic cities of Plymouth and Exeter. Occasionally special holidays are offered with walks laid on, or visits to National Trust houses, of which there are a great many in this region.

Readers' comments: Comfortable and well fed. Wonderful host and hostess. Warm, friendly; excellent food. Decor, food and friendly atmosphere exceptional. Peace and tranquillity with exceptional views.

Library at the Haven (see page 134)

Main Street, Chideock, west of Bridport, Dorset, DT6 6JH
Tel: 0297 89368

5 **bedrooms** (double or family) from £13. Less for 3 nights. Rooms have central heating or electric heaters; views of country or garden; tea/coffee facilities. Continental breakfast in bed is available. Most rooms have shower. (Laundering facilities available.) No smoking.

Dinner £7.95–£9.95 for 4 courses and coffee with liqueur, at 7.30pm (5 days a week). Special diets if ordered. Non-residents by prior arrangement. Drinks can be ordered. No smoking.

Sitting-room with central heating, log fire, TV and video, books; bar. No smoking.

Garden

Nearest main road A35 from Axminster to Bridport.

This pretty thatched cottage in its old-fashioned garden is on the road between Georgian Bridport and the historic town of Lyme Regis. Built in the 17th century, the guest-house has been furnished in keeping with its age. The sitting-room and bar are beamed and with log fires in winter. Two bedrooms have four-posters, and several are beamed (the ones at the back are quiet, front ones are double-glazed).

For dinner you might get a home-made soup, pork chop in orange sauce, ice cream made with Cointreau, cheese, Rombouts coffee (and free liqueur), on a table with lace cloth, cut glass and Royal Worcester china. For breakfast, try the coddled eggs or one of many other imaginative options. Cream teas sometimes available.

Mr and Mrs Hardy lend visitors Ordnance Survey maps and give advice. For example, they can tell you where to find fossils easily plucked from the Blue Lias clay, or where the best walks are on clifftops or through valleys – and if you want a lift back at the end of a walk, they are willing to come and fetch you in their car. They also show a film of Dorset.

Car washing and vacuuming facilities free.

Chideock itself is a very pretty village of thatched cottages, in a fold of the west Dorset hills designated an 'area of outstanding natural beauty'. The sea is close and much of the coastline hereabouts belongs to the National Trust. Within a short distance are Lyme Regis, Charmouth, Abbotsbury (swannery and subtropical gardens), Chesil Beach, Portland and Weymouth – all on the coast. Among the hills and vales, the farmlands and streams, are Sherborne (castle and abbey), Parnham House and Cricket St Thomas, Cerne Abbas (abbey and the giant cut in the chalk hills nearly two thousand years ago) and Beaminster (Georgian houses). There are fine gardens at Forde Abbey and Clapton Court. This part of Dorset has rolling chalk hills through which streams have created picturesque valleys. There are fine views from high tracks created by prehistoric man.

Readers' comments: Beautifully appointed house, historic without detracting from 20th-century comforts, comfortable, friendly, good food. Very helpful and pleasant, well prepared food but not too exotic. Charming house and owners. A delight; meal was exceptionally good value, owners have warmth and humour. Comfortable room, excellent meals, many little extra touches.

CHISWICK HOUSE

C

Meldreth, north of Royston, Hertfordshire, SG8 6LZ   Tel: 0763 260242

4 bedrooms (single or double) from £14. All have own shower; TV; tea/coffee facilities; central heating; views of garden. No smoking.

Sitting-room with central heating, log fire, TV, books.

Small garden

Nearest main road A10 from Cambridge to Royston.

Elbourns have lived in this house for a century. When the latest generation, John and Bernice, set about renovating it, they uncovered beams with drawings and lettering from the 15th century. It originally had no chimney or fireplaces: these 'mod cons' came in during Tudor times. Over one fireplace is the coat-of-arms of James I: it is believed he used the house as a hunting-lodge (he had a palace at nearby Royston, of which fragments still remain), and the panelling in the dining-room dates from his reign.

The house, although modernized, still has a very historic look, with old oak beams, polished woodwork and flowers in every room. Carved chairs surround a refectory table, there is a Knole sofa, and brass-studded leather chairs. One of the beamy bedrooms opens onto the terrace. Bed-and-breakfast only: visitors dine at the Swan (Fowlmere), Royal Oak (Barrington) or Red Lion (Grantchester – immortalized in Rupert Brooke's poem).

Many people stay here as a base from which to visit Cambridge, but north Hertfordshire is itself worth exploring. Royston, a town of narrow streets and old inns, has a strange man-made cave beneath its streets with carvings of the Crucifixion. Baldock, with many 18th-century houses, is distinguished by a main street lined with trees and grassy banks. Ashwell's Roman origins are shown in its unusually spacious planning, and the traces of a Roman road can still be seen nearby; there are fine 17th-century houses with decorative plasterwork (pargetting) and ash trees still grow around the spring which gave it its name. (South Hertfordshire has been described elsewhere.)

From Meldreth it is no distance to the borders of three other counties – Cambridgeshire (Cambridge itself, Newmarket of racing fame, and St Neots – its market square flanked by the river Great Ouse and its church adorned with wonderful carvings; Gog Magog Hills for a view of the university spires; stately Wimpole Hall); Essex (mediaeval Saffron Walden and further south the picturesque Rodings – eight waterside villages, the great 17th-century house of Audley End, much-photographed Wendens Ambo and Finchingfield, the three historic Bardfield villages); and Bedfordshire (Bedford itself, Whipsnade Zoo park, stately homes such as Luton Hoo, Ampthill's park, Houghton House ruins – Bunyan's 'House Beautiful', the water gardens of Wrest Park, Sandy's RSPB reserve, historic aircraft at Biggleswade). Altogether, this is an area of great variety and yet one which many tourists merely pass through on their way to more famous places, quite unaware of what they are missing.

Readers' comments: Unassuming, hospitable hostess; homely, comfortable rooms. How relaxed we felt!

CHITHURST FARM

CS

Chithurst Lane, Smallfield, Horley, north of Gatwick, Surrey, RH6 9JU
Tel: 034284 2487

3 bedrooms (single, double or family) from £12. Much less for 7 nights. Rooms have electric heaters; armchairs; views of country or garden. Coffee, tea, snacks, for a charge. Non-smokers preferred.
Sitting-room with central heating, open fire, TV, books.
Garden and farmland.
Nearest main road A23 from Redhill to Crawley.
Closed in December and January

Despite being so near Gatwick (and even London is only 35 minutes from the nearest rail station), this farm seems truly remote, reached by a long and winding lane. Built in the 16th century, it has tile-hung walls of mellow red brick against which the japonica flowers in spring.

Inside are low beams and a twisting staircase leading to simple but spacious bedrooms. These have double-glazing so that the sound of aircraft (numerous only during the day in summer) is not disturbing, with air-conditioners providing fresh air. In the visitors' sitting/dining-room, armchairs and a rocking-chair are grouped around a huge inglenook fireplace (with log stove), its original spit-rack still in place.

Visitors are welcome to watch cows being milked, and to buy home-made jams. This is a good area for walking in the North Downs. There are several stately homes, gardens (such as Ardingly and Wakehurst), and bird or wildlife parks nearby. Even Brighton in one direction, and the Kentish Weald in the other, are soon reached. Nearby, several old towns like Horsham and Dorking are worth exploring. Churchill's house (Chartwell), the Bluebell steam railway, Hever Castle, Box Hill, Tunbridge Wells and Ashdown Forest are all very popular as are the many pick-your-own fruit farms.

Some people stay at the farm before flying from Gatwick, and if necessary Mrs Tucker will leave early breakfasts ready. A nearby garage will house your car, with free transport (24 hours a day) to and from the airport – where parking would cost you far more.

Mrs Tucker does not provide evening meals, but has a list of recommended local restaurants etc. which do, such as the Plough Inn at Smallfield. Chithurst Farm is remarkably good value for this area.

Readers' comments: Charming. Pleasant attention.

Inclusive terms for dinner, bed-and-breakfast (particularly for a week) can be much lower than those quoted here for these items taken separately. For short-notice bookings you may be able to get a reduction.

No proprietor wants to have a room standing empty. This particularly applies to Sunday nights. Some hotels make a discount if you want only two courses from a three-course menu.

CHURCH FARM

C D PT X

41 High Street, Roxton, north-east of Bedford, MK44 3EB
Tel: 0234 870234

2 bedrooms (double or family) from £12. Tea/coffee facilities; central heating; views of garden. (Washing-machine on request.)
Sitting-room with central heating, open fire, TV, books.
Large garden
Nearest main road A428 from Bedford to Huntingdon.

It is a surprise to find such a peaceful village (a thatched church as well as thatched cottages) so close to the busy Great North Road, the A1, and in it this house – part 16th- and part 18th-century. One bedroom has a royal coat-of-arms carved in the wall, dating from Stuart times.

A beautiful breakfast-room has a Chippendale-style table and a sideboard with its original brass rails. Bedrooms in the guest wing are large (one has a particularly handsome wardrobe); all rooms are furnished with an informal mixture of family antiques. There is a pleasant sitting-room in shades of cream and brown with a log fire. (For dinner, Janet Must recommends restaurants in either St Neots or Bedford, both a few miles away, or else local village inns.)

Visitors who stay here are often surprised to discover Bedfordshire's little-publicized charms, particularly its pretty villages, many of which are sited on wandering streams. Popular outings include not only Bedford (with the John Bunyan museum, the art collection in the Cecil Higgins gallery, a church with carved angels in the roof and pretty riverside lawns) and Cambridge, but Shuttleworth's historic aircraft collection, the Swiss Garden, stately homes (such as Luton Hoo, Woburn and Hinwick House), Grafham Water and Olney (for its antique shops and boutiques). Sandy has the RSPB's headquarters and bird reserve, Huntingdon its Cromwell associations. In 15 towns or villages of Bedfordshire there are antique shops; there are also a number of pick-your-own fruit farms.

Almost the whole of Bunyan's life was played out in Bedfordshire, and it is possible to follow a Bunyan trail, starting at Elstow (where he was born in 1628 and grew up to follow his father's trade – a tinker, a mender of cooking pots and suchlike). It was at Lower Samshill that he was first arrested for preaching; and at Bedford that he spent much of his life in prison. Mementoes (including his portable anvil) are in the Bunyan Museum, near the meeting-house which has scenes from *The Pilgrim's Progress* in bas-relief on its doors.

Bedroom at the Old Rectory, Standlake, near Witney (see page 212)

CHURCH FARMHOUSE

C D PT

**3 Main Street, East Ayton, west of Scarborough, North Yorkshire,
YO13 9HL** Tel: 0723 862102

6 bedrooms (single, double or family) from £16.50. Tea/coffee facilities; central heating; views of country or garden; TV. No smoking. (Washing-machine on request.)
Dinner £10.50 for 3 courses (with choices) and coffee, at 7pm. Non-residents not admitted. Vegetarian or special diets if ordered. Lunches, packed lunches, snacks. Tea, coffee, extra. Wine can be ordered.
2 sitting-rooms with central heating, open fire, TV, books, record-player. Games room.
Small garden
Nearest main road A170 from Thirsk to Scarborough.

Not in the countryside but in the middle of a picturesque village, this 18th-century farmhouse has rooms at the back which are quiet and all of them have character. In the thick-walled, pink sitting-room, there is a log fire on the brick hearth, pink and green velvet armchairs surround this, and 'country Chippendale' chairs are at the dining-table. A second sitting-room has an unusual ceiling of wood boards. There is a flowery courtyard at the back, with pool and fountain; and a landscaped garden. Here a stone outbuilding houses a games room with table tennis and snooker.

With the help of some young part-timers from the village, Sally Chamberlain produces excellent home-cooked dinners and sometimes bakes her own bread. Said one visitor: 'The pudding trolley fairly groans'. Cakes and tea are free on arrival. Sometimes she serves mushroom vol-au-vents as a starter or hot, spiced grapefruit as an alternative to home-made soups. The main course could be an 8-oz steak, fish straight from nearby Filey, pork in orange sauce, or lasagne accompanied by garlic bread. Popular puddings include pavlovas, Bakewell tart, strawberry mousse and a gâteau with oranges, ginger and brandy in it. Sally likes children and encourages them to join in with the cooking if they enjoy this.

East Ayton is well placed to visit both the superb Yorkshire coast, where safe sandy beaches alternate with towering cliffs, and the North Yorkshire Moors (national park). There are excellent walks by the River Derwent and in lovely Forge Valley. Within an hour's drive is a choice of beaches (at Filey, Sandsend and Whitby, for instance, as well as at nearby Scarborough); abbeys at Rosedale and Rievaulx; castles at Helmsley and Pickering; Flamingoland zoo park; and great Castle Howard. There is a steam railway right across the moors. Theatres and other entertainments are available at Scarborough which is also a good shopping centre. York is within driving distance.

Roads southward go to Flamborough, a great chalk headland the sheer cliffs of which accommodate thousands of seabirds; on the way, one passes 18th-century Sewerby Hall, and the road goes through the middle of a prehistoric promontory fort. The seaside resort of Bridlington is near here (sands, harbour and a notable priory church) and the old town of Beverley with its lovely minster.

Readers' comments: Comfortable and well furnished, excellent cooking. A splendid, comfortable bedroom. Nothing was too much trouble for Mrs Chamberlain. Delighted. Food fantastic; delicious. Cooking excellent.

CHURCH HOUSE

C(12) X

Grittleton, north-west of Chippenham, Wiltshire, SN14 6AP
Tel: 0249 782562

4 bedrooms (single, double or family) from £17. Less for 8 nights or winter bargain breaks. Rooms have central heating; own bathroom; TV with remote control, armchairs; views of country or garden; tea/coffee facilities.

Dinner £11 for 4 courses, wine and coffee, at 8pm. Vegetarian or special diets if ordered. Lunches, packed lunches, snacks. Coffee, tea, for a charge. Drinks can be brought in.
2 sitting-rooms with central heating, open fire, TV, books, indoor games (including indoor boules, table skittles), piano, record-player. Sun-bed.
Garden with croquet, trampoline, swimming-pool (80°).
Nearest main road M4 (junction 17 or 18).

This little-known but very beautiful village lies just off the M4 midway between London and Wales: a cluster of elegant houses, a great Tudor mansion and church, all built from golden Cotswold limestone.

Church House began life in 1740 as a huge rectory, which it took six servants to run. Around it are lawns with immense copper beeches (floodlit at night), an orchard, fields of sheep and a swimming-pool, well heated in summer – as well as a walled vegetable and fruit garden which provides organic produce for the kitchen, where Anna Moore produces imaginative meals if these are ordered in advance. A typical menu might comprise sorrel soup, chicken in a creamy apricot-and-curry mayonnaise, a tart of fresh peaches, English cheeses, fruit and wine (included in the price). Anna can also cater for special dietary needs.

She and her family treat all visitors as house guests. If you want to meet Grittleton people, she will invite some to dinner, and she often escorts overseas visitors on sightseeing tours. Some she takes to the Royal Shakespeare Theatre (Stratford is 1½ hours away), with a champagne picnic supper on the banks of the Avon afterwards. The Moores are a musical family, and occasionally arrange music evenings – there is one huge room with a grand piano used for this purpose. Watching polo can be arranged.

The house has handsome and finely proportioned rooms. In the yellow sitting-room (which has an immense bay window overlooking the garden) are antique furniture, interesting paintings and a large log stove. The dining-room is equally handsome: raspberry walls, an Adam fireplace of inlaid marble and, on the long mahogany table, silver candelabra and Victorian Spode Copeland china. The most impressive architectural feature is the graceful staircase that curves its way up to the second floor, where the guest rooms are (and also a kitchen for making tea etc. at any hour). These bedrooms are furnished with antiques.

There is an immense amount to see and do in the neighbourhood. Close by is Badminton (celebrated for the annual horse-trials, attended by the royal family); Bath is only 12 miles away; and the many historic (and prehistoric sites) of Wiltshire, such as Avebury, are all around. Both the West Country and the Cotswolds are accessible from Grittleton. Malmesbury Abbey, Castle Combe, Westonbirt Arboretum and the gardens at Bowood, Broadleaze and Sheldon Manor are favourite sights. Antique shops abound (Swindon has monthly sales) and so do pick-your-own fruit farms.

63

CHURCH HOUSE

CPT

Lyonshall, west of Leominster, Herefordshire, HR5 3HR Tel: 05448 350

3 bedrooms (single, double or family) from £12. Less for 3 nights and bargain breaks. Some have own bath; all have tea/coffee facilities; central heating; views of country or garden. (Washing-machine on request.)
Dinner £7 for 3 courses (with choices) and coffee, at 7.30pm. Non-residents not admitted. Vegetarian or special diets if ordered. Tea, coffee, free. Drinks can be brought in.
Sitting-room with central heating, open fire, TV, books.
Large garden
Nearest main road A44 from Leominster to Kington.

Venture into the barn here and you may be tempted to order a unique creation: a pin-tucked blouse, lace- or ribbon-trimmed in Edwardian style, each specially designed for its recipient by Eileen Dilley (formerly a London fashion designer). Now she uses the barn as a display centre for these and other crafts – all in Edwardian style: other garments (including children's), lavender bags, dolls, cushions.

The 18th-century house, too, is filled with her work and with Edwardiana she and her husband have collected. All the furnishings are from that period, with bedrooms named after celebrities of the time such as Baden-Powell, Nellie Melba and Conan Doyle (who lived near here while writing *The Hound of the Baskervilles*, using a well-known local name in its title). Every room has frilled curtain-ties or cushions she has made; fans, fashion prints or Valentines she has collected. In one of the large bedrooms is a four-poster; and in the dining-room each lace-covered table has its own distinctive pattern of Edwardian bone china. Her traditional teas are served to the public (winning Eileen 'Tea Place of the Year' award in 1987); dinners are for residents only. The latter may comprise a tuna-and-sweetcorn starter, pork in mustard sauce and peach meringue, for instance. There is much emphasis on local produce and recipes.

Outside are donkeys in a paddock, many trees including a specimen copper beech in the garden, spring lambs and fine views beyond the haha.

Whichever way you drive there is plenty to see. Hereford (cathedral), Leominster (market town, with many antique shops), hilly mid-Wales, the Elan Valley, Llandrindod Wells (old-fashioned spa), Welsh seaside resorts, the black-and-white villages typical of Herefordshire, several stately homes (Croft Castle, Berrington Hall and Burton Court, for instance). Clee Hill is a well-known beauty-spot in the direction of historic Ludlow and the outstanding castle of Stokesay. Symonds Yat is a celebrated viewpoint above the Wye Valley. Walkers head for Offa's Dyke, bookworms for Hay-on-Wye, garden-lovers for Hergest Croft.

Readers' comments: Excellent quality. Highly recommended, excellent food; I have been four times in one year. Superior to lots of hotels.

All prices are inclusive of any VAT or service charge. They are minimum prices: superior rooms or high-season bookings may cost more.

THE CITADEL
Weston-under-Redcastle, north of Shrewsbury, Shropshire, SY4 5JY
Tel: 063084 204

3 bedrooms (double or family) from £18. Less for 3 nights. All have own bath/shower; central heating; views of country or garden. (Washing-machine on request.)
Dinner £10.50 for 3 courses (with choices) and coffee, at 7.30pm. Non-residents not admitted. Vegetarian or special diets if ordered. Packed lunches. Tea, coffee, free. Drinks can be brought in.
Sitting-room with central heating, open fire, TV, books, piano.
Large garden
Nearest main road A49 from Shrewsbury to Whitchurch.
Closed November–March

The castellated turrets of this unusual red sandstone mansion have never known a shot fired in battle. Erected in 1820 when the fashion for mock-Gothic architecture was at its peak, it was built as the dower house for Lady Jane Hill – the Hills lived in nearby Hawkstone Hall.

The interior is equally striking: some rooms – including one guest bedroom – are round, windows are deep-set, and ceilings are particularly decorative. From the cobbled terrace there are views of the Welsh hills and of Hawkstone Park (now a golf course). Among its trees are follies (a tower and an obelisk) and caves.

One enters through a round hall with an inlaid octagonal table; the ceiling has decorative ribs and bosses. In the celadon-green dining-room the coffered ceiling is embellished with plasterwork vines. There is a sitting-room (chocolate and white) which houses a grand piano; as well as a billiard room with terracotta ceiling. An unusual stone staircase leads up to the turret bedrooms; one of the bathrooms is of Edwardian splendour.

Sylvia Griffiths serves such dinners as cheese and asparagus flan to start with, jugged pheasant and chocolate roulade.

Apart from the scenery of one of England's loveliest and most peaceful counties, the greatest attraction of the area is historic Shrewsbury – perched on a hill almost islanded by a great loop of the River Severn. It deserves repeated visits to explore twisting lanes (with such curious names as Dogpole, Shoplatch or Coffeehouse Passage), the castle, the main square with flower-baskets hung around an open-pillared market hall, and all the exceptionally decorative black-and-white houses with carved figures of warriors and other characters. Wealthy wool-merchants built impressive homes here, and helped to enrich the colourful church with stained glass and carved angels. Among the zigzag alleys are craft and curio shops.

The house of Clive of India is open as one of Shrewsbury's many museums (a good china collection); and between the town walls and the river are the Quarry Gardens. Percy Thrower designed these.

Other places of interest in north Shropshire include Georgian Ellesmere and its surrounding lakes (seven of them); the little market town of Wem; the curiously named Ruyton-XI-Towns (11 small hamlets decided to unite in 1301, resulting in a main street over a mile long); Hodnet, particularly rich in black-and-white houses and with fine gardens around Hodnet Hall; Market Drayton, where Clive was born and where canal cruises are now popular; and Oswestry – castle and historic houses.

CLANDON MANOR FARM

C(12) **PT**

Back Lane, East Clandon, east of Guildford, Surrey, GU4 7SA
Tel: 0483 222357 and 222765 (Fax: 0483-223-585)

3 bedrooms (twin or family) from £10. Rooms have central heating; TV; views of farmland or garden.
Small sitting-room with central heating, TV, books.
Nearest main road A246 from Leatherhead to Guildford.

When financial disaster struck Sir Freddie Laker, this immaculately kept farm was one of the properties he had to sell. Its purchaser, surprisingly, was Sally Grahame, who hitherto had led a typically Kensington life as an interior designer. But inside Sally the townee there was clearly a country-girl struggling to get out, and she took to this life like one of her newly-acquired ducks to water.

On the farm are a hundred cattle; innumerable pigs, free-range chickens, geese, Khaki Campbell ducks and rabbits; and fifty horses. The horses include some pale mink-coloured Norwegian Fiords, rare in this country, with manes of black-and-white – velvety to stroke, gentle and at their superb best when pulling the maroon Victorian landau which Sally hires out for weddings and suchlike, complete with green-uniformed coachman and groom. Riding lessons are available.

The black-and-white beamed cottage which contains guests' bedrooms (simply furnished and without washbasins), one downstairs, is surrounded by lawn, farmyard and flint barns hung with baskets of geraniums and often crammed with hay, oats or barley. Mrs Haines, wife of Sally's farm manager, comes in to cook breakfast. For other meals, most visitors go to the Queen's Head opposite.

East Clandon, itself a very lovely old village, is well placed for exploring the many others hidden in the folds of the North Downs – much of the landscape protected by the National Trust which also owns a large number of the stately homes near here. Beauty-spots (many accessible to motorists as well as walkers) have great variety: the spectacular summit of Box Hill, the woods of Leith Hill, the blue Silent Pool near Albury, clock with automaton at Abinger Hammer.

Readers' comments: Very good; friendly. Excellent value; and excellent food at the Queen's Head.

Also in this area is **Hazelgrove** at West Horsley, a comfortable and well-kept 'twenties house with lovely garden and sun-room, on the road to Leatherhead. Jean Green can provide snack meals as well as breakfast. (Tel: 048 65 4467.) Visitors watch her occasional dog-training classes and can buy orchids from her greenhouse. No smoking.

CLAY LANE HEAD FARM

C D PT S

Cabus, Garstang, north of Preston, Lancashire, PR3 1WL   Tel: 09952 3132

rear view

3 bedrooms (single, double or family) from £10. Less for 7 nights. Rooms have electric heaters; armchairs; views of country or garden.
Dinner £6.50 for 4 courses and coffee, at 6.30pm. Coffee, tea, free. Non-residents not admitted. Drinks can be brought in.
2 sitting-rooms with open fire, TV, books, piano, record-player.
Garden and fields. Riding available.
Nearest main road A6 from Preston to Lancaster.

Though hardly off the beaten track – it stand on the A6 – Clay Lane Head Farm could easily be missed as one sped by, on the way to or from Scotland or the Lake District. It would be a good place to break a long journey, though it deserves more than a brief overnight visit, for both the house and the surroundings have much to offer visitors who like an easygoing atmosphere.

The stone house, which is more characterful than it appears to be from the outside, is basically 16th century, and some of the internal walls are of plastered reeds. It is a rambling, beamy old place, full of family antiques and Victoriana, with a book-lined sitting-room to sprawl in (it has a log fire); and it has not been modernized. The rooms face away from the main road.

Joan Higginson, a pharmacist, dispenses good food home-made from fresh ingredients, including plenty of cream from the Jersey cow. A typical dinner might be creamy carrot soup, steak braised with mushrooms and lemon meringue pie. There are goats too, and ponies for children to ride; and though this is no longer a working dairy-farm, there are cattle, hens and sheep. Bicycles on loan.

The immediate surroundings are not exciting, but there is good reason to investigate the hinterland – notably the Trough of Bowland, which is like a miniature Lake District without the lakes. The steep, heather-covered hills here are excellent for walking and picnicking, and there are picturesque stone villages and mansions to visit. One such is Browsholme Hall, a little-altered Jacobean house still in the possession of the family which provided the hereditary Bow-bearer of Bowland. Historic towns such as Lancaster and Clitheroe are not far, and the Lake District and the resorts of the Lancashire coast are within an easy day-trip. Other popular outings include Lancaster Castle, Cockersand Abbey, Sunderland Point, Beacon Fell country park and Brock Bottom nature trail.

Readers' comments: Very enjoyable. Excellent cooking and attentive service. Concerned for our every comfort, spotless rooms, excellent dinner. Interesting place, excellent food. Very satisfactory.

Prices are the minimum *per person* in a double room at the beginning of the year.

2 bedrooms (double) from £15. Rooms have own bath/shower (one); tea/coffee facilities; central heating; views of country or garden. (Washing-machine on request.)

Dinner £9.50 for 3 courses, aperitif, wine and coffee, at 8pm. Non-residents not admitted. Vegetarian or special diets if ordered. Tea, coffee, free.

Sitting-room with central heating, open fire, books, piano.

Large garden

Nearest main road A361 from Frome to Shepton Mallet.

Closed mid-December–mid-January

Jacqueline George has two outstanding talents. She is a professional cook of high calibre, and she has a flair for combining beautiful colours. Her early 18th-century home is a perfect setting for both her skills.

The big sitting-room is memorable. Duck-egg blue walls and the mellow patina of walnut furniture contrast with the brilliance of apricot chairs grouped round a stone fireplace – their colour echoed in Warners' pheasant and peony fabric on the sofas. (When I was there Jackie had put a great bowl of matching peonies on a table.) Big casement doors open onto a sloping lawn, flowerbeds and water-garden. The dining-room has Chippendale-style chairs (Prince of Wales' feathers decorate their backs) with tapestry seats made by her aunt; and on the coral walls are marine paintings. Here Jackie serves such dinners as cheese mousse in smoked trout; lamb en croûte (or game shot by Ryan) with garden vegetables; chocolate meringues; and cheeses (pre-dinner drinks and wine are included).

Bedrooms, too, are charming with little rosebuds on one bedspread, crochet (made by Jackie) over a pink lining in another, for example.

Claybatch used to be part of the Longleat estate. The great Elizabethan mansion of Longleat is one of England's stateliest of homes, full of art treasures and famous for its free-ranging lions in part of the grounds landscaped by Capability Brown. Stourhead, too, is near: a Palladian mansion with fine gardens.

Somerset is a county of great beauty, its landscape punctuated by impressive church towers from the resplendent Perpendicular period of mediaeval architecture, big stone barns and little stone villages, with Bath itself just over the county boundary to the north and mysterious Glastonbury still drawing pilgrims to its holy places. Geology is what accounts for its great variety, with buildings made of stone that ranges from lilac to gold (for every quarry is different), and a landscape of hills and levels contrasting with one another. Monks drained marshes (still crisscrossed with their ancient ditches) between hills of great beauty but quite dissimilar from one another – the Mendips, the Quantocks and Exmoor stretching into Devon. Where streams carved their way through rock there are gorges and caves. Somerset is an agricultural county unscarred by industry.

Readers' comments: Made most welcome, delicious meals, beautiful home.

CLEAVERS LYNG

C D PT S

Herstmonceux, east of Hailsham, East Sussex, BN27 1QJ   Tel: 0323 833131

8 bedrooms (single or double) from £12.60. Less for 7 nights. Rooms have central heating; armchairs; views of country or garden; balcony (some). Tea/coffee facilities.

Dinner £5.90 for 3 courses and coffee, at 7pm. Special diets if ordered. Lunches, packed lunches, snacks. Coffee, tea, for a charge. Non-residents admitted for lunch only. Drinks can be ordered.

Sitting-room with central heating, TV, books.

Garden with play area.

Nearest main road A271 from Hailsham to the A269.

The unusual name means a woodcutter's (cleaver's) hill by a marsh (lyng). Many centuries ago this was a yeoman's house – with a tile-hung exterior typical of Sussex, and an interior given character by beams, and an inglenook fireplace in the dining-room. Marylin Holden and her son have been running it for many years as a small hotel, and often have visitors to nearby Herstmonceux Castle – its beautiful gardens and moat can be seen in summer.

The bedrooms are prettily furnished, and have views of the garden and its apple trees with the far distant hills beyond.

Good meals with plenty of choices – home-made soups or seafood cocktails, roasts or game pies, lemon chiffon or mincemeat tarts, are just examples. Home-made preserves are on sale. On Sundays there is always a traditional lunch with a choice of two roasts.

Herstmonceux village is the centre of Sussex trug-making (trugs are traditional garden baskets made from slats of willow), one of many pretty Downland villages around here. It is an area in which valleys alternate with wooded ridges that have panoramic views when the leaves thin out. Many craftsmen work here and wrought iron is a local speciality. Popular sights include Michelham Priory, Batemans (Kipling's home), Battle Abbey, Pevensey Castle and picturesque Alfriston. The coast is near, with such resorts as Hastings and Eastbourne.

Readers' comments: Very welcoming. Excellent, have stayed many times. Beautiful position, and a comfortable stay.

In the picturesque old town area of Hastings, Dorothea and Stanley Pelling (at **105 High Street**) take bed-and-breakfast guests in their attractive little Tudor house. At the back, a tiny garden (all steps and terraces, clinging to the steep hillside) is an afternoon sun-trap. Tel: 0424 424894.

Readers' comments: Charming house, cosy and well-loved, unpretentious. Gracious and helpful hosts. Great value.

69

CLEY MILL

C D S-C

Cley-next-the-Sea, west of Cromer, Norfolk, NR25 7NN   Tel: 0263 740209

4 bedrooms (single, double or family) from £16. Less for 3 nights. Rooms have central heating; shower or bathroom (some); views of sea and country; tea/coffee facilities on request: One has balcony.

Dinner £10 for 3 courses and coffee, at 7pm. Vegetarian or special diets if ordered. Packed lunches, snacks. Coffee, tea, for a charge. Drinks can be brought in.

Sitting-room with central heating, open fire, TV, books, indoor games.

Nearest main road A149 from Wells-next-the-Sea to Cromer.

On the enthusiastic recommendation of a friend, I made my way to this most unusual of guest-houses – not, in fact, next to the sea (for centuries of silting up followed by land reclamation have left Cley a little way inland) but overlooking a rivulet winding its way through salt marshes where cattle graze.

Once Cley was a principal port of East Anglia, and great ships came to collect wool, and flour from the mediaeval windmill (the present structure dates from the 18th century). Milling ceased in 1921, since when generations of the Blount family have lived in it: one of the most celebrated visitors was the Duchess of Bedford who learned to fly when she was about seventy, and was lost flying at sea in 1937.

Only a few years ago, it was completely renovated. One enters through the beamy dining-room. The circular sitting-room has big armchairs around the brick fireplace, where Toby jugs are arranged, and window-seats overlooking the marshes. Upstairs, bedrooms are named according to the original purpose which they served: for instance, in the Wheat Chamber flour was sifted; in the Stone Room above it the flour was ground. Lace bedspreads and wildflower curtains contrast with brick walls, now painted white, and soft green carpet. One room has a balcony running all round the mill, with views on one side to Blakeney Harbour and on the other to the pantiled roofs and chimney-pots of Cley, its flint gables and its walls with hollyhocks peering over the top. Higher still are observation and information rooms, with telescope. (Book well ahead in summer, otherwise you will not find a vacancy.)

The Mill is run by Carolyn Hederman, who produces such meals as roast lamb, casseroles, or fish with hollandaise sauce; followed by lemon soufflé or mousse.

Cley is in the centre of the north Norfolk coast; a shoreline of cliffs and sands now officially protected for its beauty and its wildlife. Inland are woods, heath and pretty villages of flint walls or (eastward) red carr stone, with inns where crab salads are as common as ham sandwiches. The National Trust owns a number of stately homes which, along with castles and almost cathedral-like churches, innumerable craft studios and wildlife reserves, provide plenty of opportunities for sightseeing. Blakeney's waterfront is always lively with boats; Cromer is a family seaside resort in the old-fashioned style. Holkham Hall, Felbrigg, Blickling Hall are near and the royal gardens at Sandringham a little further. At Walsingham are two famous shrines.

Readers' comments: Cooking and hospitality could not be faulted. Comfortable; food very good. Excellent. Shall return. Interesting and friendly. High praise for standards and culinary expertise.

COACH HOUSE C D H S S-C
Crookham, Cornhill-on-Tweed, east of Coldstream (Scotland), Northumberland, TD12 4TD   Tel: 089082 293

8 bedrooms (single, double or family) from £17. Less for 3 nights. Rooms have central heating or electric heaters; shower or bath-room (most); armchairs; views of country or garden; tea/coffee facilities. (Clothes-washing facilities available.)
Dinner £10.50 for 4 courses and coffee with petits fours, at 7.30pm. Special diets if ordered. Tea with home-made cakes is free on arrival. Non-residents not admitted. Drinks can be ordered. Occasional bar-becues.
2 sitting-rooms with central heating, open fire, TV, books, record-player. Also a billiard room with darts, table tennis room.
Grounds Terrace, paddock, orchard and fields. Escorted riding or birdwatching.
Nearest main road A697 from Morpeth to Coldstream.
Closed in winter

This is almost on the border of Scotland, and very close to the site of Flodden Field, where in 1513 Henry VIII's armies slaughtered the King of Scotland and 10,000 of his followers: the very last mediaeval battle with knights wearing armour, and swords or arrows the principal weapons. Each August there is a tremendously emotive spectacle commemorating it, with 200 horsemen bearing down at a canter after being led by the Coldstream Guards across the old bridge.

The Coach House is a group of several old farm buildings forming a square around a courtyard which traps the sun. What was the coach house itself is now a highly individual sitting-room, with lofty beamed ceiling and great arched windows where there used to be doors for the carriages. One looks onto an orchard. Colours are light and cheerful, and there is a log fire in an enormous brick fireplace. The dining-room was once a smithy and the forge still stands at one end.

An old dower house is now used for a daytime restaurant, and a games room. It has panelled doors of stripped pine, pointed 'gothick' windows, rare chestnut beams, an old Victorian kitchen-range, and two immensely high attic bedrooms.

In the main part, some of the ground-floor bedrooms look onto paddocks where goats graze. All are light and airy, with interesting paintings and a file of leaflets on the many local places worth visiting. They have fridges which guests find useful for a variety of purposes (baby's feeds, dog's meat, insulin or soft drinks) and toasters: there are reduced prices for people who make their own breakfast.

The owner, Lynne Anderson, used to travel a great deal when she was a singer, and so has a lot of practical ideas about what travellers need – disabled travellers in particular. She had doorways made wide, and steps eliminated.

Porridge is properly made from pinhead oatmeal, and breakfast includes bacon from an Edinburgh smokery, beef sausages from a local butcher, and free-range eggs. Dinner has a choice of starters; a roast or casserole; puddings like lemon meringue pie or almond ice cream with damson sauce; cheese and coffee.

Readers' comments: Very friendly and welcoming, exceptionally well organized; most impressed. Warm and friendly owner; professional efficiency. A great success! Wonderful. So much room, the very best breakfast, and Lynne is exceptionally good at making guests at ease with one another.

71

COACH HOUSE
Scotland Road, Dry Drayton, north-west of Cambridge, CB3 8BX
Tel: 0954 782439

4 bedrooms (single or double) from £17.50. Rooms have central heating; own bathroom; armchairs; views of garden; tea/coffee facilities. No smoking.
Sitting-room with central heating, TV, books. No smoking. (Also a room for group meetings.)

Large garden
Nearest main road A604 from Huntingdon to Cambridge.
Closed mid-December–February

Not so very long ago, what is now an immaculate reception room (with pink walls and chinoiserie curtains) contained mounds of dung, for it had been stables. The transformation wrought by Catherine Child and her builders was as total as it had been swift – here and in the rest of the building. In the grounds, too: now turned into a very pretty landscaped garden, with moorhens in the lily-pool and a Victorian summerhouse.

The rector who, a century ago, stabled his horses here must have been a man of considerable substance, keeping several carriages and maintaining his own forge. The forge fire still burns, built into a corner of the entrance hall.

A new and handsome pine staircase rises to the bedrooms but offers temptations to linger on the way up, for one large window and a blocked-up doorway have been filled with shelves to display small bits of Victoriana (for sale – they are provided by antique-dealer friends of Catherine). Bedrooms are light and pretty, with excellent bathrooms (in one, a shower). The best has a king-size brass four-poster, its valance beribboned and its quilt and draperies matching the pink bathroom.

Guests have the use of a large dining-room with mahogany tables for breakfast, which includes an array of home-made preserves, and of a small television room – both south-facing, with sunny views of the garden. (And there's a lovely room to hire for groups, music-making and suchlike.)

In the folders of local information provided for guests Catherine lists recommended eating-places (such as Trinity Foot or the Three Horseshoes inn at nearby Madingley or the Plough at Coton, and many in nearby Cambridge, of course). She can arrange for private guided tours round Cambridge. Go to Huntingdon for the Oliver Cromwell museum (this was his birthplace) and to St Ives; there are several stately homes within easy reach; and close by is the American Cemetery, which is well worth a visit. Grantchester and Duxford aircraft museum are also close. All around are wide, windswept skies and marvellously clear light.

Readers' comments: Very warm welcome, such pretty bedrooms, a lovely outlook. A lovely house. Every conceivable care given to visitors' requirements. Totally impressed by it all! Has great character, most peaceful, will stay again.

COASTGUARDS

St Agnes, Isles of Scilly, TR22 0PL   Tel: 0720 22373

2 bedrooms (double and family) at £12.
**Discounts are offered to readers of this
book, except in high summer.** Rooms have
views of sea. (Laundering facilities.)
Dinner 2 or 4 courses for £5 or £7.50, and
coffee, at 6.30pm. Special diets if ordered.
Packed lunches. Coffee, tea, free. Non-
residents not admitted. Drinks can be
brought in.
Dining/sitting-room with open fire, books.
Small garden
Closed in winter

There are very few coastguards living in the many coastguard cottages still left
around the shores of England: electronic surveillance has taken over from the man
with the spyglass. Needless to say, such cottages were always well sited for sea
views, on coasts where high seas and jagged rocks make spectacular scenery, but
are hazards for ships, and where coves and inlets were an attraction to smugglers.

One such group of cottages stands on a high point of St Agnes, a little island in
the Scillies so unspoilt that there are no cars, no hotel, no commercialism at all. It is
a paradise for those who want nothing more than sunshine early or late in the year,
wildflowers, walks, birdwatching, going about in boats and perfect peace.

Wendy and Danny Hick live in one of these cottages, with a couple of rooms for
guests. They have furnished the rooms simply but attractively, with interesting
objects around. (No washbasins.) The sitting-room has a William Morris sofa and
brown tweed curtains, polished board floors, many books on the shelves and an
open fire for chilly evenings. The pieces of iron-studded furniture are from
Curaçao, where Danny's father was a mining engineer. The collection of old
bottles (from inkwells to flasks that contained sheep-cures) are mostly local finds.
Danny makes ship models sold in London's West End galleries.

The food is all of a very good, homely style: bread is home-baked, soups
home-made, clotted cream is from a friendly neighbourhood cow, fish (of course)
straight out of the sea, and new potatoes from the fields around.

Visitors reach St Agnes via St Mary's from which boats take them in 15 minutes
to the little quay at St Agnes. (Mrs Hick will supply all the times etc. for getting to
the Scillies by rail and boat or helicopter.) Luggage is conveyed for them up the
steep track that leads to the few cottages; past the Turk's Head inn (for a really
succulent Cornish pasty, pause here!); and past Rose Cottage and Covean which
serve Cornish cream teas and light lunches. Whatever track you follow, there is a
superlative view at every turn. This is a great place for birdwatchers, particularly
in autumn when rare migrants arrive. But even at other times it is a pleasure to
watch the red-legged turnstones, for instance, scuttling like busy mice among the
rock-pools on the shore. Around the lighthouse (built in 1680) are fields from
which daffodils and narcissi are sent early in the year to mainland florists. There
are strange rock formations and islets, deserted sandy coves and pools, a simple
church (built from money raised by salvaging a wreck), and – a mystery – the
centuries-old Troy Town maze by a remote cliff edge.

Readers' comments: Excellent in every respect. Good food, lovely scenery, such
nice people. Warmly welcomed, well looked after, delicious food, excellent value;
beautiful and peaceful place.

COBBLERS

South Creake, north-west of Fakenham, Norfolk, NR21 9PF
Tel: 032879 200

2 bedrooms (double) from £16. Rooms have central heating; views of garden; tea/coffee facilities; showers.
Dinner from £11 for 4 courses and coffee, at 7.30pm. Drinks included.

Sitting-room with central heating, open fire, TV, books.
Garden
Nearest main road A148 from Cromer to King's Lynn.

The U-shaped house encloses a particularly pretty little garden that comes as a surprise when one turns in from the main road. Arches and hanging baskets of flowers surround the lawn and a sun-trapping patio, stone hounds guard a lily-pool (lit up at night), there are tubs of marigolds, and one can open a narrow wrought-iron gate to watch trout and ducks in the clear stream flowing by.

Ian Dow was formerly a theatrical production manager – hence the many theatrical designs, photographs and posters around the house. The small sitting/dining-room is crammed with other interesting objects – from samplers and old jigsaw pictures to portraits of his Scottish ancestors. Here his wife Mardi serves generous meals that may comprise, for instance, avocado with smoked trout, followed by duck or another roast, and home-made ice creams, then cheeses.

The bedrooms are attractively furnished with, for instance, both furniture and walls painted dark billiardcloth green to contrast with the shaggy rust carpet in one room; ivy trellis paper in another which has fabrics striped in cobalt blue.

South Creake is centrally placed for enjoying many of Norfolk's contrasting areas – the scenic coast lies six miles north; there are bird reserves; several great houses lie near (Oxburgh, Blickling, Felbrigg – all National Trust – and also Holkham, Houghton and royal Sandringham) and picturesque Walsingham with two shrines.

Readers' comments: Lovely imaginative cooking, generous portions. Very friendly atmosphere. The Dows spoil their guests. Absolutely delightful. The meals were a highlight of the holiday. Friendly and helpful.

A little further west is Docking, where Margaret Robinson caters inexpensively for bed-and-breakfast guests in her immaculate 18th-century **Holland House** (tel: 04858 295), with peaceful garden. Most dine at the Pilgrim's Reach.

COCKETT'S HOTEL   D X

Market Place, Hawes, Wensleydale, North Yorkshire, DL8 3RD
Tel: 09697 312

7 bedrooms (double) from £14.75. Less for 3 nights. Rooms have central heating; own bathroom; TV, armchairs; tea/coffee facilities. (Clothes-washing facilities.) No smoking.
Dinner from £13 for 4 courses (with choices) and coffee, from 7.45pm. Vegetarian or special diets if ordered. Packed lunches. Coffee, tea, for a charge. Drinks can be ordered. No smoking.
Nearest main road A684 from Sedbergh to Leyburn.

'God being with us Who can be against' is carved deep into the stone lintel of a door, together with the date 1668. It was the main entrance to a hostel once used by Quakers travelling to distant meeting-houses.

Things are different now. One steps from the paved forecourt into a snug little bar with leather chairs and racing-prints all over the walls – most visitors much prefer this to the larger, pine-panelled sitting-room elsewhere. Adjoining it is a dining-room where, on lace-covered tables, are served imaginative meals. There is always plenty of choice at each of the courses, with many French specialities such as lamb Argenteuil (it is cooked with asparagus and cream), or chicken Marika (cottage cheese and green peppercorns go into the sauce), or duck-breasts stuffed then braised in lettuce leaves. The cheeseboard usually includes a rarity – local Swaledale cheese.

John Oddie's hotel is something of a gallery, with over two hundred pictures on its walls. Every room has interesting furniture, too: one four-poster, with barley-sugar posts, is covered in a scarlet dragon fabric; another, of pine, has pale green chintz. One's eye is caught by interesting details everywhere: satinwood bedside cupboards, art nouveau fingerplates on the doors, for example.

In the annexe (over an art gallery) are the two least expensive bedrooms, which would make an ideal suite for a family wanting to be self-contained.

Hawes, its buildings clustered around a stream, is near the head of Wensleydale from which the spectacular Buttertubs Pass leads to very different Swaledale (described elsewhere): the 'butter tubs' are curious holes in the rock. The dale's crags and waterfalls, castles and history museums, attract visitors from all over the world. Hardraw Force, a 100-foot waterfall, has a footpath that goes behind the gushing torrent – take your showercoat! At the next village, Bainbridge, cottages huddle round a big, steep green with Brough Hill rising above it.

Readers' comments: Food excellent, rooms comfortable, Jackie and John really made the week for us. Felt very welcome, interesting food and rooms, friendly staff. High standard. Cuisine excellent. Delightful. Excellent dinner. Friendly.

COCKLE WARREN

36 Seafront, Hayling Island, east of Portsmouth, Hampshire, PO11 9HL
Tel: 0705 464961

central heating; views of sea or garden. No smoking. (Washing-machine on request.)
Dinner £17.50 for 4 courses (with choices), wine and coffee, at 8pm. Non-residents not admitted. Vegetarian or special diets if ordered. Lunches, packed lunches, snacks. Tea, coffee, free. Drinks can be ordered or brought in.
Sitting-room with central heating, open fire, books, piano, record-player.
Large garden
Nearest main road A27 from Southampton to Chichester.

4 bedrooms (single or double) from £17. Rooms have own bath/shower (some); TV;

Much of Hayling Island is built up but if you know where to go there are waterfront byways, birdwatching haunts, and quiet lanes to be discovered. Cockle Warren is on the south side with only a road between it and the sea – shallow and therefore relatively warm here, with golden sands and a view across the Solent to the Isle of Wight.

It is quite difficult to find any small hotels or guest-houses right on the seafront of the south coast which have attractive furnishings and good food: this house has both.

David and Diane Skelton were both Portsmouth people. They bought a piece of land here and built this house only a few years ago, furnishing it agreeably. There are buttoned velvet sofas in the sitting-room and some bedrooms; clear, light colours and white walls give the rooms an airy look; and in one room is a four-poster. There is a pretty ground-floor room in an annexe.

Their own hens and ducks, and local produce (especially fish), provide the kitchen with fresh ingredients for meals served on bone china. In order that every dish shall be freshly prepared, guests are asked to choose at breakfast-time what they want for dinner, from a menu that runs to 15 main courses. Starters include such things as cream of salmon soup or seafood au gratin; meat dishes, duckling with a sauce of orange, cranberry and wine or pork in cider and cream.

Hayling Island is connected to the mainland by a bridge, and acts as a divider between two natural harbours, Langstone and Chichester. Its reputation for summer sunshine, coupled with its sands, have made it very popular for family holidays (and for sea-sports), with a funfair and so forth at one end. But there are also quiet stretches of heath and sand, as well as wild spots on the Chichester Harbour side which only birds, fishermen, walkers and small sailing boats frequent. A car is not essential: I explored the island when writing *England by Bus & Coach* (Sphere).

Using the ferry, one can cross Langstone Harbour to Eastney (beyond this lie historic Portsmouth and Southsea, described elsewhere). The Royal Marines have their outstanding museum here (a palatial and very colourful building with fascinating exhibits and a vivid audiovisual of the Battle of Zeebrugge, 1918). Also worth a visit is the splendid Victorian pumping-station when it gets up steam and the brass pistons of the beam-engine pound away.

Other nearby places of interest include Emsworth Quay (where swans glide on the millpond and there is a waterfront inn).

COLLEGE FARMHOUSE

Thompson, north of Thetford, Norfolk, IP24 1QG   Tel: 095383 318

4 bedrooms (single or double) from £13.
Rooms have central heating and electric
heaters; electric blankets; TV, armchairs;
views of country or garden. Coffee, tea, free.

Large garden
Nearest main road A1075 from Thetford to
Watton.

Over six centuries ago, colleges (meaning residential communities) of some
half-dozen priests were established in various parts of East Anglia, to serve local
communities. This house was built for one of them. When these colleges were (like
the monasteries) disbanded by Henry VIII, it became a private house: the new
owner had his coat-of-arms put above the main fireplace. Later, carved oak
panelling with fluted pilasters was put into the dining-room; a second storey was
added; and then all manner of Victorian or later accretions followed. These last
have been gradually removed, revealing forgotten fireplaces and beams masked by
hardboard. A tremendous task; and when it was begun the only running water was
from leaks in the roof. The house is therefore full of curious architectural features
– Gothic windows blocked up, walls (some three feet thick) with odd curves, steps
up and down.

Lavender Garnier has collected together interesting pieces of furniture and
some ancestral portraits (including a great-grandfather who took part in the first
Oxford and Cambridge boat-race, and selected dark blue as Oxford's now famous
colour). Bedrooms have pleasing fabrics – brilliant nasturtiums on the bed of one
room, for instance; yellow linen bedheads in another white-panelled room – and in
one the basin is set in a thick, handsome plank of polished elm. Each bedroom has
armchairs and TV, as there is no sitting-room for guests' use.

Outside, a lovely old garden slopes down to eel ponds, and flint walls make a
perfect background to the roses, herbaceous borders and a great beech.

Breakfast is the only meal served, but there is good inn food at the thatched
Chequers, a mile away.

Thompson is in an attractive, leafy part of Norfolk, where the landscape
undulates and villages are pretty. There are varid options for day-outings – from
the very beautiful Norfolk coast to Cambridge, from Norwich and the Broads to
Bury St Edmunds (described elsewhere in this book). Breckland is an area of heath
and meres, with little population now but a considerable history (explained in
Thetford's museum, in a Tudor house). Visit Brandon to see the variety of ways
flints are used in building; and Grimes Graves where prehistoric man mined the
chalk to find these, for use as tools and weapons. Castle Acre lies within Norman
earthworks (the priory remains are impressive); near Denver is an unusual
windmill, and the 15th-century Oxburgh Hall is moated.

COOMBE FARMHOUSE

C(5) D H

Widegates, north-east of Looe, Cornwall, PL13 1QN   Tel: 05034 223

9 bedrooms (single, double or family) from £14.50. Less for 2 nights half-board and for families. Rooms have central heating or electric heaters; shower (some); TV in most; armchairs; tea/coffee facilities; views of sea, country or garden.

Dinner £10 for 4 courses and coffee, at 7–8pm. Special diets if ordered. Lunches, packed lunches, snacks. Drinks can be ordered.

Sitting-room with central heating, open fire, TV, books. Games room with snooker, table tennis, video films.

Grounds Lawns, meadows, woods and ponds; with croquet, swimming-pool (73° in summer).

Nearest main road A387 from Looe to the A374.

Closed November–February

Built on a marvellous site with a distant sea view between hills, this very spacious and comfortable 'twenties house had long been coveted by Alexander Low, who used to bring his family regularly to Looe for holidays. When at last it came up for sale, it had deteriorated into a seedy guest-house, gaudily decorated, with barbed wire and a cow-field outside. But within a year he and Sally transformed it and its grounds, and every year sees still further improvements (a swimming-pool and a stone-walled games room for snooker and table tennis are the most recent).

Alex frequents salerooms to find additions to the already rich array of antiques, paintings and interesting objects with which he has filled the house.

The dining-room extends into a glassed-in verandah from which there are views of terraced lawns where peacocks roam, and of a pond (one of several) frequented by ducks and coots. Elsewhere, geese and ponies graze, there are woods with rhododendrons, and camellias grow wild.

All rooms have an abundance of pot-plants, flowers are put on each green-clothed dining-table and in each bedroom, and on cool nights log fires crackle on two hearths: all part of the considerable attention to detail.

My bedroom (like several, very big indeed) opened straight onto the garden. Others upstairs have armchairs or, in one, a big sofa from which to enjoy the view.

As a professional photographer and one-time picture editor of the *Telegraph* magazine, Alex used to travel a lot and knows what makes guests feel truly at home. They are welcome to take picnic lunches into the garden, for instance; and to help themselves to drinks, writing down in a book what they have had.

A typical dinner prepared by Sally may comprise something like home-made soup, roast duck and a fruit sponge accompanied by Cornish clotted cream – freshly cooked from local produce, and served in generous quantities.

As to sightseeing, there are twenty mansions and gardens within motoring distance, plenty of coast or moorland walks and river trips, a wide choice of sandy bays or coves, and such special attractions as a monkey sanctuary and another for seals. There is a huge choice of unusual museums or exhibitions: mechanical music, miniature villages, smuggling, steam rail, air history, mining, shire horses, local history, tropical birds, historic pottery and much more.

Readers' comments: Excellent! Friendliness and warmth. A wonderful experience. Place superb, hospitality gracious. A haven of peace. Excellent food.

CORNER ELM

Netton, Salisbury, Wiltshire, SP4 6AW   Tel: 0722 73 314

4 bedrooms (single or double) from £14. Less for 7 nights and bargain breaks. All have tea/coffee facilities; central heating; views of country or garden. No smoking. (Washing-machine on request.)
Dinner £12 for 4 courses (with choices) and coffee, at 7.30pm (offered on Monday and Wednesday evenings only). Non-residents not admitted. Tea, coffee, free. Drinks can be brought in.
Sitting-room with central heating, open fire, TV, books.
Small garden
Nearest main road A345 from Amesbury to Salisbury.

Once called the Wool House, this was a wool-collecting depot for the area; drovers going from the Marlborough Downs to Wilton Sheep Fair used to pass the door. In 1854 it became a dwelling, being converted into a rambling house and re-named for the great elm outside (now a colossal hollow trunk prettily draped with flowery Russian vine); this was one of a series of elms known as 'mile elms' that used to mark the way from Durnford to Salisbury. Diana Howard has furnished all rooms to very high standards. In the sitting-room, for instance, are velvet chairs in blue and deep rose, toning with the carpet, which look well against a deep pink marbled wallpaper; at deep-set sash windows with white shutters are pretty blinds matching the wallpaper and appliquéd with flowers from the curtain fabric, their colours echoing those of her huge velvety gloxinias. There is an open fireplace with log fire.

One of the bedrooms, blue and cream, has frilled curtains and a lace bedspread. In the low-beamed dining-room Diana serves breakfast and dinner (on Monday and Wednesday only). A typical meal: mackerel pâté, chicken Marengo with garden vegetables, raspberry bavarois and cheeses. The house is beautifully situated midway between Salisbury and Stonehenge in the scenic Woodford Valley. Wilton's historic carpet factory and Wilton House – well worth a visit – are just over the hill. Old Sarum with the ruins of its Norman castle and Stonehenge are also near. The New Forest makes a pleasant, leisurely excursion with lovely walks; the famous ponies graze freely.

Don't complain if –
 – because you booked at short notice, you do not get the best room
 – because you did not order a meal in advance, you get something plucked from the freezer
 – because you do not arrive on time, your room is let to someone else
 – because you bring a dog without asking, it is refused entry
 – because you don't express your wishes (for more heat, a second helping or whatever), you don't get what you want!

THE COTTAGE

C H S-C X

Westbrook, Bromham, south of Chippenham, Wiltshire, SN15 2EE
Tel: 0380 850255

5 bedrooms (double) from £15. Rooms have central heating or electric heaters; shower or bathroom; TV, armchairs; views of country or garden; tea/coffee facilities.
2 sitting/breakfast-rooms with central heating, open fire, TV, books.

Large garden and paddock with 9-hole putting.
Nearest main road A3102 from Calne to Melksham.

Converted stables, weatherboarded and pantiled, provide the accommodation here, in a quiet hamlet once the home of Thomas Moore, the Irish poet. The adjoining mediaeval cottage was originally a coaching inn.

Inside, the roof beams are still visible. The bedrooms have been furnished in keeping with the style of the building and Gloria Steed has added such decorative touches as patchwork cushions and pincushions which she made herself. Through the bedroom windows one can sometimes see deer and rabbits, with a distant landscape created by Capability Brown in the 18th century.

At breakfast (in a room with rough white walls, small William Morris armchairs and beautifully arranged flowers) there will be, in addition to the usual things, home-made muesli and some very special jams from France. For other meals, Gloria can show you menus from inns and restaurants within a few miles (I ate very well at the Lysley Arms). Occasionally she invites guests to a barbecue.

This is very lovely walking country, and with lots of sightseeing possibilities too (Lacock, Devizes, Avebury and Bath are all within a few miles; and Bowood House is close – an Adam building in superb grounds, with lake and cascade). Chippenham and Calne are historic market towns, with fine churches and other buildings of golden stone. Castle Combe is a much-photographed village in a dramatic setting – woods above it, stream through it, mellow stone cottages and fan-vaulted church. Corsham Court, and the waterside at Devizes, are well worth visits. This part of Wiltshire is very rustic but with fine limestone houses built in the centuries when wool brought wealth. Riverside pastures contrast with hills and wooded dells. Sheldon Manor and Stourhead have exceptional gardens. A good area for hunting antiques, or buying farm produce.

Readers' comments: Full of charm and character. We couldn't have asked for more.

COTTESWOLD HOUSE   PT
Market Place, Northleach, Gloucestershire, GL54 3EG   Tel: 0451 60493

4 bedrooms (single, double or family) from
£13.50. Less for 3 nights. Rooms have
central heating.
Sitting-room with central heating, TV,
books.
Nearest main road A40 from Oxford to
Cheltenham.

This is not strictly 'off the beaten track', being in the centre of the historic little
town, but now that heavy traffic has been diverted, Northleach is quite a quiet
place. The house has tremendous character, after being carefully restored by Mrs
Powell a few years ago. Zigzagging passages lead to roomy bedrooms with rugged
stone walls and low oak beams now exposed. She has furnished all the rooms with
good carpets and folkweave or similar fabrics. Guests breakfast in a dining-room
with oak furniture, including a vast carved chest, and can use the sitting-room and
its comfortable yellow armchairs – big and velvety. There are plenty of good places
for dinner within a few yards, such as the Union Inn. Plenty of antique shops in the
area – and a celebrated clock and music-box restorer.

There is plenty of interest within easy motoring distance. For example,
Cirencester still has a lively market (I recommend the farm cheese stall) outside its
almost cathedral-like church. The Corinium Museum is one of the country's
best-displayed Roman museums, and there is a flourishing craftsmen's market in a
former brewery. The most picturesque villages and lanes of the Cotswolds are
close – stately homes, gardens, a Roman villa, the source of the Thames,
handsome Cheltenham, Gloucester's cathedral and the colleges of Oxford are all
easily accessible.

Readers' comments: Eminently satisfied, thoroughly enjoyed it.

When to go? Seaside resorts or other places suitable for children will be at
their busiest (and dearest) in July–August and during half-term holidays
(especially in late May, which is also a bank holiday period). Other peak
periods are, of course, Easter, Christmas, New Year and the bank holiday
in late August. (The bank holiday in early May is not usually a peak,
because it comes rather soon after Easter, but much depends on the
weather.) There are local peaks, too (the Gold Cup races at Cheltenham or
the regatta at Henley, for instance, are apt to fill hotels for miles around),
and local troughs (Brighton, a conference centre, is least busy in high
summer). You won't get much personal attention when hotels are full to
bursting.

4 bedrooms (single, double or family) £25, including dinner. Tea/coffee facilities; central heating; views of river, country or garden. Some have own bathroom. No smoking. (Washing-machine on request.)
Dinner (see text) at 7.30pm. Non-residents not admitted. Vegetarian or special diets if ordered. Tea, coffee, extra (but free on arrival). Drinks can be brought in.
Sitting-room with central heating, open fire, TV, books.
Large garden and farmland.
Nearest main road A356 from Crewkerne to Dorchester.
Closed mid-October–April

In the 'thirties, a mansion that had belonged to Sheridan's family was demolished. Materials from it – such as the limed oak staircase and the window frames – went into the construction of this handsome house. The buff-and-white dining-room, has rush ladderback chairs around oval tables and William Morris curtains. In the conservatory bamboo sofas invite one to linger among the bougainvillaea and fuchsias. The gold-and-cream sitting-room has windows on three sides. One bedroom is huge, with a magnificent walnut suite complemented by frilled bedlinen; carved gilt pelmets top windows at each end (like others, it has a very good, carpeted bathroom). In another, there is much *trompe l'oeil* maple and gilt.

The garden is a particularly attractive spot in which to take tea. It has a long pool with weeping-willow island (reached by footbridge), once a monastic fishpond; a stream; and woods with delightful walks. Waterfowl and peacocks roam at will.

Peggy Lazenby produces gourmet-class meals for visitors. A typical dinner: avocado mousse in a prawn dressing, followed by lamb with garlic sauce, a bavarois, and cheeses.

Readers' comments: Made to feel at home, lovely memories, cordon bleu cooking. A cosy, intimate quality; beautifully landscaped gardens, flawless meals.

On the opposite side of Dorchester is West Knighton and picturesque **Yoah Cottage** (tel: 0305 852087), all whitewash and thatch. On every window-sill are terracotta images of country life, which Furse and Rosemary Swann sculpt in their garden studio. The garden is a romantic spot, flagged paths wandering among cottage flowers. Rosemary produces not only imaginative dishes of her own (for instance, pork tenderloin with water chestnuts in a sweet-sour cream sauce or trout fillets with ginger and dill) but also a number of Swedish specialities. Indoors, the 17th-century cottage has a mixture of antique and modern furniture, 18th-century glass and 20th-century paintings.

Readers' comments: Most beautiful and characterful. Warm and welcoming, most interesting people. Comfortable and extremely well fed.

COURTNEY COTTAGE

C D S S-C

Iwerne Courtney, north of Blandford Forum, Dorset, DT11 8QA
Tel: 0258 860650

3 bedrooms (double or family) from £16.10. Less for 7 nights. All have own bath; TV; electric heating; views of country or garden. Free early morning tea served. (Washing-machine on request.)
Dinner £10.35 for 3 courses and coffee, at 7.45pm. Vegetarian or special diets if ordered. Snacks by arrangement. Tea, coffee, extra. Drinks can be brought in.
2 sitting-rooms (one with open fire); books.
Small garden
Nearest main road A350 from Shaftesbury to Blandford Forum.

The cottage is in a village with two names (on some maps it appears as Shroton): by either, this is an attractive spot, with a large green. In the 17th century this cottage was the village school, possibly the first such in England.

Today, the ambience – and the food – are far removed from these humble beginnings. When Tacina Rae-Smith turned her home into a guest-house, it soon secured a reputation for exceptional meals and these are what bring most visitors to stay – together with the particularly attractive, old rooms with family heirlooms. Now it is her daughter Emma who does most of the cooking, to the same high standards: she used to cook for the British Minister in Paris.

For example, you might be offered for dinner cheese aigrettes, paupiettes of beef in red wine, raspberry and almond iced bombe, coffee with home-made chocolates.

This will be served in a dining-room furnished with unusual antiques (a painted Korean chest, for instance), shelves of plates and a number of family portraits. (There is a separate dining-room for families who want to be on their own.) By contrast, in the library there are Dufy prints. The pretty blue sitting-room with log fire has a bay window in its thick walls.

Bedrooms, too, are very pleasant and the attic suite, under the eaves, would particularly suit a family or friends travelling together. Views are of hills, one topped by a prehistoric fort.

Eastward lies scenic Cranborne Chase, described elsewhere. Most visitors here also like exploring the area's Roman remains, and great houses such as Longleat, Montacute and Wilton. Stourhead has particularly lovely gardens and lakes. The Dorset coast is near, so are the Purbeck Hills and many picturesque Dorset villages. The nearest town, Blandford Forum, is a remarkably complete 18th-century town (because in 1731 fire destroyed earlier buildings) with an exceptionally grand church of the period. The lovely River Stour flows languidly by; on the bridge is a warning that anyone damaging this will be transported! Other popular destinations include Dorchester, Corfe Castle, Kingston Lacy house, and a famous silk and butterfly farm. East Dorset is a very varied area: bleak hills, forests, valleys, heaths and sea cliffs contrast with each other and with rich cornfields and pastures.

Readers' comments: Cooking superb, wonderful views and walks on the very doorstep.

COVE HOUSE   C D
Ashton Keynes, north-west of Swindon, Wiltshire, SN6 6NS
Tel: 0285 861221

3 bedrooms (double or family) from £17. Less for 2 nights or bargain breaks. Discounts for repeat bookings. Rooms have central heating or electric heaters; shower or bathroom; TV, armchairs; views of garden; tea/coffee facilities.
Dinner £12 for 3 courses and coffee, at 7.30pm. Garden fruit free (when available) for picnics. Drinks can be brought in.
2 sitting-rooms with central heating, open fire, TV, books. Videos of local attractions.
Large garden
Nearest main road A419 from Swindon to Cirencester.

The narrow trickle running through this little village is in fact the infant Thames; you can walk right to its source from here. All around is a chain of large pools (originally gravel-diggings) now known as the Cotswold Water Park, which more or less encloses Ashton Keynes as if it were an island: birdwatchers come here to view the waterfowl.

Here Peter and Elizabeth Hartland live in one half of a 17th-century manor house (with later alterations) surrounded by a particularly lovely and secluded garden which has a succession of lawns and a paved carriage-yard with barbecue beside its lily-pool. One of its previous owners was Puritan John Richmond, who had a part in founding Taunton, Massachusetts.

Indoors is a large, friendly sitting-room; a dining-room that has interesting wallpaper, antiques and huge heirloom paintings; and Elizabeth's lovely flower arrangements everywhere. In the small library is an alcove lined with a large-scale, illuminated map of the area. Here Peter keeps a collection of packs for visitors, each full of carefully compiled information about various day-outings and his own 'good food guide' to local eating-places. Yet another sitting-room, upstairs, is for TV.

Bedrooms have individuality – one green-and-white sprigged; another full of clematis; a third (turquoise, with brass bedheads) has an unusual domed ceiling. Flowers are usually present.

Elizabeth uses garden produce for meals, at which the Hartlands dine with their guests. You might start with gazpacho or home-made pâté, perhaps; to be followed by a roast or salmon mayonnaise and then perhaps fruit sorbets or rhubarb-and-orange pudding.

Ashton Keynes is on the edge of the Cotswolds. Among other sightseeing possibilities the following are within an easy drive: Cheltenham, Oxford, Burford, Avebury, Bath, Stratford-upon-Avon, Marlborough, Blenheim, Cirencester, Malmesbury, Bibury village – also the gardens of Hidcote, Barnsley House and Kiftsgate. Ashton Keynes has an outstanding farm shop (meat etc.) with fruit and trout farms nearby. Antique shops are numerous.

Readers' comments: Stayed several times. Excellent in all respects.

Book well ahead: many of these houses have few rooms. Do not expect dinner if you have not booked it.

CRAB AND LOBSTER INN

Foreland, east of Bembridge, Isle of Wight Tel: 098387 2244

5 bedrooms (single, double or family) from £11.50. Less for 7 nights. Rooms have central heating; armchairs; views of sea or country; tea/coffee facilities.
Dinner A la carte, from 7pm. Lunches, packed lunches, snacks. Coffee, tea, for a charge. Drinks can be ordered.
Sitting-room with TV and sea views. Bars.
Nearest main road A3055 from Ryde to Shanklin.

This old inn perched on a clifftop provides simple accommodation and spectacular views over the Channel. David Hill will tell you the inn was not named after the plentiful local shellfish but a New Zealand shrub (Puniceus) which has flowers that look like crab or lobster claws and which grows by its walls. Before he took over the inn he used to have the job of advising hotels on their wine, so naturally his are good value. Good straightforward food – big lobsters straight from the sea.

The inn started in 1810 as tea-rooms, but one day the clifftop garden fell into the sea. The dining-room, with big windows is very attractively decorated (as is the adjoining bar); its walls are white-painted boards, and there are pot-plants everywhere. In the main bar are casks of sherry, peach and apricot wine, mead and scrumpy alongside more conventional drinks. There is a second bar with darts etc.

Outside are the weatherboarded watchtower of the coastguards who keep a careful eye on the reef below, footpaths along the clifftop or down to the sands, and, out in the sea, the enormous old Nab Tower that was built in Southampton and towed to its site in the days when French invasion was feared, later to be used for suspending anti-submarine nets across the approaches to the Solent. David and the coastguards who frequent the bar are full of anecdotes about such local oddities, and about some of his past visitors ('we get prince and pauper here'), who have included the French Ambassador on one occasion, and Edward Heath with the crew of *Morning Cloud* on others. The inn is very busy in high summer.

Bembridge itself is an interesting little place with a lifeboat house open to the public, sailing harbour and a particularly good maritime museum. Coast and rolling countryside are equally lovely here. Although it is at the east end of the island where most of the resorts are, it is not difficult to get to the wilder west end. There is a lot to visit here: many stately homes, fossils around Sandown (visit the geology museum to identify your finds), a first-rate wildlife park, botanical gardens with an intriguing museum of smuggling, Queen Victoria's house outside the sailing centre of Cowes, beautiful Blackgang Chine with one lovely garden after another, a centre with dozens of craftsmen at work, Carisbrooke Castle.

Readers' comments: Food excellent; service most attentive.

CRIB FARM

Luddenden Foot, west of Halifax, West Yorkshire HX2 6JJ
Tel: 0422 883 285

4 bedrooms (single or double) from £10. Some have own bath/shower; central heating; views of country or garden. No smoking.
Dinner £6 for 3 courses (with choices) and coffee, at 6.30pm. Non-residents not admitted. Vegetarian or special diets if ordered. Lunches, packed lunches. Tea, coffee, free. Drinks can be ordered.
Sitting-room with central heating, open fire, TV, books, piano; bar.
Large garden
Nearest main road A646 from Hebden Bridge to Halifax.

A necessary break to change horses on the long cross-Pennine journey from Lancashire to Yorkshire brought this 17th-century moorland house into being, for originally it was a coaching inn. Centuries later it became – and still is – a dairy-farm, though its role as a haven for travellers continues too, even though they now arrive by car, by train (to Halifax) or even by air (to Leeds). The Hitchen family have been here since 1815.

The old house has a warm and hospitable atmosphere, with rooms decorated in light and cheerful colours. Comfortable and unpretentious, it has been recommended to me by friends who also praise Pauline's cooking. A typical menu: melon or home-made asparagus soup, home-reared turkey with garden vegetables, a choice of puddings from strawberries and cream to applie pie, or cheeses.

Luddenden Foot, which lies below the farm, once had a railway station, where Branwell Brontë worked as a clerk, and the village will be familiar also to viewers of Thora Hird's 'In Loving Memory'. From the farm there are sweeping views to the wild uplands of Midgley Moor, but down below Branwell found his station dank and depressing – 'hacked out of a great black rock-face', as Lynne Reid Banks describes it in *Dark Quartet*. He, the rich son of a local mill-owner, and Irish labourers together drank themselves silly at local inns; and it was at Luddenden that he first took drugs too, stealing money from the station till to pay for them.

Beyond Ripponden lies the best-preserved Roman road in Britain, running across the Blackstone Edge: its big stone setts have survived nearly 2000 years of wind and weather some 1500 feet up on the desolate moors.

Not much further afield are Haworth (the Brontës' home), the Worth Valley steam railway, the villages where 'Emmerdale Farm' and 'Last of the Summer Wine' have been filmed for television, and Bingley of the five-rise locks. Bradford is well worth several day-trips for its splendid architecture, the outstanding National Photographic Museum, bargains at the many woollen mills and much else. But above all, the moors and the dales can be explored from here, with their great crags, tremendous views, waterfalls and streams. Some people come to them for the climbing, golf, riding, angling or other sports; many simply for the peace.

Prices are the minimum *per person* in a double room at the beginning of the year.

CROSS LANE HOUSE
Allerford, near Minehead, Somerset, TA24 8HW   Tel: 0643 862112

3 bedrooms (single, double or family) from £11. Tea/coffee facilities; views of country and gardens.
Dinner A la carte from 7pm (except Sundays in summer). Advance bookings Thursday–Saturday in winter; optional Indonesian on Thursday. Vegetarian dishes if ordered. Packed lunches. Drinks can be ordered.

Sitting-room with log stove and electric heater, TV, books, record-player.
Small garden
Nearest main road A39 from Minehead to Porlock.
Closed usually in November

At picturesque Allerford, on the other side of Minehead, is Cross Lane House, its restaurant well known to gourmets in the area (and, although on the A39, it has fairly quiet rooms, inexpensive and with country views). Lawrie Pluck's gourmet cooking began in a tent on safari when he lived in Kenya and when camping near here as a student. He and his Dutch-born wife Ida honeymooned here. Then he had a career in computers until, at 48, he at last realized his ambition to start a first-rate restaurant in the area.

Inside the old farmhouse, a small sitting-room is filled with African carvings among a host of other objects, and leather sofas. An old wig-cupboard has survived the centuries. The dining-room is furnished with spindleback chairs and gingham cloths on the tables. All rooms are simple and unpretentious.

As to the most important thing at Cross Lane, the food, the menu is extensive and contains some surprises. Some dishes are very English – such as watercress soup, salmon mousse, local venison (simmered in wine, cream and herbs) or the cider syllabub from a recipe of 1600. But, from travels, Lawrie has also collected a number of exotic recipes. Loempia is a pancake with chicken and beanshoots in a spicy sauce. He does an Indonesian rijstaffel once a week in winter. Lamb comes with a peanut sauce. And, an indication of his attention to detail, when he cooks a Kenyan curry he often offers Kenyan beer with it. All this in a setting of incomparable National Trust landscape, between Exmoor and coast.

15th-century **Old Manor** at Dunster (tel: 0643 821216) stands on marshes that lead to the sea. There is a chapel over the front porch, its barrel-vaulted roof decorated with carved bosses.

Gillian Hill's bedrooms differ, the most striking being a huge room with the wood pegging of the cruck-beamed roof open to view. Some other rooms (for self-catering) are in a Victorian

addition. (B & B only.) *Reader's comments:* A most enjoyable two weeks.

CROSSWAYS FARM

C D PT

Abinger, south-west of Dorking, Surrey, RH5 6PZ   Tel: 0306 730173

3 bedrooms (double or family) from £12. Rooms have electric heaters; armchairs; views of country or garden; tea/coffee facilities. (Laundering facilities.)
Dinner £6 for 3 courses and coffee, at 7pm. Packed lunches. Drinks can be brought in.
Sitting-room with log fire, TV, books.
Garden with croquet and putting.
Nearest main road A25 from Guildford to Dorking.

Meredith's *Diana of the Crossways* (one of those books most people have heard of and few have read) took its title from this historic building of unusual architectural interest, which featured in a television film about the 17th-century diarist John Evelyn.

One steps through the arched door in a high wall to find a small, enclosed garden with a flagged path leading to the wide front door of the house. In its façade decorative brickwork combines with local sandstone, and Dutch-style arches curve over the small-paned windows. There is an immense chimney-stack towering above – 30 feet in circumference. But the most striking feature of all is the great oak staircase inside, its two flights leading up to large, beamed bedrooms, simply but comfortably furnished; the banisters and newels are handsomely carved.

The house has had many owners since it was built about 1620. For the last quarter-century, the Hughes family have farmed here, producing beef and corn. Sheila Hughes serves homely farmhouse meals (like Irish stew, fish pie, roast chicken etc.) usually with garden vegetables; or you can eat outstandingly well at, for instance, nearby Wootton Hatch. Breakfast options include, if ordered in advance, such extras as fishcakes or kidneys.

Crossways is attractive to many people: walkers, because both the Pilgrims' Way and the Greensand Way are near (and you need no car – buses can be picked up only yards away); continental visitors, because it is a good half-way stop en route to the West Country or to Wales. And for Londoners, it's an ideal weekend retreat: a drive of only half an hour or so. Leith and Box hills are near; Polesden Lacey and Clandon Park; also gardens at Wisley, Chilworth and Ockley; and countless antique shops.

Readers' comments: Warm welcome. Comfortable.

Undercroft at Swalcliffe Manor (see page 291)

CROWN INN

C(14) PT

Downham Market, south of King's Lynn, Norfolk, PE38 9DH
Tel: 0366 382322

rear view

10 bedrooms (single or double) at £15. Bargain breaks. Rooms have central heating; own bathroom (most); TV (on request), phone, armchairs; tea/coffee facilities.
Dinner A la carte, 6–10pm. Vegetarian or special diets can be prepared. Lunches, packed lunches, snacks. Coffee, tea, free. Drinks can be ordered.
Nearest main road A10 from Ely to King's Lynn.

The unassuming and small façade of this inn, facing the market square, gives no hint of what lies behind. The 17th-century building straggles far back, and when you pass under the high arch (built for coaches) you come first to the bars, with rooms above, and beyond them to what were once a considerable range of stables – since converted into restaurant and kitchens: black-and-white pantiled buildings, with hanging baskets of flowers. This was once a yeomanry centre. John Champion (formerly a civil engineer) keeps the bar more or less as it has been for the last century or so – oak-panelled, jugs hanging from its beams, a brick hearth at each end. The bar is made from sherry casks, and on the walls are wartime photographs of the famous Pathfinders air squadron who, based nearby, used this bar as their 'local'.

The stable restaurant has been discreetly converted: floors and walls are of brick, solid elm tables stand in each former loose-box. A chef works in full view at one end, cooking griddled steaks or chops, for instance. Gâteaux, pâtés and everything else are made in the kitchens. Breakfasts are served elsewhere – in a low-beamed Dickensian parlour, beyond which are two very handsome Jacobean staircases leading to the bedrooms (and a residents' sitting-room). These are spacious and furnished to a much higher standard than is usual in country inns: most have beautiful bathrooms. (Ask for a quiet bedroom at the back.)

From Downham Market one can tour north Norfolk. Royal Sandringham is a few miles in one direction, Ely Cathedral in the other. King's Lynn itself certainly needs more than a flying visit because its mediaeval quarter alongside the river holds so much of interest. Just walking along the quays, through courts and alleys, into the cathedral-like church and to the immense market square is pleasure in itself. In addition, there are museums, art gallery, theatre in a historic building and snug inns to visit. Eastward lies one of East Anglia's finest coastlines (an area of outstanding natural beauty) with a string of bird reserves and natural shoreline. One can visit Houghton Hall and three older National Trust mansions from here, the Norfolk lavender fields, the fens, the Caithness glass factory (with bargains), Castle Rising, the cliffs of Hunstanton, Nelson's birthplace, and also the Peterborough area. The fens have a strange, wild beauty all their own. Peterborough's cathedral is one of the great splendours of the area, but its museum, riverside gardens and old byways are well worth visiting too. Go to Wisbech for a Dutch-style town (and Peckover House) and the surrounding tulip-fields in spring; to Spalding for the flower festival; to Thorney for its abbey.

Readers' comments: Most welcoming. Comfortable character, friendly.

CRYER HOUSE

C D

Castle Street, Castleton, west of Sheffield (Yorkshire), Derbyshire, S30 2WG
Tel: 0433 20244

2 bedrooms (double or family) from £10.50.
Rooms have central heating; TV, armchairs;
views of country or garden.
Garden
Nearest main road A625 from Sheffield to
Chapel-en-le-Frith.

Castleton's main claim to fame is its range of huge underground caves (several can be visited), from one of which is mined a very pretty stone, unique in the world, called Blue John – elegant trinkets made from it are lovely souvenirs to take home. Another would be a painting by actor-artist Terence Skelton, whose excellent local landscapes are extremely popular.

Wisteria-covered Cryer House (named after a 17th-century rector who owned it) is where he lives with his wife Felicity, a former theatrical director, and their children. They have furnished the house with great flair: excellent colours and well chosen furnishings in every room. On the ground floor is a tea-room (board floor, pine tables and benches, green trellis wallpaper). Breakfast is served either here or in the new conservatory adjoining it. Packed lunches are available, but for other meals there is a choice of six eating-places in the village (I found the food at the inn next door excellent); then after dinner one can join the Skeltons' Burmese cat to relax in their little cottage garden, brimming with flowers, and watch the world go by.

The High Peak of northern Derbyshire is in complete contrast to the rest of the county. Here the crags that rise from windswept heather moors are wild and challenging. No towns – only stone hamlets sheltering below the towering ridges. This is where you will see climbers and pot-holers (hang-gliders too), and where even the less intrepid can explore winding footpaths or go down to caves of stalactites and stalagmites, some visited by boat. Some of the loveliest hamlets are Abney (with gorge), Baslow (mediaeval bridge), Castleton itself (and Peveril Castle), Edale (gorges, crags and a path up Kinder Scout, over 2000 feet high), Eyam (in wild, open country with superb views and a prehistoric circle). Eyam is 'the plague village': to prevent infection spreading, in 1666 the heroic villagers deliberately cut themselves off to die alone. Grindleford is celebrated for sheepdog trials on the moors and for Longshaw Park (1000 acres, NT). Axe Edge Moor and the Goyt Valley are two areas of outstanding scenery; so is the Snake Pass; and the chain of reservoirs starting with Lady Bower.

Readers' comments: A warm welcome; comfortable, spacious rooms, lovely conservatory.

> When writing to me, if you want a reply please enclose a stamped addressed envelope.

CUMBERS HOUSE

Rogate, east of Petersfield, Hampshire, GU31 5EJ   Tel: 073 080 401

rear view

2 bedrooms (double) from £15. Rooms have central heating or electric heaters; showers; TV, armchairs; views of country or garden, tea/coffee facilities.
Dinner £8.50 for 3 courses and coffee, at 7.30pm (Monday to Friday only). Non-residents not admitted. Drinks can be brought in.
Sitting-room with central heating, open fire, TV, books, piano.
Grounds Woodland and lawns with croquet.
Nearest main road A272 from Midhurst to Petersfield.

A large woodland garden screens this comfortable brick house from the road, and beyond are fine downland views. Every bedroom is spacious, has large casement windows, and is pleasantly furnished – for instance, white bedspreads and curtains contrasting with coral walls and chair-covers, flowers and bowls of pot-pourri on handsome mahogany or walnut furniture. In the green-and-grey sitting-room, there are pretty trifles around: ivory-framed miniatures, pots of velvety gloxinias or delicate streptocarpus, old china. Guests are welcome to play on the mellow and well-tuned Schiedmeyer, and to pass idle hours on the swing-seat in the garden, surrounded by varied firs, catalpa, magnolia and a fruitful fig-tree, chatting with Jon Aslett, who served with the Gurkhas. From the surrounding woods a deer occasionally wanders in, to be chased away by the tiny but ever-vigilant Licky, a Lancashire heeler.

Prue Aslett is an excellent cook and produces imaginative meals – for instance, fish cocottes followed by chicken en papillote and hazelnut gâteau. Bread is home-baked; eggs are home-produced, too. Breakfast options include home-made fishcakes.

Non-smokers preferred. Bicycle on loan.

Apart from the Georgian towns of Petersfield and Midhurst, both very near, Rogate is within a short drive of Chichester (cathedral, theatre, harbour, Roman palace); Petworth and Uppark, stately homes belonging to the National Trust; Broadlands (the Mountbatten home); Arundel (castle, river trips, antiques market, three museums, wildfowl trust); and even Portsmouth (for HMS *Victory* and Henry VIII's *Mary Rose*) and Brighton (the Regency Pavilion). There is polo to be watched at Midhurst; racing at Goodwood; a vineyard at Singleton. Among several gardens, West Dean is outstanding; there are antique shops in which to browse, and at least one good fruit farm in which to pick-your-own.

Petersfield is worth exploring on foot to discover the fine old houses in its streets; and Midhurst is even more attractive – an old market town on the River Rother along which are pleasant walks.

Readers' comments: Full of praise – maximum stars! Thoroughly enjoyed the welcome, and the cooking. Delightfully warm welcome, pretty rooms, delicious food, a great deal of trouble taken for our comfort. Excellent value. A charming and gracious hostess; house magnificent and peaceful. Very good home and grounds; excellent dinner, beautifully presented. Very comfortable, homely, lovely!

DAIRY FARM

Cranford St Andrew, east of Kettering, Northamptonshire, NN14 4AQ
Tel: 053678 273

C S X

3 bedrooms (single, double or family) from £16. Less for 4 nights. Rooms have central heating or electric heaters; bathroom (in one); armchairs; views of country or garden. TV on request.
Dinner £8.50 for 3 courses, at 7pm. Special diets if ordered. Lunches, packed lunches, snacks. Coffee, tea, for a charge. Non-residents not admitted. Drinks can be brought in.
Sitting-room with central heating, open fire, TV, books, record-player.
Garden with croquet.
Nearest main road A604 from Kettering to Huntingdon.

This is not in fact a dairy-farm but arable and sheep. Its name derives from the old dairy around which the manor house was built, in 1610. It is a fine building with mullioned lattice windows in limestone walls and a thatched roof. Its noble chimney-stacks, finials on the gables, dormer windows and dignified porch give it great character. In the grounds stands a circular stone dovecote (mediaeval) with unique rotating ladder inside, used for collecting the birds from the 400 pigeonholes that line it.

Audrey and John Clarke have hung old family portraits in the sitting-room, and furnished the house with things like an oak dresser, chests and ladderback chairs that are in keeping with it. Some bedrooms overlook church and mansion nearby.

Meals consist of straightforward home cooking – soups, roasts, fruit pies – using fruit and vegetables from the garden. Mrs Clarke also does a cordon bleu menu, which costs a little more and has to be ordered ahead.

Visitors enjoy local walks (beside a willow-fringed stream, across-country, or simply to the Woolpack Inn). This is good cycling country, too. Sightseeing possibilities include Burleigh House, Rockingham Castle, the mediaeval stone town of Stamford, Althorp (home of the Princess of Wales's father), Lamport and Kirby Halls, Peterborough Cathedral, Cambridge, Uppingham and Oundle. And at Kettering, Wicksteed Park is an ideal place to take children. Oundle is as attractive as many old Cotswold towns, for the local stone is the same, but much less frequented by tourists. The buildings of its famous public school are like an Oxford college. One can take boat trips on the River Nene, and visit watermills and a country park just on the outskirts, or the gardens at Coton Manor.

Readers' comments: Very special, will return. Delicious food; peaceful; attentive hosts. Very kind, food plentiful, peaceful.

Inclusive terms for dinner, bed-and-breakfast (particularly for a week) can be much lower than those quoted here for these items taken separately. For short-notice bookings you may be able to get a reduction.

No proprietor wants to have a room standing empty. This particularly applies to Sunday nights. Some hotels make a discount if you want only two courses from a three-course menu.

DAISY BROOK
Forest Lane, Lacock, south of Chippenham, Wiltshire, SN15 2PN
Tel: 024973 257

2 bedrooms (double or family) from £12.50. Less for 7 nights and bargain breaks. Both rooms have tea/coffee facilities; central heating; views of country or garden. (Washing-machine on request.)
Dinner £6 for 3 courses and coffee, at 7pm. Non-residents not admitted. Vegetarian or special diets if ordered. Tea, coffee, free. Drinks can be brought in.
Sitting-room with open fire, TV, books.
Small garden
Nearest main road A350 from Chippenham to Melksham.

It is rare for an entire village of such beauty as this to have been preserved (by the National Trust) just as it was in the 18th century, and with many buildings much older than that.

On the outskirts, in rural seclusion, stands this 18th-century stone cottage, behind a low wall on which stonecrop and other sedums grow in profusion. On sunny days, Joy Ames will welcome you with tea in the garden, beyond the petunias and lobelias of which is a far view of Bowden Hill (also National Trust property).

Go in through the low porch and you will find small, beamed rooms with Liberty's Iolanthe fabric (an art nouveau pattern) used on the sofa and for curtains, a log stove and pot-plants. There's a white and green dining-room with mahogany tables; and, up a steep stairway, fresh-looking bedrooms that are pale and trim.

When Joy serves dinners (not in high season) you might be offered such a meal as salad niçoise, tarragon chicken with lyonnaise potatoes and home-grown vegetables, followed by a pavlova.

In Lacock's winding streets are grey stone houses with gothic arches, half-timbered cottages, a lovely church, big mediaeval barn and the cloistered abbey which, after the dissolution of the monasteries by Henry VIII, was converted into a mansion – here, in Victorian times, lived Fox Talbot, pioneer of photography.

Just within the village is the **Old Rectory** (tel: 024973 335), built for a newly appointed rector and his bride-to-be in 1866. But on the wedding-day it was revealed that – shock! horror! – he already had a wife overseas.

This less than virtuous life-style had not inhibited him, however, from filling the house with sanctimonious detail. One enters through an ecclesiastical-style oak door within a pointed arch; to either side are stained glass windows. A particularly fine yew staircase leads up to very well equipped bedrooms which Margaret Addison has

furnished with style, using chinoiserie fabrics, pink moiré (in a four-poster room) or Laura Ashley prints. Each has an immaculate modern bathroom. Breakfast only (visitors dine at, for instance, the George Inn).

DAMSELLS CROSS (AND DAMSELLS LODGE)   D H S PT
The Park, Painswick, north of Stroud, Gloucestershire, GL6 6SR
Tel: 0452 813197 (Cross) and 0452 813777 (Lodge)

The following details refer to Damsells Cross:

3 bedrooms (double) from £15. Less for 2 nights. Rooms have central heating or gas heaters; TV, armchairs; views of country or garden; tea/coffee facilities. One en suite bathroom.

Sitting-room with central heating, open fire, books.

Large garden with tennis court and unheated swimming-pool.

Nearest main road A46 from Stroud to Cheltenham.

Mrs Pointer and Mrs Cooke are sisters-in-law, living in houses next to one another. The first is a stone mansion in traditional Cotswold style (mullioned windows with leaded panes, solid oak doors that have iron fittings which were specially made by a local blacksmith, wide corridors and elegant arches indoors), and the second is a smaller but still very comfortable house, originally the lodge to the mansion. Both are in a peaceful rural lane and have truly spectacular views from every window. The Lodge has a small garden of lawns, stone terrace and flowering shrubs; Damsells Cross is surrounded by (at the front) a sunken garden with drystone walls and stone troughs of flowers and (at the back) terraces, tennis court and a swimming-pool, all against a backdrop of fine trees. At both only breakfast is provided – guests eat dinner at the nearby Royal William or in one of Painswick's restaurants: the Royal Oak or Country Elephant, for instance.

At the big house, Mrs Pointer has chosen very pretty fabrics for the large bedrooms – lacy bedspreads, or white flower-sprigged ones matching the wallpaper. The breakfast table of figured mahogany is in a bay window overlooking the garden, swimming-pool and leafy view beyond. (Sandwich suppers available.)

Mrs Cooke is a welcoming hostess who soon makes friends with her visitors. She has made the Lodge immaculate and very comfortable. The huge sitting-room has windows on three sides, and a big log stove. Everywhere there are thick carpets and good furniture (even the bathroom is pretty luxurious). In my view, the best bedroom is one separate from the house: it is in a one-floor garden cottage, with huge sliding windows through which to step straight onto the lawn or to view the distant hills while still in bed, and ideal for anyone who finds stairs difficult. Peter is a landscape gardener; and some shrubs and conifers are for sale.

Painswick church is famous for its 99 enormous yews, centuries-old, clipped into arches or other neat shapes, and for its fine peal of twelve bells. When the September yew-clipping takes place, children dance and sing round the church. The village has many antique shops. To the north lies the cathedral city of Gloucester, and to the south the wooded Cotswold Hills, with particularly spectacular views from Minchinhampton and Rodborough commons (National Trust land). Go west for the Severn estuary with its throngs of seabirds and geese.

Readers' comments: Mrs Pointer is a delightful hostess – good breakfast, lovely garden. The Cross is the finest house we stayed at. Excellent accommodation at the Lodge; the place and the owners delightful. A luxurious night at the Cross: will return. Lodge immaculate; lovely setting, gorgeous view; helpful.

DEDHAM HALL
Dedham, north of Colchester, Essex CO7 6AD   Tel: 0206 323027

12 bedrooms (single, double or family) from £16.50. Less for 7 nights. Rooms have central heating or electric heaters; shower or bathroom; armchairs; views of country, lake or garden; tea/coffee facilities.
Dinner £12 for 4 courses, at 7.30pm. Special diets if ordered. Non-residents not usually admitted. Drinks can be ordered. No dinner on Wednesdays.

2 sitting-rooms with central heating, open fire, TV, books. Bar.
Large garden and paddock; with croquet.
Nearest main road A12 from Ipswich to Colchester.
Closed mid-December–February

Set back from the village, beyond a large green (where sheep graze) and a big duckpond, stands this lovely old house, with a wide-spreading magnolia tree in front of it and gardens all around. Wisteria and clematis clamber up its pink walls. Just beyond the barns and lawns is Dedham's fine mediaeval church.

When the Slingos moved here there was an immense amount to do. The house, which developed in stages from the 14th to 17th centuries, had once been the miller's house and a bakery (the watermill itself has been turned into flats). Now it is elegantly furnished with antiques, decorated in lovely colours and filled with flowers from the garden. Every room, from the beamed hall to the carpeted and wallpapered bathroom, is attractive. In the sitting-room, a log fire is lit on chilly evenings.

The food in the beamed dining-room is very good; home-grown vegetables are served and home-made bread. A typical dinner might consist of avocado and walnut mousse, outstandingly good roast beef with Yorkshire pudding, and meringues. Home-made jam, chutneys and honey are on sale.

Picturesque Dedham is, of course, celebrated for its Constable connection, and there are art holidays at Dedham Hall (a 15th-century barn is now a studio). This means vacancies for other visitors are limited.

Readers' comments: Most enjoyable. Food and accommodation excellent.

Don't complain if –
- – because you booked at short notice, you do not get the best room
- – because you did not order a meal in advance, you get something plucked from the freezer
- – because you do not arrive on time, your room is let to someone else
- – because you bring a dog without asking, it is refused entry
- – because you don't express your wishes (for more heat, a second helping or whatever), you don't get what you want!

DERWENT COTTAGE

Portinscale, west of Keswick, Cumbria, CA12 5RF   Tel: 07687 74838

C(12) PT

5 bedrooms (double) from £17. All have own bath/shower; TV; tea/coffee facilities; central heating; views of garden.
Dinner £10 for 4 courses and coffee, at 7pm. Vegetarian or special diets if ordered. Packed lunches, snacks. Tea, coffee, free. Drinks can be ordered.
2 sitting-rooms with central heating, open fire, books; bar.
Large garden
Nearest main road A66 from Penrith to Keswick.
Closed November–March

The house is, despite its name, no mere cottage – for the original 17th-century dwelling was greatly extended in Victorian times in the picturesque but rather grand style favoured by those who built retreats in the Lake District in those days. The result is high-ceilinged and spacious rooms oriented to take advantage of the site, which is set back above the main street of a village.

It is conventionally and comfortably furnished, with one sitting-room and a bar. In the colourful dining-room, with crisp linen and sparkling glassware, Sue Hoffmann and her partner Edward Compton serve a choice of soup or other first course (all home-made); a dish of the day, which might be a joint with a good sauce, beef Wellington or guinea-fowl; a pudding; and cheese.

A previous owner, an Austrian, amassed a collection of paintings which sold for millions after his death years ago. None of them remains in Derwent Cottage, nor does the statuary which he had in the garden, but this still contains the unusual trees he planted – stately conifers for the most part, around terraced lawns. The extensive grounds give a splendid view across to Skiddaw, the highest mountain in the northern Lake District.

Portinscale is a good base for those keen on sailing, boating and other water-sports, which can be pursued on Derwentwater (there are launch trips for the less active). On the lake shore are Lingholm Gardens, best known for rhododendrons and azaleas and for fine trees in the woodland area. At the foot of the lake is Manesty Park, one of the first acquisitions of the National Trust, which was founded in the Lake District. Above the east side is the National Trust village of Watendlath. The narrow, twisting road to it, which gives spectacular views of the lake and its islands, crosses Ashness Bridge, which must be the most-photographed in the country.

Above Keswick (a pleasant enough town but crowded during the tourist season) is Bassenthwaite Lake, the most northerly of the lakes and the only one with the word 'lake' in its name. By it lies Mirehouse, one of the least intimidating of mansions. Children have been known to be led to find a sweet in a secret drawer in a bureau, and the sound of the grand piano is heard on occasion. It is still in the possession of the family whose ancestor entertained Tennyson and Carlyle there. As well as maintaining a domestic atmosphere in the house itself, they have provided a good adventure playground in the grounds.

Readers' comments: Delightfully surprised by the superb standard of the cuisine, the pleasant atmosphere, and the character of the place. Quite excellent. Very attentive service. Food excellent, and all comforts.

DORNDEN

C D

Church Lane, Old Sodbury, north-east of Bristol, Avon, BS17 6NB
Tel: 0454 313325

9 bedrooms (single, twin, double or family) from £17. Less for 4 nights and bargain breaks. Some have own bath/shower; all have TV; central heating; views of country or garden. (Washing-machine on request.) **Dinner** £6.50 for 3 courses (with choices of dessert) and coffee, at 6.45pm. Non-residents not admitted. Vegetarian or special diets if ordered. Packed lunches, snacks. Tea, coffee, free. Drinks can be brought in. **Sitting-room** with central heating, TV, books, piano.
Large garden
Nearest main road A432 from Bristol to Old Sodbury.

An immaculate garden surrounds the big guest-house – flowerbeds and box-hedges in trim and neat array, with a large vegetable and fruit garden to supply the kitchen. From its lawns and grass tennis court, set high up, there are splendid views.

This is the place for a quiet stay, well placed for exploring the scenic counties of Avon, Somerset, Wiltshire and Gloucestershire around it. All the rooms are sedate and comfortable in a style appropriate to what was, in mid-Victorian days, a vicarage and with features of the period still retained – from the beautifully polished tiles of the hall to the terrace onto which the sitting-room opens.

Daphne Paz serves traditional favourites at dinner – such as pork chops or trout with almonds, followed by a choice of two puddings (rice, trifle, plum-and-almond tart or cheesecake, for instance) and then cheeses.

Old Sodbury is conveniently near a motorway yet is a quiet retreat at the south end of the Cotswolds. In its immediate vicinity are 17th-century Dyrham Park (which the National Trust regards as one of its most spectacular properties – its tapestries and its gardens are outstanding), Tudor Thornbury Castle and other stately homes as well as Westonbirt Arboretum.

Quickly reached from, for instance, London, it is also well placed as a centre from which to go sightseeing in several of England's most scenic counties. Bath and Bristol are near, and Wales only a short hop across the Severn estuary; while, using the M5, one can quickly arrive in Somerset, Devon and the rest of the West Country. But there is no need to go far.

Close by is Castle Combe – a most picturesque village, nestling in a valley around which wooded hills climb high (it's a place of mellow stone houses, a turreted church with lovely fan-vaulting, canopied market cross, and a twisting brook that flows under its ancient bridge). And other lovely villages (Biddestone and Badminton in particular). Two things contributed to the beauty of north-west Wiltshire: the fact that wealth (from wool weaving) was amassed during a period of fine architectural style, and the availability of lovely gold or creamy stone with which to build. Rivers watered fertile pastures and carved out valleys where woodlands flourish.

The Romans left remains in Bath and elsewhere; in mediaeval times, great churches were built throughout the region.

Readers' comments: Strongly recommended. Cooking of high standard. Excellent value. Very friendly.

97

EASTON HOUSE

C D S

Chidham, west of Chichester, West Sussex, PO18 8TF   Tel: 0243 572514

3 bedrooms (double or family) from £12. Rooms have central heating and electric heaters; washbasin, shower or bathroom; armchairs; views of sea, country or garden; tea/coffee facilities; laundering available. No smoking.
Sitting-room with central heating, open fire, TV, books, piano.
Garden
Nearest main road A259 from Chichester to Portsmouth.

Every corner of this Tudor house has been filled by Mary Hartley with unusual furniture and trifles. A modern white-and-red poppy wallpaper contrasts with old beams, oriental rugs with stone-flagged floor, scarlet folkweave curtains with antique chandeliers. Jim Hartley collects mirrors (Spanish, art deco, rococo – every conceivable kind) and pictures of cats; Mary makes patchwork; guests play on the Bechstein if so inclined. It's a free-and-easy atmosphere, a house full of character and cats. Even the bathrooms are pretty, with sprigged wallpapers.

Although only breakfast is served (one can dine well in Chichester, particularly at Thompson's, at the Old House at Home in Chidham, or in nearby waterfront inns), visitors are welcome to linger in the comfortable lime-green sitting-room with its log stove (where tea is served on arrival); or in the garden, under the shade of magnolia and walnut trees.

Peaceful Chidham looks across an inlet to ancient Bosham, one of the most picturesque sailing villages on the winding shores of Chichester's lovely natural harbour (with boat trips): very popular and therefore very crowded in high summer. Chichester itself is near. It has a mediaeval cathedral, Georgian houses and a festival theatre of considerable renown.

Wherever you drive or walk there is fine scenery; and plenty of interesting sights within a few miles – such as the Weald and Downland Open-Air Museum (acres of ancient buildings reconstructed), the huge Roman palace of Fishbourne, a brass-rubbing centre in Chichester and crafts complex in Bosham (which also has an open-air theatre), fine gardens at West Dean, a fascinating 'live' museum of mechanical music (organs, pianolas etc.), military aircraft at Tangmere, rose nursery at Apuldram, Kingley Vale nature reserve, Goodwood House, the gardens of Chidmere House and Chilsdown vineyard. Arundel, Petworth, Portsmouth Beaulieu and the New Forest are near.

Readers' comments: Peaceful house with great character, very reasonably priced. A marvellous place. Mrs Hartley anticipates her guests' every need. Excellent.

Further down the lane is the **Old Rectory** (tel: 0243 572088), built in 1830 and now well-furnished by Anna Blencowe in traditional country-house style. The large garden has a swimming-pool (unheated) and the sitting-room a grand piano. Bed-and-breakfast only.

EBURY HOTEL

C D H PT S-C

65–67 New Dover Road, Canterbury, Kent, CT1 3DX   Tel: 0227 68433

15 bedrooms (single, double or family) from £18.75. Bargain breaks. **15% discount**

offered to readers of this book who stay for **2 nights or more (other than bargain breaks)**. Rooms have central heating; shower or bathroom; remote-control TV, phone, armchairs; tea/coffee facilities.
Dinner £9.50 for 3 courses and coffee, at 7–8.30pm. Special diets if ordered. Packed lunches, snacks. Coffee, tea, for a charge. Drinks can be ordered. No dinner on Sundays.
Sitting-room with central heating, TV, books.
Large garden
Nearest main road A2 from Dover to M2 (junction 7).

This is a very big Victorian mansion (run by Jane and Anthony Mason), set back from a main road out of Canterbury, with a large garden at the rear. The food and furnishings are conventional, with much emphasis on comfort and space. The sitting-room is huge and, like the other rooms, immaculately kept. An unusual feature is Anthony's collection of *oeil de boeuf* clocks. There is an undercover swimming-pool and spa bath in the garden.

As to dinner, there are eight choices at each course – mainly classic dishes like salmon mayonnaise, steak Bercy or roast duck.

The city centre is within walking distance. The Ebury Hotel, being on the road to Dover, is a useful place to stay before or after a ferry-crossing to the continent – or as a base from which to explore the historic south Kent coast, the Cinque Ports, Dover Castle and Dover's famous Roman 'Painted House' or the Kent countryside, the garden of England. Other attractions are Chilham Castle, Howlett's Zoo, the Romney miniature railway, and Sissinghurst's gardens.

There is a tremendous amount to do in this county – dozens of stately homes or castles to visit; craft workshops, wildlife parks, vineyards, a pinetum, old towns like Tunbridge Wells, Finchcocks (a 'live' museum of old musical instruments in a Queen Anne house) and the countryside itself. Many of the beaches of Kent are within motoring distance.

As to Canterbury itself, its treasures are world-famous: superb cathedral (stained glass and monuments in particular), St Augustine's abbey, lanes of ancient houses and even older town walls with fortified gateway, museums, gardens and the River Stour.

Readers' comments: Very friendly and helpful, good meals. Very good food, lovely room. Very comfortable, immaculate.

There is a particularly pretty little cottage at Eastling, in the Faversham direction: **Plantation House** (tel: 079589 315), where Dany Fraser takes visitors for bed-and-breakfast only. Half-timbered and with low beams, brick hearth and French provincial furniture, it has an unusually large and wandering garden concealed behind it.

EDENBRECK HOUSE

C(3) **D PT**

Sunnyside Lane, Lancaster, LA1 5ED   Tel: 0524 32464

5 bedrooms (double or family) from £12.50. Rooms have central heating; TV, armchairs; views of country or garden; tea/coffee facilities; bathrooms.
Sitting-room with central heating and open fire, TV, books, record-player.
Large garden
Nearest main road A6.

To find this secluded house, with views of fields and hills, actually *in* the city of Lancaster is one surprise. Another is that, though it aims at all the detail and dignity of an 1860s mansion, it was built only a few years ago. Margaret Houghton and her husband wanted to recreate the style of a 'gentleman's residence' of that era – with all that implies in terms of quality, comfort and spaciousness – and the thought and care they put into it are impressive. They sought out furniture of the period too; but into old marble washstands modern basins have been fitted, and in the largest suite, running from front to back of the house and equally suitable for a honeymoon couple or for a family, is an outsize Jacuzzi bath and a bidet. The pink double bed is on a pink-carpeted dais. One room has a four-poster. As the house is hard to find, the Houghtons will escort your car (from the station), or give you a lift.

Only bed-and-breakfast is served but Lancaster has many eating-places: Elliot's restaurant is very popular with visitors. Among popular local sights are Lancaster Castle and church, Hornsea pottery, Blackpool and the Lake District. At Barton Grange is a good garden centre. Lancaster itself is a historic city, often overlooked by tourists. Even its name is historic, describing its role as a Roman fort (*castra*) on the River Lune. It is well worth visiting the quay, no longer busy and with its handsome Custom House (portico and pillars) now turned into a maritime museum. The wealth of trade conducted via the river in the 18th century accounts for the multitude of fine houses from that period which still make Lancaster an attractive city.

A leafy lane leads steeply up from the quay to the Norman castle looming overhead, and the 15th-century church which has finely carved choir stalls (and a café, where its silver is displayed). There are splendid views over the rooftops from here, towards great Morecambe Bay in one direction and in another to the hill where the enormous copper-domed Ashton Memorial dominates the skyline. Parts of the castle (including dungeons) are open to view; the rest is a prison. Celebrated trials have been held in its courtroom. It still has a portcullis. The pedestrian town centre has good shops.

There are cobbled byways to explore, interesting museums in historic houses, antique shops, a notable covered market, the canal (with boat trips), a lovely park on the hill around the Ashton Memorial, and in adjoining Morecambe an immensely long promenade overlooking sands which, when the tide is out, seem to stretch to infinity.

Readers' comments: Beautiful house and setting; luxurious; unsurpassed hospitality. Beautifully decorated, outstanding value. Excellent in every way. Well kept, pleasant, outstanding value. Very comfortable.

100

EDGCOTT HOUSE

C D S X

Exford, south-west of Minehead, Somerset, TA24 7QG   Tel: 064383 495

4 bedrooms (single, double or family) from £12. Less for 7 nights and bargain breaks. Some have own bath/shower; central heating; views of river, country or garden. (Washing-machine on request.)
Dinner £7.50 for 4 courses (with choices) and coffee, at 7.30pm. Vegetarian or special diets if ordered. Packed lunches, snacks. Tea, coffee, extra. Drinks can be brought in.
Sitting-room with central heating, open fire, TV, books, piano.
Large garden
Nearest main road A396 from Tiverton to the A39.

Trompe l'oeil murals, in 'Strawberry Hill gothick' style, cover the walls of the long dining/sitting-room. They were painted in the 1940s by George Oakes, who is now a director of the distinguished interior decorating firm of Colefax & Fowler. The tall bay windows of this room open onto a tiled terrace from which there is a fine hill view beyond the old, rambling garden where yellow Welsh poppies grow in profusion, and wisteria clambers over the pink walls of the house. In the long entrance hall (red quarry-tiled floor contrasting with whitewashed stone walls) are Persian rugs and unusual clocks. Bedrooms are homely; throughout there is a mix of antique and merely old furniture, with more *trompe l'oeil* alcoves or doors.

Gillian Lamble's style of cooking is traditionally English and she serves such meals as mackerel pâté, roast lamb, lemon meringue pie and cheeses.

Exford is right in the middle of Exmoor, a national park that was once, a thousand years ago, a royal hunting forest. It is a region of varied scenery – part of the moor is green and pastoral, part wild heath, and to the north it goes to the sea.

Readers' comments: Mrs Lamble is kindness itself. A house of character.

Outside nearby Luckwell Bridge is an 18th-century farm with apricot walls: **Cutthorne** (tel: 064383 255), where Ann Durbin – who once ran a restaurant – can produce anything from simple to gourmet candlelit dinners. Bedrooms in the house vary, some homely but one with a carved and tapestry-hung four-poster. In the sitting- and dining-rooms are antique rugs, log fires and brass-rubbings.

There is also a courtyard where chickens roam, a pond with exotic species of ducks and geese, and swings in a children's play area. (Very good value.)

101

EDGEHILL HOTEL

High Street, Hadleigh, Suffolk, IP7 5AP   Tel: 0473 822458

C D PT

9 bedrooms (single, double or family) from £16; less in new annexe. Less also for 2 nights or bargain breaks. Rooms have central heating, double glazing; shower or bathroom; TV, armchairs. Laundering available. One four-poster.
Dinner £10 for 3 courses (with limited choices) and coffee, at 7pm. Special diets if ordered. Packed lunches, snacks. Coffee, tea, for a charge (free on arrival, with cakes). Drinks can be ordered.
Sitting-room with central heating, books.
Walled garden
Nearest main road A1071 from Ipswich to the A134.

Hadleigh, once a rich wool town, went through bad times but is now prospering again. As a result, its very lengthy High Street is full of shops enjoying a new life as wine bars, antique shops and so forth. It is a street of colourful façades, gables, pargetting (decorative plasterwork), overhanging bay windows, carved wood details, ornamental porches and fanlights over the doors. Behind lie meadows and a river.

One of the High Street's many fine historic buildings to have been rejuvenated is a Tudor house with Georgian façade which is now this private hotel. Rodney Rolfe, formerly the manager of a motor dealer's, took over Edgehill Hotel in 1976 and began to convert it. The well-proportioned rooms have been furnished in good taste, and attractive wallpapers chosen for each one. In all the spacious bedrooms there are thick-pile carpets and good furniture. The large sitting-room has glass doors opening onto the walled garden where there are some annexe bedrooms.

Angela Rolfe, previously a teacher, and her mother do all the cooking and use home-grown raspberries, strawberries, vegetables and other produce from the kitchen garden. She serves soup, roasts and 'good, old-fashioned puddings' like plum duff, rice or bread-and-butter pudding (not on Sunday; and always ordering ahead is necessary). She is not only a good cook, but also makes and sells crafts.

This is a good base from which to explore the very pretty countryside and villages nearby, and such well-known beauty-spots as mediaeval Lavenham, Dedham, Woodbridge on the Deben estuary, Kersey, Long Melford and many others. There are stately homes to visit nearby and the castle at Colchester, Flatford Mill, gardens at East Bergholt and Kentwell Hall, two garden centres and any number of antique shops.

Readers' comments: Absolutely excellent. High standard.

Some readers tell me they have stayed at lots of places from *Staying Off the Beaten Track*. I wonder who has stayed at most? A free copy of the next edition awaits the reader who sends me his/her comments on the greatest number!

ELDOCHAN HALL
Willimoteswyke, Bardon Mill, west of Hexham, Northumberland, NE47 7DB Tel: 04984 465

C D H PT S

2 bedrooms (double or family) from £11.50. Less for 3 nights and bargain breaks. All have own toilet; tea/coffee facilities; central heating; views of river, country or garden. No smoking. (Washing-machine on request.)

Dinner £7.50 for 3 courses and coffee, by arrangement. Non-residents not admitted. Vegetarian or special diets if ordered. Packed lunches, snacks. Tea, coffee, free. Drinks can be brought in.

Sitting-room with central heating, open fire, TV, books, piano, cassette-player.

Large garden

Nearest main road A69 from Haltwhistle to Haydon Bridge.

No stranger would guess that an extraordinary enclave lies just to one side of the busy Newcastle–Carlisle road, reached only by an inconspicuous turning or, from the east, by a network of narrow roads which lead to nowhere. It is where the rushing River Allen slows down to meet the South Tyne in its valley bottom. To reach Eldochan Hall, you will drive through old mixed woodland, pass a bastle house (an old fortified farmhouse – bastle is the same as *bastille*) and a miniature hamlet with a picture-postcard church and graveyard, and at the end of this winding road, probably having taken a wrong turning or two, you will see a half-ruined castle built into a farmstead. Eldochan Hall, which lies below the castle, is perhaps two centuries old, probably built on the site of another bastle.

The stone-slated porch leads into a dining-room with an old kitchen range, now with a wood stove incorporated. Here, teacher's wife Elaine MacDonald serves meals (such as melon, pork casserole, and chocolate pudding) when the house is full. When guests are few, they eat in what amounts to a private sitting-room, off which opens the best bedroom. This, like the upstairs rooms, has a pleasant mixture of antique and modern furniture. Much of the neat modernization of the house was the MacDonalds' own work. A stream rushes past the garden.

For walkers, there are footpaths and the wooded Allen Banks estate; for the carless, a railway station is only half a mile away over a footbridge. Photographers and naturalists will make the most of the nearby nature reserve, the tree-lined river banks, and the picturesque buildings at Beltingham and along little-used lanes.

A few miles eastward, and more accessible for a short stop, is **Geeswood House** (tel: 043484 220), an efficiently run guest-house on the outskirts of the town of Haydon Bridge, with a very large hillside garden containing a small waterfall. Doreen Easton's food is home-made, including the bread. It is a short walk from the station, with regular services to Carlisle, Newcastle, and points in between (connections for Scotland and west Cumbria).

ELM FARMHOUSE

Fulbrook, north of Burford, Oxfordshire, OX8 4BW   Tel: 099382 3611

7 bedrooms (single, double or family) from £15.50. Less for 3 nights or more and bargain breaks. Some have own bath/shower; all have TV; tea/coffee facilities; central heating; views of country or garden. No smoking preferred.

Dinner £13.50 for 4 courses (with choices) and coffee, at 7.30pm. Non-residents not admitted. Vegetarian or special diets if ordered. Tea, coffee, extra. Drinks can be ordered.

2 sitting-rooms with central heating, open fire, TV, books, record-player; bar. No smoking in one sitting-room.

Garden

Nearest main road A361 from Burford to Chipping Norton.

Closed late December and January

Although built only in 1897, this handsome house is in traditional Cotswold style – constructed of golden limestone, with gables, two-foot thick walls, mullioned windows that have shapely dripstones above them, and a roof of stone slates. Sue and David Catlin have furnished its large rooms handsomely. The south-facing sitting-room has damask wallpaper, chrysanthemum-patterned sofas and a brass-legged coffee table drawn up by the Minster stone fireplace; and in the dining-room Royal Worcester china on pink tablecloths. Bay windows overlook a croquet lawn, herbaceous borders sheltered by stone walls, and a paved terrace from which there are views of fields, stream and some fine specimen trees. Off the hall, a bar leads to a television room.

A great Jacobean staircase sweeps up to well-equipped and agreeably furnished bedrooms – the blue room has a particularly attractive garden view.

Dinners here have imaginative touches (and choices at several courses). One example: courgette and fennel soup, lamb with such vegetables as cucumber in herbs or baked aubergines, black cherry jelly with Kirsch cream, cheeses.

The northward part of the Cotswolds, not greatly frequented by tourists, has very fine views across the Evenlode Valley. All the famous beauty-spots like Bourton-on-the-Water and the Tews are within easy motoring distance.

Readers' comments: Beautiful house. Most friendly and helpful. Will go there again. Pleasant, comfortable rooms and good food.

At Westhall Hill, Fulbrook, is the **Dower House** (tel: 099382 2596), another handsome house of golden stone, which Diana Westall has furnished with flair. You might sleep in a four-poster with honeysuckle draperies or a brass bed with porcelain panels in a room with panoramic views on two sides and a bathroom which, like other rooms, has William Morris wallpaper. (B & b only: plenty of restaurants in Burford.) Parked outside is likely to be the Westalls' 1938 Alvis tourer.

ELM HOUSE

C D PT S

Upper Holt Street, Earls Colne, north-west of Braintree, Essex, CO6 2PG
Tel: 0787 222197

4 bedrooms (double or family) from £12. Some have own bath/shower; tea/coffee facilities; central heating; views of garden. (Washing-machine on request.)
Dinner From £9 for 4 courses (with choices) and coffee, at 7.45pm. Non-residents by arrangement. Vegetarian or special diets if ordered. Lunches, packed lunches, snacks. Tea, coffee, free. Drinks can be brought in.
2 sitting-rooms with central heating, open fire, TV, books.
Small garden
Nearest main road A604 from Colchester to Halstead.
Closed in December and January

This gracious 18th-century house has been furnished with suitable elegance. The moss-green and pale gold sitting-room, where a log fire crackles behind a high brass fender is furnished with antiques (its high French doors open onto a large garden where meals are occasionally served). In the dining-room, which is sage-green, the mahogany table is laid with white-and-gold Spode and silver candelabra at dinner time; breakfast is eaten in the big L-shaped kitchen made cosy by a log stove. There is also a reading/writing-room for guests who want complete quiet.

Although on a main road, the house provides quiet bedrooms at the back, overlooking the walled garden (windows are double-glazed). I liked the coffee-and-white room with William Morris curtains; another is huge, with windows on three sides. There are pretty antique iron beds (painted white or black, with bright brass knobs) coupled with the modern comfort of warm duvets. Details like brass curtain-poles and decorative fanlights catch one's eye.

Lady Larcom so much enjoyed entertaining that she started to run a private catering service and to take guests in Elm House. Dinners here are therefore rather special. They may begin with bouillabaisse, for example, followed perhaps by stuffed peppers (baked in tomato and mushroom sauce, topped with sour cream, and served with wild rice and salad), then may come iced coffee soufflé and cheeses.

Earls Colne is in one of the best parts of Essex – the north-east. This is a region of peaceful water-meadows with willows, outstanding churches and great historic interest. Colchester is an exceptional Roman/Norman city, described elsewhere. All down the coast are winding creeks and wildernesses that attract migrant waterfowl. Where once the Vikings sailed in to plunder, boat enthusiasts now go yachting. There is very varied scenery to explore inland: heaths, woods and villages that once prospered from weaving wool and which still remain beautiful today.

> Prices are the minimum *per person* in a double room at the beginning of the year.

ENFORD HOUSE

C D PT S

Enford, south-east of Devizes, Wiltshire, SN9 6DJ   Tel: 0980 70414

3 bedrooms (double or family) from £12.50; tea/coffee facilities; central heating; views of country or garden. (Washing-machine on request.)
Dinner (when available) £10 for 4 courses and coffee, at 7–8pm (must be ordered by lunchtime). Packed lunches. Tea, coffee, free. Drinks can be brought in.
Sitting-room with central heating, open fire, TV, books.
Large garden
Nearest main road A345 from Marlborough to Salisbury.

The latest in telecommunications and 4000-year-old mysteries oddly combine in the telephone number of this house – Stonehenge* 70414: this world-famous monument is only a few miles away. In fact, Enford (being in Salisbury Plain) is surrounded by prehistoric remains of many kinds.

The 18th-century house (once a rectory) and its garden are enclosed by thatch-topped walls – a feature one often finds in those parts of Wiltshire where, stone being non-existent, a mix of earth and dung with horsehair or else chalk blocks were used to build walls (which then needed protection from rain). The house has pointed 'Gothick' windows on one side, glass doors to the garden on another. Antiques furnish the panelled sitting-room, which has a crackling fire on chilly nights. Bedrooms are conventionally furnished.

Sarah Campbell serves, on pretty Watteau china, soups that she makes from garden vegetables, roasts, puddings such as gooseberry fool or lemon soufflé, then cheeses. The Campbells tell their guests a great deal about the area – not just its historic sights for they are knowledgeable about its wildlife (Salisbury Plain has a tremendous variety of wildflowers as well as larks and lapwings), where to go for the finest views from the surrounding downs, the best walks (paths beside the historic Kennet & Avon Canal are level and the scene very pretty) and the best inns. The Avon rises in the downs north of here, flows through an exceptionally lovely valley all the way into Salisbury and thence through Hampshire to the sea at historic Christchurch – it would be possible to follow its course by car, passing through many pretty villages along the way.

The vast green undulations of Salisbury Plain have changed little over the centuries; its grandeur is as imposing as ever, its fields of grain sweeping to the horizon like a prairie.

Near Enford is the lovely Vale of Pewsey: Pewsey itself (under an hour from London by train) is a small town of thatched cottages and 18th-century houses with a statue of Alfred the Great near the river. At the other end of the Vale is the market town of Devizes (its museum holds many of the prehistoric remains found in the Plain) and beyond it Trowbridge, the handsome stone buildings of which were built by rich cloth-merchants descended from Flemish weavers who fled here during periods of religious persecution. Another weavers' town is Westbury, near which is one of Wiltshire's many famous white horses, cut through the turf.

* The number 0980 quoted above is the dialling code for Stonehenge.

ESHTON GRANGE

C PT S S-C X

Gargrave, north-west of Skipton, North Yorkshire, BD23 3QE
Tel: 0756 749 383

4 bedrooms (double or family) from £15. Rooms have central heating, electric heaters; shower (some); TV, armchairs; views of country or garden; tea/coffee facilities. (Clothes-washing facilities.)
Dinner £8 for 3 courses and coffee, at 6.30–8pm. Vegetarian diets if ordered. Packed lunches. Drinks can be brought in.
Sitting-room with central heating, open fire, books.
Nearest main road A65 from Skipton to Settle.

Inquisitive brown eyes watched my arrival: two of the Eshton Grange stud of tiny Shetland ponies were in a paddock overlooking the courtyard.

Judy and Terry Shelmerdine have created a comfortable, informal atmosphere in their home even though it is furnished with fine antiques and good paintings, many by Judy. It has stone inglenooks, chintz or tapestry chairs and deep-set windows.

The beamed bedrooms are on two floors – at the top is a big attic room ideal for a family, for children shin up a ladder to their beds in the apex of the roof, tucked away above the king-post which supports it. It's a higgledy-piggledy room, with pretty trellis wallpaper, a circular window, and in one corner a cooker useful for preparing the children's supper.

Dinners are traditionally English – home-made soup, roast chicken with all the accompaniments, sherry trifle, and cheese, for example. You help yourself to as much as you want. (Must be ordered in advance.)

Eshton is surrounded by beautiful views. It is near Malham (in Airedale) famous for its massive crags, tarn (lake) belonging to the National Trust, and cove – a huge circular cliff. Go to Gordale Scar for the sight of twin waterfalls in a 300-foot gorge. There is a moorland road through wooded Littondale to Arncliffe and Litton, villages with quaint houses, ancient churches, swirling rivers – and few tourists.

Readers' comments: Owners, room, food and views fantastic! A good place, very reasonably priced. Bang on! – have stayed twice.

Shetland ponies at Eshton Grange

For explanation of code letters (**C, D, H, PT, S, S-C, X**) see page xxvi

ETCHILHAMPTON HOUSE

C D

Etchilhampton, south-east of Devizes, Wiltshire, SN10 3JH   Tel: 0380 2927

rear view

4 bedrooms (single, double or family) from £12.50. Rooms have electric heaters; TV, armchairs; views of country and garden; tea/coffee facilities.
2 sitting-rooms with open fire, TV, books, piano.

Large garden and paddock, with tennis, croquet and heated (75°) swimming-pool.
Nearest main road A342 from Devizes to Andover.

A gracious house (surrounded by lawns, fine trees and the herbaceous borders of a walled garden), built by a local merchant in the 18th century, this is now the home of Priscilla and Michael Maude, both widely travelled. Priscilla used to work in the British embassies of Rome and Paris, there developing a taste for the arts. She provides bed-and-breakfast only, but there is a plentiful choice of eating places in Devizes (five minutes away).

There is a yellow sitting-room with alcoves full of books; and from the big hall a fine staircase rises to spacious bedrooms – their large sash windows have garden views. Flowery wallpapers and simple furniture predominate.

Guests are welcome to use the garden, the croquet lawn, tennis court and heated, covered swimming-pool. The best view of the wisteria-covered house is from the back: to one side of the door, with pretty fanlight under its arch, is a great wall-sundial ('I only tell ye sunnie hours'). There is a sunken rose garden.

Visitors staying here (only 2 hours from London) find the local scenery delightful, but can go further afield to visit Bath, Longleat and other stately homes, prehistoric Avebury and Stonehenge, Salisbury Cathedral. This is good cycling and walking country (with views of the famous white horses carved into the chalky downs), and one can go on the historic Kennet & Avon Canal. Other interesting places are Lacock Abbey, Devizes Museum and the gardens of Bowood.

Readers' comments: Could not have been made more welcome or comfortable. Delightful.

> **Book well ahead:** many of these houses have few rooms. Do not expect dinner if you have not booked it.

108

FAIRFIELD HOUSE
C(5) **H PT X**

44 High Street, Corsham, south-west of Chippenham, Wiltshire, SN13 0HT
Tel: 0249 712992

5 bedrooms (single or double) from £12. All have TV; tea/coffee facilities; central heating. (Washing-machine on request.)
Small garden
Nearest main road A4 from Bath to Chippenham.

Within a peacock's cry of Corsham Court (a palatial Elizabethan mansion with a famous collection of paintings and other treasures) is a quiet and picturesque street which, in the 17th century, was lined with the cottages and workrooms of Flemish weavers. Fairfield House is one of few to have survived from then, for an explosion of gunpowder stored nearby (during the building of Brunel's Box Hill railway tunnel, one of his greatest feats) devastated much of the street.

During the building of the two-mile tunnel (1836–41), every spare bed in Corsham was occupied by railway navvies working on the 'monstrous and extraordinary, most dangerous and impracticable tunnel'. Men and horses were the only power available to get through the rock (solid Bath stone for much of the way), working by candlelight; every week, a ton of candles and a ton of gunpowder were used; and, in all, 30 million bricks to line the tunnel which the sceptics said Brunel could never complete. Today's high-speed travellers whisk through it with little thought of how it was built.

At Fairfield House, one steps straight into a low, white breakfast-room with jade paintwork and curtains, beyond which lie two bedrooms and bathroom, with more upstairs. Christine Reid has furnished all of these with exceptional grace – using either silky cream duvets or pretty patchwork (made by her mother) on the beds, wallpapers patterned with small roses or with Chinese-style pheasants. White-shuttered windows are set in deep embrasures; fresh or dried flower arrangements are everywhere. This is altogether an exceptionally attractive small house, and very good value. (Breakfast only; for dinner, visitors go to the Weaver's Loft, Methuen Arms or other restaurants in the little High Street.)

Wiltshire is, I feel, an undervalued county, for in addition to its rolling countryside there is so much to see – outstandingly, its 4500 prehistoric sites (of which Stonehenge may be the most famous but is less impressive than Avebury). Great houses include Wilton, Stourhead, Mompesson House (within the precincts of Salisbury Cathedral); even nearer, Bowood, Lacock Abbey and Longleat. In fact, the county has more listed buildings than any other, and many of its villages are little beauties.

Readers' comments: Delightful; great food; very welcoming.

When writing to me, if you want a reply please enclose a stamped addressed envelope.

109

FELDON HOUSE
Lower Brailes, west of Banbury, Oxfordshire, OX15 5HW   Tel: 060 885 580

4 bedrooms (double) from £17.50 with central heating; armchairs; views of garden or country; bathrooms. Bargain breaks.
Dinner £16.50 for 4 courses and coffee, served whenever required (not Sunday). Lunches, packed lunches. Special diets if ordered. Tea, coffee, free. Drinks can be ordered.
2 sitting-rooms with central heating, log fires, TV, books.
Garden
Nearest main road A34 from Oxford to Stratford-upon-Avon.

It is not only the outstanding cooking of Allan Witherick which brings visitors to this lovely and peaceful house by the village church. The leafy Cotswold views, a particularly pretty cottage-garden and the care with which Maggie has furnished every room all add up to something very special.

One approaches this mainly Victorian house up a long stone-flagged path, columbines and lupins brimming over the beds on either side and a huge lime tree shading the lawn. There is a south-facing terrace of herringbone bricks where guests often take their pre-dinner drinks (always served with crudités and a dip).

Inside are two dining-rooms (and two sitting-rooms) so that when there are separate parties of guests they can remain separate if they prefer. One dining-room (furnished, like all rooms, with well-chosen Victorian antiques) has redcurrant walls; and adjoins an older sitting-room, brick-walled and with views of the rear garden (it has an alcove with television). The other is in a former conservatory, now carpeted and with Aztec-patterned curtains; its adjoining sitting-room is decorated in sandalwood, against which the Withericks' collection of Victorian watercolours shows well.

Bedrooms (and bathrooms) are equally attractive; and all rooms are full of Maggie's personal touches – like her constantly growing collection of eggs (glass, alabaster or decorated), pot-plants or nosegays, masses of books, well-chosen pictures and, in winter, log fires.

In the adjoining coach-house two large bedrooms have been created, one with a four-poster and one in Chinese style.

As to Allan's meals, not only is he an outstanding chef but the presentation of each dish is done with style. A typical dinner menu: lovage soup; salmon; chicken breast stuffed with pine kernels; peach with strawberry sauce. The vegetables are particularly imaginatively prepared – it's the only place where I've been served new potatoes with lavender leaves! The food is complemented by Chartreuse china, crystal glasses and candlelight; coffee is accompanied by a dish of petits fours. Breakfasts are both ample and varied.

This part of Oxfordshire is described under other entries.

Readers' comments: Our favourite. Food excellent. Congenial helpful hosts. A glorious, peaceful house. Delightful friendly owners. Perfect in every respect. Could not have wished for a better place. We were extremely comfortable in the coach house. A very happy atmosphere.

FITZ MANOR

Fitz, Bomere Heath, north-west of Shrewsbury, Shropshire, SY4 3AS
Tel: 0743 850295

3 bedrooms (single, double or family) from £15. Less for 7 nights and bargain breaks. Rooms have tea/coffee facilities; central heating; views of country or garden. (Washing-machine on request.)
Dinner £10 for 4 courses (some choice) and coffee, at times to suit guests. Vegetarian or special diets if ordered. Lunches, packed lunches, snacks. Tea, coffee, free. Drinks can be brought in.
2 sitting-rooms with central heating, open fire, TV, books, record-player.
Large garden
Nearest main road A5 from Shrewsbury to Llangollen.

This outstanding manor house was built about 1450 in traditional Shropshire style – black timbers and white walls. It is at the heart of a large farm where vegetables and grain are grown.

The interior is one of the most impressive in this book. A vast dining-room with parquet floor and Persian carpet overlooks rosebeds, pergolas and yew hedges. It is furnished with antiques, paintings by John Piper and a collection of Crown Derby. In the oak-panelled sitting-room there are damask and pink velvet armchairs around the log fire (or guests can use the glass sun-room). Between these two rooms are the arched hall and a winding oak staircase; one door here is carved with strapwork and vines, on the walls are ancestral portraits, and on the tiled floor Persian rugs and oak chests.

Bedrooms differ in size. For instance, adjoining one huge room with armchairs from which to enjoy views of the Severn Valley and Welsh Hills is a white cottage-style bedroom – a useful combination for a family (and Fitz Manor has a playroom with toys for children).

Dawn Baly's candlelit dinners often start with home-made pâté or soup; casseroled pheasant or wild duck sometimes appear as the main course, with home-grown vegetables; puddings may be fruit pies, meringues or chocolate mousse; and then there are cheeses – unless visitors want only a salad or shepherd's pie supper.

The garden is still much as it was when laid out in Tudor times, although now there is a heated swimming-pool and croquet lawn. Guests are encouraged to use the land – for barbecues, picnics, swimming or fishing in the river. Though Fitz Manor is a stately home in miniature, the atmosphere is very friendly and easygoing.

(Shrewsbury and north Shropshire are described elsewhere).

Some hotels and even farms offer special Christmas holidays; but, unless otherwise indicated (by the code letter **X** at top of entry), those in this book will then be closed.

FLEUR-DE-LYS INN

Cranborne, south-west of Salisbury (Wiltshire), Dorset, BH21 5PP
Tel: 07254 282

7 bedrooms (double) from £15.50. Less for 6 nights. Rooms have own bath/shower; TV; tea/coffee facilities; central heating; views of country.
Dinner A la carte at 7–9.30pm. Vegetarian menu, and special diets if ordered. Lunches, packed lunches, snacks. Tea, coffee, extra. Drinks can be ordered.
Small garden
Nearest main road A384 from Salisbury to Blandford Forum.

> 'Where is the food, in toil's despite?
> The golden eggs? The toast? The tea?
> The maid so pretty and polite?
> These things are at the Fleur-de-Lys.'

Rupert Brooke (he of the 'honey still for tea') was also inspired to write a long poem about quiet pleasures and good food when he visited Cranborne's Fleur-de-Lys inn (in 1914 he was stationed at the barracks of nearby Blandford Forum).

The inn's history goes far back – to the 11th century – and mediaeval stones uncovered during building work may have come from a monastery that once stood where the church is now. Other finds included 17th-century documents, copies of which are on show. Infamous Judge Jeffreys (notorious for sending to the gallows hundreds of rebels in the revolt against James II led by the Duke of Monmouth) stayed here, and so did Hardy. In *Tess of the d'Urbervilles* Hardy describes a dance in the inn's barn; how one haymaker said 'the maids don't think it respectable to dance at the Flower-de-Luce'; and how Alec d'Urberville accosted Tess there.

Today, Charles Hancock provides comfortable bedrooms for travellers; and good food (including vegetarian choices) is served in the inn's very traditional, panelled bar, on tables covered with green cloths. You can either have substantial bar snacks or choose from a full à la carte menu featuring traditional English dishes such as whitebait, venison and meringues.

Cranborne is in the middle of Dorset's lovely countryside, with the ancient wooded hills close by. Trout streams wander through the landscape, there are historic houses in plenty and countless gardens (and Lady Salisbury's garden centre, which specialises in old roses). Within easy motoring distance are the cathedral city of Salisbury, the big seaside resort of Bournemouth, the New Forest, impressive Wimborne Minster, and picturesque Fordingbridge.

For a good day-drive, explore Cranborne Chase, one of England's most scenic but little frequented areas, on the steep and winding road from Tollard Royal.

Readers' comments: Most enjoyable. Excellent meals.

112

FOLDGATE FARM

C PT S X

Corney, near Millom, Cumbria, LA19 5TN   Tel: 06578 660

3 bedrooms (single, double or family) from £9.50. Less for 2 nights. Rooms have electric heaters; electric blankets; washbasin; armchairs; views of country or garden. (Clothes-washing free.)
Dinner £5.50 for 4 courses and coffee, at 6pm. Special diets if ordered. Lunches, packed lunches. Coffee, tea, free. Drinks can be brought in. Snack suppers available.
Sitting-room with open fire, TV, books.
Nearest main road A595 from Millom to Whitehaven.

A real Cumbrian farm, and well outside the main tourist areas, it covers 100 acres on which are kept Swaledale and Herdwick sheep as well as some cattle. The approach to the farm is through a cobbled courtyard, with a great stone byre and stables at one side, Muscovy ducks perching on a dry-stone wall, and sundry old iron pots and kettles filled with stonecrop, London pride or primroses. A stream slips quietly by. Pat, the sheepdog, comes bounding out to greet visitors.

The rooms have old furniture. Guests sometimes eat with the family, by a dresser where mugs hang, the clothes airer suspended overhead and a grandfather clock ticking in one corner. There are bacon-hooks in the ceiling, old horn-handled shepherds' crooks stacked in the hall, and a bright coal fire in the evenings.

Mary Hogg does most of the talking as she serves guests a proper farmhouse meal, and her husband is glad to tell visitors about his sheep and all the local goings-on – guests are welcome to watch the life of the farm, and to join in at haymaking time in July or August.

You'll get real country fare here: Cumberland sausage, 'tatie pot', plum pudding with rum sauce, farm duckling, Herdwick lamb or mutton, rum butter on bread, currant cake with tea on arrival and at bedtime, and jams made from local bilberries, pears, or marrow and ginger. There are free-range eggs for breakfast. This is a thoroughly unpretentious, homely and friendly place to stay – but not for those who want everything shiny as a new pin.

As to the countryside around, there are the moors of Corney Fell close by and roads winding up and down, with sea views. An unusual attraction is a smokery (for meats) where visitors are welcome.

Close to Corney are Wastwater, Eskdale, the 'Ratty' railway, Muncaster Castle and its gardens, Coniston and Ravenglass.

Readers' comments: Excellent food, good company. Good food. Lovely welcome.

Single people may find more company in houses that have a shared dining-table, a bar, and no TV in the sitting-room. As my descriptions indicate, some owners mingle more with their guests than others do. Houses marked **S** charge singles little or no more than half a double.

FORD FARMHOUSE

Harberton, south of Totnes, Devon, TQ9 7SJ   Tel: 0803 863539

C(12) **D S X**

3 bedrooms (single or double) from £14.50. Less for 7 nights and bargain breaks. Some have own shower; central heating; views of garden. (Washing-machine on request.)
Dinner £9 for 3 courses and coffee, at 7pm. Non-residents not admitted. Vegetarian or special diets if ordered. Lunches, packed lunches, snacks. Tea, coffee, free. Drinks can be brought in.
Sitting-room with central heating, TV, books.
Small garden
Nearest main road A381 from Totnes to Kingsbridge.

In this little village are two houses of outstanding excellence. For years, **Preston Farm** has been one of the most popular places in this book (see elsewhere); now I am glad to include another, at the other end of the village, which will be of particular appeal to gourmets.

Within the white walls are a low-beamed dining-room with stone fireplace (furnished with country Chippendale chairs and a dresser with pretty plates), an upstairs sitting-room, and delightful little bedrooms, one with patchwork spread, some with flowery views of the small, wandering garden and its stream.

Mike Edwards (a Master Sommelier) and Sheila (who trained at the Cordon Bleu school in Paris) previously owned a restaurant and so the food here is rather special. She will produce dishes you request, or else her own specialities such as lamb prepared with a garlic-and-mustard marinade (which she may accompany with clove jelly, and cabbage in a creamy onion sauce) or gammon with sultana and cider sauce. She sometimes serves meringues with rum-and-chestnut purée or brandied peaches. Starters might include local mackerel with a lemon-and-horseradish sauce, or celery-and-cucumber soup. Meals must be ordered in advance.

On those nights when dinner is not available, Mrs Edwards recommends the Church House Inn as an excellent alternative. It is only two minutes' walk away.

Each day's breakfast is different, with options such as particularly tasty sausages, kidneys or liver, teacakes or croissants.

The dilemma is to choose which of Harberton's houses to stay at!

Within a short drive one can reach Exeter, all the resorts and beaches of Torbay, Plymouth and innumerable beauty-spots in the countryside and along the coast. Dartmoor has a wild beauty all its own – a vast expanse of open country (one of the National Parks) with market towns and villages here and there, streams in the valleys and rocks high on the hills where sometimes mist or rain are dense. Nature trails, prehistoric remains, Buckfast and Buckland abbeys, steam railway, butterfly farm, Shire Horse Centre, Dartington Hall, great gardens, six garden centres, museums and historic buildings are among the sightseeing possibilities.

In holiday areas, travel on any day other than a summer Saturday if you can. Make ferry, Motorail or coach/train reservations well in advance if travelling at such periods.

114

FORTITUDE COTTAGE

C D PT

51 Broad Street, Old Portsmouth, Hampshire, PO1 2JD   Tel: 0705 823748

3 bedrooms (single, double or family) from £12.50. Less for 3 nights. Rooms have central heating; shower or bathroom; TV; views of sea; tea/coffee facilities.
Nearest main road A3 from Portsmouth to Petersfield.

Carol Harbeck's little cottage – one room piled on top of another – backs onto her mother's (also a guest-house), with a flowery little courtyard and fountain between the two. Hers is named for the Fortitude Inn, which was once next door; itself named for HMS *Fortitude*, a ship-of-war which ended its days as a prison hulk in the harbour – overlooked by the big bay window of Carol's first-floor sitting-room. This is Portsmouth's most historic area. From here, Richard Lionheart embarked for the Crusades, Henry V for Agincourt, and the first settlers for Australia. It's a place of ramparts and bastions, quaint buildings and byways, much coming-and-going of ships and little boats. Now the waterbus leaves from the quay just outside the cottage in summer and autumn.

All the rooms in the cottage are prettily furnished – even the bathroom; and Carol (who provides only bed-and-breakfast) can recommend a dozen good eating-places nearby. Handy as a stopover for people using Portsmouth's port, Fortitude Cottage deserves a longer stay. For Portsmouth (and its adjoining Victorian resort, Southsea) have so much to offer: HMS *Victory*, the *Mary Rose*, HMS *Warrior*, the Royal Navy's museum and that of the Marines, cathedral and historic garrison church, Henry VIII's Southsea Castle, the D-Day museum, Hayling Island and the wild places of Chichester Harbour, clifftop Victorian forts, Roman/Norman Portchester Castle, submarine museum at Gosport, a big new leisure centre, other museums (including Dickens's birthplace), the Searchlight Tattoo every September, trips to the Isle of Wight, and a fine downland country-side to explore inland. Southsea has outstanding seafront gardens. There are boat trips to Spitbank Fort and Southsea is an antique-hunter's paradise. Fishing trips arranged.

Readers' comments: Excellent accommodation, spotless. Absolutely excellent, high standard. Delightfully unusual.

Near the city is Denmead and **Forest Gate** (tel: 0705 255901), the graceful 18th-century house of Torfrida Cox and her husband, with a large garden. It is an informal home, furnished with antiques. Meals (which have to be ordered in advance), include such dishes as Armenian lamb pilaff or moussaka, mousses or lemon meringue pie.

115

THE FOX   C D X
Ansty, west of Blandford Forum, Dorset, DT2 7PN   Tel: 0258 880 328

14 bedrooms (double or family) from £19. Much less for bargain breaks. All have own bath/shower; TV; tea/coffee facilities; central heating; views of country or garden. No smoking in some. (Washing-machine on request.)
Dinner A la carte or from £5.50 for 2 courses (with choices) and coffee, at 7–10pm. Vegetarian or special diets if ordered. Lunches, packed lunches, snacks. Tea, coffee, extra. Drinks can be ordered.
Sitting-room with central heating, open fire, piano, record-player. Bars.
Nearest main road A354 from Salisbury to Dorchester.

Although not particularly old (it started its flint-and-brick life as a Victorian home), the Fox is full of character and has a great reputation for food – from its cold carvery to its charcoal grill. Thirty salads; fourteen meats which include pheasants and ham on the bone; jacket potatoes with unusual fillings; pies, granary bread and home-made soups: this is exactly what authentic pub food should be but so rarely is. And, on top of this, the Fox is in one of the most rural parts of Dorset, surrounded by exceptionally fine scenery.

There is a succession of bars, used by locals at least as much as tourists. One has a huge collection of Toby jugs (800 at the last count), and another hundreds of plates. Among the inn's nooks and crannies are a children's games room, a skittle alley, and even a heated swimming-pool. A busy convivial pub.

Kathryn Witheyman has made the bedrooms very comfortable – some have sofas which is a thoughtful touch. I particularly liked a large coral-and-white room which has an excellent view of the hills.

Ansty is well placed for visiting Dorchester and the Dorset County Museum, Athelhampton House, Chard and Forde Abbey, Corfe Castle, the swannery at Abbotsbury, the old market town of Blandford Forum, picturesque Milton Abbas and its great abbey church, the giant of Cerne Abbas, Shaftesbury and Sherborne – a particular jewel, often passed by. The Blackmoor Vale is undulating country threaded by streams, spreading northward into Wiltshire. Eastward is Cranborne Chase, less well known than some of Dorset's beauty-spots yet well worth exploring because there are exceptionally fine views from its hills with pretty valleys and villages in between. To the south lies Dorset's heritage coast, and the old-fashioned resorts of Weymouth and Swanage.

Don't complain if –
- – because you booked at short notice, you do not get the best room
- – because you did not order a meal in advance, you get something plucked from the freezer
- – because you do not arrive on time, your room is let to someone else
- – because you bring a dog without asking, it is refused entry
- – because you don't express your wishes (for more heat, a second helping or whatever), you don't get what you want!

FOXHILL

C(5) S

Kingsey, south-west of Aylesbury, Buckinghamshire, HP17 8LZ
Tel: 0844 291650

3 bedrooms (double) at £14. Rooms have central heating; shower (in two); armchairs; views of country or garden. No smoking.
Sitting-room with central heating, TV, books. No smoking.
Large garden and paddock, with heated swimming-pool.
Nearest main road A4129 from Princes Risborough to Thame.
Closed in December and January

The instant impression is delightful: sparkling white house beyond green lawns where Muscovy ducks waddle with their young towards a pool crossed by an arching stone bridge. The gnarled remains of an immense 500-year-old elm tree stand beside the drive. At the back of the house is a large garden with swimming-pool, against a distant view of the Chiltern Hills.

The interior is just as attractive. The house having been the home of architect Nick Hooper and his family for many years, it is not surprising that its modernization was done with imagination and with care to respect its 17th-century origins. In the hall, floored with polished red quarry-tiles, a wrought-iron staircase leads up to bedrooms with beamed ceilings, attractive wallpapers and rugs, and restful colour schemes. Board doors have the original iron latches. The breakfast-room (which also serves as a sitting-room) has brown gingham tablecloths and rush-seated chairs. Here Mary-Joyce – a warm, gentle hostess – serves only breakfast, recommending for other meals restaurants in the ancient market town of Thame, only a few minutes away.

Thame is a lively place in autumn when the mile-long market place at its heart is filled with stalls for the annual fair, and is a mecca for gourmets; beyond lie all the attractions of Oxfordshire described elsewhere in this book. In west Buckinghamshire, too, there is plenty – from the wooded hills of the Chilterns down into the fertile Vale of Aylesbury. Early in the year there are bluebells and cherry blossom; in autumn the beech woods blaze with colour.

The centre of Aylesbury is picturesque, threaded with pathways and courtyards to explore on foot (one of the many inns, the King's Head, belongs to the National Trust). Of many villages worth visiting, go to Long Crendon not only for the nearby lovely bridge and rose-covered cottages but for two 15th-century houses (one belonged to Catherine of Aragon and is now owned by the National Trust). At Waddesdon is the Rothschild mansion, looking like a French château (also National Trust property); at Upper Wichendon, high up, a dramatic view of the Thames; Cuxham, in good walking country, has a stream through the middle. Hughenden Manor was Disraeli's house. Waterperry's gardens are outstanding.

All these are very near. Visitors staying for some time can also from here explore Oxford, West Wycombe, old Amersham, Henley and other Thames-side towns (even Windsor), and any number of castles, stately homes, museums, antique shops etc. London is only an hour away.

Readers' comments: Wonderfully kind hosts, lovely home, top of our list! Beautiful house, meticulously kept; charming, friendly and helpful. The Hoopers and their home are charming.

117

FRIAR HALL FARM C S
Caldbeck, south of Wigton, Cumbria, CA7 8DS   Tel: 06998 633

3 bedrooms (single, double or family) from £11.50. Less for 5 nights. Rooms have central heating or electric heaters, electric blankets; washbasin, shaver-point; armchairs; views of country/farmland or garden. **Dinner** £7 for 3 courses and coffee, at 6pm. Special diets if ordered. Coffee, tea, for a charge. Non-residents not admitted. Drinks can be brought in.
Sitting-room with open fire, TV, books.
Nearest main road A595 from Carlisle to Cockermouth.

As the name suggests, this farmhouse has a long history. The Prior of Carlisle built a hospital here, which was dissolved in the reign of King John. The 12th-century part of the house was once the monks' refectory (hence the name 'hall'), with the hospital proper next door.

Today it is the centre of a 140-acre sheep- and dairy-farm. Caldbeck Fells rise up above the village where John Peel was born and is buried (the little churchyard is right opposite Friar Hall, across a tiny humpback stone bridge spanning a tumbling stream with a weir). The Blencathra foot-hounds still roam these fells in winter, just as they once did with John Peel – but now hang-gliders go up there too.

Guests use a snug sitting/dining-room with big leather armchairs, crimson velvet curtains and, on wintry evenings, logs blazing in a fireplace made of greenish Buttermere slate, casting a flicker on the gleaming brass fire-irons. The ceiling is beamed, the walls are thick.

All the bedrooms look across the tiny garden and the stream to the far hills beyond, and to a sky of scudding clouds when the wind blows. Fresh paint and light colours make them attractive; carpets are good; colour schemes simple.

Dorothy Coulthard serves farm food, using plenty of home-grown vegetables and other produce for dishes such as egg mayonnaise, roast lamb and fruit pies with cream.

Caldbeck is one of the Lake District's prettiest villages, with a pond (used by Muscovy ducks), an old inn, and a Wesleyan chapel carved with the reminder, 'Remember NOW thy creator'. The approach from the north is particularly lovely, driving across a heath with gorse towards a view of a green valley, with bracken-coloured hills beyond.

Apart from all the obvious attractions of the area, visitors often enjoy going to the October auctions (in Wigton) of horses and Shetland ponies, although the spectacle of foals being separated from the mares can be distressing. Bassenthwaite Lake, Carlisle Castle and Cockermouth are other attractions.

Readers' comments: Beautiful view; comfortable bedroom. Good home cooking; made very welcome; pretty view of the beck. Thoroughly enjoyed our visit, well looked after. Food excellent, house delightful, shall return. Most enjoyable, excellent food, will return.

> All prices are inclusive of any VAT or service charge. They are minimum prices: superior rooms or high-season bookings may cost more.

GAISGILL FARM

Gaisgill, south of Penrith, Cumbria, CA10 3UA   Tel: 05874 634

C(7) **D S X**

3 bedrooms (single, double or family) from £11.50. Rooms have central heating or electric heaters; armchairs; tea-making facilities; views of country or garden.
Dinner £5 for 3 courses and coffee, at 7.30pm. Packed lunches, snacks. Coffee, tea, free. Drinks can be brought in.
Sitting-room with central heating, open fire, TV, books, record-player.
Garden and farmland.
Nearst main roads M6 (exit 38) and the A685 from Tebay to Kirkby Stephen.

People who zip along the M6 to Scotland miss a lot that is just a little way off the highway – like the long stone village of Tebay with the River Lune's gorge to the south of it. Nearby is Gaisgill with the 18th-century farmhouse of a shepherd.

The huge living-room with low-beamed ceiling, odd nooks and windows set deep in thick stone walls, is welcoming even in winter – with comfortable armchairs and sofas grouped around a blazing fire at one end and two big dining-tables at the other, with patchwork place-mats and small bowls of flowers.

The patchwork is Joyce Leak's; during winter she keeps busy on this and other needlework, sold to summer visitors. The Afghan rugs and cushion-covers are hers too; and she was teaching herself to spin while I was there.

Among the antique furniture, the books and records, is a huge display of silver trophies and another of colourful rosettes – awards won by Alan and his dogs.

Although Alan has sheep on his own nine acres, he is largely occupied in training other farmers in the handling of their border collies. His father was a celebrated shepherd who went sheepdog trialling until he died at 82. And so was his grandfather, until his farm was sold to Beatrix Potter, who lived at Troutbeck.

This is walking country, and Joyce cooks generous meals for appetites sharpened by the fells: home-made soups followed by a roast, and then an array of help-yourself puddings (perfect pastry!) and cheeses. (Not on Thursdays.)

After dinner, there are those fireside armchairs; while Alan, wearing a sweater his wife has spun and knitted, may reminisce about 'the worst spring in memory' when the force of the wind drove sheep before it and fifty were dug out of just one snowdrift, with hundreds more perishing; or he may explain the mysteries of 'gimmer hogs' and 'shearlings'.

Readers' comments: Charming house, lovely people – hospitality itself. Superb food. The best we have stayed at; a lovely position. Super atmosphere. Very comfortable, most enjoyable, everyone praised Joyce's cooking.

If you prefer a small 18th-century guest-house, only a few miles away is the **White House** at Clifton (tel: 0768 65115), now run by the Broadbent sisters who use much garden produce. Light, pleasant rooms; and children particularly welcomed. No smoking.

119

THE GRANARY

Fenny Compton Wharf, south-east of Leamington Spa, Warwickshire, CV33 0XE Tel: 029577 214

3 bedrooms (double) from £15. Less for 3 nights. Rooms have central heating; shower and wc; armchairs; views of country or garden; tea/coffee facilities. No smoking.
Sitting/dining-room with central heating, TV, books.
Large garden
Nearest main road A423 from Coventry to Banbury.
Closed December

On the banks of the Oxford Canal, where colourful narrowboats pass by, the Cotterills – local farming people – inherited a derelict 18th-century warehouse, and completely rebuilt it to make a new home for themselves (upstairs) and rooms for guests (on the ground floor).

Everything indoors has been very neatly done, with pale colours predominating, while the garden outside is (though only a few years old) beautifully landscaped, rock plants and flowering shrubs grouped round a smooth lawn where one may sit to watch the boats glide by. All around are fields.

Dinner can be had at the waterside George & Dragon near the house, or at other restaurants (June Cotterill gives guests a list of eating-places which she recommends).

The hamlet is close to where three counties meet, Warwickshire, Oxfordshire and Northamptonshire. Favourite day-trips for visitors include Coventry Cathedral, Northampton, the colleges of Oxford, Stratford-upon-Avon, Warwick Castle, the Cotswolds and the fruitful Vale of Evesham as well as the gardens of Hidcote and Kiftsgate.

A 'hostess of the year' award was once won by Deborah Lea – the most unassuming of people – who with her brother runs **Crandon House** at Avon Dassett (tel: 029577 652) as a guesthouse on a smallholding where a few Jersey cows, sheep and poultry roam free. One can sit in the glass sun-room to watch the geese and ducks enjoying life, with a view of hills beyond. There is a separate television room with log stove, and terrace outside; in another direction, the small disused quarry (now overgrown) from which Crandon stone was hewn is a picturesque feature. Everything about this house, built in the 1950s, is solidly comfortabie. The pink or blue bedrooms have nice pieces of furniture (a walnut suite, for instance, and a shell-back brocade

chair) and large windows. Deborah produces, as she says, 'plain old-fashioned food' which her visitors love – a variety of soups, roasts and casseroles, bread-and-butter pudding, for example.

Readers' comments: We felt extremely welcome, no detail was overlooked.

120

THE GRANGE

C(5) **D S X**

Sunderland Hill, Ravensden, north of Bedford, MK44 2SH
Tel: 0234 771771

rear view

3 bedrooms (single or double) from £15. Less for 7 nights and bargain breaks. Some have own bath or shower; TV; tea/coffee facilities; central heating; views of country or garden. No smoking. (Washing-machine on request.)

Dinner £11.50 for 3 courses (with choices) and coffee, at 6pm. Non-residents not admitted. Vegetarian or special diets if ordered. Lunches, packed lunches, snacks. Tea, coffee, free. Drinks can be ordered/brought in.

Sitting-room with central heating, open fire, TV, books. No smoking.

Large garden

Nearest main road A428 from Bedford to the A1.

This large manor house has been divided into three dwellings, of which No. 1 is the handsome home of Patricia and Peter Mort, with views downhill of terraced lawns and great cedars, flowering shrubs and a copper beech. Patricia has furnished the rooms in keeping with the architectural style. Good paintings (some by her daughter) hang on silky coral walls; silver, big velvet armchairs and Chippendale furniture are in one room; in another the tulips and pinks of curtain and sofa fabric have inspired the colour scheme for the whole room. Even the bathrooms are carpeted and have flowery wallpaper. The snug little dining-room is in fact a book-lined alcove behind a blue satin curtain (sometimes another is brought into use when there are two families being accommodated).

Meals are very attractively presented. Salmon and pheasant often appear on the menu but guests can have whatever they like if it is ordered in advance. Beans, asparagus, strawberries and spinach are among the produce grown in the garden; honey comes from their own hives; and, because Peter runs a health-food shop in Bedford, vegetarian or other special diets are no problem.

Patricia has much information to share about sightseeing in Bedfordshire, and about the best places in which to hunt for antiques (Ampthill and Olney – even on Sundays – for instance).

It is still possible to identify, in and around Bedford, places which inspired passages in Bunyan's *The Pilgrim's Progress*. Bedford has, in addition to its Bunyan Museum and a notable church, a good traffic-free shopping centre, twice-weekly market and fast trains to London. There are long garden walks beside the lovely River Ouse (boat trips, too). All around the town are pretty villages. At Cardington one can see ballooning and the giant sheds which once housed airships. Elstow (Bunyan's birthplace) has an old moot hall with museum, and half-timbered houses; Felmersham is a boating centre; Harrold has an ancient bridge and country park, Odell castle grounds, Podington old cottages and Hinwick Hall. A nature reserve in gravel-pits is at Sharnbrook, bird gardens at Stagsden, a windmill at Stevenington, an extraordinary Tudor dovecote (for 1500 birds) at Willington, and plenty of fine mediaeval churches throughout the area. A little further afield, Woburn Abbey (and safari park), Whipsnade Zoo, Dunstable Downs (to watch gliders), Wrest Park Gardens, Luton Hoo (art treasures), Castle Ashby and Chicheley Hall are other sights well worth half a day each. With so much of interest it is surprising that Bedfordshire is rarely thought of as a holiday destination – particularly by Londoners (only ¾ hour away).

121

GRASSFIELDS

CDPTS

Pateley Bridge, north of Harrogate, North Yorkshire, HG3 5HL
Tel: 0423 711412

9 bedrooms (single, double or family) from £18. Less for 3 nights. Most have own bath/shower; all have TV; central heating; views of country or garden.
Dinner £9 for 3 courses and coffee, at 7pm. Vegetarian or special diets if ordered. Packed lunches. Tea, coffee, extra. Drinks can be ordered.
3 sitting-rooms with central heating, open fire, TV, books; bar.
Large garden
Nearest main road A59 from Harrogate to Skipton.
Closed in winter

This country house is set back from the road, in its own gardens: it is a handsome Georgian building surrounded by lawns and trees. All the rooms are spacious, well maintained and comfortably furnished. Barbara Garforth studies her visitors' interests and provides helpful information on local areas of interest, including many local walks. There is a tranquil and informal atmosphere.

Meals are prepared from local vegetables and produce wherever possible, including free-range eggs and Nidderdale lamb. A typical menu: grilled grapefruit, braised steak and fresh fruit salad in generous quantities. There is a wide selection of wines.

Pateley Bridge is an interesting small town (in 1982 it won the award for Europe's best floral village), with a number of good shops, set on a junction of several roads, which makes it a fine centre from which to go sightseeing. Grassfields is in the heart of Nidderdale, where there are crags, glens, lakes and How Stean gorge.

A number of Yorkshire's most historic towns are within easy reach: Harrogate (elegant spa), Ripon (cathedral and market), Skipton (castle), for example. There are many pretty villages, particularly in nearby Wharfedale. Fountains Abbey is probably the most spectacular sight in the neighbourhood but there are many other abbeys and castles too, caverns like Stump Cross and strange rock formations like Brimham, rivers and lakes, interesting shops, old inns, nature trails and much else.

Harrogate has its spring flower show as well as Harlow Car gardens; Newby Hall gardens are particularly attractive too.

Readers' comments: Stayed twice: excellent. Most comfortable and quiet. Most helpful.

Inclusive terms for dinner, bed-and-breakfast (particularly for a week) can be much lower than those quoted here for these items taken separately. For short-notice bookings you may be able to get a reduction.

No proprietor wants to have a room standing empty. This particularly applies to Sunday nights. Some hotels make a discount if you want only two courses from a three-course menu.

GRATWICKE HOUSE

9 Gratwicke Road, Worthing, West Sussex, BN11 4BH   Tel: 0903 213000

4 bedrooms (single or double) from £15. Less for 7 nights. All have TV and tea/coffee facilities; central heating. No smoking.
Sitting-room with central heating, open fire, TV, books, piano. No smoking.
Nearest main road A24 from Dorking to Worthing.
Closed November–March

Royalty put Worthing on the map nearly 200 years ago, when Princess Amelia (youngest daughter of George III) visited what was then merely a fishing village. Amelia, 15, had TB and it was thought the sea would do her good. Her adored and adoring brother (Prince Regent) rode daily from his Brighton Pavilion to see her here – her mother would not allow her to go to Brighton. (She died when only 27.)

This patronage immediately made Worthing fashionable as a seaside resort, but not many buildings survive from that period, except in watercolours displayed in the town's museum. However, there is still an old quarter away from the modern razzmatazz; and it is here that Gratwicke House (1878) is found, in a sidestreet only a minute from the sea.

From the outside it looks just like many another. But Barbara and Rupert Webb, previously an actress and a county cricketer, have decorated the interior with great flair – Rupert did all the work himself. There is a shell-pink sitting-room with gilded mirrors, grand piano, Victoriana, leafy plants and open fire – rather as it may have looked when the house was first built. In total contrast is the pine dining-room where swags of dried flowers and a trellis ceiling give a country air to the room. Photos from Barbara's theatrical past and Rupert's cricketing high days hang on the walls here. The window, with festoon blinds, overlooks a tiny courtyard garden. Breakfast is served on Royal Worcester china (no dinners, but this part of Worthing is an enclave of restaurants, such as La Difference).

Every room is a pleasure to look at, with inspired combinations such as a pheasant wallpaper with a watermelon carpet; poppy pictures and poppy cushions contrasting with a cool colour scheme of moss green and white; pink and white lacy fabrics in a bedroom with stripped pine. One very charming single room has flowers and butterflies painted on the built-in cupboard and bedhead; in another, the patchwork bedspread is in glowing colours. All bedrooms have very good armchairs.

Some people come to Worthing because it is so sunny; or because it is a good centre from which to tour (there are many coach excursions); or because it is an international centre for bowls. The town itself has plenty to see and do: bathing beaches, pier, promenades, several theatres or concert halls, huge swimming-pools and other sports, day-trips to France, a costume museum.

West Sussex, described in more detail under other entries, has lush, rich countryside; hills and valleys give the scene great variety.

Readers' comments: Charm itself, warmly welcoming, and a sense of freedom.

GREY GABLES
C D

Norwich Road, near Cawston, north-west of Norwich, Norfolk, NR10 4EY
Tel: 0603 871259

6 bedrooms (single, double or family) from £16. Less for 7 nights, full board or bargain breaks. Rooms have central heating; bathroom; TV, armchairs; views of country or garden; tea/coffee facilities; phone.

Dinner £13 for 3 courses (with choices) and coffee, from 7pm. Vegetarian or special diets if ordered. Lunches, snacks. Coffee, tea, for a charge. Drinks can be ordered.

Sitting-room with central heating, open fire, books.

Large garden Orchard and paddock. Lawn tennis.

Nearest main road A140 from Cromer to Norwich.

Every year James and Rosalind Snaith travel in Europe looking for interesting new wines and recipes to add to their repertoire, for this former rectory is no ordinary guest-house. There is a choice of a three-course dinner or five-course feast that may include, after an hors d'oeuvres, creamed salmon or Italian bean soup, chicken Wellington with apricots in puff pastry, or fillet steak with Marsala sauce, choux filled with lemon curd and cream, and then cheeses.

They have rung the changes on blue-and-beige colour schemes in nearly every room from the Victorian-style sitting-room and up the elegant mahogany staircase to the bedrooms. Dinner is eaten at mahogany tables with velvet-upholstered chairs; silver, rosy Royal Albert china and candles make it an elegant occasion. I was looking at a needlework sampler made by Rosalind's great-aunt in the 'twenties when her mother told me embroidery had been a family tradition through at least four generations of craftswomen ('We never buy anything if we can embroider it ourselves!'): Rosalind herself continues it.

My favourite bedroom is no. 1: pretty fireplace, big bay windows.

Readers' comments: Excellent; marvellous food. Very friendly, good food.

The big landscaped garden is the main attraction at **Glavenside**, Letheringsett (tel: 0263 713181), restored by John Cozens-Hardy. There are lawns and rosebeds, streams with ponds and waterfalls, a rock garden and an area of heathers. He has got the old hydraulic ram to raise water; and the waterwheel (1802) of the mill turns again (you can buy stone-ground flour there). It is safe for children to paddle in the River Glaven, or to take out a boat on the millpond; visitors can also play croquet or deck tennis on the lawns, or walk by the river. The house is handsome; the furnishings homely; prices moderate. (Bed-and-breakfast only.)

Readers' comments: Comfy beds, a relaxed holiday.

GREYS

Margaret Roding, north-west of Chelmsford, Essex, CM6 1QR
Tel: 024531 509

3 bedrooms (double) from £12. Rooms have central heating; views of country or garden. No smoking.
Sitting-room with central heating, books. No smoking.
Large garden
Nearest main road A1060 from Bishops Stortford to Chelmsford.
Closed November–March

Once a pair of farmworkers' cottages, Greys became the Matthews' home when they moved out of their large farmhouse to let their son take over management of the farm. They painted the exterior apricot – in typical East Anglian style – and furnished the rooms simply (a mixture of Habitat and antiques) and with light, clear colours. The beamed breakfast-room has pine furniture and clematis-patterned curtains; from the sitting-room, glass doors open onto the large garden.

'It's lovely when guests book in for one night and then stay for several,' says Joyce. This often happens because so many people think Essex consists of Dagenham's motorworks, Southend's trippers and little else – then, when they come here, find a revelation.

The eight Roding villages include some of England's prettiest, in an area of winding streams and lanes, flowery inns, colour-washed houses with pargetted walls (decorative plasterwork) under thatched roofs. Many visitors arrive at Harwich or at Stansted airport, then base themselves here to visit London (¾-hour by train from Epping), Cambridge, Roman Colchester and the rest of East Anglia. But there is much to enjoy close by including picturesque Thaxted (which has music festivals and a church of cathedral-like splendour), old Dunmow which still has the four-yearly award of the Dunmow Flitch (bacon) to happily married couples – the next ceremony, complete with bewigged judge, will be in 1992, Greenstead (unique Saxon church made of wood), and the attractive towns of Saffron Walden and Bishops Stortford. Audley End is one of England's most splendid Jacobean mansions.

These are only a beginning. Go to Waltham Abbey for the enormous church where King Harold was buried after defeat by William the Conqueror. To Maldon to see great russet-sailed sailing-barges along the picturesque waterfront. To Mersea for the oysterage. To Clacton for the pleasures of an old-fashioned seaside resort. At Mountfichet Castle you might find a wildflower festival in full swing or a herbal weekend; in one of many fine manor gardens, a typical country fête; on village greens, Morris dancers; windmills in full sail; great shire horses on show at Toppesfield; displays of sheep-shearing; exhibitions by the many local craftsmen and artists; guided walks. The area also has the Imperial War Museum's collection of historic aircraft, etc. (at Duxford), two wildlife parks and numerous National Trust properties within easy reach. Saffron Walden has a museum internationally renowned for its 'worlds of man' gallery, particularly the Aborigine exhibits.

Every night you could dine at a different, excellent local inn: the Black Bull at Fyfield, the Cock & Bell at High Easter, and many others. This is a fruit-growing area with plenty of pick-your-own opportunities for the last day of one's visit, too. (Whoever said Essex is dull!)

GROVE HOUSE

C D

Hamsterley Forest, west of Bishop Auckland, County Durham, DL13 3NL
Tel: 0388 88203

3 bedrooms (single, double or family) from £15. Less for 7 nights. Rooms have central heating; armchairs; views of country or garden; tea/coffee facilities. (Clothes-washing facilities.)
Dinner £8.50 for 4 courses and coffee, at 7.30–8pm. Vegetarian or special diets if ordered. Lunches, packed lunches, snacks.

Coffee, tea, free. Drinks can be brought in. No smoking.
2 sitting-rooms with central heating, TV, books, record-player.
Large garden and woodland; croquet. Bicycles on loan.
Nearest main road A68 from Darlington to Consett.

Hamsterley Forest is a 5000-acre Forestry Commission holding in the hills of County Durham. Much of it consists of commercial conifers, but down one side lie 1000 acres of old mixed woodland, which the Forestry Commission manages for recreational purposes, with drives, waymarked walks, two rivers, a visitor centre, and so on. A few houses are buried in this beautiful forest, among them Grove House, which was once an aristocrat's shooting box. (Another is the home of David Bellamy, the television naturalist.)

Grove House is now the home of businessman Russell Close, his wife Helene, and their three children. It is a peaceful place, surrounded by its own big gardens and reached only by a forest road (private but metalled). The windows of the prettily furnished guest rooms look across the lawn into the forest, where you can see woodpeckers at work. Birdsong is the loudest sound you will hear.

The downstairs rooms have a touch of aristocratic grandeur, with the addition of some unusual fittings brought from Germany by Helene's grandparents, from whom she inherited them (notice the art deco doorhandles). Settees and armchairs in the enormous sitting-room are covered in William Morris fabrics.

Helene prepares all the food from fresh ingredients. Meals usually consist of a first course such as a fish gratin; home-made soup; followed by a main course which is often game from the forest; and then a cold sweet such as meringues with ice cream and hot chocolate sauce. She discusses guests' preferences beforehand.

Should you tire of walking, driving, or simply sitting in the forest, there is a huge expanse of deserted heather moorland a few miles away. The other attractions of this little-known county include High Force waterfall, Raby Castle, the magnificent Bowes Museum (château-style), Beamish open-air museum and of course Durham Cathedral.

Readers' comments: Delicious, imaginative food. Fairytale house in beautiful setting. Good value. Greeted as old friends.

GUNNARSGILL HALL

C S X

Gunnerside, west of Richmond, North Yorkshire, DL11 6LA
Tel: 0748 86213

3 bedrooms (single or double) from £27.50 with dinner. Much less for 2 nights or more.

Rooms have central heating or electric heaters; views of country, farmland or garden; tea/coffee facilities; two have showers.
Dinner 4 courses (with choice of starters) and coffee, at 7pm. Special diets if ordered. Lunches and packed lunches. Coffee, tea, free. Non-residents not admitted. Drinks can be ordered.
2 sitting areas with central heating, open fire, TV, books, record-player, semi-grand piano.
Garden
Nearest main road A6108 from Leyburn to Richmond.

The main room here, a huge beamed space like the nave of a church, with mullioned and latticed windows, was a schoolroom 130 years ago. One end is now a studio, for Ken and Lesley Jones are respectively an enameller and a painter. In the middle is the dining area, with an oak settle, elm tables, and farmhouse chairs. At the far end, under a gallery, the floor is covered with oriental rugs; and comfortable armchairs face a log fire.

Lesley, who loves cooking, prefers to use organically grown produce, and she has a network of local suppliers of fresh vegetables and eggs and a butcher who knows the quality of meat she insists on. You might perhaps choose soup made from local artichokes; chicken stuffed with pâté and mushrooms (served in a wine-and-garlic sauce); and pears in red wine (with chocolate-and-brandy sauce) – plus farm cheeses and coffee. Breakfasts are imaginative, and so are the vegetarian menus.

It is Ken's and Lesley's paintings that hang on the white-painted walls of the old schoolroom, where she and Ken can sometimes offer courses in painting. Enamelling as well as silverwork are done in a studio-workshop.

At one side of the building, in what was the schoolmaster's home, are the bedrooms, furnished mostly with stripped pine and cotton prints. All give views of Gunnerside Gill, in which tumbles a tributary of the River Swale that you can follow on foot to its source. Many of the plants and trees in the pretty garden (with stream) were gifts from guests.

The house is reached by a narrow lane alongside the gill from Gunnerside, one of the picturesque stone villages which are a feature of Swaledale. Waterfalls, woodlands, streams, fells and the ruins of old lead mines give the area its distinctive character. There is plenty more to see: ancient churches and abbeys, prehistoric remains, strange geological formations (including crags and caves).

Readers' comments: Genuine friendly service, outstanding cooking (including breakfast and imaginative packed lunches). Impossible to better it! Wonderful food, lovely people. Memorable experience. Fascinating building and location. Delicious meals. Remarkable personal attention. A warm and lovely home, food superb, the best place we have ever stayed. Absolutely marvellous; perfect hosts. Lovely house, beautiful location, excellent dinner. Outstanding hospitality. Gastronomic delight.

GUY WELLS

C

Eastgate (road), Whaplode, east of Spalding, Lincolnshire, PE12 6TZ
Tel: 0406 22239

3 bedrooms (single, double or family) from £12. Less for 5 nights. Rooms have central heating; armchairs; views of country or garden; tea/coffee facilities.
Dinner £8 for 3 courses (with choices) and coffee, at 7pm. Special diets if ordered. Snacks. Coffee, tea, free. Drinks can be brought in.
Sitting-room with central heating, log stove, TV, books.
Large garden
Nearest main road A151 from Spalding to King's Lynn.

Springs in the land around this Queen Anne house are what gave it its name. It is in a lovely and secluded position, surrounded by a traditional garden, trees, and beyond that the fens. The Thompsons have daffodil and tulip fields as well as glasshouses where they cultivate spring flowers and lilies.

The interior of the house is full of imaginative touches – like the addition of an alcove with domed top and scallop-edged shelves to one side of the brick hearth where a log stove stands. Raspberry velvet tub chairs contrast with homely stripped-pine doors. And there is no sound louder than a slow-ticking clock.

Hall and staircase are pretty (with sprigged wallpaper, prints and bouquets of flowerheads dried by Anne), leading to the bedrooms – one of which is huge, with antique bedhead and an old cedar chest. The best one of all has a spread with tucks and pink ribbons, and windows on two sides. One has a half-tester bed.

Visitors who choose Guy Wells do so in order to explore the superb churches of the county, to enjoy its bird life or the spring flowers, for the easy cycling (it's a level area) or just for the peace.

And for Anne's wholefood cooking (using their own vegetables and eggs). She makes all her own pâtés, soups, quiches or ratatouille for starters; a traditional roast or casserole may follow; and puddings like raspberry pavlova, cheesecake or (a speciality I found delectable) a crème brûlée in which yogurt combines with cream as a topping to brandied grapes. (Non-smokers preferred.)

From Whaplode, one can easily explore most of Lincolnshire and much of Cambridgeshire, too – Peterborough, in particular, is worth a day for its cathedral, river trips, local museums and shopping centre, all described elsewhere. There is a butterfly park nearby. Great churches, Springfield bulb gardens, windmills, Burleigh House and many garden centres add to the interest of the area.

Readers' comments: Lovely people. Enjoyed the cooking so much. Delightful lady, friendly, excellent cook, very pleasant house. Lovely place, superb food, nice lady. Very warm welcome, happy atmosphere, glorious food. Interesting part of the country, have visited twice.

For explanation of code letters (**C, D, H, PT, S, S-C, X**) see page xxvi

THE HALL   C(5) D

Great Hucklow, Tideswell, east of Buxton, Derbyshire, SK17 8RG
Tel: 0298 871175

3 bedrooms (single, double or family) from
£13. Less for 3 nights. Rooms have electric
heaters; armchairs; views of country or gar-
den.
Dinner £8.50 for 3 courses and coffee, at
7pm. Vegetarian or special diets if ordered.
Packed lunches. Coffee, tea, free. Non-
residents not admitted. Drinks can be
brought in.
Sitting-room with open fire and books.
Large garden and field.
Nearest main road A623 from Chapel-en-le-
Frith to the A621.
Closed December–February

This, like many Derbyshire villages, is famous for summer 'well-dressings': huge
mosaics of flower-petals depicting religious themes, each ushered in by a blessing
of the well. To enjoy this floral event, stay at The Hall, where you can also see the
Whatleys' south-facing garden when it is at its most colourful (Angela grows the
vegetables, her mother-in-law – who lives in the Hall's converted barn – the
flowers).

The sandstone Hall was built – on mediaeval foundations – soon after Charles I
became King. Like **Highlow Hall** (see elsewhere), it was one of several in similar
style which a Derbyshire farmer (Bagshaw, in this case) provided for each of his
sons. Rows of small, mullioned windows give it particular charm, and in the
former kitchen (now a sitting-room) the original fireplace, which would have
housed a great spit, has been exposed. Walls three feet thick, which keep the house
warm in winter and cool in summer, have here been painted cream, a good foil to
the handsome furniture and unusual mirrors (some for sale) which John makes in
his spare time. He has restored an unusual, very narrow, cellar-to-attic window
(diamond-paned) which lights the staircase.

His craftsmanship is evident in the bedrooms too. For instance, in one of the
very big family rooms there is a huge cockerel he carved, as well as stools and
bedside tables made by him. The bath- and shower-rooms (cork, pitch-pine and
unusual tiles) have more of his decorative mirrors. (No washbasins in bedrooms.)

Angela is a discriminating cook, using fresh garden produce, local game, and
imaginative recipes. A typical dinner might comprise her own liver-and-bacon pâté
(with watercress and toast); chicken pie accompanied by ratatouille, boulangère
potatoes and other vegetables; then unusual water-ices (such as gooseberry and
elderflower, or blackcurrant-leaf) accompanied by home-made biscuits.

All around are the hills and lovely valleys of the Peak District and such sights as
Chatsworth (and its garden centre), Haddon Hall, and Monsal Dale. Lea Gardens
are noted for rhododendrons. Buxton, over 1000 feet up in the hills, is a spa that
was laid out in the 18th century to rival Bath. You can drink the waters (palatable –
unlike many!) which well up, hot, from underground springs; attend the opera;
peer at insects in the unique micrarium; or walk in the fine gardens and shopping
streets.

Readers' comments: More than satisfied. Dinner one of the most superb meals I
have ever had, quite perfect. Most friendly welcome. Most enjoyable. Excellent
food.

129

HALL BANK HOTEL

Beck Lane, Bingley, West Yorkshire, BD16 4DD   Tel: 0274 565296

C(3) **H PT**

10 bedrooms (single or double) from £18 with bath/shower; TV; tea/coffee facilities; phone; central heating; views of country or garden. (Washing-machine on request.)
Dinner £7.75 for 3 courses (with choices) and coffee, at 6.30–7.30pm. Non-residents not admitted. Vegetarian or special diets if ordered. Packed lunches, snacks. Wine can be ordered. No smoking.
Sitting-room with central heating, TV, books.
Garden
Nearest main road A650 from Bradford to Keighley.

The peaceful country surroundings come as a surprise to many. This Victorian house of brown stone ('millstone grit'), once the residence of an American consul, is perched high in its own grounds overlooking the Aire Valley, woods and moors: from its sun-parlour or its paved terrace visitors often enjoy spectacular sunsets. The hotel is now run by Emmie and Jack Wright; with meals cooked by their son-in-law, a professional chef. All rooms have been refurnished to a high standard of comfort if not elegance.

A typical dinner might (from several choices) comprise turnip soup, a roast or trout, and a gâteau.

There's plenty to see and do in this part of Yorkshire: moorland walks, a nature trail, the spectacular five-rise and three-rise locks on the canal which descends steeply near the hotel: hang-gliding, golf, riding, boating; Shipley Glen (ravine and stream); Saltaire model village – a very early little garden city (the woollen mill has a shop with sweaters and tweeds at half price, and canal cruises start here); stately homes like Harewood and the National Trusts's Jacobean mansion, East Riddlesden Hall; Haworth (the Brontës' home); the Worth Valley steam train; Skipton (castle); ruins like Bolton Abbey and Kirkstall; several museums. York, Harrogate and the Dales are within reach.

The city of Bradford (J. B. Priestley's 'Bruddersford') has some unusual museums. Of national importance is that of photography, film and television, which has done much to help the city's recent and rather unlikely growth as a tourist centre. There is also a colour museum, an industrial one devoted to the city's past greatness as a textile centre, and one of rocks and gems, which also includes a walking-stick hall. Cartwright Hall is an art gallery with works by Reynolds and local lad David Hockney.

Bedroom at Northleigh House (see page 196)

HAMPSTEAD VILLAGE GUEST-HOUSE C H PT S-C X
2 Kemplay Road, Hampstead, London NW3 1SY Tel: 01 (or 071 after 6th May)-435 8679

6 bedrooms (single, double or family) £18 or £15 without breakfast. All have own TV; tea/coffee facilities; central heating. No smoking. (Washing-machine on request.)
Small garden
(1–2 days' payment in advance required.)

Both the house and the professional family who live there are very typical of Hampstead. Solidly Victorian, with many of the original features retained, the mansion is now furnished in a slightly bohemian style: homely, hospitable, totally unpretentious.

In the breakfast-room a big pine dresser is laden with jugs and pots, old English china rubbing shoulders with Mexican peasant crockery. The table overlooks a flowery paved patio (where breakfast is sometimes taken). Of the bedrooms, I particularly liked the blue room (even the television and anglepoise desk-lamp are blue, and on the mantelpiece are blue Delft pots), spacious and light, overlooking lime-trees. In another, family room, a ladder goes up to a child's bed on a gallery behind the parents'. Small drinks-refrigerators, many books, a cordless telephone, writing-tables and comfortable chairs are useful touches. In addition to these rooms, there is a basement one with its own door to the garden; and a self-contained suite in the garden.

Annemarie van der Meer does not do evening meals but Hampstead has a number of bistros and restaurants – along with boutiques, antique or craft shops, and bookshops. By Underground, central London is only 10 minutes.

Hampstead village is a conservation area, well worth walking round to see the 18th-century architecture, and houses where so many famous historic or literary people have lived – or still do. Local sights include Keats' House, Fenton House (old musical instruments), Kenwood (Adam mansion, famous paintings, grounds with lake), the elegant 18th-century parish church and Constable's grave, gardens with rose pergola at Inverforth House, Pavlova's house, and of course the famous Heath. Downhill is Camden Lock. Annemarie recommends the guided walks run by 'Footloose in London' (01-435 0259) and can send a leaflet describing these.

Readers' comments: Warm, comfortable and homely. Look forward to a return visit. Would certainly go there again. Secluded and reasonably priced.

Inclusive terms for dinner, bed-and-breakfast (particularly for a week) can be much lower than those quoted here for these items taken separately. For short-notice bookings you may be able to get a reduction.

No proprietor wants to have a room standing empty. This particularly applies to Sunday nights. Some hotels make a discount if you want only two courses from a three-course menu.

131

HARE AND HOUNDS INN

C PT S-C

Talkin, south of Brampton, Cumbria, CA8 1LE   Tel: 06977 3456/7

4 bedrooms (single, double or family) from £13.50. Less for 4 nights. Rooms have central heating or electric heaters; shower or bathroom in some; armchairs; views of country; tea/coffee facilities.
Dinner £7 for 3 courses and coffee, at 7–9pm. Lunches, packed lunches, snacks. Coffee, tea, free on arrival. Drinks can be ordered. Vegetarian diets.
4 sitting-rooms or bars with central heating, open fire, TV, books.
Beer garden
Nearest main road A69 from Carlisle to Brampton.

You could easily pass by this unassuming little inn in the middle of a quiet village – but there is more to it than meets the eye. Even the public bar is a bit different from the average, with heavy elm tables, logs in stone fireplaces at each end, and over the bar itself heraldic panels of stained glass. There is a separate family room, still with the old black-leaded kitchen range and brass fender, where children's menus are served.

Tucked away behind all this are peaceful, beamed bedrooms, and a farm-cottage annexe, quite attractively furnished and with pretty duvets on the beds. One has a four-poster.

As this edition went to press, the inn was taken over by a friendly young couple, who plan to make few changes and to maintain its reputation for good, simple food at modest prices and for interesting breakfasts (a variety of waffles, for example).

Talkin itself is situated in an interesting part of the country, surrounded by fells that are popular with walkers and near a large, unspoilt tarn with various water-sports. Hadrian's Wall is quite near: the most interesting parts at this end of it are the Banks Burn stretch and the fort at Birdoswald. The Scottish border-country and the Lake District are easily reached, too, and the beautiful Eden Valley lies to the south. Brampton is an old market town; Alston and the city of Carlisle are not far. Talkin used to be a stopping-place for monks making their way to Lanercost Priory: part of it is in ruins, but the very lovely nave is still used as a church and what was the guests' solar is a village hall.

For farmhouse accommodation at its most comfortable, **Hullerbank** (tel: 06976 668) is only half a mile from Talkin. Prices in this neat 17th-century house are moderate, especially since all rooms have their own bath or shower. The setting is sheltered and peaceful, and the food, which includes lamb produced on the smallholding, fruit and vegetables from the garden, and trout from a local fish farm, is all home cooked by Sheila Stobbart.
Readers' comments: Comfortable facili-

ties, friendly hosts, a lovely part of the country, and a reasonable price. We are definitely planning a return visit . . . Very friendly. I can definitely recommend Hullerbank.

132

4 bedrooms (double or family) from £15. Less for more nights by agreement. Some have own bath/shower; all have TV; tea/coffee facilities; central heating; views of moat, country or garden. (Clothes-washing facilities.)
Large garden
Nearest main road A41 from Chester to Whitchurch.

A moat dug by Normans surrounds this large 18th-century house, at the heart of a big dairy-farm. Once there was even a drawbridge.

The bedrooms are beautifully decorated and particularly well equipped (bathrooms quite luxurious). Australian-born Shirley Woolley likes, for instance, traditionally rosy cretonnes, countrified Chippendale chairs, antique bedspreads of white crochet. One room has a chair from the Prince of Wales' investiture at Caernarfon Castle at which Shirley's father-in-law (Lord Woolley, former president of the NFU) was a guest.

Visitors dine in Chester or at the Pheasant Inn, Burwardesley, as Shirley serves only breakfast (though for women travelling alone, she will do dinners), which includes unusual home-made jams (such as sloe-and-ginger or strawberry-and-loganberry) as well as honey 'which I steal from my bees at great risk to my person!' On the table will be flowers and fine china.

Beyond the garden and the rose-bordered moat are stables with a dozen horses (trained to compete at horse shows) as well as geese and free-ranging chickens ('I would use my own eggs if only I could find them!'). The Cheshire Hunt meets here every year.

Chester, described elsewhere, is only a few miles away as is (in the opposite direction) little Malpas where old houses overhang steep streets; in its mediaeval church of red sandstone are carvings, stained glass and a superb parish chest. Buy farmhouse Cheshire cheese here. The town is close to the Welsh border, and to Shropshire. The peaceful, pastoral countryside around is low and rolling (unlike east Cheshire with its ridges and crags), the weather often dry and sunny when other parts are wet. Centuries of prosperous farming means there are a number of substantial or even stately homes on large estates and some richly decorated churches; turbulent times have left their mark in castles that still stand.

Interesting places to visit include Tarporley with its gabled houses and notable church monuments, the Delamere Forest, the hilltop ruins of Beeston Castle, the pretty villages of Bunbury and Peckforton (the latter with an imposing Victorian 'castle') among the Peckforton Hills.

When writing to me, if you want a reply please enclose a stamped addressed envelope.

HAVEN

Hardwicke, west of Hereford, HR3 5TA   Tel: 04973 254

C D H PT S

6 bedrooms (single, double or family) from £15.75. Less for 2 nights. Some have own bath/shower; TV; tea/coffee facilities; central heating; views of country or garden. No smoking. (Washing-machine on request.)
Dinner £7.50 for 3 courses (with choices) and coffee, at 7.30pm. Non-residents not admitted. Vegetarian or special diets if ordered. Lunches, packed lunches, snacks. Tea, coffee, extra. Drinks can be ordered. No smoking.
2 sitting-rooms with central heating, open fire, books, piano, record-player; bar. Smoking in one, only.
Large garden
Nearest main road A438 from Hereford to Brecon.
Closed in December and January

'The long-talked-of Hardwick Bazaar for the Home Missions . . . Mary Bevan was radiant with her beautiful eyes and brow. Everybody was buying everything at once. The Volunteer Band banged and blasted away. Persons ran about in all directions with large pictures and other articles, bags, rugs, cushions, smoking caps, asking everyone they met to join in raffling for them.'

Thus Kilvert (a frequent visitor when this house was a vicarage and its garden much used for charity fêtes) wrote in his now famous diary, on 29 August 1870 – with an eye, as usual, for a pretty girl. Kilvert says that paintings done by the vicar's wife were auctioned – but her flowers and birds still adorn the door to one of the sitting-rooms. Here, through shuttered windows, are views of the Radnor Hills, and alcoves are filled with china. In the other sitting-room, books and old local maps line the walls; and there is a cabinet of fifty little drawers which Mark Robinson has filled with information for visitors and labelled 'archaeology', 'crafts', 'maps', 'tapes', etc.

There is a ground-floor bedroom (with bathroom) equipped to suit disabled people – even a wheelchair for use under the shower – and with a view of the unheated swimming-pool in the garden. Janet Robinson has stencilled the walls with a waterlily pattern to match the Liberty fabrics used in the furnishings.

In the dining-room she has stencilled cornflowers to match the festoon blinds of the bay windows; a collection of childhood birthday cards from the 'thirties is a feature elsewhere; and in every room her flair for decoration is evident – a pretty chinoiserie wallpaper here, a sweet-pea paper there, cane bedhead in one room and a huge four-poster in another. One bathroom (raspberry and gold, with sunken bath, bidet and two basins) is not so much a bathroom as an event.

Because Janet enjoys cooking (and studied traditional country recipes at Hereford Technical College), meals are unusually imaginative. A nut-and-herb roulade might be followed by beef casseroled with ginger and then a creamy fool.

The Robinsons occasionally run special activity weekends on such subjects as Kilvert's diary, book-collecting (Hay-on-Wye is near) or 'hidden treasures' (visits to little-known or private houses of historic interest).

Beyond the large garden are paddocks brilliant in spring with snowdrops, miniature daffodils, frittillaries, cowslips and bluebells growing wild.

134

HAZEL TREE FARMHOUSE   C H S
Hassell Street, Hastingleigh, east of Ashford, Kent, TN25 5JE
Tel: 023375 324

5 **bedrooms** (single, double or family) from
£15. Less for 3 nights and bargain breaks.
Rooms have tea/coffee facilities; central
heating; views of country or garden. One
double has own W.C. and washbasin.
(Washing-machine on request.)
Dinner £7 for 3 courses (with choices) and
coffee, at 7.30pm. Non-residents not
admitted. Vegetarian or special diets if
ordered. Lunches, packed lunches, snacks.
Tea, coffee, free. Drinks can be brought in.
Sitting-room with central heating, open fire,
TV, books, piano.
Large garden
Nearest main road A20 from Folkestone to
Ashford.
Closed November–February

Small though this is, it is a true hall house: that is to say, an early mediaeval
structure in which the ground floor consisted of one high communal room, with
only a screen wall separating it from the dairy, now used as the kitchen.

Christine Gorell Barnes and her artistic family have contributed greatly to the
character of the old house, filling it with their paintings, tapestries and the results
of a lifetime of collecting. There are old chests in a corridor, patchwork curtains
and spreads on old brass beds, bunches of dried flowers and hop bines over a brick
inglenook, books everywhere, and on the landing many generations of dolls, dolls'
house and toys which young visitors are allowed to play with. One unusual
treasure is an old dulcitone – a keyboard instrument in which the hammers strike a
graduated row of steel tuning-forks, with bell-like sounds. Bedrooms are furnished in simple cottage style: I particularly liked a ground-floor one with pine
walls. Outside is a willow-fringed pool and a field with Christine's 14 sheep.

Meals are, like the old house itself, out of the ordinary. When I called, Christine
was preparing borscht (beetroot soup), chicken baked with courgettes and
accompanied by dauphinoise potatoes, and a spicy pumpkin pie.

Walnut Tree Farmhouse at Lynsore
Bottom has one of the prettiest ex-
teriors in Kent. Inside, too, it is full of
charm. Gerald Wilton makes furniture, very decorative carved sign-
boards, colourful decoy ducks and
much else in the house – including the
long oak table which looks as if it, like
the house itself, dates from the 14th
century; and the painted clock with a
picture of the farm on its face.

Guests' bedrooms (some in the house
and others in a former apple-loft) are
reached by broad step-ladders. Every
wall and floor slopes a little. Crisp
white fabrics, flower-sprigged, and
pine fitments combine to give rooms an
airy, cottagey feel. An attic one with
low windows has the ancient king-post
that supports the whole structure. (B &
b only. Tel: 022787 375.) Self-catering
available.

Readers' comments: Have returned
many times, most exceptional. A lot of
thought and care; made most welcome.
Beautifully furnished. Made to feel like
guests of the family.

135

HEAVERS

Ryarsh, West Malling, west of Maidstone, Kent, ME19 5JU

Tel: 0732 842074

C D PT S

3 bedrooms (double) from £15. Much less for 2 nights. Rooms have central heating; armchairs; views of country or garden.
Dinner £10 for 4 courses and coffee, at 7.30pm. Special diets if ordered. Packed lunches, snacks. Non-residents not admitted. Drinks can be brought in.
Sitting-room with central heating, open fire, TV, books, record-player.
Large garden and fields.
Nearest main road A228 from Tonbridge to Rochester.

Perched on a hilltop, this red brick farmhouse with dormer windows in the roof and clematis around the porch is at the heart of a smallholding which provides much of the produce that Jean Edwards (once a health visitor) enjoys cooking for her guests. Until a few decades ago, the old house was occupied by generations of the same farming family which built it in the 17th century. All around are country lanes, fields, woodlands and two long-distance footpaths.

The little sitting-room has very comfortable armchairs grouped around the brick hearth (stacked with logs), which still has the old bread oven alongside. It's a cosy room, with the soothing sound of clocks ticking, Gem (the Edwards' Jack Russell terrier) snoozing on the hearth, a collection of china pigs and good books.

Jean enjoys cooking a wide repertoire of dishes (whenever she and her husband travel in the wine regions of France, she always returns with new recipes). She bakes her own bread; honey, eggs, geese and lamb are home-produced.

Beamed bedrooms with white-boarded, latched doors are prettily furnished with Laura Ashley fabrics and attractive colour schemes (pink- or blue-and-white, or moss-green with red-and-white). The Edwards have collected stuffed birds and maps for the walls, and pot-plants for every window-sill. Through the windows are views of the Downs or of the garden which, even in winter, is colourful with witch hazel, holly berries and winter-flowering cherry trees. There's an old pump in it, a swing-seat on the brick patio, and a children's swing. Rooms are small.

Although only an hour from South London (Heathrow and Gatwick airports are even closer), this is a good centre from which to explore rural Kent, the mediaeval bridges of the upper Medway, and any number of castles – Allington, Leeds, Hever, Rochester – and historic buildings – Boughton Monchelsea house, the friary at Aylesford, Sissinghurst with its famous gardens, the Archbishop's Palace at Maidstone, Chartwell (Churchill's home) and Ightham Mote. There's county cricket, boating and sailing, and a famous collection of carriages at Maidstone. But the scenery is the main thing: hills, orchards, streams, hop gardens with their conical oast houses (you can visit Whitbread's hop farm), half-timbered cottages, picturesque villages like Loose (a stream threads its way among the houses). West Malling itself is largely Georgian, with Norman remains; while Mereworth has an unusual classical church. Canterbury and Dover are under an hour away. Gardeners appreciate Great Comp, Sissinghurst, Bedgebury Pinetum and the herb gardens of Ightham and Staplehurst. Plenty of pick-your-own fruit farms.

Readers' comments: Very good indeed. As charming as could be; convivial hosts; mouth-watering and plentiful food. Charming house, food delicious.

HERMITAGE MANOR

Canon Pyon, north-west of Hereford, HR4 8NR   Tel: 0432 760317

4 bedrooms (double) from £17.50. Rooms have central heating; bathroom or shower; armchairs; views of garden or hills; tea/coffee facilities.
3 sitting-rooms with central heating and electric or open fire; one with TV. Baby grand piano. No smoking in music room.
Large garden and orchard.
Nearest main road A4110 from Hereford to Knighton.
Closed mid-December–February

An *escalier d'honneur* sweeps grandly up to the front door which opens into a room of baronial splendour, its ceiling decorated with Tudor roses and strapwork, motifs which are repeated on the oak-panelled walls. Through stone-mullioned bay windows are some of the finest views from any house in this book. There is also a very lovely music room (damask walls and velvet chairs are in soft blue; the limewood fireplace has carved garlands). Throughout, carpets and other furnishings are of equal quality to the architecture.

The recently converted bedrooms, and their bathrooms, are of the highest standard and very large. No. 6 has a view of a hillside spring flowing through stepped pools of pinkish limestone (from a quarry in the area) which Shirley Hickling created when she was converting this exceptional house. She serves bed-and-breakfast only – but there are good inns nearby, and Hereford is only ten minutes away.

Walking and watching the deer or birds are main attractions in this scenic area – the Wye Valley (with Symonds Yat viewpoint), Malvern Hills, Welsh border, Offa's Dyke path, Brecon Beacons and Black Mountains are all accessible. This is a county of woods and streams. In addition there are historic houses such as Berrington Hall to visit, rural museums, Croft and other castles and abbeys. Hereford and Weobley, the 'golden valley' and Wyevale garden centre are also popular.

Judy Seaborne's very good home cooking is the principal attraction of **Stone House Farm**, Tillington (tel: 0432 760631). The setting is very peaceful, with fine views, and children in particular enjoy spring visits when there are lambs, calves and foals to be seen. A typical meal: home-made soup, a roast (the farm's own meat), fruit pie – served from Royal Worcester dishes, in a dining-room with open fire. (Milk, butter and cream are also usually from the farm.) Made of solid stone, the house is well away from any road, and has fine greenery beyond its small orchard. There is an old pump in the front garden.

Readers' comments: Well fed and received with great friendliness. Food of high quality and ample. Most welcoming; excellent cook.

HIGH GREEN HOUSE

C D H S X

Nowton, south of Bury St Edmunds, Suffolk, IP29 2LZ   Tel: 0284 86293

6 bedrooms (single, double or family) from £13.50. Less for 7 nights or bargain breaks. Rooms have central heating or electric heaters; shower or bathroom (some); TV; views of country or garden; tea/coffee facilities. Laundering.
Dinner £8 for 4 courses and coffee, from 7.30pm. Special diets if ordered. Tea free. Drinks can be ordered. Packed lunches.

Sitting-room with central heating, open fire, TV, books.
Large garden
Nearest main road A134 from Bury St Edmunds to Sudbury.

Part Tudor and part Victorian, this delightful house is truly secluded – surrounded by brimming herbaceous borders, a paddock of geese and an old well, with wheat fields beyond. There are a lily-pool (it is all that remains of a moat), troughs of begonias and fuchsias, and, where only the great frame of a mediaeval barn survives, Rosemary Thew has created a suntrap in which to sit, training scented roses and wisteria over the timbers, and placing seats to face the view.

The interior of the house is full of nooks and crannies, cabinets of old china and glass, antique furniture and low beams. There are oriel and mullioned windows, a brick fireplace, and wrought-iron hinges on bedroom doors. Some bedrooms are small and simple; but one has a four-poster, windows on three sides, a carved chest and a cheval mirror with painted flowers. Rosemary (who worked with physically handicapped people until her retirement) has also provided a downstairs bedroom ideal for a disabled person.

Dinner can comprise a chicken vol-au-vent as a starter, then a good roast joint, profiteroles and cheese. She is a genial, informal lady with whom one immediately feels at home; and, because she was formerly clerk to the local council, she is a mine of information about the area (and its people).

Bury and its environs are described elsewhere. Also within easy reach are Lavenham; the great houses of Ickworth, Kentwell and Melford; pretty villages like Clare and Cavendish; the gardens at Bressingham – and antique shops everywhere.

Readers' comments: Warm welcome and excellent food. Most tranquil house. Miss Thew is delightful. Charming building; a bargain; Miss Thew is a character. Peaceful and friendly, nothing too much trouble. Warm welcome and personal attention. Took a lot of trouble; fed us royally.

All prices are inclusive of any VAT or service charge. They are minimum prices: superior rooms or high-season bookings may cost more.

138

HIGH GREENRIGG HOUSE

C(5) D H S X

Caldbeck, south-east of Wigton, Cumbria, CA7 8HD   Tel: 06998 430

8 bedrooms (single, double or family) from £18. Less for 7 nights. Some have own bath/shower. All have central heating and views of country or garden. No smoking. (Washing-machine on request.)
Dinner £10 for 4 courses (with choices) and coffee, at 7pm. Vegetarian or special diets if ordered. Packed lunches. Tea, coffee, free. Drinks can be ordered.

3 sitting-rooms with central heating, open fire, TV, books, piano, record-player; bar.
Small garden
Nearest main road A595 from Carlisle to Cockermouth.
Closed November–February

Hidden in the moors above the village, this 17th-century house has great character, with low doorways and stone lintels. Inside, modern furnishings have been well chosen to suit the beamed interior with no attempt at a 'ye-olde' effect. Pine and cane predominate in the dining-room; in the sitting-room, once a cow byre, ceilings and floor are cork-covered, and there is a self-service alcove where visitors can make unlimited tea and coffee. The bedrooms (which include some on the ground floor) have pine fittings and bedheads, and they give fine views of the surrounding fells. Good food is a speciality of Robin and Fran Jacobs (who used to be an engineer and a social worker respectively). They share the cooking and make their own bread and marmalade. A typical dinner might comprise marinated mushrooms, beef goulash, Lancaster lemon tart, and Stilton.

There is plenty of room for quiet relaxation in the evening; or one can go to a games room with a mezzanine bar, where plate glass has replaced the barn doors. This being an outstanding area for walkers, well away from the crowded part of the Lake District, the Jacobs, with the help of a National Park ranger, have prepared a well-produced booklet of recommended routes.

The Caldbeck area has attracted a number of celebrities to live (Chris Bonington, Margaret Forster, Sir Fred Hoyle, for example) and a lot of craftspeople. A fairly recent addition to what was always a very pretty village is, in a converted watermill, a group of shops for books, antiques and various crafts, and a wholefood restaurant. The nearest places of any size are Carlisle (cathedral, castle, and shops of all kinds) and Wigton (home of Melvyn Bragg and subject of his book *Speak for England*).

> **Book well ahead:** many of these houses have few rooms. Do not expect dinner if you have not booked it.

HIGH WINSLEY COTTAGE

C(5) **X**

Burnt Yates, north-west of Harrogate, North Yorkshire, HG3 3EP
Tel: 0423 770 662

5 bedrooms (twin, double or family) from £14.50. Less for 7 nights and bargain breaks. Rooms have own bath or shower; tea/coffee facilities; central heating; views of country or garden.
Dinner £5 for 3 courses and coffee, at 7pm. Non-residents not admitted. Vegetarian or special diets if ordered. Packed lunches. Tea, coffee, free. Drinks can be ordered.
2 sitting-rooms with central heating, open fire, TV, books, record-player. No smoking.
Large garden
Nearest main road A61 from Harrogate to Ripon.

Weird shapes loom above the moors – a 50-acre outcrop of stone which wind and rain have carved into surreal forms: Brimham Rocks.

Off the road leading to these is a one-time farm cottage now much extended, which has been modernized with care by Clive and Gill King. From the parquet-floored dining-room one steps down to a sitting-room where rosy sofas face a log fire and sliding glass doors open onto a terrace with views to the far hills. Lawn, flowers, orchard and a population of bantams and guinea-fowls add to the charm of the setting.

Colour schemes have been well chosen, here and upstairs. A blue-and-white bedroom with matching bathroom has bedspreads of pin-tucked satin; Laura Ashley briar-roses predominate in another, furnished with antiques; and I particularly liked a large room with windows on two sides and comfortable armchairs from which to enjoy the views.

Gill was once one of 'Miss Gray's young ladies' at the Bay Tree, Burford: those readers who knew the cooking standards there will rightly guess that High Winsley Cottage, too, can be depended upon for good and imaginative food. Gill also lived, and cooked, in Paris for a while.

She puts as much care into making shepherd's pie, for instance, as into a dinner such as lemons with a stuffing of smoked fish, pork in a spiced orange sauce and apple jalousie. Her own or local produce is used; bread is home-baked.

Burnt Yates is not only in the middle of a very scenic area (Nidderdale is among the loveliest yet least frequented of the Yorkshire Dales, and popular Wharfedale is not far away) but is also close to several traditional spa towns – Harrogate (described elsewhere), Ripon (with cathedral), and, one of my favourites, Ilkley, a delightful little town in the valley of the River Wharfe. It is particularly pretty in spring when the cherry-blossom is out on the trees that line its shopping streets, and the riverside gardens are coming into flower. The town has excellent restaurants, tea-rooms and bakers; a grocer specializing in cheeses and ham on the bone for picnics; plenty of bookshops, antique and craft shops; and historical interest, from ancient Saxon monuments to Tudor and 18th-century buildings. The invaluable local guide (free from the Tourist Information Centre in the library) gives maps for walks, short and long; tells you where to watch fell-racing, hang-gliding or international tennis. It lists other places for outings: caverns, ruins, picturesque villages and much else. North Yorkshire is a county that offers great variety to the visitor.

HIGHLOW HALL

C D

near Hathersage, west of Sheffield (Yorkshire), Derbyshire, S30 1AX
Tel: 0433 50393

6 bedrooms (single, double or family) from £15. Less for 7 nights. Rooms have electric heaters; armchairs; views of moors or garden; tea/coffee facilities.
Sitting-room with open fire, TV.
Garden and farmland.
Nearest main road A625 from Sheffield to Chapel-en-le Frith.
Closed mid-November–mid-March

At the heart of this huge farm (raising sheep and cattle) is a castellated, stone manor house of considerable historic interest – complete with not one but four ghost stories. It is one of several similar ones in the Peak District built by a 16th-century farmer for each of his sons: his name, Eyre, is now famous because Charlotte Brontë, who stayed at Hathersage vicarage, took it for her heroine Jane Eyre. (And in the locality was a house which had burned down with, reputedly, a mad woman in it – inspiration for Thornfield Hall.) In the square porch is a massive front door with old iron studs and hinges; the windows have stone mullions and small panes; and above the rugged walls of gritstone is a roof of dark stone slates. It is as if the house grew out of the land itself, for this is the northern (or 'dark') part of the Peak District, in contrast to 'white' limestone peaks further south.

The sitting-room was added in Georgian times, so it has large sash windows with views of the far moors, where the Wains' sheep graze, rising to slopes brilliant with heather in September and rusty bracken in October. The house is 800 feet above sea level (its name derives from 'high hlaw', meaning 'high hill'). Deep, velvety chairs are grouped round a blazing fire on cold days. Adjoining is the dining-room, with comfortably upholstered chairs around each table. Bed-and-breakfast only; most visitors dine at the Poacher's Arms or Hathersage Inn.

Bedrooms are roomy and comfortable, some with ancient stonework and all with fine views – not another building is in sight. One may wake in autumn to frost-sugared grass and grazing sheep; and, beyond, a line of graceful pines.

Margaret Wain will show you the most ancient part of the house (unused at present): the huge stone-flagged hall with great oak staircase. This was once the kitchen, and it still has an old stone sink, stone cheese-press, and ancient chest.

Many visitors come here simply for the scenery and the peace; but there are plenty of places worth visiting (and, of course, glorious walks – the Pennine Way starts in the Peak District). There are the Blue John caverns, stately homes such as Chatsworth and Haddon Hall, the summer 'well-dressing' ceremonies in the many historic villages, interesting old towns such as Buxton and Bakewell, and the city of Sheffield – a great deal more than just an industrial centre (its art gallery, cathedral and theatre are all good, and it has a working 'industrial hamlet'). In hilly Buxton are plenty of interesting places to visit. In its heyday as a spa it emulated Bath, so there are splendid Georgian crescents and squares, a superb Assembly Room (now housing the library) and flowery parks.

Readers' comments: Quite delightful; beautifully furnished; friendly and obliging; very impressed – made most welcome. Very hospitable; comfortable, quiet and in beautiful countryside. A wonderful experience; a beautiful setting.

141

HILL FARMHOUSE

C D

Hitcham, north-west of Ipswich, Suffolk, IP7 7PT   Tel: 0449 740 651

4 bedrooms (double or family) from £13. Less for 5 nights. Some have own bath; TV; tea/coffee facilities; views of country or garden.
Dinner £7.50 for 3 courses (with choices) and coffee, at hours to suit guests. Vegetarian or special diets if ordered. Tea, coffee, free. Drinks can be brought in.
Sitting-room with central heating, open fire, TV, books, piano.
Large garden
Nearest main road A45 from Bury St Edmunds to Ipswich.
Closed November–March

Part Tudor, part early Victorian, this handsome house provides a choice between the spacious, traditional bedrooms at the front of the house (with cornfield views); or the snug low-beamed ones at the back, with little oak-mullioned windows and rugs on brick floors. The latter share a kitchenette for guests' use, while the brick oven and hearth of Tudor times are now a decorative feature, which Pippa McLardy fills with arrangements of dried flowers.

One enters the main house through a hall of powder-blue and white, with cherry-carpeted staircase. Pale pink sitting- and dining-rooms have mahogany antiques, a carved pine fireplace and views of countryside or garden (there are duckponds, a freestanding swimming-pool and slides etc. for children). Pippa is an imaginative cook: for dinner one might choose between fennel Mornay or stuffed vineleaves; pork normande or Scotch salmon; raspberry-and-cream choux or lemon sorbet. Eggs and vegetables are mostly home-produced.

Hitcham is centrally placed within a triangle of historic towns (Bury St Edmunds, Sudbury – Gainsborough's birthplace – and Ipswich) and surrounded by very lovely countryside, ideal for walking as well as touring. The great mediaeval 'wool' churches of the area are justly famous, as are such picturesque villages as Lavenham, Kersey and Long Melford, and the valley of the River Stour – 'Constable country'. When visiting Ipswich, call at Christchurch Mansion (in a fine park) to see Gainsboroughs, Constables and an excellent museum of domestic arts; and at the Buttermarket for the Ancient House.

This unspoilt region is a patchwork of farmland and fens, low hills and a varying shoreline (much favoured by birdwatchers), secretive valleys and wild heaths. Sunny and dry, though sometimes windy, it is nevertheless relatively free of traffic and tourists – by comparison with, say, the West Country – and over all is that wonderful sky, the light of which inspired so many famous landscapes.

On the other side of Hitcham is **Mill House** (tel: 0449 740 315) where once lived the miller whose windmill – long gone – is depicted on the front of the house. Judith White has furnished the bedrooms with rose-sprigged fabrics and velvet bedheads, the stone-walled dining-room with maple furniture (there is no sitting-room). Outside is a large landscaped garden, tennis court,

self-catering cottages – and peacocks as well as ducks. A typical dinner: pâté, chicken chasseur and trifle.

HOLEBROOK FARM

C H S-C X

Lydlinch, Sturminster Newton, south-west of Shaftesbury, Dorset, DT10 2JB   Tel: 0258 817348

shower; TV; tea/coffee facilities; central heating; views of country or garden. (Washing-machine on request.)

Dinner £6.50 for 3 courses and coffee, at 7pm. Tea, coffee, free. Drinks can be brought in.

Sitting-room with central heating, open fire, TV, books.

Small garden

6 bedrooms (single or double) from £12. Less for 3 nights. Some have own bath/

Nearest main road A357 from Sturminster Newton to Stalbridge.

A long track brings one into the yard of this large farm; on one side are stables handsomely converted into bedrooms, and on the other the back of the stone house itself where there are more bedrooms. You are likely to enter via the big old kitchen, with its original flagged floor and stone ovens carefully preserved – it is here that Sally Wingate-Saul serves dinner. (The main course may be anything from lasagne to – once a week – pheasant; puddings include such calorific treats as chocolate roulade or treacle tart with sultanas and lemon; and there are always prize-winning local cheeses too.)

From a gracious sitting-room (shell-pink walls, pale blue damask chairs, log fire) deep-set, pine-shuttered windows overlook the lawn at the front of the house beyond which are apple trees and a kitchen garden. Clematis and a grape-vine clamber up the walls. The house is full of interesting objects which the Wingate-Sauls acquired on travels to the Seychelles, the Pitcairns and Australia; and in a huge attic bathroom is a varied collection of hats (to which visitors have contributed).

The stable rooms include some that are enormous, each with sitting-room and bathroom. Stripped pine has been used a lot, and old horse-stalls retained as room dividers. Small concealed kitchens are useful for visitors who want to prepare any meals themselves, and there are plenty of armchairs.

At Shaftesbury, King Canute died; and the remains of King Edward (martyred at Corfe Castle) were brought here. This ancient town is perched high on a hilltop overlooking the lovely Blackmoor Vale, and from its centre the picturesque cobbled street of Gold Hill makes a steep descent. Church, museum of curiosities and the Grosvenor Hotel are all well worth a visit – the last because it houses (upstairs) an incredible sideboard depicting the Battle of Otterburn carved from one massive piece of wood.

All around Sturminster Newton are other places of scenic or historic interest – Blandford Forum, Milton Abbas, Dorchester, Sherborne, Cerne Abbas and the villages in between.

Some readers tell me they have stayed at lots of places from *Staying Off the Beaten Track*. I wonder who has stayed at most? A free copy of the next edition awaits the reader who sends me his/her comments on the greatest number!

HOLLY TREE

East Witton, south-east of Leyburn, Wensleydale, North Yorkshire, DL8 4LS   Tel: 0969 22383

4 bedrooms (single or double) from £14. Less for 7 nights. Rooms have central heating; bathroom; armchairs; views of country or garden. (Clothes-washing facilities.) No smoking.

Dinner £10 for 5 courses and coffee, at 7.30pm. Vegetarian or special diets if ordered. Coffee, tea, for a charge. Wine can be ordered. No smoking.

2 sitting-rooms with central heating, open fire, TV, books.

Garden

Nearest main road A6108 from Masham to Leyburn.

This is in one of Wensleydale's more peaceful villages, a pretty group of cottages around a green, where sometimes strings of racehorses trot by on their way to exercising on the moors. All around is some of England's most magnificent scenery – the Yorkshire Dales – and towns which are honeypots for antique collectors. In the 12th century, part of the house provided stabling for the horses of monks travelling between the great Cistercian abbeys which are a feature of this area. A curiously shaped breakfast-room, with built-in settle and window-seat was the 'snug' when the house used to be an inn.

Beyond the sitting-room, which has a crackling fire and huge grandfather clock, are two small garden-rooms with glass doors opening onto terrace and lawn with seats from which to enjoy the far view. The formal dining-room has scarlet walls and curtains contrasting with white shutters, green alcoves filled with flowers, antique furniture. Everywhere there are steps and odd angles.

Bedrooms are particularly pretty. One, for instance, has a brass bed with white and apricot draperies; in its bathroom (blue poppy wallpaper, pale blue curtains) are two basins and a bidet. Another has a rose-swagged frieze, pink-and-white beds, and a green chaise longue skilfully upholstered by Andrea Robson herself.

But Andrea Robson's greatest skill is cookery (she won the Gas Boards' 'Cook of the Year' award in 1981). Typically, one of her dinners (preceded by free sherry) might comprise salmon mousse and then her own recipe for chicken breast en croûte (it has a mushroom stuffing and a coat of pâté and ham, inside a flaky-pastry crust). The pudding might then be pears – stuffed with walnuts and cherries, coated with chocolate and brandy, and served with cream.

Altogether, this is a house that has everything – memorable food, attractive rooms, and very lovely surroundings.

Wensleydale is described more fully elsewhere. The nearest small town is Middleham: 18th-century houses cluster around the market place, there's a ruined castle, and racehorses can be seen exercising on the surrounding moors. Well worth a visit are Wensley's riverside church, Ushaw bridge, Jervaulx Abbey and an inn (at Carlton, in Coverdale) with a Saxon burial-mound in its yard. Richmond (with castle), Ripon (cathedral) and Newby Hall are all near – the last with fine gardens. A good area for antiques.

Readers' comments: More than comfortable. Food truly excellent. A lovely home. Very warm welcome. Wonderful food and accommodation. Very comfortable, superb cuisine, delightful house. Cannot be faulted.

144

HOLMHEAD

C PT S-C(4)

Greenhead, west of Haltwhistle, Northumberland, CA6 7HY
Tel: 06972 402 (to be changed to 0697747 402 during 1990)

4 bedrooms (double or family) from £16.50. Less for 3 nights or bargain breaks (20% discount). Rooms have central heating; showers; armchairs; views of river, country or garden; tea/coffee facilities. Laundering facilities available. No smoking. **Dinner** £9 for 3 courses and coffee, at 7.30pm. Special diets if ordered. Lunches, packed lunches, snacks. Coffee, tea, free. Non-residents not admitted. Drinks can be ordered. No smoking. **Sitting-room** with central heating, TV, tape recorder, books, piano, record-player. Games room (snooker, table tennis). **Large garden** with badminton, cricket, swingball, and swing. Helicopter flights over the Roman Wall start from the garden. **Nearest main road** A69 from Brampton to Haltwhistle.

Beside a salmon river, just where the walkers' Pennine Way crosses the Roman Wall, this remote house has the ruins of Thirlwall Castle looming overhead (Edward I once stayed there). Just outside are the remains of a Roman turret, somewhere under the lawn or sunken garden, awaiting excavation; and some Roman stones were re-used when the house was built. All this, with the distant moors, is within view through the windows of the guests' large and comfortable sitting-room upstairs – copiously equipped with games, toys and facilities to make unlimited hot drinks. Pauline Staff used to be a tour guide, and so is immensely helpful with advice on sightseeing. She occasionally gives visitors talks with slides, or may even show them around. Pre-Christmas party weekends are run; and discounts on tickets to local museums are available.

There are all kinds of unexpected 'extras' in this out-of-the-way house: a solarium; foot-massager for weary walkers; pure spring water; table tennis; snooker; snacks at any hour; the freedom of the kitchen – and the company of Rex, a Hungarian visla hound. Pauline likes to cook local dishes and has even experimented with Roman recipes cooked in the area around AD 300 (one favourite is honey-roast ham in pastry). She makes all the preserves, chutneys, cakes and scones. A typical dinner might comprise: melon with kiwi fruit; trout with hollandaise sauce; almond meringue with wild raspberries in whipped cream.

Breakfast choices include haggis, black pudding, kedgeree, muffins, crumpets and occasionally a Scandinavian buffet.

This is a splendid area for walks (with or without a National Park guide). Holmhead and **Beggar Bog** (see elsewhere) offer a holiday with a few days at each house. Visitors walk from one to the other, and their luggage is transported. The Northumberland National Park starts here; there are associations with Walter Scott and Catherine Cookson. You can look at working shire horses, Roman forts or prehistoric remains (including rock carvings), four castles, Hexham Abbey, Lanercost Priory, Beamish's celebrated open-air museum, stately homes. Some of the most popular sights include the Roman Army Museum, Naworth Castle and Talkin Tarn. But it is, of course, Hadrian's Wall that is the biggest attraction of all and at Holmhead you can get guided tours, and certain free tickets.

Readers' comments: Food very good, Mrs Staff a marvellous help. Enjoyable. Well cared for and well fed. Fell for it completely. Orderly and civilized.

145

HOME FARM

Church Lane, Old Dalby, north-west of Melton Mowbray, Leicestershire, LE14 3LB   Tel: 0664 822622

3 bedrooms (single, double or family) from £11. Less for 5 nights. Rooms have central heating, electric heaters; rural views; tea/coffee facilities.
Sitting-room with central heating, open fire, TV, books, piano.
Garden with swingball and swing.
Nearest main road A46 from Leicester to Newark-on-Trent.

Set in an idyllic garden and facing the church, this 18th-century house (extended in 1835) has great charm and an atmosphere of peace. Clematis and quinces grow up its walls. Beyond espaliered apples and herbaceous beds are lawns, a kitchen garden, and for children a separate play area with tree-swing. (It is no longer a farm.) Some plants are for sale.

Indoors, every room has old furniture, pot-plants and white walls. Country-style dining-chairs surround the long table where breakfast is served, a fire crackling on chilly mornings. Val Anderson's collection of 'twenties and 'thirties photographs of local hunting personalities hangs here (including one of the then Prince of Wales, who first met Mrs Simpson at nearby Burrough Court).

Normally, Val serves only breakfast as the snug little Crown Inn nearby is popular for other meals: 'the best food in the Vale of Belvoir', Val says.

Guests at Home Farm find plenty to do in the area (both Nottinghamshire and Lincolnshire are close), visiting Belton and Burghley houses, Belvoir Castle, Newstead Abbey (Byron's house), Wollaton Hall, Whatton Gardens and the Donington Motor Museum. The National Watersports Centre, Trent Bridge and Rutland Water are other attractions.

When to go? Seaside resorts or other places suitable for children will be at their busiest (and dearest) in July–August and during half-term holidays (especially in late May, which is also a bank holiday period). Other peak periods are, of course, Easter, Christmas, New Year and the bank holiday in late August. (The bank holiday in early May is not usually a peak, because it comes rather soon after Easter, but much depends on the weather.) There are local peaks, too (the Gold Cup races at Cheltenham or the regatta at Henley, for instance, are apt to fill hotels for miles around), and local troughs (Brighton, a conference centre, is least busy in high summer). You won't get much personal attention when hotels are full to bursting.

HURDON FARM

south of Launceston, Cornwall, PL15 9LS   Tel: 0566 772955

C D H S

6 bedrooms (single, double or family) from £11. Less for 3 nights. Rooms have bath-rooms (some); armchairs; views of country or garden.
Dinner £7 for 4 courses and coffee, at 6.30pm. Special diets if ordered. Snacks. Coffee, tea, free unless brought upstairs. Non-residents not admitted. Drinks can be brought in. Free tea on arrival.
Sitting-room with open fire, TV, books.
Garden and farmland.
Nearest main road A30 from Launceston to Bodmin.
Closed November–mid-April

The 18th-century stone house is in a picturesque area, not far from Dartmoor and Bodmin Moor (both the north and south coasts are within reach, too). It has large sash windows with the original panelled shutters and built-in dressers in the dining-room. The sitting-room has large and comfortable chairs and a great log stove. The most interesting room is, however, the big kitchen-scullery where an old slate sink and pump stand alongside the modern washing machine, and in the granite fireplace is an array of old jacks, trivets, and a built-in Dutch oven.

Upstairs, all is spick-and-span with fresh paintwork and light, bright colour schemes in the bedrooms. There is also a family suite (made pretty by an old-fashioned rosebud wallpaper) on the ground floor, where the dairy used to be.

Meals, prepared by Margaret Smith and her daughter, are above average 'farmhouse fare', with imaginative starters, in particular. Her soups are accompanied by home-made rolls; lamb or coq au vin by such vegetables as courgettes au gratin, cabbage cooked with onion and bacon, potatoes lyonnaise (with milk and cheese) or creamed turnips; her puddings include raspberry pavlovas, chocolate rouleau and home-made ice creams – always followed by cheeses. She uses the farm's own produce and clotted cream. Visitors can join in farming activities.

From Launceston you can visit the majestic and romantic north Cornish coast, described elsewhere in this book, or head inland to wild Bodmin Moor to discover hidden, unspoilt villages. The coast has stark cliffs, waterfalls and wide sands; the moor, high tors that can be reached only on foot or horseback. Don't miss the elaborately carved church (St Mary's) in Launceston itself, an old-world market town. The area is full of Arthurian legends; and Daphne du Maurier's Jamaica Inn is on the moor. An otter park, a steam railway, Lydford Gorge, Launceston Castle and a rare breeds park add to the varied interest of the region, together with garden centres and gardens open to visitors.

Readers' comments: Charming lady. Recommended for value, friendliness and atmosphere. Fantastic, very good value. Lovely room. Superb atmosphere. Idyllic – we were spoilt! Excellent meals, very comfortable, very reasonable. Enjoyable and relaxing. We return year after year. Well above average farm cooking. Food of the highest standard. Everything immaculate.

Prices are the minimum *per person* in a double room at the beginning of the year.

INVERLODDON

Wargrave, west of Maidenhead, Berkshire, RG10 8ET   Tel: 073522 2230

2 bedrooms (single or double) from £14.50. Both have own bath or shower; tea/coffee facilities; central heating; views of river, country, garden. (Washing-machine on request.)
Sitting-room with central heating, open fire, TV, books, piano, record-player.
Large garden
Nearest main road A4155 from Reading to Marlow.

This 18th-century house is a combination of two flint cottages, one of which started life as a beer-house for passengers awaiting the ferry across the Thames. The ferry is no more, but the Hermons keep a dinghy in which one can explore this lovely reach of the river – frequented by herons as well as ducks and swans.

Past the hall with its array of Toby jugs on an inlaid dresser is a sitting-room with old-fashioned sofas (big and comfortable), oriental rugs on a wood block floor, mementoes of Eton (hatbands and the House Rules of the 1920s), and an open fire. The dining-room has unusual chairs, each carved with an English monarch, around a large circular table. Other unusual antiques include a cockfighting chair in one bedroom that is attractively furnished with waterlily bedspread and curtains (the large, well-equipped bathroom has swan towels, and there are swans on doorknobs and fingerplates too). In a charming little single room even the cupboard doors are decoratively wallpapered. There are views of rosebeds, a summerhouse and the river. (The summerhouse is used for teas.)

There are four good places in the village at which to dine.

Wargrave is surrounded by the Chiltern Hills (famous for their beech woods), close to Windsor, Henley (for its regatta), Oxford, Blenheim and many pretty villages. The Royal County of Berkshire is a historic area, and one of great beauty. Windsor Castle is the largest inhabited castle in the world, with Eton just across the river and Tudor Dorney Court nearby. Walkers enjoy the Great Park and the Savill Garden, children Thorpe water park and the Windsor safari park.

Events of national importance include polo at Smith's Lawn, racing at Ascot, horse and rose shows, and carriage-driving championships. Go to Maidenhead for shopping, picturesque river locks, and the shire horse centre, Cliveden for landscape and the Astor mansion (now a hotel), picturesque Cookham (Stanley Spencer gallery). Marlow and Hurley are other riverside spots worth visiting. Plenty of entertainments, too – the Wilde Theatre is an outstanding arts centre, for instance. Stately homes are numerous, and scenic drives into the hills lead to some fine viewpoints.

It is also an area of countless good restaurants, antique shops and crafts – with all the riches of Oxfordshire and Buckinghamshire only a few miles further. (Bicycles on loan.) This winding stretch of the Thames (Sonning to Maidenhead) is the finest – in summer, made lively by the launches, punts and canoes that pass by the riverside inns and houses with trim gardens, and throng the locks.

The M4 motorway to London and Heathrow is near; good trains and coaches, too, to London.

KARSLAKE HOUSE HOTEL

C D S

Winsford, south of Minehead, Somerset, TA24 7JE   Tel: 064 385 242

7 bedrooms (double) from £17; bargain breaks. Rooms have electric heaters; armchairs; views of country or garden; most have bathrooms, and one a four-poster. TV and tea/coffee facilities.

Dinner £10 for 4 courses (with choices) and coffee, at 7.30pm. Vegetarian or special diets if ordered. Packed lunches. Coffee, tea, for a charge. Drinks can be ordered.

Sitting-room with fire and books.

Garden

Nearest main road A396 from Minehead to Exeter.

Closed November–March

This one-time malthouse (parts of it date from the 15th century) is now run by Fred Alderton and Jane Young. Spring is an ideal time to visit, when it is surrounded by daffodils and azaleas in bloom.

Beyond the large, light dining-room is a small bar; and, for residents, a sitting-room. Narrow, scarlet-carpeted passages twist and turn. Upstairs are pleasant bedrooms – two of the nicest have views of the garden lawn and herbaceous borders. The bathrooms are attractive.

There are always choices on the 4-course menu, which features such things as baked crab followed by fillet steak cooked with port and peaches, strawberry pavlova and cheeses.

Winsford, an ancient village (and birthplace of Ernest Bevin), has eight bridges over the several streams which converge here, thatched cottages, a crafts centre in an 18th-century chapel, and the Royal Oak inn (12th century) which provided material for Blackmore's book *Lorna Doone*. It is a good centre from which to explore Exmoor: quite near are the Caractacus Stone, a 5th-century memorial to a nephew of Caradoc, one of the most valiant defenders of Britain against the Romans; prehistoric burial mounds; and Tarr Steps, a prehistoric bridge.

Readers' comments: High standards, we were delighted. Charming and hospitable, food excellent, rooms spotless and comfortable.

Inclusive terms for dinner, bed-and-breakfast (particularly for a week) can be much lower than those quoted here for these items taken separately. For short-notice bookings you may be able to get a reduction.

No proprietor wants to have a room standing empty. This particularly applies to Sunday nights. Some hotels make a discount if you want only two courses from a three-course menu.

KIMBERLEY HOME FARM

Wymondham, south-west of Norwich, Norfolk, NR18 0RW
Tel: 0953 603137

3 bedrooms (single, double or family) from £25 with dinner. Rooms have central heating or electric heaters; armchairs; views of country or garden.
Dinner 3 courses and coffee, at 7–9pm. Special dishes if ordered. Coffee, tea, free.
Sitting-room with central heating, open fire, TV, books.
Large garden with hard tennis and meadows.
Nearest main road A11 from Norwich to Thetford.

This is a beautifully furnished farmhouse with stables at the front and a large garden at the back, onto which the glass doors of the large sitting-room open. There is a pond with ducks. Apart from the hundreds of acres of crops, the main activity at Kimberley is training and racing horses.

The bedrooms are particularly pretty, the bathroom excellent, and the dining-room has a long Regency table. Jenny Bloom is not only an excellent cook but a generous one, leaving pheasants, guinea-fowl or joints of meat on a hot-tray from which guests may help themselves, and apt to whisk away a half-demolished chicken merely in order to replace it with a fresh one. Starters are imaginative (avocado mousse, for instance), and puddings delicious.

You can have the exclusive use of rooms if you wish, or get more involved with the family and the activities of the farm. Jenny is a charming hostess.

Norwich is one of the most beautiful of mediaeval cities, complete with castle and cathedral, full of craft and antique shops in cobbled byways. The county has a great many stately homes and even statelier churches, wonderful landscapes and seascapes, and, of course, the Broads. The Sainsbury Art Centre outside Norwich is exceptional. The Norfolk coast, King's Lynn and Cambridge are all about one hour away.

This is an excellent spot from which to explore in all directions. Bressingham Hall has fine gardens and steam engines. Beyond Diss (market on Fridays) are the very colourful villages of Burston and Shelfanger. East Dereham has an unusual town sign (two legendary does), an interesting church, an archaeological museum in cottages with decorative plasterwork. Go to the Norfolk Wildlife Park to see bears and otters, to Harleston for spring blossom or summer roses and the River Waveney. Further afield, in Suffolk, there are historic Bungay and Earl Soham, riverside Debenham, Framlingham Castle, Heveningham Hall and a museum of rural life at Stowmarket. Yoxford village is famous for its cottage gardens. Farming is done on a prairie-size scale, but villages with their little greens, and occasional windmills, are a pretty sight.

Readers' comments: Total peace, comfortable rooms, delicious food.

When writing to me, if you want a reply please enclose a stamped addressed envelope.

KING'S LODGE

C D S X

Andover Road, Whitchurch, Hampshire, RG28 7AS   Tel: 025689 3644

rear view

2 bedrooms (double) from £16. Both have own bath/shower; tea/coffee facilities; central heating; views of river, country or garden. (Washing-machine on request.)
Dinner £12 for 4 courses (with choices) and coffee, at any specified time. Non-residents not admitted. Vegetarian or special diets if ordered. Lunches, packed lunches, snacks. Tea, coffee, free. Drinks can be brought in.
2 sitting-rooms with central heating, open fire, TV, books, piano.
Large garden
Nearest main road A34 from Newbury to Winchester.

On 20 October 1644, King Charles I wrote to his nephew urging him to bring more troops here quickly: it was at this house that he penned his desperate letter and visitors can go up the great oak staircase to sleep in the 'King's room'. (A week later the King successfully resisted Cromwell's advance at the second Battle of Newbury.)

Some may prefer the big blue room, however, for its windows on two sides and view of the famous River Test.

Downstairs is a large and handsome sitting-room and the dining-room, with an 'upright grand' piano, country Hepplewhite chairs at a table in a big bay window, comfortable old armchairs around a log stove and innumerable family mementoes – some from China where Hermione Goulding's father was stationed, and others from Hong Kong and Singapore where her husband served.

Outside are lawns, fruit trees, flint walls, herbaceous flowerbeds and a riverside walk. Also a kitchen garden from which come peas and beans for soups, vegetables to accompany such main courses as steak-and-kidney pie, and fruit for raspberry fool and to serve with the cheeses.

Whitchurch is the home of Lord Denning (who lives next door) and of Richard Adams ('Watership Down' is nearby). Its other claim to fame is the riverside silk-mill which wove the fabric for the Princess of Wales' wedding-dress.

Also in the vicinity are war paintings by Stanley Spencer (at Sandham Memorial Chapel), Winchester Cathedral, Hilliers' aboretum (the world's largest collection of temperate trees and shrubs), Mottisfont Abbey (rose gardens), Exbury (rhododendrons), Windsor and the Savill Gardens. Many visitors go to such stately homes as Stratfield Staye (Duke of Wellington's home), Littlecote, Broadlands (Lord Mountbatten's home), Wilton and the Vyne, as well as Jane Austen's home at Chawton. Whitchurch is also on the edge of the Wiltshire Downs with their many prehistoric remains, including Stonehenge.

The scenery around here is high and open; big fields with white flints are covered with golden grain in summer. By contrast, paths lead to a riverside where rushes and other waterplants grow green, and on the banks purple loosestrife and willow-herb flourish.

Readers' comments: Wonderful food, so welcoming, made us feel like family friends.

151

KING'S LODGE

C D S S-C

Long Marston, south-east of Stratford-upon-Avon, Warwickshire, CV37 8RL
Tel: 0789 720705

4 bedrooms (single or double) from £14. Less for 3 nights. Rooms have central heating; views of country or garden; TV. (One with bath.)
Dinner £8 for 3 courses and coffee, at 7 pm. Special diets if ordered. Packed lunches, snacks. Coffee, tea, for a charge. Non-residents not admitted. Drinks can be ordered.
Sitting-room with central heating, TV, books.
Large garden and parkland, with croquet.
Nearest main road A46 from Stratford-upon-Avon to Cheltenham.
Closed December and January

With his father beheaded and Cromwell ruling England, young Charles II (only twenty-one) made a desperate attempt in 1651 to regain the throne. Badly defeated at Worcester, however, he became a fugitive on the run – for weeks eluding escape by means of disguises and hiding-places, as he made his way to the coast and France.

To get through Stratford-upon-Avon, swarming with Cromwellian troops, he dressed himself as the manservant of Miss Jane Lane (sister of one of his colonels), and together they rode to Long Marston and the house of her kinsman, John Tomes. This was on 10 September; and I stayed there on almost the same date, dining in the hall with great inglenook fireplace where he had a narrow escape: on being asked by the cook to wind up the jack that operated the roasting-spit, his ignorance of this homely task nearly gave the game away. Although other parts of the Tudor house have changed, this room is much as it was when he stayed here – and outside, too, the scene has altered very little. Probably, the willow-fringed duck pond and the mulberry and pear trees are very like what he saw.

When the house came up for sale many years ago, George and Angela Jenkins (who lived locally) could not resist buying it, even though it was very neglected and rather too large for their family. To pay for its restoration and upkeep, they decided to take paying guests.

After dinner (plain home cooking, often with produce from the garden) at a big refectory table by the famous fireplace, visitors can sit in a sitting-room or out in the large garden. One bedroom has a four-poster made from elms felled in the grounds and a fine stone fireplace on which the Tomes children inscribed their initials over three centuries ago. The house is full of old pictures and trifles which the Jenkins have collected, many relating to Charles II or the Tomes family who sheltered him.

The house is ideally placed for visiting the beauty-spots, gardens and historic sights of three counties – Warwickshire, Gloucestershire (the Cotswolds), and Oxfordshire. Head for Evesham if you want pick-your-own fruit and to Stratford for its Shakespeare sights. Close to King's Lodge is an antiques warehouse.

Readers' comments: Delighted with situation, food and hospitality. Enjoyable and interesting. Very good value. Have returned because of friendly, unassuming service. Lovely house, good accommodation and food. Very nice people.

152

LAMB INN
D PT

Great Rissington, north-west of Burford (Oxfordshire), Gloucestershire, GL54 2LP   Tel: 0451 20388

7 bedrooms (single or double) from £16. (**Reduction to readers.**) Less for 7 nights, bargain breaks and winter discounts. Rooms have central heating; shower; armchairs; views of country or garden.
Dinner A la carte, at 7pm. Lunches, packed lunches. Coffee, tea, for a charge. Drinks can be ordered.
Sitting-room with fire, TV. Also bars.
Large garden with swimming-pool.
Nearest main road A424 from Burford to Stow-on-the-Wold.

This is exactly what one asks of a typical old Cotswold inn! The interior is a place of little windows, zigzag corridors, quaint oak doors and thick stone walls; outside, magnificent views of the countryside, looking across to some of the highest Cotswolds. Kate and Richard Cleverly have furnished the bedrooms with care – restful colours, everything neat, a pretty tulip wallpaper in one room, and in the dining-room pine chairs at lace-covered tables with candle-lamps lit at night. The menu is à la carte, with such dishes as Stilton-topped fillet steaks, veal-and-sweetcorn pies, salmon-and-prawn mousse, lamb with apricots. Outside is a landscaped garden from which to enjoy the summer view with a glass of 'real ale' in hand; a covered swimming-pool (heated to 80°) and a summerhouse-cum-aviary. In cold weather, there is a log fire in the bar, and in the attractive residents' sitting-room. A recent addition is a restaurant extension created from an old barn and furnished with Laura Ashley fabrics.

Richard is an imaginative as well as skilled craftsman: the carving of a lamb over the sitting-room fire is his, and so are the conversions of old doors, pews and even school desks to new uses. When I last visited the Lamb, he was making a four-poster with carved decorations.

The Lamb is midway between two famous Cotswold villages (Bourton-on-the-Water and Burford, described elsewhere in this book). Most people come here simply for the scenery, but also in the vicinity are the Cotswold Wildlife Park, a rare breeds farm, and – only a little further – Oxford, Stratford-upon-Avon, Warwick and Woodstock (with Blenheim Palace). Stow-on-the-Wold and Broadway are picturesque villages. For gardens, go to Sezincote and Hidcote (and to Burford's garden centre) and nearly every village has antique shops. A good area, too, for pick-your-own fruit.

Readers' comments: Excellent.

> All prices are inclusive of any VAT or service charge. They are minimum prices: superior rooms or high-season bookings may cost more.

153

LANGAR HALL

C D S X

Church Lane, Langar, south-east of Nottingham, NG13 9HG
Tel: 0949 60559

10 bedrooms (single, double or family) from £17.50. Less for 7 nights. Rooms have central heating; shower or bathroom; TV, armchairs; views of country or garden; tea/coffee facilities. (Clothes-washing facilities.) **Dinner** £15 for 4 courses (some choice) and coffee, at 7.45pm. Vegetarian or special diets if ordered. Lunches. Coffee, tea, free. Drinks can be ordered.
2 sitting-rooms with central heating, open fire, TV, books; bar.
Garden and park with croquet.
Nearest main road A46 from Nottingham to Grantham.

Imogen Skirving's great-grandmother bought the house thirty years after it was built in 1830, a fine country mansion of apricot stucco built on the site of an earlier one which had associations with many names famous in English history (particularly Admiral Lord Howe). When it came into Imogen's possession, she and her art-dealer husband had to refurnish it – which they have done with unusual antiques and well-chosen colours in each room. And every wall is hung with paintings of great interest (mainly 19th- and 20th-century pictures, some family heirlooms). Imogen is a picture restorer, and is willing to demonstrate to interested visitors. There are some paintings for sale.

The pillared yellow-and-white dining-room has tables that are covered with cloths of embroidered voile and tall, fluted, silver candlesticks. Across the stone-flagged hall is the all-white sitting-room with alcoves of china and tall sash windows. Some of the paintings here were bought by Imogen in her teens – she used to save up all her pocket-money to buy pictures. A second sitting-room, book-lined, is for TV and smoking. (Visitors help themselves to pre-dinner drinks, recording what they take in a notebook.)

Some bedrooms are very grand (one has a four-poster with Nottingham lace), others are simple and cottagey (prices vary accordingly). One with a half-tester bed, lilac-and-roses fabrics, antique bamboo furniture and lemon walls has a dressing-room adjoining, containing sofa, desk and TV. The simpler rooms are in another wing of the house. Dinner, which Imogen and her chefs prepare, may include such dishes as marinated kipper fillets – the genuine thing, oak-smoked and delicate in flavour – as a starter; chicken breast with a stuffing that contains lobster and prawns; and orange ice cream with Cointreau and peaches.

The large garden is dotted with urns and statues among the ancient trees, a path leads to the chain of fish-ponds, and lime trees line the long drive.

Langar is in the best part of the famous Vale of Belvoir. Scenery is not the only attraction of this area, however. Next to the house is the village church, known as 'the cathedral of the Vale' (well worth a visit). There are many great houses: Belvoir Castle, Belton House, Holme Pierrepont Hall, Doddington Hall.

Readers' comments: One of the most delightful weeks I have ever had. Quite exceptional. Fascinating hostess, fine house. Delicious dinner beautifully served. Interesting ambience.

154

LANGLEY WOOD

D

Redlynch, south-east of Salisbury, Wiltshire, SP5 2PB Tel: 0794 390348

3 bedrooms (double) at £14. All have views of garden.
Dinner A la carte. Sunday lunches. Tea, coffee, extra. Drinks can be ordered.
2 sitting-rooms with heating, open fire, books; bar.

Large garden
Nearest main road A36 from Southampton to Salisbury.

A restaurant of distinction is the principal *raison d'être* of Langley Wood, but it has comfortable bedrooms too – overlooking the surrounding lawns and woods. The house began life as three 17th-century cottages, but was transformed at the turn of the century. Panelling, Georgian doors and other handsome details were added. It still retains the sedate, old-fashioned style of that period, with dinners enjoyed by candlelight and, on chilly evenings, a log fire blazing.

David and Sylvia Rosen used to run a bistro near London's Camden Town, an area much populated by connoisseurs of good food; and many of the favourite dishes from those days are now enjoyed at Langley Wood – things like baked carrot and Gruyère with fresh tomato sauce, roast stuffed fillet of beef, hazelnut meringue filled with strawberries and cream; and vegetarian dishes.

Visitors who stay here can quickly reach Salisbury in one direction or the New Forest in the other: Redlynch is close to the border of Hampshire, and of Dorset too – for descriptions see other entries.

Wiltshire, despite its low population (which makes it a quiet and attractive place in which to travel), has a number of great houses such as Wilton and Stourhead, and great prehistoric remains too (Stonehenge and Avebury in particular). There is magnificent scenery on its chalk hills and by its many rivers and streams, where undisturbed villages are to be found.

Don't complain if –
- because you booked at short notice, you do not get the best room
- because you did not order a meal in advance, you get something plucked from the freezer
- because you do not arrive on time, your room is let to someone else
- because you bring a dog without asking, it is refused entry
- because you don't express your wishes (for more heat, a second helping or whatever), you don't get what you want!

155

LANNARDS
Okehurst Lane, Billingshurst, south-west of Horsham, West Sussex, RH14 9HR Tel: 040 381 2692

3 bedrooms (single or double) from £12.50. Rooms have TV; tea/coffee facilities; central heating; views of garden. No smoking.
Sitting-room with central heating and books. No smoking.
Small garden
Nearest main road A29 from London to Chichester.
Closed November–March

This is one for collectors of modern art – paintings, ceramics or silver; for adjoining the house of cedar shingles where guests are accommodated is an octagonal gallery of pine and glass where a discriminating display of fine arts is exhibited for sale. It is the brainchild of Betty Sims, herself an accomplished potter, on whose husband's farm is this unusual gallery-cum-guest-house.

Lannards is also an ideal place at which to stay if antiques or music interest you, for within yards is an outpost of Sothebys (a Tudor mansion where auctions are held), and not much further afield a new music school in Slinfold Manor, where concerts are held from time to time.

All bedrooms are on the ground floor – neat modern rooms with pale colours and built-in cupboards. And at the back is the studio of potter Robert Gibbs, where visitors are welcome if they want to see him at work. There is a comfortable sitting-room, lawn with tables and rural views all round. (Bed-and-breakfast only. For dinner Sheila recommends a local Italian restaurant.)

Nearby Billingshurst is one of many pretty Sussex villages, sited on the road the Romans called Stane Street (it ran from London to Chichester). It is well placed to visit – to the south – Brighton (Pavilion, etc.) and other coastal resorts beyond the South Downs, Arundel (castle, wildfowl reserve) and Chichester (cathedral, outstanding theatre, Roman palace, natural harbour); and also innumerable stately homes such as Goodwood, Petworth, Parham and Hever Castle.

The long River Arun meanders through this part of Sussex, rising in St Leonard's Forest (part of the Weald) and winding through lovely countryside to the sea at the resort of Littlehampton, roads crossing it on old bridges from which there are lovely views of the river.

In pretty Billingshurst itself, right by the mediaeval church, is a beamy 17th-century house, **Churchgate** (tel: 040 381 2733) which Sheila Butcher has furnished in traditional country-house style. Views from its windows are of a flowery little garden and the church. Dinner (to be ordered in advance) might typically be pâté, coq au vin, home-made ice cream and cheeses. In the sitting-room is a piano which guests are welcome to play, television and a good selection of books.

Readers' comments: Excellent, personal service.

156

LANSDOWNE HOUSE

C(5) **PT S X**

Clarendon Street, Leamington Spa, Warwickshire, CV32 4PF
Tel: 0926 450505 or 421313

13 bedrooms (single, double or family) from £18.50. Less for bargain breaks. **If included in a 3-night half-board stay, Sunday's accommodation is free to readers of this book except at peak periods.** Most rooms have central heating; shower or bathroom; TV, armchairs; tea/coffee service. Laundry and cleaning service (8-hour).
Dinner £13 for 3 courses (with choices) and coffee with home-made petits fours, from 6.30pm. Special diets if ordered. Lunches, packed lunches, snacks. Coffee, tea, free. Drinks can be ordered.
2 sitting-rooms with central heating, TV, books; bar.
Nearest main road A425 from Warwick to Daventry.

A pretty creeper-covered house built in the 18th century, this small hotel cannot be described as truly 'off the beaten track' for it stands at a crossroads not far from the centre of Leamington. But bedroom windows are double-glazed to reduce any sound from traffic – and the hotel is of such excellence that I wanted to include it.

David and Gillian Allen took it over only a few years ago and have furnished it to a very high standard and in keeping with its architecture. There is a particularly pretty sitting-room with sea-green and strawberry Victorian sofas, for example; in the small dining-room, meals are served on fluted Rosenthal china and wine in elegant glasses; the bar has cherry buttoned seats; and every bedroom is attractively decorated in soft colours with well chosen fabrics, stripped-pine furniture and thick, moss-green carpet. (No. 2 is the quietest, with roof-light not windows.)

The same care goes into the food. David, who trained as a chef in Switzerland, is a perfectionist. He sends to Scotland for his steaks, to the Cotswolds for his trout, has coffee specially blended to his taste, and damson and other sorbets made for him on a fruit farm nearby. Connoisseurs will appreciate some little-known wines among his very good selection, and the range of malt whiskies.

There are always several choices of good English dishes at dinner. Starters include particularly imaginative soups (such as celery-and-walnut or cream of parsnip), while main courses are likely to be such things as roast pork with freshly chopped rosemary or liver-and-bacon with fresh sage. Puddings might include walnut and chocolate fudge pudding or fruit cobbler.

Royal Leamington Spa is a health resort with a saline spring. It has fine Georgian terraces and lovely riverside gardens. A good base from which to visit not only Warwick and Kenilworth castles, described elsewhere, but also Coventry (modern cathedral, some historic buildings), Southam (old market town), Stoneleigh (mediaeval village and the great National Agricultural Centre) and fine countryside towards Stratford-upon-Avon. The Mill gardens in Warwick and Jephson gardens in Leamington are worth seeking out.

For residents there are discounts at Warwick Castle and many other sights. Free guided local walks.

Readers' comments: Excellent. Charming features, food excellent.

157

LASKILL HOUSE FARM

C D S S-C

Hawnby, north of Helmsley, North Yorkshire, YO6 5NB Tel: 04396 268

6 bedrooms (single, double or family) from £13.50. Rooms have central heating; armchairs; views of country or garden.
Dinner £9 for 4 courses and coffee, at 6.30pm. Lunches, packed lunches, snacks. Coffee, tea, for a charge. Non-residents not admitted. Drinks available. Free tea on arrival.
Sitting-room with central heating, open fire, TV, books. Games room.
Garden and farmland.
Nearest main road B1257 from Stokesley to Helmsley.
Closed November–March

This stone farmhouse lies in a hilly, wooded area of great scenic splendour ('Herriot country'), and close to famous Rievaulx Abbey. Its courtyard is made pretty with stone troughs, flowers and rocks; and around lie 600 acres with cattle and sheep or wheat. There are white iron chairs for guests in the garden and a duck-pond. Children are welcome to help feed the calves and to hold the lambs.

In the sitting/dining-room is oak furniture hand-carved by local craftsmen, each of whom 'signs' his work with his own particular symbol – an acorn, a beaver or a stag's head. Here Sue Smith serves home-made soup or pâté before a main course which is likely to comprise meat and vegetables from the farm, followed by (for instance) lemon meringue pie or a fruit fool, and then an interesting selection of cheeses. Often there is a chance to see James Herriot himself, as he sometimes opens fêtes or gives talks.

The bedrooms vary in style: I particularly liked 'the blue room' with its sprigged wallpaper, thick carpet and cretonne fabrics. Two, with bathrooms, are in a beamy outbuilding and open onto the lawn.

The North York Moors are one of England's finest national parks: whether you walk or drive, the views are spectacular, particularly when the heather blooms.

Readers' comments: Comfortable, welcoming, and good food. Excellent meals, complete relaxation. Charming and considerate hostess. Delightful; everything perfect. Mrs Smith was so welcoming and easy to get on with. Food excellent. Beautiful location. Comfort, good food and congenial company. Delightful room.

A little further south is **Newton Grange Farm** (tel: 04393 262) where Sue Ward's immaculate rooms have exceptionally fine views – and a few miles away is one that James Herriot described as the finest in England. Sue serves simple, generous meals (pâté, stew and steamed pudding, for example), or there are good pub restaurants nearby for a change. The house is a good choice for those who want a genuine and unpretentious farm holiday.

Readers' comments: Careful attention to detail, like clean towels daily and excellent breakfast. Excellent value.

LAWYER'S REST

C(10) **D PT S X**

Undercliff Drive, St Lawrence, west of Ventnor, Isle of Wight, PO38 1XF
Tel: 0983 852610

rear view

8 bedrooms (single or double) from £28 with dinner. Less for 3 nights or short-notice reservations. Rooms have electric heating; shower or bathroom; armchairs; views of sea, country or garden.
Dinner 3 courses (with choices) and coffee, at 7pm. Vegetarian or special diets if ordered. Lunches, packed lunches or snacks. Coffee, tea, for a charge. Drinks can be ordered.
Sitting-room with gas fire and books. Cocktail bar. Wine bar.
Terraced garden
Nearest main road A3055 from Ventnor to Niton.
Closed November–February

This 1840 house is set among terraced gardens on a steep slope leading down towards the sea – one of many fine mansions which wealthy Victorians built along a coast they called 'the English Madeira'. In its grounds are mimosa, figs, vines and palms.

Previously in this book as Woody Bank, the name was changed by Ann Dex (a former entertainments agent) and Geoffrey Phillips when they retired early from their respective professions to start a new joint career. Geoffrey Phillips was a Lincoln's Inn solicitor (hence the legal theme of the hotel). There is a fine collection of porcelain legal figures and a number of splendid clocks.

The bar has window-seats and superb sea views. The sitting-room is furnished in Victorian style; but the dining-room is in complete contrast with bamboo chairs and sliding glass walls that can be opened wide to the garden. Bedrooms vary greatly in style: the best has fine walnut beds, a huge mahogany wardrobe and dressing-table, and a double frontage from which to enjoy the sea view. Bedrooms at the back overlook a heavily wooded nature reserve, across a road (little used at night).

A typical menu might comprise smoked haddock in cheese sauce, veal escalope and apple strudel, and there is a very good wine list.

St Lawrence has not only the tiniest church in England (12th century) but another with exceptional pre-Raphaelite stained glass. It has a tropical bird park, internationally known glass-making studios, and a network of undercliff footpaths among rocks where subtropical plants grow wild, with small bays and coves down below. Most visitors make for Queen Victoria's Osborne House, Carisbrooke Castle, the Botanical Gardens, Arreton Manor, St Catherine's lighthouse and the gardens at Barton Manor vineyard (its wine is on the hotel's list). Those who prefer the quieter west end of the island head for Freshwater Bay, Tennyson Downs, the wildlife reserve at Newtown, the Needles fort and Alum Bay with its sand in a myriad of colours.

Ferry-taxi-hotel packages can be arranged (to include golf and clay pigeon shooting, if required).

Readers' comments: Marvellous environment of graciousness, warmth and genuine hospitality. Excellent cooks, who share their wine expertise. One of the best.

159

LEIGH COURT

C D S-C

Leigh, west of Worcester, WR6 5LB   Tel: 0886 32275

3 bedrooms (twin, double or family) from £13. Less for 3 nights. Rooms have central heating and electric heaters; armchairs; views of country and garden; tea/coffee facilities.

Dinner £9 for 4 courses and coffee, at 7pm (except on Wednesdays). Vegetarian or special diets if ordered. Non-residents not admitted. Drinks can be brought in.

2 sitting-rooms with central heating, open fire, TV, books, indoor games (including snooker, darts).

Large garden and farmland; coarse fishing in river.

Nearest main road A4103 from Worcester to Hereford.

Closed mid-October–mid-March

Passers-by often pause here, just to look – not only at the 16th-century manor house of mellow brick, with gables in both Dutch and Flemish style, but also at the 14th-century cruck barn, the biggest of its kind in the world.

Sally Stewart's ancestors were bailiffs here when, before Henry VIII dissolved the monasteries, the abbots of Pershore were lords of the manor.

She and her civil engineer husband modernized the comforts of the house when they inherited it in 1960, but have carefully preserved all the fine architectural detail. The entrance hall is particularly striking, a tiled floor and traditional acanthus-patterned wallpaper (blue-and-white) setting off the white staircase, handsome sash windows and fanlight over the door. The sitting-room has a pretty fireplace, all curlicues and swags, round which velvet or cretonne chairs are drawn up, while portraits of ancestral aunts adorn the walls. In the dining-room (in fact, in all rooms) there are family antiques; sprigged blue cloths cover the tables; and from the bay window there is a fine view of a weeping ash, the nearby 13th-century church and a huge copper beech. Throughout the house, there are good wall-papers, homely old-fashioned furniture and (from room 3 in particular) fine views.

This is a good place for anyone who enjoys dogs and other animals for Sally breeds pedigree pugs, Cavalier King Charles spaniels and golden retrievers. (If you want to bring your own dog, it must have been vaccinated.) In the grounds, where hens range free, you will find a variety of rare farm breeds.

Sally serves such dishes as fish mousse, pot-roast pheasant and apple Charlotte.

In the grounds, a riverside walk appeals to many visitors (there is another good, level walk along the track where once a railway ran). In autumn, you can see the farm's cider mill in action, and taste the results.

People touring by car use Leigh Court as a base to visit Malvern, Worcester (with china factory, cathedral etc.), Upton-on-Severn, Ledbury, Stourport-on-Severn and Evesham.

Readers' comments: Very comfortable; food delicious. Most enjoyable. A delightful week. Excellent food; peaceful. Enjoyed it so much I returned for a further eight days. Friendliness, hospitality and food delightful. A splendid stay.

LEWORTHY FARM

C H PT S S-C X

Leworthy, east of Bude (Cornwall), Devon, EX22 65S   Tel: 0409 253488

12 bedrooms (single, double or family) from £14. Less for 2 nights or bargain breaks. Rooms have central heating or electric heaters; shower, wc; armchairs; views of country or garden; tea/coffee facilities. (Clothes-washing facilities.)

Dinner £8 for 4 courses and coffee, at 7pm. Special diets if ordered. Lunches, packed lunches, snacks. Afternoon or bedtime coffee, tea etc. for a charge. Drinks can be ordered. No smoking.

3 sitting-rooms with central heating, open fire, TV, books, indoor games (including table skittles, snooker, table tennis, darts, badminton), piano, record-player. Video films. Bar.

Grounds Lawns, farmland and lake, with rough and clay pigeon shooting, croquet, tennis, trout fishing, archery and pony riding.

Nearest main road A388 from Bideford to Launceston.

Genial Eric Cornish deservedly won the AA's 'Farmhouse of the Year' award in 1981. His guests are greatly appreciated by him, and he goes to considerable lengths to give them a good time – young children in particular. Dozens of their drawings and letters to him are pinned up around the bar.

He has added to the rooms in the farmhouse to provide more accommodation in a bungalow close by, and sometimes has as many as forty people staying – laying on for this huge house-party all kinds of evening entertainments (games, dancing, conjuror, film) for which there is no extra charge. This is obviously appreciated by families tired of the spend-spend-spend involved in keeping the youngsters entertained in most resorts. Eric also takes visitors on tractor-drawn hay-rides (dogs following) to see his crops, sheep, beef-cattle, lake, river and woods, while explaining to them what work is going on. It's a place where parents can leave their older children to go their own way – they find plenty to do, like organizing table tennis, or badminton competitions. There are deer, herons and even otters to be spotted; abundant wildflowers; and lots of good picnic spots within the farm estate. In low season, crafts including patchwork and farm activity courses are run; the latter include wine-making, clay pigeon shooting, fishing and pub skittle matches. And there is a wheelchair.

Something new is always afoot, so Eric and Marion keep in touch with past guests by means of a circular letter with news of what has been happening to the stock, the pets and the family. Cormorants steal the trout, Sarah returns from world travels, 'Willigrub' gets booked for next season – it's all reported in these letters. Many guests become lifelong friends, and most get involved in Leworthy Farm in one way or another (the gumboot rack was made by a group of dads).

The bedrooms, like all the other rooms, are comfortable and unfussy: I liked those in the converted farm building called Leeside. Marion produces typical farmhouse meals such as soup, roast beef, fruit pie and cream, cheese, coffee.

There is so much going on that many people hardly stir. However, within a short drive are the beaches of Bude and superb clifftop views, Hartland's dramatic reefs and lighthouse and quaint Clovelly. Holsworthy is only three miles away.

Readers' comments: Very much enjoyed the Cornishes' company; they make you feel welcome. A delightful couple who spared nothing to see that everyone had a good time. We had a high time! So genial and helpful; constant laughter.

LINDISFARNE HOTEL
Holy Island, south of Berwick-upon-Tweed, Northumberland, TD15 2SQ
Tel: 0289 89273

7 bedrooms (single, double or family) from £15. Less for 7 nights and bargain breaks. Some have own bath/shower; TV; tea/coffee facilities; central heating; views of garden. No smoking. (Washing-machine on request.)
Dinner £9.50 for 4 courses (with choices) and coffee, at 7–8pm. Vegetarian or special diets if ordered. Lunches, packed lunches, snacks. Tea, coffee, extra. Drinks can be ordered.
Sitting-room with central heating, books; bar.
Small garden
Nearest main road A1 from Alnwick to Berwick.
Closed November–March

It is a great pity that this island, so beautiful and so full of history, is ill-provided with good accommodation.

One drives across a causeway (impassable at high tides). Sir Walter Scott described it:

'Dry shod, o'er sands, twice every day,
The pilgrims to the shrine find way.
Twice every day the waves efface
Of staves and sandalled feet the trace.'

It was at this holy place that monks illuminated the Lindisfarne Gospels over twelve centuries ago, made mead from honey (you can still buy this on the island) and built a priory the ruins of which to this day soar majestically. It is – except when coachloads of summer trippers ruin it – a place of beauty and mystery. Over all presides Lindisfarne Castle, topping a steep rock. This was built in Tudor times, a rather cosy little castle. Well modernized in 1903 by Sir Edwin Lutyens, it is filled with furniture and textiles chosen to harmonize with their surroundings. There is now an outstanding museum of Saxon history, too.

The Lindisfarne Hotel is unpretentious, well kept, and furnished in conventional style. From the choices on Susan Massey's 4-course dinner menu, one might perhaps choose, for instance, grapefruit with crème de menthe, seafood casserole, roast lamb or Holy Island crab, and a creamy dessert. Based here one could enjoy not only the tranquillity of the island and its wildlife after the coachloads have gone home, but also explore much of mainland Northumberland by day.

For instance, the border town of Berwick-upon-Tweed is only a little way further north. Its three bridges bestride the estuary, there are fine walks along the Tudor fortifications encircling it – some of Europe's best mediaeval walls and bastions, and the busy market is frequented by Scots as well as the English. Other attractions in the region are Norham Castle, Heatherslaw watermill, quaint little Ford – a model village of the Victorian era, still with smithy and a village hall lined with murals painted by the Marchioness of Waterford. Near Wooler, centre of good walking country, is the site of the Battle of Flodden; and round Chillingham Castle roam the famous white cattle, sole survivors of a wild breed once common in Britain. Along the coast to the south is a succession of spectacular castles, Craster (for kipper teas) and the little harbour of Seahouses – boats go from here to the Farne Islands where seals and puffins are to be seen at close quarters.

162

LINK HOUSE

Bassenthwaite Lake, east of Cockermouth, Cumbria, CA13 9YD
Tel: 059681 291

8 bedrooms (single or double) from £17.50. Less for 7 nights and bargain breaks. All have own bath/shower; TV; tea/coffee facilities; central heating; views of country or garden. (Washing-machine on request.)

Dinner £9 for 5 courses (with choices) and coffee, at 7–8pm. Vegetarian or special diets if ordered. Lunches, packed lunches, snacks. Tea, coffee, free. Drinks can be ordered.

2 sitting-rooms with central heating, open fire, books; bar.

Small garden

Nearest main road A66 from Keswick to Cockermouth.

Closed in December and January

Teacher May Smith so much enjoyed cookery as a hobby that eventually she gave up her career to start a new one, running a guest-house. That is why Link House, outwardly similar to many others in the Lake District, is in fact very different in the kind of meals that are served.

The small Victorian house stands in a garden near the north end of the lake. Everything inside is spick-and-span. One bay-windowed sitting-room has a log fire and comfortable chairs; the other, a conservatory bar, is attractively furnished, with cane seats and tiled floor. Beyond this is the dining-room where tables are laid with pink linen napkins, Wedgwood china, decorative silver and Cumbria crystal goblets; it is a light room with windows on two sides. The bedrooms are equally pleasant: pine woodwork and pale shades in one, modern furniture and cheerful colours in another, and so on. All around are fells and forests.

Dinner is a five-course meal with coffee. Prawn, celery and apple cocktail might be followed by a herby tomato soup (home-made), lamb roasted with rosemary, strawberry meringues, and then cheeses (with choices at most courses). Bread is home-made.

The lake is in a valley overlooked by the great peak of Skiddaw and by Thornthwaite Forest. Leafy Cockermouth has Wordsworth's birthplace and is, like most places in the northern Lake District, less crowded than the south. Loweswater and Ennerdale Water are particularly peaceful; go to Wastwater for wild grandeur. Ullswater, Buttermere and Borrowdale are particularly beautiful. Keswick is near: full of shops, craft studios, museums and theatre. All around are fells (with hunting on foot just as in John Peel's day).

Readers' comments: Could not have been more helpful; food ample and delicious. Food, service and friendly atmosphere truly excellent.

Bedroom at Monk Soham Hall (see page 3)

LISLE COMBE

St Lawrence, west of Ventnor, Isle of Wight, PO38 1UW   Tel: 0983 852 582

C PT S S-C

4 bedrooms (single, double or family) from £10. All have tea/coffee facilities; views of sea, country or garden.
Sitting-room with open fire, TV, books.

Large garden
Nearest main road A3055 from Ventnor to Niton.
Closed in December and January

'East of the garden, a wild glen glimmers with foxgloves,
And there, through the heat of the day,
In a fern-shadowed elf-ring of sand, with pine logs round it,
Three bird-voiced children play,
With a palm to shelter their golden heads from the sun,
When the noon-sun grows too strong . . .'

One of Alfred Noyes' 'bird-voiced children' about whom he wrote this poem in 1936 now owns that garden, glen and the family home. Hugh Noyes grew up to become *The Times* parliamentary correspondent until 1982, but is now occupied in dairy-farming and breeding rare species of waterfowl, with plans for a farm park, where the public will be able to enjoy the sight of these as well as rare breeds of mainly domestic animals.

Visitors staying at Lisle Combe see not only the scenes which inspired so many poems but many of the poet's possessions, such as a series of watercolours by Frederick Weld (who became New Zealand's first Prime Minister); and all his papers are preserved in his still intact library.

The house itself is exceptional. It was built in the early 19th century – but in Elizabethan style, by the same Lord Yarborough whose monument dominates one of the island's hills (he was a considerable landowner on the island – Pelham Woods, opposite the house, carries his family's name).

It has barley-sugar chimneys and lozenge-paned bay windows, many overlooking the English Channel; and a paved verandah with grapevine where breakfast is sometimes served. Hugh's mother brought to the house some very exceptional furniture and paintings that were salvaged when, in the 'thirties, her former home – Lulworth Castle (in Dorset) – was burnt down. One of the most attractive rooms is a small, pale-blue sitting-room with sea views. Through the garden and among palm trees, pools and streams a path leads down to the sandy beach: an idyllic spot for generations of children.

(No dinners: Judy recommends such nearby inns as the Crown at Shorwell or the New Inn at Shalfleet, or the Seaview Hotel. See also other Isle of Wight entries.)

Lisle Combe is close to Ventnor's botanical gardens, full of subtropical flowers, and with an excellent museum of smuggling through the centuries. This south-facing part of the coast is the warmest, and Ventnor itself looks rather Mediterranean because the houses are built on terraces zigzagging steeply down to the sea.

164

LITTLE LODGE FARMHOUSE   C(6)
Broughton Green, Hanbury, east of Droitwich, Worcestershire, WR9 7EE
Tel: 052784 305

3 bedrooms (double) from £15. Less for 3 nights. Rooms have own bath/shower; tea/coffee facilities; central heating; views of country or garden. No smoking. (Washing-machine on request.)
Dinner £13.50 for 4 courses and coffee, at 7pm on Tuesday, Wednesday and Thursday only. Non-residents not admitted. Sand-wich suppers available. Tea, coffee, free. Drinks can be brought in.
Sitting-room with central heating, open fire, TV, books. No smoking.
Large garden
Nearest main road A38 from Birmingham to Worcester.
Closed November–March

Once there was a great deer forest all around a mere woodland clearing where this secluded house, originally a hunting-lodge, was built about 1650. Now, nearly all the oaks gone, its surroundings are a patchwork of farmlands and fields for the thoroughbred horses which the Chuggs breed (Robert used to be a jockey), with a distant view of the Clent Hills. In the grounds is a tiny building that was once a school-room for local children.

The beamed sitting-room with inglenook fireplace is on two levels and, like all rooms here, has very lovely fabrics to complement the antique furniture. There are hedgerow fruits in the dining-room fabrics, Warner peonies in the coral and green sitting-room, Colefax roses in one bedroom and Jane Churchill garlands in another.

In a very pretty attic room, Jackie herself stencilled the ribbons that decorate the walls. Everywhere she has placed decorative arrangements of dried flowers.

Another of her talents is cookery (she trained at the celebrated Tante Marie School), and at each meal she offers – if it is arranged in advance – a choice of such dishes as egg-and-prawn mousse, duck with Morello cherry sauce and gâteau Diane (which is chocolate-filled meringue). Even breakfasts are rather special, with such options as *fromage frais* to accompany fruits, granary bread, black pudding from Stornoway, etc.

Worcestershire is one of England's loveliest counties (particularly to the south). The highest point is in the Clent Hills, rising to 1000 feet, among which you can drive or walk to explore their woodlands and pools; and there are hills to the west, too. The Severn is a lovely river to follow down from Stourport to where, beyond the cathedral city of Worcester, it joins the pretty River Teme in an area well-known for its orchards, hops, dairy-cattle and lush meadows. At Droitwich, water saltier than the Dead Sea is pumped up from subterranean sources 200 feet down – so buoyant that visitors bathing in it float unsinkably. It was these baths that turned the market town into an elegant little spa, still functioning.

Readers' comments: A marvellous place. I could not find fault anywhere.

165

LITTLE PARMOOR

LITTLE PARMOOR C(7) **X**
Frieth, north-east of Henley-on-Thames, Oxfordshire, RG9 6NL
Tel: 0494 881447

3 bedrooms (single, double or family) from £15. Less for 4 nights. Rooms have tea/coffee facilities; central heating; views of country or garden. No smoking. (Washing-machine on request.)
Sitting-room with central heating, open fire, TV, books, record-player.
Large garden
Nearest main road A40 from Oxford to High Wycombe.

Within a mere half-hour of Heathrow (and little further to London) is a peaceful spot among the lovely Chiltern Hills, and in it this attractive house built in 1724. (It used to be the house of the estate manager who looked after the lands of Sir Stafford Cripps' father, Lord Parmoor, when he occupied the nearby great house, now a convent.)

Inside are pale green and white panelling, log fires and watercolours painted by Wynyard Wallace's grandfather. An elegant pine staircase leads to one pretty white-panelled bedroom and another, single, that is very good – unlike so many single bedrooms. Children particularly like the attic rooms above, with circular windows and sloping ceilings. Julia provides only breakfast (sometimes taken under the vine outside) because within five miles are ten inns all of which serve good food.

Although so many busy roads skirt this area, it is very secluded and few motorists explore its narrow lanes where boughs reach overhead, pheasants dart from hedges or vanish into the glades, beech woods turn to fiery colours in autumn, and one finds unknown villages tucked away, built in the mixture of flint and brick which is traditional in these parts.

Southward is one of the finest and most winding stretches of the River Thames – from Sonning through Henley (of regatta fame) and Maidenhead to Windsor, best explored by boat – arguably at its best in uncrowded autumn when the hills descend to the river in a blaze of colour. The scene constantly changes: weirs, bridges, locks and islands along the way; meadow banks dotted with historic mansions, abbeys, boat-houses and inns. From summits of hills there are superb views of it all. Along the river itself, visit Sonning and Shiplake, Cookham for Stanley Spencer's paintings and for its backwaters, Hurley, Marlow, the beech woods of Cliveden, picturesque Boulter's Lock (well-described in Jerome K. Jerome's *Three Men in a Boat*), busy Maidenhead with two fine bridges, and Bray (the village of the turncoat Vicar of Bray). Then come the splendours of Windsor Castle and Eton College. Edwardian houses and well-kept gardens line the banks, and here are the willows of Kenneth Grahame's *Wind in the Willows*, together with the summer wildflowers he described – 'purple loosestrife shaking luxuriant tangled locks; willowherbs, tender and wistful like a pink sunset cloud; comfrey, the purple hand-in-hand with the white; and the diffident dog-rose . . . June at last was here.'

All prices are inclusive of any VAT or service charge. They are minimum prices: superior rooms or high-season bookings may cost more.

166

LOW GREEN HOUSE

C D S S-C

Thoralby, Bishopdale, east of Hawes, North Yorkshire, DL8 3SZ
Tel: 0969 3623 (to be changed to 0969 663623 during 1990)

2 bedrooms (double and family) from £14. Less for 5 nights. Rooms have central heating; showers; TV, armchairs; tea/coffee facilities; views of country or garden. No smoking.
Dinner £8 for 4 courses and coffee, at 6.45pm. Vegetarian or special diets if ordered. Packed lunches, snacks. Drinks can be brought in.
Sitting-room with central heating, open fire, books, record-player.
Small garden
Nearest main road A684 from Leyburn to Hawes.

This stone house in a tiny hamlet is the home of Tony and Marilyn Philpott, who are founts of information on where to walk and what to see.

Within rugged walls are particularly comfortable and pretty rooms. I had a pink-and-white bedroom with deep brown carpet; the bathroom was excellent; and in the sitting/dining-room (which runs from front to back of the house, with a picture window looking towards Wensleydale) soft colours, deep armchairs around a log fire and plentiful books provide a relaxed atmosphere. For dinner Marilyn served – with decorative flourishes – local smoked trout, pork cooked with cream and mushrooms, blue Wensleydale cheese, and raspberry torte. With the coffee came a dish of chocolates. (All carefully prepared, and remarkably good value.)

The Yorkshire Dales have many peaks over 2000 feet high: wild and windy, with lonely farms on their foothills, sheep on the moors and waterfalls rushing down to the valleys. Wensleydale is only five minutes away. Bishopdale itself follows a stream south, the road rising high up at Kidstones Pass, to join Langstrothdale (see other entries) and, much more tourist-ridden, Wharfedale. Sights worth seeing include Aysgarth Falls, Malham Cove, Hardraw Falls, Jervaulx Abbey, Fountains (Abbey and gardens), the Settle-Carlisle scenic railway, Newby Hall gardens, Thorpe Perrow arboretum, Bolton Castle. (Bicycles, including mountain bicycles, for hire locally.)

This would be a good place for a touring bibliophile. The first stop would be nearby Hawes, where there is a small and crowded secondhand bookshop specialising in fine bindings (not always open). (The ropeworks in Hawes is also well worth a visit, both to see ropes being made and to buy anything from a bellrope to a lead for the dog: once in danger of closing, it is now flourishing thanks to a combination of traditional craft methods and modern technology.) From Hawes, a drive over the bleak spine of the Pennines takes one to Sedbergh, where there is a bookshop specialising in valuable collectors' items and works of local interest.

And from Sedbergh, Kendal is only a short distance away: here is also a big antiquarian bookshop on several floors.

Readers' comments: Comfort, hospitality and value cannot be bettered. Lovely hosts.

167

LOW HALL

C(10) **D S**

Brandlingill, south of Cockermouth, Cumbria, CA13 0RE Tel: 0900 826654

6 bedrooms (single or double) from £17. Less for 3 nights and bargain breaks. All have own bath/shower; tea/coffee facilities; central heating; views of river, country or garden.

Dinner £10.25 for 4 courses (with choices) and coffee, at 7–7.30pm. Non-residents not admitted. Special diets if ordered. Packed lunches. Tea, coffee, free. Drinks can be ordered.

2 sitting-rooms with central heating, open fire, TV, books, piano; bar. No smoking in one.

Large garden

Nearest main road A66 from Keswick to Cockermouth.

Closed December–March

David and Dani Edwards gave up other careers to renovate this farmhouse, which is mostly of 17th-century origin but was enlarged to accommodate a big Victorian family. In carrying out this task, they uncovered a huge fireplace in what was the dairy and is now the dining-room where candlelit dinners are accompanied by classical music. They have decorated it with sprigged wallpapers and some attractive old furniture.

There is one big sitting-room for non-smokers, and a smaller one for smokers and television addicts – a problem for people with only one of these vices!

The bedrooms, most of which are spacious, give views of the Lorton fells on the north-western corner of the Lake District or of the grounds of the house, through which a stream runs. This is an area of great beauty, wooded rather than rugged, where the Cumbrian mountains start their descent to sea level. It is never overrun by tourists, yet the well known parts of the Lake District are only a short drive away. Cockermouth – birthplace of Wordsworth and among the most pleasant of Cumbrian towns – is three miles away. Buttermere and Ennerdale Water (the only lake with no road along it, and approachable only from the west) are near. The historic port of Whitehaven, one-time fishing villages such as Allonby, and the sandstone cliff of St Bees Head are all close as well.

Dani's menus always include a vegetarian alternative to the meat course. A typical menu: potted broccoli; soup; roast loin of pork with fig, apple and cheese stuffing, or sweet-and-sour almonds; and either cheese or a choice of puddings – one light, one richer, and one hot. Breakfasts are much more interesting than the usual egg-and-bacon routine. Preserves, rolls and ice cream are home-made.

Readers' comments: My favourite guest-house . . . fulfils all your criteria and more. Extremely comfortable.

A few miles away, on the edge of the village of High Lorton, Mrs Roberts provides bed-and-breakfast at **Owl Brook** (tel: 090085 333). This architect-designed bungalow of green lakeland slate with pine ceilings was built a few years ago, and all the airy bedrooms have fine views. It lies at the end of Whinlatter Pass, the least alarming of the Lake District passes. The accommodation is suitable for disabled visitors.

Readers' comments: Beautiful views and utter tranquillity. Breakfasts were superb. Very friendly family atmosphere.

LOXLEY FARMHOUSE   C D
Loxley, south-east of Stratford-upon-Avon, Warwickshire, CV35 9JN
Tel: 0789 840265

3 bedrooms (double or family) from £15.
Less for 3 nights. Rooms have central heating; armchairs; tea/coffee facilities; own bathrooms. Two with use of small kitchen.
2 sitting-rooms with central heating, open fire, TV, books.

Garden and paddock, with Shetland ponies.
Nearest main road A422 from Stratford-upon-Avon to Banbury.

Loxley is a hilltop village with diminutive church. From a seat on its sloping green, where crab-apple trees are bright in autumn, there are far views across woodland and fields of red earth. Just downhill from here Loxley Farm is tucked away: a picture-postcard house of half-timbering and thatch, parts dating back to the 13th century. Perhaps Robin Hood ('Robin of Loxley') knew the house; there's a worn stone in the churchyard on which, tradition has it, he and his companions used to sharpen their arrow-tips. And certainly Charles I stayed here after the nearby Battle of Edgehill.

Inside, everything is in keeping with the style of the ancient house: low ceilings with pewter pots hanging from the beams, flagged floors, small-paned windows, log fires, oak doors. You can see the cruck construction of the house – at its heart, the unhewn trunks of two trees support the roof timbers. There is not a single straight wall or floor. Anne Horton has furnished the rooms in appropriate style. In the dining-room, leather chairs surround a large oak table; in the sitting-room are a grandfather clock and wing armchairs, with Staffordshire figures and old silver on the shelves, lavender and dried flowers.

The bedrooms differ in size and style, the largest having a shaggy carpet, antiques and a sofa; the smallest, flowery frilled bed linen. Two are in a newly converted, thatched barn.

Breakfast only – with home-made buns – and supper trays; but there are many good restaurants in Stratford; the Bell Inn at Alderminster is also good.

The broad River Avon gives character to the peaceful countryside: cattle grazing in green meadows where once Shakespeare's Forest of Arden spread for miles around – only remnants survive. It is very easy to visit Stratford-upon-Avon from here, and the rest of Warwickshire, the Cotswolds, and Oxford. Warwick Castle, Blenheim Palace, Charlecote, Hidcote (and many other great gardens) make this area a tourist honeypot.

Readers' comments: Idyllic surroundings. Much care and attention. Generous, flavoursome fare. Most welcoming and comfortable. Not a jarring note.

MAINS HALL

C D PT X

Mains Lane, Little Singleton, east of Blackpool, Lancashire, FY6 7LE
Tel: 0253 885130

9 bedrooms (single, double or family) from £15. Less for 7 nights. Rooms have central heating; shower or bathroom; TV, phone, armchairs; views of river, country or garden; tea/coffee-facilities. One with four-poster, two have half-testers.
Dinner £11 for 3 courses and coffee, at 7pm. Special diets if ordered. Packed lunches, snacks. Coffee, tea, for a charge. Drinks can be ordered.
2 sitting-rooms with central heating, open fire, TV, books, indoor games (including table tennis); bar; garden room.
Large garden Meadow with riverside walk.
Nearest main road A585 from Fleetwood towards Preston.

A long drive through fields brings one to a vista of this historic house, white with leaded windows, at the end of its shrub-lined drive. Built in the time of Henry VII or VIII, it remained a manor house until the turn of the century.

Robert Owen knew and loved it as a boy. When the opportunity came he bought it; and his wife Beryl, who used to have a catering service, runs it as a country hotel. (He is a lecturer in technical communication.) Its outstanding feature is the exuberant wood-carving: Jacobean garlands and nymphs abound, in the panelling of the hall and up the staircase.

It has a history of romance and plots, with secret hiding-places used by Cardinal Allen and Jesuit priests who were attempting the overthrow of Elizabeth I. The old barn, which carries the date 1686 in its brickwork, housed an illicit chapel. Jacobite rebels stayed here in 1745, and later the Prince Regent – wooing Catholic Mrs Fitzherbert, a connection of the family. All around are other ancient remains – an octagonal brick dovecote (from the time when pigeons were 'farmed' for their meat), pool and fountain.

At the back is the River Wyre, and the grounds are full of wildlife – kestrels, woodpeckers, tawny and barn owls. There are two old walnut trees, and Beryl uses the nuts in the meals she cooks. A typical menu is Stilton soup, lamb in honey and orange, and syllabub. (No dinner on Sundays.) Popular breakfast options include smoked haddock and creamed mushrooms.

My bedroom was spacious and comfortable, with a view right along the drive.

The house stands in an attractive area of countryside, and is within easy reach of plenty of other interesting places to visit such as Blackpool, Fleetwood (port and fishmarket), Beacon Fell, Salmesbury Hall (for antiques), Garstang's canal and farming museum and Barton Grange garden centre.

Readers' comments: Excellent. Will stay again.

Prices are the minimum *per person* in a double room at the beginning of the year.

THE MALTINGS

C(10) S

Aldwincle, south of Oundle, Northamptonshire, NN14 3EP Tel: 08015 233

3 bedrooms (single or double) from £17. Less for 3 nights. Rooms have central heating; armchairs; views of country or garden. (Clothes-washing facilities.) No smoking. Coffee, tea, free.
Sitting-room with central heating, open fire, TV, books.
Large garden and paddock.
Nearest main road A605 from Thrapston to Oundle.

As soon as you enter the courtyard to park, you get an enticing glimpse through a stone arch (framed in honeysuckle and jasmine) of a particularly lovely walled garden. Pebble and flagstone paths pass between stone troughs of flowers, and baskets of begonias hang overhead. Beyond is an alpine bed.

This is a long, low, 16th-century house with very thick stone walls. Its barn used to provide the warmth needed to make heaps of barley sprout – the malting process which is at the heart of brewing.

Its dining-room has a Persian carpet on the wood-block floor, and antique furniture, as does the sitting-room where, from a pale green sofa, you can enjoy logs blazing in the stone fireplace or a garden view through French doors. The walls of the house are lined with portraits or animal paintings which Margaret Faulkner collects (she used to work for an art dealer).

Upstairs, a long and wavering passage leads to bedrooms that have rose chintzes or pink patchwork, for instance, and to equally attractive bathrooms. Their 17th-century doors are of stripped pine; and, like all the rooms in the house, they are very light.

As only breakfast is served, most visitors go for other meals to the Falcon Inn at Fotheringhay; the Snooty Fox at Lowick; or the Pheasant at Keyston.

In his childhood, the poet Dryden grew up in and around this village, a breezy spot but well placed for touring.

There are 14 stately homes in the vicinity including Burghley and Boughton (gardens too), as well as Rockingham Castle, historic Stamford, Huntingdon for its associations with Oliver Cromwell, bird reserves, Notcutt garden centre, and steam railways. London is less than an hour by train. (More about Northamptonshire under other entries.)

Don't complain if –
- because you booked at short notice, you do not get the best room
- because you did not order a meal in advance, you get something plucked from the freezer
- because you do not arrive on time, your room is let to someone else
- because you bring a dog without asking, it is refused entry
- because you don't express your wishes (for more heat, a second helping or whatever), you don't get what you want!

MANOR FARM
S

Crackington Haven, south-west of Bude, Cornwall, EX23 0JW
Tel: 084 03 304

5 bedrooms (single or double) from £17. Less for 2 nights and bargain breaks. All have own bath/shower; central heating; views of country or garden. No smoking. (Washing-machine on request.)
Dinner £8 for 4 courses and coffee, at 7pm. Non-residents not admitted. Drinks can be ordered.

2 sitting-rooms with central heating, open fire, TV, books, organ; bar. No smoking. **Large garden** and farmland. **Nearest main road** A39 from Bude to Camelford.

Muriel Knight so much enjoys cooking and looking after guests that she gave up her job as a teacher in order to concentrate on this, in her outstandingly beautiful home near the sea (the garden of which provides fruit and vegetables).

It is a historic manor house (named in Domesday Book), much of the present building three centuries old, and furnished with taste. Past a stone-flagged hall is a beamed sitting-room with mullion windows, stone pillar, and wrought-iron screen concealing a log stove. Pinkish armchairs are grouped on a slate-grey carpet and there is a help-yourself bar. In the dining-room lyre-backed chairs with yellow seats surround the mahogany table which Muriel lays with silver, cut glass and starched napkins. There is also a room with TV and organ (with earphones!). Equal care has gone into bedrooms that have such things as 17th-century antiques, Berlin-work window-seats, lattice windows, elegant bathrooms. (One has a Sitz bath which some elderly people appreciate.) I particularly liked the rose room.

In the grounds are a sloping lawn with herb border and, beside an old waterwheel, a games room with full-size billiards and table tennis.

Muriel's pleasure in cooking shows itself in the dinners she provides. Here is just one example. Choux-pastry swans with a filling of avocado and cream; Coronation chicken (that is, in an apricot and curry sauce) accompanied by jacket potatoes stuffed with cheese and basil, *and* cauliflower and date salad *and* rice, prawns and eggs in prawn sauce; a lemon and orange pavlova. It hardly needs saying that Manor Farm is a good choice for gourmets.

In such an idyllic spot, there is little temptation to go elsewhere. However, the resort of Bude is very near and the border of Devon. Bude is more sedate than many West Country resorts, in a setting of grassy downs and golden sandy beaches on which the Atlantic thunders in. There is a historic quarter by the port, where an old canal enters the sea via a lock.

Readers' comments: Gracious and warm, a beautiful ambience. Delightful place. We were looked after superbly. Super place, nice hosts. Peace, quiet, good food, comfort.

MANOR FARM

C S-C X

**Kelmscott, north-west of Faringdon (Oxfordshire), Gloucestershire,
GL7 3HJ**   Tel: 0367 52620

2 bedrooms (double or family) from £12.
Bargain breaks. Rooms have central heating;
armchairs; views of country or garden; tea/
coffee facilities. (Clothes-washing facilities.)
No smoking.
Sitting-room with central heating, open fire,
TV, books. No smoking.
Small garden and farmland.
Nearest main road A417 from Faringdon to
Lechlade.

This Cotswold stone house (at the centre of a dairy-farm belonging to the National
Trust) stands on the outskirts of a carefully conserved village – utterly peaceful,
for it is not on the route to anywhere else. Outside is a pigeon-house as old as the
rest of the buildings; paddocks with a pony, pet lambs and calves; pollarded
willows and cherry trees that flower prettily in spring.

The 17th-century windows, stone-mullioned and with panelled shutters, are a
handsome feature of rooms which Anne Amor keeps immaculate as well as
comfortable; with, in winter, a crackling fire framed by the Adam mantelpiece
and, in summer, chairs on the lawn. Some people go to a riverside inn, the Trout,
for dinner (or to the Tavern at Clanfield). Anne will, however, produce packed
lunches.

Kelmscott's greatest claim to fame is William Morris's big manor house, still
with tapestries and embroideries made by him and his wife; paintings by Rosetti;
wallpapers, tiles and textiles which Morris designed. Occasionally, one-day
embroidery courses are held here; and you can buy things made from William
Morris fabrics. The house is rarely open, but Anne can usually arrange visits.

The Thames (merely a stream here) is 5 minutes' walk away. In addition to
lovely countryside, visitors enjoy days spent at the Cotswold Wildlife Park,
Cogges living farm 'museum', the steam railway centre at Didcot; touring
Cotswold villages like Bourton-on-the-Water and Burford; and visiting Filkins
(woollen weavers) or stately homes (Coleshill, Buscot, Pusey House and gardens,
and Blenheim Palace). Oxford and Cheltenham are not far away.

Readers' comments: Very comfortable and welcoming. A lovely time; highly
recommended.

Four-poster at Vauld Farmhouse (see page 307)

MANOR FARM HOUSE

C(5) **D S X**

Wormington, south-west of Broadway, Worcestershire, WR12 7NL
Tel: 038673 302

rear view

3 bedrooms (single or double) from £13.50. Rooms have central heating; views of garden; shower (two). No smoking.
Sitting-room with central heating, open fire, TV, books.
Small garden
Nearest main road A46 from Broadway to Cheltenham.

Once this house was known as Charity Farm because 'dole' was dispensed to wayfarers. The farm was connected with Hailes Abbey (in the 13th century, its phial of Christ's blood made it a centre of pilgrimage; now there are only ruins), hence some ecclesiastical touches like the pointed arch beside the log fire – possibly it was a leper window. There are leaded casements in the comfortable sitting-room, a stone inglenook in the hall, slabs of Welsh slate on the floor, steps and turns everywhere on one's way up to beamy all-white bedrooms well furnished with mahogany pieces. There's still a cheese room dating from the time when this was a dairy-farm.

What was once a cattle-yard is now a very attractive court with lawn, fountain and stone sinks planted with flowers. To one side is an old granary of brick and timber which dates, like the house itself, from the 15th century. From his stable door Monty, a big hunter, watches visitors' comings and goings.

Pauline Russell serves only breakfast, recommending for other meals Goblets wine bar in Broadway – that world-famous showplace, best known of all the picturesque villages hereabouts and once called 'the painted lady of the Cotswolds' because the colour of the golden stone glows so vividly here. Flower-filled, perfectly groomed gardens do their bit too.

From here one can drive to the fruitful Vale of Evesham (loveliest in spring), high Bredon Hill ringed by pretty villages, Tewkesbury to see the abbey, historic Evesham for boat trips on the Avon, Pershore (abbey church and 18th-century houses), or little Ripple with old houses around its green and quaint carvings on the misericord seats in the church.

Through the region runs the River Avon, watering the rich fields and orchards around it.

The area is a source of endless pleasure to anyone who enjoys discovering little-known villages and their individual treasures. Examples are Bosbury, surrounded by hop gardens and dominated by a detached church tower fortified as a refuge from the Welsh raiders of the 12th century; Bredon, full of black-and-white houses and, in its church, a treasure-house of carved tombs and monuments – it also has an immense mediaeval tithe barn; Bretforton, where the ancient and picturesque inn – just one of many fine buildings here – is owned by the National Trust (look for the 'witch marks' on the floor and the splendid collection of 17th-century pewter); Colwall which has a huge stone said to have been hurled there by a giant in pursuit of his faithless wife (the scenic Jubilee Drive high up in the hills starts here); and the two Combertons, Great and Little (the latter is in fact the bigger one, but both are beautiful) at the foot of high Bredon Hill.

MARINA HOTEL

C D PT S

The Esplanade, Fowey, Cornwall, PL23 1HY   Tel: 072683 3315

rear view

11 bedrooms (double) from £18 (**this price exclusive to SOTBT readers**, and for one room only). Much less for 2 nights. Rooms have central heating; shower or bathroom; TV, armchairs; views of sea or garden; balcony (some); phone.
Dinner About £12 for 4 courses (with choices) and coffee, at 7–8pm. Special diets if ordered. Lunches, packed lunches, snacks. Coffee, tea, for a charge. Drinks can be ordered. No smoking.
3 sitting-rooms with central heating, books; bar.
Riverside lawn with sailing, fishing, wind-surfing etc. Boat users can moor.
Nearest main road A3082 from St Austell to Fowey.
Closed November–March

Built in 1830 as a seaside retreat for the Bishop of Truro, this fine house has been furnished with the elegance it deserves. The handsome mouldings, arches and panelling of the hall and octagonal landing are now decorated in brown and cream; and each bedroom is different – a pale colour scheme in one; sprigged covers and pine in another (its rounded window overlooking the sea); four with covered verandahs of lacy ironwork facing the tiny walled garden and waterfront beyond it. The dining-room has Indian Tree china on peach tablecloths, with spectacular views from the big picture-window; the bar, rosy armchairs and a thick pale carpet. Recently, 8-foot marble pillars were uncovered in one bedroom!

David Johns gives equal attention to the standard of the food. Dinner is priced according to your choice of main dish, from a selection that includes (for instance) boned chicken in a sauce of mushrooms and cider, escallopes of veal with mushrooms and cream flamed in Madeira, and local fish in a variety of ways, cooked by Stephen Vincent.

Fowey (pronounced Foy) is on that mild stretch of the coast known as the Cornish Riviera. It is an old and picturesque harbour of steep, narrow byways (parking is difficult; a hotel car will take you to the town carpark), its waters busy with yachts and fishing boats. Some people arrive by car ferry. It is easy to find secluded coves and beaches nearby, or scenic walks along clifftops. The little town is full of antique, book and craft shops; historic buildings; restaurants and good food shops. Easily reached from here are Lanhydrock House and gardens, Restormel Castle, Charlestown, Wheal Martin China Clay Museum, Probus gardens. Cornwall has a spring gardens festival – ask the Marina for a leaflet about the 55 gardens that participate.

Readers' comments: Excellent; super room. Extremely helpful. Have never experienced such professional yet personal attention.

When writing to me, if you want a reply please enclose a stamped addressed envelope.

175

MARSHGATE COTTAGE

C D H PT X

Marshgate, west of Hungerford, Berkshire, RG17 0QX   Tel: 0488 82307

9 bedrooms (single, double or family) from £14.75. Most have own bath/shower; TV; tea/coffee facilities; phone; central heating; views of canal, country or garden.
Sitting-room with central heating, open fire, books.

Small garden
Nearest main road A4 from Marlborough to Newbury.

The marshes which give this cottage its name stretch down to the 18th-century Kennet & Avon Canal, a haven for birds and wildflowers. The cottage (used as a pest-house during the plague of 1640) is even older than the canal, its thatched roof descending almost to ground level; and although it has been skilfully modernized and extended everything is in keeping with its original character. Most rooms overlook the marshes, which are a sheet of yellow in buttercup-time. Wild orchids grow there, frogs croak in spring, and among the network of little streams kingfishers can be spotted hunting, or redshanks on their nests.

Mike Walker, once a journalist, did most of the conversion himself, re-using old handmade bricks and wrought-iron locks; laying floors of beautiful chestnut boards. His Danish wife Elsebeth, a biochemist, has furnished the rooms with Scandinavian taste, hunting for finds such as mirrors or stained glass in the area's many antique shops. The breakfast-room is in white and pine; dried flowers are strung along the beams; hand-thrown pots contrast with curios such as an old mangle. From a quarry-tiled hall an open-tread staircase goes up to some bedrooms (others are on the ground floor), furnished with a pleasing simplicity.

In the grounds are goats and ducks – also a 'dipping hole' (that is, the point where an underground stream pops up – watercress grows in it). You can stroll along the canal path into old Hungerford.

Only breakfast is provided (a chance to sample fresh duck eggs and goat's milk if you wish) because Hungerford has excellent restaurants such as the Bear.

Around Hungerford there is scenic downland in every direction, and a great many stately homes or other sights described elsewhere in this book. Nearby Newbury's Watermill Theatre is one of many interesting spots (the wheel is still to be seen). Thatcham Moors are relatively unknown even though they have an almost unique feature, a huge inland reed-bed. Walkers make for the high Ridgeway Path which is of prehistoric origin. Donnington has castle ruins.

Readers' comments: Agreeably cosy. Delightful river setting.

MELLINGTON HOUSE

C S S-C

Broad Street, Weobley, north-west of Hereford, HR4 8SA
Tel: 0544 318537

5 bedrooms (single, double or family) from £12.50. Rooms have own bath/shower (some); TV; tea/coffee facilities; central heating. No smoking.
Dinner £7.50 for 3 courses (with choices) and coffee, at 7pm. Non-residents not admitted. Vegetarian or special diets if ordered. Tea, coffee, free.
Sitting-room with central heating, open fire, TV, books, piano, record-player.
Large garden
Nearest main road A4112 from Leominster to Brecon.

Once, mediaeval houses were considered old-fashioned and so many householders had new façades put on them. That is why Mellington House has a front in Queen Anne style, but its real age is revealed at the back where the original half-timbering is still exposed – typical of most buildings in Weobley, which is a particularly fine mediaeval village set in the lovely Herefordshire countryside. Although the house is in the centre of the village, it is quiet because its walls are thick and the big sash windows double-glazed (not that Weobley gets heavy traffic).

Ann Saunders has furnished the house very pleasantly (for instance, brass beds and wildflower duvets), the sitting-room is large and comfortable, and there is a downstairs bedroom which Ann (a physiotherapist) provides for people who have mobility problems. The dining-room opens onto a large, old, walled garden where, on sunny mornings, she serves breakfast.

Although there are good restaurants in Weobley (also a craft centre, shops and art gallery) Ann will prepare such meals as: melon, roast beef with garden vegetables, home-made cheesecake, and cheeses.

From Weobley, there are plenty of sightseeing options. The picturesque black-and-white village of Eardisland is close. There are a dozen bookshops (most belonging to Richard Booth) in Hay-on-Wye, now nicknamed 'Book City'. Brecon, Offa's Dyke and numerous stately homes provide other destinations for a day out; and, as this is an area of orchards and nursery gardens, many people return home laden with pot-plants and pick-your-own soft fruits. The Malvern Hills and the Black Mountains are close, and several market towns are nearby. Add to these the Brecon Beacons, Radnor Forest, the 'Golden Valley', Welsh and Shropshire market towns, a motor museum, a lovely drive along Wenlock Edge, Ironbridge Industrial Museum, the Wye Valley and innumerable garden centres.

Travel northward for Worcestershire, which has a tremendous amount to see. Fine scenery, historic buildings (including churches), hill walks, waterside dairy-farms, a magnificent cathedral in Worcester itself, hop fields and orchards, woods, and sights which include Elgar's birthplace (Broadheath), an outdoor museum of salvaged ancient buildings (at Avoncroft), the Royal Worcester porcelain museum and factory (bargains to be had!) and a variety of stately homes. River trips, the Three Choirs festival, delightful villages and beautiful gardens add to the interest of the area.

Readers' comments: Could not praise more.

177

MEVAGISSEY HOUSE

C(7) **PT** S-C

Vicarage Hill, Mevagissey, south of St Austell, Cornwall, PL26 6SZ

Tel: 0726 842427

rear view

6 bedrooms (double or family) from £14. Less for 7 nights and bargain breaks. Some have own bath/shower; TV; tea/coffee facili-

ties; central heating; views of sea, country, garden. No smoking preferred. (Washing-machine on request.)

Dinner £9 for 4 courses (with choices) and coffee, at 7.30pm. Non-residents not admitted. Vegetarian or special diets if ordered. Salad lunches, packed lunches, snacks. Tea, coffee, extra (free on arrival). Drinks can be ordered.

Sitting-room with central heating, open fire, TV, books, record-player; bar.

Large garden

Nearest main road A390 from St Austell to Truro.

Closed November–February

Perched on a hillside above this very popular resort is a handsome 18th-century house (once a vicarage), looking south across garden and countryside towards the sea. A great picture-window in the large sitting-room makes the most of this view.

In the dining-room, dinner is served by candlelight, with Doulton daisy plates on green cloths that match the green carpet. Diana Owen's dinners are based on the best of traditional English cookery – mackerel pâté or chicken-and-leek soup might be followed by steak pie or sole stuffed with prawns. After a pudding such as chocolate fudge cake, petits fours will be served with the coffee.

I particularly liked the king-sized brass bed with crochet cover in one of the bedrooms, and the huge size of the carpeted bathroom: very good value.

At the end of June, the annual 'Mevagissey feast' week takes place here, with the Cornish floral dance through the streets. Mevagissey is still a fishing harbour though tourist shops predominate. There are a small museum of model railways, an aquarium, and shark-fishing trips. The nearest sandy beach is at Porthpean.

Readers' comments: Charming hosts who do everything possible to make your holiday a time to remember. Delighted; have booked again. Excellent value.

In Mevagissey itself, up a steep lane is **Anchor Cottage**, Cliff Street (tel: 0726 842089). A 200-year-old fisher-man's cottage, it is only a minute from the harbour which tends to be packed with tourists on summer days and therefore best enjoyed in the evening (Cliff Street itself is peaceful). Virginia Dale-Stephenson has chosen William Morris fabrics to contrast with the slate walls and floor; the little dining-room overlooks a flowery courtyard.

Dinner may comprise fish soup, chicken with four vegetables, and apple pie with clotted cream (she also serves cream teas). Crafts, made by her

sister, are on sale. Accommodation here is very good value indeed.

Readers' comments: Very comfortable, well furnished and as good as any place we have found.

THE MILL

CDH

Mungrisdale, west of Penrith, Cumbria CA11 0XR   Tel: 059683 659

7 bedrooms (single, double or family) from £26 with dinner. Less for 5 nights. Rooms have central heating, electric heaters; shower or bathroom, wc; TV, armchairs; views of country or garden; tea/coffee facilities. (Clothes-washing facilities.)
Dinner 5 courses (with choices) and coffee, at 7pm. Vegetarian or special diets if ordered. Packed lunches, snacks. Coffee, tea, for a charge. Drinks can be ordered. No smoking.
2 sitting-rooms with central heating, open fire, TV, books; table tennis, snooker, darts.
Garden and woods.
Nearest main road A66 from Keswick to Penrith.
Closed November–February

It is little more than 20 years since the watermill in this Lake District valley stopped working. By the old stone building which used to house the saw which it powered is the sawyer's cottage, now a private hotel. It is a peaceful spot, with little more than the sound of the Glenderamackin River rushing down its rocky bed.

The Mill (which is next to, but not connected with, the Mill Inn) is a simple white house with moss on the slate roof and a small conservatory, facing a stone terrace and a lawn with seats by the water's edge. Eleanor and Richard Quinlan came here after years in big hotel management, having fallen for the place when they stayed as guests. Their aim is to give the polished attention to detail expected in a big establishment, combined with a less impersonal atmosphere. So Richard looks after the 'front-of-house' and the wines (on which he is an expert), while Eleanor exercises her talent for cooking. She has found sources of ingredients not usually associated with the Lake District, which explains the presence on the menu of such things as stuffed vine leaves, as well as excellent home-made soups accompanied by fresh soda bread (the last a fixture by popular demand). The main course might be quail with orange, brandy and thyme; or roast beef with mustard puddings and claret gravy. And there are four or five sweets on the trolley (cheese follows).

The main sitting-room is pretty (the stone surround to the log fire bears the date 1651), and there is a small TV room with well filled bookshelves. In the dining-room each small oak table has blue linen napkins, willow-pattern china, candles and a nosegay. Bedrooms are trim and simple, with restful colours.

Mungrisdale itself is a tiny village sheltered within a setting of blue-grey crags and slopes, and well placed for excursions to all parts of Cumbria. Close by are plenty of good walks (and even six-year-olds can take the fells in their stride for an hour or two, when not paddling in the stream).

A great variety of places can be reached from here. Some people go trout-fishing, some watch the hang-gliders, some explore the strange rock formations.

Readers' comments: Beautiful, quiet, excellent food. Service attentive and friendly.

179

MILL HAY HOUSE

C PT X

Snowshill Road, Broadway, Worcestershire, WR12 7JS   Tel: 0386 852498

6 bedrooms (single, double or family) from £17.50. Less for 3 nights. Rooms have central heating or electric heaters; shower or bathroom (some); armchairs; views of country or garden; tea/coffee facilities.
Sitting-room with central heating, open fire, TV, books.

Large garden
Nearest main road A46 from Stratford-upon-Avon to Cheltenham.
Closed January and February

Picturesque Broadway, now world-famous, can get unpleasantly crowded with tourists – but Mill Hay House, in the oldest part, lies well away from all that, a very lovely house of Cotswold stone with a mossy roof and leaded windows. At the front is a formal garden of rosebeds and clipped yews; at the back, terraced lawns are surrounded by flowering shrubs, more roses and yew hedges, and a rock garden through which a tiny rivulet trickles down to where an old watermill still stands, its great wheel spotlit at night. From some of the yews a bower has been created, sheltering a seat.

Not only is the garden, with its millpond, quite exceptional but the building too is very special. To the stone part, brick additions were made in Queen Anne's reign; there are stone-mullioned windows, and curious carved heads built in here and there.

The furnishings are of the same high order – I was very pleased to find that there is a *single* four-poster (18th-century) in one of the rooms, since singles often get the most meagre rooms. One bedroom (with king-size bed) has a view of the mill and garden. Others (one with four-poster and balcony) overlook the rose garden and pond. There is also a separate family suite with two rooms and its own bathroom. Room prices vary a good deal.

Bed-and-breakfast only; for dinner, the Snowshill Arms is recommended.

The owner, Hans Will, also owns nearby Broadway Tower and its surrounding country park. From the top of this 18th-century folly there are fine views and inside is a museum, including displays about William Morris who once lived in the tower. In the park (famous for spring wildflowers and autumn colours) are a barbecue, with meat on sale, wildlife trails, and animals for the children as well as an imaginative play centre. It's worth a whole day for the family.

Not only is there the whole of the Cotswold area to explore, but three of England's most popular tourist cities or towns are equidistant – Stratford-upon-Avon, Oxford and Cheltenham, their environs all described elsewhere.

Readers' comments: Beautiful building, wonderful food, exquisite garden. A real find, most comfortable.

180

MILL HOUSE

Berwick St James, north-west of Salisbury, Wiltshire, SP3 4TS

C(5) S

Tel: 0722 790331

5 bedrooms (single, double or family) from £17. Less for 3 nights and bargain breaks. Some have own bath; TV; tea/coffee facilities on request; central heating; views of river, country or garden. No smoking. (Washing-machine on request.)
Sitting-room with central heating, open fire, TV, books.
Large garden
Nearest main road A303 from Andover to Wincanton.

One crosses the little River Till by a footbridge in the garden to reach this 18th-century house, next to the old watermill itself (still in use for pumping water and generating electricity). Trout and grayling frequent its clear waters (dry fly fishing available), and a terrace has been built by Diana Gifford-Mead's son, a woodwork teacher, where visitors can sit at the waterside. In the garden, peaches grow – and an abundance of old-fashioned roses and hollyhocks. The best time for a waterside walk through the local nature reserve is in late June when, among many other wildflowers, the southern marsh orchid blooms.

From some of the bedroom windows, with leaded panes, there are views of the stream, lawn, tables made from old millstones and rambling herbaceous beds. In some rooms are patchwork bedspreads made by Diana's great-aunt. (One is on the ground floor.) Family photographs and pictures of horses line the walls of the comfortably furnished sitting-room (with log stove). The large breakfast-room, flint-walled, has blue Chatsworth pottery for the table and antique plates displayed.

Diana serves only breakfast. For other meals, visitors go to the noted Dove Inn at Corton or to one of the excellent nearby pubs. Diana has lived in the village all her life (her father owned it and the surrounding estate) and therefore is very knowledgeable about places to visit in the area.

Berwick St James lies between two lovely river valleys: the Avon (described elsewhere) and the Wylye, with the Nadder further south. All converge at Salisbury. Along the Wylye Valley are a number of interesting villages such as Great Wishford (look on the churchyard wall for a record of the price of bread since 1800, and wander in nearby Grovely Wood), Steeple Langford (some thatched cottages, some of chequered flint), streamside walks to Hanging Langford), and Wylye (more chequered stone and flint). One can also walk to Stonehenge. In the Nadder Valley lies pretty Tisbury with its huge thatched tithe barn; Chilmark (17th-century houses and bridges of local stone – this stone was also used in the building of Salisbury Cathedral); Teffont Magna, where each cottage has its own little bridge over the stream; Dinton (three stately homes around it), and the great house of Wilton. (Wilton was the capital of Wessex a thousand years ago.)

For explanation of code letters (**C, D, H, PT, S, S-C, X**) see page xxvi

MILNE HOUSE

C(5) S

Millers Dale, east of Buxton, Derbyshire, SK17 8SN   Tel: 0298 871832

6 bedrooms (single, double or family) from £9. Rooms have central heating or electric heaters; views of garden; tea/coffee facilities. One has a shower. No smoking.
Dinner £7.50 for 4 courses and coffee, at 7pm. Vegetarian or special diets if ordered. Lunches, packed lunches. Drinks can be brought in.
Sitting-room with central heating, wood stove, TV, books.
Small garden
Nearest main road A6 from Bakewell to Buxton.

Soon after the watermill here ceased to function, Nick and Fran Davidson moved in, converting it into a home for themselves and for their business: from this out-of-the-way corner of England they run the world's largest supplier of specialist tools and materials for hand craftsmen in wood. Just across the little road is this pale stone house, clematis rambling up its walls, where the mill-owner once lived – now providing separate accommodation for visitors. (Some of these come to attend the 2-day courses in wood-turning run at Milne House for beginners who go home with at least five small items completed in that period. There are other courses for experts.)

The visitors' rooms are white-walled and simply but pleasantly furnished. A family room is conveniently situated on the ground floor, and outside is a small paved terrace (racks of timber from all over the world behind it) on which to sit and enjoy the view of wooded hills opposite and the sound of water.

A local lady comes in to cook dinner (typically, this might consist of home-made soup, beef bourguignonne and trifle). Otherwise, visitors go to any of several good eating-places nearby.

They are welcome to go through the mill (its former wheelroom now displays woodware and woodworking supplies) to the very pretty garden beside the river, great crags rising up on the opposite bank.

Mid-Derbyshire is famous for its dales (river valleys) among wooded peaks: those of the rivers Dove, Wye and Derwent in particular. Wildlife, historic buildings, archaeological remains and old customs survive the years largely unchanged.

This is a limestone area, dotted with pure springs around which small spas were built (Matlock and Buxton, for instance – the latter with some crescents like Bath) and caves (Matlock and Castleton). Places to visit include Ashbourne (markets, and a very fine 13th-century church with striking monuments); old Bakewell, of Bakewell pudding fame; Birchover village, surrounded by unusual rock formations; Chatsworth House, with the Duke of Devonshire's world-famous art treasures, and gardens designed by Paxton; Crich – a collection of vintage trams (you can ride in a horse-drawn one); the gorge known as 'little Switzerland', through which the Dove flows – Izaak Walton fished here; Matlock, with dramatic crags – a cable-car will take you to the Heights of Abraham.

Haddon Hall is near Rowsley, a moorland walking centre. Historic stone towns include Wirksworth (of 'Adam Bede' fame) and hilly Youlgreave.

182

MILTON FARM

C S

East Knoyle, north of Shaftesbury (Dorset), Wiltshire, SP3 6BG
Tel: 074783 247

2 bedrooms (double or family) at £16. Rooms have central heating; shower or bathroom; TV, armchairs; views of country or garden; tea/coffee facilities.
Dinner £11.50 for 3 courses and coffee, at 7pm. Coffee, tea, free. Wine can be ordered. Vegetarian dishes if ordered.
Sitting/dining-room with central heating, open fire, books.
Garden with heated (80°) swimming-pool.
Nearest main road A350 from Shaftesbury to Warminster.

This is a truly picturebook farmhouse – a stone-flagged floor in the entrance hall, glimpse of a kitchen with pine table and a gun-case beside the gleaming Aga, narrow oak staircase. In the sitting-room, which has a boarded ceiling, logs hiss gently on the stone hearth. There are old oak furniture, deep chairs, silver and flowers everywhere (including the bedrooms).

The Hydes removed a lot of later accretions to reveal the original beams in this mainly Queen Anne house, and then added comfortable furniture and elegant fabrics (such as Sanderson's 'Country Trail'). Janice Hyde serves candlelit dinners – she is a superb cook – which consist of interesting dishes using local produce. One example: onion quiche, followed by a huge trout from the River Nadder (stuffed with almonds, mushrooms, lemon and I-know-not-what) and then the lightest of mousses. Clotted cream, milk and butter are from the farm's cows; pheasant, hare and rabbits are local. Her breakfasts are equally excellent.

Outside is a paved area with chairs facing a view of the hills, and total silence.

East Knoyle is a tiny old village with just one claim to fame: Christopher Wren was born there (his father was rector). So was Edward Strong, who became Wren's master mason and worked on St Paul's. In 1674, Strong built the cottage opposite, and possibly parts of Milton Farm too. Janice Hyde can sometimes show visitors a fascinating scrapbook of village history compiled by the local Women's Institute, including the memories of the local blacksmith and of the postman who used to deliver the letters on horseback. Every summer, there is a music festival in two local castles. Just wandering around here is a pleasure in itself, enjoying willows or magnolias or buttercups, and details like the old stone troughs or a well, and looking for the Victorian 'bun' penny set in the wall of Penny Cottage or the fire-bell on Bell Cottage.

There are views over the Blackmoor Vale, a windmill, bluebell woods, and the Seymour Arms where Jane Seymour once lived.

Salisbury and Wilton House lie in one direction and in the other the ancient, cobbled, hilltop town of Shaftesbury, followed by Sherborne – one of England's jewels, and much underrated. It has two castles, a golden abbey, a quaint museum, and a nearby butterfly and silkworm centre in a historic house. Longleat and the Palladian mansion and gardens of Stourhead are within easy reach.

Readers' comments: Janice Hyde is a delight; countryside and house are beautiful. Very welcoming; delicious dinner; very comfortable. Welcoming and comfortable. Excellent service. Welcoming; superb cooking.

MOATENDEN PRIORY

C D PT

Headcorn, south-east of Maidstone, Kent, TN27 9PT   Tel: 0622 890413

4 bedrooms (single, double or family) from £12.50. Bargain breaks. Rooms have central heating; armchairs; views of country or garden. No smoking.
Dinner (weekends only) £10 for 3 courses, wine and coffee, at 7.30pm. Special diets if ordered. Drinks can be brought in.
Sitting-room with central heating, open fire, books.
Large garden
Nearest main road A274 from Maidstone to the A262.

The house includes the moated remains of a monastery, the monks of which used to raise money to ransom crusaders. The walls are of thick stone, the oak doors fit into arched doorways, pointed windows are deep-set. After Henry VIII dissolved the monasteries, the Priory was owned by a succession of famous people – among them, Thomas Cromwell (Henry's chancellor) and the court poet Sedley, whose daughter became James II's mistress. Then for many years the building was used as a farmhouse.

Guests eat at the big table in Jessie Barclay Deane's dining-kitchen, under a ceiling of great oak timbers. The floor is of quarry tiles, the seating consists of old wood benches and chairs. The big sink is the original stone one. A typical dinner might consist of egg mayonnaise, casseroled chicken, cheeses and fruit.

The sitting-room has comfortable tapestry chairs and a Persian carpet; its walls are painted a soft terracotta and its paintwork white. There is a small conservatory and an outstandingly interesting garden with unusual plants.

Bedrooms are equally attractive and peaceful: beamed ceilings, antique furniture, warm colour schemes, pretty cast-iron fireplaces, and interesting furnishings (a fur spread from India and a woven wall-hanging from Peru, for instance). Jessie makes and sells distinctive knitwear.

Some visitors come for the peace, some for the many sightseeing possibilities in Kent, and many to visit Vita Sackville-West's famous garden at Sissinghurst (before she bought Sissinghurst she nearly decided to take Moatenden Priory, but it did not have enough land for her needs). The Priory's exceptional garden, surrounded by high beech hedges, has two ancient pillars over which honeysuckle clambers and an old orchard where mallards, moorhens and sometimes partridges wander.

Within easy reach are many of Kent's spectacular mansions and castles (Knole, Leeds and Hever, for example, or Scotney with its lovely gardens), and historic cities (such as Canterbury and Maidstone) and towns (Tenterden, Cranbrook). The country lanes are particularly beautiful in apple-blossom time (usually May) or even earlier, when the cherry trees are in flower. In September, the hops are gathered and taken to the oast houses for drying – a few allow visitors. There are several good garden centres, and, of course, Sissinghurst's garden.

Readers' comments: A delightful place. Beautiful, peaceful, hospitable: very good value. A gracious hostess. Very pleasant and welcoming. Friendliest and most cosy of all; charming building, warm welcome. Delightful, visited twice. Comfortable, food very good.

184

MOORLANDS
Levisham, north-east of Pickering, North Yorkshire, YO18 7NL
Tel: 0751 60229

rear view

6 bedrooms (single, double or family) from £14. Some have own bath/shower; all have tea/coffee facilities; central heating; views of country or garden. No smoking.
Dinner £6 for 4 courses (with choices) and coffee, at 6.30pm. Non-residents not admitted. Vegetarian or special diets if ordered. Lunches, packed lunches, snacks. Tea, coffee, free. Drinks can be ordered. No smoking.
2 sitting-rooms with central heating, open fire, TV, books; bar. No smoking.
Large garden with putting green.
Nearest main road A169 from Pickering to Whitby.

Once a vicarage, this is now a comfortable small hotel run by John and Rita Bean. Built in 1906 (the year when Galsworthy's *Man of Property* was published) the house is redolent of the secure and prosperous Edwardian era, with such handsome details as the mahogany staircase and galleried landing above. I particularly liked bedroom no. 3 which has windows on two sides to make the most of the fine views (the house is perched high up above a valley).

Outside are terraced gardens with rhododendrons and a putting green: they were laid out by Italian landscape gardeners brought here specially when the house was built. In a part that has deliberately been left natural, foxes and badgers can sometimes be spotted; and from the terrace one can see right across to the Yorkshire Wolds.

Rita's cooking is traditionally English – joints, pies, etc. She uses vegetables from the garden, fish fresh from Whitby and Lockton-reared meats. Afterwards, if the evening is chilly, guests relax by a crackling log fire in the sitting-room or, if sunny, take their coffee in the garden.

Levisham is a particularly peaceful moorland village, hardly altered by time and right within the North Yorkshire Moors National Park. It has a station on the celebrated Moors Steam Railway; and from Moorlands' gate escorted horse-riders set off into the wilds. It is easy to get from here to the 'heritage' coast in one direction and the historic city of York in the other.

Well worth visiting in the vicinity are such sights as the Beck Isle Museum of Rural Life, in one of Pickering's fine 18th-century houses (in its seventeen rooms are old village shops reconstructed, a Victorian photography room, and agricultural exhibits); Eden Farm (a working farm with walks around it, a display explaining farm work, animals and a barn tea-room); the Ryedale Folk Museum; many abbey and castle ruins; the Yorkshire Museum of Farming; palatial Castle Howard and its art treasures; and many other activities and places described in a holiday information pack obtainable from Ryedale House (in Malton).

The limestone hills of the moors (where Swaledale and Blackface sheep wander) sweep down to the fertile Vale of Pickering and Vale of York throughout which fields of cereals or livestock predominate. Villages become colourful with flowers in spring (Farndale is famous for its wild daffodils), and the fields in summer when rapeseed is in bright yellow flower and wheat or oats are ripening to shades of gold. The vales are among the richest agricultural areas in the country.

MORAR FARM

C(6) **PT**

Weald Street, Bampton, west of Oxford, Oxfordshire, OX8 2HL
Tel: 0993 850162 (Telex: 83343, Morar)

3 bedrooms (double) from £12.50. Less for 2 nights and winter breaks. **Reductions to** readers of this book staying 7 nights; and for winter bookings by over-60s. Rooms have central heating; views of country or garden; tea/coffee facilities. No smoking.
Dinner (winter only) £10.50 for 4 courses and coffee, at 6.30pm. Vegetarian or special diets if ordered. Lunches (in low season only) and packed lunches. Coffee, tea, free. Non-residents not admitted.
Sitting-room with central heating, open fire, TV, books, piano. No smoking.
Large garden and paddock.
Nearest main road A4095 from Witney to Faringdon.

This modern stone house, comfortable and trim, stands in an attractive garden; but what makes it a particularly nice place at which to stay is the personality of its owners. Janet and Terry Rouse are a lively couple, numbering among their accomplishments Morris-dancing, bell-ringing, barn-dancing and spinning (their pet sheep provide the fleece); and they gladly involve their guests too. One reader described Morar as the best place he had ever stayed at, because of the helpful hospitality and excellent food.

Janet takes quite exceptional care of her visitors, with much attention to detail – for instance, two fresh towels are provided every day; there are unlimited fruit juices at breakfast and a wide range of home-made preserves, as well as help-yourself strawberries and raspberries or figs, stewed fruits etc.; she does washing free for visitors who stay two weeks; and has plenty of maps on loan, fills vacuum flasks free, and gives refrigerator space to chill drinks visitors bring in.

For dinner Janet may, during winter, serve a menu such as soup made from home-grown vegetables; their own beef with Yorkshire pudding and six vegetables including red cabbage cooked with honey and juniper berries; Bakewell pudding and cream; a wide choice of cheeses and fruit. (In summer most visitors eat at the Clanfield Tavern.)

Bampton, a pretty village, is famous for its spring festival of Morris dancers when the village children all make wildflower garlands. It is well placed to visit Oxford, the Cotswold villages, Cheltenham, Blenheim Palace and gardens, Bladon (Churchill's grave), Cirencester (Roman museum), Avebury stone circle, and the Berkshire Downs. There's a wildlife park, rare farm breeds centre, arboretum, trout farm, restored watermill and farm museum all within easy reach. For garden-lovers, Puzey and Waterperry are of particular interest.

Readers' comments: Excellent!

Some readers tell me they have stayed at lots of places from *Staying Off the Beaten Track*. I wonder who has stayed at most? A free copy of the next edition awaits the reader who sends me his/her comments on the greatest number!

MULBERRY HALL

Burstall, west of Ipswich, Suffolk, IP8 3DP   Tel: 047387 348

shower; tea/coffee facilities; heating; views of country or garden. No smoking. (Washing-machine on request.)
Dinner £11 for 3 courses and coffee, at 7.45pm. Non-residents not admitted. Vegetarian or special diets if ordered. Lunches, packed lunches, snacks. Tea, coffee, free. Drinks can be brought in.
Sitting-room with central heating, open fire, TV, books, piano, record-player.
Large garden
Nearest main road A1071 from Ipswich to Sudbury.

3 bedrooms (single or double) from £15. Less for 3 nights. Rooms have own bath/

Cardinal Wolsey owned this house in 1523. Son of an Ipswich butcher, he had had a meteoric rise under Henry VIII (a cardinal and Lord Chancellor of England while still in his thirties) and he used his consequent wealth to commission fine properties and works of art. But in 1529, having failed Henry in the matter of divorcing Catherine of Aragon, he was stripped of nearly all his honours.

It is Henry VIII's colourful coat-of-arms which embellishes the inglenook fireplace in the big sitting-room – pink, beamed and with a grand piano. From this a winding stair leads up to well-equipped bedrooms. There is a small dining-room (green curtains and wallpaper in a sprigged Laura Ashley pattern, wheelback chairs round an oak table) where Penny Debenham serves such meals – to be ordered in advance – as trout mousse with a watercress purée; pork au poivre accompanied by dauphinoise potatoes, broccoli, courgettes and salad; fruit tartlets with elderflower cream; and cheeses. Breakfasts, too, are good, with such pleasant options as local apple-juice, chilled melon, home-baked bread and smoked haddock in addition to the usual bacon and eggs.

Outside is an exceptional garden – or series of gardens, enclosed within walls of yew or beech. Beyond a brick-paved terrace is a lawn with long lavender border, and a pergola leads past a rose garden to the tennis court with old hay-wain alongside.

Nearby Ipswich, a port even in Saxon times, has a plethora of mediaeval churches with fine monuments. The traffic in the town is heavy, so exploring is best done on foot. Wolsey made it a twin to Oxford, such was its reputation for learning – but only the gateway of his uncompleted college remains, near the quays where old inns and a classical Custom House survive. The town museum includes replicas of two local Saxon treasures now in the British Museum, the Sutton Hoo and Mildenhall finds; Christchurch Mansion (in a park) is a Tudor house with a collection of furniture and toys, as well as paintings by Constable and Gainsborough. Stroll down the Buttermarket to find the Ancient House, its façade covered in elaborate 17th-century plasterwork representing the (then) four continents: it is now a bookshop.

The surrounding scenery is of open farmland, dotted with particularly pretty villages.

Readers' comments: Beautiful house, outstanding food and service; will visit again. A lot of loving care. Bedrooms light and airy, extremely comfortable; excellent food, breakfast a highlight.

MUNK'S FARMHOUSE
Smarden, west of Ashford, Kent, TN27 8PN   Tel: 023377 265

3 bedrooms (double) from £14. Less for 4 nights and bargain breaks. Some have own bath/shower; all have central heating; views of country or garden. No smoking.
Dinner £10 for 3 courses and coffee, at 7.30pm. Non-residents not admitted. Vegetarian or special diets if ordered. Snacks. Tea, coffee, free. Drinks can be brought in.
Sitting-room with central heating, open fire, books. No smoking.
Large garden
Nearest main road A274 from Maidstone to Tenterden.

You had better behave yourself if you stay here for in the garden is a prison-cell. The old wood lock-up (double-walled and with tiny barred window), now a 'listed building', was moved here in 1850 from the village for, once the railway had been built, there was no longer a stream of drunk and brawling railway navvies needing to cool their heels in it.

The house itself has an even longer history. Weatherboarded in typically Kentish style, it was built nearly three centuries ago. Inside are beams, inglenook fireplaces, iron-latched doors, the original built-in cupboard and a very wide oak staircase: clearly the yeoman-farmer who originally lived here was a man of substance. Even the quarry tiles he laid were so large and thick that they are still as good as new. These are in the dining-room (formerly the kitchen) where guests now eat at a big refectory table. Josephine Scott serves such dinners (if these are ordered in advance) as corn-on-the-cob or melon, roast duck or whole plaice from Rye (in a creamy sauce), and gooseberry fool or raspberries with meringues.

There is a sitting-room with log fire and William Morris sofa, and pretty bedrooms with attractive 'Vanitory' units and sloping ceilings; the attic room has exposed rafters and good views.

In the garden is a large swimming-pool (a solar blanket keeps its temperature up to 70° or 80° in midsummer) where ducks gather to watch you swim.

Readers' comments: Really attractive and comfortable place, pretty garden, amiable hostess, excellent dinners.

The 15th-century **Bell Inn** at Smarden (tel: 023377 283) has a façade of chequered brickwork overhung with scalloped tiles. Inside are Ian Turner's bars, two with inglenooks and all paved or brick-floored. Here one can eat very well, seated on oak settles under beams strung with hop-bines. Outdoors an iron spiral staircase, wreathed in honeysuckle, leads up to the bedrooms, still with the original board ceilings and white brick walls but immaculately furnished in soft colours. (No wash basins.) Visitors are provided with the wherewithal to make their own continental breakfast.

3 bedrooms (single or double) from £18 (**this price exclusive to SOTBT readers and for one room only**). Rooms have central heating; bathroom or shower; armchairs; views of country or garden; tea/coffee facilities; TV (some).

Dinner £12.50 for 4 courses and coffee, at 7.30pm. Coffee, tea, free. Drinks can be brought in.
Sitting-room with central heating, books.
Nearest main road A6 from Lancaster to Kendal.

So close to the busy M6 motorway and yet so rural, this is a place of absolute peace. The oak beams and stone walls that are features of most rooms date from the 17th century when the house was built as a farm. Now, surrounded by lawns, it is simply the home of Peter and Sally Townend, who are both teachers. They moved north, to this house, when Peter got a deputy headship locally and they say frankly that it was only when the cost of central heating soared that they began, a little doubtfully, to take paying guests – and then found they really enjoyed the experience. Sally encourages people to treat the house as if it were their own home. After serving breakfast, she leaves for her work at the nearby primary school while her helpers get busy; she returns at 3.30 to cook an excellent dinner which could consist of avocado with prawns, roast turkey, a choice of two puddings (meringues, chocolate gâteau etc.), cheese, fresh fruit and coffee.

Meals are eaten in what was once the dairy, now furnished with Ercol elm chairs and table. In the sitting-room, velvet armchairs and sofa contrast with the rugged stone of fireplace and walls. Bedrooms have doors of dark wood with brass knobs, attractive colours and Edwardian-style pine furniture. There are cane armchairs.

Capernwray not only lies in attractive countryside but is midway between the Lake District and the Yorkshire Dales, neither much more than a half-hour in a car. Scenic walks, pretty villages, market towns and inns abound.

Other areas 'of outstanding natural beauty' are the Lune Valley, Arnside and Silverdale, and the Trough of Bowland. Canal cruisers can be hired by the hour or day, there are bird reserves, stately homes, castles and a steam railway museum. Morecambe's beaches are near, so is historic Lancaster and its quaint little port at Glasson Dock with salmon smoke-house. Mediaeval Thurnham Hall has a permanent exhibition about the mysterious Turin Shroud. Other attractive places are Kirkby Lonsdale, Levens Hall (and gardens), and Barton Grange.

Readers' comments: Every bit as comfortable as you describe it, if not more so! Food and friendliness first class. Four very happy nights. A real gem, superb food. Particularly enjoyable.

NEW MOOR HOUSE C D H S
near Edlingham, south-west of Alnwick, Northumberland, NE66 2BT
Tel: 066574 638

5 **bedrooms** (single, double or family) from £12.50. Less for 7 nights and bargain breaks.

All have tea/coffee facilities; central heating; views of country.
Dinner £7 for 4 courses and coffee, at 7pm or by arrangement. Non-residents not admitted. Vegetarian or special diets if ordered. Lunches, packed lunches, snacks. Tea, coffee, free. Drinks can be brought in. **Sitting-room** with central heating, open fire, TV, books, piano.
Large garden
Nearest main road A697 from Morpeth to Wooler.

Travelling north, one rounds a curve in the road and comes to a view of New Moor House, once a coaching inn. In dramatic scenery of moorland and forests, the house is set against a backdrop of the Cheviot Hills. It is bounded by Rimside Moor, once notorious for its highwaymen and subject of many songs and poems, notably the ballad of the 'Black Sow of Rimside and the Monk of Holy Island'.

When Hilary and Peter Harcourt-Brown took the house over, they refurbished it to its present comfortable standard, with antiques in keeping with the age of the house. One steps into a dining-room furnished with high-backed pews salvaged from a disused church. The beamed sitting-room, with cretonne armchairs and an open fire, is upstairs.

Hilary prepares the home-cooked meals in generous portions. A typical meal might be home-made soup, a roast with fresh vegetables, then apple pie with cream. The house has its own soft, filtered, spring water which makes a very good cup of tea. Hilary gives herself one evening off a week (Wednesday) but can recommend good restaurants in the area for dinner then.

Peter and Hilary, who breed prize-winning collies and Afghan hounds, are keen on accommodating visitors with dogs, if inoculated. (Their own dogs do not frequent the house.)

People who pause here for a night on the way to Scotland have sometimes got no further, for the area is so full of interest that one could easily spend a fortnight exploring it all. The best part of the Northumbrian coast is nearby, with its castles (Bamburgh, Dunstanburgh, Warkworth); its islands – the Farnes for seabirds, Lindisfarne for its ancient history, priory ruins and castle; and Craster where the kipper teas are so luscious that they stand comparison with treats like smoked salmon. You can find beaches with firm 'sugar' sands and rock-pools, or go on walks – strenuous or gentle – in, for instance, Coquetdale, the Ingram Valley and Langleeford or along clifftops. National Trust properties include Cragside (best at rhododendron time, early summer) and Wallington Hall (tapestries, dolls' houses and a lovely garden). Alnwick Castle, Brinkburn Priory, Chillingham's wild cattle or hang-gliders: take your pick!

At Cambo is a garden centre specializing in cottage-garden and windy-site plants.

Readers' comments: Most comfortable, delicious food. Warm welcome, comfortably furnished. Well ordered; they take pains to accommodate the varying whims of guests. Substantial servings.

NEWBARN   C D S S-C X
Wards Lane, Wadhurst, south-east of Tunbridge Wells (Kent),
East Sussex, TN5 6HP   Tel: 089288 2042

5 bedrooms (single or double) from £15. Less for 3 nights and bargain breaks. Some have own bath/shower; central heating; views of lake, country, garden. No smoking. (Washing-machine on request.) Packed lunches. Tea, coffee, free.
2 sitting-rooms with central heating, open fire, TV, books, piano, record-player. No smoking.
Large garden
Nearest main road A267 from Tunbridge Wells to Heathfield.

Sitting on the brick terrace with the blue lake view below and hills beyond, I could have imagined I was in the Lake District – but this was Sussex, and London only an hour away. There was a solitary angler in a boat, rabbits and wagtails on the lawn – perfect peace!

In the 18th century this was a farmhouse, lattice-paned and tile-hung in traditional Sussex style. Indoors, knotty pine floorboards gleam with polish, there are low beams, and the wood-latched doors were specially made by a local joiner for Christopher and Pauline Willis, who took great care, when renovating the house, to ensure that every detail was in harmony.

Bedrooms are light and flowery, pale buffs and sandy colours predominating. The sitting-room, which has an inglenook, is decorated in cream and coffee. There is a games room in one barn, and one day they hope also to have a swimming-pool in another. Bicycles on loan.

Only breakfast is served (with Pauline's preserves to follow – marmalade made with treacle, gooseberry jam with elderflowers, for instance) because the area is well supplied with good restaurants.

The landscaped garden descends right to the edge of the lake, which is in fact man-made: Bewl Water reservoir. Around its perimeter and many inlets is a 15-mile footpath: there are boat cruises, a visitor centre, watersports, a wooden ark for children and picnic spots. Sometimes Morris dancing or crafts shows are to be seen. Birds from the nature reserve can be spotted.

Bewl Water is on the Kent/Sussex border and there is so much of interest in this historic area that one could happily spend a week or two without going far afield. Beyond the reservoir is a cluster of interesting mansions. At Finchcocks, a Queen Anne house, is a collection of early pianos and other instruments which visitors can hear played. Scotney is a decorative, turreted castle with particularly lovely waterside gardens. Bayham Abbey's ruins are beautifully sited by a river. Sissinghurst has not only the Court but also Vita Sackville-West's gardens around its castle. There's a pinetum at Bedgebury, a great windmill at Cranbrook. Crittenden House is a mansion with outstanding gardens – Great Dixter, too.

Tunbridge Wells is the nearest major town, with true spa elegance, tempting shops in the Pantiles and elsewhere, curious 'twittens' (footpaths) twisting behind the backs of elegant houses; and, on its large common, strange rock formations that challenge the skills of even experienced climbers. Antique shops abound.

Readers' comments: Views and peace superb. A pleasure to stay in. Warm, comfortable and excellent decoration. Friendly and helpful.

191

NEWLANDS FARMHOUSE

Aston Magna, north of Moreton-in-Marsh, Gloucestershire, GL56 9QQ
Tel: 0608 50964

rear view

3 bedrooms (double) from £13. Less for 2 nights. Rooms have central heating; armchairs; views of farmland or garden. (Clothes-washing facilities.) Coffee, tea, for a charge. No smoking.

Sitting-room with central heating, TV, books. No smoking.
Garden
Nearest main road A429 from Warwick to Stow-on-the-Wold.

The spacious and well kept rooms inside this Tudor house do justice to its handsome stone exterior, a feature of which is the big archway through which wagons entered when this was a farm.

The white hall has polished flagstones on the floor and a big dough-chest as old as the house; and off it is a very comfortable sitting-room (hung with rugby photos – Jim Hessel was president of the local club). Beamed bedrooms are roomy and the bathroom is huge, with handsome basin units. From stone-mullioned windows one can see the village and hills beyond. Everywhere are pot-plants and flowers.

Pat Hessel serves only breakfast, but collects menus of local eating-places for dinner – from the popular Bakers' Arms at Broad Campden, and the Crown Inn at Blockley, to Annie's Restaurant at Moreton-in-Marsh.

Moreton-in-Marsh is one of the Cotswolds' show towns: a wide street of handsome and historic houses, with many antique shops. All around are gently rounded hills and wooded valleys with bright streams, quiet villages of the famous Cotswold stone (don't miss Bourton-on-the-Water), the two Slaughters, Broadway, Bibury, Chipping Campden and Stow-on-the-Wold), rich farms with sheep grazing, and superlative churches and manor houses built on wealth created by the mediaeval wool trade and richly embellished. Garden-lovers enjoy Batsford, Hidcote Manor and Kiftsgate in particular; pick-your-own fruit abounds in the Vale of Evesham, antique shops in the Cotswolds.

Readers' comments: Exceptionally friendly and welcoming. Very peaceful. Attractive and comfortable rooms. Most hospitable and helpful.

Prices are the minimum *per person* in a double room at the beginning of the year.

192

THE NODES   C D H PT S

**Alum Bay Old Road, Old Totland, south-west of Yarmouth,
Isle of Wight, PO39 0HZ**   Tel: 0983 752859

11 bedrooms (single, double or family) from
£14. Less for 7 nights or bargain breaks.

Rooms have central heating; shower or bathroom; TV on request, armchairs; views of
sea, country or garden; tea/coffee facilities.
Dinner £6.50 for 4 courses (with choices)
and coffee, at 6.30–7pm. Vegetarian or
special diets if ordered. Lunches, packed
lunches, snacks. Coffee, tea, for a charge.
Drinks can be ordered.
2 sitting-rooms with central heating, open
fire, TV, books, indoor games (including
table tennis, darts), piano; bar.
Large garden with golf practice, putting-
green and badminton.
Nearest main road A3054 from Yarmouth
to Freshwater.

At the far west end of the island (with spectacular marine sunsets to enjoy after
dinner) is a handsome mid-Victorian mansion standing in its own grounds: it is
now a small hotel run by Kevin Harris, very suitable for family holidays.

Some of the bedrooms are in the original part of the house; while others (more
modern and compact; each with its own front door) line a courtyard at the back.
The one in the house that particularly appealed to me was the blue room, which
has a magnificent sea-captain's bed and a view of the Solent. The dining-room is
rustic in style: Italian pine and rush chairs, pink candles on chocolate or pink
tablecloths; I thought the decor elsewhere less harmonious.

There are a number of choices at dinner – one might select, for example,
fisherman's pie, roast beef and hazelnut meringue. There is a long wine list.

The foothills of Tennyson Downs extend into the grounds (which include
lawns, a play area for children and a golf practice-net).

This end of the island and its superb coastline are unspoilt (much of it is
controlled by the National Trust): an area of pretty little villages, lanes and
country inns; with sandy beaches ideal for children. Visitors particularly enjoy the
Tennyson trail, Alum Bay, the Needles, Blackgang Chine and (further east)
Osborne House and Carisbrooke Castle.

Between the island and the mainland is the Solent where there is always a busy
scene of small sailing boats and of big ships making for Southampton.

Readers' comments: Thoroughly enjoyed our stay; staff always smiling; Kevin
made us all feel like one big happy family. Peace and tranquillity. Thoroughly
enjoyed it; food excellent; staff could not do enough for us.

Also at this end of the island, and within two minutes of sand and sea, is
Rockstone Cottage, Colwell Bay,
which Sheila Reason runs as an immaculate and comfortable guest-house
with good home cooking. (Tel:
0983 753723.)

Readers' comments: Very good value.

NORTH COURT

C PT S S-C

Shorwell, south-west of Newport, Isle of Wight, PO30 3JG
Tel: 0983 740415

3 bedrooms (double or family) from £10. Less for 3 nights and bargain breaks. Rooms have own bath; tea/coffee facilities; central heating; views of stream, country or garden. No smoking. (Washing-machine on request.)
Sitting-room with central heating, open fire, TV, books, piano.
Large garden
Nearest main road A3055 from Totland to Ventnor.
Closed mid-December–mid-January

Swinburne and his girl cousin used to play the organ that stands in the hall of this great 17th-century manor house – a big stone-flagged room with pale blue walls, logs piled high around the stove.

The house is now the home of John and Christine Harrison, portraits of whose ancestors hang on the walls of the large dining-room with mahogany tables and marble fireplace. The great staircase was reputedly designed by Grinling Gibbons, and nearly every room has handsome detailing from that period – arched or scallop-framed doorways, egg-and-dart mouldings, shuttered windows in thick stone walls. At the top of the house is an attic suite (and games room), very suitable for family use; but the prettiest bedroom is perhaps the blue-and-white one with bay window overlooking the tennis court.

Impressive though the house is, the really outstanding feature is the large and undulating garden with many plants of botanical interest. You can wander through woodlands or down terraces to a stream with water-plants, try to tell the time from a sundial in the knot garden, look down into the ancient bath-house, wander through arches of wisteria or lilac . . . As only breakfast is served, dinner for most people always involves a stroll through this lovely garden (opened to the public occasionally) to reach the nearby Crown Inn.

The island's coastline, its inland scenery and pretty villages appealed to the Victorians' love of the picturesque, and it was they who established it as an ideal holiday destination. Some feel that this has now ruined parts of the coast but, in a village such as this, one is well away from the summer crowds and yet so central that every part is within easy reach. Small though the island is, the scenery is extraordinarily varied – and at its best in spring or autumn, when visitors are few. You could stay a month and every day find a different 'sight' to visit, as varied as Carisbrooke Castle or Osborne House on the one hand and the ferny chines (ravines) or wildlife reserves on the other. Some of the least famous places are the most attractive – unspoilt villages such as Calbourne, Mottistone, Yaverland and Kingston, for instance.

When writing to me, if you want a reply please enclose a stamped addressed envelope.

NORTHLANDS FARMHOUSE
**Ketches Lane, Sheffield Park, east of Haywards Heath,
East Sussex, TN22 3RX**   Tel: 0825 790958

3 bedrooms (single, double or family) from £16. Less for 7 nights and bargain breaks. All have own bath/shower; tea/coffee facilities; central heating. No smoking.
2 sitting-rooms with central heating, TV, books.
Large garden and paddocks.
Nearest main road A275 from Lewes to the A22.

This is a low-beamed 16th-century house typically Sussex in style (tile-hung walls and roses round the door) surrounded by ancient barns, in an area of outstanding natural beauty.

Pat Frank has furnished it very attractively – for instance, oak chairs have rosy tapestry seats, there are violet-patterned curtains in one room, another has a blue and green colour scheme against which pine beds show well. Where breakfast is served depends on the weather: it may be on the terrace outside, in a sun-room with bamboo and glass tables, or cosily by an inglenook fireplace in the dining-room.

For dinner most visitors go to local inns. One, the Piltdown Man, gets its name from the famous hoax of 1912, the alleged discovery nearby of a 150,000-year-old skull: the fraud was not unmasked until forty years later. In this part of Sussex there are a great many gardens to visit, most notably Borde Hill, Leonardslee (best in spring), Nymans (NT) and Sheffield Park (NT), which has five big lakes linked by cascades – near this is the Bluebell Line steam railway which goes to the Tudor village of Horsted Keynes. There are castles and stately homes, too. The wooded ridge to the north is a remnant of the once huge Forest of Anderida, part of the Weald. It became denuded of oaks by the 17th century because these were felled to supply the furnaces of the Sussex iron-smelters. Many ponds were created at this time, the dammed waters being used to drive hammers in their forges. A number of rivers rise in these woods and then make their way south to the sea. The most extensive remnant of Anderida is Ashdown Forest where there is a mixture of woods, heath, moor and rocky outcrops: a varied area well worth exploring (a number of footpaths or drives start out from Wych Cross and Forest Row). In the other direction is West Hoathly, once populated by the iron-workers – and by smugglers. At Ardingly is a National Trust mansion, Wakehurst Place, with gardens under the control of Kew. Much of Cuckfield is still as it was in the 13th century, and one of the region's beautifully naturalized reservoirs is at Weir Wood, perfect setting for a picnic. The whole area is a good one for antique-hunting.

For explanation of code letters (**C, D, H, PT, S, S-C, X**) see page xxvi

195

NORTHLEIGH HOUSE C
Fiveways Road, Hatton, north-west of Warwick, CV35 7HZ
Tel: 092687 203

5 bedrooms (single, double or family) from £16. All have own bath/shower; TV; tea/coffee facilities; central heating; views of country or garden. No smoking. (Washing-machine on request.)
Dinner £12 for 3 courses (with choices) and coffee, by arrangement. Non-residents not admitted. Vegetarian or special diets if ordered. Snacks. Tea, coffee, free. Drinks can be brought in.
Sitting-room with central heating and books.
Small garden
Nearest main road A41 from Warwick to Solihull.

A former dress designer, Sylvia Fenwick – a vivacious personality – has turned her creative talents to decorating every bedroom with elegance – each is different, each memorable, and many verge on the luxurious (for instance, double rooms have two washbasins). They are all very well equipped and heated.

The L-shaped blue suite (with kitchenette in cupboard) has a sofa, bamboo tables and a carved bed in a silk-curtained alcove. There's a huge poppy room, also with bamboo furniture, in which the pale green wicker-patterned wallpaper is matched by the carpet. Another room, Victorian and frilly in style, has a cocoa-and-white colour scheme; while yet another (the least expensive) is in Chinese style. On two sides of the big sitting-room are garden views; the room has comfortable furniture, pleasant colours and an ornate little wood-burner.

Sylvia serves supper trays, or dinners (by arrangement) at which you might get something like avocado salad, pork chops in a sauce of mustard, sugar and almonds – served with five vegetables; and a rich strawberry trifle ('I go mad with the cream!'). But she also provides guests with a map showing a dozen local inns that do good food. Because she keeps rare breeds of sheep and poultry, her own produce sometimes features in these meals.

Rural quiet surrounds the house – and yet it is only a few miles from Birmingham's National Exhibition Centre and international airport; the National Agricultural Centre; and the bustling towns of Warwick and Coventry.

Readers of Edith Holden's *Country Diary of an Edwardian Lady* will be familiar with a number of place-names around here. Knowle, a historic village on a hill, with half-timbered houses. Packwood House (N.T.) which has a lovely garden, conical yews representing Christ and the disciples (and fine furniture inside): Edith did many sketches here. Mediaeval Baddesley Clinton is moated.

Readers' comments: Very superior, one of the best I have found, bedrooms spacious and breakfasts excellent.

OLD BAKEHOUSE

33–35 High Street, Little Walsingham, north of Fakenham, Norfolk,
NR22 6BZ   Tel: 0328 820454

3 bedrooms (double) from £14.50. Less for bargain breaks. All have tea/coffee facilities; central heating; one with shower.
Dinner A la carte or £10 for 3 courses and coffee, at 7pm. Vegetarian or special diets if ordered. Drinks can be ordered.
Nearest main road A148 from Cromer to King's Lynn.
Closed in January

Above a restaurant renowned for good food are excellent bedrooms, some very secluded at the back (with views of a paved garden and ancient cottages that have higgledy-piggledy pantiled roofs and flint walls).

From 1550 until recent times, part of this house was a bakery and the old ovens are still to be seen. Above an ancient cellar bar is a large, lofty dining-room – in the 18th century it was a corn exchange. There is a great brick fireplace at one end, and huge iron-hinged doors. When Chris and Helen Padley took over, they painted the walls pale pink and furnished the room with pine and rush furniture. Here they serve such delectable table d'hôte meals as fresh peaches baked with cheese and herbs (for a starter), banana-stuffed chicken with a mild curry-and-almond sauce, and ice-cream coffee-cake; with a wider à la carte choice too.

The bedrooms are very pleasantly furnished in pale colours such as mushroom and beige, with pine furniture, flowery or William Morris fabrics and wallpapers, pot-plants, bowls of pot-pourri and festoon blinds in some; excellent bathrooms.

Little Walsingham is full of mediaeval charm: few villages are so well preserved. It was a pilgrims' shrine before the Norman Conquest – and still is (both Catholics and Protestants come here). Really big pilgrimages fill the village three times a year, but at other times it is peaceful. Walsingham Abbey's riverside grounds are open at certain times, there is an ancient Franciscan friary, a museum of bygones, and a light railway which children enjoy. The sea shore is near, and also a great many stately homes and impressive churches for which Norfolk is famous. Chris Padley is an enthusiastic birdwatcher and this is an area of outstanding interest for its birds.

Readers' comments: Gourmet food; friendly and efficient.

Some hotels and even farms offer special Christmas holidays; but, unless otherwise indicated (by the code letter **X** at top of entry), those in this book will then be closed.

OLD BAKERY

C(12) **D S**

Milton Abbas, south-west of Blandford Forum, Dorset, DT11 0BW
Tel: 0258 880327

5 bedrooms (single or double) from £10. Less for 7 nights and bargain breaks. Some have own bath/shower; tea/coffee facilities; central heating; views of country or garden.
2 sitting-rooms with central heating, open fire, TV, books, piano.
Large garden (also woods and fields).
Nearest main road A354 from Blandford to Dorchester.

Milton Abbas looks almost too good to be true, as if it had been created specially for a picture on a chocolate-box. Indeed, it is a special creation; for in the 18th century it was laid out as a 'model village' when the Earl of Dorchester razed a nearby mediaeval settlement to build himself a mansion (Milton Abbey) and resited its inhabitants here. The broad village street, grass-verged, slopes steeply down, lined all the way with trim white-and-thatch cottages.

One of these is the Old Bakery: the huge ovens are still there, in a vast sitting-room where guests now relax. Margaret Penny has a decorative touch, so all the bedrooms (and even the toilet) are attractive. There are small but pretty single rooms – pink and lacy. She has found interesting wallpapers – poppies for one room, wildflowers in another, navy-and-white for a third – to complement twirly cane bedheads, board doors, neat pine cupboards within which basin and shower are concealed in one room, and the antiques that feature in every room. Behind the house are woods, pasture and stables for visitors who bring horses – this is a great area for riding and walking. There is an inn nearby for evening meals.

Some of Milton Abbey (now a school) can be visited, notably the huge chapel and its striking monuments: part of a 15th-century church of cathedral-like proportions which the Earl retained when he demolished most of the original monastery to make his great house. The Abbey is celebrated for its music weeks. The countryside all round is wholly unspoilt and tranquil, part of Hardy's Wessex: nearby Dorchester was his 'Casterbridge'. There are great contrasts, for in only a few miles one can find wild heaths, lonely hills, sea, and lush valleys.

Across the pretty Piddle Valley, is Cerne Abbas and, in Duck Street, **Sound o' Water** (tel: 030 03435), a former inn which Jean and Doug Simmonds have modernized to provide a comfortable guest-house. Some rooms are in an annexe opening onto a pretty garden that wanders down to the winding River Cerne. B & b only; all Cerne's inns do good food. Cerne is a lovely village with the famous giant on its hillside.

OLD COURT

Newent, north-west of Gloucester, GL18 1AB   Tel: 0531 820522

4 bedrooms (single, double or family) from £12.50. Less for 2 nights or bargain breaks. Rooms have central heating, electric heaters; shower or bathroom; TV, armchairs; views of garden; tea/coffee facilities.
Dinner £9 for 3 courses and coffee or à la carte, from 7pm (not on Sundays). Veg-etarian or special diets if ordered. Lunches, packed lunches, snacks. Coffee, tea, for a charge. Drinks can be ordered.
Sitting-room with central heating, open fire, books.
Large garden
Nearest main road M50 (junction 3).

A high wall and big garden give this handsome William-and-Mary house seclusion. One steps straight into a particularly fine hall – coral walls, white arches and a big chandelier, with the sun and moon revolving above the face of a grandfather clock which warns 'Time is Valuable'.

In the elegant dining-room, panelled in soft greens and with alcoves, a pretty skirted lamp hangs above the tables laid with Copenhagen china, heavy silver and crystal. Margaret Reece serves interesting, very English food: things like artichoke soup, pheasant casserole (with four vegetables, which may include such unusual combinations as sprouts and mushrooms braised together with mustard seed), and a raspberry soufflé, followed by cheeses. Much garden produce.

Architecturally, the sitting-room is outstanding. One end is curved; there are fluted pillars, prettily arched windows, and the plaster garlands on the ceiling have been picked out in soft colours. Margaret chose an acanthus wallpaper and velvet-covered Victorian sofas to complement this; and in the carved pine fireplace logs crackle on chilly evenings.

I particularly admired one of the bedrooms, the lofty walls of which are covered in a butterfly wallpaper. It has windows on two sides, velvet bedheads, armchairs and tables with crochet covers and a big indigo bathroom which is luxuriously carpeted.

Old Newent (only 5 minutes from the M50) is at its best when spring brings out the thousands of daffodils. It is close to the Forest of Dean (20 million oak, beech and other trees) where sheep graze and ancient rights allow miners and quarrymen to take coal and stone free. Drives and walks take you into the heart of the forest. Newent has a world-famous falconry centre where you can see flying displays, the young in their nests and lovely gardens. Within easy reach are the Wye Valley, Cheltenham, Bath, Malvern, the Cotswolds and the many beauty-spots in Wales.

Readers' comments: Excellent. Wonderful bedroom. A special and refined atmos-phere but relaxed. Lovely house, excellent dinner. Very nice atmosphere, well presented menu.

OLD FARMHOUSE

C D

Raskelf, north of York, YO6 3LF   Tel: 0347 21971

10 bedrooms (single or double) from £17. Less for 4 nights and bargain breaks. All have own bath or shower, and central heating.
Dinner £10 for 4 courses (with choices) and coffee, at 7–7.45pm. Vegetarian or special diets if ordered. Packed lunches. Tea, coffee, free on arrival. Drinks can be ordered.

2 sitting-rooms with central heating, open fire, TV, books.
Small garden
Nearest main road A19 from York to Thirsk.

Bill and Jenny Frost have established a reputation for very good food at their 18th-century guest-house, which has immaculate accommodation and decorative touches like a bouquet of silk flowers in the brick hearth whenever a log fire is not burning; a four-poster in one of the bedrooms; and, for sybarites, a particularly luxurious bathroom adjoining another.

But it is the outstanding dinners which bring most visitors here (for which reason advance bookings for bed-and-breakfast only are not usually accepted). At every course there are several choices, from which one might select (for example) deep-fried Camembert with cranberry compote as a starter; quail en croûte with gooseberry jelly; home-made coffee and Tia Maria ice cream; and finally the most interesting selection of a dozen English cheeses I have come across for some time, ranging from yarg (mild and low-fat, wrapped in edible nettle-leaves) to potted Stilton (buttery and port-laden); blue Wensleydale to snow-white Ribblesdale. Bread and preserves are home-made; local produce used wherever possible.

Nearby are the Hambleton Hills – splendid touring or walking country. It is a good base from which to explore both the North York Moors and the scenic coastline. York, Harrogate, the Dales, many stately homes and several spectacular abbey ruins (such as Rievaulx) are all within a comfortable drive, as are James Herriot's house, the Hambleton white horse, Newborough Priory, Beningbrough Hall and the 'mouse-man' workshops for oak furniture. Easingwold is a good hunting-ground for antiques.

A lovely but little-known part of the county, the Yorkshire Wolds merit exploration: gentle hills, Hornsea mere, fine churches, mediaeval Beverley and an outstanding coastline beyond.

Readers' comments: Wholehearted recommendation. High standard. Excellent and varied food, very amiable and faultless service. Spotless and comfortable accommodation. Quite outstanding. Our favourite: so friendly, and food is first class. Will go again.

OLD FARMHOUSE HOTEL   C D H

Lower Swell, west of Stow-on-the-Wold, Gloucestershire, GL54 1LF
Tel: 0451 30232

13 bedrooms (double or family) from £18.50. £25.75 with dinner. Less for 2 nights. Very good bargain breaks. Rooms have central heating; shower or bathroom; TV, armchairs; views of country or garden; tea/coffee facilities.

Dinner £11.25 for 3 courses (with choices), at 7–9pm. Vegetarian or special diets if ordered. Lunches, packed lunches. Drinks can be ordered. No smoking.

Sitting-room with central heating, open fire, books; bar.

Large garden

Nearest main road A429 from Cirencester to Stratford-upon-Avon.

Closed Christmas and January

A typical Cotswold stone house, dating from the 16th century, this small hotel lies in a pleasant valley right in the middle of England's most popular tourist sights – Stratford, Oxford and Cheltenham. Nearby runs the little River Dickler – its waters help to give the local Donnington ale its reputation, and they serve the Donnington Trout Farm too.

There is a series of pleasant downstairs rooms running into one another – from bar at one end to dining-room at the other, some with stone walls, one with old panelling. Here, as in the bedrooms, restful shades of pink, green or apricot predominate.

There is a particularly good pair of family rooms under the eaves, which children love; and two bedrooms with four-posters (in one, apricot moiré silk and, in the other, aquamarine clothe the bed). Most rooms are spacious and light, one of them with view of the stone-walled, sheltered garden – a lawn surrounded by roses. Some are in the former stables behind the house, together with a big sitting-room.

Eric Burger sets high standards in the kitchen: vegetables are not only fresh but freshly cooked for each customer, to accompany such dishes as whole poussins served with a creamy pepper sauce; pork fillet with apricots, brandy and cream; or venison simmered in wine and juniper berries.

Walking or motoring in the Cotswolds is a pleasure in itself, but there are many other things to do too – the Roman villa at Chedworth, Sudeley Castle, the Cotswold Wildlife Park, horse-racing, shopping for antiques or country clothes, visiting gardens such as those at Hidcote, Kiftsgate or Batsford (it has a Japanese-style arboretum) or the many stately homes and even statelier churches for which this county is famous.

Stow itself merits exploration: it's a little town of antique and craft shops, restaurants and byways – one of many picturesque villages. And there are plenty of places at which to buy farm produce.

OLD GRANARY

PT

The Quay, Wareham, Dorset, BH20 4LP   Tel: 0929 552010

4 bedrooms (double) from £17. Rooms have central heating; bathrooms (some); TV, phone, armchairs; views of river or country; tea/coffee facilities.
Dinner £11 or à la carte, from 6.30–9pm. Special diets if ordered. Lunches, packed lunches, snacks. Coffee, tea, for a charge. Drinks can be ordered.
Sitting-room with bar and open fire.
Riverside terrace
Nearest main road A351 from Poole to Swanage.

Standing right on the quay by the River Frome, this 18th-century brick building was once a warehouse for grain that went by barge to Poole, and it still has much of its old character.

Derek and Rose-Marie Sturton run a restaurant on two floors, with good food served on flowery china in two dining-rooms furnished with cane chairs and attractive colours.

A typical meal might comprise, for instance, haddock Mornay, duckling, and raspberry mousse. There is a riverside terrace with seats, for cream teas and drinks (the terrace is lit up at night), and a bar with open fire. Upstairs are two floors with pretty, beamed bedrooms, their windows giving a view of the river, swans and the Purbeck Hills beyond. The local landscapes on their walls are for sale.

Wareham is a most interesting old town, encircled by great earth banks built by the Saxons to fortify their village against Viking raids. The roads within this were laid out, Roman-style, on a grid. St Martin's church is Saxon and contains, rather oddly, a memorial to Lawrence of Arabia (whose home at Clouds Hill is open to the public).

Wareham is a great mixture of history and of architectural styles. One of its noblest buildings, the Priory, is now a particularly lovely hotel – too expensive for this book, alas, but people staying at the Old Granary could at least enjoy its lovely Tudor rooms and waterside garden for the price of a first-rate meal or even tea on the stone terrace, surrounded by roses.

All around this area are marvellous places to visit – the following is merely a selection. Poole Harbour, the second largest and loveliest natural harbour in the world, the Blue Pool, Corfe Castle, Lulworth Cove, the Purbeck Hills; Arne – heathland nature reserve; Swanage, old-fashioned resort with sandy bay and architectural curiosities salvaged from London; Durlston Head – cliffs, birds, country park, lighthouse; Studland's beaches with Shell Bay beyond; Wool and Bere Regis (with Thomas Hardy associations); Bindon Abbey; the army Tank Museum at Bovington; Bournemouth, Compton Acres gardens, and any number of pretty villages down winding lanes.

Readers' comments: Superb in every respect; a real find; haven't words to describe food, room and attention to detail; absolutely professional but very personal; welcoming and friendly, spotlessly clean, excellent food. Lovely situation, a personal touch. Food superb. Pretty bedrooms, high quality food. Unique place, very comfortable. Wonderful! Exceptionally friendly and welcoming. Very pretty dining-rooms.

OLD JORDANS

C H X

Jordans, east of Beaconsfield, Buckinghamshire, HP9 2SW   Tel: 02407 4586

30 bedrooms (single, double or family) from £18. Less for 7 nights and bargain breaks. Rooms have central heating; armchairs; views of country or garden. Tea facilities. **Dinner** £6.50 for 3 courses and coffee, at 7pm. Special diets if ordered. Lunches, packed lunches, teas.

4 sitting-rooms with central heating, electric fire, TV, books.
Garden Orchards and fields.
Nearest main road A40 from London to High Wycombe.

A place of beehives and belfry, granary and lily-pool, flagstoned paths bordered by lavender and honeysuckle clambering over old walls. The house was a farm when Elizabeth I was on the throne, and a deed of purchase, 'signed' by thumbprints and dated 1618, hangs in one of the rooms. A brick-floored kitchen added in 1624 is now a dining-room, with Windsor chairs and elm tables, chintz curtains and a big inglenook with James I fireback and built-in bread oven.

The farm became a meeting-place for Quakers (including Fox and Penn), though many were arrested for gathering here; Penn's grave is at the 17th-century Quaker meeting-house just beyond the orchard. In 1910 the almost derelict farm was bought by the Quakers, repaired and turned into a guest-house.

Its Mayflower barn (built from the timbers of the historic *Mayflower* that carried the Pilgrim Fathers to America) is used for art exhibitions, concerts and so forth.

All told, this is a most unusual guest-house, open to all as a 'well from which to draw waters of peace'. Inside the house, winding corridors lead to simple but comfortable bedrooms and prettily decorated bathrooms. Board doors have wrought-iron latches and decorative hinges, each slightly different in design. Old furniture, pictures and other details in the sitting-rooms are all in character. Some carvings are from the *Mayflower*. It is run by a warden, Carole Hamer.

Meals are plain and wholesome: home-made soup, a roast or stew, gooseberry flan or pears in wine might be on the menu, followed by good coffee.

The neighbourhood is very interesting with beautiful scenery (typical of the chalk Chilterns, with beech woods on the hills, far views, and wooded valleys with tumbling streams). The village of Penn has a Norman church with the tomb of William Penn's grandchildren. Milton's cottage is at Chalfont St Giles, as is the Chiltern Open Air Museum, where ancient buildings (some 500 years old) have been saved from destruction and re-erected to provide a view of life in the Chilterns from past centuries. The area has innumerable antique and craft shops. Windsor is near, and London and Heathrow are soon reached.

Readers' comments: Have stayed many times, very pleased with standards and friendly service. Quite wonderful.

OLD MANOR FARMHOUSE

Norton Fitzwarren, north-west of Taunton, Somerset, TA2 6RZ
Tel: 0823 289801

7 bedrooms (double) from £18. Less for bargain breaks. Rooms have central heating; shower, or bathroom; TV, phone; tea/coffee facilities.
Dinner 3 courses from £9, at 7pm. Special diets if ordered. Drinks can be ordered.
Sitting-room with central heating, books; bar.
Kitchen garden and orchard.
Nearest main road A361 from Taunton to South Molton.

This building is neither old nor a manor; and the farmlands passed into other hands long ago. Now it is a small hotel run by Eric and Vera Foley. I found a comfortable bedroom, well-prepared food, everything very spick-and-span.

Norton Fitzwarren is not in itself a very interesting village (although there is a cider factory which can be visited), but it is close to Taunton, a historic town of such interest (once you get away from the hustle of the main streets) that it is an excellent stopover on the way to the far West Country.

At breakfast as well as dinner there is much emphasis on wholefood, with a wide range of imaginative vegetarian dishes (as well as meat) – such as pear with tarragon cream, cashew paella and home-made damson ice cream; but steaks, lamb and venison are available too. There is an excellent selection of very good value wines.

The River Tone winds through Taunton and there are attractive riverside paths. The historic heart of the town lies around the castle remains (with excellent county museum inside). There are two notable churches and, after walking along pedestrianized shopping streets, one can wander through a particularly fine park which was where monks once had their fish-ponds.

The surrounding countryside is not only beautiful but varied: the Quantock Hills are gently rolling and well wooded, with small villages (Combe Florey, for instance, which is as pretty as its name suggests) and sparkling streams. Red sandstone is used for many buildings here. Eastwards are the limestone Mendips – far more gaunt, with gorges and crags. The Vale of Taunton Deane is a fertile land, with apple orchards supplying the cider-makers. The sea is within easy motoring distance, and the little port of Watchet. There is fen country too; and Exmoor is quite close. As well as scenery, there are a number of stately homes in the area; numerous country shows and festivals; and excellent walks, easy or strenuous. Particularly attractive gardens surround Hestercombe House, Killerton and Barrington Court; more are in Taunton's Vivary Park. Not only are there antique shops but a Monday antiques 'fair'.

Readers' comments: Pleasant, good food, good value. Very pleasant; very good food. Very comfortable, well looked after. Excellent fresh vegetables.

All prices are inclusive of any VAT or service charge. They are minimum prices: superior rooms or high-season bookings may cost more.

OLD MILL
Little Petherick, south of Padstow, Cornwall, PL27 7QT   Tel: 0841 540388

7 bedrooms (double) from £14.50. Less for 7 nights and bargain breaks. Some have own bath/shower; tea/coffee facilities; central heating; views of river or country. (Washing-machine on request.)
Dinner £6.50 for 3 courses and coffee, at 7pm. Vegetarian or special diets if ordered. Drinks can be ordered.
2 sitting-rooms with central heating, TV.
Small garden
Nearest main road A389 from Padstow to the A39.

This picturesque 16th-century watermill is beside a stream that winds its way into the Camel estuary, along a coastline celebrated for its many beautiful beaches (a number of them are protected by the National Trust).

Michael and Pat Walker have furnished the Mill very attractively. The beamy sitting-room has white stone walls, one with a mural of ploughing. William Morris sofas and Berber carpet contrast with the green slate of the floor. All around are unusual 'finds': an ancient typewriter and sewing-machines, clocks, and old tools such as planes and picks. The paved terrace by the stream is enclosed by suntrapping walls. Bedrooms are homely (very nice bathrooms); quiet ones at back.

For dinner, at tables covered with homespun cloths, you may be offered such choices as chicken in a Stilton-and-pineapple sauce or lamb with ginger and orange; or there is a more conventional table d'hôte available.

Little Petherick is a pretty village with (just across the road from the Mill) a beautiful church; close to Padstow which is still agreeably antiquated. Narrow, crooked lanes lead down to Padstow's harbour, a pretty group of houses encircles the quay, and there are several outstanding buildings including the Court House where Sir Walter Raleigh dealt out judgments when he was Warden of Cornwall. The world-famous Hobby Horse street dance takes place on May Day here. There are idyllic, golden beaches around here (go to Treyarnon to see surfing). Near St Columb Major (impressive church) is an Iron Age fort called Castle an Dinas; St Mawgan is a pretty village in a woodland valley while, by contrast, St Wenn is a wild and windy moorland spot; by the lighthouse on Trevose Head you can see the whole coast from St Ives to Lundy Island.

On the whole, north Cornwall is far less touristy than the south, its greatest attractions being scenery (not only coastal but inland too) with fewer commercial entertainments, sights, etc.

Readers' comments: Beautifully furnished. Could not be more pleasant and helpful.

Some readers tell me they have stayed at lots of places from *Staying Off the Beaten Track*. I wonder who has stayed at most? A free copy of the next edition awaits the reader who sends me his/her comments on the greatest number!

OLD MILL HOTEL
Town Path, West Harnham, Salisbury, Wiltshire, SP2 8EU
Tel: 0722 27517

7 bedrooms (single, double or family) from £16.50. Less for 7 nights. Rooms have electric heaters; views of river and garden; tea/coffee facilities. One has a shower.
Dinner £10 for 3 courses and coffee, from 7–10pm. Lunches, teas and snacks in summer; special diets and packed lunches to order.

Bar and TV room.
Nearest main road A3094 from Salisbury to Wilton.
Closed December–March (except for restaurant).

It was by this ancient watermill that John Constable painted his famous view of Salisbury Cathedral seen across the water-meadows, and little has changed since then. The mill dates back to the 12th century, and was used to house the church records while the cathedral was being built. It is now a hotel run by Jerry Such. The bedrooms are simply furnished but some are pretty, with William Morris wallpaper and river views.

The meals served in the much better furnished restaurant (in the oldest part) are traditionally English: kidneys, pheasant, braised rabbit and so forth (cooked by Steve Jackman). This is an unpretentious place to stay, in an idyllic setting and well placed for touring. The hotel can arrange day-permits for trout or coarse fishing, and squash.

In addition to Salisbury's ancient streets and cathedral, and the historic site of Old Sarum, there are such outstanding places of interest as Wilton House, Stonehenge, Salisbury Plain (wide open spaces, changing skies and mossy villages), Marlborough and its downs, innumerable prehistoric sites, old Amesbury (where Queen Guinevere is said to have been buried), Devizes with its noble market square and Norman church, Shaftesbury (abbey and cobble lanes) and, of course, the coast with Bournemouth and its sandy beaches. Weyhill Hawk Conservancy and Broadlands (Mountbatten's house) are very popular and there are at least eight fine gardens to visit. Breamore is a Tudor mansion; and picturesque villages, a Roman villa at Rockbourne and the New Forest are not far away.

Readers' comments: Our room was enormous and comfortable (but suffered noise from the bar below); very pretty surroundings; delicious meals. Accommodation and food excellent. Very welcoming – great service. Most obliging. Idyllic!

> Prices are the minimum *per person* in a double room at the beginning of the year.

OLD PARSONAGE FARMHOUSE   D

Hanley Castle, south-east of Malvern, Worcestershire, WR8 0BU
Tel: 0684 310124

rear view

3 bedrooms (double or family) from £17. Less for 7 nights. All have own bath; central heating; views of country or garden. No smoking. (Washing-machine on request.) **Dinner** £12.50 for 4 courses (with choices) and coffee, from 7pm. Vegetarian or special diets if ordered. Tea, coffee, free. Drinks can be ordered.

2 sitting-rooms with central heating, open fire, TV, books, record-player; bar.
Large garden
Nearest main road A38 from Worcester to Tewkesbury.
Closed mid-December–mid-January

It is not just the surrounding views of the Malvern Hills or the handsome 18th-century house of mellow brick which makes this worth seeking out: Ann Addison has a flair for both cookery and interior decoration, while Tony is a wine expert. He runs wine-tastings in the one-time cider mill adjoining the house.

You enter the house via a vaulted entrance-hall (with Edwardian fireplace), then through double doors into the sandalwood sitting-room with its small library and television. On the right is the elegant, pale sea-green drawing-room with its arched Georgian windows and marble Adam fireplace. To the left is the sunflower-yellow dining-room which has the original brick hearth and bread oven.

Damask cloths and Rorstrand china from Sweden create an appropriate setting for the kind of meals Ann serves, such as mushrooms and herbs in puff pastry, chicken breasts with prawns in a cream and brandy sauce, bramble mousse, cheeses.

Upstairs are elegant bedrooms (for instance, one has waterlily fabrics complemented by daffodil walls, another has a vast bathroom with oval chocolate bath).

Readers' comments: Very impressed. Warm and friendly welcome, helpful and charming. Extremely comfortable. High standard of imaginative food.

The road from Hanley leads to Malvern Wells and the **Old Vicarage** (tel: 06845 2585), a handsome Victorian villa. Pointed arches and cruciform detailing are reminders of its original purpose, but now there are pale flowery curtains at the stone-mullioned windows, with duvets to match. The L-shaped sitting-room overlooks lawn and sweeping cedar trees. Michael and Maureen Gorvin serve such meals as seafood vol-au-vent, tarragon chicken and fresh strawberry flan.

rear view

Readers' comments: Extremely welcome; standard of cuisine very high; strongly recommended. Lovely people and house, an appealing atmosphere.

OLD PLACE

Cuckfield Road, Ansty, west of Haywards Heath, West Sussex, RH17 5AG
Tel: 0444 451464

2 bedrooms (double and family) from £15. Rooms have own shower (one); TV; tea/coffee facilities; phone; central heating; views of country or garden. No smoking. (Washing-machine on request.)
Sitting-room with central heating, wood burners, TV, books. No smoking.
Large garden
Nearest main road A23 from Brighton to Crawley.

A long track between banks of wildflowers leads to this half-timbered and tile-hung house, built in the year when Richard III was slain at the Battle of Bosworth.

When the Newmans were renovating it, they discovered that an old brick outhouse had been the original toilet – very sociable, for it was complete with a three-holed bench! Upstairs and down are shapely Tudor fireplaces of stone, and over a large brick inglenook the original spit-rests still remain. Stairs are winding, oak doors have ancient latches, there is a 60-foot well.

From the windows are views of wooded hills and lawns (there is a swimming-pool, too), to be enjoyed from the sitting-room or from the bedrooms, the biggest of which has windows on three sides and a beamed ceiling. For the dining-room curtains and seats, Selina Newman chose a particularly attractive William Morris fabric in blue to complement the huge refectory table and chairs specially made for the house from the old oak timbers of Lewes Theatre (now demolished). On many of the walls are watercolours by a well-known artist and playwright, James Forsyth, who lives in the next house.

Breakfast only; for dinner, visitors go to nearby Cuckfield, a steep mediaeval village, where there is plenty of choice. Look for the cuckoo on the village sign, which is what gave the place its name – pronounced 'Cookfield' – and for the noble church which is worth a visit.

This is a good area for antique shops and for visiting outstanding gardens (such as Borde Hill, Sheffield Park, Nymans, Wakehurst and Leonardslee – all within a few miles). In Roman times the great forest of Anderida stretched for over a hundred miles along the Wealden ridge of north Sussex and traces still remain. Most of the oaks were, however, burnt in the furnaces of the Sussex ironmasters during the 17th century: the furnace ponds you discover here and there were created by them (they dammed streams to provide power for the hammers that forged their iron). How rich those ironmasters grew can be guessed from nearby Ockenden Manor, for example, the house of one of them. The largest surviving tract is Ashdown Forest where woods (much devastated in the hurricane of 1987) alternate with stretches of heath. There is a network of lanes and paths to explore, by car or on foot, between here and East Grinstead. The lane from Balcombe to Ardingly is especially pretty: all curves, rising and falling, with willow-fringed duckpond along the way. Go to Turners Hill or Handcross for superb views. Westward is St Leonards Forest, with tales of smugglers and highwaymen; drifts of lilies-of-the-valley; and the high village of Colgate. Brighton is only 20 minutes away.

OLD RECTORY   C
Byford, west of Hereford, HR4 7LD   Tel: 098122 218

3 bedrooms (double or family) from £12. Less for 3 nights. Rooms have shower (some); TV; central heating; views of river, country or garden. No smoking (Washing-machine on request.)
Sitting-room with central heating, TV, books. No smoking.
Large garden
Nearest main road A438 from Hereford to Brecon.
Closed December–March

An enormous cedar of Lebanon dominates the garden outside the Rectory, a handsome brick house which, though built in 1830, is Georgian in style – having big, well-proportioned rooms and great sash windows which make the most of the very fine views of hills and church. Audrey Mayson and her husband have put a great deal of loving care not only into the restoration of the big house but also the landscaping of the formerly neglected garden.

Themselves parents of a growing family, the Maysons welcome children and therefore run the house in an informal, caring way: comfortable and spacious, a place in which to relax completely.

The sitting/dining-room has pale green walls, deep pine-shuttered windows and pine-panelled doors, and their collection of unusual Escher pictures. There is a big family bedroom with sofa, and good views.

Audrey does not cook evening meals, unless specially arranged, so most visitors go either to the local Portway Inn or to one of the many restaurants in Weobley – six miles away.

Byford is on the way to Wales, but there are many reasons to pause here for more than a stopover. Nearby are Hereford and its cathedral, Hay-on-Wye for its multitude of bookshops, the hills of the Brecon Beacons (a National Park), picturesque black-and-white villages, the lovely River Wye with footpaths along-side it, innumerable churches and castles.

Because Monica Barker previously lived in India, **Appletree Cottage** (at nearby Mansell Lacy), built of half-timbering and brick in the reign of Henry VI, is full of exotic touches such as Kashmiri crewel bedspreads and curtains. These nevertheless assort well with Laura Ashley fabrics, antique oak furniture, and chairs covered in traditional tapestry or velvet. Previously two cottages, then a cider-house, the building still has many of its original features, such as low beams and small, deep-set windows; and when Monica had to put in a new, twisting staircase, she had it wood-pegged in the traditional way. By

arrangement, she will cook such meals as: cucumber and yogurt soup, steak pie (or nasi goreng, an Indonesian spe-ciality) and meringues – using wholefood ingredients. The cottage stands at the foot of a hill popular with walkers and birdwatchers alike. (Tel: 098122 688.)

209

OLD RECTORY **D S**

Patrick Brompton, east of Leyburn, Wensleydale, North Yorkshire, **DL8 1JN** Tel: 0677 50343

5 bedrooms (single or double) from £11.50. Less for 7 nights. Rooms have central heating; TV, armchairs; views of country or garden; tea/coffee facilities; bathrooms (some). (Clothes-washing facilities.) No smoking.

Dinner £8.50 for 4 courses and coffee, at 7.30pm. Vegetarian or special diets if ordered. Packed lunches, snacks. Non-residents not admitted. Drinks can be brought in. No smoking.

Sitting-room with central heating, open fire, books. No smoking.

Garden

Nearest main road A684 from Bedale to Leyburn.

Closed December and January

David and Felicity Thomas have furnished their home in keeping with its period (it was built early in the 18th century), complementing comfortable chintz sofas with a soft green colour scheme, the mahogany furniture of the dining-room with peach walls (the table is laid with Minton china and good silver). Bedrooms (on two floors, reached by a twisting staircase) are spacious and immaculate, some overlooking a walled garden with lawns beyond. There are alcoves, bay-windows and low doorways.

Felicity enjoys cooking. A typical dinner might comprise stuffed eggs, pork dijonnaise with wine sauce, and blackberry mousse, followed by cheeses.

The village is surrounded by small market towns (there's at least one market on the go every weekday), great mediaeval abbeys such as Jervaulx, two cathedral cities and two spa towns, waterfalls (at Aysgarth in particular), famous crags and viewpoints, and the Dales – both Wensleydale and more rugged Swaledale are close by. Wensleydale (famous for cheese) is the broadest and most fertile of the Dales – heather-clad hills enclose fields marked by dry-stone walls, with stone cottages and prosperous 18th-century houses. Bolton, Richmond and Middleham have castles. The North York Moors and even the Lake District are accessible for a day's outing. Constable Burton Hall has a fine garden, Thorpe Perrow an arboretum. Antique sales and shops attract many visitors; and there is plenty of farm produce to buy or pick. In winter, there are activity weekends at the Old Rectory – painting, crafts, history, etc.

Readers' comments: Delicious meal, pretty rooms. The best yet! Beautifully furnished, genuine welcome, superb dinner, wonderful hosts. Outstanding. Very pleasant rooms. Delightful owners. Wonderful hospitality, excellent food, most relaxing. A marvellous week. Most comfortable, so welcoming. House beautiful and food delicious.

Book well ahead: many of these houses have few rooms. Do not expect dinner if you have not booked it.

St Keyne, south of Liskeard, Cornwall, PL14 4RL   Tel: 0579 42617

8 bedrooms (double) from £18. Rooms have central heating, bathroom; TV; views of country or garden; tea/coffee facilities. **Dinner** from £10 (or à la carte) for 4 courses and coffee, at 7–8 pm. Special diets if ordered. Packed lunches. Coffee, tea, for a charge. Drinks can be ordered.

Sitting-room with central heating and open fire. Bar.
Large garden
Nearest main road A38 from Bodmin to Plymouth.

Throughout this house, there is an air of calm and dignity, with furnishings chosen to complement the early 19th-century architecture. Features like a fine fireplace of black marble, handsome staircase (with barley-sugar balusters and ruby glass in its windows) and panelled pine doors have fortunately survived the years intact.

There are handsome cushioned chairs around the tables in the dining-room (pale blue predominates in carpet and damask wallpaper) where, on fluted Wedgwood china, Ron and Kate Wolfe serve such 4-course meals as Stilton and celery soup, chicken in red wine, chocolate fudge-cake, plus cheese. Their fish comes straight from nearby Looe.

In the sitting-room (which has glass doors to the garden) are capacious velvet sofas; and separated from it by a curtained archway is a turquoise and cherry bar. Bedrooms are equally distinctive. Two have lacy, four-posters; another, on the ground floor, would particularly appeal to anybody who finds stairs difficult.

St Keyne, being fairly high up, has panoramic views and is surrounded by varied scenery: moors, beaches, cliffs and woodland paths are all at hand. There are over 40 places to visit, which include unusual museums and collections, steam rail, fishing villages, gardens, seal sanctuary, tin mines, tropical bird gardens, waterfall, Shire Horse Centre, watermills, river trips, craft centres and many National Trust houses.

Readers' comments: Excellent cooking with quality ingredients; warm and welcoming. Charming atmosphere of true repose and Victorian elegance. Food exceptional.

Two-thirds of the houses in this book have bargain breaks or other discounts on offer, some exclusive to readers. Only a third raise prices at the peak of summer.

211

OLD RECTORY   **C**

Standlake, south of Witney, Oxfordshire, OX8 7SG   Tel: 0865 300559

4 bedrooms (single, double or family) from £15. All have own bath/shower; TV; tea/coffee facilities; central heating; views of river, country or garden. (Washing-machine on request.)
Dinner £15 for 4 courses (with choices) and coffee; time by arrangement. Non-residents not admitted. Vegetarian or special diets if ordered. Lunches, packed lunches, snacks. Tea, coffee, free. Drinks can be brought in.
2 sitting-rooms with central heating, open fire, books.
Large garden
Nearest main road A415 from Witney to Abingdon.
Closed in December and January

Once Magdalene College, Oxford, owned this house of Cotswold stone, the hall of which dates back to the 13th century. At the end of this is what an old inventory called 'the dark entry', leading to lawns with a seat beside the River Windrush (fishing and canoes available) and with tall beech hedges sheltering them. There are pine trees, a 500-year-old yew and a stew-pond (that is, one where fish were bred for the pot). The 15th-century dining-room had several big sash windows added later to take advantage of this view. Throughout, there are features of architectural interest: old ogee-arched fireplaces of stone, lattice-paned windows with stone mullions, odd angles and steps everywhere.

The house was in decay when Pat and Bob Claridge started on the long task of restoring and then furnishing it to a very high standard. Even the least expensive room (nicknamed 'the curate's quarters'!) is attractive; while others are really beautiful, the most luxurious being a suite with four-poster draped in a silky, pale blue fabric with a pleated pink canopy above, figured mahogany wardrobe, a delicately patterned Louisiana wallpaper, pink and gold bathroom and river view.

By arrangement, Patricia will serve dinner, a typical menu being prawn cocktail in a half-melon, chicken and chilli casserole, raspberry pavlova.

Around the village are lakes, and the beginning of the Cotswold Hills with sights such as Blenheim Palace, the Oxford colleges, historic Burford and Cogges Farm Museum easily reached.

At Witney itself (a blanket-making town) is a great green with handsome lime trees and a wide main street, flanked with houses of Cotswold stone, and with a gabled, pillared and turreted Butter Cross built in the 17th century – among other notable buildings.

When and if the local Cotswold sights (which include the beautiful ruins of Minster Lovell Hall) are exhausted, it is easy to reach Bath, Stratford, Stonehenge, Cheltenham and even London from here. Garden-lovers appreciate Hidcote, Pusey, Kiftsgate, Sezincote and Mattocks' rose nurseries.

Readers' comments: Warm and friendly. Beautifully appointed. Superb breakfast. A delightful weekend. Sympathetically and beautifully restored. Faultless food and service.

212

OLD RECTORY
Wetherden, north-west of Stowmarket, Suffolk, IP14 3RE   Tel: 0359 40144

2 bedrooms (single or double) from £15. Both have own bath or shower; TV; central heating; views of country or garden. (Washing-machine on request.)
Sitting-room with central heating, open fire, TV, books, piano.
Large garden
Nearest main road A45 from Stowmarket to Bury St Edmunds.
Closed mid-December–mid-January

Readers who used the first edition of this book may have stayed with Pamela Bowden when she lived near Hadleigh. Now she has an equally elegant house here, into the decoration of which she has put the same tremendous amount of care.

The house, which dates from the 18th century, stands in extensive grounds. One steps into a hall with stone floor, a piano in one alcove and pot-plants all around.

Up the deep pink and white staircase one finds elegant bedrooms – I particularly liked one decorated in apricot with an antique brass bed and comfortable armchairs. Fine paintings, graceful curtains and Persian carpets are features of the house, even in the television room. In the sitting-room is a wallpaper patterned with classical medallions; the raspberry dining-room has an Adam fireplace of pink marble and a most unusual table – immensely long, it was made in Renaissance Italy from a single piece of walnut. Pamela, a member of the Embroiders' Guild, has made many of the furnishings herself: cushions, curtains, bed-hanging and sheets with broderie anglaise, for example.

Bed-and-breakfast only. For other meals, Pamela recommends such local inns as the King's Arms at Haughley, the Bull at Woolpit or Trowel & Hammer at Cotton.

Central Suffolk, once forested, is now an area of wide open fields with prairie-size farms. Villages cluster around greens, big mediaeval houses like that at Parham are often moated – less for defence than to drain the site and provide a water-supply for the inhabitants (rainfall being low in this part of England). The area has had a turbulent history, hence the presence of so many castles (the one at Framlingham is outstanding, and so are the monuments in the church: it is a pleasant town with a good bookshop).

The many attractive villages include Debenham, threaded by a pretty stream and with rush-weaving to be seen; Eye, for the fine roodscreen in its church and the Minstrels' Gallery at the White Lion; Hoxne, scene of St Edmund's martyrdom at the bridge. Earl Soham, unusually leafy for this largely treeless region, has a great variety of architectural styles from every period; Saxtead Green, a working windmill; Heveningham, stately mansion in a park laid out by Capability Brown. Yoxford is called 'the garden of Suffolk' because of the abundance of spring flowers at every cottage.

From Wetherden, so centrally situated, it is easy to motor to the coast and Aldeburgh, celebrated for its music festivals, historic Bury St Edmunds, the mediaeval showpiece of Lavenham, Ipswich (and beyond it the seaside resort of Felixstowe), and even to Cambridge, Norwich and Colchester in adjacent counties. In Stowmarket, a small market town, is Abbot's Hall which has a museum of rural life – crafts, old farm implements and so forth.

OLD SCHOOL HOUSE

St James' Street, Castle Hedingham, south-west of Sudbury (Suffolk), Essex, CO9 3EW   Tel: 0787 61370

5 **bedrooms** (single or double) from £18.50. **For readers of this book substantial reductions for 2 nights or more.** Most rooms have central heating; shower or bathroom; armchairs; views of village or garden. (Clothes-washing facilities.) No smoking.

Dinner £12.50 for 3 courses and coffee, served when requested. Coffee, tea, free. No smoking.

Sitting-room with central heating, open fire, TV, books. No smoking.

Garden

Nearest main road A604 from Halstead to Haverhill.

Garden-lovers in particular should go out of their way to stay here, for the Crawshaws have created – within a remarkably few years of taking over what was then a rough field – an elegant and lovely garden. Its several lawns are surrounded by shapely and brimming beds of shrubs and flowers, all grown from seed. Steps lead up to a lily-pool with koi carp, and at the end is hidden a neat vegetable garden which supplies the kitchen. And there's a population of little toads – hundreds of them – which come out at night.

Through the street door of the terracotta-and-white house, built in the 18th century, one steps straight into a quarry-tiled hall/dining-room. Between its ceiling beams is a trap-door, known as a coffin door – necessitated by the narrowness of the staircase – and a former inglenook is filled with flowers. There are Chippendale chairs around the dining-table, and silver candlesticks on it. Here, Penny may serve, on Sundays and Mondays only (if ordered well in advance), such dinners as haddock soufflé in spinach leaves, rack of lamb and a choice of puddings – chocolate pots, lemon pie, etc. (she makes no charge for pre-dinner drinks). Some guests, however, dine at the many good restaurants in or near Castle Hedingham: the Moot House, the Trading Post and the White Hart, in particular. There is a second sitting-room (brick-walled and with a copper-hooded fire), opening onto a paved terrace made colourful and appealing by a dozen huge plant-pots.

The principal bedroom is attractively decorated, with colourful quilted bedhead and spread, while the other has roses on walls and bed. The view from either is of the public tennis court across the street which leads into the centre of the village (picturesque, and with interesting shops), over which the castle itself looms high. A cottage in the garden provides extra, pretty bedrooms and its own sitting-room.

This is a very scenic part of Essex, near the Suffolk border, with a great deal to enjoy, crisscrossed by footpaths and bridleways. Audley End and a large number of other stately homes are in the neighbourhood, as well as many very pretty half-timbered villages and towns: Saffron Walden and Thaxted in particular (the latter has music festivals). Mole Hall Wildlife Park is another attraction. Colchester and Dedham Vale deserve at least one whole day. Cambridge is little more than half an hour away (it, and Suffolk villages such as Lavenham and Long Melford, are described under other entries.)

Readers' comments: Charming house and garden, excellent cooking.

OLD VICARAGE

S

Affpuddle, east of Dorchester, Dorset, DT2 7HH   Tel: 0305 848315

3 bedrooms (double) from £15. Rooms have central heating and electric heaters; bathroom (one); TV, armchairs; views of country or garden; tea/coffee facilities on request.
Garden with croquet.
Nearest main road A35 from Dorchester to Bere Regis.

Before Anthea and Michael Hipwell moved here, it was an ambassador's country home: a handsome Georgian house with fine doorways, windows and fireplaces – surrounded by smooth lawns and rosebeds within tall hedges of clipped yew, the old church alongside.

Anthea has a flair for interior decoration. Even the corridors are elegant, with portraits and flower-prints on walls of apple-blossom pink which contrast with the cherry carpet. In my bedroom, the curtains were of ivory moiré, the bedspread patterned with rosebuds.

Breakfast is served in the prettiest dining-room in this book. Taking as the starting-point her collection of aquamarine glass (housed in two alcoves) and a series of modern lithographs in vivid turquoise, Anthea decorated the walls to match, and chose a dramatic turquoise curtain fabric reproduced from a Regency design in Brighton's Royal Pavilion. Against this all-blue colour scheme, the pale furniture shows to advantage. As no evening meal is provided, many visitors go to the Brace of Pheasants at Plush, the Fox at Ansty or the Frampton Arms at Moreton.

The Old Vicarage is well placed for a stopover on the long journey (by A35) to the West Country; when arriving or departing on the Weymouth-Cherbourg ferry; or while learning to fish for trout at the nearby angling school (tel: 0305 848450).

The Hipwells lend walkers Ordnance Survey maps, and will advise them on sightseeing possibilities, including less obvious ones – such as the huge bric-à-brac market held at Wimborne every Friday, or little-known beaches (one favourite is at Ringstead, surrounded by National Trust land). In addition, there are such favourites as Hardy's cottage and T. E. Lawrence's; Kingston Lacey House; Maiden Castle and Corfe Castle; Studland beach and the Purbeck Hills; and several garden centres – one specializing in old roses. And, at the end of the day, you are welcome to relax in the Hipwells' garden chairs under sun umbrellas.

Readers' comments: Very pleasant. Excellent service.

When writing to me, if you want a reply please enclose a stamped addressed envelope.

OLD VICARAGE

Church Square, Rye, East Sussex, TN31 7HF   Tel: 0797 222119

5 bedrooms (double) from £16. Bargain breaks. Rooms have central heating, electric heaters; TV; tea/coffee facilities. Some have own showers.
Sitting-room with central heating and books. Packed lunches.
Nearest main road A259 from Folkestone to Hastings.

This pink-and-white, largely 18th-century house is virtually in the churchyard, a peaceful spot since it is traffic-free and the only sound is the melodious chime of the ancient church clock (its pendulum hangs right down into the nave of the church). One steps straight into a very pretty sitting-room, yellow sofas contrasting with grass-green walls. Curved windows, antiques and copious pot-plants complete the scene. Beyond is the breakfast-room.

The bedrooms are prettily decorated, mostly with pine furniture and flowery fabrics. Two have elegant four-posters. Those at the front have views of the church and its surrounding trees; others, of Rye's mediaeval roofscape. Henry James wrote *The Spoils of Poynton* while living here in 1896 with his fat dog, servants and a canary, before moving to nearby Lamb House. He said in a letter '. . . the pears grow yellow in the sun and the peace of the Lord – or at least of the parson – seems to abide here' (no pears now, but the rest is still true).

As only breakfast is served (and cream teas in the garden on sunny weekends), for dinner Julia Lampon recommends – out of Rye's many restaurants – the Landgate bistro, Flushing Inn or Old Forge.

Rye has a celebrated church at the heart of its narrow mediaeval streets, lined with antique and craft shops. There is a weekly sheep market and a general market. Romney Marsh (famous for its autumn sunsets and its spring lambs) attracts painters and birdwatchers. Rye itself was the setting for E. F. Benson's 'Mapp and Lucia' stories. Benson lived in Georgian Lamb House after Henry James (it is now a National Trust property).

The town deserves a lingering visit to explore its cobbled byways, antique and craft shops and historic fortifications, for there are few places where a mediaeval town plan and original houses have survived so little altered. In addition there are in the area 20 castles, historic houses such as Kipling's Batemans, Ellen Terry's Smallhythe and (with fine gardens) Great Dixter, Sissinghurst and Scotney. Battle Abbey and Camber's miles of sandy beaches are other attractions.

Readers' comments: Charming house, pretty rooms, friendly welcome. Outstanding. Charm and helpfulness of the owners gave us a perfect weekend.

For explanation of code letters (**C, D, H, PT, S, S-C, X**) see page xxvi

OLD VICARAGE   **C D S-C X**
Higham, north of Colchester (Essex), Suffolk, CO7 6JY   Tel: 020637 248

4 bedrooms (single, double or family) from £17. Less for 3 nights. Rooms have central heating and electric heaters; bathroom (some); TV, armchairs; views of river, country or garden; tea/coffee facilities. Packed lunches, snacks. Coffee, tea, free.
2 sitting-rooms with central heating, open fire, TV, books, record-player.
Large garden and fields, with tennis, swimming, boating and fishing.
Nearest main road A12 from Colchester to Ipswich.

One of the most elegant houses in this book, the Old Vicarage stands near a tranquil village and is surrounded by superb views, with the old church close by. Everything about it is exceptional, from the Tudor building itself (its walls colourwashed a warm apricot), and the lovely furnishings, to the pretty south-facing garden – which has unheated swimming-pool, tennis and safe river boats (it's surprising that few families with children have discovered it, particularly since the coast is near; Felixstowe and Frinton have sandy beaches).

Colonel and Mrs Parker have lived here for many years, and their taste is evident in every room. Lovely colours, pretty wallpapers and chintzes, antiques, flowers and log fires all combine to create a background of great style. In the breakfast-room, eight bamboo chairs surround a huge circular table (of mock-marble), and the walls have a trellis wallpaper the colour of watermelon. Bedrooms are equally pretty: one green-and-white with rush flooring; another has mimosa on walls and ceiling (its tiny windows are lattice-paned); the family room is in lime and tangerine. There are lace bedspreads, Indian watercolours, baskets of begonias – individual touches everywhere.

Bed-and-breakfast only; most visitors dine at the Angel, Stoke-by-Nayland.

Lynne, from the village, comes in to help and (herself a lively source of information) is evidently as greatly impressed as the visitors themselves with all that the Parkers do to help people enjoy their stay – from information on sightseeing and eating-places or where to watch local wildlife, to offering a mother the use of their own washing-machine.

Higham is very well placed for a great variety of activities and outings. One could easily spend a fortnight doing something totally different each day. There are Roman Colchester (lovely gardens on the ramparts), Constable's Flatford Mill and Dedham, the seaside, racing at Newmarket, sailing, music festival at Aldeburgh, the mediaeval villages and great churches of central Suffolk, tide-mill at Woodbridge, market and Gainsborough's house at Sudbury, and lovely villages (like Lavenham). Beth Chatto's garden, Ickworth and East Bergholt Lodge attract garden-lovers. And everywhere superb scenery, with few people on the roads.

Readers' comments: Lovely house, very calm, beautifully appointed, charming staff. A firm favourite; superb and beautiful; hospitality outstanding. Perfect! Delightful weekend; privileged to be there. Excellent in every way. Most beautiful house. Very friendly. Thoroughly enjoyed it, superb. Very helpful. Food of highest standard, attention to detail outstanding.

217

OLD VICARAGE

C(7)

Muker, west of Richmond, North Yorkshire, DL11 6QH   Tel: 0748 86498

4 bedrooms (double or family) at £32.75 with dinner (if you stay 2 nights). Rooms have central heating; bathroom; TV, phone, armchairs; views of country; tea/coffee facilities. No smoking.
Dinner 5 courses and coffee, at 7.30pm. Vegetarian or special diets if ordered. Packed lunches. Non-residents not admitted. Drinks can be ordered.
Sitting-room with central heating, open fire, books.
Large garden
Nearest main road A6108 from Leyburn to Richmond.
Closed November–mid-March

At the head of lovely Swaledale, this house (filmed in the TV series 'All Creatures Great and Small') provides accommodation that is furnished with comfort and in character with the age of the house. King-size beds, good carpets, fruit and flowers in the bedrooms, and open fires all contribute to its comfort; and from every room there are fine views – for close by is Great Shunner Fell (2400 feet), the famous Buttertubs Pass, and Kisdon Hill. Good walking country.

Marjorie Bucknall's five-course meals are based on fresh produce; and all the bread (both white and brown) is home-baked. A typical menu might comprise home-made tomato soup, eggs mimosa, chicken casseroled in white wine with yogurt, pears in ginger syrup, local cheeses, and coffee with mints. If you want a daytime TV programme videoed for evening viewing, the Bucknalls will do it.

Muker is the largest of the villages of Swaledale. It houses a shop for woollens hand-knitted by a team of 40 farmers' wives and daughters, mostly from the wool of the breed of sheep to which the dale has given its name. From it, you can also visit the rest of the Yorkshire Dales, the Yorkshire Moors and the Lake District.

There is plenty of scenery to enjoy in Swaledale but, for a change, the nearest town is Kirkby Stephen, westward over the watershed of the Pennines in Cumbria. Its rather grand church contains the tomb of the man reputed to have killed the last wild boar in England. It is reached from the market square, where the area once used for bull-baiting is still marked, through the picturesque classical cloisters. There are some good walks along the River Eden, and castles to visit include the remains of one supposed to be the birthplace of Uther Pendragon, King Arthur's father. One could return to Muker via the Buttertubs Pass, having taken a look at Hardraw Force, the highest single-drop waterfall in England. Brass bands used to use the natural amphitheatre here for performances.

Readers' comments: Warm welcome, excellent value. Cannot praise too highly; rooms excellent, food superb, owners very attentive. Lovely people, went out of their way to make us feel at home; and the food . . . ! A delight; the Bucknalls are welcoming and perceptive; food excellent. Warm welcome, excellent food and value, we will visit again and again! Lovely house, superb views, quiet.

All prices are inclusive of any VAT or service charge. They are minimum prices: superior rooms or high-season bookings may cost more.

OLD VICARAGE

C D PT S

Parc-an-Creet, St Ives, Cornwall, TR26 2ET   Tel: 0736 796124

10 bedrooms (single, double or family) from £13. Less for 3 nights. Rooms have central heating; washbasin, shower or bathroom (some); TV, armchairs; views of country and garden; tea/coffee facilities.

Dinner £9 for 4 courses (with choices), and coffee, at 6.45pm (weekends only). Bar meals mid-week. Vegetarian or special diets if ordered. Packed lunches, snacks. Coffee, tea, free. Non-residents not admitted. Drinks can be ordered
Sitting-room with central heating, open fire, TV, books, indoor games (including snooker), record-player and records. Also a bar with piano and bar skittles.
Garden with swing, putting, badminton and swing ball.
Nearest main road A30 from Redruth to Penzance.
Closed November–February

Although part of the once extensive grounds (on the outskirts of this steep little town) were sold off long ago to build modern houses all round, the trees in the remaining garden shut most of these (and the church) from view.

The house itself, built of silvery granite in the 1850s, is entered via a small conservatory and a great iron-hinged door of ecclesiastical shape, which opens into a hall with red-and-black tiled floor. Mr and Mrs Sykes have done their best to preserve this period ambience, furnishing the bar with crimson-and-gold flock wallpaper and all kinds of Victoriana. There's a piano here, which occasionally inspires visitors to join in singing some of the old songs of that period. In addition there is a sitting-room, and blue-and-white dining-room. Big windows (some with floor-length velvet curtains on poles) and handsome fireplaces feature throughout; and the Sykeses have put in excellent carpets, along with good, solid furniture – a 'thirties walnut suite in one bedroom, and velvet-upholstered bedheads. There is a refurbished Victorian loo, preserved in all its glory of blue lilies and rushes.

Jack Sykes, formerly an engineer, did all the modernization himself, even the plumbing; while Irene, who used to be a confectioner and later took a hotel management course, is responsible for the meals. She provides such dishes as Stilton-and-walnut mousse, haddock Wellington, and pineapple in kirsch with Cornish cream; then cheeses and coffee.

There are chairs and sun umbrellas in the garden; and a path leads down (in 10 minutes) to the sandy beach where there are beach chalets for hire. A bus will bring you uphill again. Another will take you out to the moors and rugged cliffs that lie between St Ives and Land's End.

The colourful, one-time fishing village of St Ives, famous for its artists' colony, is now a crowded tourist centre in summer. Beyond it lie (on the north coast) some splendid scenery, outstanding prehistoric remains, tin mines and lighthouses. The sheltered south coast has sandy coves like Porthcurno and Lamorna, the cliffside Minack theatre, wildflowers in abundance and historic fishing harbours (Mousehole and Newlyn in particular). The byways and curio shops of Penzance, as well as its subtropical gardens, are well worth exploring on foot and from here there are day-trips to the lovely Isles of Scilly and to the castle on the little islet of St Michael's Mount. Much of the land around here belongs to the National Trust.

Readers' comments: Beautifully restored; excellent in all aspects. Pleasant, and good value. Excellent in every way; superb home cooking.

OLD WHARF FARM

C D S S-C

Yardley Gobion, south-east of Towcester, Northamptonshire, NN12 7UE
Tel: 0908 542454

3 bedrooms (single, double or family) £13. Less for 4 nights. Rooms have central heating; views of canal and country. (Clothes-washing facilities.) No smoking.
Sitting-room with central heating, open fire, books, record-player.
Grounds Farmland and croquet lawn.
Nearest main road A508 from Milton Keynes to Northampton.

'It's Arcadian!' and 'It's rather tatty': both comments are true, and both were made by the Bowens themselves who live here. The 18th-century house has had many lives – as farm, then inn, then wharfmaster's house and back to a small-holding before they took over. The Duke of Grafton helped to pioneer the canal system in this area and he used French prisoners-of-war to build the stables for horses to tow the boats along – now turned into a self-catering cottage.

The wharf alongside is still in use, servicing colourful narrow-boats that use the Grand Union canal.

One enters through a tiled and beamed hall with an Orkney chair (made like the old straw beehives), interesting pictures and rugs. There's a deep green parlour for meals, with mahogany furniture, and a red-tiled sitting-room where old armchairs covered in William Morris fabrics are gathered round a log stove in the big inglenook. Board stairs lead to the bedrooms: one has a brass bed with ribbon-trimmed duvet and a grapevine peering through the window, while in a particu-larly pretty family room sugar-pink duvets match the walls. Lying casually about are such oddly assorted family treasures as the Bowens' own childhood teddybears and Bonzo, and the plush top-hat of showman C. B. Cochrane: John's father was a ballad singer in some of his variety entertainments. Other mementoes include a bust of John's father topped by the actual flying helmet he wore as an aviator in the First World War. Quadraphonic stereo is available for guests to use.

Outside there's a view of water-meadows, and a miscellany of animals ranging freely about, which children in particular enjoy: a donkey (which they can ride), goats, chickens, ducks, geese, pigs, some calves and two Jersey cows. The Bowens keep a herd of beef-cattle.

A rowing boat can be borrowed, for fishing, exploring or picnicking. Old farm machines, the original Victorian weighbridge (for carts delivering coal, etc., to the barges), and a rope-ladder up into a spreading willow tree all contribute to the scene.

Only breakfast and snacks are provided by Susie: most visitors go for meals to the Coffee Pot inn or the White Horse in the village (there are other choices of dining-places nearby). Tea and coffee are free – help yourself in the kitchen.

The southern part of Northamptonshire has agreeable countryside, easily reached from the M1 (use junction 15 for Yardley Gobion), with attractive stone villages among the folds of the hills. A special feature of the scene is water – rivers, canals, lakes and reservoirs abound (and on many of these watersports and boating are possible). The area was the scene of major battles in both the Wars of the Roses (15th century) and the Civil War (17th century). Sulgrave Manor is where George Washington's ancestors lived; other sights include the Waterways Museum at Stoke Bruerne, Turner's organ museum, and Castle Ashby and its park.

OLDFIELDS PT
102 Wells Road, Bath, Avon, BA2 3AL   Tel: 0225 317984

14 bedrooms (single, double or family) from £15. Less for 4 nights or bargain breaks. Rooms have central heating; shower or bathroom; TV, armchairs; views of town or garden; one has a balcony; tea/coffee facilities. For quiet, ask for a room away from the main road.
Sitting-room with central heating, open fire, books.
Terraced garden
Nearest main road A367 from Bath to Radstock.

Although this late Victorian house (or, rather, two) of honey-coloured stone stands just off the steep main road out of Bath to Exeter, I spent a quiet night; and in a particularly attractive and spacious bedroom (pine-louvred doors to cupboards, a terracotta-and-cream colour scheme, sprigged Laura Ashley wallpaper, attractive modern pictures and lots of pot-plants). The big sitting-room is decorated in soft browns and mossy greens, with a marble fireplace (crackling fire in winter) and lace curtains from ceiling to floor at the high windows with their fine views of the city. But what I liked best about Oldfields were the owners, Anthony O'Flaherty and his wife Nicole, who are great fun. Breakfasts are generous (with herbal teas, if you like) with much emphasis on wholefoods.

Care is taken over every detail. Says Anthony: 'We buy muesli at a holier-than-holy wholefood shrine called Harvest, in a restored Victorian factory by the Avon, with the statutory Greenpeace poster alongside the statutory Employers' Public Liability notice. We buy butter from a Somerset farm, and eschew the miniscule foil-wrapped jobs. The bread from a local baker is unsliced wheatmeal which means more work at breakfast-time but it makes better toast: it's delivered to us the morning it is baked.'

Apart from Bath itself (which deserves at least a week-long stay with Wednesday reserved for the influx of antique dealers and Saturday for the 'flea market'), you can visit the cathedral city of Wells, the Cheddar Gorge and the lovely Mendip Hills, the sea at Weston-super-Mare, old market towns like Warminster, Chippenham and historic Bristol (a lively city, with plenty to interest tourists, theatre-goers etc.) And, of course, the beauties of Devon, the South Wales coast and hills, and the Cotswolds are not far away; also delectable villages like Lacock, Bradford-on-Avon, Biddestone and Castle Combe, as well as the gardens at Stourhead.

Readers' comments: Wonderful! Exceptionally nice people. Warmth and charm. Spacious comfort.

Some readers tell me they have stayed at lots of places from *Staying Off the Beaten Track*. I wonder who has stayed at most? A free copy of the next edition awaits the reader who sends me his/her comments on the greatest number!

ONE-EIGHT-FOUR
West Malvern Road, Malvern, Worcestershire, WR14 4AZ
Tel: 06845 66544

5 bedrooms (double) from £16. Rooms have central heating, electric heaters; shower or bathroom; armchairs; views of country. (Clothes-washing facilities available.) No smoking.
Sitting-room with central heating, open fire, books; bar; TV. No smoking.
Nearest main road A449 from Worcester to Great Malvern.

The house is in an undistinguished road, but its steep site is superb: from the back windows, there is an uninterrupted rural view to the hills of Wales over thirty miles away, with glowing sunsets. The rooms are on five floors but, fortunately for the less agile, there are ground-floor bedrooms available.

The previous owner was an interior designer, and the Kelletts have retained much of her style – sparkling colour schemes, well chosen wallpapers and curtains, unusual antique bedheads in many rooms, pine shelving and corner cupboard in the sitting-room – while steadily combing antique shops themselves for such touches as unusual condiment sets, embroidered linen napkins and so on. There are always fresh flowers on the scarlet-clothed breakfast-tables.

Only breakfast (and light suppers) are provided but an album of menus from the many local restaurants is kept. For breakfast Jan serves all the usual things, plus such imaginative options as fruits already peeled and sliced, fresh-baked scones and muffins, raspberries when in season, and vegetarian selections.

The Kelletts have varied interests: Dennis is a leather chemist producing high-quality saddlery and a keen golfer; Canadian-born Jan's great enthusiasm is calligraphy (she belongs to the Society of Scribes and Illuminators).

A footpath leads walkers to the Malvern Hills. Malvern itself has been described elsewhere in this book, as well as the surrounding cathedral cities of Hereford, Worcester and Gloucester, each giving its name to counties that are amongst the loveliest in England. Elgar's birthplace, the Royal Worcester china factory, Malvern Priory and Little Malvern Court are popular sights.

Readers' comments: So welcoming and restful. Good value.

Don't complain if –
- – because you booked at short notice, you do not get the best room
- – because you did not order a meal in advance, you get something plucked from the freezer
- – because you do not arrive on time, your room is let to someone else
- – because you bring a dog without asking, it is refused entry
- – because you don't express your wishes (for more heat, a second helping or whatever), you don't get what you want!

THE ORCHARD

C(11) PT

Bathford, north-east of Bath, Avon, BA1 7TG   Tel: 0225 858765

4 bedrooms (double) from £17.25. Less for 7 nights. Rooms have central heating and electric heaters; bathroom; TV, armchairs; views of country or garden. No smoking.
Sitting-room with central heating, open fire, books.
Large garden with croquet.
Nearest main road A4 from Bath to Chippenham.
Closed in winter (except for house-parties of friends).

All the pleasures of Bath are within about ten minutes by car (or bus), yet this little village perched on a hillside seems deep in the countryside. There are stunning views over the River Avon to the far countryside and all around is peace.

The Orchard is a luxurious Georgian house standing in its own grounds. Sometimes one sees balloonists drifting by. The bedrooms are amongst the most elegant in this book, with private bathrooms and big windows overlooking the garden; and the other rooms are equally handsome with attractive colour schemes and antique furniture. Breakfasts include home-made muesli, free-range eggs and locally baked wholemeal bread. For dinner, the nearby Crown Inn is excellent.

Bath, described elsewhere, is full of interest as is the whole region – with innumerable stately homes and gardens, such as Stourbridge, the Westonbirt Arboretum and much else.

Readers' comments: House and appointments are a delight. Complete peace, beautiful surroundings, everything done perfectly. Went out of their way to make us feel welcome. Rooms fabulous. Delightfully furnished. Outstanding. A privilege to stay there.

When to go? Seaside resorts or other places suitable for children will be at their busiest (and dearest) in July–August and during half-term holidays (especially in late May, which is also a bank holiday period). Other peak periods are, of course, Easter, Christmas, New Year and the bank holiday in late August. (The bank holiday in early May is not usually a peak, because it comes rather soon after Easter, but much depends on the weather.) There are local peaks, too (the Gold Cup races at Cheltenham or the regatta at Henley, for instance, are apt to fill hotels for miles around), and local troughs (Brighton, a conference centre, is least busy in high summer). You won't get much personal attention when hotels are full to bursting.

223

ORCHARD HOUSE C
High Street, Rothbury, Northumberland, NE65 7TL Tel: 0669 20684

6 bedrooms (double or family) from £14.25. Less for 7 nights. Rooms have central heating and electric heaters; TV; tea/coffee facilities; views of country or garden. Some have shower and toilet.
Dinner £9 for 4 courses and coffee, at 7pm. Special diets if ordered. Packed lunches. Coffee, tea, free. Non-residents not admitted. Drinks can be ordered.
Sitting-room with central heating, books; bar.
Garden
Nearest main road A697 from Morpeth to Wooler.

Rothbury, a pleasant little market town with some interesting shops, stands in the very centre of Northumberland; so many of the pleasures of that large and underestimated county are within an easy drive: the Roman wall to the south, Holy Island to the north, and in between countryside which can change from open moorland to woods and arable fields within a few miles, with picturesque villages and historic monuments for punctuation. Castles and peel towers (fortified farmhouses) remind one of border raiders.

The Orchard is a Georgian house standing aside from Rothbury's bustling main street. Jeff and Sheila Jefferson took it over several years ago when Jeff left the RAF after years as an engineer (some of them spent in Malaysia) and have turned it into a comfortable and unpretentious place to stay. Like many people who provide good accommodation in relatively unknown spots, they have found that guests who stayed a night or two while passing through have returned for a longer holiday.

Sheila's four-course menus are out of the ordinary and varied, the only fixture being roast beef every Sunday. Otherwise you might get (for instance) French onion soup, pork scallopine, strawberry meringue and cheese (local produce is used whenever possible). There is no choice except when fish is on the menu. Coffee is included, and there is free tea on arrival. In the lounge is a cabinet well stocked with miniatures of drinks for you to help yourself and enter in a book.

The sight closest to Rothbury is Cragside, the mansion which Norman Shaw (best known, perhaps, for his government buildings in London) designed for Lord Armstrong, the armaments king. It is one of the most complete late-Victorian houses there are. Among the oddities are a Turkish bath and a hydraulic lift, but its main distinction is that it was the first house in the world to be lit by electricity. The elaborately landscaped grounds are also notable.

Brinkburn Priory, Alnwick Castle, Wallington Hall and gardens are all near. At Cambo is a garden centre specializing in cottage-garden and windy-site plants.

Readers' comments: Very impressed. A delightful couple, friendly and helpful. Outstanding food; rooms sparkling clean and spacious. Excellent food – first-rate value. Comfortable, spotless; we thoroughly endorse all you say. Excellent in every way. Exceptionally helpful, excellent food, very good value. Very good food, everything of the highest standard. Marvellous food and accommodation. Thoroughly endorse all you say: excellent.

OTLEY HOUSE
Otley, north-west of Woodbridge, Suffolk, IP6 9NR Tel: 047339 253

4 bedrooms (double) from £15. Rooms have central heating; shower or bathroom; armchairs; views of garden. (Clothes-washing facilities.) No smoking.
Dinner £14 for 4 courses (with choices) and coffee, at 7.30pm. Vegetarian or special diets if ordered. Coffee, tea, for a charge. Non-residents not admitted. Drinks can be ordered. No smoking.

Sitting-room with central heating, open fire, TV, books, piano. No smoking, except in billiard room.
Large garden with croquet.
Nearest main road A1120 from Stowmarket to Yoxford.
Closed December–mid-February

It's a story frequently told about houses in this book: lovely old buildings, once occupied by a large family with many servants, prove too big and expensive for today's needs, and fall into sad neglect – until someone sees their potential for a new life sustained by paying guests who occupy rooms surplus to family needs.

When the Hiltons moved to mainly 18th-century Otley House, it was very run down and the grounds (once tended by seven gardeners) so overgrown with brambles that, when clearing them, they fell into a pool before realizing it was there. Within a few years all this was transformed. High French windows now open onto immaculate lawns and the two lakes that were part of a moat round the house. Wild ducks frequent these and a small island with marguerites and astilbes.

The sitting-room's wood block floor is scattered with oriental rugs, and on its off-pink walls hang some of the Hiltons' collection of watercolours. Many of these, like other objects around the house, come from Denmark – Lise's home country. The large hall (with handsome details such as arches and panelled doors) houses early Chinese porcelain which she has restored, and one of Michael's ship models.

Chippendale chairs surround the long mahogany dining-table with its crystal chandelier and family silver where Lise serves such meals as salmon mousse or a herby Danish pâté to start with; chicken in tarragon sauce; Danish lemon mousse or chocolate mousse with Grand Marnier; then Stilton. After dinner, a grand piano awaits – or the billiard room, with big leather armchairs around a coal fire.

Up the curving staircase with barley-sugar balusters are very attractive bedrooms, one with stripped pine four-poster and fabrics printed with old vegetable dyes; another that has windows in two of its cobalt blue walls, and a pale pink carpet.

From Otley, beautiful stretches of the coast are only a few miles away and Aldeburgh (celebrated for its music festivals, started by Benjamin Britten).

Readers' comments: Delighted. Dinner excellent, room well above average; first-class. Impeccable standard of cooking. Relaxed excellence, meticulous attention to detail and concern for every guest. Immaculate. Delicious food.

225

OTTERBURN TOWER HOTEL   C D X

**Otterburn, north-west of Newcastle-upon-Tyne (Tyne & Wear),
Northumberland, NE19 1NB**   Tel: 0830 20620

12 bedrooms (single, double or family) from £20 but very much less for 2 nights and bargain breaks. Some have own bath/shower; TV; tea/coffee facilities; central heating; views of country or garden.
Dinner A la carte or £9.50 for 3 courses (with choices) and coffee, at 7–9.30pm. Vegetarian or special diets if ordered. Lunches, packed lunches, snacks. Tea, coffee, extra. Drinks can be ordered.
2 sitting-rooms with central heating, open fire, TV, books, piano; bar.
Large garden
Nearest main road A696 from Newcastle to Jedburgh.

Though most of this battlemented 'castle' dates only from the last century, it has a much longer history. The first tower was built by one of William the Conqueror's cousins, given the estate 'to hold by the service of defending that part of the country forever from wolves and enemies'. It had a turbulent history, the most epic conflict in which it was involved being the Battle of Otterburn, 1388.

Despite baronial splendour, the Hardings have created a relaxed family atmosphere. The interior lives up to the impressive exterior, with oak-panelled rooms, leaded windows carrying coats-of-arms of past owners, tapestry seats in the bar (a wide range of malt whiskies here), mock-noble decorations, and no less than five log fires. An upstairs sitting-room has murals of the Battle of Otterburn – occasionally re-enacted locally in August – and there is a library with buttoned leather armchairs. Bedrooms have been decorated with pretty wallpapers and matching curtains (some with four-posters, others cottagey – prices vary).

Classic English dishes make up the dinner menu (cooked by Peter), the main courses of which usually include such things as sirloin of local Bellingham beef, haunch of venison, loin of pork and leg of Northumbrian lamb – served with interesting cream-based sauces freshly prepared for each person.

A few miles westward and, close to Kielder Water (the biggest man-made lake in Europe), is the Kershaws' **Pheasant Inn** at Stannersburn (tel: 0660 40382) which is everything one wants a country inn to be – nearly four centuries old, stone-walled and low-beamed and in particularly lovely countryside. The Kershaws are determined to keep it unspoilt. The bedrooms, however, are modern, in a former hemel (farm implements store) and barn; many of them are on the

ground floor. Food is freshly prepared – one interesting starter is avocado with grapefruit and Stilton; trout comes with a sauce of yogurt and herbs; venison appears often.

OVERCOMBE HOTEL   C D H PT S X
Horrabridge, north-west of Yelverton, Devon, PL20 7RN   Tel: 0822 853501

rear view

11 bedrooms (single, double or family) from £17. Less for 7 nights or bargain breaks.

Rooms have central heating; shower or bathroom (some); TV, armchairs; views of country or garden; tea/coffee facilities.
Dinner £9.75 for 4 courses and coffee, at 7.30pm. Special diets if ordered. Lunches, packed lunches, snacks. Coffee, tea, for a charge. Drinks can be ordered.
2 sitting-rooms with central heating, open fire, TV, books; and a bar.
Large garden with swing-ball.
Nearest main road A386 from Plymouth to Tavistock.

Conveniently placed for one to explore Dartmoor and the coast, the Overcombe Hotel (now run by Brenda and Maurice Dumell) consists of two houses joined in one to make a very comfortable small hotel. You can relax in either of the sitting-rooms, according to what you want – a bar in one, TV in another, log fires, pleasant views. From the bay window of the dining-room, one looks across to the moors. The walls are hung with local paintings, some of which are for sale.

There is always a selection of dishes on the menu with such choices as pear and parsnip soup, salmon in filo pastry, apple mousse and cheeses.

Visitors come here for a variety of reasons (the least of which is that it's a good staging-post if you are on that long slog to furthest Cornwall). The Dartmoor National Park attracts people touring by car, anglers, riders, golfers and – above all – walkers (for them, Maurice organizes special two- to seven-day bargain breaks, with experienced guides accompanying visitors on walks of eight miles or more, and illustrated after-dinner talks about the moors). Plymouth is near; and among visitors' favourite outings are Cotehele, Buckland Abbey and Saltram House (all National Trust), Morwellham Quay and the Shire Horse Centre.

Further east lie the delectable South Hams: flowery valleys, sands, mildest of climates. To the west is the Cornish coast: dramatic cliffs, sandy coves and some harbours so picturesque (Polperro, Looe, etc.) that popularity threatens to ruin them. But go inland, and you will still find undisturbed villages and market towns.

Plymouth was heavily bombed, which means that its shopping centre is very modern. But the old quarter, the Barbican, which Drake and the Pilgrim Fathers knew so well, survived, and it is to this that visitors throng. Here are the old warehouses and the harbours full of small boats, the narrow alleys with beguiling little shops and restaurants, the mediaeval houses now turned into museums, the fish market and, high above, the 17th-century citadel. Plymouth has an outstanding aquarium, Drake's Island out in the Sound (to be visited by boat), the naval dockyard and the famous clifftop – the Hoe – with its unique seascape, memorials and flowers.

Readers' comments: A wonderful stay. Made us very welcome and could not have been more delightful hosts. Excellent food, fresh vegetables daily. Comfortable and warm. We will go again.

> All prices are inclusive of any VAT or service charge. They are minimum prices: superior rooms or high-season bookings may cost more.

PARADISE HOUSE   *(illustrated on cover – rear view)*   C PT
88 Holloway, Bath, Avon, BA2 4PX   Tel: 0225 317723

9 bedrooms (single, double or family) from £18.50. Less for 5 nights. Rooms have central heating; shower or bathroom in seven; TV, armchairs; views of city, country or garden; tea/coffee facilities; phone.
Sitting-room with fire, central heating, books.
Garden with croquet and swing-ball.
Nearest main road A367 from Bath to Radstock.

It stands half way up a steep, curving road which was once indeed a 'hollow way': a lane worn low between high banks by centuries of weary feet or hooves entering Bath from the south: the last lap of the Romans' Fosse Way. It is now a quiet cul-de-sac in the lee of Beechen Cliff, with panoramic views over the city, the centre of which is only 7 minutes' walk away – downhill. (As to uphill – take a taxi! Or else a bus to the Bear Flat stop.) Look the opposite way and all is leafy woods.

The house itself was built about 1720, with all the elegance which that implies: a classical pediment above the front door and well-proportioned sash windows with rounded tops in a façade of honey-coloured Bath stone.

David and Janet Cutting took it over several years ago and have restored it impeccably throughout, stripping off polystyrene to reveal pretty plasterwork ceilings, for instance, and gaudy tiles to expose a lovely marble fireplace in which logs now blaze. They stripped dingy paint off the panelled pine doors and put on handles of brass or china. They have furnished to a very high standard indeed, with both antique and modern furniture, elegant fabrics, and well chosen colours, predominantly soft greens and browns. The sitting-room is especially pretty, with Liberty fabrics and wallpaper, pictures in maple frames and a collection of Coalport cottages.

The bedrooms have been given as much care as the rest. They vary in size and amenities; therefore prices vary too.

At the back, beyond a verandah with ivy-leaf ironwork, is quite a large walled garden (a suntrap in the afternoon), with lawns, fish-pool, a rose-covered pergola and marvellous views of the city and hills all around. This secluded setting extends behind the mediaeval Magdalen Chapel next door, which was once a hostel for lepers banned from the city. In 1982 David and Janet acquired the adjoining Georgian house, which they then completely restored, furnished and decorated to the same elegant standards as the main house.

As to Bath itself – which attracts more visitors than any other place in England except London – the attractions are so varied that they can hardly be compressed into one paragraph. Just wandering among the Georgian perfection of its streets and squares, which spread from the historic centre right up the sides of the surrounding hills, and in its award-winning gardens, is a pleasure in itself, and it would take many days to explore them all (the best method is to take a bus to each hilltop in turn and walk back downhill, with far views succeeded by discoveries of lovely houses, streets, alleys or gardens all the way).

There is more about Bath in other entries.

Readers' comments: Top-class! Truly excellent. Ideal, with excellent facilities. Superbly equipped, very attractive. Outstanding hotel.

228

PARK HOUSE

C(10) **PT S**

20 Macduff Road, Battersea, London SW11 4DA
Tel: 01 (or 071 after 6th May)-622 4757

3 bedrooms (double) from £12.50. Less for 7 nights. Rooms have central heating. No smoking. (Washing-machine on request.)
Dinner £6 or £7 for 3 courses and coffee, at 7.30pm. Vegetarian diets if ordered. Tea, coffee, free. Drinks can be brought in. No smoking.
Sitting-room with central heating and open fire, TV on request, books, piano. No smoking.
Small garden
Closed mid-December–mid-January

Just across the river from Chelsea stood the ancient village of Battersea which later became a fashionable suburb, declined, and is now on its way up again. One of its pleasures is Battersea Park (200 acres of flowers, lake and woodland) which was laid out in 1853 where previously there was only a marsh; eventually to be flanked by blocks of mansion flats and terraced villas – the developer of which selected this one for his own home. Now artist Christine Fremantle lives here, and has transformed it with light and colour.

She has extended the kitchen (equipped with pale oak and white fitments) into a conservatory where meals are served. This opens onto a small courtyard garden where, among wisteria and laburnum, fish lead a tranquil life in her lily-pool, fringed with slender irises. On the sitting-room's blue walls are Christine's roofscapes and other paintings, and a striking tapestry of a griffin which took her seven years to make. Oriental rugs are scattered on the shining woodblock floor, on chilly nights flames dance in the small fireplace, and all around are antiques, alcoves of books and pot-plants.

The quiet, airy bedrooms are cottagey in style (simply but comfortably furnished). In a children's room, one of the two beds is up a ladder, with play-table below.

Although Christine will provide a homely dinner if requested (such as avocado, roast lamb and ice cream) this part of London has several French restaurants frequented by gourmets and, very close, a particularly good Greek one, Jason's.

The house is well placed as a centre from which to visit London because a car can easily be parked and nearby buses go in a few minutes to Chelsea, Kensington and Oxford Street (for fashionable shops, national museums, the Chelsea Flower Show and Hyde Park, for instance). Also easily accessible are main rail and coach termini (Victoria and Waterloo), the South Bank (Festival Hall, National Theatre, Hayward Gallery etc.), Clapham Junction (a new shopping complex), Westminster (Abbey and Houses of Parliament), the Strand (theatres and Covent Garden) and boat trips on the Thames.

Battersea's attractive riverside church deserves a visit (it has fine 17th-century monuments and royal portraits in stained glass).

Christine helps to organize the park's colourful Easter Parade; and can tell you whereabouts in it to find the children's zoo, waterfowl on the lake, wildlife reserves (guided walks with a naturalist are available), sports events and open-air concerts. She is a many-sided lady – a linguist, Jungian counsellor and (how useful at the end of an exhausting day's sightseeing!) reflexologist.

PARKFIELD HOUSE

Hogben's Hill, Selling, south of Faversham, Kent, ME13 9QU
Tel: 0227 752898

5 bedrooms (single, double or family) from £13.50. Less for 2 nights. Rooms have central heating; armchairs; views of country or garden. Evening coffee, tea, free. No smoking.
Sitting-room with central heating, open fire, TV, books. No smoking.
Small garden
Nearest main road A251 from Faversham to Ashford.

There were Hogbens on this hill in 1086 (they are named in the Domesday Book) . . . and there still are!

It is Mr and Mrs Hogben who own Parkfield, a largely modern house with a pretty garden, as well as the small joinery works alongside – John Hogben's principal activity. It is worth staying at Parkfield House simply to listen to him talk about Kentish ways and history (especially his stories of past Hogbens, who were blacksmiths, farmers, wheelwrights and smugglers). Next door there used to be an inn, called Ye Olde Century in memory of a John Hogben who lived there until he was 101.

The house, built in 1820, had become run down until about 30 years ago when Mr Hogben renovated and extended it. Now it is immaculate and very comfortable.

Although only bed-and-breakfast guests are taken (they can dine, very well indeed, at the old village inn – the White Lion), there is a sitting-room for their use in the evening, with television and big, velvet armchairs in which to relax by a log fire.

And if you want something special for breakfast (fish, fresh fruit, ham, cheese) Mrs Hogben will get it – and will do packed lunches.

Selling is in a very beautiful and tranquil part of Kent, well situated for touring, walking and sightseeing. It is, of course, the cathedral which brings most visitors to nearby Canterbury: one of Britain's finest and most colourful, with many historical associations, the site of Becket's martyrdom (commemorated in some of the finest stained glass in the world), the splendid tomb of the Black Prince, and much more.

The ancient walled city still has many surviving mediaeval and Tudor buildings, the beautiful River Stour, old churches and inns, Roman remains, a very good theatre, and lovely shops in its small lanes. It is in the middle of some of Kent's finest countryside, with a coast of great variety quite near (cliffs, sands or shingle; resorts, fishing harbours or historic ports) and ten golf courses. Howlett's Zoo and mediaeval Faversham are very popular, and the whole area is full of fine gardens and garden centres. It would be very easy to spend a fortnight here without discovering all there is to see in one of England's most beautiful and most historic counties, rich in towns with antique shops and fields of fruit where you can pick-your-own.

In blossom-time there are car 'trails' marked out among the orchards.

Readers' comments: Excellent in all respects, exceptional hospitality. Excellent service, well cared for. Warm welcome. Spotless. Attractive bedroom.

PEACOCK FARM GUEST-HOUSE

Redmile, west of Grantham (Lincolnshire), Leicestershire, NG
Tel: 0949 42475

9 bedrooms (single, double or family) from £12.50. Bargain breaks. Rooms have central heating; some have shower or bathroom; views of country or garden; tea/coffee facilities. (Clothes-washing facilities.)
Dinner £9 for 3 courses (with choices) and coffee, at 7.30pm. Vegetarian or special diets if ordered. Lunches, packed lunches, snacks. Coffee, tea, free. Drinks can be ordered.
Sitting-room with central heating, open fire, TV, books. Snooker, table tennis and piano elsewhere.
Large garden (small swimming-pool).
Nearest main road A52 from Nottingham to Grantham.

This guest-house with restaurant (built as a farm in the 18th century and later a canal bargees' inn) is ideal for a break when doing a long north-south journey on the nearby A1, particularly with children – or as a base from which to explore the many little-known attractions of Nottinghamshire and adjacent counties.

It is in the outstandingly beautiful Vale of Belvoir, with the Duke of Rutland's Belvoir Castle (full of art treasures) rearing its battlemented walls high above a nearby hilltop: an unforgettable sight. The topiary yew peacock on the front lawn, started in 1812, was inspired by the peacock in the crest of the Duke.

The Needs have created a happy family atmosphere here. Most rooms are simple and comfortable (two en suite rooms are very nicely equipped), and two are ideal for families: a self-contained pine cabin and a coach-house outside the main building. Children can safely play in the garden which has a large lawn, hammock, swings, small covered swimming-pool, playroom, pool-room, bicycles, barbecue, horse, goat and dogs. All around are wheatfields.

Food (much of it cooked by daughter Nicky) is above average, with home-made bread and soups, herbs from the garden and much local produce. Starters may include stuffed tomatoes or pan-fried sardines; main courses, salmon or trout with sorrel sauce or game pie; puddings, chocolate and rum nut loaf.

There are many popular sights in this region: Belvoir Castle, Belton House, Stapleford Park, Rutland Water and Wollaton Hall in its park; also Holme Pierrepont Hall, Doddington Hall, and Newstead Abbey (Byron's home). Eastwood has D. H. Lawrence's birthplace. Lincoln (cathedral), Southwell (minster), Sherwood Forest (Robin Hood display) and Nottingham are also near – the last a much underrated city. I recommend the arts museum in the castle and others at its foot (the lace museum is fascinating), river trips and walks through the Georgian quarter. The historic market towns of Stamford (in particular) and Newark are of great interest. One can shop for local Stilton, crafts and Nottingham lace to take home – Melton Mowbray is famous for pies and other pork delicacies. Well worth a detour is Burghley House, near Stamford.

231

...west of Stratford-upon-Avon,

...el: 0789 205889

7 bedrooms (double or family) from £12.50. All have own bath/shower; TV; tea/coffee facilities; central heating; views of country or garden. (Washing-machine on request.)
2 sitting-rooms with central heating, TV, books.
Small garden
Nearest main road A34 from Stratford-upon-Avon to Birmingham.

Mary Arden, Shakespeare's mother, grew up in the big half-timbered house which overlooks this cottage of much the same date, and it is quite possible that Shakespeare visited here when calling on his grandparents across the way. Now there is a museum of rural life in the Arden house.

Pear Tree Cottage, too, is half-timbered. From its flowery garden one steps onto a stone-flagged floor with an oak settle, other antiques and bunches of dried flowers. The flagstones are of blue lias, once quarried at Wilmcote, and to be seen also in Stratford's famous Clopton Bridge and the steps of St Paul's Cathedral in London.

In the beamed sitting-room, the yellow and green armchairs and colourful Staffordshire pottery figures show well against rugged stone walls. There is a little breakfast-room with country Hepplewhite chairs; and bedrooms (reached by steps and turns all the way) have very pleasant colour schemes – in one is a specially made Windsor bedhead. From the shower-room of another there is a perfect view of Mary Arden's house: an ideal, if unusual, place from which to photograph it!

Outside are two gardens, a stream, a pool with pink waterlilies, stone paths and seats under old apple trees. As Margaret Mander does not serve evening meals, most people stroll to the nearby Swan or Mason's Arms for dinner.

The cottage is right in the middle of 'Shakespeare country' with the Cotswold Hills to the south. The cities of Oxford, Worcester and Warwick – and their counties – are all within easy reach.

There is an attractive cross-country drive from Wilmcote to visit Charlecote Park, an Elizabethan house on a terrace overlooking the River Avon. The outside is more beautiful than the interior (much altered in Victorian times) and in the gatehouse is a museum of sporting life.

In the other direction, a rural drive will bring you to Coughton Court – another gatehouse, with Gunpowder Plot and Civil War associations and good furniture and paintings in its rooms. Beyond this lies the elegant old town of Alcester where two rivers meet, and Ragley Hall – a classical stone mansion on a hilltop (one of its treasures is a great, new mural in *trompe l'oeil* covering the wall of its big hall).

To the south the River Avon meanders on its way. Shakespeare is known to have frequented the inn at Bidford-on-Avon (which has a 14th-century bridge) and at Welford-on-Avon are a great many thatched and half-timbered cottages, each with its colourful flower-garden.

The countryside in this part of Warwickshire is pleasant rather than dramatic, but there are attractive woodland walks and picnic spots.

Readers' comments: Ideal in all respects. Have always received most kind and courteous attention and a wonderful breakfast. Thoroughly enjoyed every stay.

232

PEAT GATE HEAD

Low Row, west of Richmond, North Yorkshire, DL11 6PP   Tel: 0748 86388

C H S X

rear view

6 bedrooms (single or double) from £30 with dinner. Much less for 2 nights. Rooms have central heating; three have shower; armchairs; views of river and moor; tea/coffee facilities.
Dinner 4 courses and coffee, at 7pm. Special diets if ordered. Drinks can be ordered. Packed lunches.

2 sitting-rooms with central heating, wood burner, open fire, TV, books; bar. No smoking in some rooms.
Garden and meadows.
Nearest main road A6108 from Richmond to Leyburn.

It sometimes seems that anywhere north of Leeds now calls itself Herriot country, what with almost countless books, films, and television series. Though the author actually practises to the east of the county, much filming of his books was done in the Yorkshire Dales, and Peat Gate Head is just along the moor road (with watersplash) where the opening sequence of every television episode was recorded.

Alan Earl had long loved Peat Gate Head, a 300-year-old Swaledale farmhouse built of the local limestone, and when his job as a history lecturer ended with the closure of the training college where he worked, he decided to buy it and to turn his enthusiasm for cooking to good use by opening it as a guest-house. From several choices at each course one might select, for instance, salmon mousse, chicken breasts in orange-and-tarragon sauce, and queen of puddings.

The beamed house is pleasantly furnished. There is a vast stone chimneypiece in the dining-room, and in the sitting-room a wood-burning stove pleasantly scents the air. Two bedrooms are on the ground floor (one with own shower and toilet). The bathroom is on the ground floor (but with a toilet upstairs).

Outside the door, a summerhouse on the lawn looks across a sweep of Swaledale, a textbook illustration of a valley, from the river running along the flat bottom, through stone-walled fields, to open moorland. From the bedrooms on the opposite side of the house, you are at eye level with peewits and curlews. Richmond and other castles, especially Barnard Castle, are extra attractions, along with waterfalls and the Dales scenery. There is more on these on other pages of this book.

Readers' comments: Made us so welcome and entertained us non-stop; delicious meals; peaceful atmosphere. Great charm, most acceptable dinner, massive breakfast. Very good value, most entertaining too. Three unforgettable days . . . the quality of everything. A fine man, a character! Took a great deal of trouble. Excellent cuisine. Food interesting, well cooked and presented. Delightful premises; high standard of comfort. Totally relaxed mood.

233

PENNINE LODGE

D S

St John's Chapel, Weardale, west of Stanhope, County Durham, DL13 1QX
Tel: 0388 537247

5 bedrooms (double or family) from £13.50. Reductions for 3 nights. Bargain breaks. Rooms have central heating; shower or bathroom; views of country; tea/coffee facilities. **Dinner** £6.50 for 3 courses and coffee, at 7pm. Vegetarian or special diets if ordered. Packed lunches, snacks. Drinks can be ordered. No smoking.
Sitting-room with central heating, TV, books.
Large garden
Nearest main road A689 from Stanhope to Alston.
Closed November–mid-March

Pennine Lodge was built in the 16th century, and it has the long and narrow shape typical of a Weardale farmhouse. Just below the windows of the corridor which connects the bedrooms is the upper River Wear, rushing over a small waterfall backed by trees, a beautiful spot. The rooms themselves are full of interest, with lots of timber and stone, antiques and bric-a-brac: in one a grandfather clock (silent!), in another a real Durham quilt.

Guests dine in a long, low-ceilinged room next to the garden, with a stone inglenook at one end. There are three courses: a starter (or else cheese), with a main course which is quite likely to be a casserole of pheasant or other game from the Raby estates, and, for example, rhubarb pie and cream. All is home-made by Yvonne Raine, including jams and bread; afternoon tea is available.

Raby Castle is one of the best of its kind, and High Force is England's highest waterfall. Killhope Wheel is a huge waterwheel which, with its associated buildings, is being very well restored to display the history of lead mining, the mainstay of the north Pennines for centuries. Over the highest road in England is the isolated town of Alston, and beyond that the lovely Eden Valley and the Lake District. Hadrian's Wall, the Beamish open-air museum, Bowes Museum and Durham Cathedral are other outstanding day-trips.

Northward is the picture-postcard village of Blanchland. Westward is the village which gave its name to Frosterley marble – actually a kind of puddingstone – which, in worked and polished form, can be seen in some of the columns of Durham Cathedral. Another village, Rookhope, was written about by W. H. Auden. Rookhope Burn, which joins the Wear near Eastgate, is of interest both botanically and geologically, and by one of its waterfalls a Roman altar was found a century ago.

Readers' comments: It's so good I've been back repeatedly. Lovely position, comfortable without being pretentious. Delightful old house, competent and delightful hostess, food excellent.

Prices are the minimum *per person* in a double room at the beginning of the year.

PENSCOT FARMHOUSE HOTEL

C(8) **D H**

Shipham, north of Cheddar, Somerset, BS25 1TW   Tel: 093 484 2659

18 bedrooms (single, double or family) from £14.50. Less for long stays. Discounts to people after a second visit. Rooms have central heating; shower and wc; armchairs; views of country or garden; tea/coffee facilities; TV for hire.
Dinner £6 for 3 courses and coffee, at 7pm. Vegetarian meals if ordered. Lunches, packed lunches, snacks. Coffee, tea, for a charge. Non-residents not admitted to dining-room (but there is a restaurant too, Wed.-Sat. only). Drinks can be ordered.
2 sitting-rooms with central heating, open fire, TV, books; bar.
Large garden and orchard.
Nearest main road A38 from Bristol to Taunton.
Closed December

Built in the 15th century as farm cottages, Penscot became an inn on the village green, and still retains much of that character. It is a long low building, white-walled and with low beams and log fires inside. The atmosphere is informal and comfortable. Bedrooms are simple, the sitting-room well provided with plenty of deep armchairs and doors to the garden where one can sit in the sun. There is a small conservatory with a flourishing vine and hanging baskets of flowers.

There are two dining-rooms. The one (non-smoking) for residents has pine alcoves and Scandinavian-style chairs. Here the Tildens serve a set meal such as home-made soup, chicken casserole with local vegetables, and cheesecake. In a converted barn there is an à la carte menu too: mainly conventional food such as trout, duck, steaks etc., with many vegetarian dishes.

Most of the bedrooms are quite simple but two (on the ground floor) have special features. One very attractive room has a four-poster, plus an extra bed; and the other would be ideal for a family as there is a children's room adjoining.

From peaceful Shipham there are far views to Bridgwater Bay and the Welsh Hills. It lies on the edge of the beautiful Mendip Hills (and half way along the walkers' Mendip Way which winds from the coast to Wells). In the neighbourhood are facilities for riding, golf, caving and painting. Plenty of sightseeing, too: castles, stately homes, gorges, woods, viewpoints, museums, wildlife, gardens, the Wookey Hole caves and innumerable churches of architectural interest. Plenty of gardens, too, including those at Longleat and Cricket St Thomas; and antique shops. The Tildens have produced a book of local walks.

Readers' comments: Delightful. Tasty home cooking. Every comfort, good service, happy atmosphere. Good food and welcoming atmosphere. Nice to see everyone smiling. Warm welcome, enjoyable atmosphere and food, very good value. Delightful rooms; food was great; personal attention. So friendly, so peaceful. Gracious hosts, food wonderful. Cheerful, willing staff made us feel so welcome.

235

PICKFORD HOUSE

C P T S X

Bath Road, Beckington, south of Bath (Avon), Somerset, BA3 6SJ
Tel: 0373 830329

3 bedrooms (double or family) from £12. Less for 4 nights and bargain breaks. Rooms have own bath/shower; TV; tea/coffee facilities; central heating; views of river, country or garden. No smoking. (Washing-machine on request.)

Dinner A la carte or £8 for 4 courses (with choices) and coffee, at 7pm or later. Vegetarian or special diets if ordered. Lunches, packed lunches, snacks. Tea, coffee, free. Drinks can be ordered.

2 sitting-rooms with central heating, open fire, TV, books, piano, record-player; bar.

Small garden

Nearest main road A36 from Bath to Warminster.

Closed around Easter

Sometimes parties of friends take the whole of this hilltop house for a gourmet weekend together – for Angela Pritchard is a cordon bleu cook (and cookery teacher) while Ken is a great wine enthusiast. (Every year, they go to a different region of France or Germany to bring back little-known wines and local recipes to accompany them.)

On such weekends, the guests are invited to enjoy a Somerset cream tea to be followed later by a candle-lit dinner of 6 courses with appropriate wines. On the next day, they explore the area's attractions (on their own or with the Pritchards at the helm), which include Bath, Wells and innumerable stately homes, before another gourmet meal. On Sunday morning, there is the heated swimming-pool behind a wall in the garden or picturesque Beckington in which to pass the time before a traditional roast lunch.

Even on everyday occasions Pickford House food is exceptional. Angela offers the choice of a 4-course dinner or what she calls a 'pot-luck' one of 3 courses. An example of the former: mushroom roulade, lamb en croûte, mulberry mousse (made from garden fruit) and cheeses (wine included). And of the latter: fish au gratin, liver-and-bacon casserole, bananas baked with Kirsch (wine included).

As to the house itself, this is one of a pair that were built from honey-coloured Bath stone for spinster sisters in 1804. The furnishings are comfortable rather than elegant, with some bedrooms in a garden annexe. In addition to the principal sitting-room, there is a family room which has television and toys to keep children occupied; and outside is a large walled garden with views across the Frome Valley.

All visitors dining at Pickford House are offered a free pre-dinner drive around little-known sights in the vicinity, and the Pritchards will advise on other sightseeing, book you into the local theatres, or help in other ways.

The area is not only very beautiful but full of historic interest. Go to Bath, of course, for its Georgian crescents and streets, elegant shops, abbey, Roman temple, baths and museums (especially the museum of American history). Wells has an outstanding cathedral and Bishop's Palace; Glastonbury, the famous Tor as well as abbey. Castle Combe claims, with good cause, to be the prettiest village in England and is probably the most photographed. Devizes, Bradford-on-Avon, Frome and Malmesbury are each worth a leisurely visit. The area has some of England's most famous mansions, filled with art treasures and surrounded by noble parks or gardens: Longleat, Stourhead, Dyrham Park, Lacock Abbey, Kingston Lacey, Corsham Court, Montacute and Bowood.

236

PILLMEAD HOUSE

C D H

North Lane, Buriton, south of Petersfield, Hampshire, GU31 5RS
Tel: 0730 66795

central heating; views of country or garden. No smoking. (Washing-machine on request.)

Dinner £8 for 3 courses (with choices) and coffee, at 7.30pm. Non-residents not admitted. Vegetarian or special diets if ordered. Lunches, packed lunches, snacks. Tea, coffee, extra. Drinks can be brought in.

Sitting-room with central heating, open fire, TV, books, record-player. No smoking.

Large garden

Nearest main road A3 from Petersfield to Portsmouth.

2 bedrooms (double) from £17. Both have own bath/shower; TV; tea/coffee facilities;

Sarah Moss used to run a kitchenware shop of distinction, and so she is particularly well equipped with things to produce, for instance, home-made pasta or ice cream – and she sometimes demonstrates their use to interested visitors who end up in the big kitchen after they have enjoyed the gourmet results. She grows much of the produce that is used in the kitchen for such meals as game soup followed by roast lamb with a gratin of courgettes and then French apple tart, for example. Dessert grapes come from John's greenhouse.

The house overlooks a valley, its lawn and rock garden descending steeply among terraced beds of roses and lavender. To the side is a tree-swing for children. Sometimes breakfast is served out here so that visitors can enjoy a view of the Queen Elizabeth country park while eating eggs from the free-range hens.

The sitting-room's bow windows, too, make the most of the view. This is a pretty room, with pink wildflower curtains and sofas, and Victorian tapestry chairs.

Upstairs, white walls contrast with moss-green carpets. One bedroom, cottage-style, has pink fabrics and patchwork cushions; in another apricot predominates, there is a patchwork bedspread and bow window.

Adjoining the house is a building that was once a schoolroom. John now uses it in connection with his work, which is renovating old buildings, a subject on which he is a mine of information. Pillmead House is itself of interest: its lozenge-paned windows and brick-and-flint walls are typical of many houses in this area, but the Tudor chimneys – very elaborate, and 8 feet high – came from a mansion.

There really are toads at **Toad's Alley** in South Lane on the other side of Buriton, home of interior designer, Patricia Bushall (tel: 0730 63880). They can sometimes be seen heading to the stream which lies between the garden and the crest along which walkers follow the South Downs Way. The secluded house comprises three tiny farmworkers' cottages built in the 15th century, with brick-floored hall and low-sloping ceilings upstairs. A sitting-room for guests is attractively fur-

nished, like the other rooms, with pale colours.

(Bed-and-breakfast only; both the village inns do good evening meals and are only two minutes' walk away.)

237

PIPPS FORD

Needham Market, north of Ipswich, Suffolk, IP6 8LJ   Tel: 044979 208

C H P T S

6 bedrooms (single or double) from £16. Winter discounts. Rooms have central heating or electric heaters; shower or bathroom; armchairs; views of country or farmland/garden; tea/coffee facilities; TV on request. **Dinner** £13 for 4 courses and coffee, at 7.15pm. Drinks can be ordered. Vegetarian meals if ordered. Afternoon teas. No dinner on Sundays.

Sitting-room with central heating, open fire, books, record-player. TV room. Piano. **Garden** with unheated swimming-pool, croquet lawn; river, meadow and woodland, with coarse fishing; and a tennis court. **Nearest main road** A45 from Ipswich to Bury St Edmunds.

On a stretch of the River Gipping that has been designated an 'area of outstanding natural beauty' stands a large Tudor farmhouse. Raewyn Hackett-Jones has made patchwork quilts or cushion-covers for every room and searched out attractive fabrics (Laura Ashley, French ones and so on) for curtains or upholstery. She puts flowers in each bedroom. Many of the beds are collectors' pieces: a four-poster, a French provincial one and several ornamental brass beds. Oriental rugs cover floors of wood or stone. Even the bathrooms attached to each bedroom are attractive. One is spectacular, with a huge oval bath. Some bedrooms are in newly converted stables, with sitting-room.

This is a house of inglenook fireplaces, sloping floors, low beams and historic associations, for it once belonged to Tudor chronicler Richard Hakluyt. Visitors who use the sitting-room, with log fire, can enjoy the family's huge collection of classical records. Meals are served in a flowery conservatory.

Breakfasts are exceptional. From an enormous choice, you could select exotic juices; home-made sausages or black pudding; home-made yogurt, croissants or cinnamon toast; waffles, crumpets, muffins; kidneys, mackerel, fishcakes.

Popular dinner dishes include kidneys in a sauce of mustard, sherry and cream; pears and Stilton in filo pastry; a roulade of salmon, turbot and spinach; pork with ginger and orange sauce; tropical fruits with *fromage frais* and blackcurrant sauce.

Beyond the garden, there is coarse fishing in the river, where cricket-bat willows grow, and a Roman site. Interesting places to visit by car are Sandringham, Constable country, Lavenham, Aldeburgh, Southwold, Norwich, Ipswich and Bury St Edmunds. The area is full of pretty villages and ancient churches.

Readers' comments: Most impressed; made very welcome; food absolutely super; most hospitable place; relaxed and informal, thoroughly happy and comfortable; delightful house, beautifully furnished; food and service outstanding; one of the best holidays ever; friendly good humour. A fitting climax to our wonderful trip with 'SOTBT'. Charming and talented hostess, food beautifully garnished.

238

POACHERS' INN

C D

Piddletrenthide, north of Dorchester, Dorset, DT2 7QX Tel: 03004 358

6 bedrooms (single, double or family) from £16. Less for 7 nights. Rooms have own bath/shower; TV; tea/coffee facilities; central heating; views of river, country or garden.

Dinner A la carte. Lunches, packed lunches, snacks. Tea, coffee, extra. Drinks can be ordered.

Sitting-room with central heating, open fire; bars.

Large garden

Nearest main road A352 from Dorchester to Sherborne.

A mass of colourful flowers against white walls caught my eye when passing through the village, and I stopped to visit this pretty inn. At the back, one crosses a footbridge over the tiny River Piddle (after which the village is named) to enter the pleasant beer-garden of the inn, parts of which date back to the 18th century. To one side of this is a modern wing of ground-floor bedrooms in pink-and-white or other fresh colour schemes; and to the other a solar-heated swimming-pool enclosed for privacy by wood fencing. There are also bedrooms (rather larger) inside the inn.

The bars are all you might expect of a busy village inn; the dining-room, with turquoise leather chairs, is set apart from their bustle (there is also a barbecue in the garden).

Here Dennis Fox and his family provide typical English pub food such as prawn cocktail or soup, steak or salmon.

Nearby Dorchester is the 'Casterbridge' of Hardy's novel (and his birthplace, a cottage at Higher Bockhampton, can be visited). The town is still full of farmers doing business, inns selling local beer and handsome buildings of Portland stone with which he was familiar. It was here that the Bloody Assize took place (when Judge Jeffreys condemned to death so many who took part in the 1685 Monmouth Rebellion), and also the 1834 trial of the Tolpuddle Martyrs, transported for their attempts to set up a trade union.

West of the village is Cerne Abbas, famous for its white giant cut into the green turf of the hills, a pagan fertility symbol, and for the ancient abbey remains behind its small streets of Tudor houses. Nearby Sydling St Nicholas has an old smithy and a church with a multitude of gargoyles and monuments. To the south is Stinsford, a mecca for Hardy enthusiasts because his heart is buried here (his ashes are in Westminster Abbey). Puddletown's church has fine monuments, Athelhampton a battlemented mansion surrounded by a series of lovely gardens, and Tolpuddle the same great sycamore under which the 'martyrs' held their illegal meetings.

The church at Bere Regis is remarkable for its carved roof and life-size apostles.

For another day's outing, head in the direction of picturesque Milton Abbas (described elsewhere) and its abbey church; and Blandford Forum, an elegant 18th-century market town with good opportunities to buy books and paintings. If you go from here to Shaftesbury, avoid the direct road in favour of scenic lanes at the end of Cranborne Chase because there are fine views from the downs here.

POLETREES FARM
Brill, west of Aylesbury, Buckinghamshire, HP18 9TZ   Tel: 0844 238276

2 bedrooms (double or family) from £13. Tea/coffee facilities; central heating; views of country or garden. No smoking.
Dinner £10 for 4 courses and coffee. Drinks can be brought in.
Sitting-room with central heating, open fire, TV, books.
Large garden with swimming-pool.
Nearest main road A41 from Aylesbury to Bicester.

There is clematis round the porch, baskets brimming with begonias and lobelias hang on the walls, and all around are roses, apple trees and views of fields: a scene of total peace. But in the 16th century this was a coaching inn on the principal road (Roman in origin) from Oxford to Buckingham. Now that road is nothing but a grassy track, for the traffic goes another way.

Inside, stone walls, oak beams and an inglenook with a rare 15th-century window beside it – tiny oak mullions and wood-pegged shutters – have survived the centuries, though some features were plastered over or boarded up until the Coopers did careful restoration work. The water for the house still comes from a spring.

So ancient is the area that King Lud – that prehistoric (or mythical?) figure for whom London's Ludgate is named – is reputed to have hunted boar here when all was forest. Hence the name of a nearby village, Ludgershall; which is where Wycliffe started his great work of translating the Bible into English for the first time.

Anita has furnished her ancient home well. In the dining-room a thick blue carpet is complemented by chair and curtain fabric of flowery blue and bedrooms are pleasantly decorated too, with handsome walnut furniture. She caned the bedheads herself. On a wall of one room is a collection of keys – all from the old Brill railway, closed in 1926; and also what looks like a huge horseshoe but is in fact an ox shoe, from the time when oxen were used to draw carts.

For dinner you might be offered such dishes as stuffed tomatoes, roast beef, spotted dick and cheeses. Occasionally Anita cooks a local speciality, 'bacon clanger', which is a rolypoly made with bacon.

Apart from livestock (sheep, cattle, ducks, geese – and a donkey) the farm produces a rather unusual 'crop' – turf, sold to garden centres. And in the garden is another pleasant surprise, a swimming-pool.

Buckinghamshire is one of the loveliest counties around London: in the south are the Chiltern Hills, with dense forests of beech – a handsome sight; and in the north the broad Vale of Aylesbury threaded by little streams – it is here that most of the stately homes and fine churches are to be found; great mansions include Ascott (outstanding furniture and paintings), Claydon (with Florence Nightingale museum), Hughenden (Disraeli's home), Stowe (by Vanbrugh) and Waddesdon (the Rothschild house of French Renaissance splendour).

The Thames runs along the southern edge of the county – with beauty-spots like Boulter's Lock, Bray (famous for punting), the spectacular reach by Cliveden (stately home, now an expensive hotel), Marlow, Medmenham and Hambleden.

Brill itself is of interest. It has a hilltop windmill, good buildings of the 15th to 17th centuries, and nearby is a mediaeval gatehouse, Boarstall Tower.

240

POND COTTAGE

C(6)

Brandsby Road, Stillington, north of York, YO6 1NY   Tel: 0347 810796

2 bedrooms (double or family) from £11. Rooms have central heating; views of country or garden. No smoking.
Sitting-room with central heating, open fire, TV, books. Tea, coffee, free. No smoking.
Garden with croquet, badminton and barbecue.
Nearest main road A19 from York to Thirsk.
Closed December and January

In a barn adjoining this tiny primrose-yellow cottage is a treasure-trove of domestic bygones – from kitchen tools to antique bottles and cans, woodware to chamber-pots. For the Thurstans are antique dealers, specializing in 'kitchenalia' and pine furniture.

The 18th-century house itself is furnished with antiques, and its shelves and nooks are filled with curios. There are collections of coronation mugs and Staffordshire dogs in the low-beamed sitting-room, where high-backed wing chairs are grouped around an inglenook fireplace. This is a house of twists and turns, unexpected steps and low windows. Its pleasant bedrooms overlook a terrace with stone troughs of flowers, a croquet lawn and a natural pond. The only drawback is the distance of the bath from the guests' bedrooms, a minor inconvenience considering the modest price charged.

Dianne serves only breakfast because (the citizens of nearby York being great diners-out) the area is very well supplied with eating-places.

Stillington is almost equidistant from the city of York, the coast, the North York Moors and the Dales – each described elsewhere in this book, and each offering totally different holiday experiences needing many days to explore. It is in the middle of the great Vale of York, a fertile area watered by the River Ure and its tributaries, unspoilt by industry. All around are traces of history, from prehistoric man and later the Romans to the Civil War, and onward. The nearest stately home is Sutton Park which has art treasures and furniture once in Buckingham House (precursor of Buckingham Palace) and gardens laid out by Capability Brown; the nearest market town is cobblestoned Easingwold.

The area is scattered with pretty villages, built of warm red brick and yellow stone and roofed with clay pantiles. A typical one is Coxwold, where Laurence Sterne was the incumbent. His house, called Shandy Hall after the house in his most famous book, is open to the public during the summer months. Now run by a trust, its rescue from neglect was the work of a single enthusiast for the author, and it is filled with his collection of Sterne memorabilia. The brick skin conceals a much older structure, and there is a curious Tudor wall-painting uncovered during restoration.

York itself, one of the most-visited cities in the country, hardly needs description: the newest draw, among its many attractions, must be the recently completed restoration work in the minster, which has put right the extensive damage caused by the lightning strike of a few years ago.

Readers' comments: Wonderful! Enjoyed very much. A warm welcome. Delightful house, hospitable and sensible hostess, cosy and comfortable, delicious and plentiful breakfasts. Will go again.

POND COTTAGE S

The Green, Warmington, north-west of Banbury (Oxfordshire), Warwickshire, OX17 1BU Tel: 029589 682 (*evenings best*)

2 bedrooms (single and double) from £15. **10% less for readers of this book if they stay a week.** Rooms have central heating; views of village green or garden; double room has a shower.

Dinner £9 for 3 courses and coffee, at 7pm, or by arrangement. Coffee, tea free. Non-residents not admitted. Drinks can be ordered or brought in.

Sitting-room with central heating, open fire, TV.

Nearest main road A41 from Banbury to Warwick.

Closed November–March

This village, though near the A41, is so tucked away that, beauty-spot though it is, few tourists find it. Around a sloping village green with duck-pond and waterlilies, dominated at one end by a Tudor manor house, are ranged rows of charming cottages built from warm local stone, roses and honeysuckle climbing up their walls. Mrs Viljoen's home is one of these.

She has furnished its small rooms with great elegance. Gleaming antique furniture and silver contrast with the rugged stones of the sitting-room walls and hearth. She has chosen browns and lemon to harmonize with the colour of the stone. One pretty bedroom is all blue – from the silk spread and the cover of the armchair to the flowery Victorian wallpaper.

At the back is a tiny garden with a seat among roses and nasturtiums climbing up the walls.

Vi asks visitors to say what kind of food they like. A typical menu might include home-made soup, chicken with almond sauce, and a tart of her own fruit, or home-made ice cream.

Vi Viljoen is a Tourist Board guide – so is well qualified to advise visitors on sightseeing.

Pond Cottage has appeared on the cover of *Forever Ambridge* by Norman Painting (who plays Phil Archer in the radio series), a resident in the village. Within a few miles of it are: the castles of Broughton, Warwick and Kenilworth; Stratford-upon-Avon; Sulgrave Manor (home of George Washington's ancestors); sixteen stately homes belonging to the National Trust, a number of antique shops, and also fine gardens. The Cotswolds, Althorp, Oxford and Blenheim are also easily accessible.

Readers' comments: A delightful stay. A pleasure to see so many lovely things in the house. Welcomed us like friends, and made our wedding anniversary dinner a feast. Delicious food, extremely good value. Most friendly and helpful; food memorable; pretty garden. Lovely little place. Delightful little cottage. Most enjoyable and relaxing. Charming house, warm welcome. Like staying with a friend, every need anticipated.

For explanation of code letters (**C, D, H, PT, S, S-C, X**) see page xxvi

POOL HOUSE HOTEL   C

Hanley Road, Upton-upon-Severn, south of Worcester, WR8 0PA
Tel: 06846 2151

rear view

9 bedrooms (single, double or family) from £14. Less for 7 nights or bargain breaks. Rooms have central heating or electric heaters; most have shower or bathroom; armchairs; views of country or garden.
Dinner £8.50 for 4 courses (with choices) and coffee, at 6.30pm. Vegetarian or special diets if ordered. Packed lunches, snacks. Coffee, tea, for a charge. Drinks can be ordered.
Sitting-room with central heating, open fire, books. Also a TV room; bar.
Large garden with fishing and croquet.
Nearest main road A4104 from Pershore to the A449.

I have included this hotel for its superb river-bank setting, with gardens that make the most of this. Herbaceous borders wander among lawns with fruit trees, sloping down to the waterside. The 18th-century house is simply furnished. I thought bedroom 2 particularly attractive: it has a rose-and-white colour scheme and a good view of the river. Jill Webb's flower arrangements are a feature of the house.

Meals are traditional: home-made soup or a prawn cocktail might be followed by roast beef (with fresh local vegetables) and a rhubarb-and-raisin crumble, for instance. Beyond the peach dining-room is a hexagonal TV room with big armchairs and a door leading to the garden; and then a sitting-room with log fire.

From the house one enjoys views of the Malvern Hills. Not far off is the River Avon, the Cotswolds, 'Shakespeare country' and the lovely Wye Valley. Other sightseeing possibilities include Tewkesbury Abbey, Cheltenham spa, Worcester Cathedral (and the Royal Porcelain factory), Hereford and Gloucester (two more cathedrals). Upton itself is a delightful old market town, as is Ledbury. The Malverns have a spring garden show, Hidcote is near, and Pershore Agricultural College grounds are well worth visiting. Racing, fishing, cricket and birdwatching at the waterfowl sanctuary are other pursuits which bring visitors here.

In Upton-upon-Severn itself (a small town that needs to be explored on foot and by boat), there are plaques dotted about on sites of historic events – the most photographed one describes how, on that spot, Cromwell was acclaimed in 1651 'with abundance of joy and shouting' after his victory at the Battle of Upton. The town's history, which goes back to Saxon times, is displayed in its heritage centre (in the old cupola-topped church tower). You can go as far as Tewkesbury on the pleasure-cruiser, or simply stay in Upton to make the most of its little shops, bistros and byways. The 'Three Counties' agricultural show takes place nearby.

Readers' comments: Most helpful. Food and accommodation excellent. Very enjoyable week's stay. The loveliest garden; friendly people. Beautiful setting.

When writing to me, if you want a reply please enclose a stamped addressed envelope.

PORTWELL HOUSE

C D H PT

Market Place, Faringdon, Oxfordshire, SN7 7HU   Tel: 0367 20197

7 bedrooms (single, double or family) from £15. Less for 4 nights or bargain breaks. Rooms have central heating; own bathroom; TV, armchairs; tea/coffee facilities. (Laundering facilities available.)
Sitting area with central heating, books.
Nearest main road A420 from Oxford to Swindon.

David and Margo Manning run a small and friendly guest-house.

The curiously wedge-shaped house is well over 300 years old. Inside, all is fresh and neat. Up two winding staircases are bedrooms (each with bathroom) which have colourful curtains and duvets, comfortable chairs from which to watch television and, in some cases, views of the weekly market below. There is a ground-floor bedroom too, and a sitting area with pot-plants, aquarium, armchairs and books. B & b only, but there are many good eating-places in and around the Market Place – including the Crown Inn which adjoins Portwell House.

Faringdon is a pretty town – a place of mossy roofs, old inn signs, swinging lamps and clocks on brackets, with a colonnaded buttermarket. Brickwork, stone and colourful stucco give the streets variety, and there is an ancient church half-hidden behind great yews (one of many in this area). A good centre for public transport and for many sports, it is at the heart of an area full of interest with plenty to explore. In the spring, the grounds of nearby Faringdon House produce a wonderful display of flowers. This was the home of Lord Berners (the model for Lord Merlin in *The Pursuit of Love*), who also built the Folly Tower on the nearby hill. In his will, he asked to be stuffed and placed on top of it, but his executors thought otherwise.

In the surrounding Vale of the White Horse there are plenty of good canalside walks (with revitalizing little inns along the way); Uffington church, which has memories of Tom Brown (of *Tom Brown's Schooldays*); the prehistoric white horse itself, cut out of the turf on the chalk downs; and adjacent earthworks with far views. The old Ridgeway Path runs here, with Wayland's Smithy close by. Great Coxwell has a superb tithe barn; Coleshill and Buscot Park are two National Trust properties, and Ashdown and Littlecote are not much further. Then there are the wilder reaches of the Thames – Lechlade, the source, and Kelmscott (William Morris's lovely house). The theatres of Oxford, Swindon and Newbury are accessible. Pusey gardens, Blenheim, the Cotswold Wildlife Park, old Burford and the Lechlade garden centre (for fuchsias) are top attractions. In fact, from here you can easily reach a number of interesting areas described elsewhere: Hungerford, Cirencester, Marlborough and the Chilterns, for example.

Readers' comments: Kindness, attention and hospitality. Pleasant and comfortable; the best bargain for a long time. Excellent standards, friendliness, very happy atmosphere. Outstanding. Excellent in every way. Cannot praise too highly, warm welcome. Attractive, roomy bedrooms. Excellent atmosphere.

PRESTON FARM

Harberton, south of Totnes, Devon, TQ9 7SW   Tel: 0803 862235

3 bedrooms (double or family) from £11.50. Rooms have central heating or electric heaters; shower; armchairs; views of country or garden; tea/coffee facilities. (Washing-machine available.)
Dinner £6.50 for 4 courses and coffee, at 6.45pm. Snacks. Coffee, tea, free. Non-residents not admitted. Drinks can be brought in.
Sitting-room with central heating, open fire, TV, books, record-player.
Garden and fields.
Nearest main road A381 from Totnes to Kingsbridge.
Closed to visitors in winter

It's unusual to find a working farm with its house right in a village (a very quiet one), but there used to be several such clustered together in Harberton. The Steers' house, built in 1680, has been in the same family for generations. All the rooms are comfortable, and there is good home cooking at dinner-time, with dishes as varied as pancakes stuffed with salmon au gratin, chicken Marengo, roasts, pies, baked Alaska, treacle pudding. The ingredients are mostly home-grown or local. One bedroom is in 'Country Diary' fabrics; another has a matching pink-and-cream bathroom. Breakfast comes on 'help-yourself' platters – conventional bacon and eggs or more unusual things like hog's pudding or smoked haddock.

Harberton is a picturesque cluster of old cottages with colourful gardens, set in a valley. Its 13th-century church has a magnificent painted screen and stained glass windows. The local inn is of equal antiquity. Preston Farmhouse was once a manor house, which is why rooms are spacious.

Most visitors head for historic Totnes and its castle, or to Dartmouth and Salcombe, for example, via country lanes. Dartmoor lies to the north, the coast to the south, and neither is far off. Modbury is one of many picturesque towns near here, its Georgian or slate-hung houses clinging to a steep hill. Buckfastleigh (with abbey built in 1938; notable stained glass) is where the Dart Valley steam trains go, along a lovely route. At Dartmeet, one of the most famous of beauty-spots, two rivers join – there is a pretty 'clapper' bridge of stone slabs nearby. Totnes itself has, in addition to the 13th-century castle, steep lanes beside the River Dart; historic buildings such as the Guildhall; arguably the finest rood-screen in England, in St Mary's church; and a quaint Butterwalk.

A little further is Widecombe-in-the-Moor with its huge old church, its September fair and 'Uncle Tom Cobleigh an' all'. Exeter, Plymouth and Torbay are easily accessible by car. River trips, Dartington Hall, the Shire Horse Centre, innumerable gardens and garden centres add to the interest of this area, as do its many antique shops, markets and fairs (e.g. every Tuesday in Totnes).

Readers' comments: Far more than we had hoped for; made most welcome; meals were excellent, good variety and generous helpings. Warm welcome, excellent accommodation, superb cooking. Absolutely marvellous. Everything perfect – especially the fish pie! Very comfortable; delicious meals; perfect company. Excellent accommodation, super meals, everything delightful. First-class in every way. Happy atmosphere. A delight to be there – visited twice.

PRIORY COTTAGE

C(5) **D S X**

Butley Low Corner, east of Woodbridge, Suffolk, IP12 3QD

Tel: 0394 450382

3 bedrooms (single and double) from £12.50. Less for 2 nights and bargain breaks. Rooms have central heating and views of river, country or garden. No smoking. (Washing-machine on request.)
Dinner £9 for 4 courses (with choices) and coffee, at 7pm. Non-residents not admitted. Vegetarian or special diets if ordered. Packed lunches. Tea, coffee, free. Drinks can be brought in.
Sitting-room with central heating, open fire, TV, books, record-player. No smoking.
Large garden
Nearest main road A12 from Ipswich to Lowestoft.

Cats, cats and more cats (lifelike pottery ones) inhabit every room of this country cottage, some for sale. On arrival, visitors are greeted by a Muscovy duck who has made the well-head his own throne; all around is a prettily landscaped garden.

The entrance hall has an unusual floor of polished 'pamment' tiles, sofas and arrangements of dried flowers. There are velvet chairs in the lime green L-shaped sitting-room, and a log stove. In the dining-room (pine table, dresser and Windsor chairs) Rosemary Newnham serves dinner – if ordered in advance by four or more people – which may comprise sherry, soup or mousse, a casserole or pie, fruit fool or meringues, and cheeses. Alternatively, there are several inns and restaurants in the area: at one inn, Suffolk folk songs can be heard on Sundays.

Upstairs, rooms with clear bright colours, flowery wallpaper friezes, pine doors and beds, and louvred built-ins are neat and cheerful: some have views of Butley Creek and the bird reserve on Havergate Island. I particularly liked the blue-and-white one which has a prettily draped bed and linen trimmed with broderie anglaise. A small box of chocolates greets new arrivals.

The cottage is in an area designated as being of outstanding natural beauty, and completely unspoilt. It is virtually on the Suffolk Coast Path (50 miles of footpath and bridleway) which wanders through forests where deer roam and along a shore much frequented by migrant wildfowl and by small yachts. Beyond the elaborately carved gatehouse of Butley Priory lies Orford – celebrated for its oysterage and for its huge polygonal castle (early Norman). Further up the coast is the old-fashioned resort of Aldeburgh (made famous by Britten's opera, 'Peter Grimes'), with an internationally famous music festival centred on the Maltings at nearby Snape and with events in numerous churches too. From the waterfront here are views of small craft bobbing on the estuary and, at times, avocets and oystercatchers combing the marshy banks at low tide. Inland lies Framlingham and another outstanding castle. South of the sailing centre of Woodbridge is the only big resort, Felixstowe: sedate and orderly, with well-tended flowerbeds along the seafront.

The sunny, breezy coast here has been much eroded (entire towns have vanished into the sea after floods or storms) and so the principal road lies some way inland (through heaths and across estuaries), with only lanes penetrating to the shore, which means the area is undisturbed by traffic or crowds. There are any number of outings: horse-drawn wagon rides, walks with a naturalist, a cruise in a motor launch, a cordon bleu picnic with champagne, clay-pigeon shooting and much else.

246

PROSPECT HILL HOTEL   C
Kirkoswald, north of Penrith, Cumbria, CA10 1ER　　Tel: 076883 500

rear view

11 bedrooms (single, double or family) from £17. Less for 2 nights. Special breaks include honeymoons (with champagne), group bookings, etc. Rooms have central heating; shower or bathroom; armchairs; views of country; tea/coffee facilities. TV available. (Clothes-washing facilities.)
Dinner A la carte, from 7.15–8.30pm. Special diets if ordered. Packed lunches, sandwich suppers. Coffee, tea, for a charge. Drinks can be ordered.
2 sitting-rooms with central heating, open fire, TV, books; bar.
Grounds Lawns and fields. Maps, gumboots and cycles for hire.
Nearest main road A6 from Penrith to Carlisle.

A group of 18th-century farm buildings close to a village that feels remote (though the M6 is only 9 miles away) has been turned into a hotel with great individuality by Isa and John Henderson (he was formerly a television designer).

They reconstructed a rare gin case, a half-round room, within which ponies walked round and round powering wheels to grind grain.

A collection of old farm implements is displayed on the sandstone walls in the bar (once a byre, with low-beamed ceiling and flagged floor).

Every bedroom is individually decorated, and traditional materials have been used. Many rooms still have walls of rugged stone, and a number have brass bedsteads with patchwork quilts. Homespun curtains, thick carpets and country colours like peat or moss are all in keeping with the character of the place. The former coach house has been turned into an annexe where one room is ideal for a family. There is a glassed-in porch with cane furniture and a terrace.

A typical dinner: leek-and-mushroom soup, lamb steak with honey and rosemary, strawberry shortcake and good, plentiful coffee. There is a vegetarian menu. Breakfast includes such things as green figs and smoked haddock.

John has produced his own leaflets of walks from evening strolls to half-day hikes with notes about where deer can be seen, a spectacular waterfall in a gorge, riverside paths, a forest nature reserve with hide for watching badgers and hares or wildfowl, caves, old quarries and castle ruins. The neighbourhood is full of ancient villages, the prehistoric stones of 'Long Meg' and a traditional pottery still using a Victorian steam engine. Kirkoswald is a good choice for a winter break.

Readers' comments: Comfortable and well organized; good cuisine; excellent amenities; nothing was too much trouble; very good in all respects; well decorated rooms; good and thoughtful service; value for money. Attractively converted and with good food. Thoroughly enjoyed our stay, food excellent. Full marks for service, cuisine and superb farmhouse conversion and lovely surroundings.

PYKARDS HALL FARM
Rede, south-west of Bury St Edmunds, Suffolk, IP29 4AU   Tel: 028489 229

2 bedrooms (single or double) from £14.50. Rooms have TV; tea/coffee facilities; central heating; views of country or garden. No smoking. (Washing-machine on request.)

Sitting-room with central heating, open fire, books, piano.
Large garden
Nearest main road A143 from Bury St Edmunds to Haverhill.

One of William the Conqueror's followers was rewarded with the gift of this land on which he built a hall with moat (now filled in). The present building dates from 1500: a terracotta house with white dormers, in a large garden with a willow-fringed duck-pond.

Young Louise Drayton has decorated its rooms very attractively. In the low-beamed sitting-room, a pink-skirted table contrasts with the mulberry carpet, and armchairs are drawn up by the brick fireplace. The dining-room has Windsor chairs around a circular table and a dresser loaded with china. Outside there are seats on a paved terrace facing rosebeds.

An elegant welded staircase leads up to cottagey bedrooms with such pretty touches as a lace bedspread on a brass bed, a modern basin fitted into an old pine washstand, Laura Ashley fabrics used for festoon blinds.

Louise, being rather busy with her children, does not serve full dinners but is happy to provide simple family dishes like chicken pie or lasagne with salad. Otherwise, most visitors go to the Beehive at Horringer to dine.

Rede is very close to the historic abbey town of Bury, a place of mediaeval ruins and churches, fine gardens, Georgian byways, and some good shops for antiques or crafts. It has a Regency theatre (belonging to the National Trust) and some unusual museums. Newmarket and its races are near, too.

The famous mediaeval wool villages of Suffolk are within a short distance (see descriptions on other pages of Clare, Cavendish, Lavenham etc.), all with half-timbered houses and richly decorated churches. Georgian Ickworth Hall stands in grounds landscaped by Capability Brown. Among the undulating hills are pretty streams, mills, country parks and inns.

Readers' comments: A delightful place. Very hospitable.

If you want your hosts to post you things you have accidentally left behind, send them the cost of postage. (The trouble they take is free.)

248

RECTORY FARM

C D

Sulgrave, north-east of Banbury (Oxfordshire), Northamptonshire, OX17 2SG   Tel: 029 576 261

5 bedrooms (single, double or family) from £12. Less for 7 nights. All have tea/coffee facilities; central heating; views of country or garden. (Washing-machine on request.)
Dinner £6 for 3 courses and coffee, at 7pm. Packed lunches, snacks. Tea, coffee, free. Drinks can be ordered.
Sitting-room with central heating, open fire, TV, books, piano.
Large garden
Nearest main road A43 from Oxford to Northampton.

The stars-and-stripes flies over Sulgrave, its design inspired by the stars and bars in the family coat-of-arms over the porch of the manor house. For this was the home (built in the reign of Elizabeth I) of Lawrence Washington – ancestor of George Washington, some of whose possessions are on show at the house, which is now a museum.

Rectory Farm is equally old, and it overlooks the manor. Under its thickly thatched roof are walls of golden stone – the same stone which gives the Cotswolds their particular charm continues into Northamptonshire. Yet, when the famous Cotswolds are over-busy with tourists, this little-known area remains undisturbed, even though it is not far west of the M1. Winding lanes go up and down, passing picturesque villages like Moreton Pinkney, ancient churches and some outstanding buildings – Canons Ashby, for example.

Rectory Farm is, both inside and out, in harmony with this scene. Downstairs are stone-flagged floors and a stone fireplace, deep-set windows giving a view of the walled garden at the back. An old rocking-horse stands in the hall, a dresser laden with china in the sitting-room. Up a substantial oak staircase are the bedrooms – doors and floors alike have become crooked with age. Rebecca Trace has furnished these in appropriately cottagey style: walls are in pale colours, curtains sprigged, most furniture is of stripped pine. One has a view of the adjoining farmyard: the Traces keep a few sheep, chickens and horses.

For dinner you may be offered a home-made soup, pâté or egg dish to be followed, perhaps, by roast beef or chicken in a sweet-sour sauce of green peppers and pineapple (accompanying vegetables are likely to be from the garden). Puddings tend to the traditional: fruit pies, soufflés or mousses, for instance.

Sulgrave is well placed for visiting both Oxford and Stratford-upon-Avon, but I recommend it also as a base from which to explore less well-known beauty-spots (in Northamptonshire, particularly). It is close to the Grand Union Canal and its pleasure-boats – the River Nene, too. At Badby is not only a hilly village of thatched cottages but also a very lovely bluebell wood. Towcester – a steeple-chasing centre – has the Saracen's Head inn which Dickens described in *The Pickwick Papers*:

'The candles were brought, the fire was stirred up . . . In ten minutes' a waiter was laying the cloth, the curtains were drawn, everything looked (as everything always does, in all decent English inns) as if the travellers had been expected, and their comforts prepared, for days beforehand.'

RED HOUSE

Sidmouth Road, Lyme Regis, Dorset, DT7 3ES   Tel: 02974 2055

C(6) **PT**

3 bedrooms (double or family) from £16. Less for 7 nights. Rooms have central heating and electric heaters; bathroom; TV, armchairs; drinks refrigerator; views of sea or garden; tea/coffee facilities. Supper trays (not in summer), £5.50.
Garden
Nearest main road A3052 from Lyme Regis to Exeter.
Closed December–February

Delightful old Lyme has many claims to fame – the profusion of fossils (including dinosaur bones) found along its beaches; the landing of the rebel Monmouth in 1685 to start his abortive rebellion; Jane Austen's *Persuasion*; and most recently *The French Lieutenant's Woman*, the author of which, John Fowles, lives locally.

When Geoffrey Griffin retired, he and his wife Elizabeth, a journalist, decided to move here and (inspired by reading previous editions of *Staying Off the Beaten Track*) run a bed-and-breakfast house. It wasn't any olde worlde cottage that they fell in love with but this handsome 'twenties house that had been built for Aldis (inventor of the famous signal-lamps which bear his name) on a superb site with a 40-mile sea view south-east as far as Portland Bill. It is a house with handsome features – iron-studded oak doors, leaded casements and window-seats, for example. On sunny mornings (occasionally even in late autumn), you can take breakfast on the wide verandah and enjoy sea breezes while you eat – at your feet, sloping lawns with colourful rhododendrons, camellias, fuchsias and wisteria. On chilly mornings, breakfast is served in an attractive room with a fire.

The bedrooms are excellent. Mine was 20 feet long, very comfortably furnished in period with the house, with a thick carpet. By contrast, there is an even larger family room in scarlet-and-white. Each bedroom is equipped with armchairs, TV, a refrigerator, flowers and books – the aim being to provide individual bed-sitters for guests, as there is no communal sitting-room, only a large landing which has seats and a supply of leaflets, maps and local menus.

This is a perfect base from which to explore the locality. Sandy beaches with their shrimp-pools are ideal for children. There are excellent walks (in Marshwood Vale or along the coast) including nature trails; drives along lanes of primroses, bluebells and subtropical wildflowers in the downs; Hardy villages; National Trust houses. You can watch or take part in sea-sports and cider-making.

Readers' comments: Just perfect, equal to the best hotels, excellent value. Kindness itself, so caring. The best ever. Good value. Splendid views and pleasant gardens. Comfort and charm. Could not have been kinder, a marvellous place.

An 18th-century house recommended by the Griffins when the Red House is full is **Springfield**, Woodmead Road (tel: 02974 3409), where Mrs Culpan provides inexpensive bed-and-breakfast, no dinners. It, too, is surrounded by a garden and has sea views.

250

REGENCY HOUSE

C D PT X

Neatishead, north-east of Norwich, Norfolk, NR12 8AD   Tel: 0692 630233

5 bedrooms (double or family) from £13. Less for 3 nights or bargain breaks. Rooms have electric heaters; TV, armchairs; views of country or garden; tea/coffee facilities.
Meals Packed lunches or snacks. Coffee, tea, for a charge.
Garden
Nearest main road A1151 from Norwich to the A149.

Former Manchester bank-manager Alan Wrigley was so touched by the friendliness of Neatishead people towards a newcomer that, after a few years here, he began planting wayside trees as a 'thank you': the total has already reached 2000. He and his wife Sue, previously a *Daily Express* reporter, run not only this 18th-century guest-house to an immaculate standard but also the village stores adjoining it, in the heart of the Norfolk Broads area.

The breakfasts are outstanding: standard issue is 2 sausages, 4 rashers of bacon, 6 mushrooms, 2 whole tomatoes, 2 slices of fried bread and as many eggs as you request! But if you prefer it, she will produce a vegetarian breakfast instead. This is served in a fresh, white room with stoneware crockery on tables that were specially made by a local craftsman. On the walls are photographs of bygone Neatishead. Bedrooms have Laura Ashley fabrics (the bed in no. 6 is king-size) and, in some cases, garden views. (As to dinner, there are two good places in the village to choose from, and others at popular Horning – such as the Swan. The White Horse serves a local speciality, wild duck.)

Pretty little Neatishead, at the centre of the Norfolk Broads, fortunately does not attract the crowds which sometimes ruin Horning, Wroxham and other villages.

There is a staithe (mooring) here for fifteen boats – and the Wrigleys have a 14-foot dinghy which visitors can use for fishing – and pleasant picnic-spots by the waterside at, for instance, Burton Turf. Some families choose to divide themselves between cabin cruisers (for the younger generation) and Regency House (for older members, who prefer to sleep on shore and boat with their family only by day). There is good cycling around here, too; wildlife and birdwatching; and plenty of sightseeing in mediaeval Norwich and elsewhere. The sandy beaches are easily accessible, too. Rose nurseries, and the gardens at Blickling, Hoveton Hall and Burnt Fen interest flower-lovers; antiques-hunters head for Holt and Norwich.

The Broadland Conservation Centre is worth seeking out at Ranworth (which also has a very fine church interior): a nature trail leads to a thatched, floating building with an exhibition about the Broads and their wildlife, and a hide from which to watch the waterfowl. Sue will give you leaflets with maps of two interesting walks – the Weavers' Way and Marriott's Way.

Recently the Norfolk Broads have been declared a National Park, which means they will now be protected from harmful development.

Readers' comments: Welcoming, friendly, good breakfast.

RICHMOND LODGE

C(10)

Mursley, south-west of Milton Keynes, Buckinghamshire, MK17 0LE
Tel: 029672 275

3 bedrooms (single or double) from £12.50. Rooms have own bath/shower (some); TV; tea/coffee facilities; central heating; views of country or garden. No smoking.
Dinner from £9.50 for 3 courses and coffee, at 7pm. Non-residents not admitted. Tea, coffee, free.
Sitting-room with central heating, open fire, TV, books. No smoking.
Large garden
Nearest main road A421 from Bletchley to Buckingham.

Just before the First World War, this house was built as a hunting-lodge for a wealthy London butcher who frequented the area when buying beef-cattle and decided to make his weekend retreat in this high, windswept spot. The whole atmosphere is still one of sedate, solid comfort; and even the garden retains its original Edwardian formality. From an immaculate lawn, with a stately blue cedar, there are views right down the Vale of Aylesbury with a glimpse of Waddesdon Manor, High Wycombe and Dunstable Downs.

Chris Abbey used to be a hotel manager and so her standards are very professional. Rooms have well-chosen fabrics and are spotless: for its view of the lily-pool, I thought the green-and-white bedroom the most attractive. Chris sometimes serves breakfast on a sunny patio where there are fuchsias and clematis. For dinner (if this is ordered in advance) she might cook you salmon mousse, pork chops with a celery and pineapple sauce, and (she loves doing puddings) summer pudding.

Buckinghamshire is a county of contrasts – leafy in the south, rising up into the Chiltern Hills where great beech trees flourish on the chalky soil, and then turning into a great fertile plain northwards (the Vale of Aylesbury). Here the landscape is threaded with little rivers. This is not an area for many spectacular views – that from Richmond Lodge is exceptional – but rather for the pleasures of making small, private discoveries of its beauties which include a wealth of ancient and interesting churches, for instance, and quite a lot of stately homes.

Don't complain if –
 – because you booked at short notice, you do not get the best room
 – because you did not order a meal in advance, you get something plucked from the freezer
 – because you do not arrive on time, your room is let to someone else
 – because you bring a dog without asking, it is refused entry
 – because you don't express your wishes (for more heat, a second helping or whatever), you don't get what you want!

RIVER PARK FARM

C S

Lodsworth, west of Petworth, West Sussex, GU28 9DS Tel: 07985 362

5 bedrooms (single, double or family) from £10.50. Less for 3 nights. Rooms have central heating and electric heaters; views of country or garden; tea/coffee facilities.
Dinner £4.50 for 2 courses (with choices) and coffee, at 7–8pm (not on Wednesdays). Packed lunches. Non-residents not admitted. Wine can be brought in.
Sitting-room with central heating, open fire, TV, books.
Garden (mainly lawn) and farmland, with coarse fishing, table tennis.
Nearest main road A272 from Petworth to Midhurst.
Closed November–Easter

The farm (of 340 acres of corn, bullocks, sheep and poultry) is in a secluded position among woods where, if you are up early enough, you may encounter deer. There is a 4½-acre lake with plentiful carp and ducks, and in front a pretty garden. The house itself, built in 1600, is old and beamy with comfortable bedrooms along twisting passageways, and outside are golden roses and wisteria clambering around the door. Altogether it is a pretty and tranquil spot, full of nooks and crannies – amazing, visitors think, because it is so close to London.

Pat Moss does not do full-scale dinners (available elsewhere locally) but has a list of homely dishes like shepherd's pie or macaroni cheese, and for puddings like banana split she uses rich Jersey cream from the farm's own cows. Bread is home-baked and eggs free-range. There are flowers in every room.

People come for the local walks and birdwatching (Pat has pinned up bird-identification charts and gives visitors field notes on the crops and wildlife in each season, with map, and her own daily nature notes); or to visit the many outstanding sights in this neighbourhood – beginning with one of England's greatest houses at Petworth; or the polo or point-to-points at Cowdray; or to see the local game of stoolball played at Midhurst. There are many small country towns around here, streams running down into the River Rother, woodlands and picturesque villages with greens and duck-ponds, old inns and ancient churches, Arundel Castle, wildfowl reserves, Goodwood House and Roman remains. Turner knew and loved this area, staying at Petworth House where many of his paintings can be seen. It's a good area for antique shops, too. Garden-lovers head for West Dean and Denmans; and there is the open-air Weald and Downland Museum.

Pat also makes and sells marmalade and dried flowers.

Readers' comments: Warm hospitality, generous home cooking. Enjoyed ourselves so much that we have twice visited for a week. Marvellous setting and house, kind hosts, good food. Outstanding. Very relaxed atmosphere.

Some readers tell me they have stayed at lots of places from *Staying Off the Beaten Track*. I wonder who has stayed at most? A free copy of the next edition awaits the reader who sends me his/her comments on the greatest number!

ROCK HOUSE

Alport, south of Bakewell, Derbyshire, DE4 1LG   Tel: 0629 636736

3 bedrooms (single or double) from £14. Some rooms have central heating, gas heaters; bath or shower; armchairs; all have views of country or garden; tea/coffee facilities. (Clothes-washing facilities.) No smoking.

Sitting-room with gas fire, TV, books.
Small garden
Nearest main road A6 from Bakewell to Matlock.

The rock for which the Stathams' house is named is a great crag of tufa (a type of volcanic stone, perforated like Gruyère cheese, which was formed 300 million years ago) rearing up alongside it.

Only a few yards from the 18th-century house two rivers join, splashing over weirs constructed long ago to contain trout downstream – you can watch these drifting in water so transparent that the locals call it 'gin-clear' (its purity is due to the limestone bed over which it runs). Lathkill Dale is a National Nature Reserve: Tony and Jan are first-rate sources of information about the wildlife and history of this most beautiful of valleys. They will lend maps, tell you the best riverside walks, and where to find river pools (created for washing sheep).

The front door opens straight into the stone-flagged sitting-room, its walls now painted mushroom, with grey buttoned velvet armchairs, where you will be served tea on arrival. Glass doors lead through to the breakfast-room.

By pre-arrangement, Jan may serve supper platters, beautifully presented (but most visitors go to the nearby Druid Inn or other pubs). Breakfast possibilities include muffins, poached fruit, Staffordshire oatcakes, home-made jams and some vegetarian dishes. All bedrooms are well furnished.

Alport is well placed for touring either the wild and dramatic 'Dark Peak' (the stone there is millstone grit) or the more benign 'White Peak' (limestone), a fertile and verdant region. It is close to Chatsworth House and park with garden centre (the autumn colours there are glorious), Dove Dale, Haddon Hall and Hardwick Hall – a great Tudor mansion, the Norman splendours of Southwell Minster – famous for its botanical carvings, Castleton (remarkable caves), the market town of Bakewell where the original Bakewell puddings are still to be had, Haddon Hall (mediaeval), the spa of Buxton, Melbourne's stately home, the Crown Derby porcelain museum, historic trams at Crich, the canal at Cromford, a cable car to the heights outside Matlock, Kedleston Hall (designed by Adam), and Alton Towers for its gardens and leisure park. Many mansions have fine gardens. This part of Derbyshire has some of England's finest river valleys.

Readers' comments: Very comfortable and a warm welcome. Breakfast excellent, rooms large and comfortable. Beautiful house, much pampering, what breakfasts! One of our favourites, lovely house; thoughtful and friendly people.

ROCK WINDMILL

C D

The Hollow, Washington, north of Worthing, West Sussex, RH20 3DA
Tel: 0903 892941

2 **bedrooms** (double or family) from £12. Less for 7 nights. All have tea/coffee facilities; central heating; views of country or garden. (Washing-machine on request.) Packed lunches, snacks. Tea, coffee, free.
Sitting-room with central heating, TV, books, record-player.
Large garden with swimming-pool (heated).
Nearest main road A24 from Horsham to Worthing.

The composer John Ireland lived here until his death in 1962: much of his music was inspired by the surrounding landscape (for instance, the *Downland Suite*, *Equinox* and *Amberley Wild Brooks*). It had ceased to function as a mill long before – and the sails have gone – but part of the original building (1820) remains, further modernized in recent years: the octagonal sitting-room, for instance, which is now decorated in a restful celadon green and has modern leather armchairs. This opens onto a garden with swimming-pool (heated to 80°F). Bedrooms are in a modern extension, neatly furnished with pine and cane fitments.

Janice Langley provides only breakfast but she or David give visitors lifts to the Frankland Arms (immortalized in Hilaire Belloc's 'West Sussex Drinking Song' which is sometimes sung at the pub), where there is very good food and from which it is a pleasant walk back to the mill. Or drive to Barn Owls, see below.

Chanctonbury Ring is within sight and accessible by steep footpath from the village: a striking landmark, it consists of beech woods within the earthworks of an Iron Age hill fort; superb views all round. In this part of the lovely South Downs are such attractive villages as Findon (flint-walled cottages and three racing-stables), Steyning (mediaeval gabled houses and an outstanding church), Bramber (castle ruins, and a museum of pipes) and Ashurst (well preserved and with far views). The River Adur runs through this area to the sea at the small port of Shoreham, and everywhere there are good walks to be found – the long-distance South Downs Way goes by Washington on its way from Hampshire to Beachy Head (80 miles), and this is one of its most scenic, hilltop stretches. The nearest coastal resort is Worthing; the stateliest homes are Petworth and Parham.

At another village near here, Coldwaltham outside Pulborough, is **Barn Owls** (tel: 07982 2498), basically a restaurant in a Victorian house but with some bedrooms. Not 'off the beaten track', for it is on a road to London, but popular for Pat Hellenberg's cooking. As well as a standard menu, there are often 8-course feasts available, a traditional Victorian dinner, regional specialities, vegetarian dishes and special events (Hawaiian, Moroccan, farmhouse etc.): send for brochure of

all these. Cream teas are served in the rock garden.

ROSE-IN-VALE HOTEL

C D H S S-C

Mithian, east of St Agnes, Cornwall, TR5 0QD   Tel: 087255 2202

15 bedrooms (single, double or family) from £25 with dinner. Less for 2 nights off-season. Rooms have central heating or electric heaters; shower or bathroom; phone, TV, armchairs; views of country or garden; tea/coffee facilities. Balconies (some). One four-poster.
Dinner 4 courses (with choices) and coffee, at 7–8pm. Also à la carte sometimes. Special diets if ordered. Lunches, packed lunches, snacks. Coffee, tea, for a charge. Drinks can be ordered.
3 sitting-rooms with central heating, open fire, TV, books, indoor games (darts, table tennis, bar billiards in separate games room); bar. Solarium.
Large garden Woodland and pasture; with croquet lawn, badminton and swimming-pool.
Nearest main road A3075 from Newquay to the A30.
Closed November–April

This handsome 18th-century mansion was originally the home of a local mine captain. A regular visitor to the Nankivel family here was the artist, John Opie, who grew up nearby and painted Joyce Nankivel, 'the belle of Mithian'.

The Arthurs, who honeymooned here several years ago, made many discoveries after they took over and began making improvements.

In what is now the bar at the back, they uncovered a most unusual stone fireplace with a fringle (bread oven) built into what had been an inglenook fireplace in an old cottage adjoining the 18th-century house. They have added fire-baskets welded by Tony himself: he says his past experience as an engineer has come in handy! He installed central heating himself, too.

There are two large sitting-rooms, now fully refurbished to a high standard, with fine details preserved, such as sash windows with folding shutters. The curving staircase has a decorative window. In a modern extension at the back is a third sitting-room and a very long dining-room with huge windows giving a view of the lawns and rosebeds, with a primrose-banked stream behind. There is a small, sheltered swimming-pool heated by solar panels which, in a good summer, keep the water temperature at 78°. Some smaller, modern bedrooms open onto this, but for one with outstanding views from its four windows choose no. 1 upstairs with a four-poster, in the main house. There is also a family suite. (Special activity weekends in winter.)

The Arthurs have a good chef – Philip Simms was once at the Imperial Hotel, Torquay, and now lectures part-time at Camborne Catering College. He prepares such à la carte specialities as fish mousse in crab sauce; game or local fish as a main course – or perhaps duck in a sauce of Grand Marnier served with little pancakes containing orange segments and zest; and delicious puddings like an iced soufflé of peaches, surrounded by a purée of raspberries and cream. Take your mother here for the mid-March weekend when he does a special Mothering Sunday luncheon.

Beyond the sheltered valley and quaint village of Mithian are the well-known surfing beaches of St Agnes and Perranporth (a quieter one is at Trevellas), seal sanctuary, country park, and six National Trust houses (with gardens).

Readers' comments: Hospitality beyond reproach; extremely high standard. Very pleasant; comfortable but not luxurious; friendly and helpful owners. Very pleasant – return visit planned. Food excellent.

ROWE HOUSE

C(12) D

Horton-in-Ribblesdale, north of Settle, North Yorkshire, BD24 0HT
Tel: 072 96 212

7 bedrooms (double) from £14.50. Less for 4 nights and bargain breaks. Some have own shower; all have tea/coffee facilities; central heating; views of country or garden.
Dinner £9 for 4 courses and coffee, at 6.30pm. Vegetarian or special diets if ordered. Packed lunches. Tea, coffee, extra. Drinks can be ordered.
Sitting-room with central heating, open fire, TV, books.
Large garden
Nearest main road A65 from Settle to Ingleton.
Closed December–February

In the 18th century this started life as a wealthy wool merchant's shooting-lodge – hence some of the impressive details such as the very handsome window and decorative ceiling of the staircase, and a fireplace of local marble in the sitting-room. It stands just above the banks of the River Ribble and over it looms the great bulk of Penyghent – one of the famous 'Three Peaks' (each some 2000 feet high). All around is the spectacular scenery of the Yorkshire Dales National Park and only a few miles away is Lancashire's less celebrated but just as fine Forest of Bowland (moors, woods, valleys and rivers).

Bob and Ann Jones now run the lodge as a guest-house, with simply but agreeably furnished bedrooms and much emphasis on good cooking (Bob qualified at a catering college), using their own eggs, honey, fruit and vegetables. A home-made soup or pâté might be followed by roast pork, perhaps, and then a pudding such as walnut-and-treacle flan or sherry trifle, and cheeses. There is a garden which Bob was improving at the time when I visited.

Lying so far to the east of the National Park, Ribblesdale's charms are sometimes overlooked but this means it may be less crowded than more famous parts such as Wharfedale, for instance. From Settle runs a famous scenic railway (to Carlisle), saved by a mere whisker from closure a few years ago – there is a station at Horton – and there are also several preserved steam railways in the region.

The history of this area is one that goes back through aeons of geological time, when two million years ago this part of the Pennine rocks cracked and the whole landscape slipped, creating such striking features as the roadside cliff known as Giggleswick Scar and a great gap through the high hills which enabled invaders or traders, railways or roads, to penetrate the high and lonely places around. Eventually villages grew up on the valley floors, some developing into little market towns. One sees extraordinary cliffs or terraces of stone among the greenery, while down below are warrens of subterranean tunnels and pockets which bring pot-holers here: the biggest underground cave is Gaping Gill (larger than a cathedral), entered through an opening on Ingleborough Hill.

The long-distance Pennine Way – it goes from Derbyshire all the way to Scotland – wanders across the hilltops; for the less energetic, there are breathtaking car drives to follow (for instance to Hawes and then over the Buttertubs Pass).

The Lake District to the west, and pretty little Dentdale to the north are accessible – Dent is an exceptionally attractive little cobbled town.

RUTLAND COTTAGES

C H S S-C

Cedar Street, Braunston, south-west of Oakham, Leicestershire, LE15 8QS
Tel: 0572 722049

5 bedrooms (single, double or family) from £14. Rooms have central heating, electric heaters; shower or bathroom; TV, armchairs; views of country or garden; tea/coffee facilities. No smoking in one.
Sitting-room with central heating, open fire, TV, books. No smoking.
Garden
Nearest main road A6003 from Oakham to Kettering.

A 17th-century bakehouse is the home of John and Connie Beadman (she taught music); and in addition they own nearby cottages let either for self-catering or on a bed-and-breakfast basis. All b & b guests take breakfast together in the beamed dining-room of the house. Those who do not want to cook their own dinner (in their cottage) can eat at the Old Plough in this pretty conservation village of golden stone. (Packed lunches can be provided; tea and coffee are free.)

Guests have the use of the Beadmans' huge and beautifully furnished sitting-room (it has a see-through stone fireplace in the middle, and a 'curfew window' through which the village watchman could check that the baker's fires had been properly extinguished for the night). Its windows open onto a heather garden with a view of stately cedars beyond.

Bedrooms in the cottages are more homely, but guests have the advantage of self-contained accommodation including fully equipped kitchens: particularly suitable for families.

John and his sons are keen bell-ringers, willing to take visitors on guided tours up into the bell-towers of local churches. This is a good area for walks or cycling (maps on loan), and other country pursuits, and for sightseeing too: the historic schools at Uppingham and Oundle, the mediaeval town of Stamford, castles at Rockingham and Belvoir as well as Oakham, the stately homes of Burghley and Belton – at the former, horse trials take place each September. The former county of Rutland (now absorbed into Leicestershire) still has its own rural museum and farm park.

Man-made reservoirs when naturalized can be as beautiful as any lake. Rutland Water, greater in area than any reservoir in northern Europe, is particularly fine. There are paths around its wandering perimeter, pleasure boats on it, a nature reserve and trail, and areas devoted to watersports. The road around the south side is the more scenic one. At Normanton, a classical church on a causeway seems almost to float on the water (it is now used as a water museum); the village of Upper Hambleton is picturesquely sited too, on a spur of land projecting into the reservoir.

Readers' comments: Most friendly. Cottage excellent.

Book well ahead: many of these houses have few rooms. Do not expect dinner if you have not booked it.

ST CHRISTOPHER'S

C(11) D S X

Boscastle, north of Camelford, Cornwall, PL35 0BD   Tel: 08405 412

9 bedrooms (single or double) from £14. Less for 7 nights or bargain breaks. Rooms have central heating; some have shower or bathroom; armchairs; views of country or sea; tea/coffee facilities.

Dinner £8 for 4 courses (limited choice) and coffee, at 7pm. Special diets if ordered. Packed lunches. Coffee, tea, for a charge. Drinks can be ordered.

Sitting-room with central heating, open fire, TV, books.

Nearest main road A39 from Bude to Wadebridge.

Closed January–March

This 18th-century house is in an unspoilt harbour village (a conservation area) and now belongs, after many changes of owner, to Brenda and Brian Thompson who used to run a local restaurant.

One enters it through a slate-floored hall with roughcast walls. There is a large sitting-room, well furnished with damask wallpaper and a big velvet sofa. It is heated by an open fire, while a log stove warms the cottage-style dining-room that adjoins it. Bedrooms have well-chosen colour schemes: no. 2, for instance, which is L-shaped, is decorated in celadon and white, with cane chairs.

A typical dinner might comprise a mushroom-and-wine savoury, then tenderloin of pork in a cream sauce, syllabub and cheeses.

Boscastle lies on one of the most scenic parts of the rugged north Cornwall coast, with Tintagel and its King Arthur associations nearby. This is an area of great contrasts. Castles, sandy beaches, glens, traditional crafts, moorland or coastal footpaths, National Trust houses or gardens and quaint inns all abound. There are fine gardens to visit, slate quarries and St Juliot's church (Thomas Hardy).

Readers' comments: Very good. Pleasant welcome and good food. Excellent hospitality, very relaxing. Very good value. Excellent food with plenty of variety.

When to go? Seaside resorts or other places suitable for children will be at their busiest (and dearest) in July–August and during half-term holidays (especially in late May, which is also a bank holiday period). Other peak periods are, of course, Easter, Christmas, New Year and the bank holiday in late August. (The bank holiday in early May is not usually a peak, because it comes rather soon after Easter, but much depends on the weather.) There are local peaks, too (the Gold Cup races at Cheltenham or the regatta at Henley, for instance, are apt to fill hotels for miles around), and local troughs (Brighton, a conference centre, is least busy in high summer). You won't get much personal attention when hotels are full to bursting.

Boxgrove, east of Chichester, West Sussex, PO18 0DY   Tel: 0243 773173

1 bedroom (double) from £13, with own shower; TV; tea/coffee facilities; central heating; view of garden. (Washing-machine on request.)
Small garden
Nearest main road A27 from Chichester to Worthing.

There is an increasing trend, of which this is a good example, to provide accommodation which is a mix of 'bed-and-breakfast' with self-catering. Visitors have their own self-contained suite (including cooking facilities) but breakfast and service are provided.

In the case of St Hugh's, the accommodation is in a separate annexe in the garden. A spacious bedsitting-room – well and newly furnished – opens onto a private patio with cushioned chairs. There is an excellent shower-room; and cooking facilities are hidden away in pine fitments. For breakfast, visitors enter the house and its dining-room (lined with ancestral portraits of Cornish farmers). No dinners: Edwina Tremaine recommends the Nicodemus restaurant in nearby Chichester or the Anglesey Arms at Halnaker.

Boxgrove itself deserves a visit because, when other great monastic churches were being destroyed by Henry VIII, the one here was saved by the protests of the Lord of the Manor and is now the parish church: its great Norman nave is quite outstanding. Walkers can follow the rural track of the Roman's Stane Street which was once the main route from Chichester to London: it goes across the Downs and passes near the Roman villa at Bignor. At West Dean (where the great house is now a college for arts and crafts) is a superb park with botanical gardens; with the Weald and Downland Museum near – an open-air collection of very ancient buildings rescued and re-sited here. Goodwood House is famous not only for its fine furniture and art treasures but for the racecourse. There are interesting villages such as Chilgrove and (for sea views) Selsey, the Hartings (with Uppark, a Queen Anne mansion belonging to the National Trust), yellow-painted Cocking and Apuldram from the waterfront walks of which flocks of migrant ducks and geese can be seen. Turner painted seascapes at Birdham. The cathedral city of Chichester and its lovely natural harbour have been described elsewhere.

Readers' comments: Wholly recommended, beautifully furnished.

Inclusive terms for dinner, bed-and-breakfast (particularly for a week) can be much lower than those quoted here for these items taken separately. For short-notice bookings you may be able to get a reduction.

No proprietor wants to have a room standing empty. This particularly applies to Sunday nights. Some hotels make a discount if you want only two courses from a three-course menu.

ST JAMES'S HOUSE C(12) **PT**

The Green, Thirsk, North Yorkshire, YO7 1AQ   Tel: 0845 22676

4 bedrooms (double or family) from £13.50. Less for stays of 7 nights. Rooms have central heating; two have shower or bathroom; TV; tea/coffee facilities. No smoking.

Sitting-room with central heating and TV. **Nearest main road** A19 from Middlesborough to York. **Closed November–March**

Barry Ogleby being an antique dealer, it is not surprising that every part of his 18th-century house is well endowed with period pieces. You may sleep in a room with a bedstead of prettily turned spindles or in a genuine Victorian four-poster; and in corridors as well as rooms there are such interesting pieces as inlaid blanket-boxes or unusual chairs. On the ground floor is a particularly convenient family room, looking onto the flower beds, winding paths and lily-pool of the enclosed garden.

Only two minutes' walk from the quiet green, a conservation area, is Thirsk's busy market place and many restaurants (only breakfast is served by Liz Ogleby, who recommends the Carpenters' Arms for other meals). This is where the world's most famous vet, writing under the name of James Herriot, has his surgery. There are local guides who will accompany you on car tours, pointing out sites associated with Herriot, his books or the films (much filming was done not here but in the Dales); one shows videos en route.

In the immediate vicinity are landscaped gardens and an arboretum, more market towns, the stupendous view from Sutton Bank, great ruined abbeys (the beautifully laid out terraces above Rievaulx Abbey provide a bird's-eye-view of it), Castle Howard (famous even before 'Brideshead Revisited'), thriving Ampleforth Abbey and its school, the pretty villages of Coxwold and Kilburn – the latter associated with 'the mouse-man' and his furniture, the former with Shandy Hall (home of Laurence Sterne). A few miles away is Northallerton, a town of fine houses, with characterful villages all around. Fountains Abbey, Newburgh Priory, the white horse of the Hambleton Hills, Byland Abbey, Helmsley (old market town), arboretum at Bedale and Harlow Car gardens are other attractions.

> Two-thirds of the houses in this book have bargain breaks or other discounts on offer, some exclusive to readers. Only a third raise prices at the peak of summer.

SAINT MARIE'S GRANGE   C PT S
Alderbury, south-east of Salisbury, Wiltshire, SP5 3DJ   Tel: 0722 710351

3 bedrooms (double or family) from £17.50. Less for 2 nights and bargain breaks. Rooms have tea/coffee facilities (on request); central heating; views of river, country or garden. No smoking. (Washing-machine on request.)

Dinner £17.50 for 4 courses, wines and coffee, at 7.30 or 8 pm (must be ordered in advance). Vegetarian or special diets if ordered. Tea, coffee, free.

Sitting-room with central heating, open fire, TV, books, piano. No smoking.

Large garden

Nearest main road A36 from Salisbury to Southampton.

Pugin, whose most celebrated work was done as architect (with Barry) of the Houses of Parliament, was largely responsible for the Gothic revival of the early 19th century, a style that was to dominate the building not only of churches but even libraries and prisons for decades to come. Saint Marie's was the first house that he built for himself, in 1835 when he was only 23, and it has many typically Puginesque features: the iron-studded front door, stained glass (some with Pugin's initials and motto), open-joisted and coffered ceilings, pointed windows with stone mullions, and a great fireplace of chamfered stone in the former library. Originally there was even a drawbridge; and there is still a bell-tower (though it now houses a shower). It is said that Mr Pecksniff in *Martin Chuzzlewit* was based on Pugin – Dickens once stayed at the Green Dragon in Alderbury, and later as the guest of another owner of Saint Marie's.

Peter Higgins says he is still making new Pugin discoveries hidden under layers of paint and other accretions, some in bedrooms used by visitors – for instance, a little alcove with pointed window framing an attractive view of the River Avon. Below the house are terraced lawns and lovely trees descending towards the water-meadows; and in an outbuilding are Peter's vintage Humber cars.

Gina Higgins is an accomplished artist (her pictures hang on many of the walls) and cook too, producing such imaginative meals as courgette and Brie soup or a grapefruit sorbet with mint and prawns by way of a starter; lamb cooked with garlic, marjoram and rosemary; a rum-and-ginger trifle – followed by cheeses. Aperitifs, wine and liqueurs accompany the meals (these include local Fonthill wines). There is much emphasis on wholefood; and vegetables are steamed. At or after dinner the Higgins join their guests in the blue sitting-room with its William Morris fabrics and grand piano, and its bay windows through which to enjoy the valley view as night falls.

Outside Alderbury is one of England's oldest follies: a hexagonal 'pepperbox' built in 1606, high on the downs. Britford has another Gothic revival house, with moat, and Longford Castle which contains fine paintings. Salisbury, described elsewhere, is very close and Alderbury is well placed for visiting other historic cities too (Winchester and Southampton, for instance) as well as the New Forest and resorts such as Bournemouth. Romsey and its abbey are soon reached, and Broadlands – the Mountbatten home. Mottisfont Abbey (part Norman, part 18th-century) has paintings by Rex Whistler; Broughton is a pretty village with flowers against half-timbered cottage walls.

262

ST MARY'S HOUSE

C D H PT S-C X

Kintbury, west of Newbury, Berkshire, RG15 0TR   Tel: 0488 58551

7 **bedrooms** (single, double or family) from £13. Less for 7 nights. Some have own bath/shower; TV; central heating; views of river, country or garden.
Dinner £7 for 4 courses (with some choice) and coffee, at 7–8.30pm. Vegetarian or special diets if ordered. Packed lunches, snacks. Tea, coffee, extra. Drinks can be ordered.
Sitting-room with central heating, open fire, books; bar.
Small garden
Nearest main road A4 from Marlborough to Newbury.

Old-fashioned roses and a grapevine up the walls add to the picturesque look of this unusual house. Its pointed windows are lozenge-paned, and little dormers punctuate the roof: it used to be a school.

Some bedrooms are on the ground floor, one of them opening onto a paved terrace with lavender hedge. The sitting-room is furnished with antiques, and the dining-room with a great, 17th-century refectory table surrounded by leather chairs.

Margaret Barr prepares (if given adequate notice) such meals as fish mousse, chicken in a variety of exotic sauces, and meringues or fruity desserts, followed by cheese. Alan has a well-stocked wine cellar to complement her cooking.

The lovely Kennet & Avon Canal is only a hundred yards away, for Kintbury lies midway between Hungerford and Newbury – towns described elsewhere in this book (along with the rest of Berkshire). Only a few miles south are the Hampshire Downs; and, westward, Wiltshire's Vale of Pewsey, both of which are also scenic areas which take days to explore. Northward is a region rich in prehistoric remains – hill forts, barrows, ancient tracks and so forth. The valley itself is quite different: woodland, commons and meadows as the backdrop to villages of flint, brick and thatch with narrow lanes and some richly decorated churches. Birdwatchers and walkers love the whole area (as do anglers). A good way to enjoy the waterways is on a horse-drawn barge, for which Kintbury is a starting-point. Favourite outings include Littlecote House, Avebury (prehistoric ring), Marlborough, Newbury (racecourse), Bowood House and Highclere Castle.

Picturesque Hungerford is famous for its scores of antique shops (many open even on Sundays). Nearby are the windswept heights of the Berkshire Downs where racehorses train, and you can walk along the prehistoric Ridgeway Path. The sites of Iron Age forts or burial mounds dot the area. The Kennet Valley is in complete contrast – fertile meadows with birch and oak woods beyond, a great area for birdwatchers.

The villages in this area have flint-and-brick cottages roofed with thatch. In and around both Lambourn and Newbury are historic buildings (the latter has a racecourse and a theatre in a converted watermill), stately homes and pretty villages. Savernake Forest is well worth visiting.

263

SAXELBYE MANOR HOUSE   C

Saxelby, north-west of Melton Mowbray, Leicestershire, LE14 3PA

Tel: 0664 812269

3 bedrooms (double or family) from £11.75. Less for 4 nights. Rooms have central heating, electric heaters; armchairs; views of country or garden; tea/coffee facilities. (Clothes-washing facilities.)

Dinner £7 for 4 courses and coffee, at 7pm. Vegetarian or special diets if ordered. Packed lunches, snacks. Coffee, tea, free. Non-residents not admitted. Drinks can be brought in.

Sitting-room with central heating, open fire, TV, books, piano.

Large garden and farmland.

Nearest main road A6006 from Melton Mowbray to the A6.

Closed in winter

In this little hamlet is an especially attractive farmhouse, tucked within a garden where willows and fuchsias flourish. Parts of it are 800 years old. Margaret Morris has furnished it with a fascinating collection of Victoriana (even in the cloakroom): little velvet chairs and chaises longues, old prints and pot-plants in abundance. Narrow passages lead to a grand staircase constructed four centuries ago in the old stone stairwell. There's even a big Victorian bath in the huge bathroom. She provides traditional 4-course dinners as well as bed-and-breakfast, all at a very modest price. One might, for instance, eat prawn cocktail, the farm's own lamb with four vegetables, sherry trifle and a cheeseboard that includes Stilton and other local cheeses.

Melton Mowbray is a pleasant market town (from which you can go home laden with its famous pork pies and other products of the pig), and is well placed for visiting other historic Leicestershire towns such as Loughborough and Oakham (as well as Grantham and Stamford in Lincolnshire, and Nottingham for its castle and other historic buildings). Belvoir Castle and Rutland Water are well worth a visit. The tiny county of Rutland still keeps its identity even though it was incorporated into Leicestershire decades ago, a region in which sheep graze on green wolds. Roads wind up and down past cottages of pinkish stone, many of which have fine views across the great Vale of Belvoir to its castle. Villages worth touring include Bottesford (for its church monuments), Burley (for views), Lyddington (old almshouses, etc.), Uppingham (famous 16th-century boys' school), Wing (a mediaeval maze). There is a steam railway.

Readers' comments: Have stayed repeatedly.

SCOTT ARMS
Kingston, south of Corfe Castle, Dorset, BH20 5LH   Tel: 0929 480270

7 bedrooms (double or family) from £15. Tea/coffee facilities and central heating.
Large garden
Nearest main road A351 from Swanage to Wareham.

This creeper-covered country inn is in one of the most beautiful parts of Dorset, on a hilltop with magnificent views of Corfe Castle. There is a stone-walled family bar, fire blazing in inglenook, leather-upholstered fender; and tables both inside and out – some on stone-walled, terraced lawns with superb views. Bedrooms are neat and homely (choose Room 8 for its view, Room 7 for a stair direct to the garden).

Mrs Stansfield cooks traditional bar food; Dorset crabs and apple-cake are two local specialities. There are farmhouse wines and ciders, and real ales. And, to make the most of those superlative views, a former milking-shed has been converted into a lounge bar with panoramic windows. (No meals on Sunday night or winter Mondays.)

Kingston stands nearly 500 feet high, overlooking Corfe Castle, the lovely Isle (no longer literally an isle) of Purbeck, and Poole Harbour – described elsewhere in this book. It's only two miles from the sea; 10 miles west of sophisticated Bournemouth.

Inland Dorset is less frequented by tourists than its justly celebrated coast, but it is a region of great beauty and with many stately homes or small unspoilt villages and inns to visit. The scenery is varied: chalk streams meander through secretive valleys. Some parts, by contrast, are all stone and thatch. There are lush pastures in the Vale of Blackmoor, wild moorland further south, few major roads to disturb the peace, and market towns – including Dorchester itself – which still have some of the character that Hardy described in so many novels or poems. Many lanes must still be very much as he saw them when he wrote:

> 'I went by footpath and by stile
> Beyond where bustle ends,
> Strayed here a mile and there a mile
> And called upon some friends.'

SHEARINGS

C(12) **PT**

Rockbourne, south of Salisbury (Wiltshire), Hampshire, SP6 3NA
Tel: 07253 256

3 bedrooms (single or double) from £19.50;
10% discount to readers of this book. Less

for 7 nights. All have own bath/shower; tea/coffee facilities; central heating; views of stream or garden. (Clothes-washing facilities on request.)
Dinner £12.50–£19 for 2–3 courses (with aperitif and wine) and coffee, at 8pm. Non-residents not admitted. Vegetarian or special diets if ordered. Packed lunches, snacks. Tea, coffee, free. Drinks can be ordered or brought in.
Sitting-room with central heating, open fire, TV, books. Piano.
Small garden
Nearest main road A354 from Salisbury to Blandford.
Closed mid-December–January

The house may look familiar, for it has been photographed many times for calendars and greetings cards. Its thatched roof and porch overlook a clear stream (in hot summers this tends to dry up, alas); the cottage has its own footbridge. It was built in the 16th century (from oak beams that are even older), and when Colin and Rosemary Watts came here they took great care to decorate and furnish it appropriately. One pink-carpeted sitting-room has rosy cretonne sofas facing the inglenook fireplace; another, with chintz-covered chairs, is for television. The dining-room with ladderback chairs overlooks the twinkling stream; its table converts to billiards. Most meals are eaten, however, in the beamy kitchen/dining-room. (Bedrooms are rather simply furnished.)

The garden at the back is particularly pretty: sloping lawn, brick summerhouse, a suntrapping brick patio. Here there is an annexe to the house that could be particularly suitable for youngsters, with upstairs bedsitter; 'Portaloo' below.

Mr and Mrs Watts are interesting people to meet – she, musical and artistic; he, a retired brigadier. Rosemary is an excellent cook – of such meals as iced cucumber soup, beef, éclairs, cheeses; aperitifs and wine included.

The village itself is picturesque, and has a Roman villa. Within a very short distance are the New Forest, Breamore House and Salisbury.

Readers' comments: Excellent. Made very welcome. Truly beautiful and peaceful. Top marks.

Woodgreen is another village near here, where at **Cottage Crest** (tel: 0725 22009) the Cadmans provide bed-and-breakfast in a Victorian drover's cottage – no dinner. Bedrooms are of a very high standard (and moderately priced). A great brass bed with pink-and-white lacy linen is in one; it has an L-shaped room with windows on two sides from which to enjoy superb views of the River Avon in the valley below. One can sit on a paved terrace with a

little pool, or take a zigzag path down to a lower garden, to look for badgers.

SHIELDHALL

C D S

Wallington, west of Morpeth, Northumberland, NE61 4AQ Tel: 0830 40387

6 bedrooms (single, double or family) from £16. Less for 2 nights and bargain breaks. All have own bath/shower; tea/coffee facilities; central heating; views of garden. (Washing-machine on request.)
Dinner £8 for 3 courses (with choices) and coffee, at 6.30pm. Non-residents not admitted. Vegetarian or special diets if ordered. Tea, coffee, free. Drinks can be ordered.
Sitting-room with central heating, open fire, TV, books.
Large garden
Nearest main road A696 from Newcastle to Otterburn.

18th-century stone buildings enclose a courtyard where white fantails strut, the former barns to left and right providing very well-equipped ground-floor bedrooms for visitors – each with its own entrance. Meals are taken in a beamed dining-room in the centre, furnished with antiques and an inglenook fireplace (a typical dinner might be home-made soup, a roast or lasagne, and blackcurrant tart – with produce from the smallholding); and to one side is a sitting-room for visitors. From a patio with chairs one enjoys a serene view.

Stephen Robinson-Gay is an accomplished cabinet-maker, happy to show visitors the workshop where he makes or restores furniture. Many of the bedrooms have examples of his work. For example, beyond the arched doorway of the mahogany room is a colonial-style bed with very fine inlay, and in the oak room a four-poster with carved canopy, copied from a Flemish bed in Lindisfarne Castle (on Holy Island), complete with a secret cupboard to hold a shotgun – necessary bedside equipment in the troubled times of three centuries ago.

Celia is a fount of information on local history and what to see. Close by is one of the National Trust's biggest houses, Wallington Hall (very fine grounds), with others not far afield – Cragside, Belsay and a great number of castles. Capability Brown was born in the area, there are Pre-Raphaelite associations, and the whole region is one of impressive landscapes – from the hills and valleys of the Cheviots to the dramatic coastline more fully described elsewhere.

Flemish bed

SHOTTLE HALL FARM

C D H PT S-C

Shottle, north-west of Belper, Derbyshire, DE5 2EB   Tel: 077 389 276

9 bedrooms (single, double or family) from £15. Discount for over 65s or long stays. Rooms have central heating; armchairs; views of country or garden. Tea/coffee facilities available. No smoking.
Dinner £8.50 for 4 courses (limited choice) and coffee, at 7pm. Special diets if ordered. Packed lunches, snacks. Coffee, tea, free. Drinks can be ordered.
Sitting-room with central heating. Games room with snooker and TV; bar.
Garden and farmland.
Nearest main road A517 from Ashbourne to Belper.

The house is over a century old and has all the solid Victorian quality of that period: big rooms, fine ceilings and doors, dignity in every detail. Not only the bedrooms but even the bathrooms are large and close-carpeted, with paintwork and everything else in pristine condition. As well as a sizeable sitting-room, there are two dining-rooms – one is used for breakfasts because it gets the morning sun. From both, the huge windows have views of hills and of the fertile valley stretching below the house – much of it is the Matthews' land. There are a rose garden and lawns – and not another house in sight.

Philip is a former county chairman of the National Farmers Union and an extremely interesting person with whom to discuss agricultural politics, Common Market affairs and so forth. Occasionally, vintage cars rally here. Her guests enjoy Phyllis's straightforward home cooking. A typical dinner menu might include: salmon mousse, chicken in apricot sauce, meringue with raspberries, English cheeses, and coffee with cream. Phyllis collects antique cheese dishes; and has other antiques for sale.

Shottle is in the middle of a rural area of fine landscapes. Close by are the Derbyshire Dales and the Peak District (described elsewhere). The Matlocks are a hilly area with pretty villages to be found. The old spa of Matlock Bath has interesting places to visit (stately gardens, wildlife park, model village, a museum of mining, and the tower, terraces and caverns of Abraham's Heights). Cromford is both attractive and historic, with Arkwright's first mill, old waterside buildings, a good bookshop etc. At Crich is a tramway museum. There are six stately homes (including Chatsworth), a museum of childhood and innumerable good walks in the Peak District, the famous Alton Towers gardens and leisure park, Shipley country park and a cable-car up the Heights of Abraham.

Readers' comments: Lovely room, excellent dinner: a winner. Good and friendly. Wonderful! Delightfully warm and friendly couple. Superb cook. Thoroughly enjoyed our stay, charming and friendly people. Very impressed; could not have been more helpful.

All prices are inclusive of any VAT or service charge. They are minimum prices: superior rooms or high-season bookings may cost more.

SHOULDER OF MUTTON INN

C(3) D

Kirby Hill, north of Richmond, North Yorkshire, DL4 7JH Tel: 0748 2772

5 bedrooms (double) from £13.80, or £23 including dinner. Less for 3 nights or bargain breaks. Rooms have central heating; shower or bathroom; TV, armchairs; views of country; tea/coffee facilities.
Dinner 7.30–9pm. Special diets if ordered. Bar lunches and packed lunches. Drinks can be ordered.
Nearest main road A66 from Scotch Corner to Brough.

The Shoulder of Mutton is the sort of ivy-covered village inn to stay in if you like talking to the locals in a beamy, stone-walled bar in the evening – in fact, holiday-makers have been known to flee here from the formal atmosphere of a nearby hotel of the grander kind. There is no sitting-room, however, but a pool room. Now run by Hylton and Shirley Pyner, the inn has been extended to create a restaurant where you can order such dishes as steaks, guinea-fowl (in a sauce of asparagus, mushroom and cream), or plaice stuffed with smoked salmon and prawns. They have decorated rooms with attractive fabrics, Turkey carpets, and jolly Victorian pictures; and there is a log stove in the bar.

Kirby Hill is a small village, complete with green and old church. As the name suggests, it stands on a hill giving impressive views of the valley, which extends as far as the North York Moors. It is in a quiet spot close to the A1 and also to the historic town of Richmond, with its Georgian theatre and Norman castle. The Shoulder of Mutton is popular with race-goers, for Catterick is also within a few miles. You can do day-trips to Hadrian's Wall, Durham Cathedral, York and the superb coastline of Northumberland and North Yorkshire.

Barnard Castle, a few miles away, is a small town which deserves half a day or more of one's time. Best known for the market cross in the centre and the riverside castle from which it takes its name, it is a good place to shop for antiques, and there is a choice of restaurants. Perhaps the most surprising thing there is an old textile mill by the river, which is now a supermarket-size remainder bookshop: there is no knowing what you will find there at knockdown prices, from a history of horror films to obscure technological works or classical authors.

Another surprising attraction of Barnard Castle is the Bowes Museum, just outside the town (not at nearby Bowes). This château-style pile was built in the 19th century by a distant relative of the Queen Mother's family, (the Bowes-Lyons), to house the family's big collections of ornate French furniture, musical instruments, minor old masters, and ceramics, as well as toys, model ships, butterflies – and a two-headed calf. There is also a silver automaton of a swan which does its fish-swallowing performance every hour, and travelling exhibitions are mounted periodically. It is not what you would expect to find in such a spot.

Inland are some pleasant villages, many with good pubs: specially recommended is the Fox & Hounds at Cotherstone. Sample if you can Cotherstone cheese, a genuine local speciality which is excellent but elusive in shops.

Readers' comments: Super position, nice people. Idyllic; view from our corner room was magic; good food and attentive owners. Exceptional value, superb meal. Very welcoming, food splendid, enjoyed the Monday singalong!

SINGLETON LODGE

C D PT X

Lodge Lane, Singleton, east of Blackpool, Lancashire, FY6 8LT
Tel: 0253 883854

10 bedrooms (single, double or family) from £18. Less for 2 nights. Bargain weekends. Rooms have central heating; shower or bathroom; TV; views of country or garden; tea/coffee facilities.
Dinner from £8 for 5 courses (with choices) and coffee, or à la carte, from 7pm. Special diets if ordered. Snacks. Coffee, tea, for a charge. Drinks can be ordered.

4 sitting-rooms with central heating, open fire, TV, books; bar.
Large garden with croquet and swing, and pastures.
Nearest main road A585 from Preston to Fleetwood.

The early 18th-century house has played many roles – a vicarage, a school, the home of Fleetwood admirals, a farmhouse (as it was when I first included it in this book) and now – though Alan Smith still owns and farms from it – a hotel.

Beyond the handsome panelled doorway of the mellow brick front is now an elegant sitting-room with silvery-blue armchairs of buttoned velvet, cream walls hung with Victorian watercolours and big sash windows overlooking a lawn with rustic seats.

There is a pink-and-pine bar with log fire; and in the dining-room are laceclothed tables with peach velvet chairs.

Bedrooms are now of a similar standard – specially made frilled and flowery bedlinen features in most of them, colour schemes are restful (cream-and-pink or cream-and-blue, for instance), one has fine inlaid furniture and another a romantic, canopied bed. Upstairs is a second, small sitting-room for quiet reading.

Ann's chef now produces meals with such classic dishes as veal in a sherry and cream sauce, duckling with Madeira and cherries, scallops Mornay or salmon in cucumber sauce.

It's a tranquil place, yet Blackpool is easily accessible for its sands and entertainments, or the quieter resort of Lytham St Anne's. There are plenty of stately homes to visit, the port of Fleetwood, Lancaster's historic streets, old Glasson Dock, the great sandy bay of Morecambe, Garstang (market town) and the magnificent, wild Trough of Bowland. The Lake District is within easy motoring distance.

In the immediate neighbourhood are plenty of good walks. Nearby Poulton-le-Fylde has an ancient church, stocks and fish stones. For garden-lovers: Stanley Park, Jubilee Gardens at Fleetwood and Barton Grange at Preston.

Shooting and fishing can be arranged.

Readers' comments: Very welcoming. Remarkable value.

THE SKAKES   C D PT
Glewstone, south-west of Ross-on-Wye, Herefordshire, HR9 6AZ
Tel: 098 984 456

have central heating; views of country or garden.

Dinner £5.50 for 3 courses and coffee, at 6.30pm. Vegetarian or special diets if ordered. Packed lunches. Non-residents not admitted. Drinks can be ordered. No smoking.

2 sitting-rooms with central heating, open fire, TV, books.

Grounds Grassland.

8 bedrooms (double or family) from £11. Less for 3 nights or bargain breaks. Rooms

Nearest main road A4137 between the A40 and the A49.

An expressive Norse word, skakes means 'a place of twisting tracks' – which well describes this part of the Herefordshire countryside. The 18th-century house is now the home of Raymond Vivian and his wife Beris whose love of cooking was a prime reason why they decided to run a guest-house.

A typical meal might comprise mushroom soup and rolls (both home-made), followed by spatchcock – a Tudor recipe for baking chicken with a crisp coating of crumbs – with peas and potatoes in a mustard-and-cream sauce, then Austrian coffee-cake. Meals are served in a former barn, overlooking a herb garden. Like other rooms, it has chunky stone walls. Interesting objects give the house character – an heirloom grandfather clock 8 feet tall, horse harness and pitchforks found on the land, a collection of old bottles and jars (to which visitors contribute); outside, a working pump and an old stone cider-press. Bedrooms are pleasantly decorated, with louvred cupboards. There is a well-planned family room on the ground floor, the children's end curtained off from the rest.

Most visitors come to enjoy walking and birdwatching, but there is plenty of sightseeing too. Hereford and its cathedral are near, also Chepstow (castle) and Bath (elegant spa town). Some of England's most scenic areas are round here: Symonds Yat, the Wye Valley, Brecon Beacons and the Black Mountains.

An interesting drive southward could take one via Goodrich Castle (its impressive red ruins stand high on a hill overlooking the River Wye) into the Forest of Dean to visit Clearwell Caves: 1000-year-old passages dug in the quest for minerals have created a vast honeycomb to be explored. One huge cave holds 500 people. There is a forest railway with preserved steam locomotives; and a heritage centre in a former watermill which also houses craft workshops. Onward the road goes through deep valleys of pines and up to fine viewpoints, past Littledean Hall and its Roman temple excavations, with a pause at Newnham to watch the spectacular Severn bore (tidal wave) if your timing is right, and so to Westbury Court water-gardens in Dutch style.

Some readers tell me they have stayed at lots of places from *Staying Off the Beaten Track*. I wonder who has stayed at most? A free copy of the next edition awaits the reader who sends me his/her comments on the greatest number!

271

SLIPWAY HOTEL   **S**
Port Isaac, north of Wadebridge, Cornwall, PL29 3RH   Tel: 0208 880264

10 bedrooms (single, double or family) from £18. Some have own shower; views of harbour; balcony; all have central heating; phone; tea/coffee facilities.
Dinner A la carte or £10.95 for 3 courses (with choices) and coffee, at 7.30pm. Vegetarian or special diets if ordered. Lunches, packed lunches, snacks. Tea, coffee, extra. Drinks can be ordered.
Sitting-room with central heating, TV, books; bar.
Nearest main road A39 from Bude to Camelford.
Closed in January and February

Slate pillars and great beams give character to the dining-room – the most important room in this small harbourside hotel, for the food is its particular attraction. The room is on two levels with gallery.

Once, this was a ships' chandlery shop and, in running it as a restaurant-cum-hotel, Barry and Angela Smith have preserved most of the old features (some of which date from 1527).

Dinners here offer such choices as leek and Stilton soup, kidneys chasseur, and apple pie with clotted cream. Afterwards, a comfortable sitting-room awaits upstairs.

The bedrooms here vary – some have harbour views; some, stone walls and beamed ceilings. A few are tucked under the eaves.

Port Isaac, at the foot of a steep lane, is still a fishing village of slate-hung cottages (it supplies crabs, for instance, to the hotel), and from it run footpaths along the coastline, which is spectacular hereabouts and frequented by a great variety of seabirds.

Resorts like Newquay and Bude are soon reached, as well as tourist honeypots such as Tintagel (castle ruins and Merlin's cave) and Polperro. But in the immediate vicinity there is plenty to see, and with fewer people about: Tregeare Rounds (an Iron Age fort), for instance; Rock, with ferry to ancient Padstow and Prideaux Place (a Tudor house with carvings by Grinling Gibbons); inland, Bodmin Moor – some of it really wild and little-visited, with peaks rearing up dramatically, and at other places green and flowery; Bodmin, market town; Lanhydrock, a 17th-century NT house; attractive villages like Blisland and Bolventor, the latter with Daphne du Maurier's Jamaica Inn, or Altarnum which has 'the Cathedral of the Moor'. Everywhere there are legends connected with King Arthur (Dozmary Pond is said to be where the sword Excalibur was thrown in, and Camelot was reputedly at Camelford).

Many of the houses in this area incorporate local slate as well as Cornwall's ever-present granite, from which the hundreds of Celtic crosses that dot the countryside also are made, many of them from the era when Irish saints sailed here in such numbers to convert the Cornish to Christianity. Centuries later, Wesley was to come on a similar mission, leaving a trail of small Methodist chapels in his wake.

But the greatest attraction is, of course, the spectacular shoreline – black headlands, golden sands, white-foamed waves rolling in from the Atlantic – and the inland scenery where moors contrast with lush valleys.

SLOOP INN

Bantham, west of Kingsbridge, Devon, TQ7 3AJ Tel: 0548 560489

5 bedrooms (single, double or family) from £16. Less for 2 nights and bargain breaks. Some have own bath; TV; tea/coffee facilities; central heating; views of sea, river or country. (Washing-machine on request.)
Dinner A la carte, at 7–10pm. Vegetarian or special diets if ordered. Lunches, packed lunches, snacks. Tea, coffee, extra. Drinks can be ordered.
Nearest main road A379 from Kingsbridge to Plymouth.
Closed mid-December–mid-January

It goes without saying that this 400-year-old inn by the sea has a history of smuggling.

One of its owners was in fact a notorious wrecker, luring ships (by means of false lights) onto rocks in order to plunder them. Since the law was that 'if any man escape to shore alive, the ship is no wreck' – and so plundering it would be theft, wreckers were murderous wretches too. Neil Girling can tell you many stories of the smugglers and point out places in the village where they hid their kegs of French brandy. Once, the Sloop minted its own coins (some are now in the interesting museum at Kingsbridge) with which to pay for goods and services – the coins were usable only to buy drinks at the Sloop: good business!

The inn is unspoilt: everything one hopes that a lively waterfront inn will be but rarely is, low-beamed, stone-flagged and snug. Some walls are of stone and some panelled.

One of its several bars is made from old boat-timbers. Here you can take on the locals at a game of darts or table-skittles after enjoying an excellent bar meal; or stroll down to the sandy dunes to watch the sun set over the sea. Bathing, building sandcastles and exploring rock-pools delight children; and there is surfing. Many of the unpretentiously furnished bedrooms have a view of the sea or River Avon. There is a yard and well at the back with seats.

Soups are home-made and ham home-cooked; smoked salmon, crabs and steaks are all local produce; granary bread is served. Fish is, of course, particularly good and fresh. All portions are generous.

Bantham is one of Devon's most ancient villages (the remains of prehistoric dwellings were laid bare in an 18th-century storm, and there was a Roman camp here later). Once, its main livelihood was pilchard-fishing but there are no more pilchards now.

The whole area is remote, peaceful and unspoilt with good walks through particularly beautiful countryside or along the coastal footpath; and yet the historic cities of Plymouth and Exeter are within reach, and the great resort of Torquay. In early spring, wildflowers are everywhere and the blue waves are already beginning to be dotted with boating enthusiasts. This is a rich farming area ('the fruitfullest part of Devonshire'), with villages full of well-kept colourwashed cottages thickly thatched.

On the other side of the Avon is Bigbury where a strange, long-legged 'tram' takes people across the sea to Burgh Island and further still is Newton Ferrers on the Yealm estuary, a medley of gabled houses and thatched cottages in steep lanes. On May Day, Noss Mayo still has a traditional procession.

SNOWFORD HALL FARM

C

Hunningham, east of Leamington Spa, Warwickshire, CV33 9ES
Tel: 0926 632297

4 bedrooms (single, double or family) from £11. Rooms have central heating; two have shower; armchairs; views of country or garden. No smoking.
Dinner £9 for 4 courses and coffee, from 6.30pm. Coffee, tea, free. Non-residents not admitted. Drinks can be brought in. No smoking.
Sitting-room with central heating, TV, books, piano.
Garden and farmland.
Nearest main road A423 from Coventry to Banbury.

A very long drive through fields leads to this spacious 18th-century house at the heart of a 300-acre farm (cattle and crops) with fine views around it. One enters through an interesting hall with old china on a big dresser and polished wood floor. The huge sitting-room is very attractively furnished. Here and there around the house are many things made by Rudi Hancock herself, a skilled craftswoman – samplers, for example, and corn dollies; and furniture which she has restored.

Dutch-born, she was previously a cookery teacher and so (except at harvests, when she has no time to cook evening meals) you can expect a good dinner, if booked in advance. She uses many home-grown vegetables and fruit, and makes her own jam.

The most interesting of the bedrooms has a very unusual and decorative Dutch bed of solid mahogany, handsomely carved.

Snowford Hall is near Leamington Spa and its environs, described elsewhere, and such sights as Warwick and Kenilworth castles, Stratford-upon-Avon, Coventry Cathedral and Draycote water country park. Packwood House has an exceptional garden, and the National Centre for Organic Gardening is near. Southam is an old market town; Stoneleigh a mediaeval village (with the great National Agricultural Centre outside it). The National Exhibition Centre is within easy reach, so are Warwick University and Rugby School. And all around are some of England's finest landscapes.

Hunningham is close to the ruler-straight Fosse Way which goes all the way from Devon to Lincolnshire, built by the Romans to link their most important forts. Though not even a 'B' road now, it still survives the centuries, so well was it engineered, on the line of a prehistoric trail which was an important trade route linking the mines of the south-west to ports that traded with Scandinavia. Now trade travels by other roads and the Fosse Way sees little traffic.

Leamington (it gained the prefix 'Royal' when the young Queen Victoria stayed there only a year after coming to the throne) is still an active spa, its baths supplied by underground springs of saline water: it is the only spa to which you can bring your rheumatism on the National Health Service. Fine 18th- and 19th-century squares and terraces give the town a discreet charm. There are some outstanding gardens in the area – including the public Jephson Gardens in Leamington and those of the Mill House by the river at the foot of Warwick Castle.

Readers' comments: Lovely rooms; gorgeous, silent countryside. Wonderful reception, beautiful house, plenty of very good food, wholly pleasurable.

274

SOMERSET HOUSE

C(9) D H PT S X

35 Bathwick Hill, Bath, Avon, BA2 6LD   Tel: 0225 466451

9 bedrooms (single, double or family) from £19.35, or £33.85 with dinner. Less for 5 nights. Rooms have central heating; bathroom; phone, armchairs; views of city or garden; tea-making facilities. No smoking.
Dinner 4 courses and coffee, at 7pm (not on Sundays). Vegetarian and special diets if ordered. Lunches on Sundays. Drinks can be ordered. No smoking.
2 sitting-rooms with central heating, open fire, TV, books, piano. No smoking.
Large garden
Nearest main road A36 from Bath to Southampton.

The Seymours moved to this handsome Georgian mansion from a smaller house down the steep hill. Above the Doric-columned portico is a decorative iron verandah; wisteria and roses climb up the walls of honey-coloured stone.

The entrance hall (marble-tiled and with a Greek key border round the ceiling) leads to a sitting-room, with conservatory opening onto lawn, grand piano, fire and abundant books and records. There is one bedroom on the ground floor. The dining-room is below stairs (it, too, has an open fire), furnished with pine dresser.

On the first floor is another sitting-room with a particularly pretty plasterwork ceiling and very old Venetian glass chandelier. The original panelled shutters flank the hugh sash windows; outside is the long verandah, with fine city views.

Bedrooms are large and pleasantly furnished, many with antique fireplaces (one has an antique loo) and attractive views. Some have Laura Ashley fabrics.

Malcolm (once director of a regional tourist board) is a mine of information on what to see in the neighbourhood. Throughout the year he arranges weekends with special themes: Georgian Bath, exploring the Mendip and Cotswold Hills, Brunel, or opera whenever the Welsh National Opera Company visits nearby Bristol. Jean, formerly a teacher, enjoys finding recipes appropriate to each of these occasions, assisted by three other members of the family.

At breakfast, few people opt for the full cooked version because there is such an array of home-baked breads (nutty, spicy or fruity), preserves, muesli, freshly squeezed fruit juice and so forth; often haddock, kidneys, Cumberland sausage or muffins are offered. As to dinner, when nothing more exotic is afoot, Jean may produce something like (for example) game soup, her own 'rolypoly, gammon and spinach' recipe with home-grown vegetables, and apples in cider served with home-made ice cream.

Perhaps the greatest glory is the garden. Every tree flowers at a different season, and the centrepiece is a great 300-year-old Judas tree – at its purple best in May. All around, between beds of peonies and columbines, is a 7¼-inch rail track installed by a former owner. Adjoining is a herb and fruit garden. All within a 12-minute walk of the city centre.

Readers' comments: The best establishment I've stayed at, where people count; the cooking reinvigorates the taste-buds. Superb comfort and food. Excellent accommodation; the most interesting and nicest food we have ever experienced. Particularly delighted. A favourite. The Seymours make guests welcome; one meets interesting people there. We stay regularly. Comfortable; very good food.

SOUTH FARM
East Meon, west of Petersfield, Hampshire, GU32 1EZ   Tel: 073 087 261

3 bedrooms (single, double or family) from £15. Some have own bath; tea/coffee facilities; central heating; views of river, country or garden. No smoking. (Washing-machine on request.)
Sitting-room with central heating, open fire, TV, books.
Large garden
Nearest main road A272 from Winchester to Petersfield.

The approach to the farm is delightful. There are specimen trees on a lawn (ash, viburnum, chestnut), an old granary and a grapevine under glass. In the 500-year-old house is a brick-floored dining-room with huge inglenook, rush ladderback chairs and a big oak table. The very large sitting-room has carved furniture and chinoiserie curtains in gold-and-blue. Bedrooms have been very agreeably furnished by Jane Atkinson: one with poppy fabrics, for instance; in another are purple-and-white clematis curtains and a lace bedspread. An oak-panelled room has William Morris's chrysanthemum fabric.

Jane serves only breakfast. For other meals, there are two historic inns in East Meon – The George (where I chose an excellent game pie from their bar snacks) and the Izaak Walton, of *Compleat Angler* fame.

The Meon Valley amid the South Downs has churches that go back to Saxon times, flint-walled houses, and prehistoric burial mounds. To the south are woodlands, remnants of the once-great Forest of Bere, and then comes Portsmouth Harbour. Despite heavy traffic on roads into the port, this is well worth a visit – to see Nelson's *Victory*, Henry VIII's *Mary Rose* and his Southsea Castle, Victorian forts up on the hills and Norman Portchester Castle down by the waterfront. There are boat trips and ferries to the Isle of Wight; excellent museums (don't miss the Royal Marines one); Dickens's birthplace; much ceremonial on Navy Days; and waterfowl on the wilder shores of the two natural harbours here. Queen Elizabeth Forest contrasts with all this (drive to Georgian Buriton, up Butser Hill, or visit the recreated Iron Age village). There's a mediaeval palace at Bishop's Waltham. Hambledon has a vineyard.

When to go? Seaside resorts or other places suitable for children will be at their busiest (and dearest) in July–August and during half-term holidays (especially in late May, which is also a bank holiday period). Other peak periods are, of course, Easter, Christmas, New Year and the bank holiday in late August. (The bank holiday in early May is not usually a peak, because it comes rather soon after Easter, but much depends on the weather.) There are local peaks, too (the Gold Cup races at Cheltenham or the regatta at Henley, for instance, are apt to fill hotels for miles around), and local troughs (Brighton, a conference centre, is least busy in high summer). You won't get much personal attention when hotels are full to bursting.

276

SPION KOP

C D S X

Spring Lane, Ufford, north of Woodbridge, Suffolk, IP13 6EF
Tel: 0394 460277

3 bedrooms (double) from £13. Less for 7 nights and bargain breaks. Rooms have own bath/shower; TV; tea/coffee facilities; central heating; views of country or garden. (Washing-machine on request.)
Dinner £7 for 3 courses (with choices) and coffee, at 7pm. Non-residents not admitted. Vegetarian or special diets if ordered. Lunches, packed lunches, snacks. Tea, coffee, free. Drinks can be brought in.
Sitting-room with central heating, open fire, TV, books, record-player.
Large garden
Nearest main road A12 from Ipswich to Lowestoft.

When Colonel Walters returned from the Boer Wars he built himself a house reminiscent of his years on the veldt, with an almost conical roof of thatch and a wide-eaved verandah. Its site must have reminded him of the hill on which 300 British died at the hands of the Boers, for he named it after this.

The Fergusons have added their own distinctive touches to what was already a very unusual house. Along the verandah (hung with brimming baskets of lobelias and begonias) are life-size marble nymphs – the Four Seasons – with more among the flowerbeds. Indoors, along with much other Victoriana which surely would have delighted the colonel, are bronzes and paintings of turn-of-the-century beauties well displayed against the pale pink walls of sitting- and dining-rooms, through the lattice windows of which (or from the glass sun-room) there are wooded valley views more typical of Devon than of Suffolk. There is a meadow brilliant with kingcups and wild orchids in spring.

Bedrooms are spacious and elegantly furnished; and Susan's meals are delicious. One example – a herby soup with croûtons was followed by pork in a sauce of mushrooms, cream and wine (with vegetables cooked to perfection); raspberry meringues; cheeses, and a glass of wine included.

Spion Kop is one of about 50 houses, mostly in Suffolk, in a scheme under which one-third of whatever you pay is given to Oxfam. The participating proprietors choose a particular project to support (at the time when I stayed, it was a college in Kampuchea to train young men in irrigation systems), and between them over £9000 a year is raised. The scheme was originated by Rosemary and Robin Schlee (he is an accountant), at whose own very lovely home – with equally lovely garden – visitors are also welcomed. I looked at this and two others nearby (Four Elms at Ufford, and No. 29 Ipswich Road, Woodbridge) and was very impressed with their high standards and – at the latter – a spectacular view of the Deben estuary from one of the bedrooms. All charge similar prices (other, simpler houses in the scheme charge less); and all have been inspected. On departure, every visitor is given a special receipt for the one-third that goes to Oxfam.

Readers can book into Spion Kop direct – telephone number above; or phone Mrs Schlee to book into others: her number is 03943 2740.

SPORTSMAN'S ARMS
C D PT

Wath-in-Nidderdale, Pateley Bridge, west of Harrogate, North Yorkshire, HG3 5PP Tel: 0423 711306

6 bedrooms (double or family) from £18. Less in winter for bargain breaks. Rooms have electric heaters; shower, wc; TV, armchairs; views of country or garden; tea/coffee facilities. No smoking.

Dinner £9 for 3 courses and coffee, from 7.30–9.45pm. Special diets or vegetarian dishes if ordered. Lunches, packed lunches, snacks. Coffee, tea, for a charge. Drinks can be ordered.

3 sitting-rooms with open fire, TV, books; bar.

Garden

Nearest main road A59 from Harrogate to Skipton.

A delightful place, in a delightful setting: Wath is a hamlet tucked away beside the River Nidd.

A pine-panelled bar leads to the dining-room (and, beyond this, sitting-rooms) which has palms, pink-and-grey colour scheme and bentwood chairs, reflected by the light of cut-crystal candle-lamps in the big mirror of a carved Victorian sideboard. Jane Carter has chosen blue/green/beige colour schemes for bedrooms in which curtains and bedspreads match. Huge Victorian baths have been retained. Ray, who used to be catering lecturer, cooks all the meals, assisted by a team of enthusiastic young people. A typical summer dinner: salad with scallops and sweetbreads; salmon filled with prawns, and Hollandaise sauce; and summer pudding with cream. The cooking is exceptional, and much produce is local. Wines are outstanding and reasonably priced.

Lovely Nidderdale, being outside the National Park area, is less frequented than some other dales. It has some very old reservoirs created by damming the River Nidd, now well naturalized and full of ducks, geese, herons and other birds (200 species have been recorded, including some rare migrants). The effect is reminiscent of the Lake District. How Stean is a romantic gorge with a stream cascading into a rocky cleft 70 feet deep (good home-made cakes at the modest café nearby). From the churchyard at Middlemoor, high up at the head of the dale, there are spectacular views down the length of it.

From here one can easily motor to York, Ripon spa (with gardens and cathedral), and a great array of spectacular abbeys – Fountains, Bolton, Jervaulx, Rievaulx and Byland. Also Harewood Hall, Newby Hall and garden, and half a dozen castles; as well as the strange natural formations of Brimham Rocks.

Readers' comments: Food fabulous, staff well trained and friendly. Food very good, and staff appeared to be one largish happy family. Delightful; good food, excellent value. Could not be faulted; food, rooms and surroundings all outstanding in every detail. Very friendly.

278

SPRING END

CDSX

Low Row, west of Richmond, North Yorkshire, DL11 6NL
Tel: 0748 86341

11 bedrooms (single, double or family) from £22 with dinner. Less for 7 nights and bargain breaks. Rooms have central heating or electric heaters; shower or bathroom; TV, armchairs; views of country; tea/coffee facilities.
Dinner 4 courses (with choices) and coffee, at 6.30pm. Vegetarian dishes if ordered.

Packed lunches, snacks. Coffee, tea, free. Drinks can be ordered.
3 sitting-rooms with central heating, open fire, books; bar.
Small garden
Nearest main road A6108 from Leyburn to Richmond.
Closed January and February

Swaledale is a place for active holidays: the roads are too narrow, steep and twisting for relaxed motoring, and there are few contrived 'attractions' for the passive holiday-maker. So the Thompsons have organized their guest-house with walkers in mind.

After a day on the fells, you can have a drink at the bar, eat a meal of generous and fairly simple food (such as leek soup, chicken casserole and chocolate gâteau), and then collapse in a comfortable sitting-room, where there are shelves of books – guides, local history, and fiction – but no television to kill conversation. On sale is a huge selection of books of local interest as well as some well chosen souvenirs.

Spring End is a long and rambling house, with bedrooms in a modern annexe. The house is furnished for comfort rather than effect, and Marion and David Thompson radiate unpretentious hospitality.

Spring End takes a little finding – it is perched on fellside with spectacular views, with a village far below – but, once there, visitors tend mainly to abandon the car until it is time to go home again. They enjoy visiting various waterfalls, Kisdon Hill, and art galleries at Reeth. There is more about Swaledale under other entries.

Readers' comments: Very comfortable, marvellous food, good company. Homely and casual, ideal for walkers.

Inclusive terms for dinner, bed-and-breakfast (particularly for a week) can be much lower than those quoted here for these items taken separately. For short-notice bookings you may be able to get a reduction.

No proprietor wants to have a room standing empty. This particularly applies to Sunday nights. Some hotels make a discount if you want only two courses from a three-course menu.

SPURSHOLT HOUSE

C D S

Salisbury Road, Romsey, north of Southampton, Hampshire, SO51 6DJ
Tel: 0794 512229

4 bedrooms (single, double or family) from £12. Less for 4 nights and bargain breaks. Rooms have own bath/shower; tea/coffee facilities; phone; central heating; views of river, country, garden. No smoking. (Washing-machine on request.)

Sitting-room with central heating, open fire, TV, books. No smoking.
Large garden
Nearest main road A31 from Bournemouth to Winchester.

The house had originally been built for one of Cromwell's generals. It came into the hands of the Palmerston family who lived at Broadlands; and in the 1830s was extended for occupation by Lord and Lady Cowper. Emily Cowper became one of Lord Palmerston's many mistresses (the prime minister was nicknamed Cupid!); and then, after her first husband's death, his wife.

The result of those additions is the imposing mansion one sees today, surrounded by a magnificent garden. There are paved terraces with urns of geraniums, overlooking a lawn, impressive topiary, and a view of Romsey Abbey. Beyond flowerbeds, yew hedges enclose a succession of further pleasures – one garden leading into another, rose beds followed by apple trees, and a lily-pool. There is a tennis court too, and dovecote with fantails.

Rooms have been furnished by Anthea Hughes in keeping with the character of the house. A few have stained glass originally in the Palace of Westminster. One bedroom is oak-panelled, and all contain antiques. Two have open fireplaces, extra-large beds, elegant sofas and garden views; another two are far less grand.

Downstairs is a dining-room handsomely furnished in Victorian style, just as Palmerston might have known it; and a spectacular sitting-room with Knole sofa in silvery damask, a turquoise love-seat and a carved fireplace: like nearly every room in the house, it is impressive.

Bed-and-breakfast only: for dinner, Anthea recommends the Manor House restaurant or a number of local inns.

The house is close to Broadlands, ancestral home of the Palmerston family and later of Lord Mountbatten; and to the fine abbey church of Romsey, built by the Normans. The abbey of Mottisfont, a few miles away, was converted into a stately home during the 18th century (it stands in fine riverside grounds notable for their old roses; and inside is a big *trompe l'oeil* drawing-room painted by Rex Whistler). The quiet river here is the Test, crossed by numerous hump-back bridges and world-famous among anglers for trout. Following its meandering route one can detour to King's Sombourne, which has an arts centre, and Middle Wallop for its museum with exhibits from a century of army flying. By walking to the top of Danesbury's Iron Age hill fort, one can enjoy tremendous views. For another day tour, go to Salisbury; also to Winchester (yet another cathedral), pausing en route at Farley Mount for wooded walks in the nature reserve and hilltop views.

280

THE STABLES

C PT S

Bootle village, near Millom, Cumbria, LA19 5TD   Tel: 06578 644

2 bedrooms (single, double or family) for £21 with dinner. Less for 7 nights. Rooms have central heating; own bathroom and wc; armchairs; views of country or garden.
Dinner 4 courses and coffee, served by arrangement. Special diets if ordered. Drinks can be brought in. Free tea on arrival.

2 sitting-rooms with central heating, open fire, TV, books.
Garden
Nearest main road A595 from Millom to Whitehaven.

Where four horse-drawn coaches were once parked is now a huge sitting-room, with picture windows on three sides. This was the carriage-room of stables which used to serve the great house of a family that grew rich from the manufacture of candles (their tallow was made from sheep fat). The original beams and doors have been kept and the fireplace is simply an opening in the old brick wall, so the room retains something of the character of the original building. Similarly, when the tack-room was converted into a dining-room, the hooks on which harness used to hang were kept.

All this transformation was the work of Pete and Mary Walker, who now run the old stables as a guest-house. They used to come to this part of Cumbria for their holidays, and fell in love with it.

The deep-carpeted bedrooms are attractive. One, decorated in a coffee-and-cream colour scheme, has a huge circular window opposite the bed.

The same menu is never repeated within a fortnight and, as far as possible, Mary cooks whatever dishes her guests like best. A typical menu might be: salmon mousse, gammon with raisin sauce, sticky toffee pudding, cheese and coffee. As an alternative to traditional breakfasts, Mary offers kedgeree, smoked mackerel or haddock and other choices.

The two are a particularly warm, genial couple who make their guests feel at home – for instance, encouraging them to wander off with a tray of tea to where, at the end of the little bluebell copse, their bubbling stream joins the River Annas. They grow vegetables and fruit, have lawns, shrubs and an array of daffodils which brings viewers from miles. They laid a terrace of great slabs from St Bees, the red sandstone headland along the coast. There are marvellous views over lawn and fields to the hills, and you can smell the sea in the air.

Being away from the National Park area of the Lake District, this corner of Cumbria is not greatly frequented by tourists yet it has splendid scenery – from the peak of Black Combe to the excellent sands around Haverigg. There is particularly lovely countryside near Bootle.

Readers' comments: Memorable holiday. Warm and friendly welcome, excellent accommodation, beautiful situation, superb meals – a jewel of a place. Excellent accommodation, food plentiful and well cooked, warm welcome and attention.

STAPLEFORD HALL

C(5) S S-C

Tarvin, east of Chester, Cheshire, CH3 8HH   Tel: 0829 40202

2 bedrooms (single, double or family) from £18. Less for 3 nights and bargain breaks. Both have own bath/shower; TV; tea/coffee facilities; central heating; views of country or garden. No smoking.
Sitting-room with central heating, open fire, TV, books. No smoking.
Large garden
Nearest main road A51 from Chester to Nantwich.

'His table was bountiful . . . he made provision for the multitude'. This was said of John Bruen, squire of the original Hall (the present building dates from 1789). He used to hunt in nearby Delamere Forest with a dozen 'great-mouthed dogs' until converted to Puritanism, when he maintained his own preacher and chapel instead. On his estate were warrens of conies (rabbits), fish-ponds and a flight of pigeons kept for the table.

These days, Margaret Winward's table provides only breakfast for visitors: most dine in Chester, only a quarter-hour away, or at the Rising Sun in Tarporley, returning to the modern comforts of conventionally furnished and spacious bedrooms, and to enjoy either log fires indoors or else the peace of the large garden (with immense beech trees, tennis and croquet), surrounded by acres of dairy-farm.

There are views of two castles (ruined Beeston is particularly romantic, perched on a steep hill with terraced woods and overhanging rocks below it) and of the hills of Wales.

The nearest small town, Tarporley, is surrounded by woods and rich farmland, its ancient churchyard filled with roses in summer. North of it is Delamere Forest, 4000 acres of dense woodland concealing bright-gleaming meres.

Still further, in the direction of the Mersey estuary, are Daresbury (in the church of which Alice and the Mad Hatter are depicted in stained glass, for this was the birthplace of Lewis Carroll), and Helsby Hill from which there are fine views across marshes to the estuary – and of climbers practising on its rocks. Liverpool is soon reached from here, via the Mersey tunnel – well deserving of a visit to see its waterside maritime museum, two modern cathedrals, outstanding art gallery and concert hall among much else.

Also near Tarporley is 18th-century **Duddon Lodge** (tel: 082 924 372), where Dickory Joynson has furnished every room beautifully. This house would appeal to anyone interested in the arts, not only for its contents (antiques, grand pianos, artistic wallpapers, paintings, porcelain figures) but because Mrs Joynson is well informed about arts festivals, opera and similar events in the region. B & b only, which

costs much less than at Stapleford Hall. (There is a covered swimming-pool and sauna, croquet and lawn tennis.)

THE STEPPES

C(12) **D H X**

Ullingswick, north-east of Hereford, HR1 3JG   Tel: 0432 820424

3 bedrooms (double or family) from £17.50. Bargain breaks. Rooms have central heating; bath or shower; TV, telephone, armchairs; views of country or garden. Tea and coffee facilities available and drinks fridge. Laundry room (for a charge). **Dinner** £13.50 for 4 courses and coffee. Choices if ordered. Vegetarian or special diets if ordered. At 7.30pm or later on request. Lunches, packed lunches, snacks. Coffee, tea for a charge. Non-residents not admitted. Drinks can be ordered. No smoking. **Sitting-room** with central heating, log stove, TV, books. Cellar bar/sitting-room. **Large garden Nearest main road** A417 between A49 and A449.

This is one of the prettiest old houses in this book, very attractively furnished by its owners Henry and Tricia Howland. Part of the house is mediaeval, most of it 17th century. Originally, the ground floor was one great hall (the old flagstoned floor is still intact).

The dining-room has a great inglenook fireplace with its original log-irons, and there is a bread oven adjoining its chimney. In the thick walls are original built-in cupboards, and between some rooms 'borrowed lights' (that is, internal windows) with their original glass. The red-and-black tiles of the dining-room are also old.

The beamed dining-room, with a patterned rug on the tiled floor and some dried hop-bines draped across the fireplace, has great character. There are corn dollies on the white walls, flowers on each table, interesting prints, and a melodiously chiming clock.

There is a cellar bar which includes half a dozen kinds of local cider, from clear-and-sparkling to rough-and-heavy. In the sitting-room, flowery chairs and pale velvet curtains contrast with the rugged stone fireplace. Quaint pastry dolls hang on some walls – made by Tricia (a few for sale).

Each bedroom has a different and colourful style – raspberry-pink wall and rosebud fabrics in one, crisp blue-and-white in another; built-in pine storage fitments, pretty lace curtains or deep-pile carpets contribute to the individual character of each one. Each has its own shower. Views are of rounded hills, sheep or cows, hop kilns and the old garden where collared doves perch in cherry trees or lilac spreads its fragrance in early summer. The old pump still draws water to fill a stone trough.

Tricia cooks a wide range of very imaginative dishes and ensures that not one is repeated during a guest's stay. One local speciality which she serves is cheese-and-cider soup (chilled and creamy); another unusual starter is grapefruit with mint ice. The main course might be boned duck with a stuffing of beef, onions, bacon and herbs, or turkey saté (served with peanut sauce and cucumber relish – a Thai recipe). A pudding such as zabaglione, or raspberry meringue gâteau may follow.

Readers' comments: Thoroughly enjoyed it. Superb. 5-star food! Attentive and comfortable. Local food specials and the puddings were excellent. A wonderful few days; delicious and individual cooking served on lovely china; cannot praise it enough. Imaginative dishes. One of the prettiest houses, wonderful garden. First-rate, quiet, cordon bleu cooking. Enchanting house, superb food.

STOKE FARM

C PT S S-C

Broad Chalke, west of Salisbury, Wiltshire, SP5 5EF   Tel: 0722 780209

2 bedrooms (double) from £17. Rooms have central heating or electric heaters; shower or bathroom; TV, armchairs; views of farm or garden; tea/coffee facilities.
Dinner £10 for 3 courses and coffee, at 7pm. Special diets if ordered. Coffee, tea, for a charge. Non-residents not admitted. Drinks can be ordered or brought in.
Sitting-room with central heating, open fire, TV, books, indoor games (including billiards, darts), piano, record-player.
Garden with tennis and croquet.
Nearest main road A354 from Salisbury to Blandford.

A gracious house at the heart of a 1000-acre farm overlooking the Ebble Valley, this is very typical of many other such farms set among the rolling downs of Wiltshire: a mixture of arable fields and of pastures for beef-cattle and dairy-cows.

One approaches the house past mossy rickstones, old cattle-troughs now filled with flowers, and tree-stumps overgrown by periwinkles. A lovely magnolia covers the front wall. Inside, the early Victorian features have been retained – panelled doors, arches and window shutters. My bedroom had windows on three sides with pretty 'cottage garden' curtains and views across fields of cows to the hills. Late in the year, the pens immediately below are full of calves. Throughout the house, soft colours predominate, with carefully arranged flowers, baskets of trailing plants and interesting paintings well lighted (one is by Cecil Beaton, who used to live in the village). There are good carpets and attractive wallpapers everywhere, even in the bathroom. In the big sitting-room, deep armchairs are grouped around a log fire, a record-player and well stocked bookshelves. Last but far from least, Mrs Pickford is an excellent cook. Meals are served in a dining-room that still has the old built-in bread oven, with local trout and pheasant often on the menu.

Many guests go walking. The Pickfords have produced their own map of local footpaths, all well waymarked in this region, which lead down to watercress beds in the valley or up to the Ridgeway which was once a drove road for oxen being taken to market.

I first stayed here in order to visit nearby Salisbury and its cathedral. In addition there is plenty to see in the area – Elizabethan Breamore House, attractive villages (like Downton, Fordingbridge or Tilshead), the Celtic fort on top of Figsbury Hill, Old Sarum with the ruins of its Norman castle on another hilltop, the Roman villa at Rockbourne, Wilton's historic carpet factory and Wilton House, for example. Other leading sights: Stonehenge, the New Forest, two shire horse centres, and plenty of gardens (garden centres too).

Readers' comments: The best b & b in England! Everything about Stoke Farm would be difficult to fault. Very pleasant and helpful. Wonderful! Most comfortable; huge towels, wonderful bathroom. Great kindness.

For explanation of code letters (**C, D, H, PT, S, S-C, X**) see page xxvi

STONE HOUSE HOTEL

C D H S X

Sedbusk, north of Hawes, Wensleydale, North Yorkshire, DL8 3PT
Tel: 09697 571

15 bedrooms (single, double or family) from £18. Less for 3 nights or bargain breaks. Rooms have central heating, electric heaters; shower or bathroom; TV, armchairs; views of country or garden; tea/coffee facilities. (Clothes-washing facilities.)
Dinner £11 for 4 courses (with choices) and coffee, at 7.30–8pm. Vegetarian or special diets if ordered. Lunches, packed lunches, snacks. Coffee, tea, for a charge. Drinks can be ordered.
3 sitting-rooms with central heating, open fire, TV, books, billiards, piano, record-player; bar.
Large garden with tennis lawn.
Nearest main road A684 from Hawes to Sedbergh.
Closed in mid-winter

P. G. Wodehouse, with a new novel near completion, was still searching for a good name to give his principal character. On holiday here, he sat watching village cricket – and in to bat went the Stone House gardener, *Jeeves*. Problem solved!

To this day, Stone House looks exactly right for a house-party with Bertie Wooster and Jeeves drawing up in a sports car at the front door. It was built in Edward VII's reign as a country gentleman's retreat, and some of the oak-panelled rooms, the leather club chairs, 'Spy' cartoons and racehorse shoes on the wall, the billiard table, and the library with books from floor to ceiling, have changed very little.

The present owner, Peter Taplin, is an incurable collector, and on show are his many vintage slot-machines (with a supply of pre-metric pennies with which to operate them), hundreds of old 'Dinky' cars, and antique thimbles. He and Jane have furnished the house well: red chinoiserie fabric on the bar's armchairs; comfortable cushioned seats in the dining-room (which has an aquarium built into one wall); and light, immaculate bedrooms with sprigged fabrics (four are on the ground floor), their stone-mullioned windows overlooking paved terraces, neat box borders and far views. Some bedrooms have their own conservatory/sitting area, opening onto the garden.

Peter used to be a butcher, so it is not surprising that Stone House has a good reputation for straightforward English food – roast beef and Yorkshire pudding naturally being pre-eminent, perhaps preceded by crofter's soup and followed by old-fashioned trifle.

Jeeves would have approved!

For details of the Wensleydale area, see other entries. There are waterfalls (Hardraw and Aysgarth), folk museum and market at Hawes, the Settle railway and the Buttertubs Pass – both very scenic. It is easy to reach Swaledale from here – totally different scenery from Wensleydale.

STOURCASTLE LODGE C
Gough's Close, Sturminster Newton, south-west of Shaftesbury, Dorset, DT10 1BU . Tel: 0258 72320

4 bedrooms (single or double) from £16. Less for 7 nights. Some have own shower; central heating; views of country or garden. (Washing-machine on request.)
Dinner £10 for 3 courses (with choices) and coffee, at 7pm. Vegetarian or special diets if ordered. Lunches, packed lunches, snacks. Tea, coffee, free. Drinks can be brought in.
Sitting-room with central heating, open fire, TV, books.
Garden
Nearest main road A357 from Blandford Forum to Wincanton.

Although just off the market place of this little town, Gough's Close is traffic-free and peaceful: a narrow lane opening out into a green and pleasant place, with the River Stour beyond. The Lodge, which was built in 1739, has been agreeably furnished by Jill Hookham-Bassett, with soft greens and pinks predominating. Everything is very spick-and-span, the bedrooms cottagey in style, and many rooms have views of the secluded garden where one can take tea.

Ken and Jill, who achieved a gold star for cooking when she trained at Ealing Technical College, also run a catering service, so food here is well above average. A typical dinner might be: kedgeree, chicken cooked in a tarragon and mushroom sauce, and charlotte Malakoff (made with cream and almonds). An unassuming house with a lot to offer in the way of hospitality.

From the Lodge, it is easily possible to explore not only Dorset but parts of Wiltshire and even Somerset too.

Mediaeval Sherborne's superb 15th-century abbey of golden stone deserves a lingering visit because of its remarkable fan-vaulting, colourful roof-bosses and other outstanding carvings, as well as a glass reredos engraved by Laurence Whistle. There are two castles: one, Norman and perched on a steep mound; the other, built for Sir Walter Raleigh and surrounded by park and gardens – it contains a series of very fine rooms and art treasures.

Readers' comments: Friendly; eager to help and please.

Strawberry Cottage at Packers Hill, Holwell, is even older, a cottage of thatch, stone and brick, with modern furnishings of high standard. Because Vivienne Powell works at Sherborne's Tourist Information Centre, she is a mine of information about the area. B & b only (tel: 096323 629).

Prices are the minimum *per person* in a double room at the beginning of the year.

286

STRATFORD LODGE

4 Park Lane, Castle Road, Salisbury, Wiltshire, SP1 3NP Tel: 0722 25177

C(8) **PT**

4 bedrooms (double or family) at £16. Less for 2 nights and bargain breaks. All have own bath/shower; TV; tea/coffee facilities; central heating; views of park or garden. Non-smokers preferred. (Washing-machine on request.)
Dinner £12 for 4 courses and coffee, at 7pm. Non-residents not admitted. Vegetarian or special diets if ordered. Tea, coffee, free. Drinks can be brought in.
Sitting-room with central heating, open fire, TV, books. Non-smokers preferred.
Garden
Nearest main road A345 from Salisbury to Amesbury.

In a quiet byway overlooking a park stands a fine Victorian house, now a handsomely furnished guest-house. Jill Bayly has taken a lot of trouble to find good furniture in keeping with the style of the house. The sitting-room has much Victoriana and a large array of African violets; the pale green dining-room, a big mahogany table laid with pretty rosy china (napkins to match) and wildflower curtains at the windows. Bedrooms are attractive, particularly one with a cane and carved bedhead on a bed with a rosebud cover to complement the shell-pink walls. In another room, pale blue, a brass bed has a lace spread. After dark one can go on sitting in the garden which is enclosed by flowering shrubs, because Jill brings out candle-lamps. Beyond it is the vegetable plot which provides fresh produce.

Jill has a varied repertoire of dishes for dinner (not served on Sundays), and she cooks to a high standard. A typical menu: pears baked with Roquefort cheese; duckling with a sauce of port and black cherries; syllabub made with Tia Maria or apple strudel with clotted cream; then cheeses. Breakfasts, too, are generous, with options such as kedgeree and marmalade which she makes herself.

Salisbury is also known as New Sarum (new in 1220!) because the first town was elsewhere, on the hill now known as Old Sarum which began as an Iron Age fort – you can still see traces of a Norman cathedral up there. When it was decided to rebuild on a better site, two miles away by the water meadows, the new cathedral, with the tallest spire in England, was surrounded by grass and big walls to keep the township that followed at a respectful distance. Thus the cathedral can be well viewed all round, unlike some which have buildings crowding right up to them. Inside are fine tombs, the oldest working clock in the country, some fan vaulting, and immense cloisters. Historic houses surround the precincts, some open to the public. There is a big market in the town's central square.

Farthings, at 9 Swaynes Close (tel: 0722 330749), is quite central (there's a view of the cathedral spire over roof-tops) yet very quiet, and it has a garden with brimming flowerbeds. All rooms are immaculate, and pleasantly furnished. Gill Rodwell serves breakfast only (choices include fishcakes, croissants and much else). Exceptional value.

STRATHAVON
8 Charlotte Street, Bath, Avon, BA1 2NE   Tel: 0225 23068

7 bedrooms (single or double) from £15. Less for 2 nights in autumn and winter. All have central heating; some have views of garden. No smoking.
Dinner £11 for 3 courses (with choices) and coffee, at 7–9pm. Vegetarian or special diets if ordered. Packed lunches, snacks. Tea, coffee, free. Drinks can be ordered.
Sitting-room with central heating, TV, books. No smoking.
Small garden
Nearest main road A4 from Bath to Bristol.
Closed in January

It is difficult to locate a good but inexpensive hotel in the centre of Bath, so the Strathavon is quite a find. It is in a terrace of 18th-century houses, with a very small garden at the back and a road at the front (bedrooms at back are quiet). Rooms are conventionally furnished, and immaculate.

What makes the Strathavon special, however, are Tom Waugh's outstanding gifts as a chef. I have eaten at many of Bath's innumerable restaurants but – price-for-price – never better than at the Strathavon. Small though this little hotel is, he is able to offer many choices at each course by the sensible expedient of asking visitors to make their selection by midday (he will post the menu to you). That way he can shop for and prepare every dish freshly for each person – things like a particularly good seafood Mornay, as a starter, chicken breast stuffed with spinach, and delicious fresh fruit desserts.

Many of Bath's major attractions are within a short stroll. In the city centre there is much to see: the abbey, the Roman temple and baths, the botanical gardens, the shopping arcades and much else. Wells is near, as are Stourhead and Corsham.

Readers' comments: Cannot praise it too highly. Food excellent, and imaginatively presented.

Only a little further out is **Parkside**, an Edwardian villa (11 Marlborough Lane, tel: 0225 29444). From the bay window of the comfortable sitting-room (with simulated coal fire) balloonists can often be watched gliding by. The Royal Victoria Park is nearby, as well as the beautiful Botanic Gardens. The dining-room opens onto a garden with paved terrace (presided over by a teak lady from Thailand), lawn and pergola. I particularly liked bedrooms 2 and 3, on the second floor, because they are so big and airy.

Katy Putler produces not only such dinners as melon, lamb chops, blackberry parfait, and West Country cheeses but specializes in vegetarian dishes – using organic produce from one of the allotments opposite the house. Breakfast options include wholefood cereals with fruit salad, and a raw mix of celery, carrots, cucumber and onions as a refreshing change from the bacon-and-egg routine.

STREET FARMHOUSE

C D X

South Warnborough, south-east of Basingstoke, Hampshire, RG25 1RS
Tel: 0256 862225

3 bedrooms (double or family) from £14. Some have own shower; all have TV; tea/coffee facilities; central heating; views of country or garden. (Washing-machine on request.) Packed lunches and snacks.
Sitting-room with central heating, open fire, TV, books.
Large garden
Nearest main road A339 from Alton to Basingstoke.

Two 16th-century cottages were combined into one to make this attractive house, beamed and with inglenook fireplace, in an ancient village through which a stream runs. Wendy Turner's choice of furnishings admirably complements the old house. There are prettily carved chairs in the pale green dining-room; pine doors have been stripped and brick walls exposed; buttoned chairs in rust-colour covers are gathered around a log stove in the sitting-room. Bedrooms are very pleasant – for instance, furnished with chest-of-drawers of woven cane, with very good armchairs and colour schemes. One bathroom has an oval bath in peach, and a bidet. Standards throughout are high. Snack suppers only; for other meals Wendy recommends the Poacher in South Warnborough or the Hoddington Arms in Upton Grey.

North Hampshire (quickly accessible along the M3) is an area often overlooked by people hurrying on to Winchester, Southampton or the New Forest. But anyone who lingers here will find plenty of interest, not least because this is Jane Austen country (her house is at Chawton, and scenes from the area feature in her books). Farnham still has streets much as she knew them, and a hilltop castle. Not far away is Selborne where White wrote his natural history (1789) and here, too, one can still see countryside that he saw. Both his and Jane Austen's homes are open to the public – his has a museum about Captain Oates and Scott's Antarctic expedition and is surrounded by National Trust woodlands. Nearby Odiham, too, retains the appearance of an 18th-century market town, with ruined castle nearby; and there are pretty villages – Greywell, Upton Grey (houses encircling a pond), Sherborne St John (with a Tudor mansion, The Vyne – NT, and moated Beaurepaire), Basing (castle ruins). Silchester was once a great Roman fort with a road running to Salisbury – now this is a mere track in a region of woods, streams and fields. The several fast roads in the area mean that most traffic has been siphoned off to leave the lanes peaceful. South of Basingstoke are the North Downs (running into Surrey) with splendid viewpoints.

Westward lie Litchfield, a flowery village in an area of prehistoric remains; Wherwell, a real showpiece – all timber and thatch, with fine views of the famous River Test; streamside Hurstbourne Tarrant; and Highclere – castle and hilltop grave of Lord Carnarvon (who discovered Tutankhamen's tomb in 1922); Burghclere (Stanley Spencer paintings in a chapel); the two beautiful Clatford villages with pretty river bridges.

In marked contrast to all these quiet pleasures are Farnborough's air show and Aldershot's military tattoo. And if you want to go further afield there are a number of famous tourist spots within easy reach – Windsor, for instance, and of course London itself.

SUGARSWELL FARM X
Shenington, south of Stratford-upon-Avon, Warwickshire, OX15 6HW
Tel: 0295 88512

3 bedrooms (single, double or family) from £17. Less for 5 nights. Rooms have central heating or electric heaters; shower or bathroom; armchairs; views of country or garden; tea/coffee facilities. No smoking.
Dinner £14 for 3 courses and coffee, at 6.30pm. Special diets if ordered. Lunches, packed lunches, snacks. Coffee, tea, for a charge. Drinks can be brought in. No smoking.
Sitting-room with central heating, open fire, TV, books. No smoking.
Grounds Farm and woodland.
Nearest main road A422 from Stratford-upon-Avon to Banbury.

Rosemary Nunnely is a cook of cordon bleu calibre – her greatest delight is preparing meals. Visitors who stay with her are likely to get something very different from ordinary 'farmhouse fare': on the day of my first visit, she had prepared seafood gratin followed by fillet steak (home-produced) in a sauce of port, cream and garlic, with home-made lemon sorbet to finish. Rosemary uses wine and cream in many of her dishes, rum in such specialities as Jamaican torte.

The house is modern but made from old stones taken from a demolished cottage. It has big picture-windows, and a striking staircase with 18th-century portraits. Sofas are grouped round a huge stone fireplace in the sage green sitting-room. The hall, like the dining-room, has terracotta walls. Guests sit on Chippendale chairs to dine; there is good silver on the table, and one side of the dining-room consists of a see-through glass wall filled with Rosemary's collection of Crown Derby.

Upstairs are elegant bedrooms – one with a sofa from which to enjoy woodland views beyond the fields where cows graze, and a very large bathroom decorated in bright mulberry.

Included in the price is the gift of a touring map of the region, showing how to get to (for instance) Warwick, Stratford, the Cotswold towns, Woodstock (Blenheim Palace), Oxford, Silverstone (car races) and Sulgrave (the Washington ancestral home) or such stately homes as Upton House and Farnborough Hall. In Shenington itself is an outstanding garden, at Brook Cottage.

As to the curious name Sugarswell, Rosemary explained its origin: shuggers (mediaeval slang for robbers) made a settlement here, which their more respectable neighbours destroyed. Vestiges can still be seen from the air.

Readers' comments: Lovely home, superb cooking. A marvellous place. Time-capsule of the good life! Food well above average. Charming hostess, comfortable and delightful accommodation, delicious food. Very pleasant rooms and good views; lovely welcome; spacious room. Comfortable accommodation, superb cooking. A lovely place to stay. An outstanding cook. Accommodation excellent. *And from the former manager of a 5-star hotel:* We have been back nine times.

All prices are inclusive of any VAT or service charge. They are minimum prices: superior rooms or high-season bookings may cost more.

SWALCLIFFE MANOR

C(8) **D S**

Swalcliffe, west of Banbury, Oxfordshire, OX15 5EH Tel: 029578 348

4 bedrooms (single or double) from £15. Rooms have central heating or electric heaters; shower or bathroom; TV, armchairs; views of country and garden; tea/coffee facilities. One four-poster.
Dinner £14 for sherry, 4 courses and coffee, at 8pm. Vegetarian or special diets if ordered. Lunches, packed lunches. Non-residents not admitted. Drinks can be brought in.

2 sitting-rooms with central heating, open fire, TV, books, piano, record-player. Table tennis in games room.
Large garden Orchard and fields, with unheated swimming-pool.
Nearest main road A361 from Banbury to Chipping Norton.
Closed mid-December–March

Certainly the most striking entrance of any in this book is here: one passes through a 13th-century undercroft, the vaulted stone ceiling supported on massive circular pillars. Beyond is the former great hall of the house with a vast fireplace. Judith and Francis Hitching (he is the author of several books on prehistoric mysteries) have furnished this with antiques and oriental rugs, a grand piano, and a carved mediaeval chest which contrasts well with pink walls. Traces of ancient wall-paintings can be seen, Tudor roses much in evidence.

The drawing-room is completely different, for in the 18th century an extension was added in Georgian style. This classical room, decorated in pale green, has Corinthian pilasters and a very pretty fireplace of green marble in a pine surround carved with acanthus leaves. Through high sash windows, set in deep panelled embrasures, is a view of the croquet lawn and a former studio now used as a games room for children. This is part of a large garden which includes a suntrapping stone terrace, a Saxon font planted with daisies, swimming-pool (unheated) and a sunken garden with a parterre of flowers grown in Tudor times: Judith put much research as well as hard effort into re-creating this.

A gifted cook (once nominated 'Gourmet of the Year' by a London newspaper), she will cook whatever her visitors prefer, or devise the menu herself – in which case you might be served scallops cooked with ginger and leeks; very good roast meat or game, in which this area excels (accompanied by vegetables from the garden, and herby sauces); then her own Swalcliffe Pudding – a sponge with gooseberries, sultanas and honey. Food is served on flowery Portmeirion pottery.

Upstairs, bedrooms open off a broad gallery, full of pictures and antique toys. The one Georgian bedroom overlooks thatched roofs in the pretty village; while older ones have small stone-mullioned windows with church views. Pointed stone arches of the 13th-century frame baths or bathroom entrances.

Readers' comments: Charming. Nice people, interesting house, good food. Lovely welcome, splendid dinner. Excellent.

TALLY HO INN

C(8) D PT S X

Hatherleigh, north of Okehampton, Devon, EX20 3JN   Tel: 0837 810306

3 bedrooms (double) from £18. Less for 4 nights and bargain breaks. Rooms have own bath/shower; TV; tea/coffee facilities; central heating; views of country or garden. No smoking. (Washing-machine on request.)
Dinner A la carte or about £7.50 for 3 courses (with choices) and coffee, at 7–9.30pm. Vegetarian or special diets if ordered. Lunches, packed lunches, snacks. Tea, coffee, extra. Drinks can be ordered.
Small garden
Nearest main road A386 from Okehampton to Torrington.

The 15th-century inn (recommended to me by a colleague) overlooks the market place in this small historic town which was first recorded in a charter issued by King Ethelred in 981. One thousand and two years later, Gianni and Annamaria Scoz bought it, and today their cosy bar with its wooden beams and huge open fireplaces immediately conveys the feeling of hospitality and well-being that is the essence of the place.

Annamaria looks after the food which ranges from a good selection of bar snacks to a full à la carte dinner menu for the little restaurant. Essentially Italian (although there is also traditional English food for those who prefer it), this menu could not be bettered in any city trattoria – for a modest country pub in mid-Devon, it is quite outstanding. A choice of continental or full English breakfast is offered, with a glass of freshly squeezed orange juice to help you decide.

Above the bar and restaurant, three delightful bedrooms have been professionally created by one of the Scoz's three daughters, and are object lessons in how to bring modern comforts to an ancient building with sensitivity. Mellow stripped pine furniture blends happily with soft cream walls, delicate floral prints, velvet curtains and simple doors of pine that are stained a deep warm brown. In the sumptuous bathrooms, the water flows through shining brass pipes.

Gianni is rightly proud of a thatched barbecue he has built in the small garden behind the inn where summer evening meals may be enjoyed. Private fishing in season, Dartmoor and Exmoor close at hand, and the north Devon coast just a short drive away. Popular sights include Okehampton Castle, Meldon Dam, Alscott Farm Museum, the gardens of Crosspark and Rosemoor, Hartland Quay and quaint little Clovelly.

Where two rivers join, a small settlement grew up, known to the Saxons as 'hawthorn glade' – the origin of Hatherleigh's name. It expanded when the industrious Normans took it over; and from miles around farmers used to attend its markets. Later the townsfolk were given the perpetual right to gather gorse for cooking-fuel on Hatherleigh Moor (which earned them the nickname 'pot-boilers'), commemorated in an old jingle:

> 'I, John of Gaunt
> Do give and grant
> Hatherleigh Moor
> To Hatherleigh poor
> For evermore.'

Go there in November for the fiery carnival with flaming torches and tar-barrels.

THORNLEY HOUSE
C D X

Allendale, south of Hexham, Northumberland, NE47 9NH   Tel: 043483 255

3 bedrooms (single or double) from £14.
Less for 7 nights. All have tea/coffee facili-
ties; central heating; views of country or
garden. (Washing-machine on request.)
Dinner £8 for 3 courses and coffee, usually at
7pm. Vegetarian or special diets if ordered.
Packed lunches, snacks. Tea, coffee, free.
Drinks can be brought in.
2 sitting-rooms with central heating, TV,
books, piano, record-player.
Large garden
Nearest main road B6305 from Hexham to
Allendale.

Allendale town is a large village in a sheltered valley amid some of the most open
scenery in England – deserted grouse moors and breezy sheep pastures which
stretch for uninterrupted miles, punctuated only by isolated farmhouses and the
occasional relic of the lead mining which once made this area important. On the
outskirts of the village is Thornley House, a large and solid inter-war house in a big
garden. Eileen Finn runs a small language school here, so visitors may mix with a
few (adult) students from Denmark or other countries. Rooms are spacious and
light, with views of the wooded roads into the village and of the Pennines.

Mrs Finn is a keen cook, and though guests are offered conventional fare
(vichyssoise soup, breaded chicken, salad, and chocolate mousse, for example),
she needs only a little encouragement to cook a dish from Mexico, where she lived
for eight years, or from another of the many countries to which she has paid long
visits. As well as being a linguist and passionate world traveller, she is an able
pianist, and there is a Steinway grand in one of the two sitting-rooms. Visitors may
be taken on guided walks.

Allendale is Catherine Cookson's country. She lives nearby and many of her
Mallen stories are set here. It is one of the loveliest parts of the north country, wild
and rocky, in parts comparable with some Swiss scenery. Allen Banks, where two
rivers converge, is a beauty-spot. No far off is the Killhope pass (nearly 2000 feet
high) with a great wheel once used for crushing ore when these hills were mined for
lead. In Allendale town, on every New Year's Eve costumed 'guizers' parade with
blazing tar-barrels on their heads – vestige of a half-forgotten pagan fire-rite. At
Hexham is a great Norman abbey, well worth visiting, a garden centre and a lively
market every Tuesday. The Roman Wall, Kielder Forest with its vast landscaped
reservoir, and the Scottish borders are not far off.

A few miles away, Isabel and John
Wentzel offer b & b plus imaginative
cooking (for vegetarians especially) at
Crowberry Hall (tel: 043483 392), a
one-time farmhouse set in a very remote spot overlooking the valley of the
East Allen. Mrs Wentzel, who makes
preserves for sale, also runs craft
courses under experts in, for example,
lacemaking and needlepoint.

Readers' comments: Enjoyed the cooking, home-made wine and magnificent
walks.

THORNTON MANOR
Ettington, south-east of Stratford-upon-Avon, Warwickshire, CV37 7PN
Tel: 0789 740210

3 bedrooms (double or family) from £11.50. Less for 4 nights. Rooms have own bath/shower; central heating; views of country and garden. No smoking. (Washing-machine on request.)
Sitting-room with central heating, log stove, TV, piano, record-player.
Small garden
Nearest main road A429 from Warwick to Stow-on-the-Wold.

A stately home in miniature, this stone manor house, E-shaped in plan, declares its date, 1658, on a doorpost. Through an iron-studded oak door with decorative hinges, heavy bolts and locks, one enters a great hall dominated by a large stone fireplace with log stove. Overhead are massive chamfered beams; and the furniture is in keeping with this scene.

Through the leaded panes of deep-set, mullioned windows in the breakfast-room (and in a bedroom above it) there are views of the garden, woods and the fields of this farm, which is well tucked away at the end of a long drive. Little but humps in the grass show where there was once a village in view until, in the 13th century, the Black Death killed off all its 60 inhabitants. Ancient outbuildings include an old pigeon-house from the days when the birds were farmed as an important source of food.

Gill Hutsby (who occasionally sings at the Royal Shakespeare Theatre) has used old-fashioned furniture and rosy cretonnes in the bedrooms. There is a kitchen for guests' use (Gill does not provide evening meals because there are local inns and Stratford has many restaurants), and also a tennis court. Visitors can fish for trout in the Hutsbys' lake or enjoy coarse fishing in the River Dean. Stratford-upon-Avon (best visited out of season) has not only Shakespeare's birthplace but also Hall's Croft (his daughter's home), the fine mediaeval church with his tomb, Harvard House (after which the American university was named) and other mediaeval buildings.

Also at Ettington is **Grove Farm** (tel: 0789 740228), a house found at the end of a brick path, with grapevine beside it and an old pump. It is full of character, with unusual furniture and trifles Meg and Bob Morton have collected: from a spectacular carved sideboard to an old imp's head built into one wall, an elm manger to a collection of knobkerries. The chased silver pheasant-gun be-longed to Bob's grandfather and the old dough-chest to Meg's (he was a baker). Bedrooms under the sloping eaves are simple: they have old-fashioned furni-ture and Turkey carpets on board floors. Meg serves only breakfast: for other meals, I found the bar food at the

Houndshill Inn more than adequate. Meg collects elderly horses, saving them from the slaughter-house; they are to be seen grazing in the fields beyond which are deer woods and a panoramic view of the Cotswolds as far as Bourton-on-the-Water.

Readers' comments: Warm, friendly welcome. Most impressed.

TIGHE FARM

C(8)

Stone-in-Oxney, north of Rye (East Sussex), Kent, TN30 7JU
Tel: 023383 251

3 bedrooms (double or family) from £13. Much less for 2 nights or bargain breaks. Rooms have central heating or electric heaters; armchairs; views of country or garden. Coffee, tea, free.
Sitting-room with central heating, open fire, TV, books, piano.

Garden and farmland, with coarse fishing.
Nearest main road A259 from Hastings to Folkestone.
Closed Christmas–February

This 17th-century house is full of works of art and unusual antiques (collected by Jimmy Hodson's father, a sculptor before he took to sheep-farming here) and also oriental pieces (Elise's family lived in India for many years). The blue bedroom, for instance, has not only a carved mediaeval table but geisha-girl prints and Numdah rugs; a Jacobean chest has Indian paintings above it; in the oldest room, with mullioned windows, are carved marquise chairs from Paris and a Kashmir chainstitch rug. The Hodsons have retained one very curious feature – a concealed iron winch above the staircase, which they think was used when hiding contraband (Romney Marsh was notorious for smuggling).

One breakfasts at a polished refectory table with rush chairs in a particularly interesting room – hop-bines are strung across the inglenook, with a copy of a statue of the Virgin Mary in Notre-Dame; there's a carved oak sideboard and brass rubbings from the local church. In the beautiful sitting-room are unusual chests and other antiques; the old iron fireback carries the royal coat-of-arms.

The garden is equally attractive, especially a paved terrace, brimming with fuchsias and roses.

As dinner is not served (only snack suppers), Elise provides visitors with menus gathered from good local inns and restaurants – and with a series of postcards on which she has detailed routes recommended for sightseeing tours.

Being midway between Rye and Tenterden (each described elsewhere), Tighe Farm is ideally placed for exploring historic and beautiful parts of both Sussex and Kent. Guests usually visit Smallhythe (Ellen Terry's Tudor house), Sissinghurst and Great Dixter gardens, Bodiam Castle, Tenterden and its steam railway, Camber sands and the Romney Marsh churches.

Readers' comments: Very welcoming and helpful. Excellent room, peaceful. Have stayed three times: so welcome; peaceful; a stately home in miniature. Made very welcome. Mrs Hodson very helpful. Very good value for money. Wish we had stayed longer.

TOR HAVEN HOTEL

PT S X

King Street, Brixham, south of Torquay, Devon, TQ5 9TH
Tel: 0803 882281

10 bedrooms (single or double) from £16. Much less for 7 nights and bargain breaks. Rooms have electric heaters; shower, wc; TV, video films (extra), armchairs; views of sea; tea/coffee facilities.
Dinner £8.50 for 3 courses (with choices) and coffee, at 7pm. Vegetarian or special diets if ordered. Lunches, packed lunches, snacks. Coffee, tea, for a charge. Drinks can be ordered.
2 sitting-rooms with TV, books, indoor games (including darts); bar.
Nearest main road A3022 from Torquay to Brixham.

Built about 1800, this small hotel is run by Pat and Stephen Nicholls (he is a radio 'ham'). Though bedrooms are small, nearly every window has a panoramic view (across the road) of the busy fishing port, and of distant lights twinkling at night. Everywhere there are pictures of birds or landscapes, and patchwork wall-hangings by Pat (she gives weekly lessons in this craft, and runs some weekend courses too). Some rooms have exposed stone walls; the little bar is actually cut into the rock face. Steep steps lead up to the house; and at the back others rise to a small sun terrace at rooftop level. (Ask where to park nearby.)

Two readers said they did not like the proximity to the road (I myself slept undisturbed); more enthuse about the harbour views with marina opposite, and the Nicholls' friendliness.

At dinner, one of Pat's specialities is Brixham plaice; and her puddings are delicious gâteaux, meringues, summer pudding, etc. (Non-smokers preferred.)

The hotel is about five minutes' stroll from the town and harbour (with replica of Drake's *Golden Hind*), or the beach. There are many good coastal walks to the innumerable bays and beauty-spots of the area. To the north is the West Country's leading resort, Torquay (which has a slightly continental air, with sophisticated entertainments and shops), at the centre of golden sands and luxuriant gardens, yachts filling its bay with colour. Behind are lush countryside, flower-farms, and the distinctive red soil of Devon. Steep little Brixham is quite different from all this, a still-busy fishing port that has hardly changed in the last hundred years. On Berry Head are Victorian forts, you can take a ferry to Dartmouth, and the miniature gardens of the model village at Torquay are well worth seeing, as is Coleton Fishacre garden (NT).

Readers' comments: Wonderful hosts, beautiful vista. Food excellent and good value.

When writing to me, if you want a reply please enclose a stamped addressed envelope.

TREGONY HOUSE

C(7) **PT**

Tregony, east of Truro, Cornwall, TR2 5RN   Tel: 087 253 671

rear view

6 bedrooms (double). Dinner, bed-and-breakfast costs from £24 a night (for 2-night stays). Rooms have electric heaters; some with shower or bathroom; armchairs; views of garden; TV; tea/coffee facilities.
Dinner 4 courses (with choices) and coffee, at 7pm. Special diets if ordered. Coffee, tea, for a charge. Drinks can be ordered.
Sitting-room with central heating, open fire, TV, books, record-player. Also a bar.
Garden
Nearest main road A3078 from St Mawes to the A390.
Closed November–February

Behind a yellow façade is a house partly dating from the 17th century; later, additions were made – so the dining-room, for instance, is low-beamed and thick-walled while the hall and sitting-room have 18th-century elegance, particularly since the addition of well chosen fabrics, a pomegranate wallpaper in the hall, rounded alcoves crammed with books, and interesting antiques.

Bedrooms are pretty. A pink room at the back, with tiny windows, has velvet bedheads and a patchwork table-cover. Two double rooms with bathroom between make a good family suite.

In the dining-room (furnished with oriental rugs, oak tables and Windsor chairs) Mario and Verna Marin serve such imaginative meals as avocado and orange salad, boned and stuffed chicken with mushroom sauce, and pears cooked with brown sugar and lemon (plus cheeses). Herbs, raspberries etc. come from the cottage garden at the back, where you can have tea.

Because Tregony, although interesting, is not one of Cornwall's show villages, it remains uncrowded even in high summer. From it you can quickly reach the warm south coast of Cornwall, with all its coves, beaches, harbours and scenic drives in the Roseland peninsula, an area of outstanding natural beauty, with numerous stately homes and gardens to visit too. Truro and St Mawes are interesting towns, and a feature of the region are the old beam engines (for mines).

Readers' comments: Food marvellous: imaginative and beautifully cooked. The Marins are very relaxed, friendly and efficient. Meals excellent, rooms comfortable; warm and friendly. Interesting food; comfortable, friendly. Outstanding; excellent, imaginative meals attractively presented. A very happy week; accommodation excellent, comfortable, tastefully decorated; delicious food; friendly and hospitable.

Some readers tell me they have stayed at lots of places from *Staying Off the Beaten Track.* I wonder who has stayed at most? A free copy of the next edition awaits the reader who sends me his/her comments on the greatest number!

TRENT VALE FARMHOUSE

C(3) **PT S**

Hyde, north-west of Wareham, Dorset, BH20 7NX   Tel: 0929 471642

rear view

4 bedrooms (single or double) from £14. Less for 3 nights. Rooms have central heating; bathroom; armchairs; views of country or garden.
Sitting-room with central heating, TV, books.

Grounds Woodland, fields, tennis court, swimming-pool.
Nearest main road A35 from Poole to Bere Regis.

A mile-long, rough-surfaced rhododendron drive leads deep into the heart of Wareham Forest. Suddenly the scene changes: sunny meadows open out, and there springs into view a spacious modern house with wide picture-windows. This is now the secluded home of Keith and Deborah Webb and their two children.

In the grounds there is much wildlife to see – not only birds but also badgers, glow-worms, sand-lizards, and deer from the forest. Deborah Webb keeps many different kinds of animals – Jersey cows, which she hand-milks, goats, rabbits and old varieties of chickens and ducks, which she also breeds and which provide fresh eggs for breakfast.

There's a pale-carpeted breakfast-room brightly decorated and with doors to a sun-room where there are an acacia and a vine growing overhead. Bedrooms, too, are attractive. Bed-and-breakfast only (one can dine at the Silent Woman, or at several Wareham restaurants including the **Old Granary**, see earlier entry). Light suppers (from 8pm) are available.

You are welcome to wander round the grounds, which include river, lake with swans, paddocks, tennis court, birch woods and swimming-pool.

And, of course, all the other pleasures of east Dorset are within reach – Poole Harbour and Brownsea Island, Lulworth Cove and Durdle Door, Corfe Castle and old Wareham itself – described elsewhere in this book. Gardens: Compton Acres, Kingston Lacey. An excellent area for birdwatching, and there are superb walks in Wareham Forest. Keith will take visitors out in his boat or water-skiing.

Readers' comments: Idyllic. A very nice and extremely enthusiastic couple.

The old kitchen dining-room at Old Jordans (see page 203)

TREVENA HOUSE HOTEL

Alton Road, Farnham, Surrey, GU10 5ER   Tel: 0252 716908

19 bedrooms (single, double or family) at £18, weekends. 2-day breaks all through the week. Rooms have central heating; shower or bathroom; TV, phone, armchairs; views of country or garden; tea/coffee facilities.
Dinner A la carte, from 7pm. Special diets if ordered. Lunches, packed lunches, snacks. Coffee, tea, for a charge. Drinks can be ordered.
2 sitting-rooms with central heating, open fire, books; and a bar.
Large garden and orchard, tennis and swimming-pool.
Nearest main road on the A31 from Farnham to Winchester.

Mr Trimmer, a millionaire brewer, bought himself rolling acres of Surrey parkland in the 1890s on which to build an appropriate home. But Trevena House had fallen into a sorry state when Norman Levitt, formerly managing director of a flooring company, later took it over, to restore to its former handsome style. He even found great club-like oak chairs, deep-upholstered, to go with the oak panelling of the bar-lounge. This has a window-seat overlooking the lawns and stately trees such as weeping ash, cedar, mulberry and chestnut, with the lovely Surrey hills beyond. On wintry nights, guests gather round the inglenook fireplace. This is a place of thick carpets, hefty beams and solid brass fittings on the doors. In the summer, drinks can be taken out to the swimming-pool; the garden is illuminated after dark.

The dining-room, too, overlooks the lawn. Here are served, on tables with nosegays and candle-lamps, such dishes as prawns Mornay followed by beef Wellington and unusual ice creams.

The bedrooms are comfortable, furnished in conservative taste. Throughout, the accent is on spaciousness and ease. Being only one hour from London, the hotel tends to be used by executives on weekdays, but is less full at weekends.

Nearby Farnham is a lovely Georgian town (with castle), parts of it still very much as Jane Austen knew them (her house, near Alton, can be visited). It is full of antique and craft shops, wine bars and boutiques. It has a good repertory theatre, a new sports centre, a monthly country market, fortnightly auctions, weekly street market.

Close by are: Alice Holt woodlands for walks, the great lakes of Frensham Ponds (at one end, there is a sandy beach for swimming), Guildford and its cathedral, tropical bird gardens, country inns, National Trust woods and heaths. Riding, golf and Britain's largest car auction attract some guests; Winchester Cathedral and the music festivals of picturesque Haslemere (harpsichord centre) being others. The north Surrey hills make very varied scenery – oaks and holly alternating with pine and birch. Roads go up and down, streams meander. There are bulrushes and water-lilies in summer, coppery bracken and blackberries in autumn. A steam railway and the RHS garden at Wisley are other attractions.

For explanation of code letters (**C, D, H, PT, S, S-C, X**) see page xxvi

---

TREWERRY MILL

C D

Trerice, north of Truro, Cornwall, TR8 5HS   Tel: 0872 510345

6 bedrooms (single, double or family) from £12.50 with central heating and views of country or garden. No smoking. (Washing-machine on request.)
Dinner £3 for 3 courses (with choices) and coffee, at 6.30pm. Non-residents not admitted. Vegetarian or special diets if ordered. Lunches, packed lunches, snacks. Tea, coffee, extra. Drinks can be ordered.

2 sitting-rooms with central heating, open fire, TV, books, record-player; bar. No smoking in one.
Large garden (cream teas served).
Nearest main road A30 from Redruth to Bodmin.
Closed November–Easter

Trerice, owned by the National Trust, is an Elizabethan manor house of stone, with lattice-paned windows (one has 576 panes) and elaborate plaster ceilings. The watermill was built in 1639 to provide flour for the household; now it is a guest-house, the wheel stilled but a stream still flowing by. Ponds attract wildfowl.

One passes through a stone-flagged hall to two sitting-rooms, the first overlooking a lawn with millstone tables where home-made cakes are served at teatime, and the second with big leather armchairs around a log fire and a window through which there is an inside view of the waterwheel. Bedrooms are small and neat (there is one large family room), and the dining-room is simply furnished with oak tables and chairs. Here Ethel Grateley serves, for instance, turkey soup, local plaice in cheese sauce and fruit crumbles – all for a very modest price.

Readers' comments: Food plain but well cooked, bedrooms very comfortable, garden a delight. A lovely, restful weekend.

A few miles south, at Trispen (near Truro), is **Trevispen** (tel: 0872 41371): the modern home of Rita Heggie. Guests enjoy her professional skills as a home economist and cook, and she also runs 2- to 3-day courses when she demonstrates cookery. Rita says she has a love affair with food, the result of which is that visitors are treated to such meals as avocado and kiwi fruit cocktail, salmon trout coulibiac (in puff pastry) and rumptoff fruits with cream. (Immaculate bedrooms, all on ground floor.) Non-smokers preferred.

rear view

TUDOR FARMHOUSE HOTEL

C(8) **D H X**

Clearwell, Coleford, south-west of Gloucester, GL16 8JS   Tel: 0594 33046

11 bedrooms (single, double or family) from £17.50. Less for 7 nights or bargain breaks. Rooms have central heating, electric heaters; shower or own bathroom; TV; views of country or garden; tea/coffee facilities. (Clothes-washing facilities.)

Dinner A la carte or £9.95 for 3 courses (with choices) and coffee, at 7–9pm. Vegetarian or special diets if ordered. Coffee, tea, for a charge. Drinks can be ordered.

Sitting-room with central heating, log fire, books; bar. Conservatory.

Grounds Hillside.

Nearest main road B4228 from Chepstow to Coleford.

Parts of this house date back to the 13th century, and panelled walls are almost as old. Oliver Cromwell stayed here while hunting in the Forest of Dean – Clearwell is one of the prettiest villages on the edge of the forest – and may well have warmed his toes at the same inglenook fireplace round which big, flowery sofas are now grouped.

In the dining-room, rugged stone walls contrast with tables attractively laid with delicately sprigged china.

The house, still surrounded by fields with horses, now belongs to a young and lively professional couple (Sheila and James Reid). The table d'hôte dinner may start with a home-made soup, pâté or quiche; perhaps followed by beef cooked with Guinness and orange, or pork with cider and apples. Puddings are traditional favourites (crumbles, mousses, pineapple upside-down cake, etc.); and then there is a choice of cheeses.

The full à la carte menu changes monthly and has become very popular in the local area.

To reach the pleasantly decorated bedrooms you ascend either a spiral stair or a wide oak one; or go to a converted barn just outside, past an ancient stone cider-press now planted with flowers. There are low, iron-studded doors, leaded window-panes, stone mullions. Three spacious family rooms in the stone barn are particularly attractive (rather like little self-contained cottages).

Clearwell has Roman iron mines and a network of caves you can visit; a neo-Gothic castle; and mysterious Puzzle Wood – extraordinary and huge boulders from which trees sprout. Newland's impressive church is known as 'the cathedral of the forest'. Not only is there the beautiful forest to explore (in autumn, the colours are at their best) but also the nearby Wye Valley and the gorge at Symonds Yat, South Wales' beauty-spots (including Tintern Abbey's spectacular 12th-century ruins), and the market town of Ross-on-Wye. Newent's falconry centre, England's oldest house (part-Saxon), the forest's heritage exhibition and its steam railway, Lydney Park gardens and deer park, tours of the Stuart crystal glass factory, bird gardens, a model farm, a great maze, and a tropical butterfly garden are just some of the other sights which make it worth staying here for at least a week if you can.

Readers' comments: First-class accommodation, food superb, made us very welcome.

Kilmersdon, south of Bath (Avon), Somerset, BA3 5SY Tel: 0761 34452

2 bedrooms (double or family) from £15. Less for 3 nights and bargain breaks. Rooms have own bath/shower; tea/coffee facilities; central heating; views of country or garden. (Washing-machine on request.)
Dinner £12.50 for 3 courses (with choices) and coffee, at time to suit. Non-residents not admitted. Vegetarian or special diets if ordered. Lunches, packed lunches, snacks. Tea, coffee, free. Drinks can be brought in.
2 sitting areas with central heating, open fire, TV, books.
Large garden
Nearest main road A367 from Bath to Exeter.
Closed in December

> 'Jack and Jill went up the hill,
> To fetch a pail of water . . .'

The hill in question (complete with well) rises up near this house.

> 'Jack fell down and broke his crown
> And Jill came tumbling after.'

Hence the naming of the house.

It's a 17th-century stone cottage (originally four, but now turned into one) with thick walls, many steps, low beams and open fireplaces. Meriel Boileau has furnished it beautifully. The dining-room has country Hepplewhite chairs with tapestry seats stitched by a friend, an 18th-century pheasant-patterned wallpaper, alcoves of china, and turquoise curtains hanging from gilt poles. Here Meriel serves such meals as mackerel pâté, chicken florentine, crème caramel served with a compôte of oranges, and cheeses – on a candle-lit table laid with family silver.

Upstairs are not only very pretty bedrooms (for instance, one has a peony frieze all round and another tulip-patterned fabric on the bedhead) but also the guests' sitting-room with low, leaded windows and yellow silk curtains that contrast with rugged stone walls and the rafters of the roof. (Here there is a small refrigerator with milk and soft drinks, free.) The portrait of a family ancestor of the 1820s gazes down.

Outside is an attractive garden and a stream that separates the house from the quiet little village beyond.

Within a short drive are Bath (described elsewhere), Wells and Bristol, as well as such great mansions as Stourhead, Longleat and Badminton. Much of Somerset's charm, however, lies in its pretty villages tucked away in quiet valleys between the hills and in its historic associations. At Norton St Philip is reputedly England's oldest inn, the George. Hinton Charterhouse had England's second oldest Carthusian monastery, the first being at Witham Friary to the south (ruins on view at both). Midsomer Norton has Welton Manor, Combe Hay has streamside cottages and a whitewashed inn. Wansdyke, a 50-mile Roman earthwork, is at its best near Corston – a great bank with ditch intended as a boundary between the warring Mercians and West Saxons. Towards Bath are Monkton Combe, where stone cottages cluster round a stream in a deep valley.

Readers' comments: A lovely house, very comfortably furnished. Every trouble taken – we felt cossetted and cared for. Cooks with care and attention to detail.

UNICORN HOTEL
Keighley Road, Skipton, North Yorkshire, BD23 22P   Tel: 0756 4146

10 bedrooms (single, double or family) from £21.50 (or £30 with dinner) **less 10% to readers of this book** and very good week-end terms. Rooms have own bath; TV; tea/coffee facilities; phone; central heating. No smoking. (Laundering on request.)
Dinner A la carte at 7–8.30pm. Non-residents not admitted. Vegetarian or special diets if ordered. Lunches, packed lunches, snacks. Drinks can be ordered.
Sitting-room with central heating; bar. No smoking.
Nearest main road A59 from Preston to Harrogate.

You might not notice the Unicorn, hidden in a modest row of shops on a nondescript street leading into the town. You enter through a small door and go upstairs to a receptionist who takes you to your room and brings you a tray of tea or coffee with biscuits when you arrive.

What makes the Unicorn special is the quality and size of the rooms. Ours had an attractive brown-and-cream colour scheme and was more like a sitting-room than a bedroom, with comfortable armchairs and sofa (convertible into a third bed if required) grouped round the large colour TV. There were good paintings by local artists on the walls, prettily arranged flowers on a table, a pile of magazines, a folder of information (about local events and sights) and well-placed lights.

Since Paul and Jean Dolan took over, they have added an attractive pink and green dining-room with upholstered chairs. Here are served 4-course dinners that are very good value, and with a wide choice at each course: for instance, main dishes often include veal milanaise, sauté chicken with mustard sauce, pheasant normande, a roast, steaks and a vegetarian option.

The emphasis is on quality and comfort – each room has a heated, carpeted bathroom, for instance. And, although my first visit was in July, the receptionist offered to turn on the central heating because the weather was unseasonably cool.

Skipton is an old town of great character, its wide main street thronged with market stalls leading up to the castle and church at the end. Down by the bridge are interesting craft and antique shops, and historic riverside buildings. It is a good centre from which to explore Ribblesdale, Wharfedale, Wensleydale and Airedale and all the famous beauty-spots – the crags, caves, waterfalls, villages and ruined abbeys with which the region abounds.

Ilkley Moor is within reach, as are the stylish spa town of Harrogate (for shopping), and an officially designated 'area of outstanding natural beauty', the Forest of Bowland. This is largely moorland (the heather is superb in September), with parts comparable with the crags and valleys of the Lake District. Some of the finest countryside of the north-west is here. In addition there are charming villages like Bolton-by-Bowland, winding rivers, stately homes and abbeys and castles, a Roman museum, inns and markets. Boats can be hired on the canal; and, of course, this is a great area for walking.

Readers' comments: Delighted. A charming couple. Cooking, presentation and service are faultless. Blissfully quiet though in town centre. Meals well presented. An excellent recommendation.

UPPER GREEN FARM
Manor Road, Towersey, east of Thame, Oxfordshire, OX9 3QR
Tel: 084421 2496

3 bedrooms (single or double) from £14. Rooms have central heating; shower in one; TV; views of country or garden; No smoking. Packed lunches; coffee, tea, etc. **Sitting-room** with central heating, TV, books. No smoking.

Large garden Orchard, pond and farmland. **Nearest main road** A4129 from Thame to Princes Risborough.

A building of whitewash and thatch overlooking a duck-pond at the front, Marjorie and Euan Aitken's house is one of the prettiest in this book. They uncovered 15th-century beams with the original carpenters' identification marks; came across Elizabethan coins; restored the wood shutters which (window-glass having yet to be invented) were all that kept out wintry blasts five centuries ago; found a secret priest-hole where, in the days of religious persecution, a Catholic priest might have to hide for days when the search was on. In one huge chimney, there were still the iron rungs up which small boys were forced to clamber to clear the soot. In what is now the quarry-tiled breakfast-room, an old kitchen-range and adjoining copper boiler have been preserved, together with the rack on which spits for roasting whole sheep were kept, and the special hooks used for drying the farmer's smocks by the fire. In the hall is a pump (still working).

Marjorie, who used to be an antiques dealer, has filled every room with fascinating trifles – Victorian jugs and jam-pots on the sprigged brown tablecloth at breakfast, shelves of old bottles (found discarded in the garden), beadwork pincushions and watch-cases, a huge marble washstand in the downstairs cloak-room, naive Staffordshire figures, old brass scales (which she uses) and tin toys.

The Aitkens not only tell visitors about the well known sights nearby (which include Claydon House, Ryecote Chapel, West Wycombe's 'hellfire' caves, the horses' home of rest, etc.) but introduce them to other sides of local life. For instance, you may go and see the sorting and grading of sheep fleeces, join in bell-ringing, pick up bargains at local markets or auctions, chat up balloonists as they glide by only a few yards above the farm – silently, unlike the wild swans in clattering flight.

And, of course, their sheep, ducks, chickens and geese are an entertainment in themselves. Bed-and-breakfast only; plenty of options for dinner in Thame.

Readers' comments: Charming home, warm hospitality: we arrived as guests and left as friends. Much impressed by warm welcome, delightful house and excellent breakfast. Wonderful couple – it always feels like going home! Charming people, absolutely delightful house.

UPPER ORCHARD

C D PT S S-C

Hoarwithy, east of Ross-on-Wye, Herefordshire, HR2 6QR
Tel: 043 270 649

6 bedrooms (double) from £12. Bargain breaks. Rooms have central heating; views of country or garden. (One with shower.)
Sitting-room with central heating, open fire, books, piano.
Garden
Nearest main road A49 from Ross-on-Wye to Hereford.
Closed December and January

In summer, Heather – who writes books and articles on walking – provides visitors with carefully worked out routes through the lovely countryside of the Wye Valley, varying in distance from a mere 2½ to 16 miles (with wellies, maps and walking-sticks on loan). Her husband Jon Hurley, an award-winning writer on wine for several quality newspapers, runs wine-tasting weekends at other seasons. (You can send for a leaflet with full details.)

The house itself is unpretentious – in the 18th century it was an inn (its cellars now house Jon's wines). The sitting-room furniture is homely, even old-fashioned – armchairs are grouped round a log fire in winter, while in summer the focal point is a large bay window with a view of grazing cows. In the bedrooms soft pinks and greens contrast with pine furniture or handsome 'thirties mahogany.

The beamed dining-room is very pleasant, the colour of the mulberry walls repeated in china with old scenes of country life. On wine weekends only, Heather cooks such 4-course meals as home-made pâté or soup; roast meat with garden vegetables; apple crunch and thick cream; followed by English and Welsh cheeses.

Readers' comments: Old-fashioned but very comfortable. Food very good and wines superb.

Close by is **Aspen House** (tel: 043270 328), Peter Blakelock's restaurant overlooking the river meadows, which has neat, pale bedrooms (one on the ground floor; with, like others, its own bathroom); a big sitting-room opening – via a south-facing sun-room – onto a garden that is floodlit at night; and a dining-room the white stone walls of which once housed the village butcher's shop. Here – using some 400 pieces of beautiful gold-and-blue china (specially made for his family over a century ago), cut glass and lace cloths – Peter serves such dishes as halibut mousseline, carpetbag steak or veal à la crème (with shallots and sherry).

UPTON HOUSE

Upton Snodsbury, east of Worcester, WR7 4NR   Tel: 090560 226

C D S

3 bedrooms (single or double) from £18.50 but with **10% reduction to readers of this book**. Less for 3 nights. Rooms have central heating and electric heaters; bathroom; TV, armchairs; views of country or garden; tea/coffee facilities.
Dinner From £13 for 4 courses and coffee, at 7.30–8pm. Vegetarian or special diets if ordered. Drinks can be brought in. Sandwich suppers.
Sitting-room with central heating, open fire, TV, books.
Large garden and orchard, with croquet.
Nearest main road A422 from Stratford-upon-Avon to Worcester.

Part 14th-century, part Tudor and part 18th-century, this building is full of individuality. It has been furnished in character, with antiques collected by Hugh and Angela Jefferson over the years. They decided to take guests to help with the cost of educating four young children, then found how much they enjoyed entertaining them.

Their colour schemes are fresh and imaginative. In the dining-room, chairs covered in watermelon satin contrast with primrose walls (this room has a vast fireplace); in the sitting-room, sofas covered in pink or blue brocade are grouped round another log fire. A feature of this room is the pretty little bay window with wide sill, through which one looks across the lawn (surrounded by trees and rosebeds) to half-timbered cottages and the Norman church, the clock of which chimes every quarter-hour.

The pink bedroom, low-beamed, has sweet peas on curtains and duvet (and in its bathroom, a plethora of things like bath essence, talc, etc.), a moss-green carpet and violets on the Royal Albert bone china for early-morning tea. The peach room has an elegant Victorian bathroom. The blue room is almost as attractive.

Some visitors eat at the Boot (at Flyford-Flavell) or award-winning Brown's (Worcester), but menus at Upton House are good – a typical meal might comprise seafood vol-au-vent, stuffed lamb, chocolate truffle cake and cheeses.

It is hoped to get the old cider-mill at the back restored in due course. Meantime, if you want to see cider being made in the traditional way (in October) there is another mill nearby which you can visit. Children enjoy exploring the orchard, and meeting the ducks. From Upton House one can readily visit the Bredon and Malvern Hills (Hereford and the Wye Valley beyond them); such Cotswold beauty-spots as Broadway or Chipping Campden; and, in the other direction, Stratford-upon-Avon in Warwickshire. Worcester (cathedral and china factory), Spetchley gardens and several garden centres are other options. When in Worcester (best explored on foot) seek out the Commandery for Civil War exhibits, 15th-century Greyfriars, the guildhall and lovely riverside gardens (boat trips available).

Readers' comments: Excellent. Comfort and friendliness.

VAULD FARMHOUSE
Vauld, north of Hereford, HR1 3HA   Tel: 056884 898

C(5) **D PT X**

3 bedrooms (double or family) from £16.50. Rooms have own bath/shower; TV; tea/coffee facilities; central heating; views of lake, country or garden. (Washing-machine on request.)
Dinner £8.50 for 4 courses and coffee; time by arrangement. Non-residents not admitted. Packed lunches. Tea, coffee, extra. Drinks can be brought in.
Large garden
Nearest main road A49 from Hereford to Leominster.

'Sleepy hollow', the locals call this area where the ancient farmhouse lies hidden, its creamy, black-timbered walls lopsided with age (it was built in 1510, when Henry VIII had just become King). Past a lake and a stone cider-press, one steps through the front door into a great room with stone-slabbed floor, half-timbered walls, log fire and colossal beams overhead.

Those who book the granary suite (which has its own stone staircase from outside) have a private sitting-room, with deep velvet armchairs, bedroom, bathroom and a gallery with another bed; and, through windows with unusual crisscross glazing bars, a view of the lake. Other visitors may prefer the ground-floor oak room with a very impressive four-poster (this, too, has its own entrance and bathroom).

If you order dinner, Jean Bengry will prepare a meal using much local produce, for this is an area of fruit-farms; and she keeps her own poultry and goats. A typical menu: chicken liver and mushroom pâté, turkey in hazelnut sauce or beef in ale, trifle and local cheeses – served on willow-pattern china at a lace-covered table.

Readers' comments: Excellent accommodation, fine food, friendly folk.

Also in this area is **Maund Court** at Bodenham (tel: 056884 282), an old red sandstone house at the heart of a large mixed farm. Some of the bedrooms overlook the swimming-pool, heated to 76°. Although there are good eating-places in the area, Pauline Edwards will, by arrangement, provide such dinners as prawns in sherry sauce, pheasant and profiteroles.

Readers' comments: Very pleasant and welcoming, a hearty breakfast, we will go again. Friendly and welcoming atmosphere, excellent breakfast.

Prices are the minimum *per person* in a double room at the beginning of the year.

VILLAGE FARM

Sturton-by-Stow, north-west of Lincoln, LN1 2AE   Tel: 0427 788309

3 bedrooms (single, double or family) from £12. Less for 2 nights or bargain breaks.

Rooms have central heating; armchairs; views of garden; tea/coffee facilities; bathroom (one). No smoking.
Dinner £8 for 4 courses with coffee. No smoking. Drinks can be brought in.
Sitting-room with central heating, open fire, TV, books, record-player.
Garden and farmland, with hard tennis court, coarse fishing, rough shooting.
Nearest main road A15 from Lincoln to Humber Bridge.
Closed to visitors November–Easter, (except for house-parties of 6.)

In the middle of this usually quiet village stands an early Victorian house, now pleasantly furnished by Sheila Bradshaw – at the heart of a 350-acre farm where pedigree cattle and sheep are raised. For the sitting-room she chose a pale green carpet, pink velvet curtains held back in tasselled loops, and flowery chintzes; among many Victorian heirlooms are things of her own making – canvaswork or patchwork cushions, for instance. She is a keen Women's Institute member, a handbell-ringer, loves flower-arranging and has made a big sampler depicting the house itself. Her husband's family farmed in Sturton for many generations back: among his enthusiasms are Shetland ponies and growing orchids.

Guests have the use of two small dining-rooms. A typical menu: smoked mackerel, farm lamb, apricot brûlée and cheeses. Upstairs are very attractive bedrooms: one, with matching Sanderson wallpaper and fabrics, has a sloping ceiling and odd windows; in the peach-and-cream one is a rocking-chair; one of the prettiest has blue Laura Ashley sprigged linen and a Philippine cane chair. In the garden is a vast walnut tree; to one side are pantiled barns.

The Wolds, the coast and the great Humber Bridge are easily reached. Nearby sights include Doddington Hall, a country park, Gainsborough Old Hall, Tattershall Castle, Pennell's nursery gardens and Stow's cathedral-like church. The Red Arrows aerobatic team is based near here. Lincoln is described on other pages. It is full of antique shops and at Helmswell is a massive antiques centre. The county show ground is near.

Readers' comments: Very helpful, a lovely week. Sheer magic! Comfort, views and value – all very good.

An alternative in Lincoln itself is a quiet Edwardian house (5 minutes' walk from the centre), **Carline Guest-House**, 3 Carline Road (tel: 0522 530422). Immaculate and comfortable. Gill and John Pritchard provide bed-and-breakfast only. Unusually well-equipped; and very moderate prices for rooms with TV, own bathroom, etc. – eggs from their own hens.

VINES

C D PT S X

High Street, Marlborough, Wiltshire, SN8 1HJ   Tel: 0672 55333

6 bedrooms (single or double) at £18 to SOTBT readers only (also bargain breaks, available even at bank holidays). Rooms have central heating; TV, armchairs; tea/coffee facilities; phone.
Dining- and sitting-rooms (see text).
Nearest main road A4 from Newbury to Bath.

From a modest guest-house, David Ball and Josephine Scott completely transformed the Ivy House Hotel at Marlborough into a large and elegant hotel with a restaurant that has won numerous accolades. Not surprisingly, the inevitable price-rises that followed eventually took it out of the range of this book. But there is good news: David and Josey are now also running a guest-house opposite.

This is the Vines, an 18th-century terrace house converted and decorated to the same high standards as the hotel itself. Bedrooms are furnished in style, and equipped with every possible facility (remote-control TV with video films, good armchairs, mini-bars in refrigerators and – for the businessmen who comprise most of the mid-week guests – trouser-presses, telephones and radio-alarms). Those overlooking the High Street are double-glazed.

What is more, accommodation here is offered to SOTBT readers at a preferential rate, *provided that* the book is mentioned when making a reservation and shown on arrival. Further, there is a 10% discount on dinner in Ivy House Hotel; alternatively, for an all-in rate of £35 (bed, breakfast and dinner) SOTBT readers can have an unlimited choice from the à la carte dinner menu. The hotel also has a wine bar with food, where even château-bottled wines can be had by the glass. Breakfast can be taken in the hotel, or will be brought to your room in the Vines. Other hotel amenities open to Vines visitors include a smoking and a no-smoking sitting-room, bar and sun-terrace.

As to dinner, this is always a memorable occasion. Delicious and unusual canapés precede the meal, which can comprise such dishes as a gratinée of mussels on spinach glazed with Roquefort cream; then breast of duck in game sauce; and desserts created with outstanding flair by pastry chef Gary Pascoe. (Some of Gary's professional secrets are revealed on a video you can view in your bedroom.)

Marlborough is a handsome and historic town, with one of the widest high streets in the country. Many of the houses are mediaeval, though this is not immediately apparent until you explore the byways and alleys because so many frontages were rebuilt in the 18th century. It was a stage-coach centre, which accounts for the number of old inns and hotels. At each end of the broad street is a church in Perpendicular style. Its famous public school, Marlborough College, is well worth a visit when open to visitors. Every August the College runs adult summer schools (subjects range from wine appreciation to word processors, golf to country-house history) and participants can stay at the Vines.

Readers' comments: Delighted with the welcome and concern.

LATE NEWS: David is opening a country hotel, Chiseldon House: for brochure, phone 0672 55333.

WALLACE FARM

C PT S-C

Dinton, south-west of Aylesbury, Buckinghamshire, HP17 8UF
Tel: 0296 748660

3 bedrooms (double or family) from £13. Some have own bath; tea/coffee facilities; central heating; views of country or garden. (Washing-machine on request.)
Sitting-room with central heating, open fire, TV, books.

Large garden
Nearest main road A418 from Aylesbury to Thame.

When the Cooks took over this 16th-century house, they brought with them some unusual furniture collected when they lived abroad – a Chinese wedding-chest of scarlet leather, for instance, and one from the Philippines with mother-of-pearl inlay. An Indonesian dowry chest has carvings of bride, groom and dragons. Jackie has an eye for what is decorative and unusual, whether old or new – such as the hand-painted bathroom tiles which feature rare breeds of British animals.

Bedrooms differ in style – a small room in crisp white, for instance, and a very large one in pale green and pink with old pine furniture including a dresser loaded with books.

There is a tiled breakfast-room with a big, sturdy oak table and a log stove (for dinner, visitors usually go to local inns: the Bugle Horn, Stone; the Bottle and Glass, Gibraltar; the Seven Stars, Dinton); by one stone hearth, an original bread oven has survived the centuries; and the guests' sitting-room has shuttered casement doors on two sides, opening onto a terrace with seats, croquet lawn, orchard, and cows seen grazing across a haha. Also in the grounds are ponds (with coarse fishing), Jacob sheep, ducks and geese. Bicycles on loan.

This peaceful spot is roughly equidistant to Heathrow Airport and London. There is a 'Travel Card' available for only a few pounds which covers the cost of rail to London (1 hour) and unlimited bussing about on arrival, so that visiting London can alternate with tranquil country days.

The nearest town, Aylesbury, has a lively market, a 15th-century inn belonging to the National Trust, and historic houses in its byways. Other towns well worth visiting include Old Amersham – a particularly charming main street, very wide and flanked by historic buildings; Georgian Beaconsfield; Buckingham (a splendid beech avenue leads from it to Stowe, the Vanbrugh mansion that is now a famous school, grounds open to the public); High Wycombe (centre of furniture-making, with Disraeli's home – Hughenden – nearby); riverside Marlow; and Eton.

Dinton itself is a pleasant old village with stocks and whipping-post on its green, a Tudor manor house and mock ruins (look for fossils in its stones). Another attractive village is Bradenham, preserved by the National Trust.

WALLETT'S COURT   C H PT
West Cliffe, north-east of Dover, Kent, CT15 6EW   Tel: 0304 852424

7 bedrooms (single, double or family) from £18. All have own bath/shower; TV; tea/coffee facilities; central heating; views of sea, country or garden. (Washing-machine on request.)
Dinner A la carte or £13.50 for 3 courses (with choices) and coffee, at 7–8pm. Vegetarian or special diets if ordered. Snacks. Tea, coffee, extra. Drinks can be ordered.
Sitting-room with central heating, open fire, books, piano. No smoking.
Large garden
Nearest main road A258 from Dover to Deal.

Built on cellars that date back to Norman times is a magnificent 17th-century manor house. But it is not just the building, or even the surrounding scenery (protected by the National Trust), which bring visitors here: Chris Oakley is an exceptional chef who has worked with the Roux brothers, at La Gavroche.

The huge sitting-room with carved oak beams and two fireplaces, one of stone and one of brick, has deep-set, pine-shuttered sash windows with window-seats; buttoned velvet chairs and antiques furnish the room. In the elegant dining-room, tables are laid with bronze cutlery and Royal Worcester china decorated with game birds. Dining chairs are upholstered in pink, there is a log fire, brass-rubbings decorate the walls and on elaborately carved woodwork are the date 1627 and the initials of the Gibbon family (its most celebrated member was the author of *The Rise and Fall of the Roman Empire*). Bedrooms in the house are excellent (some with large, buttoned, velvet armchairs; all with antiques), bathrooms elegant. Other bedrooms, in modern pine style, are in a converted barn. (The patchwork spreads were made by Lea Oakley.) There are murals; handsome newelposts on the stairs; mellow brickwork exposed here and there. The Norman cellars are used for snooker and table tennis.

As to the meals, these are very special and people come from far afield to dine at Wallett's Court (non-residents admitted on Saturday; no meals on Sundays). The Saturday dinners often include such choices as game terrine with citrus salad followed by turbot with lobster sauce, a sorbet, haunch of venison in claret, and a wide choice of puddings. With the coffee come petits fours. Weekday dinners, though less extensive, are of similar quality.

The peaceful countryside along this coast, facing the Dover Straits, is only three miles from Dover, its castle and its harbour (for day-trips to France). One can walk along the famous white cliffs here, and there is a fine garden (The Pines) with waterfall and Nemons' statue of Churchill. St Margaret's Bay is where cross-Channel swimmers start from, and further along are Walmer and Deal – both with castles, a string of which (Norman through to Victorian) dot this coastline as it faces Europe. The white cliffs are in fact the end of the South Downs, one of the region's most beautiful features, with many good drives or walks among the hills and historic villages (Canterbury is quite near).

> All prices are inclusive of any VAT or service charge. They are minimum prices: superior rooms or high-season bookings may cost more.

311

WALLTREE HOUSE FARM   C X
Steane, north-west of Brackley, Northamptonshire, NN13 5NS
Tel: 0295 811235

10 bedrooms (double or family) from £15. All have own bath/shower; TV; tea/coffee facilities; central heating; views of country or garden. (Washing-machine on request.) **Dinner** £9 for 4 courses (with choices) and coffee, at 7pm. Non-residents not admitted. Vegetarian or special diets if ordered. Packed lunches. Tea, coffee, free. Drinks can be ordered. **2 sitting-rooms** with central heating, open fire, TV, books. **Large garden** **Nearest main road** A422 from Banbury to Brackley.

Quite a surprise to find, at the end of a long farm lane, a park-like setting in which this handsome Victorian farmhouse stands.

Pauline and Richard Harrison have transformed the house and its outbuildings to provide a large number of bedrooms, so that this is virtually a farm hotel now. Those in the former granary are very modern in style: Stag furniture in some, rosy fabrics, much bamboo and pine, very good bathrooms. One family suite is virtually a cottage, so well-equipped is it. You can be sure of ample warmth on 365 days in the year, for Richard installed a special straw-burner which means all his central heating costs him nothing but the labour of gathering straw from his fields after each harvest.

Meals are served, usually, at a great 14-foot table surrounded by Queen Anne-style chairs – except at periods when work on the farm is at its peak. A typical dinner: a half-pineapple with prawns and cream, pork in a herby tomato sauce, and chocolate mousse with toffee crunch.

If you would like to try microlight flying – or just sit and watch from the comfort of bamboo armchairs in a big octagonal sun-room – you can do so at the back of the farm, for it overlooks a mini-airfield in use only by day.

It was at Brackley that the barons negotiated Magna Carta before its sealing at Runnymede later in 1215. Today the attractive town lies around a particularly wide, mile-long main street flanked by trees and little lanes, and adorned by a very fine 18th-century town hall, historic school, old inns and quaint almshouses. The church is worth a visit for its windows and monuments are of particular interest.

The whole county is full of good things and quiet beauty, yet so many visitors merely pass through it on the way to more celebrated places of interest. It is a green county, and a county of stone – which means there are fine buildings to be found. It is a historic county, too, where many epic events took place. If you were to travel from Oxford through Northamptonshire to Peterborough you would be in a limestone area where the villages are just as lovely as those of the Cotswolds and there are scenic uplands nearly all the way. The stone varies in colour – grey, honey-gold, reddish brown – which adds to the interest of the scene. North-amptonshire is nicknamed the 'county of spires and squires', so expect fine churches and fine houses – the latter very numerous and dating from every century from the 14th onwards (a complete architectural history of England) but with the Tudor period most fully represented. The churches are notable for the number of Saxon ones that have survived. Just over the Oxfordshire border is Banbury, celebrated for its cakes and cross.

WALNUT COTTAGE   C(14) **H PT**
Old Romsey Road, Cadnam, west of Southampton, Hampshire, SO4 2NP
Tel: 0703 812275

3 bedrooms (single or double) from £14. Less for 2 nights or bargain breaks. Rooms have central heating; shower or bathroom; TV, armchairs; views of country or garden; tea/coffee facilities.
2 sitting-rooms with central heating, open fire, TV, video, books.
Garden
Nearest main road A31 from Romsey to Ringwood.

The road no longer leads anywhere (its days ended when a nearby motorway replaced it). The little white cottage, with brimming window-boxes and a red rambler-rose by the door, stands in a pretty garden (with an old well) which traps the sun. One bedroom opens onto this.

All the rooms have been attractively furnished by Charlotte and Eric Osgood, who did much of the work themselves (even the tiling of the showers, and the flowery china door-knobs on each bedroom door). There are two sitting-rooms with pale carpets, cretonne armchairs, flowers on the window-sills and interesting objects on the shelves. One has windows on all three sides. In the dining-room are Regency chairs, cupboard and mirror; a diminutive iron grate, as old as the cottage, has been preserved (though the only fireplace still in use is in the larger sitting-room). Here Charlotte serves breakfast on Royal Doulton vineleaf china, but for other meals, she recommends a thatched and whitewashed inn a few yards down the lane (the 12th-century Sir John Barleycorn).

The cottage is on the edge of the New Forest (it was originally occupied by foresters). Romsey and Broadlands are very near; Beaulieu, Breamore House, Bucklers Hard (historic waterside village), Salisbury, Winchester and Bournemouth only a little further. From Southampton (with Spitfire and maritime museums – and sometimes the *QE2*) there are trips to the Isle of Wight, and London is under a two-hour journey. The nearby motorway (M27), its hum just within earshot, makes many distant sights easy to reach.

The Osgoods not only lend maps and cycles free, but have photocopied useful hints for a selection of car outings in the area, describing the route for each, listing sights, and also recommending the best inns for lunches, good bookshops etc. They have also mapped out a 'Howards' Way' tour; and can tell you where to buy trout, venison, local fruit etc.

This is a good choice for an October break, when the forest colours are superb; but book well ahead if you want to go in September when Southampton's boat show and Beaulieu's 'auto jumble' sale are on. May is a good month for the many superb gardens such as Exbury, Furzey, Spinners, Compton Acres and various garden centres.

Readers' comments: Beautifully located . . . most helpful people. Delightful couple, charming rooms, comfortable; superb breakfasts. Excellent: a charming couple. Very impressed by their care and attention. A spacious and comfortable bedroom; helpful hosts. Their interest in the comfort and pleasure of their guests has to be experienced to be believed. Faultless accommodation and welcome. Welcome, care, attention, food – all generous.

313

WARDEN'S HOUSE

C(5) D

Lode Lane, Wicken, south of Ely, Cambridgeshire, CB7 5XP
Tel: 0353 720274

rear view

1 bedroom (twin) from £10. Less for some stays of 7 nights. Room has central heating or electric heater; views of country and garden; tea/coffee facilities. No smoking. **Sitting/dining-room** with central heating or gas fire, books. No smoking. **Garden** and orchard. **Nearest main road** A1123 from Huntingdon to the A142.

Many who visit historic Ely and its superb cathedral prefer somewhere quieter to stay overnight. This comfortable house with garden, tucked away behind high beech hedges on the edge of Wicken Fen (Britain's very first wildlife reserve), provides the answer. It is the home of naturalist Tim Bennett – head warden of the Fen – and his wife Cindy (an amateur botanist), an interesting couple with whom to stay before spending a day exploring this fen, one of the few areas of true wilderness that are still left. (Bed-and-breakfast only, using humanely produced eggs, bacon etc.; pub meals in the village at the Maid's Head.)

The fens' history is well explained in the National Trust's interpretation centre at Wicken. Once, vast areas of peaty, waterlogged land provided the perfect habitat for many wildlife species; but most has been drained for farming. Only at Wicken can you see an ancient remnant (600 acres), used in the traditional way. In one part, hay is mown and this encourages a diversity of wildflowers. The wetter sedge fields provide material for thatch, and here other plants flourish. Carr (small thickets) shelters birds among the shrubs, ferns and mossy undergrowth. Very ancient streams still thread the Fen, and also a lode (a waterway once used by barges). It is a problem now to keep the Fen from drying out, so a restored wind-pump feeds water in. You can go from a demonstration garden identifying Fen plants to woodland, ponds, areas rich in wildflowers, old brick-pits now flooded and colonized by water-plants, a stack of 4000-year-old oak trunks dug from bogs, through glades and past the ruins of a Norman abbey to a tall 'hide' from the top of which are far views beyond a mere with wildfowl and a sunny bank that attracts a host of butterflies.

Cambridge itself is within easy reach, and Anglesey Abbey (with gardens); also Saffron Walden (Essex) and Bury St Edmunds (Suffolk), both historic towns in very pretty landscapes. This is also an area of boating – for example, you can go on the Great Ouse to Huntingdon, and watch or join in watersports on Grafham Water. Ely and Peterborough have particularly fine cathedrals; March, a church with 200 flying angels; Newmarket, its heath where you can see racehorses exercising. The dykes and Roman ways throughout the county provide good footpaths for walkers.

Take the trouble to get free booklets about the area before you set off. Every habitual traveller should keep a copy of the booklet of local Tourist Information Centres issued free by the English Tourist Board (Thames Tower, Blacks Road, London W6; tel: 01-846 9000) for this purpose.

WATER HALL FARMHOUSE
Ifield Wood, Charlwood, west of Gatwick (Surrey), West Sussex, RH11 0LA
Tel: 0293 20002

7 bedrooms (single, double or family) from £18. Some have own bath/shower; all have central heating and views of country or garden.
Sitting-room with central heating, TV, books.

Large garden
Nearest main road A23 from South London to Brighton.

There are several houses in this book (in Surrey or Sussex) sufficiently close to Gatwick Airport for it to be convenient – and usually cheaper – to leave your car with them while abroad and taxi to and from the airport (some – such as this – even provide the taxi service themselves).

This one is the nearest: it takes only about 10 minutes to get to Gatwick from here. Despite the aircraft, I found I slept peacefully.

The farmhouse (parts of which are nearly five centuries old) is a traditional Sussex building, its upper storey hung with scalloped tiles up which creepers grow. There are tubs of bright busy Lizzies outside, and flowerbeds. Beyond the stone-walled and tiled hall is a sitting-room with antiques, a silvery damask wallpaper and comfortable chairs; and a breakfast-room the French doors of which open onto a lawn, more flowerbeds and beyond these fields of grazing horses (the house is full of horse pictures, among others).

Bedrooms, with double-glazed windows, are neat and pleasantly furnished: in one, for instance, an old spinet now does duty as a dressing table. I particularly liked a large blue room (called 'George's') because it has windows on three sides.

Rosalind Tilson serves only breakfast but I dined well at Limes Bistro in Charlwood just over a mile away.

The airport is not, in fact, the only reason for staying here: it is a good centre from which to explore the North Downs in one direction and the Weald in another. (It is, incidentally, a very suitable spot to which to take children for they will enjoy the Gatwick Zoo Park, the plane-viewing platform at the airport and the Bluebell Line steam railway, for example.) In the immediate vicinity are a number of old villages interesting to visit: Rusper for its church memorials to the Broadwoods (of piano fame, and associated with the folk-song movement led by Cecil Sharpe); Worth, on the edge of woodlands, which has a Saxon church and a memorial to a 17th-century worthy which boasts that he was 'discended from ye right ancient and long before ye Norman Conquest . . .'. One of England's greatest agricultural shows is held at Ardingly each June; and a little further afield is Lindfield, so famous a beauty-spot that it is best avoided in high summer: houses from every period, some colour-washed, some half-timbered.

315

THE WATERMILL

near Hildersham, south-east of Cambridge, CB1 6BS

C PT S(off-peak)   Tel: 0223 891520

1 bedroom (double or family) at £14. Central heating, electric heater; bathroom; armchairs; views of country and garden. (Clothes-washing facilities.) No smoking. **Dinner** £5 to £7.50 for 2 or 4 courses and coffee, about 7pm. Vegetarian or special diets if ordered. Lunches, packed lunches, snacks. Coffee, tea, free. Drinks can be brought in. No smoking. **Large garden** with birdwatching, trout fishing (extra) and boating. **Nearest main road** A604 from Haverhill to the A11.

A track through fields, past the stump of a windmill and by a narrow stretch of the River Granta, suddenly comes to this very large watermill – last used (for grinding wheat or sawing wood) in 1904. Its present owner, engineer David Hartland, is engaged in the long task of restoring the 7-ton waterwheel. One day he hopes it will generate enough power to run a heat-pump for the house. He has amassed a collection of old photographs and drawings illustrating the history of the mill, which dates from the 11th century (the present buildings are early 19th century).

Guests are accommodated in one-time stables (converted in the 'thirties, when a door from Cambridge Castle was salvaged and installed here). Meals are brought to their roomy bedroom (or served on the lawn by the river when the weather is sunny). The unusual bedroom (white plank walls, sloping ceiling) is furnished in cottage style: sprigged fabrics, and rugs on the floorboards. The oak bedstead dates from the 18th century. The room has views of lawn, weeping willows and the millstream, the sound of which lulls one to sleep.

The Hartlands' bees, chickens and sheep (and trout from the stream) contribute to the meals which Lynne cooks superbly – home-made game soup might be followed by lamb with fennel and scalloped potatoes; then caramelized oranges with home-made florentines; and cheeses.

Cambridge is only a few miles away. If your time is limited, the best selection of colleges to visit is perhaps King's, Corpus Christi, Queen's and Trinity – and there are also the Botanic Gardens, the great art treasures of the Fitzwilliam Museum, the lawns and gardens of 'the Backs' and an unusual house, Kettle's Yard, with beautifully arranged modern art and artefacts just as the owner left them. A boat or punt on the River Cam is a particularly enjoyable way of seeing the Backs (of colleges).

Some other sightseeing options include Saffron Walden, Newmarket, Ely, and also a number of stately homes such as Audley End, Wimpole Hall and Chilford Hall.

Readers' comments: Superb – a lovely weekend. Enjoyed very much. Warm welcome. Comfortable room, food excellent.

WAVENDEN HOUSE

C(10)

Compass Cove, Dartmouth, Devon, TQ6 0JN   Tel: 0803 833979

3 bedrooms (double) from £12.50. Less for 7 nights and bargain breaks. Rooms have central heating; views of estuary, country and garden. No smoking. (Clothes-washing facilities on request.)
Dinner £8.50 for 4 courses (with choices) and coffee, at 7.30pm. Non-residents not admitted. Vegetarian or special diets if ordered. Packed lunches. Tea, coffee, free. Drinks can be ordered.
Sitting-room with central heating, log stove, TV, books, record-player.
Large garden
Nearest main road A379 from Dartmouth to Kingsbridge.

So beautiful is the coastal scenery here (owned by the National Trust) that today no-one is allowed to build on it: Wavenden is the only house there to enjoy the superb view of the River Dart's wide estuary, jagged headlands and, across the water, 15th-century Kingswear Castle.

When Ken and Lily Gardner moved here, it was a rather ugly 'twenties bungalow which they rebuilt so sensitively that even environmentalists have congratulated them on enhancing the previous scene. And the garden too, sloping down to the shore, has been improved by them, with grassy terraces, primrose banks, well-landscaped flowering shrubs and steps down to the sea (where you can bathe).

There is a large two-level dining- and sitting-room, with huge glass doors through which to enjoy the view, and also a big fireplace of polished black slate (with wood burner). Through these doors one steps onto a paved sundeck with reclining chairs from which to watch every kind of craft go by, from sailing dinghies to submarines. This is above what was a 'Dad's Army' gun-emplacement guarding the mouth of the river during World War II, now enclosed.

From every bedroom, furnished in Laura Ashley style, are glimpses of the river and garden, colourful even in early spring because the climate here is so mild.

Ken (who used to be an award-winning investigative journalist) and Lily have always been accomplished cooks, so Wavenden is a good choice for gourmets (a typical dinner might include creamed mussels as a starter, game casserole and treacle tart). Local fish goes into their seafood chowder and other dishes.

It is a good choice, also, for walkers because the Devon Coastal Path and a network of National Trust footpaths lie just beyond the gate. In a hedge are traces of the first cross-Channel telegraph cable (about 1870).

Compass Cove lies just beyond Dartmouth Castle from which a chain used to be stretched to Kingswear Castle opposite to hold off invading ships. In hilly Dartmouth itself (a port since Roman times) is a picturesque Butterwalk with houses supported by granite pillars; 17th- and 18th-century buildings; and, on a hill high above, the imposing Royal Naval College.

317

WELLPRITTON FARM

Holne, Ashburton, west of Newton Abbot, Devon, TQ13 7RX
Tel: 03643 273

4 bedrooms (double or family), £12. Less for 7 nights. Rooms have central heating or electric heaters; shower or bath (some); views of country or garden; tea/coffee facilities. (Laundering facilities.)
Dinner £7 for 4 courses and coffee, at any time to suit guests. Special diets if ordered. Packed lunches, snacks. Non-residents not admitted. Drinks can be brought in.

Sitting-room with central heating, TV, books. Games room with snooker and table tennis.
Garden and open fields, with unheated swimming-pool.
Nearest main road A38 from Exeter to Plymouth.

Tucked away in a fold of the gentle hills south of Dartmoor is this small farm where sheep and hens are kept; donkeys, goats and rabbits too.

Sue Townsend has furnished the bedrooms very prettily, and she equips them with supplies of fruit-squash and biscuits as well as tea. There is a 'family unit' of two rooms and a shower, and a ground-floor suite. A comfortable sitting-room is available to guests.

Four-course dinners are served in the dining-room. After a starter such as melon or pâté, the main course will probably be a roast, poultry or steak pie, perhaps followed by fruit pie or flan, always accompanied by Devonshire cream, then cheese and coffee. Sue tries to cater for every guest individually. There is no charge for washing and ironing facilities, mealtimes are flexible, the welcome warm, and many extra services provided (loan of maps, hair-dryer, free tea on arrival). From the farm, which has a small swimming-pool, there are views of the moors. '

Readers' comments: We were pampered, the situation is an absolute dream. Loud praises of all aspects, especially the food. The very best: nothing is too much trouble. One of our favourites; Sue is one of the best cooks; food beautifully presented. Very enjoyable; warm welcome, good food, comfortable.

Also in the Dartmoor National Park is an exceptionally pretty, 450-year-old cottage of white walls and thatch: **Corbyns Brimley**, Higher Brimley, near Bovey Tracey (tel: 0626 833332). It has been attractively furnished by Hazel White in a style that is in keeping with its age. B & b only as a rule – most visitors eat at the Toby Jug, Bickington; the Rumbling Tum, Bovey Tracey; or the Rock Inn, Haytor Vale.

Readers' comments: Superb views, splendid accommodation, friendly and caring proprietors; shall return again and again.

WEST CROSS HOUSE

C D PT

High Street, Tenterden, Kent, TN30 6JL   Tel: 05806 2224

7 bedrooms (single, double or family) from £13. Less for 7 nights. Rooms have central heating; armchairs; tea/coffee facilities.
Dinner £7.50 for 3 courses, at 7pm. Special diets if ordered. Drinks can be ordered.
Sitting-room with central heating, open fire, TV, books.
Nearest main road A28 from Hastings to Canterbury.
Closed in winter

At the quieter end of the street stands this small Georgian house furnished with antiques, oriental carpets and well chosen wallpapers. There are attractive details, such as fanlight, arches and turned balusters – and a pretty garden of paved paths, flowers and a magnolia. The big sitting-room, which runs right through from front to back, has a huge log grate in a brick inglenook. Each bedroom, simply furnished, is different. I particularly liked one with velvet chairs and Paisley wallpaper.

A typical menu cooked by Mrs May might comprise home-made celery soup, a trout or steak pie with fresh vegetables, and home-made ice cream. Dinner must be ordered in advance.

Tenterden, an interesting old town itself, is in the middle of an area full of things to see and do and is an agreeable place in which to shop. Within easy reach are the castles of Leeds, Chilham and Bodiam; Battle Abbey; Smallhythe (Ellen Terry's home); and stately homes such as Penshurst. Canterbury is 45 minutes away. All around are the pretty villages, ancient churches and rural views typical of Kent, 'the market-garden of England'. Seaside resorts and many of the historic Cinque Ports are easily reached. Elegant Tunbridge Wells and its shops (antiques, books, crafts, clothes boutiques) lies a few miles in the other direction. This is an area where there is always something interesting afoot – notices along the country roads announce events like ox roasts and country-and-steam fairs or invite you to buy Jersey cream or to pick your own strawberries. (My favourite simply read: 'Beware. Ducks crossing'.) Tenterden has a steam railway, the Romney Marsh churches are near, and fine gardens (Sissinghurst and Great Dixter among them) are too numerous to list – as are garden centres.

Readers' comments: Excellent standards. Excellent in every respect. Considerate and efficient hosts.

Dining-room at Low Hall (see page 168)

WEST HOUSE

12 West Street, Warminster, Wiltshire, BA12 8JJ   Tel: 0985 213936

C(6) **D PT S**

2 bedrooms (single or double) from £16. Less for 3 nights. Rooms have central heating or electric heaters; shower or bathroom; armchairs; views of country or garden; tea/coffee facilities.
Dinner £11 for 3 courses with wine and coffee, at 8pm. Vegetarian or special diets if ordered. Lunches, packed lunches, snacks.
2 sitting-rooms with central heating, open fire, TV, books, piano, record-player.
Large garden
Nearest main road A36 from Salisbury to Bath.

A very graceful sitting-room extends from front to back of the 18th-century stone house: soft pink sofas and armchairs contrast with a celadon carpet, their colours complemented by those of handsome chinoiserie curtains with pheasants. White-shuttered windows are at each end. On the walls of this and other rooms are some of the sporting prints and watercolours which Charles Lane collects (and writes about). A fine staircase leads to charming bedrooms: I particularly liked one with rosebud wallpaper matching the pink slub spread on the cane-headed bed. Flowers are put in each room.

In the equally attractive dining-room, Celia Lane uses cordon bleu recipes for such meals as salmon mousse, chicken bonne femme, and the best raspberry pavlova I've ever tasted.

At the back are two large walled gardens with old-fashioned roses, herbaceous beds and an immense tulip tree (it flowers late in July).

Charles is, incidentally, a descendant of the celebrated Jane Lane whose story is told elsewhere (see **King's Lodge**).

The Lanes love to tell their guests of good places to explore – not just the famous sights (Salisbury, Bath, Glastonbury and Wells) but delightful spots such as Shaftesbury, Frome, Devizes or Bruton, for instance. Quite close by are Amesbury, Avebury ring, Stonehenge, Longleat and its famous lions, the lovely Vale of Pewsey, Wilton House, Stourhead and many beautiful but lesser known gardens. Plenty of antique shops in and around Warminster.

When to go? Seaside resorts or other places suitable for children will be at their busiest (and dearest) in July–August and during half-term holidays (especially in late May, which is also a bank holiday period). Other peak periods are, of course, Easter, Christmas, New Year and the bank holiday in late August. (The bank holiday in early May is not usually a peak, because it comes rather soon after Easter, but much depends on the weather.) There are local peaks, too (the Gold Cup races at Cheltenham or the regatta at Henley, for instance, are apt to fill hotels for miles around), and local troughs (Brighton, a conference centre, is least busy in high summer). You won't get much personal attention when hotels are full to bursting.

WESTERN HOUSE

C S X

Cavendish, north-west of Sudbury, Suffolk, CO10 8AR   Tel: 0787 280550

4 bedrooms (single, double or family) from £11. Rooms have central heating or electric heaters; views of country or garden.
Large garden
Nearest main road between the A604 and A134.

Twice made redundant, Peter Marshall decided he had had enough of industry and – his children now being grown up – would instead make a living from his best asset: his attractive 400-year-old house in the historic village of Cavendish.

He and his wife Jean (who teaches singing) are vegetarians, so at one end they started a wholefood shop, full of the good smells of dried fruit and fresh herbs, and refurnished several bedrooms to take bed-and-breakfast guests. Breakfast is served in bedrooms. Options include all kinds of good things (such as their own muesli, eggs, mushrooms, tomatoes and home-made bread) but no bacon. They will recommend good restaurants of all kinds in the village, at Long Melford or in Sudbury.

Each beamed bedroom, reached via zigzag corridors, is very pretty, and spacious – well equipped with chairs, table etc. One at the front (double-glazed, because it looks onto the main road through the village) has a fresh white-and-green colour scheme extending even to the sheets.

One of the nicest features is the large and informal garden where paved paths wander between old-fashioned flowers, elderly fruit trees, and plant troughs.

Cavendish is one of a string of mediaeval villages described elsewhere. Clare is close, so is Sudbury town, Bury St Edmunds and Long Melford – very long indeed, lined with dignified houses and antique shops. Its church and its great mansions (Melford Hall and Kentwell Hall) are well worth seeing. So are Lavenham, Kersey, East Bergholt, Dedham (Alfred Munnings exhibition), the Roman-Norman city of Colchester (with castle), Castle Hedingham, a steam railway and Beth Chatto's garden.

Readers' comments: Excellent, with very good breakfasts. Much enjoyed it; and the shop is excellent. Extremely comfortable; warm welcome. Absolutely excellent, high standard.

Don't complain if –
- because you booked at short notice, you do not get the best room
- because you did not order a meal in advance, you get something plucked from the freezer
- because you do not arrive on time, your room is let to someone else
- because you bring a dog without asking, it is refused entry
- because you don't express your wishes (for more heat, a second helping or whatever), you don't get what you want!

WESTERN HOUSE

Winchelsea Road, Rye, East Sussex, TN31 7EL   Tel: 0797 223419

C PT X

3 bedrooms (double or family) from £12.50. Bargain breaks. Rooms have central heating; shower and wc; armchairs; views of country or garden; tea/coffee facilities. Coffee, tea, for a charge.
Large garden
Nearest main road A259 from Hastings to Folkestone.

The mediaeval port of Rye was perched high on a thumb of land (almost an island) projecting into the sea. But centuries ago the sea receded, leaving behind dry land which became ideal pasturage for sheep. It is here, at the foot of Rye town, that tile-hung Western House was built in the 18th century, commanding far views – you can even see Hastings in clear weather – from its cobbled terrace (with working pump) where tea may be taken, or from the huge lawn surrounded by brilliant flowerbeds set against mellow stone walls. On summer evenings, the terrace is lit by old Victorian street-lamps.

Artist Ron Dellar is the present owner of Western House, and his paintings fill the dining-room walls. Up the staircase, and in the bedrooms are all manner of 'finds' he has amassed over the years: African masks, a parrot in a glass dome, an 1820 box of paints ('Constable was alive then', he comments), Rupert Bear books, antique toys. Melanie, his wife, sells Victorian lace, linen, baby-gowns and books which are laid out in the big entrance hall.

This is a house of character, as befits its long history. A boat-builder lived here and, later on, members of Parliament. Among its visitors (in 1913) was the impressionist artist Pissarro; and Ron has incorporated him in a mural featuring Rye church which he painted for one of the bedrooms. All these rooms are attractively decorated, with interesting wallpapers and fresh flowers, and have good views of the marshes across which you can walk to Winchelsea. There's a moated Martello tower out there, giant marsh-frogs croak throatily, you may see herons or marsh harriers flying overhead. (Although the house is on the road to Winchelsea I slept undisturbed.)

Around Rye are Camber sands, Bodiam Castle, Battle Abbey, Winchelsea and gardens at Sissinghurst and Great Dixter.

Dinner is not usually served because Rye has so many good inns and restaurants such as the Old Forge or Flushing Inn.

Readers' comments: We were particularly delighted. View magnificent.

When writing to me, if you want a reply please enclose a stamped addressed envelope.

WESTLEA   C(2) **D H PT S**

29 Riverside Road, Alnmouth, south-east of Alnwick, Northumberland,
NE66 2SD   Tel: 0665 830730

7 bedrooms (single, twin, double or family) from £13. Less for bargain breaks. Some have own bath/shower; TV; tea/coffee facilities; central heating; views of river, country or garden; balcony. (Washing-machine on request.)
Dinner £6.50 for 4 courses (with some choice) and coffee, at 7pm. Non-residents not admitted. Vegetarian or special diets if ordered. Lunches, packed lunches, snacks. Tea, coffee, free. Drinks can be brought in. No smoking.
Sitting-room with central heating, TV, books, record-player, video.
Small garden
Nearest main road A1068 from Newcastle to Alnwick.

This is a very comfortable modern guest-house facing the Aln estuary, immaculately kept by Janice Edwards. One attractive bedroom (wildflower fabrics and cane bedheads) opens onto the sunny front garden; others vary in size and style but all, even if small, are well equipped. The upstairs sitting-room has a balcony from which to enjoy the river view.

Breakfasts are imaginative; and for dinner (4 courses) there may be such dishes as beef, salmon, Cheviot lamb (with Northumbrian baked suet-puddings) or game pie. For the way she runs Westlea, Janice received a local Hospitality Award in 1989.

Nearby Alnwick is the seat of the Duke of Northumberland (and the historic Percy family whose deeds feature in so many of Shakespeare's plays), who lives in Alnwick Castle – ruined but then restored in the 18th century. This area is a good place in which to follow riverside walks; to explore the dramatic coastline and its many castles – particularly Warkworth at daffodil-time; to visit Craster for its succulent kippers (the ancient smoke-house is a listed building); and to walk to the romantic clifftop ruins of Dunstanburgh which Turner painted many times; or little Amble for its sandy beaches and island of eiderducks. Alnmouth itself is a picturesque yachting resort and has one of England's oldest golf courses (1869).

Visitors enjoy trips to the Farne Islands to watch seals and puffins, to Holy Island and to the Scottish borders. At Bamburgh is the Grace Darling museum as well as a theatrically sited castle and golden sands; inland are Rothbury and the mansion of Cragside. Although scenery – free from crowds – is the area's greatest attraction, there are plenty of other interesting things to see, such as the wild white cattle, a rare survival, at Chillingham; the farm park at Embleton; or the World Bird Research Station (very tame birds in 17th-century buildings, and an arboretum).

Blyth has one of the county's several good railway museums, there are a great many country parks, and this is a good area in which to seek out craft workshops.

Readers' comments: A most enjoyable week. Nothing was too much trouble for Janice Edwards. Hearty meals, beautifully cooked and presented. Kind and helpful. Excellent food and an amazing choice for breakfast.

WHASHTON SPRINGS FARM   C(5)
Whashton, north-west of Richmond, North Yorkshire DL11 7JS
Tel: 0748 2884

9 bedrooms (single, double or family) from £14. Less for 7 nights and bargain breaks.

Some have own bath/shower; TV; tea/coffee facilities; phone; central heating; views of country or garden.
Dinner £9 for 3 courses (with choices) and coffee, at 7pm. Non-residents not admitted. Vegetarian or special diets if ordered. Tea, coffee, free. Drinks can be ordered.
Sitting-room with central heating, open fire, TV, books; bar.
Small garden
Nearest main road A66 from Scotch Corner to Brough.
Closed Christmas–mid-January

Far more handsome than the average farmhouse, 18th-century Whashton Springs has great bow windows and other detailing typical of this fine period in English architecture. Around it is a large, mixed farm run by two generations of Turnbulls. It is high among wooded hills, with superb views of the Dales and of a stream with mediaeval bridge below.

Every bedroom is different. One, for instance, has flowery fabrics, broderie anglaise on the bedlinen, pretty Victorian antiques and a bow window; another, a four-poster with William Morris drapery and buttoned velvet chairs. Others in a converted stable-block are more modern in style (velvet bedheads, flowery duvets and pine furniture); most of these overlook a courtyard where tubs and stone troughs brim with pansies and petunias; one has a garden view. Another outbuilding houses the pottery studio of the Turnbulls' daughter-in-law Jane.

Fairlie Turnbull and her daughter Christine provide dinners except on Thursdays, always with some choice. A typical example: cheese soufflé, home-bred roast lamb, and brandysnaps. Or, a typical Yorkshire ending to a meal, Wensleydale cheese served with fruitcake. (The meals are very good value – with wine included.)

The many gardens of this region are at their best in spring, and the famous 'sights' (York, Durham, Richmond and the Dales) less crowded. One can even drive across to the Lake District from here. It's an area not only of spectacular scenery but of dramatic or romantic ruins (great abbeys and castles). Walkers seek out waterfalls and caves, fells and crags, for which the Yorkshire Dales are famous. The little cobbled villages and old inns seem hardly to change at all with the years.

Whashton's nearness to the A1 means many people use it as a one-night stopover on their London–Edinburgh journey, but it deserves better than this because there are so many good reasons to linger. Swaledale alone takes days to explore, and so does Teesdale (both described elsewhere). It is a region of contrasts. Lonely moors rise to 2000 feet (this is where to listen for curlews and plovers, and to wonder at lives passed in such few isolated farms as these are), while every dale differs – Wensleydale is wide and either pastoral or wooded; Swaledale winds between steep hills; some others are like deep clefts – Arkengarthdale, Coverdale, Bishopdale, for instance. Heather moors, houses of 18th-century dignity, the distinctive curly-horned sheep; all contribute to the individuality of this area.

Readers' comments: Very comfortable. Made very welcome. High praise. Lovely surroundings and easy access to many places.

WHEATHILL FARM   C H S

**Church Lane, Shearsby, north-west of Market Harborough,
Leicestershire, LE17 6PG**   Tel: 053758 663

4 bedrooms (single or double) from £14. Less for 7 nights. Rooms have central heating; one has shower; armchairs; views of farmland or garden; tea/coffee facilities. No smoking.
Dinner £6 for 3 courses and coffee, at 6.30pm. Vegetarian or special diets if ordered. Packed lunches. Coffee, tea, free. Drinks can be brought in.
Sitting-room with central heating, open fire, TV, books.
Large garden with boules and croquet.
Nearest main road A50 from Leicester to Northampton.

In 1823, the owners of this cottage (part Saxon, part mediaeval) put a new façade on the front: brick, with trim white paintwork. But behind this the old beamed rooms remained unchanged, with huge inglenook housing a log stove, and a twisting stair.

Sue Timms has a decorative touch, and uses pretty fabrics or beribboned net in cottage-style bedrooms, one downstairs (and even in one of the bathrooms too). The house is full of unusual heirlooms, including a 100-year-old pot-plant which originally belonged to a lighthouse-keeper (her great-uncle) on the wild Farne Islands off the Northumberland coast. Outside is an attractive garden with lily-pool and lake.

Typical of the meals which Sue prepares: grapefruit grilled with brown sugar, sirloin of beef with Yorkshire pudding, summer pudding with cream.

Shearsby is, like many others around here, a particularly pretty village, not far from Georgian Market Harborough (its lively markets date from 1200) and at the centre of rich grazing country – a tranquil region threaded by waterways with, at Foxton, ten locks packed in a tier to raise boats up a 75-foot incline.

Further north is the scenic Charnwood Forest area – a mixture of heath, crags, ridges and remnants of oak forest with fine views from its hilltops. Within a short distance are Anstey's mediaeval packhorse bridge, the pretty little spa town of Ashby de la Zouch, a particularly interesting church at Breedon-on-the-Hill, and Loughborough which has a carillon of 47 bells in a high tower in the park. Other sights include Birdland, Twycross Zoo and Stanford Hall.

Sitting-room at Wheathill Farm

WHICHAM OLD RECTORY   C S S-C
Silecroft, west of Millom, Cumbria, LA18 5LS   Tel: 0657 2954

4 bedrooms (single, double or family) from £12. Less for 2 nights. Rooms have central heating; armchairs; views of country or garden; tea/coffee facilities.
Dinner £6.50 for 3 courses (some choices) and coffee, at a time to suit guests. Vegetarian or special diets if ordered. Packed lunches, snacks. Tea, free. Drinks can be brought in.
Sitting-room with central heating, log fire, TV, books.
Large garden
Nearest main road A595 from Broughton-in-Furness to Workington.

So many people head for the heart of the Lake District that the outlying areas of the National Park remain uncrowded and uncommercialized. The south-west corner in particular is often overlooked, even though it is within an easy drive of famous beauty-spots and has its own particular attractions – uncrowded beaches, for example, and a mild maritime climate. The last accounts for the peaches and mulberries that flourish in the garden of the Old Rectory – the one appearing on the dinner-table, the other going into the wine which guests usually sample.

The house is typical of those Victorian rectories built for Trollope-size clerical families with domestic staff in proportion. David Kitchener – an ex-RAF supply officer and an accomplished woodworker – has put a lot of work into the spacious house, some of it to display intriguing family possessions – Victorian dish-covers, an ancient cast-iron pressure cooker – and other interesting bric-à-brac: a big model of a dhow he bought when on service in the Middle East, a fairground flare, woodwork from a Warwickshire church, a collection of kukris and other weapons.

He and Judy Kitchener also find time to grow most of the vegetables which she uses in her enthusiastic cooking. There is always a home-made soup, with alternative first courses, then for example coq au vin (which may be half a chicken per head), with at least three vegetables, to which guests help themselves, and a sweet such as raspberry mousse, to which the garden is likely to have contributed too. The freshly baked bread is the speciality of Judy's mother – who worries if dishes come back from the table empty, in case guests had not been offered enough.

All the bedrooms overlook the lawn, next to which is a small semi-circular conservatory which David has built onto the end of the stable, so that guests can enjoy the garden even when a sea breeze is blowing. The energetic can take a footpath to the top of Black Combe (2000 feet) for views of Scotland and Wales. The less energetic can explore the beach at Silecroft, with its sands and rock-pools. Up the coast are mansions and gardens, a narrow-gauge railway, and old seaports. Eastward are pleasant market towns, Morecambe Bay and the seabird reserve of Walney Island. Inland is, of course, the Lake District.

For explanation of code letters (**C, D, H, PT, S, S-C, X**) see page xxvi

WHITE BARN

C PT S

Crede Lane, Bosham, west of Chichester, West Sussex, PO18 8NX
Tel: 0243 573113

rear view

4 bedrooms (single, double or family) from £16. Less for 7 nights or bargain breaks. Rooms have central heating or electric heaters; shower or bathroom; armchairs; views of garden; tea/coffee facilities.
Dinner £12 for 4 courses (with choices) and coffee, at 7pm. Special diets if ordered.

Snacks. Drinks can be brought in. No dinners in August.
Sitting-room with central heating, open fire, TV, books.
Garden
Nearest main road A259 from Chichester to Portsmouth.

As interesting architecturally as any house in this book, White Barn is no barn but a very modern house indeed (single storey), designed by architect Frank Guy, and standing in the seclusion of a former orchard.

The dining-room is impressive: its principal features are a roof of exposed boards, a vast glass wall on one side (opening onto a red-tiled terrace where dinner is sometimes served).

This room is open to the big kitchen with its scarlet Aga cooker, pans hanging from brass hooks, and solid beech work-counter with old brass grocery-scales.

Then there is an oddly-shaped sitting-room, built all around the circular brick hearth on which a modern log stove stands. Its huge sofas face a narrow window 20 feet high. Throughout there are white walls and glossy scarlet doors.

Few visitors prefer a separate table for meals but join all the others at a huge pine refectory table, laid with flowery Portmeirion pottery, where Susan Trotman serves such appetite-whetting meals as stuffed mushrooms before, perhaps, chicken cooked with cream and wine (and four vegetables), then a pavlova topped with lemon curd and Jersey cream, or a Bakewell tart.

Bedrooms open onto the garden, or overlook it. One is an imaginatively planned family suite: the room with children's bunk beds is like a cabin.

Not far away is the Saxon harbour of Bosham (its church is depicted in the Bayeux tapestry), thronged with little boats. Chichester, described elsewhere, lies in one direction and the historic naval waterfront of Portsmouth in the other – where you can visit HMS *Victory*, the *Mary Rose*, the dockyard museum, old bastions and byways, Southsea Castle, and the ring of high Victorian forts. The colossal, ironclad HMS *Warrior* is an attraction. There are many Roman sites.

Readers' comments: Very comfortable, food superb. Excellent value, memorable – not to be missed! Wonderful. Warm and welcoming. A memorable stay; outstanding. Food is out of this world. Top class! Comfortable, restful, very good food in ample quantity. Charming, cheerful, considerate. Meals superb.

327

WHITE HOUSE
S-C

Grindon, east of Leek, Staffordshire, ST13 7TP   Tel: 05388 (Onecote) 250

3 bedrooms (double) from £14. Less for 2 nights. Rooms have central heating; TV, armchairs; views of country and garden; tea/coffee facilities. No smoking. Shower in two.
Dinner £12.50 for 4 courses and coffee, at 7.30pm. Drinks can be brought in.

Sitting-room with central heating, open fire, books.
Garden
Nearest main road A523 from Leek towards Ashbourne.

In the 17th century, this sparkling white cottage was a little inn, in a beautiful part of the Peak District (1000 feet up, it overlooks the very lovely valley of the River Manifold). Philomena Bunce used to teach crafts and needlework, and every bedroom reflects this – the pretty, fresh colour schemes and the hand-made lampshades, cushions, patchwork quilts and padded bedheads are her work.

Outside is a very pleasant garden with seats on a paved area with roses and cottage flowers. Drink in hand, one can watch the sunlight fading and, over a mossy wall, cows ambling on their way to be milked, while the swifts dart low.

Philomena serves dinner in her pine dining-room only at weekends (at other times, visitors walk to the nearby Cavalier Inn). She is an excellent cook. On the night when I stayed, she served a very good pâté, chicken in a sauce of apples and cream (the accompanying mange-touts and other vegetables were lightly cooked), and a feather-light raspberry pavlova – on white-and-gold china, with quilted placemats. Breakfasts include several out-of-the ordinary options, such as kippers delivered from Craster in Northumberland or a Staffordshire oatcake (like a pancake) topped with a tasty mushroom, mustard and egg mixture.

Apart from visiting the Peak District, Dovedale and the Manifold Valley from here, you can explore lesser-known Derbyshire and the much underrated north of Staffordshire. In the south the scenery is pastoral, with calm rivers. Derby city has an 18th-century quarter and other historic buildings, many parks, and Kedleston Hall – an Adam mansion. Alton Towers – an exceptional leisure park – is near.

Six towns make up the 'Ceramic City' of Stoke-on-Trent containing Coalport, Spode, Wedgwood and other well known potteries. Closer are the many antique and mill shops of the interesting town of Leek, surrounded by moorlands.

Readers' comments: Furnishings outstanding; highest standard of comfort, good food and warm welcome. Our stay one of the pleasantest ever. Absolutely superb – perfection! A wonderful find, and very reasonably priced. One of the best weekends we can remember; perfect comfort, lovely surroundings, delectable meals. A gem! Made to feel part of the family. Excellent, comfortable, friendly, a beautiful spot. Excellent accommodation, peaceful.

328

WHITE HOUSE

North Road, Widmer End, north-east of High Wycombe, Buckinghamshire, HP15 6ND   Tel: 0494 712221

1 bedroom (suite) from £14. Less for 3 nights. Has own bath/shower; TV; tea/coffee facilities; central heating; view of country and garden.

Large garden
Nearest main road A404 from High Wycombe to Amersham.

Hot in pursuit of a Buckinghamshire debutante, the Prince of Wales in 1931 persuaded his aide-de-camp, who lived in a 16th-century cottage conveniently near, to build on an extra wing for the Prince's use. It is in the Prince's self-contained but modest suite that visitors are today accommodated; and those who drop in at the village inn may encounter elderly locals who still remember the Prince's activities.

(By a coincidence, the present owner – Jane Vaughan – also has family reminiscences of the indefatigable Prince who, up in Yorkshire, had courted yet another girl, Jane's great-aunt.)

From the bedroom, with its view of grazing sheep, one descends via a staircase of exposed beams and brickwork to the breakfast-room in the old part of the cottage. No dinners (only light snacks if ordered in advance) but there is a good inn, the Hit or Miss at Penn Street; the Royal Standard at Forty Green; and plenty of restaurants in the old quarter of Amersham.

The nearby Hughenden Valley has – although only an hour from London – such fine scenery that much of it is owned by the National Trust, including the great house at its centre which was Disraeli's home. At West Wycombe there is much to see and most is very unusual, including an underground cave system open to the public, and the 18th-century church with so immense a golden ball on top of its tower that parties were held in it by Sir Francis Dashwood – leader of the 'Hell Fire Club' which held orgies in the caves and in the ruins of Medmenham Abbey. His magnificent Palladian mansion is surrounded by parkland which Capability Brown laid out.

Then there are Penn, where William Penn lived, and Jordans, associated with the Pilgrim Fathers (see entry for **Old Jordans**); Milton's Cottage at Chalfont St Giles; and High Wycombe's chair museum (from the Chiltern beech woods originated the Windsor chair, and the town is still a centre of furniture-making).

In this Chilterns area of outstanding natural beauty, it is the gentle drive through beech woods and along country lanes to the old Roman road at Ellesborough – the Upper Icknield Way – that Jane recommends most. There are fine views of Chequers, the country home of Britain's Prime Ministers, and the route passes close to the 17th-century home of parliamentarian John Hampden.

WHITE HOUSE C PT

10 High Street South, Olney, north of Milton Keynes, Buckinghamshire, MK46 4AA   Tel: 0234 711478

9 bedrooms (single or double) from £16.25. Less for 7 nights. Some have own shower; tea/coffee facilities; central heating. (Washing-machine on request.)
Sitting-room with central heating, TV, books.
Small garden
Nearest main road A509 from Wellingborough to Milton Keynes.

Although this house, dating from 1802, is on a busy road, there are quiet, modern bedrooms at the back – all immaculate. The breakfast-room overlooks a lily-pond in a small rock garden; and there is a comfortable sitting-room with big velvet armchairs. Right opposite is a good wine bar for evening meals: Ken and June Roberts serve only breakfasts (but with a varied choice). Unlimited help-yourself tea and coffee are available all day, free.

Olney is a very attractive little town with 18th-century and other old buildings, including an elaborately carved Lace Hall (Buckinghamshire was famous for its hand-made lace). The unusually wide High Street is where, every Shrove Tuesday, women race along tossing pancakes as they go. Off it are passages with antique shops open even on Sundays. As Olney is close to junction 14 of the M1, it is a useful place for a stopover (or when visiting nearby Milton Keynes) but it deserves a longer stay for in the vicinity are bird gardens, Stevington windmill and Bromham watermill on the beautiful Ouse (with milling, wildlife and art exhibits). Historic Bedford is near, described elsewhere, and there is fine scenery, particularly among the riverside villages north of the road to Bedford – Harrold has a country park, village green and lock-up; and Turvey a statue of Jonah, in the river.

Olney had one celebrated resident, Cowper: an unusual 18th-century poet. Before coming to Olney he spent many years in a mental asylum. In his home here (now a museum), he kept tame hares and birds; and he wrote in a summer-house 'not much bigger than a sedan chair which opens into the garden that is now crowded with pinks, roses and honeysuckles, and its window into my neighbour's orchards'. Here he wrote his famous ballad called 'John Gilpin's Ride' and verses about his pets:

> 'One greenhouse is my summer seat;
> My shrubs, displaced from that retreat,
> Enjoyed the open air.
> Two goldfinches, whose sprightly song
> Had been their mutual solace long
> Lived happy prisoners there . . .'

WHITESTONE FARMHOUSE   C D PT S
Staintondale, north of Scarborough, North Yorkshire, YO13 0EZ
Tel: 0723 870612

rear view

4 bedrooms (single, double or family) from £9. All have central heating; views of sea, country or garden. No smoking. (Washing-machine on request.)
Dinner £5 for 4 courses and coffee, at 6.30pm. Non-residents not admitted. Vegetarian or special diets if ordered. Snacks. Tea, coffee, free. Drinks can be brought in.
2 sitting-rooms with central heating, open fire, TV, books, record-player.
Small garden
Nearest main road A171 from Scarborough to Whitby.

'I like my guests to feel they are having a dinner-party every night!' says Pat Angus, which is one reason why many return again.

That and the position of the stone-built farmhouse just south of Robin Hood's Bay (famous for its three-mile sweep, and the constant erosion which has caused many cottages to tumble into the sea) and near National Trust coastal scenery, all with spectacular views.

There is a glass-walled sun-lounge so that you can see meadows with goats, cows and lambs in one direction and the sea in the other – from the comfort of the large curved sofa or an armchair. A steep staircase leads up to neat bedrooms which enjoy similar views.

Adjoining the farmland are woods and Heyburn Wyke nature reserve – roe deer occasionally wander in from the reserve. There are footpaths down to the rocky shore and along a disused rail track; the long-distance Cleveland Way passes by on its far journey to the North Yorkshire Moors.

As to Pat's dinner-parties, here is an idea of the kind of thing she prepares for her guests: fruit juice; tomato stuffed with walnuts, raisins, cheese and chives in mayonnaise – served with a salad and home-baked wholemeal roll; turkey breast in breadcrumbs with cranberry sauce and four vegetables; sherry trifle. Exceptional value.

Staintondale's attractions include not only the coast but also the North York Moors. To the north is Whitby (described elsewhere) and to the south Scarborough – a huge mixture of resort, fishing harbour and historic town, with superb scenery around (both cliffs and sandy bays). Some of it is now garish; but the harbour and fishmarket are as they always were, and dramatically positioned on a headland are the remains of a Norman castle overlooking Scarborough's superb bay.

Anne Brontë died and is buried at Scarborough. She wrote about 'the deep, clear azure of the sky and ocean, the bright morning sunshine on the semicircular barrier of craggy cliffs surmounted by green swelling hills, and on the smooth, wide sands, and the low rocks out at sea – looking, with their clothing of weeds and moss, like little grass-grown islands – and above all, on the brilliant, sparkling waves. And then the unspeakable purity and freshness of the air!'

Readers' comments: A lovely atmosphere, food excellent in content, presentation and quantity. A caring couple.

331

WHYKE HOUSE

C PT S-C X

13 Whyke Lane, Chichester, West Sussex, PO19 2JR   Tel: 0243 788767

rear view

2 bedrooms (single, double or family) from £15. Less for 3 nights. Rooms have bath or shower; central heating; TV, armchairs; views of garden; tea-making facilities. No smoking.
Sitting-room with central heating, books, TV. No smoking.
Small garden
Nearest main road A27 from Worthing to Portsmouth.

In an ordinary suburban cul-de-sac, very close to the historic centre of Chichester (and overlooking a grassy Roman site at the back, where children now play) is an unusual bed-and-breakfast house, ideal for families.

Here Tony and Lydia Hollis cook their guests' breakfasts (and service their rooms), give advice on sightseeing, then depart to their own home next door. There is a fully equipped kitchen which guests are then welcome to use to prepare other meals, if they do not wish to go to Chichester's many restaurants and cafés (the Nags is popular). Unlimited tea etc. is provided. Guests can also use the sitting-room and back garden (with croquet), glimpsed in the drawing. It is almost like being in a home of your own, with complete freedom.

The furnishings throughout have great individuality. Family antiques mingle with Russian folk art, local paintings (you may meet the artist) with soft furnishings made by Lydia – who also has a flair for painting furniture decoratively.

For some older guests, the ground-floor bedroom and shower are particularly convenient. Guests can be met by car at the station. Bicycle and tandem for hire.

Other entries describe the cathedral city of Chichester and its environs, which include Arundel Castle, Fishbourne Roman palace, Bosham waterfront village, Goodwood House, the open-air museum of ancient buildings and West Dean gardens. Tony, once in the antiques trade, is a good adviser on the best shops locally.

Readers' comments: The Hollises are so kind and helpful. Very comfortable; the Hollises are charming and very helpful; unpretentious and suited to young families. What good value. Comfortable and enjoyable. Comfortable, quiet, convenient; most welcoming. Pleasant weekend, comfortable; so helpful and welcoming; a real treat to stay. So welcoming, well organized. Relaxed, comfortable atmosphere. Friendly and helpful.

Some readers tell me they have stayed at lots of places from *Staying Off the Beaten Track*. I wonder who has stayed at most? A free copy of the next edition awaits the reader who sends me his/her comments on the greatest number!

WILLOW DALE

17 Carr Hill Lane, Briggswath, Sleights, south-west of Whitby, North Yorkshire, YO21 1RS   Tel: 0947 810525

3 bedrooms (double) from £13. Less for 7 nights. Rooms have own bath/shower; TV; tea/coffee facilities; central heating; views of country or garden. No smoking. (Washing-machine on request.)
Dinner £8 for 4 courses (with choices) and coffee, at 7pm. Non-residents not admitted. Tea, coffee, free. Drinks can be brought in.
Sitting-room with central heating, books. No smoking.
Small garden
Nearest main road A169 from Whitby to Pickering.
Closed October–March

Bountiful Roman goddesses Flora and Pomona adorn the sitting-room door, with swags of fruit; the front hall has stained glass; there are big sash windows throughout and handsome fireplaces of marble or decorative tiles: all redolent of the Edwardian era when this house was built. Surrounded by gardens, it looks down over the quiet Esk Valley (yet busy Whitby is quite close).

Judy Potts has boldly decorated the dining-room (which has a log fire) with a striking gold Chinese wallpaper and tasselled pelmet, while in the sitting-room are comfortable leather chairs and sofa. One bedroom has a brass bed, festoon curtains, rosebud bedlinen and pink corduroy sofa (and a really beautiful shower). The mulberry room has a frilled four-poster and an excellent bathroom with bidet.

Visitors help themselves from a drinks tray before dinner – which might, for instance, be smoked trout, chicken (with stuffing, broccoli, red cabbage Austrian-style, and jacket potatoes with cream cheese), Malvern pudding (an egg-custard and apple dish), then cheeses with celery.

Whitby is both fishing port and seaside resort, overlooked by the dramatic ruins of its 13th-century abbey on a high headland. The old part of the town is a place of steep byways, craft workshops and Captain Cook's house. There are sandy beaches further along. Briggswath is on the edge of the North York Moors; a steam railway line goes across the moors to Pickering.

Readers' comments: Most comfortable, good attention to detail. Dinner plentiful and imaginative. Peaceful.

On the other side of Whitby is 17th-century **Cross Butts Farm** which has a big bedroom that is handsomely panelled and it has an immense four-poster, seven feet wide, with barley-sugar posts. Long hours went into the making of its crochet bedspread. Other rooms are attractive: Eileen Morley has used rosebud fabrics and broderie anglaise, for instance. Willow-pattern curtains match the china on a dresser that stands against one of the stone

walls. For dinner, many visitors go to the Magpie. The farm is near sandy beaches. (Tel: 0947 602519.)

WILLOWS

S

Kingsland, north-west of Leominster, Herefordshire, HR6 9RU
Tel: 056881 529

2 bedrooms (double and small single) from £12.50, sharing bathroom; TV; tea/coffee facilities; central heating. Views of garden. (Washing-machine on request.)
Dinner £7.50 for 3 courses and coffee, at 7pm. Special diets if ordered. Tea, coffee, extra. Drinks can be brought in.

Sitting-room with central heating, TV, books.
Small garden
Nearest main road A4110 from Hereford to Ludlow.
Closed November–March

The guests' rooms, being in a separate wing of this beamy 17th-century house, are virtually a private suite: the main bedroom leads into its own sitting-room with armchairs and television. Beyond lies a private bathroom and a small bedroom for a third person (Daphne Somers lets the wing to only one family, or party, at a time). Breakfast and supper-trays can be brought up here, or served in the dining/sitting-room downstairs: a pleasant south-facing room opening onto pond and garden. For those who want a full dinner, Daphne serves such meals as home-made pâté, duck with orange sauce and meringues.

Kingsland is an attractive old village from which to explore the gentle Herefordshire landscape and the more rugged Shropshire-Wales border country, Offa's Dyke, Ludlow and Croft castles and the cathedral city of Hereford.

Leominster is an old market town that grew up centuries ago when wool from monastic herds brought wealth to the area. It sits in a river valley surrounded by hop fields and cider-apple orchards, and is the centre from which Herefordshire's famous beef-cattle (white-faced and red-coated) are exported worldwide. Many of Australia's sheep are descended from the area's distinctive wide-backed breed. The unusual Norman church – it has three naves – houses a ducking-stool, used (up to 1809) for dipping in the river women notorious for their scolding tongues. Near Bromyard, another ancient market town, are the picturesque and moated manor house of Lower Brockhampton and the gardens at Tedstone Court (occasionally open to the public).

Pretty Eardisland's timbered buildings are on the banks of a small river; Pembridge's surround a mediaeval church which (like others in a once war-torn area) has a fortified tower with arrow-slits in the walls and a detached belfry: it was used as a refuge in times of siege. At Kington (near the long earthwork of Offa's Dyke, built in the 8th century to keep the Welsh out) there are big sheep auctions every autumn. Walks up the hills are rewarded by fine views. Hergest Croft Gardens are famous for azaleas.

In general this part of Herefordshire is peaceful and lovely rather than dramatic, with broad fields of cattle or sheep, cider-apples or hops, and calm rivers.

WINCHELSEA TEA ROOM   C PT
Hiham Green, Winchelsea, south of Rye, East Sussex, TN36 4HB
Tel: 0797 226679

3 bedrooms (single, double or family) from £13.50. Less for 7 nights. All have own bath or shower; TV; tea/coffee facilities; central heating.
Sitting-room with central heating, books.
Small garden
Nearest main road A259 from Hastings to Folkestone.

Beyond a modest exterior and Edwardian-style tea-room, a surprise awaits. Fred and Linda Rankin's home is larger than it looks, rooms are spacious and immaculate, and they have furnished them with considerable style – aiming to combine modern comfort with Edwardian antiques and colour schemes.

There is a large upstairs sitting-room for visitors with pink curvaceous sofas and a handsome but ancient (1919) sewing machine – on which Linda made all the curtains in the house. Bedrooms (and bathrooms) are of a high standard. Two open onto a little garden, others are upstairs; one is virtually a suite, with kettle and refrigerator for snacks if you do not want to eat in the tea-room (light meals only) or at the nearby New Inn. Lace spreads, buttoned velvet bedheads and wildflower wallpapers are typical of the style of each.

Unlike its neighbour Rye, Winchelsea is not particularly famous and I have always found it quiet when Rye was thronged with tourists. It is a delightful, unspoilt little town in which to wander, with beautiful countryside and coast nearby.

On the road to Hastings is the 18th-century **Country House** at Winchelsea (tel: 0797 226669), surrounded by a National Trust landscape. Mary Carmichael's decorative touches include festoon blinds and cane bedheads with flowery duvets; padded blue velvet with pine bedroom furniture (this room has a sofa); in yet another room, a fabric patterned with garlands and bows. Many rooms have garden or hill views; all have bathrooms and TV. Flowering shrubs surround a lawn and brick terrace, and an adjoining brick barn is smothered in a mass of wisteria

blossom every summer. A typical meal: fish chowder, lamb in sauce with asparagus and mushrooms, baked Alaska. (There is a pool table.)

Prices are the minimum *per person* in a double room at the beginning of the year.

WINDMILL HOUSE

C PT S X

Winterbourne Monkton, south of Swindon, Wiltshire, SN4 9NN
Tel: 06723 446

Rooms have central heating and views of country or garden. (Washing-machine on request.)
Dinner (mid-week only) £6.50 for 3 courses (with choices) and coffee, at 6.15pm. Non-residents not admitted. Vegetarian or special diets if ordered. Lunches, packed lunches, snacks. Tea, coffee, free. Drinks can be brought in.
Sitting-room with central heating, open fire, books.
Small garden

3 bedrooms (single, double or family) from £11.50. Less for 7 nights and bargain breaks.

Nearest main road A4361 from Swindon to Devizes.

All but the base of the windmill vanished long ago and this, the miller's house, has been greatly modernized – although in some rooms the old walls made of chalk blocks are visible, one bearing the date 1711. All around are fields, with far views of Silbury Hill, the Ridgeway path, and Wansdyke (all prehistoric remains). This is a very ancient part of England; and the mill itself had a long history: wheat was ground there as far back as the 13th century.

A narrow spiral stair leads up to bedrooms that are simply furnished but comfortable, and the dining/sitting-room (with log stove) is unpretentious. Outside is an unheated swimming-pool. But what most impresses the walkers, game-shooting parties, and others who come here is the food. Penny Randerson, who used to be an industrial chemist, comes from a family of chefs, which may be why meals are of an order to compare with some many-starred hotels. Although one-night visitors are offered a set menu (with choices at each course), those staying longer can order ahead from her considerable repertoire of such dishes as pigeons en cocotte, seafood gratin, cheese fondue (unusually prepared with cherry brandy), fillet Chateaubriand, pork chops ardennaise, and many more. Bread is home-baked, vegetables from the garden, and there are always flowers on the table (and in bedrooms).

After a visit to Swindon to see historic locomotives in the railway museum (and its section devoted to Brunel), as well as the restored village of Victorian railwaymen's cottages, one could go to Lydiard Tregoze where there is a classical stone mansion in a great park, its rooms (which have elaborately decorated ceilings) filled with antiques and paintings. The colourful effigies in the ancient church here are well worth seeing. Beyond lie Malmesbury and its abbey and Tetbury, a particularly attractive old market town.

If you go south, you come to the prehistoric stone circles which surround Avebury village – they are even older than Stonehenge, their purpose unknown, and their construction method a mystery too, since each weighs up to 40 tons. The village has a Norman church, great thatched barn (with museum of rural life) and an old manor house currently the centre of controversy because of plans to develop it as a tourist attraction.

The road westward from here passes Silbury Hill and one of Wiltshire's many white horses cut into the chalk of the downs on the way to Calne and 18th-century Bowood House – its grounds at their most colourful when rhododendrons and then bluebells are in flower. Capability Brown laid these out.

WINDRUSH
Little Comberton, west of Evesham, Worcestershire, WR10 3EG
Tel: 038674 284

2 bedrooms (double) from £10.50. No smoking.
Sitting-room with central heating, TV, books.
Small garden

Nearest main road A44 from Evesham to Worcester.
Closed November–February

Two little thatched cottages from the 17th century have been combined as one, with a particularly pretty garden created around them – lobelias and geraniums planted in an old tree-stump, the weathered grey of rick-stones providing a good foil to colourful blooms. Rooms are low-beamed, and the inexpensive little bedrooms furnished in appropriately cottagey style. Altogether, a really 'old world' effect.

At the back are fruit trees and vegetables, with Mr Lewis a willing guide to all aspects of the garden in which he has worked for nearly 40 years – his pride and joy.

Breakfast only, but there is good food to be had at The Mill (Elmley Castle) and the Fox and Hounds (Bredon), for instance.

Evesham is a riverside market town at the centre of the fruit-growing Vale of Evesham (this is at its prettiest in spring blossom-time). A ruined abbey with bell tower, 18th-century and older houses, fine churches, and the old Almonry (now housing a museum) all contribute to its charm. Around it are innumerable pretty villages. Offenham still has that rarity, a maypole; Elmley Castle, no castle now but plenty of half-timbered cottages, a deer park and mediaeval sculpture in the church; Bredon, a huge 14th-century tithe barn to hold the grain which served as taxes paid to the church. Above looms Bredon Hill – 1000 feet high – dominating an otherwise gentle landscape of placid rivers, apple orchards and pastures where cows graze. There are prehistoric and Norman earthworks, a castellated 'gothick' folly, and from the summit a view of at least eight counties. Around the hill is an apple-blossom trail marked out for drivers to follow in the spring.

There are boat trips available on the River Avon; and within a short car-ride the showpiece village of Broadway, Malvern (spa town) and historic Pershore, famous for its plums. Other popular outings include Winchcombe, Sudeley Castle, Beckford Silk Mill, Broadway Tower, Snowshill Manor, Hailes Abbey, Tewkesbury Abbey, the sunken gardens at Kemerton and the 'minimum labour' garden at Bredon Springs.

Readers' comments: Beautifully preserved; garden a joy to behold. Mrs Lewis is charming and friendly. A gem of a find.

WINDRUSH HOUSE   C(12)
Hazleton, west of Northleach, Gloucestershire, GL54 4EB   Tel: 0451 60364

and electric heaters; shower and wc (bathroom available); armchairs; views of country and garden.
Dinner £13.50 for 4 courses and coffee, at 7.30pm. Packed lunches. Coffee, tea, for a charge. Drinks can be ordered or brought in.
2 sitting-rooms with central heating, open fire, TV, books, piano, record-player.
Large garden
Nearest main road A40 from Cheltenham to Oxford.

4 bedrooms (single or double) from £15.50. Bargain breaks. Rooms have central heating

After Mr Harrison retired from business, he and his wife Sydney extended their 1960s home of Cotswold stone in order to turn it into a small guest-house. The greatest attraction is Sydney Harrison's outstanding cooking (though she serves dinner on only three days a week). Not only is everything impeccably prepared – vegetables delicately sliced and lightly cooked, bread home-baked, breakfast orange juice freshly squeezed – but she has a repertoire of imaginative dishes that puts many an expensive restaurant in the shade. With your breakfast porridge you will be offered whisky. And all the food is served on Royal Worcester porcelain. On nights when dinner is not served, she recommends the Fosse Bridge or Frog Mill.

The Harrisons are modest, unassuming people whose only aim is to make their visitors feel at home. The friendly welcome is manifest the moment you arrive, and a free glass of sherry awaits you in your room.

As to the house itself, this is furnished with much attention to comfort, and in tranquil colours. All the rooms are immaculate, and the furnishings (conventional in style) are of high quality.

The house stands in a quiet spot some 800 feet up in the Cotswold Hills, where the air is bracing and the views are of far fields and grazing sheep. It is on the outskirts of a rambling village of old stone farmhouses with a small church nearby – part of it Saxon.

Hazleton – under 2 hours from London – is close to beautiful Northleach, which has a mediaeval church of great splendour and an excellent museum of country life; Cirencester, a lovely market town with the outstanding Corinium museum, crafts, another church as grand as a cathedral and a great park; Burford; and Cheltenham, with all the elegance of a spa, particularly at the Montpellier end of the great Promenade (another good museum and fine church). The beauty of the Cotswold Hills needs no describing, nor its showpiece villages like Bourton-on-the-Water, Bibury and Stow-on-the-Wold. There is a Roman villa at Chedworth, butterfly and bird gardens, folk and farm museums, wildlife and rare breeds parks, stately homes and gardens, castles (such as Sudeley), abbeys and walks.

Readers' comments: Food absolutely outstanding, even for a spoiled Swiss! Absolute calm. First-rate; inventive menu; highly recommended. Excellent food and genial hosts. Food outstanding; what a find! Superb cooking. The best meal we'd had – highly recommended. Excellent in every way, especially food and wine. The best cook we've found in England. Excellent food; very comfortable; welcoming. Our third visit. Excellent cook and hostess; very comfortable. One of the nicest people; outstanding cook.

WOLD FARM

Old, south-west of Kettering, Northamptonshire, NN6 9RJ
Tel: 0604 781258

7 bedrooms (single or double) from £14. Less for 3 nights. Some have own bath/shower; central heating; views of country or garden. (Washing-machine on request.)
Dinner £8 for 4 courses and coffee, at 7pm. Vegetarian diets if ordered. Packed lunches, snacks. Tea, coffee, free.
2 sitting-rooms with central heating, open fire, TV, books, record-player. Billiards.
Gardens
Nearest main road A43 from Northampton to Kettering.

This 18th-century house has particularly attractive and spacious rooms, and two delightful gardens with rose pergola, golden pheasants and swing-seat. A garden-house has recently been converted to provide more bedrooms, one of which is on the ground floor. Throughout the house are attractive fabrics and wallpapers; one bedroom in Japanese style, another with rosebuds, and a third using 'Country Manor' pattern on walls, bed and curtains. In the sitting-room are alcoves of Hummel figures, in the dining-room a carved 17th-century sideboard, and in the breakfast-room a dresser with the exhortation 'Nourish thyself with lively vivacity'. Window-seats, antiques and white-panelled doors add further character to the rooms. Throughout, standards are of the highest.

For dinner, Anne Engler serves – in an oak-beamed dining-room with inglenook fireplace – such meals as a quiche or fish salad followed by a roast joint and then perhaps profiteroles or lemon meringue pie, and cheeses – with a sherry, wine or beer included. Anne (once a 'Tiller girl') is a most warm and welcoming hostess.

A feature of the rolling agricultural landscape round here is the network of 18th- and 19th-century canals, and the reservoirs (now naturalized) that were built to top up the water in these. At Stoke Bruerne a waterways museum tells the whole story of the canals, and you can take boat trips. The many stately homes include Althorp (childhood home of the Princess of Wales) and Boughton House (modelled on Versailles). There are Saxon churches at Brixworth and Earls Barton. The county is famous for its high-spired churches and for its many historical associations: it has two 'Eleanor Crosses' erected in the 13th century by Edward I wherever his wife's coffin rested on its journey to burial in Westminster Abbey; Fotheringhay is where Mary Queen of Scots was executed; Cromwell defeated Charles I's army at Naseby in 1645 (good bar food at the Fitzgerald Arms, and a museum of the battle). In the Nene Valley is a scenic steam railway.

Looking at all the things there are to see and do – interesting to children and adults alike – it seemed to me that staying here would be a very good all-weather alternative to a traditional seaside holiday for the family. There's a live museum of roundabouts and organs, for instance, near Northampton; several water gardens and bird gardens; and Wicksteed Park is famous for its playground amusements.

In autumn Blakesley village has a soap-box 'grand prix' and Ashton world conker championships.

Northamptonshire is at the centre of England, with motorways making it quickly accessible from almost anywhere.

THE WOOD   C PT S

De Courcy Road, Moult Hill, Salcombe, south of Kingsbridge, Devon,
TQ8 8LQ   Tel: 054884 2778

rear view

6 bedrooms (single, double or family) from £16. Less for 7 nights and bargain breaks. Some have own bath/shower; TV; tea/coffee facilities; central heating; views of sea, country or garden; balcony. (Washing-machine on request.)
Dinner £10 for 4 courses (with choices) and coffee, at 7.30pm. Vegetarian or special diets if ordered. Lunches, packed lunches, snacks. Tea, coffee, free. Drinks can be ordered.
Sitting-room with central heating, open fire, TV, books, piano, record-player.
Small garden
Nearest main road A381 from Salcombe to Totnes.

One of the most spectacular sites in this book is occupied by a turn-of-the-century house which seems almost to hang in the air, so steep is the wooded cliff below it. One looks straight down onto the pale golden beach of South Sands (a small cove), and the blue waters of Salcombe estuary with the English Channel beyond. Rocky headlands stretch into the distance. To make the most of this exceptional view, some bedrooms have balconies and the elegant L-shaped sitting-room has huge windows that open onto a paved terrace (sometimes meals are served on a verandah). One can walk through the garden to a steep woodland footpath which goes down to the sands – but what a climb up again! – and from there take the ferry to Salcombe. Sometimes visitors can borrow a boat.

Bedrooms, on two floors, have different styles. No. 1 is all pink and white. No. 2 has a sensational bay window framing a view of the estuary. No. 3, a single, is very pretty: Laura Ashley festoon blinds and wallpaper, pine panelled doors. No. 4, with bamboo furniture and a turquoise-and-cream colour scheme, has a balcony; as does No. 5, with four-poster and outsize bathroom. No. 6 is level with a small lawn. Prices vary.

In the dining-room (handsomely furnished with velvet chairs, white-gold Minton china and linen napkins), Pat Vaissière serves candlelit dinners that use much local produce – such as cheese-filled eggs, lamb with apricot-and-almond stuffing, chocolate rum trifle, and cheeses. Rolls are home-baked.

Salcombe is Devon's southernmost resort, and arguably its most beautiful one. Even orange and lemon trees grow here which, together with palms, remind one of parts of the Mediterranean. The estuary is very popular for sailing, garden-lovers come to see Sharpitor (NT), walkers make for the viewpoints of Bolbery Down and Bolt Head. All along the coast from here to Plymouth are picturesque waterfront villages, such as Bantham and Newton Ferrers, described elsewhere. In the opposite direction are Kingsbridge (old market town), the long stretch of Slapton Sands (nature reserve, with lagoons), picturesque Dartmouth (of outstanding historical interest – two castles, quaint quays, elaborately carved woodwork on buildings, the Royal Naval College, river trips, two ferries).

Readers' comments: Outstanding standards. They go out of their way to provide that little bit extra at every turn. Made to feel so much at home. Worth coming for the food alone! Lovely site; delighted. Superb comfort, food and hospitality.

WOODCOTE MANOR
C S

Bramdean, east of Winchester, Hampshire, SO24 0LL   Tel: 0096 279 793

4 bedrooms (single, double or family) from £15. Less for 2 nights and bargain breaks. All have own bath; tea/coffee facilities; central heating; views of country or garden. No smoking. (Washing-machine on request.)

Dinner £12 for 3 courses (with choices) and coffee, at 8pm. Non-residents not admitted. Vegetarian or special diets if ordered. Lunches, packed lunches, snacks. Tea, coffee, free. Drinks can be ordered or brought in.

2 sitting-rooms with central heating, open fire, TV, books, piano, record-player. No smoking.

Large garden with swimming-pool and tennis court.

Nearest main road A272 from Winchester to Petersfield.

Closed November–March

In July 1554, Philip II of Spain arrived (in the pouring rain) at Winchester for his marriage to Mary Tudor. She had spent the previous night at this house; and must have been more tense than most brides, for there had been a Commons' petition against the Spanish marriage, and a plot to depose her before it could take place. (Nor was she popular with Philip's courtiers either, who called her 'old and flabby, no eyebrows . . . it would take God himself to drink this cup.') Today's visitors who occupy her room may sleep more happily than she did that night.

Woodcote Manor is one of the most outstanding houses in this book. At its heart is a 14th-century building to which additions were made in Tudor and Jacobean times, with alterations in the 18th century, and a further – very handsome – extension made in 1911. In the main part live Caroline McLaughlan and her husband (it is his paintings which hang on many of the walls) and in a wing Caroline's mother, Marguerite Morton – both take paying guests.

One enters a great hall, panelled and with elaborately plastered ceiling. On the floor of black and white marble tiles stands a huge mediaeval table which was made for the refectory of a monastery; an 18th-century Flemish cradle now nurses pot-plants. The panelled sitting/dining-room is lined with books; leather chairs are grouped round the fireplace. From this room there are good views of the grounds (which include a grass tennis court and a swimming-pool in a walled garden). The garden is opened to the public every Easter, when wild daffodils in the woods are at their best and the trees just coming into leaf. The park has a number of copper beeches and a 'handkerchief tree'.

A very long sitting-room has tall sash windows and window-seats deep-set in its pale blue walls; a marble fireplace; and Florentine cabinet with birds and flowers inlaid. Crystal sconces light the room, which has velvet sofas and a grand piano. At the back is a large dining-room dominated by a panel of Dutch oak carved with a scene of the Israelites escaping from Egypt.

A handsome staircase leads up to bedrooms including the one used by Mary Tudor before her wedding. Oak-panelled, it has a splendid fireplace that was specially installed for her visit. There is a very attractive attic suite with leaded casements which would be ideal for a family. Caroline has chosen attractive contrasts of colours and textures – white flokati rugs on polished oak floors; white cane bedheads with aquamarine walls and redcurrant curtains.

As to dinner, this is always based on the farm's own produce. A typical menu: spinach soup, roast pheasant, blackcurrant sorbet, cheeses.

WOODMANS GREEN FARM

Woodmans Green, north of Midhurst (West Sussex), Hampshire, GU30 7NF   Tel: 042876 250

3 bedrooms (single, twin, or family) from £14. Rooms have tea/coffee facilities; phone; central heating; views of country or garden. No smoking. (Washing-machine on request.)
Dinner £10 for 3 courses (with choices) and coffee, at 7.30pm. Non-residents not admitted. Vegetarian or special diets if ordered.

Packed lunches, snacks. Tea, coffee, free. Drinks can be brought in.
2 sitting-rooms with central heating, open fire, TV, books, piano, record-player. No smoking.
Large garden
Nearest main road A272 from Midhurst to Petersfield.

This Tudor house has interesting features of the period, which include a particularly grand staircase, stone-mullioned windows in the gable, low doorways (on which Mary Spreckley drapes swags of dried flowers) and, in the farmyard, an unusual roofed and brick-walled pit – a midden for farm waste. There is a barbecue and a heated (75°) swimming-pool.

Mary Spreckley has furnished the rooms with style. Bedrooms are attractive and in the elegant sitting-room, where pale colours predominate, are chinoiserie chintz sofas, a Steinway grand piano and handsome iron firebacks.

By arrangement, Mary – who is a very good cook – will prepare either a full dinner (such as carrot-and-orange soup, chicory-stuffed chicken with blue cheese sauce, and apple flan with cream) or a light supper (such as cauliflower cheese).

This very attractive area around Haslemere, Petersfield and Petworth is a good base from which to visit Chichester, Fishbourne Roman palace, Petworth House, Cowdray Park (polo), Bosham (sailing), and the Weald and Downland open-air museum of ancient buildings. Wisley (RHS gardens) is near.

Readers' comments: Friendly atmosphere, cooking imaginative and attractively served; very pleasant indeed.

A few miles to the east is Lurgashall, West Sussex, and **Little Brockhurst** (tel: 042878 296), a superbly sited turn-of-the-century mansion – stone walls, leaded casements and handsome detail throughout its spacious rooms. June Covey serves breakfast only (in a great sitting/dining-room shared with the family, or on the south-facing stone terrace outside the conservatory). Furnishings are comfortable rather than elegant. Heated swimming-pool (up to

80°) and a hard tennis court in the big garden – from which are fine views of the South Downs. (No smoking.)

WYKEHAM ARMS   CD PT
Kingsgate Street, Winchester, Hampshire, SO23 9PE   Tel: 0962 53834

rear view

7 bedrooms (single, double or family) from £16.25. Some have own bath/shower; TV; tea/coffee facilities; phone; central heating. No smoking in one of the bedrooms. (Washing-machine on request.)
Dinner À la carte from 6.45pm. Vegetarian or special diets if ordered. Lunches, packed lunches, snacks. Tea, coffee, extra. Drinks can be ordered.
Sitting-room with central heating, open fire, TV, books. No smoking.
Small garden
Nearest main road A33 from Winchester to Basingstoke.

It would be easy to pass this by without a second glance, a seemingly ordinary pub in a quiet side street near the cathedral. But ordinary it is not. Despite its Victorian-looking frontage it is one of Winchester's oldest inns, dating from 1760. (It is named after William of Wykeham, the mediaeval founder of Winchester College.)

Inside, is a series of traditional bars where real ales and malt whiskies are served, log fires blazing on chilly days ('We get through 40 tons of logs a year'), old Windsor chairs drawn up to pine tables with candles lit at night – also, a comfort which coaching travellers did not enjoy two centuries ago, thick blue carpet underfoot. There is a breakfast-room for guests, with sprigged tablecloths, large windows and (as in all rooms) flowers, and an upstairs sitting-room with pine panelled fireplace and grandfather clock. In the attic is – surprise! – a sauna. The small lawn at the back has hanging baskets of lobelias and petunias around.

Bedrooms have been attractively furnished: for instance, with Laura Ashley fabrics, antiques, pot-plants and Jane Austen pictures (and mini-bars). From some there are roofscape views with glimpses of the cathedral beyond the chimney-pots. (A family room is supplied with toys.) And I found total silence at night.

Graeme and Anne Jameson have given the inn a reputation for excellent food (served in the bars), using fresh ingredients. On the menu, which constantly changes, you might find such unusual things as sea bass soufflé, courgette and thyme soup, monkfish provençale, venison steak au poivre, honey and walnut tart and cider bavarois among more conventional dishes – all cooked by Joanne Docherty.

Winchester (so soon reached by motorway from London or Heathrow; or from Southampton or the New Forest) was once, in Saxon and early Norman times, the capital of England: it was old even then, as prehistoric and Roman finds have shown. The Norman cathedral is one of the longest in Europe, and it has seven elaborately carved chapels, royal tombs, mediaeval wall paintings. Unlike many, it is well sited on lawns that allow an unimpeded view of it. In the city itself, there are a great many old buildings, mediaeval to 18th-century, including a watermill; and there are pleasing walks not only through its lanes but on the banks of the River Itchen. Some of the ancient city walls and gates still survive, and in Castle Hall is a replica of King Arthur's round table as envisaged by Tudor antiquaries. Another survival to be seen in the streets: elderly men in gowns and ruffs. They are pensioners from the Holy Cross almshouses south of the city.

YEW TREE COTTAGE

C(6)

Baybridge, south-east of Winchester, Hampshire, SO21 1JN
Tel: 096274 254

2 bedrooms (double) from £15. Rooms have TV; tea/coffee facilities; central heating; views of country or garden. No smoking. (Washing-machine on request.)
Dinner £10 for 3 courses and coffee, at 6.30–8.30pm. Vegetarian or special diets if ordered. Packed lunches, snacks. Tea, coffee, free. Wine can be ordered or brought in.
Sitting-room with central heating, open fire, TV, books.
Small garden
Nearest main road A33 from Winchester to Southampton.

Tucked away in pretty countryside is a little lattice-paned, thatched cottage dating from the 17th century. There are – of course! – roses round the door and wood-smoke curling up from the chimney whenever a fire is alight in the big inglenook which dominates June Coombe's little sitting-room. This has carved bergère chairs, low beams and, beyond it, a small staircase winding up to two pleasant blue-and-white bedrooms with furniture painted by her daughter and a shower-room between them. Mrs Coombe does not take more than one family (or party) at a time, and they have sole use of sitting-and dining-room. She used to be a professional cook, so dinner here is well above average with menus such as trout pâté and salad, chicken breasts in wine, cream and mushrooms; and peaches with raspberry sauce.

Nearby Winchester was England's capital in the days of King Alfred (indeed, it had been a considerable town long before that, during the long Roman occupation). Kings were crowned – and buried – here. The Norman cathedral dominates all, its most famous bishop – William of Wykeham – being the founder of one of England's great public schools, Winchester College (which can be visited), and of Oxford's New College. There are the remains of two castles here, the Bishop's Palace, two of the city gates that pierced the once formidable town walls, and the chapel of St Swithin. The byways in the heart of the city are full of ancient buildings, in one of which Jane Austen lived at the end of her life. Main streets are partly colonnaded, there is a statue of King Alfred, pleasant gardens and walks to take you along the riverside or the remaining walls. And at 8pm a bell sounds curfew every day. As well as several museums there is a Great Hall housing what was once reputed to be King Arthur's round table. And all around are, as Keats said, 'the most beautiful streams I ever saw, full of trout'.

St Swithin, best known for a weather legend, was Bishop of Winchester in the 9th century when the town was capital of the kingdom of Wessex – the most important of all England's kingdoms then. A century after his death, his remains were moved from the cemetery he had chosen into the cathedral – whereupon, although it was July, a prolonged and heavy rainstorm occurred. Hence the superstition which lingers on, that if it rains on St Swithin's Day it will go on raining for forty days: improbable, even for an English summer!

Eastward, in the Petersfield direction, is rolling downland and, in one of the valleys, the very lovely village of East Meon, threaded by a clear stream and with a fine church. Northward lies the loveliest valley of all where the River Itchen wanders; and the pleasant old town of Alresford.

344

TOURING
WALES

Special needs catered for as follows (for explanation of code letters, see page xxvi).
Establishments marked with a star will accept the discount vouchers from page ii.

Bron Heulog	C	D		PT	S		X
Cefn						S-C	
Crown Inn	C				S		X
Cwmtwrch Farmhouse Hotel�લ	C	D	H				X
Cyfie Farm	C						
Dewis Cyfarfod	C(8)	D			S		
Eyarth Station✲	C	D	H				X
Fferm-y-Felin✲	C	D		PT	S	S-C	X
Glyndwr✲	C						
Gwrach Ynys	C	D					
Hendre Farm✲				PT			
Herongate					S		
Llanddetty Hall Farm	C	D		PT			
Mount Pleasant Farm	C			PT	S		X
Old Rectory	C	D			S		
Pantyfedwen	C				S		
Park Hall✲	C	D		PT	S		
Peterstone Court	C				S	S-C	
Royal Oak Farmhouse✲		D		PT			
Talbontdrain	C				S		
Tregynon Farm Hotel	C	D	H		S		X
Ty Gwyn✲	C	D	H	PT	S	S-C	X
Ty'n Rhos Farm	C(5)		H				
Ty'r Ywen	C	D					X

'You won't find much there', armchair critics told me. 'Poor food [wrong] . . . it always rains [wrong] . . . low standards [yes and no].'

We ate not one bad meal in Wales, and several outstandingly good ones; and except for half a day the sun shone while England remained grey as a floorcloth. I found many houses of very poor standards: tawdry, dingy or (in one case) smelly. Nevertheless, as the following pages show, there is an ample choice of really excellent and varied accommodation. And accommodation prices are substantially below those in England: at two-thirds of the houses described here you can stay for £14 or less.

Wales is a country of superb and varied scenery, too, with glorious beaches. There are plenty of 'sights' such as castles, steam railways, award-winning museums and so forth. Yet, even when travelling during the August Bank Holiday weekend (easily avoiding 'A' roads, large towns and the main seaside resorts), one can find it mercifully free of cars and crowds. An ideal choice for an 'off the beaten track' holiday at moderate cost and with truly hospitable hosts.

The M4 from London enters Wales through the county of Gwent. Beyond Pontypool and over the 1200-foot Garn Wen mountain by a rough and lengthy track – superb views, but not a drive for the timid! – is **Ty'r Ywen**, 'house of

Ty'r Ywen

yews', at Trevithin (Mamhilad, NP4 8TT; tel: 049528 200), which young Susan Armitage and her husband laboured for three years to transform from a derelict state to the present very attractive home. Every guest room has a four-poster (one has two), made by David with pretty draperies by Susan, and the en suite bathrooms are luxurious. Across the inglenook fireplace is a massive two-foot beam. In the huge dining-kitchen, fiddleback chairs surrounding two refectory tables, Susan serves (with the help of their vegetable garden and Jersey cows) such meals as: melon salad, chicken legs with stuffed courgettes and blackcurrant gâteau. David, a hospital engineer, drives a vintage car to and from his work, the long track notwithstanding.

Next, into the large county of Powys and following the Usk still further upstream one comes to the inexpensive 17th-century **Llanddetty Hall Farm**

347

Llanddetty Hall Farm

(Talybont, LD3 7YR; tel: 087487 267), in the heart of the Brecon Beacons National Park. All bedrooms have Welsh tapestry bedspreads and some have views of the river, while at the back runs the historic Brecon and Monmouth canal, with narrow-boats passing by (boat trips and tow-path walks are two of many local diversions and visitors can borrow the farm's canoe). Marjorie Morris is an accomplished cook: a typical menu is salmon mousse, chicken and mushrooms in wine sauce, and Eve's pudding made with Llanddetty's own raspberries or gooseberries. Just outside Brecon itself is a great 18th-century stone mansion, **Peterstone Court** (Llanhamlach, LD3 7YB; tel: 087486 666), log fires within and

Peterstone Court

a heated swimming-pool without. The rooms here are exceptionally spacious and Jean Abbott, who likes bright colours and flowery fabrics, keeps them immaculate. Plain home cooking – for instance: melon, roast lamb, charlotte russe, Welsh cheeses. On the other side of Brecon is the Victorian **Old Rectory** (Aberyscir, LD3 9NP; tel: 0874 3457), well tucked away in the hills, which Elizabeth Gould has furnished to high standards of comfort and solid quality – but prices are modest. A

Old Rectory

horse, ram and squirrel greeted our arrival, and there is poultry too. I particularly
liked the pink bedroom which has windows on two sides through which to enjoy
very lovely views of the Brecon Beacons. Imaginative dinners include such dishes
as smoked haddock ramekins, beef Stroganoff and Elizabeth's Malibu dessert –
coconut liqueur combined with tropical fruits and whipped cream. (Bicycles and
pony rides available.) *Readers' comments:* Warm and welcoming; food delicious.)

Travelling westward towards Carmarthen, in the county of Dyfed, I found one
of the very best places of all: **Cwmtwrch Farmhouse Hotel** – its name means
'valley of the wild boar' (Nantgaredig, SA32 7NY; tel: 026788 238). Jenny
Willmott and her husband have transformed a group of old farm buildings with
great sensitivity. The dining-room (open to non-residents) has stone walls painted
white, slate floor, boarded roof above, and grey Paisley cloths on the tables. At one
side, her kitchen is open to view; on the other is a glass wall overlooking the

Cwmtwrch Farmhouse Hotel

courtyard, pots of begonias and busy Lizzies, and sheep fields beyond. The food is
exceptional. Stuffed mushrooms (with garlic and cheese), followed by individual
fish pies (salmon etc. under puff-pastry) or very tender venison, with vegetables
imaginatively cooked; and a flan of grapes with sponge and almond topping were
among the varied choices when we stayed, all cooked to perfection. There are a
small bar and two sitting-rooms: all with interesting and lovely objects, paintings
and pottery (for sale). Some bedrooms (full of character) are in the old farmhouse
and others (all at ground level) in a recent conversion of stables: whitewashed stone
walls contrast with antique beds, pale blue and grey schemes echoing the colours
of the local stone. (*Readers' comments:* Superb cooking. Excellent wines.)

Also in this area is **Fferm-y-Felin** or 'mill farm' – the mill is nearby (Llanpum-
saint, SA33 6DA; tel: 026784 498 after 7pm), the 18th-century home of Anne and
David Ryder-Owen: a place of particular interest to birdwatchers. David, a keen
ornithologist, can tell you where to spot pied fly-catchers, buzzards and even the
rare red kite. He has created a small lake for emperor geese and black swans; and
throughout the house are Victorian stuffed birds and badgers. Beyond the
dining-room (furnished with antiques and with a spiral stair in one corner) is a

Fferm-y-Felin

sitting-room so large that it has a fireplace at each end; pink buttoned velvet sofas and a walnut piano contrast with rugged stone walls. Anne serves such meals as corn-on-the cob, wild trout with home-grown vegetables, and apple crumble. This would be a good place for a family holiday: the children's bedroom (with toys) has a picture-window overlooking the lake and its waterfowl, and there is a pet donkey as well as other livestock.

For anyone tracing their family history, I recommend a stay at inexpensive **Mount Pleasant Farm** (Penffordd, SA66 7HY; tel: 09916 447) because Pauline Bowen is an expert in the subject, while Peter collects vintage cars and bygones. A warm, hospitable couple, their small beamed farmhouse has been immaculately modernized and is very comfortable. Good home cooking. Further north, in the

Mount Pleasant Farm

heart of the Pembrokeshire National Park and near Fishguard, is something quite exceptional: **Tregynon Farm Hotel** (Gwaun Valley, SA65 9TU; tel: 0239 820531). Of all the places I stayed at in Wales, this remote 16th-century house had the most spectacular scenery around it, including an Ice Age ravine with waterfall, ancient oak woods, countryside where badgers and polecats or buzzards and red kites are sometimes spotted, wild moorland and a prehistoric fort. From nearby peaks of the Preselli mountains, one can sometimes see Ireland and Snowdon. Not far away are some of the sunniest sandy beaches in the country, renowned for their pure air. The meals, too, are exceptional with much emphasis on wholefood. The Heards grow vegetables organically, keep a variety of livestock, and have their own trout ponds. Their speciality breads, sausages, traditionally smoked ham, cheeses and even their own spring water contribute to the very special experience

Tregynon Farm Hotel

of eating at Tregynon, and you can relax afterwards by a log fire in the beamed sitting-room. (*Readers' comments:* Excellent host. Interesting menu.)

On Cardigan Bay is a picturesque sandy cove over-popular in high summer, but set aside from the throng here is quiet **Hendre Farm** (Llangrannog, SA44 6AP;

Hendre Farm

tel: 0239 78342 or 654342), unpretentious but very comfortable and with good home cooking by Bethan Williams, using the farm's own fruit, vegetables and other produce: a good choice for a traditional farmhouse holiday, particularly with children. Just a little further, in a wooded valley protected by the National Trust is **Park Hall** (Cwmtydu, SA44 6LG; tel: 0545 560306), one of the most interesting

Park Hall

'finds' that I made; a quite exceptional guest-house has been created in this turn-of-the-century mansion which is decorated with flair, using much Victoriana – the table linen and silver, the brass beds, the leather chesterfields and even the bath with brass claw feet are in period. Antique lace has been used quite a lot, and Laura Ashley Victorian-style fabrics. From pine-panelled bay windows, there are views of Cardigan Bay between the hills and of the picturesque valley running down to it. Dinners here are of a high order. A popular starter is, after soup such as vichyssoise, a prawn and avocado salad; main courses can include salmon poached in vermouth; with such puddings as profiteroles – and then cheeses.

Inland to the north-east of this is 17th-century **Pantyfedwen** (Pontrhydfendigaid, SY25 6EN; tel: 09745 358) home of two teachers, Ceri and Siân Davies. This

Pantyfedwen

is in the Strata Florida, 'flowery vale', just beyond very lovely abbey ruins. Behind its sparkling white façade are ancient inglenook fireplaces, a curious spiral staircase of stone and other ancient features preserved when the house was recently modernized. Siân has used attractive fabrics, white flokati rugs on board floors and furniture in keeping with the house (refectory tables, for example). There is one of the most luxurious bathrooms in this book. As to meals, which include home-grown vegetables, a typical dinner might be leek soup, carbonnade of beef and orange mousse.

Another totally different experience awaited us near Machynlleth, at **Talbont-drain** (Uwychygarreg, SY20 8RR; tel: 0654 2192). Hilary Matthews abandoned a London career as a social worker to restore this remote house, high in the hills, furnishing it simply but with attractive colours and textures. Inexpensive walking holidays are a principal attraction here (no car is needed: Hilary will pick you up at Machynlleth station and drive you up her long, twisting lane); and she provides

Talbontdrain

particularly well for children. Hilary serves such 2-course meals as bacon-and-leek flan with vegetables, followed by nectarines in a creamy sauce. Occasionally she does fungus identifying (and cooking) weekends. Her breakfasts feature Welsh specialities: I recommend 'Glamorgan sausage', a type of cheese croquette. Some guests enjoy her excellent pianola. (No smoking.) Talbontdrain is in a varied area of woodland, waterfalls, moors and sheep pastures; utterly peaceful. (*Readers' comments*: Friendly; good food and company; extremely comfortable.)

And so into the county of Gwynedd and the Snowdonia National Park. Of Wales' many lovely estuaries, the Mawddach (near Dolgellau) is perhaps the most beautiful: 'No finer view of sea and mountains', wrote Wordsworth. On the south bank, beyond a craggy oak glade, I found a very modestly priced 'b & b' house, **Herongate** (Arthog, LL39 1BJ; tel: 0341 250349), the simple but pleasant home of Pat Mallatratt whose late husband's paintings line the walls of the small sitting-room. Herons, oystercatchers and tame sheep seeking titbits can be seen from the bay windows. The house is in a small, isolated terrace built by a Victorian entrepreneur as part of a grander plan that never materialized. (B & b only: one can dine in Dolgellau or at Borthwnog Hall).

Herongate

Set on a trim lawn with flowerbeds and pines, is Edwardian **Gwrach Ynys**, 'dwarf island' (Talsarnau, LL47 6TS; tel: 0766 780742), surrounded by reclaimed saltmarshes over which the sea once swept and by the paddock of Melys, a friendly white pony. Gwynfor and Deborah Williams have restored and furnished the house to much of its original standard of handsome comfort, with open fires in marble or stone fireplaces, big sash windows with green views and Portmeirion's pretty botanical pottery on the tables. Much local produce is used for traditional meals that may start with home-made soups, pâté or salmon mousse; usually followed by a roast, beef olives or chicken pie; with puddings such as chocolate soufflé, pavlova or trifle. This is north of Harlech.

Gwrach Ynys

Just beyond Caernarfon, **Ty'n Rhos Farm** (Llanddeiniolen, LL55 3AE; tel: 0248 670489) is now almost a hotel (priced accordingly), run in a very professional way by Nigel and Lynda Kettle. A wing of modern, well equipped bedrooms and en suite bathrooms has been added. This is nevertheless still a working farm,

Ty'n Rhos Farm

which supplies produce for the table (and cheese to take home). Lynda is an excellent cook of such meals as beef soup, salmon with hollandaise sauce, and chocolate sponge with brandy sauce. (*Readers' comments:* Welcoming and efficient. Beautifully furnished. Food extremely good.)

From here it is not far to the heart of Snowdonia and to the pleasant mountain resort of Betwys-y-Coed. One can stay in a small watermill, partly 14th-century and with its wheel awaiting restoration, hidden away near the museum of vintage motors (both owned by the Houghton family): **Royal Oak Farmhouse** (Betwys-y-Coed, LL24 0AH; tel: 06902 427/632). Although so central, the mill is hidden in a little valley with a deep salmon pool close by. The lattice-paned windows, great

Royal Oak Farmhouse

stone fireplace, carved oak settle and small but very pretty bedrooms give this inexpensive guest-house great character (very good bathroom, incidentally). It was once the home of the painter David Cox, when (in the late 18th century) Betwys was an artists' colony, and his studio still stands in the garden. Elsie Houghton serves only breakfast, but there are good eating-places in Betwys – including a former coaching inn called **Ty Gwyn**, 'white house' which, although

Ty Gwyn

on a road, has quiet bedrooms at the back (Betwys-y-Coed, LL24 0SG; tel: 06902 383). Sheila Ratcliffe has a flair for interior decoration, and every bedroom – small or large – is beautiful, many with en suite bathrooms (a fact reflected in the prices). The most impressive is an attic suite with four-poster and sitting-room; the most convenient for anyone disabled, a pretty ground-floor room. Even in the ancient, beamed bar (fire glowing in the old black range, copper pots, carved oak settle) her colourful patchwork cushions are everywhere; and at the back is a very comfortable sitting-room and then another where she sells antiques and old prints. Cooking is done by chef Martin, the Ratcliffes' son, whose specialities include exotic dishes like lamb flamed in crème-de-menthe or pork in an apple and ginger sauce (the table d'hôte menu is simpler). Even the bar snacks include such imaginative options as shark with garlic butter, bulghar wheat and walnut casserole or homely rabbit pie. Trout comes from the River Conwy, which flows by the other side of the road.

Further down the River Conwy, one can head for the hills and **Cefn** (Tyn-y-Groes, LL32 8TA; tel: 0492 650233), well secluded. The white, 17th-century house is surrounded by lawns with camelias and magnolias from which to enjoy superb views of Snowdonia and of the valley below (there is also a glass-roofed verandah, and a summer-house). Sitting/dining-room (with inglenook fireplace), handsome bathrooms and most bedrooms are exceptionally spacious, well decorated and with thick carpets. Margaret Waddingham produces such meals as egg mayonnaise, roast Welsh lamb, gooseberry meringue tart and cheeses. Very good value indeed. (*Essential to phone and book: very hard to find!*)

Cefn

I, like many people, had underestimated the county of Clwyd. No national park here, but superlative scenery nevertheless in the range of Clwydian hills running south. Ruthin is an attractive little town (at its castle, really good mediaeval

Eyarth Station

banquets are held). Just south of here, a disused railway station is now an unusual – and unusually excellent – guest-house: **Eyarth Station** (Llanfair-Dyffryn-Clwyd, LL15 2EE; tel: 08242 3643). It has been imaginatively converted and furnished by Jen Spencer. Ground-floor bedrooms have such touches as broderie anglaise festoon blinds and canopied bedheads with Dollymixture fabrics; some are in what were the porters' rooms. Excellent bathrooms (even a bidet). What was once the waiting-room is now a very large sitting-room with balcony just above the fields: big sofas, log fire and thick carpet make this particularly comfortable. The dining-room – once the station platform – has sliding glass doors to a terrace and small, well-heated swimming-pool. Jen offers only snacks for supper.

Homely but sited in a really wonderful position is 17th-century **Crown Inn** (Llanfihangel-Glyn-Myfyr, LL21 9UL; tel: 049082 209) perched on the bank of the bubbling River Alwen. Tucked under a jutting crag, the inn's little beer-garden is on a series of small terraces down to the water's edge. Though bedrooms are simple (and inexpensive), there are en suite bathrooms and colour televisions. There is free fishing for brown trout, and a nature trail in the grounds.

Just across the border into Gwynedd again is beautiful Lake Bala on the way to which is one of the most attractive houses I found in Wales, **Dewis Cyfarfod** – 'the chosen meeting-place' (Llandderfel, Bala, LL23 7DR; tel: 06783 243). Drovers used to meet at this spot where road and river converge, a convenient place to water their livestock. Now the pair of 17th-century cottages is the elegant home of Peter and Barbara Reynolds, furnished with antiques and pretty chintzes, good paintings and well-chosen colour schemes. The spacious sitting-room has groups of comfortable armchairs, a log fire, and panoramic valley views through its

Dewis Cyfarfod

356

picture-windows, with the chance to spot squirrels, foxes and a great variety of birds. In one bedroom, William Morris's 'strawberry thief' fabric complements a white wallpaper with cherries, and other rooms are equally pretty – one with a walnut bed and wildflower fabric, another (in a ground-floor cottage close by) with an oyster and charcoal colour scheme. One bathroom is particularly sumptuous (two basins, royal blue and gold fittings), another has swags of flowers painted by Barbara. The Reynolds also own a celebrated restaurant in Chester (Abbey Green), and so it is not surprising that meals here comprise such feasts as celery and lemon soup, beef braised with oranges and wine (accompanied by savoyard potatoes, Polish cauliflower and mange-tout peas), *fromage frais* with strawberries and then farmhouse cheeses – unless you prefer a light supper. One can eat on the terrace in fine weather, surrounded by pots and baskets brimming with flowers, or in the elegant dining-room; with silver, crystal and candles on the table.

Glyndwr

There is an especially lovely drive through hills, moors and woods to the beautiful and little-known Tanat Valley where Enid Henderson and her niece live at **Glyndwr** (Pen-y-Bont-Fawr, SY10 0NT; tel: 069174 430) in what was once a slate-miner's cottage: the slate floor and little black cooking-range are still there. Behind is a pretty riverside garden. All rooms are homely but pleasant, there is good home cooking, and where else but in Wales would you find bedrooms with their own bathrooms for under £10 a head? (*Readers' comments:* Superb meals, cosy and warm.) A similar price is charged at **Bron Heulog** on the way to the

Bron Heulog

country's highest waterfall (Waterfall Road, Llanrhaedr-ym-Machnant, SY10 0JX, tel: 069189 521), the handsome stone house of 1861 to which the Australian-born Pashens retired from London, filling it with their collection of antiques, oil-paintings and Blüthner grand piano: the curving staircase is almost an art gallery. One bedroom, with prettily draped bedhead, looks onto the unusual tortuosa willow (as depicted on willow-pattern plates). Lorraine's dinners include dishes like avocado mousse, sweet/sour pork, and home-made rum-and-raisin ice cream. (*Readers' comments*: Rooms, food and hosts are a delight.)

Cyfie Farm

Finally, close to the English (Shropshire) border, and once more in Powys, is **Cyfie Farm** (Llanfihangel, SY22 5JE; tel: 069184 451), a picturesque hillside house of stone with a very pretty garden: as romantic a place as you could wish and near scenic Lake Vyrnwy. Inside, all is low beams, narrow stairs, nooks and crannies (except in the spacious stable suite, a more modern conversion, with its own sitting/dining-room). This is a beautifully kept house, which Lynn Jenkins has furnished attractively, with pleasant fabrics and wallpapers, pewter plates arrayed on the old dresser, pot-plants and antiques in the sitting-room. She is an excellent cook of traditional meals. Visitors have been known to stay three weeks at Cyfie – not once but repeatedly – in this surprisingly little-known part of Wales. (*Readers' comments*: An island of peace and relaxation. Affability and effort of our delightful hosts, charm and comfort of their home.)

TOURING
SCOTLAND

Special needs catered for as follows (for explanation of code letters, see page xxvi).
Establishments marked with a star will accept the discount vouchers (see page ii).

Achray House	C					
Borlum Farmhouse	C	D		PT	S-C	X
Coul House Hotel ✳	C	D	H	PT		
Cuilcheanna House	C	D			S-C	
Cuilfail Hotel	C	D			S	
Daviot Mains Farm				PT	S	
Drumbuie	C					
Dunlichity Lodge	C	D	H			
Falls of Lora Hotel ✳	C	D	H	PT		
Glen Loy Lodge	C	D			S	
Invergloy House	C(8)				S	
Kilravock Castle	C		H	PT	S	
Leny House	C			PT	S-C	
Mill House						X
Ossian Hotel	C	D		PT		
Rockhill Farm Guesthouse	C(6)	D			S	S-C
Rossmay	C	D		PT	S	
Topps Farm	C		H			
Wester Moniack Farm	C	D			S	

359

The Highlands, with their long history of hardship and strife, have relatively few guest-houses or small hotels of architectural distinction, attractively furnished, to compare with the great many found in England. But what so many of Scotland's hotels do have instead are outstanding sites with superb views of mountains or valleys (glens), sea or lakes (lochs), and access to country and watersports, birdwatching and good walking in wild country. As to food, cooking is usually very traditional but, even in the least expensive farmhouses or smallholdings (crofts), you may be served salmon or other fish straight from the sea, game (including venison) or Aberdeen Angus beef. Home baking flourishes, too. As to prices, all of the hotels or houses described below not only have good standards but come within the average price-range of this book (Coul House and Dunlichity Lodge are a bit dearer).

I arrived in the Highlands at Inverness (on the north-east coast) by Motorail and journeyed across to the west coast at Fort William, then south via Oban and Inverary, returning home by Motorail from historic Stirling, where Highlands turn to Lowlands: a route chosen for its scenic contrasts, its spectacular mountains, lochs and coastline, almost untouched by commercialism or so-called 'development'.

AROUND INVERNESS To the north-west of the town is the sunny region of Easter Ross where **Coul House Hotel** (Contin, IV14 9EY; tel: 0997 21487) is a

Coul House Hotel

typical Scottish country hotel, much used by salmon-fishers. Anne Bryan and Martyn Hill have preserved its atmosphere of traditional dignity. There are elaborately decorated ceilings; an octagonal sitting-room with large windows overlooking the rhododendrons and lawn where a piper plays every summer Friday evening; and, in the entrance hall, logs crackle on a raised granite hearth. Very good Scottish food (bar meals too), with choices at each of the four courses – some of the specialities are trout en croûte, cullen skink (smoked haddock soup) and chicken cooked with smoked salmon in brandy cream. There is a holiday

361

package which includes free entry to many local sights; ordinary b & b prices are a little high.

If you prefer a more homely atmosphere, I recommend **Wester Moniack Farm** (Kirkhill, IV5 7PQ; tel: 046383 237). It has very neat bedrooms, and an attractive setting beside a mediaeval castle that is now a winery. Mrs Munro is a good cook.

Wester Moniack Farm

To the east of Inverness, I was very impressed by the standard of bedrooms at a little cottage built shortly before the windswept moor nearby was the scene of the Battle of Culloden, 1746 (the defeat of Bonnie Prince Charlie). These rooms, equal to many modern hotels', are in a new extension; the stone-walled sitting-room and boarded dining-room are the original part. Through picture-windows is a panoramic view of the Moray Firth. Gai Hornby provides dinner as well as b & b at **Drumbuie** (Westhill, IV1 2BX; tel: 0463 791591).

Nothing could be more different from this little house than **Kilravock Castle** (Croy, IV1 2PJ; tel: 06678 258), home of the Rose family since 1460. Some of the historic bedrooms are quite exceptional – one, stone-arched, has a half-tester bed,

Kilravock Castle

prettily draped; others are in a country-style wing. Ancestral portraits, antiques and chintzes give the dining- and sitting-rooms traditional style; the library is panelled. Dinner on Sunday evening is a help-yourself buffet in the old banqueting hall. (This is an actively Christian household, with a short grace before each meal.) There are many sports facilities in the extensive grounds; and guided tours of the castle. Very good value.

My other choice in this area is **Daviot Mains Farm** (Daviot, IV1 2ER; tel: 046385 215), built in courtyard style over a century ago. The accommodation is

Daviot Mains Farm

simple but pretty, there are log fires, and Margaret Hutcheson's cooking is exceptional: a typical meal might include Stilton-and-onion quiche as a starter; chicken with mushroom and almond sauce, crisp topping; and a pudding made with yogurt, cream and strawberries. Home-made cakes etc. at bed-time – no charge.

A few miles away is one of the most elegant (and secluded) houses I found in Scotland, pink-walled **Dunlichity Lodge** (Farr, IV1 2AN; tel: 08083 282), home of Commander and Mrs Ian Wedderburn. Dinner is served at a Regency table; the carpet and hessian-covered walls of the dining-room are dark brown, contrasting with coral chintz curtains; alcoves display cut-glass decanters and silver. In the sitting-room, pink and green cretonne chairs are grouped round a fireplace of unusual green marble where logs blaze. Stripped-pine doors line the corridor in a ground-floor wing of excellent bedrooms and bathrooms. Desirée Wedderburn makes and sells little découpage boxes and miniature tapestries depicting local scenes or wildlife.

Dunlichity Lodge

INVERNESS TO FORT WILLIAM   The most direct route is through the Great Glen, where the Caledonian Canal links east coast to west via Loch Ness and Loch Lochy. Just above the west side of Loch Ness (by Urquhart Castle) is an 18th-century farmhouse quite unlike any other, for Vanessa Macdonald-Haig has a flair for interior decoration – and for finding unsuspected treasures at sales and in junkshops. As a result, this is the most imaginative and attractive of houses: **Borlum Farmhouse** (Drumnadrochit, IV3 6XN; tel: 04562 358), comfortably furnished with antiques and attractive fabrics. The summer sitting-room in the glass conservatory has panoramic views of loch and glen. The staircase, with

Borlum Farmhouse

barley-twist balusters, leads up to very pretty bedrooms and bathrooms. The focal point in one bedroom is antique, embroidered wallhangings; in another, a high Victorian bed in cream damask. Downstairs, a spacious, ochre-coloured bedroom and bathroom (suitable for handicapped visitors) has many horse prints, comfy armchairs, and the evening sun. The small wing of the farmhouse, recently converted to studio accommodation, is ideal for families. Above an attractive double bed/sitting-room and bathroom is a gallery (on three sides) housing single beds. White walls and wooden beams complement yellow, green and white furnishings. (No smoking.) The Macdonald-Haigs also have a farm (with sheep and Highland cattle) and a riding centre.

There is another route, longer but very beautiful indeed, which veers east towards the Cairngorms, along which I found the **Ossian Hotel** (Kincraig, PH21 1NA; tel: 05404 242), run by John Ramage and his family. Apart from adding some handsome items he brought from India and a sideboard topped with a single 12-foot slab of marble (from Carlisle Castle), he has retained much of the solid, old-fashioned dignity that was established during the hotel's Victorian heyday. A la carte meals (steaks, trout, salmon and game predominate) are served at tables

Ossian Hotel

laid with damask and silver – some tables are in a big bay window surrounded by trees. Bedrooms vary: no. 4 is the most interesting, for it has a 'Gothick'-style bed of carved pine and, very different, a Sheraton loveseat. Nearer to Fort William is Loch Lochy and **Invergloy House** (Spean Bridge, PH34 4DY; tel: 039781 681), hidden away in a loch-side wilderness of flowering shrubs and varied trees – for once it was the coach-house of a long-gone mansion belonging to a centenarian suffragette who employed six gardeners (also long gone – which is why the 50-acre garden is now wild, and home to a family of roe deer). One steps into a green, light dining-hall with grand piano – Margaret Cairns is a musician as well as a good home cook – off which is a sitting-room (and another piano) with a picture-window from which to enjoy the 35-mile view across lawn and loch to mountains behind which there are sometimes fiery sunsets. One bedroom, with floor-to-ceiling window, also faces this way. (No smoking.)

Invergloy House

Up Glen Finnan is a secluded guest-house, **Glen Loy Lodge** (Banavie, PH33 7PD; tel: 039781 700) run by the Ward family. I particularly liked bedroom 9 because it has a door straight into the 4-acre wild garden through which the River Loy runs. The Lodge has its own boat on Loch Arkaig. Once a week there is smoked salmon and/or salmon on the menu which typically may include such other dishes as leek soup to start with and rhubarb mousse as a pudding. Inexpensive. (This is north of Fort William.)

Glen Loy Lodge

FORT WILLIAM TO OBAN The road south runs alongside Loch Linnhe and the Atlantic coast on the edge of which is **Cuilcheanna House** (Onich, PH33 6SD; tel: 08553 226), at the heart of a 100-acre cattle farm. Parts are five centuries old. Not only is its setting superb, with loch views in one direction and the Glen Coe mountains in the other, but Margaret Dewar's reputation for good food is well known. After a home-made soup, she may serve lamb chops with garlic potatoes

Cuilcheanna House

and other vegetables, then a Norwegian cream soufflé. If you prefer the lively bustle of a traditional inn (frequented by mountaineers, particularly in February and March) press on a little to awesome Glen Coe itself, scene of the treacherous massacre of the Macdonalds by Campbells who were billeted on them in 1692.

Also in this area, down a very long, ferny track, is **Ardsheal Home Farm** (Kentallen, tel: 063174 229) which Mrs MacArthur has furnished attractively – for instance, antiques in the white-walled sitting-room, country pine furniture in a former kitchen (now dining-room), Stag furniture and tulip bedspread in a large downstairs bedroom. She provides dinner only for those who stay at least a week;

Ardsheal Home Farm

others go to the Holly Tree or the Duror Inn. This is a hill farm with cattle and sheep, surrounded by glorious scenery and wildlife (best in May or June), and with its own private beach.

Southward again, where Loch Etive joins the sea, is the big **Falls of Lora Hotel** (Connel, PA37 1PB; tel: 063171 483), owned by two sisters – Sandra Innes and Catherine Webster. It's a large hotel, built a century ago when Victorian tourists first came here by rail, and still with many features redolent of that period – sideboards loaded with Sheffield plate, stags' heads in the hall. But some rooms have been completely modernized. For instance, the bar is now all bamboo and orange plush and one bedroom has a circular bed and its own jacuzzi – others differ greatly, from small-and-simple to spacious rooms with prettily draped four-posters. Prices vary accordingly (if you don't mind the stairs, I recommend no. 59 for its loch view and low price; if you want a private bathroom, no. 53). There are plenty of choices on the conventional 4-course menu cooked by Colin Felgate but if you stay on a Thursday you will be offered (at no extra charge) a special 'Taste of Scotland' dinner of 7 courses: smoked trout, leek soup, haggis, smoked haddock in cheese sauce, roast venison, Glayva mist, Scottish cheeses.

Falls of Lora Hotel

OBAN TO INVERARY   The road south runs past the **Cuilfail Hotel** (Kilmelford, PA34 4XA; tel: 08522 274), its name meaning 'sheltered corner'. Its garden (brilliant with azaleas and daffodils in spring) lies across the road, running downhill to a stream. It was a drovers' and coaching inn when Keats stayed here, dining 'tolerably well on fowl' and watching women spinning wool. Rooms are pleasant, if unassuming (those at the back have hill views) and there is an interesting bar, stone-walled and with pews around the log fire, leading to a flagstoned dining-room with pine tables and chairs. Hilary McFadyen serves good bar snacks as well as a 3-course dinner with imaginative choices at each course which may include courgette-and-rosemary soup, rabbit and mustard casserole

Cuilfail Hotel

and brown sugar chestnut meringues. (Wide choice of vegetarian dishes.) There is a separate 2-room wing for families. This is a sparsely populated part of the country, known both for its wildlife and for several great gardens (warmed by the proximity of the Gulf Stream) which are open to the public. From nearby Oban there are sea trips to the Western Isles.

Inverary, at the head of Loch Fyne (famous for its kippers), is an attractive little resort of white houses and small shops. For a rural ambience, however, it is worth detouring to Cladich on Loch Awe, and waterside **Rockhill Farm Guesthouse** (Ardbrecknish, PA33 1BH; tel: 08663 218). The 17th-century accommodation is homely in style but well equipped and the loch-side setting is idyllic. Helen

Rockhill Farm Guesthouse

Whalley is a good cook of such meals as watercress soup, Loch Awe fish pie (it includes salmon and pike from the loch as well as other fish) and amaretto trifle or raspberries from the garden with cream from Rockhill's cows. Loch Awe's sheltered bays and its islands are accessible, there are ruined castles, and on the farm Hanoverian foals are bred – there are also sheep, goats, donkeys and a St Bernard.

AND SO TO STIRLING   Alternatively, to the south-east there is Loch Long and the Firth of Clyde. On the shores of Loch Long is a modest little guest-house-cum-boatyard, **Rossmay** (Arrochar, G83 7AH; tel: 03012 250), almost with its feet in the water. Peggy Rose (who teaches Scottish dancing) has chosen tartan carpets, and crisp, light colour schemes for the bedrooms and family suite; there's a glass verandah from which to enjoy the view; and simple meals are available – as inexpensive as the accommodation.

Rossmay

Yet another loch, Tay, is at the foot of the steep, beautifully landscaped garden of **Mill House** (Milton Morenish, near Killin, FK21 8TY; tel: 056 72 228). The house is modern, rather like a Scandinavian timber chalet, but furnished with fine

Mill House

antiques and Jean Anderson's own handiwork – a scrap-screen, Berlin-work bedheads and so forth. From the large sitting/dining-room one steps onto a wood verandah overlooking the loch. To one side of the house is a waterfall and crags where wildflowers grow. Dinner (served by Roy in his Anderson kilt) may comprise grapefruit with crème de menthe, lamb casseroled with wine, and a fruit soufflé, for example – all served on Susie Cooper china. A pre-dinner sherry is included in the price. Jean used to be a headmistress, in England, and it speaks volumes for her that a few years ago one of her former pupils chose Mill House for her honeymoon.

Loch Earn has many hotels: I recommend **Achray House** (St Fillans, PH6 2NF; tel: 076485 231). This hotel, run by the young Ross family, has very pleasantly furnished rooms – a tartan and pine dining-room (flowers, silver

Achray House

candelabra and cut-glass on the tables) and pretty bedrooms, many with loch views. There is a family suite. The bar leads to a verandah and the garden overlooking the loch, where the hotel has a private jetty. There is a good choice on the evening menu (and good bar meals as an alternative): things like melon with prawns in a cream-and-curry sauce as a starter; venison cooked with brandy and mushrooms or lamb cutlets with Pernod; and apricot/almond meringue or chocolate-and-Cointreau flan.

Travelling further south, turreted **Leny House**, a baronial pile, is near to Callander – the setting for 'Dr Finlay's Casebook' (Kilmahog, FK17 8HA; tel: 0877 31078). It stands in its own park-like grounds, looking towards one of

Leny House

Scotland's most famous beauty-spots, the woods and hills of the Trossachs, and to Glen Leny, a region of waterfalls and wildlife. From about the year 900 this site was the ancestral home of the Buchanans; the part of the house dating from 1513 was originally their fortress. This was enlarged in 1691, and again in 1845 when the handsome sitting-room was built, with pine-shuttered bay windows facing south – pale green and creamy pink predominate here, and big U-shaped sofas almost fill the room. From the tartan-carpeted hall (with concert piano) a great staircase rises to big light bedrooms, all well carpeted but varying in style. In some of the older rooms Jacobite plotters held secret meetings or stored illegal arms. (Only b & b is provided, but very good meals can be had at the nearby Lade Inn or in Callander.)

Last but far from least: **Topps Farm** (Denny, south of Stirling, FK6 5JF; tel: 0324 822471), a surprising discovery for this peaceful 1000-acre farm is in fact not far from the M80 motorway – Glasgow is less than half an hour away and Edinburgh three-quarters of an hour in the opposite direction. The house itself is modern, completely comfortable and with picture-windows from which to enjoy the views (it is on a high and breezy site). There is an excellent room for disabled visitors. But the big attraction is Jennifer Steel's cooking. Starting as an enthusiastic amateur, she later did a chef's training – and then a special course on wild mushrooms, one of her specialities (from which she makes 'fairy hoosie soup' among other things). Her research into traditional Scottish dishes means you may be offered such a menu as 'nun beads' (cheese, herbs and cream in pastry), 'wee grumphies' (pork balls made with cheese and apples), 'chappit neeps' (turnips mashed with cream), 'lillylyn pudding' (rhubarb, cream and custard). For breakfast trout or haggis will be among the many choices on offer. What better way to end a tour of Scotland?

Topps Farm

CHANNEL ISLANDS

JERSEY

Jersey's scenery has much in common with Cornwall's: wooded valleys, towering cliffs alternating with sandy bays, pink granite buildings. Although its south coast is solid with hotels and tourist-oriented shops, other areas inland and north are still unspoilt. The wildflowers are a delight, and in this mild climate palms and magnolias flourish. The principal 'sights' are the many castles and forts ringing the coast; also the gardens and nurseries (for carnations, lavender and orchids in particular). Watersports, walking and birdwatching bring many visitors; shops sell tax-free bargains (jewellery, scent, etc.); there are day-trips to France; and, above all, the choice of gourmet restaurants at moderate prices is unequalled in England – for which reason, many visitors prefer not to take dinner every night at their own hotel. Crossings by air or sea are not costly (Southampton–Jersey by air can be as little as £20 in low season); car hire and petrol are cheap. I thought accommodation often tended to be dear for what was on offer: price for price, standards of furnishing and taste are, for the most part, below those one can find in England; and I chose only one guest-house after looking at many.

Religious wars of the 13th century drove many Bretons to seek refuge in Jersey. One of these built the **Relais du St Martin**, a granite house in typical Breton style: round-arched entrance, and a massive raised hearth with a colossal slab of granite as its lintel – the dominating feature of the dining-room. By a strange turn of events, the house – after many changes – once again came into Breton hands, when Jean and Jeannine Gicquel took it over to run as a guest-house. They use only fresh produce brought from local farms or fishermen, with vegetables from their own garden. A typical dinner: terrine de campagne or chicken soup, boeuf bourguignonne or rock salmon with provençale sauce, pear belle Helene. You could

Relais du St Martin

stay a fortnight and never twice have the same soup (home-made) or potatoes cooked in the same way.

Bedrooms are neat and simple: no. 8 is particularly spacious and well equipped; there are attractive attic rooms (nos. 9 and 12) for families; and a ground-floor room for those who find stairs difficult or who want to nip out to the swimming-pool for a pre-breakfast dip. The bar (with log fire, guitars and bar-billiards) attracts the gregarious; a sun-room (with big velvet armchairs), those who want to play chess or watch television. The garden has a tree-house for children, boules, curiosities such as an ancient stone pit for salting pork – and a family of hedgehogs. (Tel: 0534 53271.) Accessible by public transport. (Self-catering accommodation too.)

GUERNSEY

March is camellia-time in Guernsey, an island I prefer to Jersey. Primroses and violets throng the banks – daffodil fields are golden. Guernsey is an ideal island, then or later, for independent travellers (no coaches or package-tours, as in Jersey), particularly for those who like fine scenery and walks (there is a 17-mile clifftop path); birdwatching (especially at migrating season); or leisurely motoring (there are only lanes, the speed limit is 35 mph, petrol and car hire are cheap). Good cooking that uses local produce, fish and cream is general, and excellent meals cost less than in England. Do not expect to find many stately homes, art galleries or theatres to visit (although there are musical events). Instead, Guernsey has some highly individual alternatives such as Victor Hugo's flamboyant house, craft workshops of a very high standard, markets, castles, folk museum, flowers, duty- and VAT-free shopping and bargain Guernsey sweaters. Swimming from the sheltered, sandy beaches beneath granite cliffs is at its warmest in September. Norman/French influence is everywhere – in place names, laws, architecture and cooking – but there are even Stone Age relics around, and a Roman ship has lately been raised from St Peter Port harbour. Recent history has left its remains, too – fortifications and underground work from the German occupation.

A car is not essential. Buses go everywhere; cycles can be hired. The cheapest of many air crossings is by Air UK from Southampton or Exeter (short-notice tickets are sold at a big discount). In my hunt for good but inexpensive accommodation, I did better than in Jersey.

In St Peter Port, but secluded, is **Les Ozouets Lodge** (tel: 0481 21288) owned by chef Yves Davy and his wife, who were born in St Malo – not surprisingly,

rear view

Les Ozouets Lodge